"Composed in the style of the great medieval *catenae*, this new anthology of patristic commentary on Holy Scripture, conveniently arranged by chapter and verse, will be a valuable resource for prayer, study and proclamation. By calling attention to the rich Christian heritage preceding the separations between East and West and between Protestant and Catholic, this series will perform a major service to the cause of ecumenism."

AVERY CARDINAL DULLES, S.J.
Laurence J. McGinley Professor of Religion and Society
Fordham University

"The initial cry of the Reformation was *ad fontes*—back to the sources! The Ancient Christian Commentary on Scripture is a marvelous tool for the recovery of biblical wisdom in today's church. Not just another scholarly project, the ACCS is a major resource for the renewal of preaching, theology and Christian devotion."

TIMOTHY GEORGE
Dean, Beeson Divinity School, Samford University

"Modern church members often do not realize that they are participants in the vast company of the communion of saints that reaches far back into the past and that will continue into the future, until the kingdom comes. This Commentary should help them begin to see themselves as participants in that redeemed community."

ELIZABETH ACHTEMEIER
Union Professor Emerita of Bible and Homiletics
Union Theological Seminary in Virginia

"Contemporary pastors do not stand alone. We are not the first generation of preachers to wrestle with the challenges of communicating the gospel. The Ancient Christian Commentary on Scripture puts us in conversation with our colleagues from the past, that great cloud of witnesses who preceded us in this vocation. This Commentary enables us to receive their deep spiritual insights, their encouragement and guidance for present-day interpretation and preaching of the Word. What a wonderful addition to any pastor's library!"

WILLIAM H. WILLIMON
Dean of the Chapel and Professor of Christian Ministry
Duke University

"Here is a nonpareil series which reclaims the Bible as the book of the church by making accessible to earnest readers of the twenty-first century the classrooms of Clement of Alexandria and Didymus the Blind, the study and lecture hall of Origen, the cathedrae of Chrysostom and Augustine, the scriptorium of Jerome in his Bethlehem monastery."

GEORGE LAWLESS
Augustinian Patristic Institute and Gregorian University, Rome

"We are pleased to witness publication of the
Ancient Christian Commentary on Scripture. It is most beneficial for us to learn
how the ancient Christians, especially the saints of the church
who proved through their lives their devotion to God and his Word, interpreted
Scripture. Let us heed the witness of those who have gone before us in the faith."

Metropolitan Theodosius
Primate, Orthodox Church in America

"Across Christendom there has emerged a widespread interest
in early Christianity, both at the popular and scholarly level. . . .
Christians of all traditions stand to benefit from this project, especially clergy
and those who study the Bible. Moreover, it will allow us to see how our traditions are
both rooted in the scriptural interpretations of the church fathers while at
the same time seeing how we have developed new perspectives."

Alberto Ferreiro
Professor of History, Seattle Pacific University

"The Ancient Christian Commentary on Scripture fills a long overdue need for scholars and
students of the church fathers. . . . Such information will be of immeasurable
worth to those of us who have felt inundated by contemporary interpreters and novel theories
of the biblical text. We welcome some 'new' insight from the
ancient authors in the early centuries of the church."

H. Wayne House
*Professor of Theology and Law
Trinity University School of Law*

Chronological snobbery—the assumption that our ancestors working without benefit of
computers have nothing to teach us—is exposed as nonsense by this magnificent
new series. Surfeited with knowledge but starved of wisdom, many of us are
more than ready to sit at table with our ancestors and listen to their holy
conversations on Scripture. I know I am.

Eugene H. Peterson
*Professor Emeritus of Spiritual Theology
Regent College*

"Few publishing projects have encouraged me as much as the recently announced Ancient Christian Commentary on Scripture with Dr. Thomas Oden serving as general editor. . . . How is it that so many of us who are dedicated to serve the Lord received seminary educations which omitted familiarity with such incredible students of the Scriptures as St. John Chrysostom, St. Athanasius the Great and St. John of Damascus? I am greatly anticipating the publication of this Commentary."

FR. PETER E. GILLQUIST
Director, Department of Missions and Evangelism
Antiochian Orthodox Christian Archdiocese of North America

"The Scriptures have been read with love and attention for nearly two thousand years, and listening to the voice of believers from previous centuries opens us to unexpected insight and deepened faith. Those who studied Scripture in the centuries closest to its writing, the centuries during and following persecution and martyrdom, speak with particular authority. The Ancient Christian Commentary on Scripture will bring to life the truth that we are invisibly surrounded by a 'great cloud of witnesses.'"

FREDERICA MATHEWES-GREEN
Commentator, National Public Radio

"For those who think that church history began around 1941 when their pastor was born, this Commentary will be a great surprise. Christians throughout the centuries have read the biblical text, nursed their spirits with it and then applied it to their lives. These commentaries reflect that the witness of the Holy Spirit was present in his church throughout the centuries. As a result, we can profit by allowing the ancient Christians to speak to us today."

HADDON ROBINSON
Harold John Ockenga Distinguished Professor of Preaching
Gordon-Conwell Theological Seminary

"All who are interested in the interpretation of the Bible will welcome the forthcoming multivolume series Ancient Christian Commentary on Scripture. Here the insights of scores of early church fathers will be assembled and made readily available for significant passages throughout the Bible and the Apocrypha. It is hard to think of a more worthy ecumenical project to be undertaken by the publisher."

BRUCE M. METZGER
Professor of New Testament, Emeritus
Princeton Theological Seminary

ANCIENT CHRISTIAN COMMENTARY ON SCRIPTURE

NEW TESTAMENT
III

LUKE

EDITED BY

ARTHUR A. JUST JR.

GENERAL EDITOR
THOMAS C. ODEN

InterVarsity Press
Downers Grove, Illinois

InterVarsity Press
P.O. Box 1400, Downers Grove, IL 60515-1426
World Wide Web: www.ivpress.com
E-mail: email@ivpress.com

InterVarsity Press® is the book-publishing division of InterVarsity Christian Fellowship/USA®, a student movement active on campus at hundreds of universities, colleges and schools of nursing in the United States of America, and a member movement of the International Fellowship of Evangelical Students. For information about local and regional activities, write Public Relations Dept., InterVarsity Christian Fellowship/USA, 6400 Schroeder Rd., P.O. Box 7895, Madison, WI 53707-7895, or visit the IVCF website at <www.intervarsity.org>.

Selected excerpts from Fathers of the Church: A New Translation, *copyright 1947-, used by permission of The Catholic University of America Press.*

Scripture quotations, unless otherwise noted, are from the Revised Standard Version of the Bible, *copyright 1946, 1952, 1971 by the Division of Christian Education of the National Council of the Churches of Christ in the U.S.A., and are used by permission.*

Cover photograph: Scala/Art Resource, New York. View of the apse. S. Vitale, Ravenna, Italy.

Spine photograph: Byzantine Collection, Dumbarton Oaks, Washington D.C. Pendant cross (gold and enamel). Constantinople, late sixth century.

ISBN 978-0-8308-1488-6

Printed in the United States of America ∞

Library of Congress Cataloging-in-Publication Data

Luke/edited by Arthur Just.
   p. cm.—(Ancient Christian commentary on Scripture. New
Testament; 3)
Includes bibliographical references (p.   ) and indexes.
   ISBN 0-8308-1488-4
   1. Bible. N.T. Luke—Commentaries.   I. Just, Arthur A., 1953- II.
Series.
   BS2595.53.L85 2003
   226.4'077'09—dc21

2002155337

| P | 28 | 27 | 26 | 25 | 24 | 23 | 22 | 21 | 20 | 19 | 18 | 17 | 16 | 15 | 14 | 13 | 12 | 11 | 10 | 9 | 8 | 7 |
| Y | 28 | 27 | 26 | 25 | 24 | 23 | 22 | 21 | 20 | 19 | 18 | 17 | 16 | 15 | 14 | 13 | 12 | 11 | 10 | | | |

ANCIENT CHRISTIAN COMMENTARY PROJECT RESEARCH TEAM

GENERAL EDITOR
Thomas C. Oden

ASSOCIATE EDITOR
Christopher A. Hall

OPERATIONS MANAGER
Joel Elowsky

TRANSLATIONS PROJECTS DIRECTOR
Joel Scandrett

RESEARCH AND ACQUISITIONS DIRECTOR
Michael Glerup

EDITORIAL SERVICES DIRECTOR
Warren Calhoun Robertson

ORIGINAL LANGUAGE VERSION DIRECTOR
Konstantin Gavrilkin

GRADUATE RESEARCH ASSISTANTS

Chris Branstetter	*Sergey Kozin*
Jeffrey Finch	*Hsueh-Ming Liao*
Steve Finlan	*Michael Nausner*
Alexei Khamine	*Robert Paul Seesengood*
Vladimir Kharlamov	*Baek-Yong Sung*
Susan Kipper	*Elena Vishnevskaya*

ADMINISTRATIVE ASSISTANT
Judy Cox

Contents

GENERAL INTRODUCTION

The Ancient Christian Commentary on Scripture has as its goal the revitalization of Christian teaching based on classical Christian exegesis, the intensified study of Scripture by lay persons who wish to think with the early church about the canonical text, and the stimulation of Christian historical, biblical, theological and pastoral scholars toward further inquiry into scriptural interpretation by ancient Christian writers.

The time frame of these documents spans seven centuries of exegesis, from Clement of Rome to John of Damascus, from the end of the New Testament era to A.D. 750, including the Venerable Bede.

Lay readers are asking how they might study sacred texts under the instruction of the great minds of the ancient church. This commentary has been intentionally prepared for a general lay audience of nonprofessionals who study the Bible regularly and who earnestly wish to have classic Christian observation on the text readily available to them. The series is targeted to anyone who wants to reflect and meditate with the early church about the plain sense, theological wisdom and moral meaning of particular Scripture texts.

A commentary dedicated to allowing ancient Christian exegetes to speak for themselves will refrain from the temptation to fixate endlessly upon contemporary criticism. Rather, it will stand ready to provide textual resources from a distinguished history of exegesis that has remained massively inaccessible and shockingly disregarded during the last century. We seek to make available to our present-day audiences the multicultural, multilingual, transgenerational resources of the early ecumenical Christian tradition.

Preaching at the end of the first millennium focused primarily on the text of Scripture as understood by the earlier esteemed tradition of comment, largely converging on those writers that best reflected classic Christian consensual thinking. Preaching at the end of the second millennium has reversed that pattern. It has so forgotten most of these classic comments that they are vexing to find anywhere, and even when located they are often available only in archaic editions and inadequate translations. The preached word in our time has remained largely bereft of previously influential patristic inspiration. Recent scholarship has so focused attention upon post-Enlightenment historical and literary methods that it has left this longing largely unattended and unserviced.

This series provides the pastor, exegete, student and lay reader with convenient means to see what Athanasius or John Chrysostom or the desert fathers and mothers had to say about a particular text for preaching, for study and for meditation. There is an emerging awareness among Catholic, Protestant and Orthodox laity that vital biblical preaching and spiritual formation need deeper grounding beyond the scope of the historical-critical orientations that have governed biblical studies in our day.

Hence this work is directed toward a much broader audience than the highly technical and specialized scholarly field of patristic studies. The audience is not limited to the university scholar concentrating on the study of the history of the transmission of the text or to those with highly focused philological interests in textual morphology or historical-critical issues. Though these are crucial concerns for specialists, they are not the paramount interests of this series.

This work is a Christian Talmud. The Talmud is a Jewish collection of rabbinic arguments and comments on the Mishnah, which epitomized the laws of the Torah. The Talmud originated in approximately the same period that the patristic writers were commenting on texts of the Christian tradition. Christians from the late patristic age through the medieval period had documents analogous to the Jewish Talmud and Midrash (Jewish commentaries) available to them in the *glossa ordinaria* and catena traditions, two forms of compiling extracts of patristic exegesis. In Talmudic fashion the sacred text of Christian Scripture was thus clarified and interpreted by the classic commentators.

The Ancient Christian Commentary on Scripture has venerable antecedents in medieval exegesis of both eastern and western traditions, as well as in the Reformation tradition. It offers for the first time in this century the earliest Christian comments and reflections on the Old and New Testaments to a modern audience. Intrinsically an ecumenical project, this series is designed to serve Protestant, Catholic and Orthodox lay, pastoral and scholarly audiences.

In cases where Greek, Latin, Syriac and Coptic texts have remained untranslated into English, we provide new translations. Wherever current English translations are already well rendered, they will be utilized, but if necessary their language will be brought up to date. We seek to present fresh dynamic equivalency translations of long-neglected texts which historically have been regarded as authoritative models of biblical interpretation.

These foundational sources are finding their way into many public libraries and into the core book collections of many pastors and lay persons. It is our intent and the publisher's commitment to keep the whole series in print for many years to come.

Thomas C. Oden
General Editor

A Guide to Using This Commentary

Several features have been incorporated into the design of this commentary. The following comments are intended to assist readers in making full use of this volume.

Pericopes of Scripture

The scriptural text has been divided into pericopes, or passages, usually several verses in length. Each of these pericopes is given a heading, which appears at the beginning of the pericope. For example, the first pericope in the commentary on Luke is "1:1-4 The Prologue." This heading is followed by the Scripture passage quoted in the Revised Standard Version (RSV) across the full width of the page. The Scripture passage is provided for the convenience of readers, but it is also in keeping with medieval patristic commentaries, in which the citations of the Fathers were arranged around the text of Scripture.

Overviews

Following each pericope of text is an overview of the patristic comments on that pericope. The format of this overview varies within the volumes of this series, depending on the requirements of the specific book of Scripture. The function of the overview is to provide a brief summary of all the comments to follow. It tracks a reasonably cohesive thread of argument among patristic comments, even though they are derived from diverse sources and generations. Thus the summaries do not proceed chronologically or by verse sequence. Rather they seek to rehearse the overall course of the patristic comment on that pericope.

We do not assume that the commentators themselves anticipated or expressed a formally received cohesive argument but rather that the various arguments tend to flow in a plausible, recognizable pattern. Modern readers can thus glimpse aspects of continuity in the flow of diverse exegetical traditions representing various generations and geographical locations.

Topical Headings

An abundance of varied patristic comment is available for each pericope of these letters. For this reason we have broken the pericopes into two levels. First is the verse with its topical heading. The patristic comments are then focused on aspects of each verse, with topical headings summarizing the essence of the patristic comment by evoking a key phrase, metaphor or idea. This feature provides a bridge by which modern readers can enter into the heart of the patristic comment.

Identifying the Patristic Texts

Following the topical heading of each section of comment, the name of the patristic commentator is given. An English translation of the patristic comment is then provided. This is immediately followed by the title of the patristic work and the textual reference—either by book, section and subsection or by book-and-verse references.

The Footnotes

Readers who wish to pursue a deeper investigation of the patristic works cited in this commentary will find the footnotes especially valuable. A footnote number directs the reader to the notes at the bottom of the right-hand column, where in addition to other notations (clarifications or biblical cross references) one will find information on English translations (where available) and standard original-language editions of the work cited. An abbreviated citation (normally citing the book, volume and page number) of the work is provided except in cases where a line-by-line commentary is being quoted, in which case the biblical references will lead directly to the selection. A key to the abbreviations is provided on page xv. Where there is any serious ambiguity or textual problem in the selection, we have tried to reflect the best available textual tradition.

Where original language texts have remained untranslated into English, we provide new translations. Wherever current English translations are already well rendered, they are utilized, but where necessary they are stylistically updated. A single asterisk (*) indicates that a previous English translation has been updated to modern English or amended for easier reading. The double asterisk (**) indicates either that a new translation has been provided or that some extant translation has been significantly amended. We have standardized spellings and made grammatical variables uniform so that our English references will not reflect the odd spelling variables of the older English translations. For ease of reading we have in some cases edited out superfluous conjunctions.

For the convenience of computer database users the digital database references are provided to either the Thesaurus Linguae Graecae (Greek texts) or to the Cetedoc (Latin texts) in the appendix found on pages 395-99.

ABBREVIATIONS

ACW	Ancient Christian Writers: The Works of the Fathers in Translation. Mahwah, N.J.: Paulist, 1946-.
AHSIS	*The Ascetical Homilies of Saint Isaac the Syrian.* Edited by Dana Miller. Boston, Mass.: Holy Transfiguration Monastery, 1984.
ANF	A. Roberts and J. Donaldson, eds. Ante-Nicene Fathers. 10 vols. Buffalo, N.Y.: Christian Literature, 1885-1896. Reprint, Grand Rapids, Mich.: Eerdmans, 1951-1956. Reprint, Peabody, Mass.: Hendrickson, 1994.
ARL	St. Athanasius. *The Resurrection Letters.* Paraphrased and introduced by Jack N. Sparks. Nashville: Thomas Nelson, 1979.
CCL	Corpus Christianorum. Series Latina. Turnhout, Belgium: Brepols, 1953-.
Cetedoc	Centre de Traitement Électronique des Documents
CGSL	Cyril of Alexandria. *Commentary on the Gospel of St. Luke.* Translated by R. Payne Smith. Long Island, N.Y.: Studion Publishers, Inc., 1983.
CPG	*Clavis Patrum Graecorum.* Edited by M. Geerard. Turnhout, Belgium: Brepols, 1974-1987.
CS	Cistercian Studies. Kalamazoo, Mich.: Cistercian Publications, 1973-.
CSCO	Corpus Scriptorum Christianorum Orientalium. Louvain, Belgium, 1903-.
CSEL	Corpus Scriptorum Ecclesiasticorum Latinorum. Vienna, Austria, 1866-.
EBT	*The Explanation by Blessed Theophylact of the Holy Gospel According to St. Matthew.* Introduction by Fr. Christopher Stade. House Springs, Miss.: Chrysostom Press, 1992.
ECTD	*Saint Ephrem's Commentary on Tatian's Diatessaron: An English Translation of Chester Beatty Syriac MS 709.* Translated and edited by C. McCarthy. Journal of Semitic Studies Supplement 2. Oxford: Oxford University Press for the University of Manchester, 1993.
EHG	St. Ambrose of Milan. *Exposition of the Holy Gospel According to Saint Luke with Fragments on the Prophecy of Isaias.* Translated by T. Tomkinson. Etna, Calif.: Center for Traditionalist Orthodox Studies, 1998.
FC	Fathers of the Church: A New Translation. Washington, D.C.: Catholic University of America Press, 1947-.
FM	*The Festal Menaion.* Translated by Mother Mary and Archimandrite Kallistos Ware. Introduction by Georges Florovsky. London: Faber, 1969.
FGFR	*Faith Gives Fullness to Reasoning: The Five Theological Orations of Gregory Nazianzen.* Introduction and commentary by F. W. Norris. Leiden and New York: E. J. Brill, 1990.
GCS	Die griechischen christlichen Schriftsteller der ersten Jahrhunderte. Berlin: Akademie-Verlag, 1897-.
HCCC	Eusebius. *History of the Church from Christ to Constantine.* Translated by G. A. Williamson. New York: New York University Press, 1966.
HOP	Ephrem the Syrian. *Hymns on Paradise.* Translated by S. Brock. Crestwood, N.Y.: St. Vladimir's Seminary Press, 1990.

JCC   John Cassian. *Conferences*. Translated by Colm Luibheid. Classics of Western Spirituality. Mahwah, N.J.: Paulist, 1985.

LCC   J. Baillie et al., eds. The Library of Christian Classics. 26 vols. Philadelphia: Westminster Press, 1953-1966.

LCL   Loeb Classical Library. Cambridge, Mass.: Harvard University Press; London: Heinemann, 1912-.

MFC   Message of the Fathers of the Church. Edited by Thomas Halton. Collegeville, Minn.: The Liturgical Press, 1983-.

NPNF   P. Schaff et al., eds. A Select Library of the Nicene and Post-Nicene Fathers of the Christian Church. 2 series (14 vols. each). Buffalo, N.Y.: Christian Literature, 1887-1894. Reprint, Grand Rapids, Mich.: Eerdmans, 1952-1956. Reprint, Peabody, Mass.: Hendrickson, 1994.

OSW   *Origen: An Exhortation to Martyrdom, Prayer and Selected Writings.* New York: Paulist, 1979.

PDCW   *Pseudo-Dionysius: The Complete Works.* Translated by Colm Luibheid. Classics of Western Spirituality. New York: Paulist, 1987.

PG   J.-P. Migne, ed. Patrologiae cursus completus. Series Graeca. 166 vols. Paris: Migne, 1857-1886.

PL   J.-P. Migne, ed. Patrologiae cursus completus. Series Latina. 221 vols. Paris: Migne, 1844-1864.

POG   Eusebius. *The Proof of the Gospel.* Translated by W. J. Ferrar. London: SPCK, 1920. Reprint, Grand Rapids, Mich.: Baker, 1981.

SC   H. de Lubac, J. Daniélou et al., eds. Sources Chrétiennes. Paris: Éditions du Cerf, 1941-.

SNTD   Symeon the New Theologian. *The Discourses.* Translated by C. J. de Catanzaro. Classics of Western Spirituality. New York: Paulist, 1980.

SSGF   *The Sunday Sermons of the Great Fathers: A Manual of Preaching, Spiritual Reading and Meditation.* Translated and edited by M. F. Toal. 4 vols. Chicago: Henry Regnery, 1958. Reprint, Swedesboro, N.J.: Preservation Press, 1996.

TTH   G. Clark, M. Gibson and M. Whitby, eds. Translated Texts for Historians. Liverpool: Liverpool University Press, 1985-.

WSA   J. E. Rotelle, ed. *The Works of St. Augustine: A Translation for the Twenty-First Century.* Hyde Park, N.Y.: New City Press, 1990-.

INTRODUCTION TO LUKE

The context of Luke's narrative raises many of the same questions for a first-century audience as for a modern audience. For whom was Luke's Gospel written? What is the setting in which the Gospel was received? How was it used in the church's life? What was Luke's purpose in writing the Gospel? Having written a modern scholarly commentary on the Gospel, I now seek to read Luke through the eyes of the early church fathers.

The process of reading Luke with the church fathers places special challenges on us. It requires that we suspend to some extent our modern understanding about what a Bible commentary must sound like and enter a world that is closer to the biblical world than our own is. Many of the questions modern commentators face are not the questions ancient commentators were addressing. Ancient commentaries on Luke were not done for the academy but for the church. The early Fathers addressed theological controversies as pastors, not as academicians, even though their analyses were deeply theological. Their exposition of Scripture demonstrated a pastoral concern for the salvation of their flock by confessing the Christian faith in its truth and purity and expressing in their interpretation the coherence of divine revelation with the apostolic kerygma. The historical and grammatical questions they faced were only a means toward the more important work of christological interpretation that led to preaching the gospel. Their exegesis of Luke is contained in sermons, theological treatises, pastoral letters and catechetical lectures and therefore is primarily theological and pastoral. Patristic exegesis of Luke's Gospel reminds us that the gospel is always heard and interpreted within a worshiping community.

Where to Find Luke Among the Fathers

To begin, where might we find explorations of Luke among the Fathers? Although it is said that certain Fathers wrote commentaries on various books of the Bible, most patristic commentaries, and this includes all the commentaries on Luke's Gospel, were compilations of homilies that the Fathers preached on Luke. And what we have of Luke is very little, and for Mark even less. When the Fathers compiled their comments on the Gospels, it was Matthew and John who were the favorites, particularly among the Eastern Fathers. For Luke there are four commentaries, all of them collections of homilies: Origen (185-254), Ambrose of Milan (339-397), Cyril of Alexandria (375-444) and the Venerable Bede (673-735).[1] Fragments of a commentary by Titus of Bostra, a fourth-century theologian, appear in later catenae, and like other patristic commentaries on Luke, this too was a compilation of sermons. The commentaries by Origen,[2] Cyril of Alexandria[3] and Ambrose[4] have all been translated into English. Other early commentaries

---

[1]Tertullian's book 4 of *Against Marcion* could have been the first Lukan commentary. See C. H. Talbert, "Gospel of Luke," in *Biblical Interpretation*, ed. John H. Hayes, 2 vols. (Nashville: Abingdon, 1999), 2:92.

[2]Origen, *Homilies on Luke, Fragments on Luke*, trans. J. T. Lienhard, in *The Fathers of the Church*, vol. 94 (Washington, D.C.: The Catholic University of America Press, 1996).

[3]Cyril of Alexandria, *Commentary on the Gospel of St. Luke*, trans. R. Payne Smith (Long Island, N.Y.: Studion, 1983).

[4]Ambrose of Milan, *Exposition of the Holy Gospel According to Saint Luke*, trans. Theodosia Tomkinson (Etna, Calif.: Center for Traditionalist Orthodox Studies, 1998).

include Theophylact, an eleventh-century Byzantine exegete, Euthymius Zigabenus, an early twelfth-century Byzantine theologian, and Walafrid Strabo, a ninth-century German theological writer, all of whom are outside the time period designated by this series.

With so few patristic commentaries on Luke, to read him with the church fathers is to read him as he is used by them in the cut and thrust of their pastoral lives. This means that one must read their sermons, catechetical lectures, letters and theological discourses. Here one sees how capable the Fathers were in using Scripture, and this is without the lexical aids that we have at our disposal today. It is very rare that one will find the Fathers using Luke without reference to other biblical texts. The whole range of Scripture was intrinsic to their theological vocabulary. Scripture found its place in their pastoral conversation whether in preaching or letters or hymnody or theological debate. To let Scripture interpret Scripture was more than a hermeneutical principle to them—it was at the heart of what it meant to use Scripture pastorally. Thus we find them constantly using the third Gospel along with other biblical passages to offer pastoral counsel and admonition to the people of God.

The Homiletical Use of Luke's Gospel Among the Church Fathers

It is in preaching that one sees the Fathers' use of Scripture most clearly and distinctly. Preaching had teaching, edifying and moral functions. It was didactic, teaching the people of God the literal meaning of the text; kerygmatic, proclaiming to them its spiritual and pastoral meaning; and paraenetic, exhorting them to live lives that reflected the Christ who dwelled among them and within them. Preaching was also liturgical as it proclaimed a living reality in a eucharistic community whose life was centered around baptism and whose homiletical traditions were biblical and rigorous. William Harmless's recent book *Augustine and the Catechumenate* not only illustrates this but also provides a window into the catechetical and homiletical life of Augustine's congregation as he uses Scripture in his teaching and preaching.[5] For example, Augustine's pastoral admonition from a sermon entitled "On the Value of Repentance," preached around 391, uses the parable of the Pharisee and tax collector from Luke 18 as the text for his sermon. Augustine weaves the text throughout his comments, and even though this is a commentary on the text, its pastoral character is self-evident. He uses the metaphor of healing to describe the effects of repentance.[6]

As we read Augustine's sermons (and this is true of all the Fathers), we must always bear in mind that we are not hearing the sophisticated and detailed argument of a theologian addressing scholarly peers. Rather, we are eavesdropping on the intimate conversation of a bishop, in his most pastoral role, as he speaks to the people of God, baptized and unbaptized, about Jesus Christ and God's intentions for them in this new creation God brings in Christ. This is pastoral care in its most primary and significant manifestation. This is why it was said that for centuries, liturgy was the most important form of pastoral care, and preaching was the primary place for the pastor to use Scripture in shaping a life in Christ for catechumens preparing for baptism and the ongoing catechetical life of the baptized. Augustine understood how his community needed to hear what the Bible had to say about life in Christ and how the primary place for

---

[5]William Harmless, *Augustine and the Catechumenate* (Collegeville, Minn.: Pueblo, 1995).

[6]Augustine, *Sermons on Various Subjects* 3.10, sermons 341-400, from *The Works of Saint Augustine: A Translation for the Twenty-first Century*, trans. Edmund Hill (Hyde Park, N.Y.: New City Press, 1995), p. 118.

Scripture in the life of the church is in the work of preaching and teaching within the church's corporate worship life.

In Augustine's sermons, there is a remarkable resonance between his thought and the Lukan text, particularly as Augustine (as well as the other early Fathers) accent Jesus' teaching on charity as the primary way in which one lives out the Christian life. Christ provided the pattern for the life of sacrifice in his sacrificial life and death, a sacrifice that is centered in his life of mercy and compassion that is so clearly expressed in his teachings about charity, almsgiving and forgiveness. This is evident in Luke's emphatic social concern as expressed in his abundant material pertaining to the proper use of possessions and his concern for the poor. This is why patristic exegesis on Luke by Augustine and others used much of Lukan material for pastoral admonition before and during the period of Lent, as the catechumens and the baptized prepared for the celebration of new life at Easter.

As one might suspect, Luke's Gospel was the obvious choice during the Christmas season because of the unique narratives associated with Jesus' infancy and childhood. This is evident from the Jerusalem lectionary, where Matthew's Gospel is most prominent throughout the year, but Luke takes a prominent place during Christmas, Easter and the major feasts of Christ's life (e.g., circumcision, presentation, annunciation); Luke's Gospel was the natural choice.[7] This is also true of the Easter week, when Luke's rich resurrection narratives are read for Easter Monday, Tuesday and Wednesday.[8] During Holy Week, the account of the Passion is read from all four Gospels.[9] Luke's text appeared in the earliest lectionaries in Jerusalem and Syria. His Gospel was as well represented as the others. For example, in Mosul, a city located on the right bank of the Tigris River in present-day Iraq, a Nestorian lectionary arises out of Syriac Christianity. Like earlier lectionaries, it follows a continuous reading of Old and New Testament books, and Luke is featured in the post-Pentecost season.[10]

The Hermeneutical Use of Luke Among the Church Fathers

Augustine's preaching is just one example of how the Fathers used Scripture in their preaching and teaching. What is remarkable about the hermeneutical approach of the Fathers is that their primary purpose was not to comment on Scripture as to its historical or grammatical significance. This does not mean that they did not consider the Scripture to be historically accurate or that they were unable to engage in grammatical analysis. Rather, the goal of the Fathers was to comment on the Scripture as to its theological or spiritual significance in the context of pastoral preaching. In this way they are following the example of the apostles, who in turn follow the pattern of the Lord's teaching. When Jesus opened the Scriptures to the Emmaus disciples and interpreted the Old Testament in terms of himself, particularly his death and resurrection, he

---

[7]See Hughes Oliphant Old, *The Reading and Preaching of the Scriptures in the Worship of the Christian Church*, vol. 2: *The Patristic Age* (Grand Rapids, Mich.: Eerdmans, 1998), p. 147, where in the Jerusalem lectionary the annunciation, visitation, birth of Jesus and circumcision are all celebrated during January with Lukan texts.

[8]Ibid., p. 158, where the texts from Luke are as follows: Easter Monday, Luke 23:50—24:12; Easter Tuesday, Luke 24:13-35; Easter Wednesday, Luke 24:36-40.

[9]Ibid., p. 154.

[10]Ibid., pp. 277-99; Old describes the Syriac lectionaries, especially on pp. 284-86, where he lists the following texts in the post-Pentecost season: Luke 10:23-42; 6:12-47; 12:16-35; 12:57—13:18; 13:22-35; 14:1-15; 15:4-32; John 9:1-39; Mark 7:1-24; Luke 16:19—17:11; 17:5-20; 18:2-15; 18:35—19:11.

set the stage for how Scripture should be read and interpreted by the emerging Christian communities. Exegesis was first and foremost christological. The evangelistic sermons of Acts and the kerygmatic and paraenetic sermons of the apostles in their letters continued this christological hermeneutic. Scripture was God's book to reveal him to the church so that in reading and interpreting his words, God's people, as Augustine says, might delight in the Trinity. As Paul says to the Galatians, Scripture is like a living being, having a mind that knows ahead of time that the gospel must be preached to Abraham (Gal 3:8). Scripture is alive because it is God-breathed, and its life is still active in the church that reads and preaches Scripture as the way Christ continues to be present among his people in the flesh.

Reading Luke's Gospel with the church fathers forces us to come to grips with what it means to read the whole of Scripture with them. The reading of Scripture in the life of early Christian communities was liturgical and pastoral. Scripture was read in the context of a worship community, and it formed the basis for the pastoral homily. The early Christian sermon was primarily expository, explaining the texts of the day to those gathered in expectation of hearing the Word of God read and proclaimed. Old Testament readings formed the core of Scripture read in worshiping communities, since New Testament documents were still in the process of collation and distribution. The Old Testament was interpreted christologically through typological exegesis that embraced a cosmology that was shot through with the Creator's presence. In the liturgy of morning and evening prayer, the Old Testament seemed to be the primary text. The reading of the Gospel was primary in the Sunday eucharistic liturgies, with readings from the Acts of the Apostles and the letters of Paul, Peter, James and John as secondary and supplementary to readings from the Old Testament and the Gospel.

Today's exegetes seem to find themselves in a context different from that of the ancient interpreter. Modern and postmodern exegesis is scientific in character and takes place primarily in academies of learning. Modern commentaries use the latest research in history, philology and literary criticism to carefully analyze texts to determine meaning. Application of texts to people's lives is a secondary matter at best and is better left to pastors and teachers in churches and parochial schools. But for the ancient church fathers, Scripture had a much different place than it does in our world.

Although no one questions that modern exegesis has provided enormous insights into the biblical text and biblical world, serious discussion is taking place within the academy about the impact of historical criticism upon the understanding of Scripture within the church. Two notable books that are exploring the effects of higher criticism on the life of the church are *Biblical Interpretation in Crisis: The Ratzinger Conference on Bible and Church* and *Reclaiming the Bible for the Church*.[11] Both books explore a return to a classic hermeneutic that George Lindbeck calls the *sensus fidelium*, the consensus of the faithful as the body of Christ that is normalized by a confession of biblical truths that are unifying and community-building. This is a call for exegesis done in a premodern ecclesial context, a hermeneutical approach that Lindbeck hopes will be recovered within the church today. Here is how he articulates his hope:

The Bible read classically but not anticritically can come to inform the *sensus fidelium*. The condition for this hap-

---

[11]Richard John Neuhaus, ed., *Biblical Interpretation in Crisis: The Ratzinger Conference on Bible and Church* (Grand Rapids, Mich.: Eerdmans, 1989); Carl E. Braaten and Robert W. Jenson, eds., *Reclaiming the Bible for the Church* (Grand Rapids, Mich.: Eerdmans, 1995).

pening is that communities of interpretation come into existence in which pastors, biblical scholars, theologians, and laity together seek God's guidance in the written word for their communal as well as individual lives. Their reading of Scripture will be within the context of a worship life which, in its basic eucharistic, baptismal, and kerygmatic patterns, accords with that of the first centuries. . . . This is a dream, a cloud no larger than a hand on the horizon, and yet if it began to be actualized, even if in only a few and scattered places, it would be living proof that Scripture is a unifying and followable text. The news would travel quickly (it always does in our day), and its influence would mushroom. Public opinion might be widely affected, perhaps even quickly, in all communions, and the transformation of the *sensus fidelium* (which takes longer) might follow in due course.[12]

This *sensus fidelium* is pastoral, and to read Luke with the Fathers is to see his pastoral use among them. To see this pastoral use of Luke in action, we begin with two of the four commentaries that we have on Luke. Both are collections of sermons, and they date from different periods in early Christian history. Origen is the first full collection of sermons, even though we have some isolated sermons from the Second Epistle of Clement (125) on Isaiah 54:1, an Easter sermon from Melito of Sardis (130-190) on the meaning of the Passover for Christians and a sermon from Clement of Alexandria (150-215) on Mark 10:17-31 about the rich ruler, for which there is a parallel in Luke 18:18-30. The other commentary is from Cyril of Alexandria, a mature theologian who is known as much for his defense of orthodox Christology and classic trinitarian theology as he is for his biblical commentaries, even though as a commentator he is perhaps the most prolific of all the church fathers.

As is the case with all early Christian preaching, these church fathers did not typically write down their sermons and read them to their congregations but preached them without a manuscript. They were recorded by stenographers who would edit them for later publication. This style of delivery followed Jewish and Hellenistic practice. In some ways, this makes their use of Scripture even more remarkable as they recalled biblical passages from memory as they were preaching their sermons. This is also one reason why their quotations of Scripture are not always as faithful to the exact wording of the biblical text as are the modern preacher's.[13] These sermons are predominately expository in nature, that is, line-by-line commentaries on the primary text of the day, with some secondary texts providing interpretive insight. The reading of Luke was based on a *lectio continua* (continuous reading) in which the reader would be responsible for deciding how far to read, and in most cases this was done in consultation with the preacher.[14] That is why compiling sermons for a commentary made sense since the preaching on a Gospel followed the orderly pattern of a continuous reading of that Gospel. Therefore some texts will overlap from one sermon to another, and a fluid commentary is possible from this homiletical and liturgical approach. The normal length of a sermon was an hour, which allowed the preacher time to develop his points exegetically and pastorally.

---

[12]George Lindbeck, "Scripture, Consensus and Community," in *Biblical Interpretation in Crisis: The Ratzinger Conference on Bible and the Church*, ed. Richard John Neuhaus (Grand Rapids, Mich.: Eerdmans, 1989), pp. 99-100.

[13]Hughes Oliphant Old, *The Reading and Preaching of the Scriptures in the Worship of the Christian Church*, vol. 1: *The Biblical Period* (Grand Rapids, Mich.: Eerdmans, 1998), p. 282 n. 67.

[14]Ibid., p. 315; also, in *Patristic Age*, pp. 135-66 and pp. 277-95, Old describes the Jerusalem and Syriac lectionaries as *lectio continua* with some exceptions. However, this is a transitional period between the earlier period, where *lectio continua* was the norm, and the time of John of Damascus, when a *lectio selecta* (selected reading) was firmly in place. For church fathers like Augustine and Cyril of Alexandria, the lectionary is a combination of both.

Origen's Thirty-Nine Homilies on Luke

The oldest commentary on Luke is a series of thirty-nine homilies by Origen, thirty-three of which cover the first four chapters (with the infancy narratives taking twenty of those sermons), and six more on various texts from the rest of the Gospel (Lk 10:25-37; 12:57-59; 17:20-21, 33; 19:29-40; 19:41-45; 20:21-40). These thirty-nine sermons were part of a larger number of sermons that covered the entire Gospel, as many as 150 or more, mostly lost. These are expository in character, preached during morning and evening prayer as part of a *lectio continua* on the Gospel. They appear to have been written during Origen's Caeasarean period and preserved in that church's library. Ambrose seems to have used them in his preaching on Luke's Gospel. Jerome translated Origen's Greek originals into Latin, and it is only Jerome's translation of Origen's homilies through the fourth chapter of Luke that survived the Justinian purge of Origen's works.[15]

Much has been written about Origen's allegorical interpretations of Scripture, and a discussion of his hermeneutical methods is best left for scholars who have made a study of Origen their life's work. As one reads Origen's use of Luke, it is striking that a literal reading of the text is more common than an allegorical one and that the goal of spiritual exegesis is to highlight its christological meaning. Robert Wilken, in *Remembering the Christian Past*, comments on the Alexandrian versus Antiochene interpretation of the prophets, particularly as these approaches are represented in Origen and Theodore of Mopsuestia. Theodore describes Origen's hermeneutics as "inebriated" exegesis, and Wilken notes that for Theodore "the presupposition for 'good exegesis of the biblical text,' that is, 'historical-grammatical' exegesis, was knowledge of the historical circumstances. Hence, the Old Testament must be interpreted in its own setting, not in relation to the New Testament."[16]

Wilken also notes, however, that "Origen cheerfully acknowledged that the words of the prophets have not been fulfilled in the way they were thought to take place." Wilken sides with Origen, not Theodore, and not because he rejects the historical-grammatical method and endorses allegory but because he sees in Origen a faithful expression of the intent of Scripture: "If Jesus of Nazareth was the Messiah, as the Scriptures taught, the prophecies about the Messianic age had already been fulfilled, and it was the task of biblical interpreters to discover what the scriptural promises meant in light of this new fact. Paradoxically, in the language of early Christian exegesis, the spiritual sense *was* the historical sense."[17]

This spiritual sense is nothing more than a christological hermeneutic that comes to fulfillment in the preaching of the Word as God's people are gathered together around that Word. Hughes Oliphant Old in *The Reading and Preaching of the Scriptures in the Worship of the Christian Church* notes that Werner Schutz, a renowned Origen scholar, "suggests that in the reading and preaching of Scripture Origen recognized a certain 'Epiphanie Jesu' ["Epiphany of Jesus"], by which he understood . . . the kerygmatic presence of Christ in worship. When the Scriptures are read and preached in worship, then Christ is present and

---

[15]This paragraph is indebted to Old, *Biblical Period*, pp. 321-22.

[16]Robert Wilken, *Remembering the Christian Past* (Grand Rapids, Mich.: Eerdmans, 1995), p. 107. It must be noted that this dichotomy between Alexandrine and Antiochene exegesis has been challenged. Wilken states, "Indeed, students of Patristics who actually read the texts associated with the ancient debate rather than a textbook synopsis often find themselves confused. . . . Sometimes Alexandrian exegesis is more literal than Antiochene exegesis and sometimes Antiochene exegetes use allegory" (quoted in John J. O'Keefe, " 'A Letter That Killeth': Toward a Reassessment of Antiochene Exegesis, or Diodore, Theodore and Theodoret on the Psalms," *Journal of Early Christian Studies* 8, no. 1 (2000): 88.

[17]Wilken, *Remembering the Christian Past*, pp. 118-19.

feeds the congregation with spiritual bread and wine."[18]

In asking how Origen read Luke, it is important to consider the liturgical context in which that preaching took place, particularly since Origen is the first large collection of sermons made into a commentary. Pierre Nautin, another noted Origen scholar, provides a valuable map for understanding the liturgical context for Origen's preaching. Here is Old's summary of Nautin's findings about the three worship settings for Origen's sermons:

1. There was the weekly service on the Lord's Day which included three readings from Scripture—one from the Old Testament; one from the apostles, that is, from one of the New Testament epistles or Acts; and finally one from one of the four Gospels—each of which was followed by a short sermon. The ministry of the Word was then followed by prayers and the Eucharist. Nautin figures that by the time of Origen the reading of a lesson from the Law followed by a lesson from the Prophets had already been consolidated into a single lesson.

2. The second type of service was the midweek eucharistic service held on Wednesday and Friday afternoons. These services concluded the weekly fast days observed by Christians at that period. At these services, according to Nautin, there was a reading from the Gospels and perhaps one from the apostles, but probably not from the Old Testament.

3. Finally there was a third type of service, the daily morning prayer service at which there was a reading from the Old Testament and, following it, an hour-long sermon, but no New Testament reading. Only these services were open to catechumens, according to Nautin.

Nautin has figured out the average length of the text for each of the sermons which has come down to us, and on the basis of that how long it would take to preach through the Old Testament and the Gospels, respectively. The whole Old Testament could be preached through in three years, Nautin estimates, as could the four Gospels. Nautin figures there was a third cycle, the apostles, which could also be preached through in three years.[19]

Old takes issue with Nautin on some of his observations—for example, that in the daily morning service only catechumens heard the preaching from the Old Testament. He also asserts that there must have been an evening service that corresponded to the morning service and that it was in this service or the Sunday Eucharist that the sermons from Origen on Luke's Gospel are handed down to us. For Old, it is likely that Origen preached through Luke's Gospel without any time constraints, since there was only a rudimentary church year in place at this time.[20] Thus to read Luke with Origen is to read him as many Christians have read him throughout the centuries—in the context of a worshiping community that has an agreed-upon method for reading Scripture.

Cyril of Alexandria's Commentary on Luke

Cyril's commentary is a compilation of 150 sermons on the Gospel of Luke which he preached from a *lectio continua*, containing more than fifteen hundred citations from Scripture. Old describes his sermons as "doctrinal preaching" as well as "the preaching of the Christian life."[21] They follow the expository tradition of the

---

[18]Old, *Biblical Period*, p. 341, citing W. Schutz, *Der christliche Gottesdienst bei Origenes* (Stuttgart: Calwer Verlag, 184), pp. 17ff., 76ff.
[19]Old, *Biblical Period*, pp. 341-42, citing P. Nautin, *Origene, sa Vie et Son Oeuvre* (Paris: Beauchesne, 1977), pp. 389-412.
[20]Old, *Biblical Period*, pp. 344-45.

Fathers, and the style of preaching resembles synagogue midrash more than Greek oration. Following rabbinical tradition, these sermons often have a secondary text that serves as the "key to his interpretation of the primary lesson."[22] Concerning their doctrinal character, Old comments:

> Cyril never missed the opportunity to point out the doctrinal implications of the passage under discussion. One must remark, of course, that this is quite in accord with the intentions of the Gospel writers themselves. One can hardly accuse Cyril of imposing doctrine on the simple story of the Gospels. He is clearly treating the Gospel texts as the original authors intended them to be treated. As the Gospel of John puts it, "These [things] are written that you may believe that Jesus is the Christ, the Son of God, and that believing you may have life in his name" (John 20:31). The Gospels intend to teach doctrine; particularly they intend to make clear who Jesus really was. That is, the Gospels are particularly concerned to teach Christology, the doctrine of the person and work of Christ.[23]

An example of Cyril's doctrinal preaching occurs in his comments on Jesus' temptations in the garden of Gethsemane, particularly concerning Jesus' grief. It is clear that Cyril sees this passage from Luke 22 as part of Luke's Christology.[24] Cyril of Alexandria's contributions to a patristic reading of Luke's Gospel in his accent on the proclamation of the Christian life conforms to a general pattern among all the Fathers. Matthew's Sermon on the Mount was a focus for the Fathers in preaching the life of Christ, but Luke's Sermon on the Plain was also foundational in the development of this theme. What is remarkable about Cyril's understanding of the Sermon on the Mount/Sermon on the Plain is that he is more inclined to interpret it christologically as gospel than as law and moral guide.

The Jewish community of Alexandria was very old and very strong in Cyril's day, and a Christian theologian in that city had to be very clear as to exactly what the difference was between the law and the gospel. One problem many Christian interpreters of the Sermon on the Mount have had is that they try to make it into a Christian law. During the Enlightenment this problem was doubly severe. It is clear that Cyril has no intention of making that error; whether he has discovered the Sermon on the Mount as gospel is another matter.[25]

Cyril's comments on the oft-quoted verse by all the Fathers from the Sermon on the Plain, "But I say unto you which hear, Love your enemies, do good to them which hate you" (Lk 6:27). He not only interprets this verse christologically but also uses the same constellation of texts from Luke and Acts that other church fathers, notably Augustine, use to demonstrate how one might be able to accomplish such an extraordinary thing: Jesus' words from the cross (Lk 23) and Stephen's words as he is stoned (Acts 7). Cyril's conclusion is pastoral, applying these difficult words to the lives of ordinary Christians, demonstrating the genius of patristic exegesis for the life of the church.[26]

Passages Unique to Luke's Gospel

As one reads Luke with the church fathers, there are many passages that one would expect them to cite.

---

[21]This section on Cyril of Alexandria is indebted to Old, *Patristic Age*, pp. 114-25.

[22]Ibid., p. 115.

[23]Ibid., p. 114.

[24]Cyril of Alexandria, *Commentary on the Gospel of St. Luke*, p. 583.

[25]Old, *Patristic Age*, p. 125.

[26]Cyril of Alexandria, *Commentary on the Gospel of St. Luke*, pp. 135-36.

Heavy emphasis is placed on the frame of the Gospel, that is, Luke's beginning and his end, since Luke 1—2 and Luke 24 are unique to his Gospel. In the infancy narratives, there are repeated references to the annunciation and the words of the angel to Mary that the Holy Spirit will come upon her (Lk 1:35). Since virginity is a strong theme among the Fathers, Mary is the model par excellence for those who have taken the vow of virginity. The words of the angels at the birth of Jesus, "Glory to God in the highest, and on earth peace among men with whom he is pleased!" (Lk 2:14), are used in many different contexts, often unrelated to the birth of Jesus, but used to illustrate the meaning of "peace among men." Simeon and Anna are of great interest to the church fathers, Simeon for his accent on the Gentiles and Anna as an example of widows, another favorite topic for sermons. Although the Emmaus story receives frequent reference (Lk 24:13-35), as well as Jesus' final words to the disciples before he ascends into heaven (Lk 24:44-49), by far the most popular passage in Luke 24, and perhaps in the Gospel, are the words of Jesus to the Eleven when they are gathered in the upper room: "See my hands and my feet, that it is I myself; handle me, and see; for a spirit has not flesh and bones as you see that I have" (Lk 24:39). For example, this is used as a proof text by Augustine against the Manicheans to demonstrate that Jesus has flesh and blood and is not simply a spirit.

Other frequently cited passages that come as no surprise are the words of Jesus from the cross that are uniquely Lukan, particularly "Father, forgive them; for they know not what they do" (Lk 23:34), used especially as an illustration of how we should forgive our enemies, as Cyril demonstrated, and the words to the penitent thief, "Truly, I say to you, today you will be with me in Paradise" (Lk 23:43). Jesus' final words to his disciples after the institution of the Holy Supper and his suffering in Gethsemane are also a rich source of material, particularly Jesus' promise to Peter that even though he will deny him, Peter will repent and strengthen his brothers, for Jesus is praying for Peter and the other disciples. And the parables of the good Samaritan, the prodigal son, the unjust steward, and the Pharisee and the tax collector are also frequently cited, with some complete sermons on these texts that explicate the entire passage. What is clear from the Fathers is a discerning recognition of what is unique to Luke among the Gospels. They use this Lukan material as a rich resource for their preaching and teaching.

There are some passages in Luke that are frequently cited but which for us seem rather obscure. Perhaps the most frequently quoted passage in Luke is from Jesus' temple teaching against the Sadducees about the resurrection, the only time in the Gospel when Jesus addresses the Sadducees by name. The part of Jesus' teaching that is highlighted is this: "The sons of this age marry and are given in marriage; but those who are accounted worthy to attain to that age and to the resurrection from the dead neither marry nor are given in marriage, for they cannot die any more, because they are equal to angels and are sons of God, being sons of the resurrection" (Lk 20:34-36). What is of particular interest to the Fathers, East and West, is that those who are faithful hearers of the Word will, in the age to come, be equal to angels. This equality with angels provided a fecund source for the Fathers' reflection on the character of our heavenly life in Christ. An equally popular verse from Luke, cited in all kinds of different contexts but clearly aimed at giving comfort to Christians who are being persecuted, are the words from Jesus in the first part of his discourse on possessions in Luke 12, where he discusses persecution, possessions and hypocrisy in the same pericope. The oft-quoted words are these from Luke 12:7: "Why, even the hairs of your head are all numbered."

Moral Instruction

Although we may be comfortable with the expository style of the Fathers, the extensive use of Luke in paraenesis makes us uneasy. This is evident by the church fathers' use of Luke 6, the Sermon on the Plain, and Luke 12, 16 and 18, the loci for Luke's record of Jesus' discourses on the proper use of possessions. The Fathers might not call this a theology of stewardship, but they clearly see the need to preach about the relationship between life in Christ and the expression of that life in works of charity. Over and over again they will exhort the people of God to be busy in living the charitable life. In some cases, this instruction is largely moralistic in tone and purpose. But the majority of the exhortations to Christians about possessions or continence or perseverance flow out of a christological foundation that demonstrates how works of charity are a natural expression of the baptismal life in Christ. And as prime examples of these Christic virtues, the church fathers appeal to biblical and early Christian saints who reflected in their lives the characteristics of Christ.

As an illustration of this and as a fitting conclusion, we listen to a conflation of two sermons of Augustine, one from Lent and the other from the first Sunday after Easter, both of them on Luke 6:37-38, which Augustine uses to equate forgiveness with almsgiving, and almsgiving with forgiveness. In Lent and Easter, almsgiving is for Augustine and all the Fathers, *the* manifestation of the Christian life:

> The season of Lent has come round again, the time when I owe you my annual exhortation; and when you also owe the Lord your good works as suited to the season; not of course that they can be any use to the Lord, but they are of use to you . . . to our prayers we must add, by almsgiving and fasting, the wings of loving kindness, so that they may fly the more easily to God and reach him. For this the Christian mind can readily understand how far removed we should be from the fraudulent filching of other people's property; when it perceives how similar it is to fraud when you don't give to the needy what you don't need yourself. The Lord says, "Give, and it will be given to you; forgive, and you will be forgiven" (Lk 6:37-38). Let us practice these two sorts of almsgiving, namely, giving and forgiving, gently and generously; since after all we pray to the Lord that good things may be given to us, and that evil things may not be repaid us.[27] . . . Notice too, my brothers and sisters, what you say just before: "Forgive us our debts," in order to carry out what follows: "as we also forgive our debtors" (Mt 6:13, 12). You give alms, you receive alms; you pardon, you are pardoned; you are generous, you are treated generously. Listen to God saying, "Forgive, and you will be forgiven; give and all things will be given to you" (Lk 6:37-38). Keep the poor in mind. I say this to all of you; give alms, my brothers and sisters, and you won't lose what you give. Trust God. I'm not only telling you that you won't lose what you do for the poor; but I'm telling you plainly, this is all that you won't lose; you will lose the rest. Come now, let's see if you can cheer the poor up today. You be their granaries, so that God may give to you what you can give to them, and so that he may forgive whatever sins you have committed. "Shut an alms up in the hearts of the poor, and it will pay for you to the Lord" (Sir 29:12, Vulg), to whom be all honor and glory forever and ever. Amen.[28]

It is an honor to be part of this landmark event of giving pastors and laity access to the voices of the church fathers. Thanks to Thomas Oden for the privilege and opportunity to participate in the project. An

---

[27]Augustine, *Sermons on the Liturgical Seasons* 3.6, sermons 184-229Z, from *The Works of Saint Augustine: A Translation for the Twenty-First Century*, trans. Edmund Hill (Hyde Park, N.Y.: New City Press, 1195), p. 107.

[28]Augustine, *Sermons on Various Subjects* 3.10, sermons 341-400, p. 350.

effort of this magnitude would not have been possible without the enormous help of two research teams. Thanks to the staff of the ACCS office at Drew University, led by Joel Elowsky, especially Joel Scandrett, Michael Glerup, Calhoun Robertson, Alexei Khamine and Hsueh-Ming Liao, who were instrumental in gathering the texts that led to the selections in this volume, as well as editing the vast number of citations into a workable text. And thanks to the Fort Wayne team at Walther Library of Concordia Theological Seminary, led by Bob Smith, including Duane Bamsch, Craig Harmon, Jeffrey Ahonen, Piotr Malysz, Jason Braaten (the servant of the last hour who was also paid a denarius) and especially John-Paul Salay. Each person on this team scanned, edited, organized, provided footnotes and undertook numerous tasks to free me to pursue the joy of reading, selecting, marking and arranging these patristic citations into a comprehensible manuscript. It is my hope that the preaching and teaching of the church today will be renewed and refreshed by their efforts to make available the living words of the Fathers.

A. A. Just Jr.
June 11, 2002
Feast of St. Barnabas the Apostle

THE GOSPEL ACCORDING TO LUKE

1:1—24:53 PRELIMINARY REMARKS ON THE GOSPEL

OVERVIEW: From the beginning, Luke's Gospel was considered a historical narrative that accents themes that are recognized as Lukan to this day. The miracles of Jesus and his teaching on morals are highlighted as examples of Luke's historical detail. Luke frames his Gospel with priestly themes, beginning with Zechariah's levitical offering in the temple and concluding with the priestly victim, Jesus, the calf offered in sacrifice on the cross. The calf is the symbol for Luke's Gospel from the Apocalypse, placing the atonement at the center of the Gospel (AMBROSE). Luke the Antiochene, a physician acquainted with healing bodies, presents us with Jesus, whose blood provides the medicine of immortality. As his traveling companion, Paul claims Luke's Gospel as his own for its healing of souls (EUSEBIUS).

LUKE, THE PRIESTLY GOSPEL. AMBROSE: St. Luke kept a certain historical order and revealed to us more miracles of the Lord, yet so that the history of his Gospel embraced the virtue of all wisdom. For what more excellent truth did he reveal concerning natural wisdom than that the Holy Spirit also gave rise to the divine incarnation?[1] . . . He taught that the powers of heaven would be shaken,[2] that the Lord alone is the only-begotten Son of God, at whose passion darkness fell during the day so that the earth was darkened as night and the sun fled.[3] . . . As compared with the other Gospels, we see greater zeal devoted to the description of the events than to the expression of rules of behavior. And the Evangelist, writing in historical mode, makes his beginning in narrative form: "There was," he says, "in the days of Herod, the King of Judea, a certain priest named Zechariah,"[4] and he continues the story with a full and orderly description. Hence, those

---

[1]See Lk 1:35. [2]Lk 21:26. [3]Lk 23:44-45. [4]Lk 1:5.

who think that the four living creatures described in the Apocalypse[5] are to be understood as the four books of the gospel wish this book to be represented by the calf;[6] for the calf is the priestly victim. This Gospel is represented fittingly by the calf, because it begins with priests and ends with the Calf who, having taken upon himself the sins of all, was sacrificed for the life of the whole world.[7] He was a priestly Calf. He is both Calf and Priest. He is the Priest, because he is our Propitiator. We have him as an advocate with the Father.[8] He is the Calf, because he redeemed us with his own blood.[9] EXPOSITION OF THE GOSPEL OF LUKE 1.4, 7.[10]

THE GOSPEL PAUL CLAIMED. EUSEBIUS: Luke was by race an Antiochian and by profession a physician. He long had been a companion of Paul and had more than a casual acquaintance with the rest of the apostles. He left for us, in two inspired books, examples of the art of healing souls that he obtained from them. These books are, namely, the Gospel . . . the Acts of the Apostles, which he composed not from hearsay evidence but as demonstrated before his own eyes. They say that Paul was actually accustomed to quote the Gospel according to St. Luke. When writing about some Gospel as his own, he used to say, "According to my Gospel."[11] ECCLESIASTICAL HISTORY 3.4.[12]

---

[5]Ezek 1:5-12, 10:14; Rev 4:6-11. [6]The original word means "ox." [7]1 Pet 2:24; 1 Jn 2:2. [8]1 Jn 2:1. [9]Heb 9:12-14; Rev 5:9. [10]*EHG* 1-5*; CCL 14:1-5; CSEL 32 4:5-6, 8-9. [11]Rom 2:16; 16:25; 2 Tim 2:8. [12]FC 19:142-43**; PG 20:219-20.

1:1-4 THE PROLOGUE

[1]*Inasmuch as many have undertaken to compile a narrative of the things which have been accomplished among us,* [2]*just as they were delivered to us by those who from the beginning were eyewitnesses and ministers of the word,* [3]*it seemed good to me also, having followed all things closely[a] for some time past, to write an orderly account for you, most excellent Theophilus,* [4]*that you may know the truth concerning the things of which you have been informed.*

a Or *accurately*

OVERVIEW: The Holy Spirit has given the church one gospel in four books (ORIGEN). The evangelist Luke does not give an unbiased, neutral narration but a persuasive, confessional one filled with christological meaning (AMBROSE). Luke is dependent on the witness of those who have seen and heard Jesus and have delivered a tradition to him of the sacraments and the person of Jesus Christ (ATHANASIUS). Luke is not only continuing this tradition but also shaping it for a church that continues to preserve in its liturgy and councils the testimony of eyewitnesses and ministers of the word centered in the incarnation and atonement of Jesus Christ (CYRIL OF ALEXANDRIA). Theophilus represents a particular audience, a community of those who love God—the baptized and those to be baptized (AMBROSE). Thus the purpose of Luke's Gospel is a fully informed, steadfast faith that endures to salvation. This faith comes through the Gospel's catechetical lectures, which is an accurate, systematic instruction in the events that are going to be narrated (ORIGEN).

1:1 A Kerygmatic Narrative

ONLY FOUR CANONICAL GOSPELS. ORIGEN: With respect to the New Testament also "many have tried" to write Gospels, but not all found acceptance.[1] You should know that not just four Gospels, but very many, were composed. The Gospels we have were chosen from among these Gospels and passed on to the churches. We know this from Luke's own prologue, which begins this way: "Because many have tried to compose an account." The words "have tried" imply an accusation against those who rushed into writing gospels without the grace of the Holy Spirit. Matthew, Mark, John and Luke did not "try" to write. They wrote their Gospels when they were filled with the Holy Spirit. Hence, "many have tried to compose an account of the events that are clearly known among us." . . .

Our doctrines about the person of our Lord and Savior should be drawn from these approved Gospels. I know one gospel called "According to Thomas," and another "According to Matthias." We have read many others, too, so that we do not appear to be ignorant of anything, because of those people who think they know something if they have examined these gospels. But in all of these questions we approve of nothing but that which the church approves, namely, only four canonical Gospels. . . .

Luke makes his intention known by the word he uses; that is, "that have been clearly shown to us," a concept that the Latin language cannot express in one word. It means that Luke knew by firm faith and by careful consideration and did not waver on any point, wondering whether it should be this way or that. HOMILIES ON THE GOSPEL OF LUKE 1.1-3.[2]

1:2 Eyewitnesses and Ministers

EYEWITNESSES AND MINISTERS OF THE INCARNATE WORD. AMBROSE: The ministry of the word is greater than the hearing of it. Not the spoken word but the essential Word is meant—that which was made flesh and dwelt among us[3]—so do not understand it as the common word but as that celestial Word to whom the apostles ministered. For one reads in Exodus that the people saw the voice[4] of the Lord, yet truly a voice is not seen but heard. For what is a voice but a sound, which is not discerned with the eyes but perceived with the ear? Truly, with the highest genius, Moses wished to proclaim that the voice of God is seen, for it is seen with the sight of the inner mind. In the Gospel, not a voice but the Word, which is more excellent than a voice, is seen.

You see, therefore, that the Word of God was seen and heard by the apostles. They saw the Lord, not only according to the body but also according to the Word. For they with Moses and Elijah saw the glory of the Word.[5] They who saw him in his glory saw Jesus. Others who could see only the body did not see him. Jesus is seen not with the eyes of the body but with the eyes of the spirit. EXPOSITION OF THE GOSPEL OF LUKE 1.5.[6]

HANDING DOWN THE TRADITIONS. ATHANASIUS: What the apostles received, they passed on without change, so that the doctrine of the mysteries (the sacraments) and Christ would remain correct. The divine Word—the Son of God—wants us to be their disciples. It is appropriate for them to be our teachers, and it is necessary for us to submit to their teaching alone. Only from them and from those who have faithfully taught their doctrine do we get, as Paul writes, "faithful words, worthy of complete acceptance."[7] With them we are back to ground level, because they did not become disciples as a result of what they heard from others. Rather, they were eyewitnesses and servants of God the Word, and they handed down what they heard directly from him. FESTAL LETTER 2.7.[8]

TRADITIONS OF INCARNATION AND ATONE-

---

[1]Cf. 2 Pet 2:1. [2]FC 94:5-6**; PG 13:1801-3. [3]Jn 1:14. [4]Ex 20:18. [5]Mt 17:3. [6]EHG 9**. [7]1 Tim 1:15. [8]ARL 65*; NPNF 2 4:512**.

ment. Cyril of Alexandria: They "who from the beginning were eyewitnesses and ministers of the Word" did not hand on to us that he was one Son and another, as I said, but one and the same, God and man at the same time, the only-begotten and the firstborn. This came about in order that he might have the first title as God and the second as man, when he "was born among many brothers,"[9] having assumed our likeness. [He had not] joined another man to himself—as it seemed good to some persons to think—but [he] really and truly [became] man and [did] not relinquish being what he was, being God by nature and impassible. For this reason he voluntarily suffered in his own flesh. He has not given the body of someone else for us. Rather, the only-begotten Word of God himself offered himself, after he became man, as an immaculate victim to God the Father. Letter 67.4.[10]

1:3-4 *The Purpose of Luke's Gospel*

Luke Written for All Who Love God. Ambrose: So the Gospel was written to Theophilus, that is, to him whom God loves. If you love God, it was written to you. If it was written to you, discharge the duty of an evangelist. Diligently preserve the pledge of a friend in the secrets of the Spirit. Exposition of the Gospel of Luke 1.12.[11]

The Truth of Luke's Instruction. Origen: "It seemed right for me, too, following the same course from the beginning." He makes his point and repeats it. He did not learn from rumors what he is going to write. He himself has grasped it from the beginning. Hence, the apostle Paul praises him deservedly when he says, "He is praised for his Gospel throughout all the churches."[12] Scripture says this about no one else. It uses the expression only for Luke. "It seemed right for me, too, following the same course from the beginning, carefully to write down all those events for you in order, most excellent Theophilus." Someone might think that Luke addressed the Gospel to a specific man named Theophilus. But, if you are the sort of people God can love, then all of you who hear us speaking are Theophiluses, and the Gospel is addressed to you. Anyone who is a Theophilus is both "excellent" and "very strong." This is what the Greek word θεοφιλος [Theophilos] actually means. No Theophilus is weak. Scripture says of the people of Israel, when they were going out from Egypt, "There was no weakling in their tribes."[13] I could say boldly that everyone who is a Theophilus is robust. He has vigor and strength from both God and his Word. He can recognize the "truth" of those "words, by which he has been instructed" and understand the Word of the gospel in Christ—to whom is glory and power for ages of ages. Amen. Homilies on the Gospel of Luke 1.6.[14]

---

[9]Rom 8:29. [10]FC 77:62*. [11]EHG 13*; CSEL 32 4:18. [12]2 Cor 8:18. [13]Ps 105:37. [14]FC 94:8-9*; PG 13:1804-5.

1:5—2:52 PRELIMINARY REMARKS ON THE INFANCY NARRATIVE

Overview: The infancy narrative receives great attention among the church fathers, particularly as a source for the defense of the incarnation. The historical events bear witness that the Holy Spirit has brought about the miraculous birth of Jesus (Cyril of Jerusalem).

THE PURE AND UNDEFILED BIRTH OF JESUS.
CYRIL OF JERUSALEM: Let us remember these things, brothers, and use them as weapons of defense. Let us not endure the heretics who teach that Christ's coming was in appearance only. Let us shun as well those who say that the birth of the Savior was from a man and a woman, daring to assert that he was begotten of Joseph and Mary, because it is written, "He took his wife."[1] Let us recall Jacob, who, before he received Rachel, said to Laban, "Give me my wife."[2] Just as Rachel was called the wife of Jacob before marriage, as a result of her betrothal Mary also was called the wife of Joseph. Note the exactness of the Gospel when it says, "Now in the sixth month the angel Gabriel was sent from God to a town of Galilee, called Nazareth, to a virgin be-

trothed to a man named Joseph," and what follows. Again, when the enrolling took place and Joseph went up to be enrolled, what does the Scripture say? "And Joseph also went up from Galilee . . . to register together with Mary his espoused wife, who was with child." Though she was with child, it does not say "with his wife" but "with his espoused wife." "God sent his Son," Paul says, not born of a man and a woman but "born of a woman"[3] only; that is, born of a virgin. We have already shown that a virgin is also called a woman. For he who makes virgin souls was born of a virgin. CATECHETICAL LECTURES 12.31.[4]

---

[1]Mt 1:24. [2]Gen 29:21. [3]Gal 4:4. [4]FC 61:246-47**.

1:5-25 THE ANNOUNCEMENT OF JOHN'S BIRTH

^{5}*In the days of Herod, king of Judea, there was a priest named Zechariah,^{b} of the division of Abijah; and he had a wife of the daughters of Aaron, and her name was Elizabeth. ^{6}And they were both righteous before God, walking in all the commandments and ordinances of the Lord blameless. ^{7}But they had no child, because Elizabeth was barren, and both were advanced in years.*

^{8}*Now while he was serving as priest before God when his division was on duty, ^{9}according to the custom of the priesthood, it fell to him by lot to enter the temple of the Lord and burn incense. ^{10}And the whole multitude of the people were praying outside at the hour of incense. ^{11}And there appeared to him an angel of the Lord standing on the right side of the altar of incense. ^{12}And Zechariah was troubled when he saw him, and fear fell upon him. ^{13}But the angel said to him, "Do not be afraid, Zechariah, for your prayer is heard, and your wife Elizabeth will bear you a son, and you shall call his name John.*

^{14}*And you will have joy and gladness,*
and many will rejoice at his birth;
^{15}*for he will be great before the Lord,*
and he shall drink no wine nor strong drink,
and he will be filled with the Holy Spirit,
even from his mother's womb.
^{16}*And he will turn many of the sons of Israel to the Lord their God,*

[17]and he will go before him in the spirit and power of Elijah,
to turn the hearts of the fathers to the children,
and the disobedient to the wisdom of the just,
to make ready for the Lord a people prepared."

[18]*And Zechariah said to the angel, "How shall I know this? For I am an old man, and my wife is advanced in years." [19]And the angel answered him, "I am Gabriel, who stand in the presence of God; and I was sent to speak to you, and to bring you this good news. [20]And behold, you will be silent and unable to speak until the day that these things come to pass, because you did not believe my words, which will be fulfilled in their time." [21]And the people were waiting for Zechariah, and they wondered at his delay in the temple. [22]And when he came out, he could not speak to them, and they perceived that he had seen a vision in the temple; and he made signs to them and remained dumb. [23]And when his time of service was ended, he went to his home.*

[24]*After these days his wife Elizabeth conceived, and for five months she hid herself, saying, [25]"Thus the Lord has done to me in the days when he looked on me, to take away my reproach among men."*

b Greek *Zacharias*

OVERVIEW: The announcement of John's birth is important for salvation history as he is prophet and martyr (MAXIMUS OF TURIN). Zechariah and Elizabeth are described in language that suggests they are a continuation of the faithful remnant of the Old Testament. Both are from priestly stock, Zechariah from the division of Abijah and Elizabeth a daughter of Aaron (AMBROSE). Elizabeth is barren, and they are too old to conceive, yet God uses Elizabeth's barrenness to bring forth the miraculous birth of a holy person, just as he did for Sarah, Rebecca, Rachel and Hannah (ORIGEN).

Luke's Gospel begins and ends in the temple, and so does the infancy narrative. The two altars of the temple signify two covenants, as the angel heralds the coming of the new covenant (BEDE). But John's advent heralds the end of Old Testament worship, the law and the priesthood (EPHREM THE SYRIAN). By beginning his Gospel with an Old Testament saint like Zechariah performing cultic acts associated with the old covenant in the temple in Jerusalem, Luke immediately shows that his narrative must be understood in connection with Israel and the Old Testament.

The angel's appearance signals a theophany in which the coming of the true priest will be announced (PSEUDO-DIONYSIUS). The angel's announcement of the miraculous birth and the name of the child is preceded by a word of comfort—"Do not fear" (ATHANASIUS). The angel comes to Zechariah as the biological father of John, whereas with Jesus, the angel comes to Mary and not to Joseph. Zechariah's prayers of supplication offered at the time of his priestly duty were for the Messiah to come (AUGUSTINE). As a priest in the temple Zechariah's prayer was answered (CHRYSOSTOM).

The angel tells Zechariah to name the child John, which means "Yahweh/the Lord has been gracious" (BEDE). John's greatness comes from the presence of the Holy Spirit even from his mother's womb (AMBROSE). John baptized the One through whom all others would be baptized (CYPRIAN). John precedes the Messiah "in the Spirit and power of Elijah" (BEDE). The Spirit is never without power (AMBROSE). The parallels between the announcements of the births of John and Jesus highlight the relationship between John and Jesus in salvation history (AUGUSTINE). Elizabeth's barrenness and Mary's virginity stand in sharp contrast, but together they announce that God is acting in a miraculous way at this climactic moment in salvation history (MAXIMUS OF TURIN).

Zechariah's silence is a sign of his doubts and that Israel has not listened to the voice of the prophets (ORIGEN). What Zechariah doubts is God's word and promise (CHRYSOSTOM). Elizabeth kept herself hidden for five months; Mary will be the first to know of her blessed state and see in it a sign of God's visitation (EPHREM THE SYRIAN). Elizabeth's modesty gives way to the recognition that, in some mysterious way, God has removed her shame (AMBROSE).

1:5-7 Time, Persons and Place

BORN FOR PROPHECY, MURDERED FOR TRUTH. MAXIMUS OF TURIN: I do not know what is the most important thing that we should preach—that he [John the Baptist] was wonderfully born or more wonderfully slain—for he was born as a prophecy and murdered for truth. By his birth he announced the coming of the Savior, and by his death he condemned the incest of Herod.[1] This holy and righteous man, who was born in an uncommon way as the result of a promise, merited from God that he should depart this world by an uncommon death—that he should by confessing the Lord lay aside his body, which he had received as a gift from the Lord. Therefore John did everything by the will of God, since he was born and died for the sake of God's work. SERMON 5.1-2.[2]

JOHN'S PRIESTLY BACKGROUND. AMBROSE: Holy Scripture tells us that not only the character of those who are praiseworthy but also their parents must be praised, so that the transmitted inheritance of immaculate purity, as it were, in those whom we wish to praise, may be exalted. What other intention is there in this passage of the holy Evangelist, except that St. John the Baptist be renowned for his parents, his wonders, his duty and his passion? Thus Hannah,

the mother of St. Samuel,[3] is praised. Thus Isaac received from his parents nobility of piety, which he handed down to his descendants. Therefore the priest Zechariah is not only a priest but also of the course of Abijah, that is, a noble among his wife's ancestors. "And his wife," it says, "was of the daughters of Aaron." So St. John's nobility was handed down not only from his parents but also from his ancestors—not exalted through worldly power but venerable through the religious succession. For the forerunner of Christ ought to have such ancestors, that he be seen to preach a faith in his Lord's advent that is not suddenly conceived but received from his ancestors and imparted by the very law of nature. EXPOSITION OF THE GOSPEL OF LUKE 1.15-16.[4]

ELIZABETH'S BARRENNESS. ORIGEN: Consider why many holy women in the Scriptures are said to have been barren, as Sarah herself,[5] and now Rebecca.[6] Also Rachel, Israel's beloved, was barren.[7] Hannah also, the mother of Samuel, is recorded to have been barren.[8] Also in the Gospels, Elizabeth is said to have been barren. In all these instances this term is used, for after sterility they all gave birth to a holy person. HOMILIES ON GENESIS 12.1.[9]

THE APPEARANCE IN THE TEMPLE. BEDE: We must note that the angel bore witness to the grace about which he had come to give the good news—not only by the power of the words which he brought forward but also by the point in time and the location of the place in which he appeared. He appeared at the time when the priest was making an offering to express the fact that he was proclaiming the coming of the true and eternal high priest, who would be the true sacrificial offering for the salvation of the world. He stood beside the altar of incense to teach that he had

---

[1]Mt 14:3-12. [2]ACW 50:22-23**. [3]1 Sam 1:2. [4]EHG 15*; CSEL 32 4:20. [5]Gen 11:30. [6]Gen 25:21. [7]Gen 29:31. [8]1 Sam 1:2. [9]FC 71:176**.

come as the herald of a new covenant. There were two altars in the temple,[10] which expressed the two covenants in the church. The first, the altar of burnt offerings, which was plated with bronze and was situated in front of the doors of the temple,[11] was for the offering up of victims and sacrifices. It signified the fleshly-minded worshipers of the old covenant. Then there was the altar of incense, which was covered with gold[12] and set near the entrance of the Holy of Holies, and was used to burn fragrant gums. This signified the interior and more perfect grace of the new covenant and its worshipers. HOMILIES ON THE GOSPELS 2.19.[13]

JOHN HERALDS THE END OF OLD TESTAMENT WORSHIP. EPHREM THE SYRIAN: John, herald of the Lord of the right, was announced from the right of the altar. It was at the time of worship that he was announced to show he was the end of the former worship. It was in the middle of the sanctuary that Zechariah became dumb, to show that the mysteries of the sanctuary had become silent, for he who was to fulfill these mysteries had come. Because Zechariah did not believe that his wife's barrenness had been healed, he was bound in his speech. COMMENTARY ON TATIAN'S DIATESSARON 1.10.[14]

1:8-17 Gabriel Appears to Zechariah in the Temple

GABRIEL ANNOUNCES THE MYSTERY OF CHRIST'S COMING. PSEUDO-DIONYSIUS: I note that the mystery of Jesus' love for humanity was first revealed to the angels and that the angels granted the gift of this knowledge to us. It was the most divine Gabriel who guided Zechariah, the chief priest, into the mystery that, contrary to all hope and by God's favor, he would have a son. His son would be a prophet of the divine and human work of Jesus, who was beneficently about to appear for the salvation of the world. Gabriel revealed to Mary how in her would be born the divine mystery of the ineffable form of God. CELES-

TIAL HIERARCHY 4.4.[15]

GABRIEL DISPELS FEAR. ATHANASIUS: Whenever the soul continues to be fearful, it is the enemy who is present. The evil spirits do not dispel the fear of their presence, as the great archangel Gabriel did for Mary and Zechariah. LIFE OF ST. ANTHONY 37.[16]

THE ANGEL COMES TO ZECHARIAH. AUGUSTINE: The angel Gabriel came to Zechariah, not to Elizabeth. Why? Because it was through Zechariah that John was going to be in Elizabeth. The angel, in announcing that John was going to come by being born, went not to the receptacle of the womb but to the source of the seed. He announced they would both have a son, but he made the announcement to the father. John, after all, was going to come from the marriage of male and female. And once more the same Gabriel came to Mary—not to Joseph. The angel came to the one from whom that flesh was to begin, from whom it was to take its starting point. SERMON 291.3.[17]

ZECHARIAH PRAYS FOR A MESSIAH. AUGUSTINE: The priest was offering sacrifice on behalf of the people. The people were expecting the Christ. John was the one who would announce the Christ. SERMON 291.3.[18]

ZECHARIAH'S PRIESTLY PRAYER. CHRYSOSTOM: This man Zechariah came into the Holy of Holies, to the innermost sanctuary, upon which he alone of all men had the right to look. Consider how he was equal in importance to all the people. When he offered prayers for the whole people, when he was making the Master propitious to his servants, he was serving as a mediator between God and men. ON THE INCOMPREHENSIBLE NATURE OF GOD 2.9-10.[19]

---

[10]Ex 27:1; 30:1. [11]Ex 27:2; 1 Kings 8:64; 2 Chron 8:12. [12]Ex 30:3. [13]CS 111:195-96*. [14]ECTD 45*. [15]PDCW 158*. [16]FC 15:169*; CWS 59. [17]WSA 3 8:132-33*. [18]WSA 3 8:133*. [19]FC 72:74*.

AND YOU SHALL CALL HIM JOHN. BEDE: Whenever in the Scriptures a name is imposed or changed . . . by God, it is indicative of great praise and virtue. It was good that our Redeemer's precursor was ordered to be called John. The name John means "the grace of the Lord" or "in whom there is grace." He received a special grace beyond other saints, that of being Christ's precursor. He came to proclaim a previously unheard of grace to the world, that of entry into heaven. Therefore he who was full of grace himself and who brought the good news of God's grace to the rest of humankind expressed even by his name a proclamation of grace. It was rightly foretold that there was to be cause for exultation for many persons at his birth, since it was through him that the Author of their regeneration was manifested to the world. HOMILIES ON THE GOSPELS 2.19.[20]

JOHN'S GREATNESS IS IN SPIRIT. AMBROSE: He here announced greatness, not of body but of soul. Greatness of soul before the Lord is greatness of virtue, and smallness of soul is childhood of virtue. . . . Thus John would be great—not through bodily virtue but through magnanimity.[21] He did not enlarge the boundaries of an empire. He did not prefer triumphs of military contest to honors. Rather, what is more, he disparaged human pleasures and lewdness of body, preaching in the desert with great virtue of spirit. He was a child in worldliness, but great in spirit. He was not captivated by the allurements of life, nor did he change his steadfastness of purpose through a desire to live. . . .

There is no doubt that this promise of the angel came true. Before he was born—still in his mother's womb—St. John depicted the grace of the receipt of the Spirit. Although neither his father nor his mother had performed any miracles previously, he, leaping in his mother's womb, proclaimed the coming of the Lord. When the mother of the Lord came to Elizabeth, the latter said, "For behold, when the voice of your greeting came to my ears, the babe in my womb leaped for joy."[22] She did not yet have the spirit of life,[23] but

the Spirit of grace. We find in another place that the grace of sanctification precedes that of the substance of living, where the Lord says, "Before I formed you in the womb I knew you, and before you were born I consecrated you. I appointed you a prophet to the nations."[24] For the spirit of this life is one, and the Spirit of grace is another. EXPOSITION OF THE GOSPEL OF LUKE 1.31-33.[25]

THOSE BAPTIZED BY JOHN. CYPRIAN: John did not merely announce the Lord in words before his coming but pointed him out for people to see. John baptized the Christ himself through whom all others are baptized. THE BAPTISMAL CONTROVERSY 73.25.[26]

HOW JOHN IS LIKE ELIJAH. BEDE: Both Elijah and John were celibate. Both wore rough dress. Both spent their lives in the wilderness. Both were heralds of the truth. Both underwent persecution for justice's sake at the hands of a king and queen—the former at the hands of Ahab and Jezebel,[27] the latter at the hands of Herod and Herodias.[28] The former, lest he be killed by the wicked, was carried up to heaven in a fiery chariot.[29] The latter, lest he be overcome by the wicked, sought the heavenly kingdom by his martyrdom, which was accomplished in spiritual combat. HOMILIES ON THE GOSPELS 2.23.[30]

IN THE SPIRIT AND POWER OF ELIJAH. AMBROSE: These words are well added because the spirit is never without power, nor power without the spirit. "In the spirit and power of Elijah," it says, perhaps because holy Elijah had great power and grace. Power so that he turned the spirits of the people back from unbelief to faith, the power of abstinence and patience, and the Spirit of prophecy. . . . Elijah divided the Jordan,[31] John made it the font of salvation. John walks with the Lord on earth, Elijah appears with the

---

[20]CS 111:197*. [21]Lk 7:28. [22]Lk 1:44. [23]See Rom 8:2; Rev 2:11. [24]Jer 1:5. [25]EHG 23-24;** CSEL 32 4:29-32. [26]LCC 5:171*. [27]1 Kings 19:1-3. [28]Mt 14:3. [29]2 Kings 2:11. [30]CS 111:230*. [31]2 Kings 2:8.

Lord in glory.[32] Elijah is a herald of the first coming of the Lord, and John of the second. Elijah after three years watered the earth with rain,[33] John after three years sprinkled the arid soil of our body with the stream of faith. Exposition of the Gospel of Luke 1.36.[34]

1:18-20 Zechariah's Response and the Angel's Proclamation

Barrenness and Virginity. Augustine: The church observes the birth of John as in some way sacred.... When we celebrate John's, we also celebrate Christ's....

John is born of an old woman who is barren. Christ is born of a young woman who is a virgin. Barrenness gives birth to John, virginity to Christ. The normal and proper age of parents was lacking with the birth of John. No marital embrace occurred for the birth of Christ. The former is announced in the declaration of the angel. With the angel's annunciation the latter is conceived. That John will be born is not believed, and his father is silenced. That Christ will be born is believed, and he is conceived by faith. First of all faith makes its entry into the heart of the virgin, and there follows fruitfulness in the mother's womb.

And yet, Zechariah used nearly the same words, when the angel announced John: "By what shall I know this? For I myself am an old man, and my wife is already advanced in her days," and by holy Mary when the angel announced that she was going to give birth: "How shall this be, since I have no husband?"[35] These are practically the same words....

Finally, John is born when the daylight begins to diminish and the night begins to grow longer. Christ is born when the night begins to be curtailed and the day begins to increase. Sermon 293.[36]

Elizabeth and Mary. Maximus of Turin: Yet ... we ought not to be so astonished that John merited such grace in his birth. For the precursor and forerunner of Christ ought to have had something similar to the birth of the Lord, the Savior. Indeed, the Lord was begotten of a virgin and John of a sterile woman, the one of an unstained girl and the other of an already exhausted old woman. John's birth, then, also has something of the glorious and the wondrous. Although it would seem to be less noble for a matron to give birth than for a virgin to give birth, yet as we look up to Mary for having given birth as a virgin we also wonder at Elizabeth for having done so as an old woman. Indeed, I think that this fact contains a certain mystery. John, who was a figure of the Old Testament, should have been born of the already cold blood of an old woman, while the Lord, who would preach the gospel of the kingdom of heaven, came forth from a woman in the flower of glowing youth. Mary, conscious of her virginity, marvels at the fruit hidden in her belly, while Elizabeth, conscious of her old age, blushes that her womb is heavy with the one she has conceived. Thus the Evangelist says, "She hid herself for five months." How wonderful it is, though, that the same archangel Gabriel performs an office with respect to each birth! He comforts the unbelieving Zechariah and encourages the believing Mary. He lost his voice because he doubted. But she, because she believed immediately, conceived the saving Word. Sermon 5.3-4.[37]

1:21-23 The People Realize Zechariah Has Seen a Vision

Zechariah's Silence a Sign. Origen: When the priest Zechariah offers incense in the temple, he is condemned to silence and cannot speak. Or better, he speaks only with gestures. He remains unable to speak until the birth of his son, John. What does this mean? Zechariah's silence is the silence of prophets in the people of Israel. God no longer speaks to them. His "Word, which was with the Father from the beginning,

---

[32]Mt 17:3. [33]1 Kings 18:1, 45. [34]EHG 25*; CSEL 32 4:32-33. [35]Lk 1:34. [36]WSA 3 8:148-49*. [37]ACW 50:23-24*.

and was God,"[38] has passed over to us. For us Christ is not silent. . . .

Christ ceased to be in them. The Word deserted them. What Isaiah wrote was fulfilled: "The daughter of Zion will be deserted like a tent in the vineyard or like a hut in the cucumber patch. She is as desolate as a plundered city."[39] The Jews were left behind, and salvation passed to the Gentiles. HOMILY ON THE GOSPEL OF LUKE 5.1, 4.[40]

ZECHARIAH DOUBTS. CHRYSOSTOM: Zechariah looked at his age, his gray hair, his body that had lost its strength. He looked at his wife's sterility, and he refused to accept on faith what the angel revealed would come to pass. ON THE INCOMPREHENSIBLE NATURE OF GOD 2.11.[41]

1:24-25 Elizabeth Rejoices in Her New Status

WHY ELIZABETH HID HERSELF. EPHREM THE SYRIAN: Elizabeth hid herself because of Zechariah's grief. Or alternatively, she hid herself because she was ashamed on account of the fact that she had resumed intercourse. So it was because of her old age that Elizabeth hid herself. But see, Moses did not write in relation to Sarah that she hid herself, when at the age of ninety she carried Isaac, nor with regard to Rebecca, who was pregnant

with twins. Elizabeth hid herself for five months, until her infant would be sufficiently formed in his members to exult before his Lord,[42] and because Mary was about to receive the annunciation. COMMENTARY ON TATIAN'S DIATESSARON 1.24.[43]

ELIZABETH'S MODESTY. AMBROSE: Elizabeth, who undoubtedly desired sons, hid herself for five months. What was the reason for this concealment if not modesty? For there is a prescribed age for each duty, and what is fitting at one time is unseemly at another, and a change of age often changes the nature of every act. . . . She, who once hid because she had conceived a son, began to carry herself with confidence because she bore a prophet—she who blushed before was blessed, she who doubted before was strengthened. "For, behold," she said, "as soon as the voice of your greeting reached my ears, the infant in my womb leaped for joy."[44] Therefore she cried out with a loud voice when she perceived the coming of the Lord, because she believed in the divine birth. There was no cause for shame when she accepted the birth of the prophet as a given, not a desired, generation. EXPOSITION OF THE GOSPEL OF LUKE 1.43, 46.[45]

---

[38]Jn 1:1-2. [39]Is 1:8. [40]FC 94:20-21*. [41]FC 72:75*. [42]Lk 1:41. [43]ECTD 52*. [44]Lk 1:44. [45]EHG 29-31*; CSEL 32 4:38, 40.

1:26-38 THE ANNOUNCEMENT OF JESUS' BIRTH

[26]*In the sixth month the angel Gabriel was sent from God to a city of Galilee named Nazareth,* [27]*to a virgin betrothed to a man whose name was Joseph, of the house of David; and the virgin's name was Mary.* [28]*And he came to her and said, "Hail, O favored one, the Lord is with you!"*[c] [29]*But she was greatly troubled at the saying, and considered in her mind what sort of greeting this might be.* [30]*And the angel said to her, "Do not be afraid, Mary, for you have found favor with God.* [31]*And behold, you will conceive in your womb and bear a son, and you shall call his name Jesus.*

³²*He will be great, and will be called the Son of the Most High;*

and the Lord God will give to him the throne of his father David,

³³*and he will reign over the house of Jacob for ever;*

and of his kingdom there will be no end."

³⁴*And Mary said to the angel, "How shall this be, since I have no husband?" ³⁵And the angel said to her,*

"The Holy Spirit will come upon you,

and the power of the Most High will overshadow you;

*therefore the child to be born*ᵈ *will be called holy,*

the Son of God.

³⁶*And behold, your kinswoman Elizabeth in her old age has also conceived a son; and this is the sixth month with her who was called barren. ³⁷For with God nothing will be impossible." ³⁸And Mary said, "Behold, I am the handmaid of the Lord; let it be to me according to your word." And the angel departed from her.*

c Other ancient authorities add *"Blessed are you among women!"*   d Other ancient authorities add *of you*

OVERVIEW: The annunciation of Jesus' birth follows upon that of John's. The Evangelist sets the scene by introducing Gabriel, which means "strength of God." The brevity of the sketch of Mary as a person is arresting; the only significant piece of information is her virginity, which she offers to God as a gift (BEDE). She is an espoused wife and a virgin who remains a virgin after Jesus' birth (JEROME). She prefigures the church that is undefiled yet wed (AMBROSE). Mary's betrothal to Joseph provides a husband for her during her pregnancy and labor (BEDE).

"Hail, full of grace" is a unique greeting for Mary (ORIGEN). The angel also announces "the Lord is with you," a greeting that is mysterious and troubling for Mary (PETER CHRYSOLOGUS) because of her modesty (AMBROSE). The new era of salvation begins with the conception of Jesus in Mary. As Eve contained in her womb all humanity that was doomed to sin, now Mary contains in her womb the new Adam who will father a new humanity by his grace (BEDE).

The angel rejoices over Mary as the place of God's glory, for God borrows Mary's flesh to lead mankind to glory (STICHERA). Mary is instructed by Gabriel concerning the child who reveals to her the divine mystery of God's action in her, for she will be a mother even though she remains a virgin (PRUDENTIUS). The Child conceived in

Mary will be both Son of God and Son of man (BEDE) The name Jesus refers to his actions rather than his nature—he will save the people from their sins (EPHREM THE SYRIAN) and bring about the re-creation of the world (EXAPOSTEILARION) for what Mary conceives in her womb is none other than the Creator of all things (STICHERA). Jesus is the culmination of the Davidic line—he is from both the house of David and the house of Levi (EPHREM THE SYRIAN). This reflects the mystery of how the timeless enters time (JOHN THE MONK). In the conception of Jesus, the house of David and Jacob now becomes the universal church (BEDE).

In continuity with the miraculous births of the Old Testament, the conception and birth of Jesus exceed all interpretation (LEO THE GREAT). But unlike Zechariah, Mary's wondering is not laced with skepticism. Mary's question arises from her vow of virginity (AUGUSTINE), pondering the divine mystery of the virgin birth (AMBROSE). It is Gabriel who should stand in awe of Mary, not Mary of Gabriel, for she now bears in her womb the eternal Son of God (THEOPHANES).

Gabriel speaks of the Holy Spirit coming upon Mary and impregnating her (PRUDENTIUS). It prefigures our rebirth to a new life and the renewal of all humanity (PETER CHRYSOLOGUS), for the water of baptism is like the Virgin's womb (LEO

THE GREAT). The virgin birth of Jesus sets us free because it is by Spirit not by carnal lust (AUGUSTINE). It is the Holy Spirit that renders her fruitful (PRUDENTIUS). This same Spirit hovered over the waters and brought forth creation.[1] The presence of Yahweh in a cloud overshadowed the tabernacle, and the glory of Yahweh filled it (EPHREM THE SYRIAN).[2]

Since Mary bears this holy child in her womb, she now represents temple, tabernacle and ark of the covenant (THEOPHANES). And as the Spirit came down upon Mary to bring about Christ's conception, so also the Spirit comes down now on the bread and wine to create the meal of the new creation, calling to the mind of early Christians the reception of the body and blood of Christ into the believer's body in holy Communion (JOHN OF DAMASCUS).

As a cousin to Elizabeth, who is of the tribe of Aaron, Mary's lineage is royal, of the house of David, and priestly, of the house of Levi, so that her Son is King and Priest (BEDE). By her obedience, she reverses the disobedience of Eve so that the first virgin's fall through the seduction of an angel is overcome by the faithful response of this virgin, who believes the word of another angel (IRENAEUS).

1:26-29 Gabriel Greets the Virgin Mary

GABRIEL, STRENGTH OF GOD. BEDE: Now Gabriel means "strength of God." Rightly he shone forth with such a name, since by his testimony he bore witness to the coming birth of God in the flesh. The prophet said this in the psalm, "The Lord strong and powerful, the Lord powerful in battle"[3]—that battle, undoubtedly, in which he [Christ] came to fight "the powers of the air"[4] and to snatch the world from their tyranny. HOMILIES ON THE GOSPELS 1.3.[5]

MARY OFFERS GOD THE GIFT OF HER VIRGINITY. BEDE: Truly full of grace was she, upon whom it was conferred by divine favor that, first among women, she should offer God the most glorious gift of her virginity. Hence she who strove to imitate the life of an angel was rightfully worthy to enjoy the experience of seeing and speaking with an angel. Truly full of grace was she to whom it was granted to give birth to Jesus Christ, the very one through whom grace and truth came.[6] And so the Lord was truly with her whom he first raised up from earthly to heavenly desires, in an unheard of love of chastity, and afterwards sanctified, by means of his human nature, with all the fullness of his divinity. Truly blessed among women was she who without precedent in the womanly state rejoiced in having the honor of parenthood along with the beauty of virginity, inasmuch as it was fitting that a virgin mother bring forth God the Son. HOMILIES ON THE GOSPELS 1.3.[7]

THE PERPETUAL VIRGINITY OF MARY. JEROME: Holy Mary, blessed Mary, mother and virgin, virgin before giving birth, virgin after giving birth! I, for my part, marvel how a virgin is born of a virgin, and how, after the birth of a virgin, the mother is a virgin.

Would you like to know how he is born of a virgin and, after his nativity, the mother is still a virgin? "The doors were closed, and Jesus entered."[8] There is no question about that. He who entered through the closed doors was neither a ghost nor a spirit. He was a real man with a real body. Furthermore, what does he say? "Touch me and see. For a spirit does not have flesh and bones, as you see I have."[9] He had flesh and bones, and the doors were closed. How do flesh and bones enter through closed doors? The doors are closed, and he enters, whom we do not see entering. Whence has he entered? Everything is closed up. There is no place through which he may enter. Nevertheless he who has entered is within, and how he entered is not evident. You do not know how his entrance was accomplished, and you attribute it to the power of God. Attribute to the power of God, then, that he was

---

[1]Gen 1:2. [2]Ex 40:35. [3]Ps 24:8 (23:8 LXX). [4]Eph 2:2. [5]CS 110:20*. [6]Jn 1:17. [7]CS 110:21-22. [8]Jn 20:19, 26. [9]Lk 24:39.

born of a virgin and the virgin herself after bringing forth was a virgin still. HOMILY 87.[10]

MARY PREFIGURES THE CHURCH. AMBROSE: And, therefore, he who had undertaken to prove the incorrupt mystery of the incarnation thought it fruitless to pursue evidence of Mary's virginity, lest he be seen as a defender of the Virgin rather than an advocate of the mystery. Surely, when he taught that Joseph was righteous, he adequately declared that he could not violate the temple of the Holy Spirit, the mother of the Lord, the womb of the mystery. We have learned the lineage of the Truth. We have learned its counsel. Let us learn its mystery. Fittingly is she espoused, but virgin, because she prefigures the church which is undefiled[11] yet wed. A virgin conceived us of the Spirit, a Virgin brings us forth without travail. And thus perhaps Mary, wed to one, was filled by Another, because also the separate churches are indeed filled by the Spirit and by grace and yet are joined to the appearance of a temporal Priest. EXPOSITION OF THE GOSPEL OF LUKE 2.6-7.[12]

WHY MARY MUST BE BETROTHED TO JOSEPH. BEDE: As to why he wished to be conceived and born not of a simple virgin but of one who was betrothed to a man, several of the Fathers have put forward reasonable answers. The best of these is to prevent her from being condemned as guilty of defilement if she were to bear a son when she had no husband. Then too, in the things the care of a home naturally demands, the woman in labor would be sustained by a husband's care. Therefore blessed Mary had to have a husband who would be both a perfectly sure witness to her integrity and a completely trustworthy foster father for our Lord and Savior, who was born of her. He was a husband who would, in accordance with the law, make sacrificial offerings to the temple for him when he was an infant. He would take him, along with his mother, to Egypt when persecution threatened. He would bring him back and would minister to the many other needs consequent upon the weakness of the hu-

manity which he had assumed. It did no great harm if, for a time, some believed that he was Joseph's son, since from the apostles' preaching after his ascension it would be plainly evident to all believers that he had been born of a virgin. HOMILIES ON THE GOSPELS 1.3.[13]

THE ANGEL'S GREETING TO MARY UNIQUE. ORIGEN: The angel greeted Mary with a new address, which I could not find anywhere else in Scripture. I ought to explain this expression briefly. The angel says, "Hail, full of grace." . . . I do not remember having read this word elsewhere in Scripture. An expression of this kind, "Hail, full of grace," is not addressed to a male. This greeting was reserved for Mary alone. HOMILIES ON THE GOSPEL OF LUKE 6.7.[14]

THE LORD'S PRESENCE MYSTERIOUS AND TROUBLING. PETER CHRYSOLOGUS: "The Lord is with you." Why is the Lord with you? Because he is coming to you not merely to pay a visit, but he is coming down into you in a new mystery, that of being born. Fittingly did the angel add, "You are blessed among women." Through the curse she incurred, Eve brought pains upon the wombs of women in childbirth. Now, in this very matter of motherhood, Mary, through the blessing she received, rejoices, is honored, is exalted. Now too womankind has become truly the mother of those who live through grace, just as previously by nature are subject to death. . . .

She soon realized that she was receiving within herself the heavenly judge, there in that same place where with lingering gaze she had just seen the harbinger from heaven. It was by a soothing motion and holy affection that God transformed the virgin into a mother for himself and made his handmaid into a parent. Nevertheless her bosom was disturbed, her mind recoiled, and her whole state became one of trembling when God, whom the whole of creation does not contain, placed his

---

[10]FC 57:217-18*. [11]Eph 5:27. [12]*EHG* 36*. [13]CS 110:20-21. [14]FC 94:26.

whole Self inside her bosom and made himself a man. SERMON 140.[15]

THE MODESTY OF THE VIRGIN. AMBROSE: Learn of character from the Virgin. Learn of modesty from the Virgin. Learn of prophecy from the Virgin. Learn in the mystery. It is the nature of virgins to tremble at every entrance of a man and to be afraid at every address by a man. Let women learn to imitate the purpose of modesty. She was alone in the inner room which none among men may see. Only the angel found her. Alone without a companion, alone without a witness, lest she be corrupted by ignoble speech, she is greeted by the angel. Learn, virgin, to shun lewdness of words. Moreover, Mary was afraid at the angel's greeting. EXPOSITION OF THE GOSPEL OF LUKE 2.8.[16]

DEATH THROUGH ONE WOMAN, LIFE THROUGH ANOTHER. BEDE: The first cause of human perdition occurred when a serpent was sent by the devil to a woman who was to be deceived by the spirit of pride. Moreover, the devil himself came in the serpent, who, once he had deceived our first parents, stripped humankind of the glory of immortality. Because death made its entrance through a woman, it was fitting that life return through a woman. The one, seduced by the devil through the serpent, brought a man the taste of death. The other, instructed by God through the angel, produced for the world the Author of salvation. HOMILIES ON THE GOSPELS 1.3.[17]

1:30-33 Gabriel Announces Jesus' Conception and His Designations

GOD BORROWS MARY'S FLESH TO LEAD HUMANITY TO GLORY. ANONYMOUS: Revealing to you the pre-eternal counsel, Gabriel came and stood before you, maid, and in greeting said, "Rejoice, earth that has not been sown; rejoice, burning bush that remains unconsumed; Rejoice, unsearchable depth; Rejoice, bridge that leads to heaven; Rejoice, ladder raised on high that Jacob saw; Rejoice, divine jar of manna; Rejoice, deliverance from the curse; Rejoice, restoration of Adam, the Lord is with you!"

"You appeared to me in the form of a man," said the undefiled maid to the chief of the heavenly hosts. "How then do you speak to me of things that pass human power? For you have said that God shall be with me and shall take up his dwelling in my womb. How shall I become the spacious habitation and the holy place of him that rides upon the cherubim?[18] Do not amuse me with deceit; for I have not known pleasure, I have not entered into wedlock. How then shall I bear a child?"

Then the bodiless angel replied, "When God so wills, the order of nature is overcome, and what is beyond humankind comes to pass. Believe that my sayings are true, all-holy and immaculate lady." And she cried aloud, "Let it be to me according to your word, and I shall bear him that is without flesh, who shall borrow flesh from me, that through this mingling he may lead humankind up to his ancient glory, for he alone has power so to do!" STICHERA OF THE ANNUNCIATION.[19]

MOTHER YET VIRGIN. PRUDENTIUS:
A heavenly fire engenders him, not flesh
Nor blood of father, nor impure desire.[20]
By power of God a spotless maid conceives,
As in her virgin womb the Spirit breathes.
The mystery of this birth confirms our faith
That Christ is God: a maiden by the Spirit
Is wed, unstained by love; her purity
Remains intact; with child within, untouched
Without, bright in her chaste fertility,
Mother yet virgin, mother that knew not man.
Why, doubter, do you shake your silly head?
An angel makes this known with holy lips.
Will you not hearken to angelic words?
The Virgin blest, the shining messenger

---

[15]FC 17:227-28*. [16]EHG 36-37*. [17]CS 110:19-20*. [18] Ps 18:10 (17:11 **LXX**). [19]FM 268. [20]Jn 1:13.

Believed, and by her faith she Christ
   conceived.
Christ comes to men of faith and spurns
   the heart
Irresolute in trust and reverence.
The Virgin's instant faith attracted
Christ into her womb and hid him there
   till birth.
THE DIVINITY OF CHRIST 566-84.[21]

JESUS IS SON OF GOD AND SON OF MAN. BEDE:
We should carefully note the order of the words
here, and the more firmly they are engrafted in
our heart, the more evident it will be that the
sum total of our redemption consists in them. For
they proclaim with perfect clarity that the Lord
Jesus, that is, our Savior, was both the true Son of
God the Father and the true Son of a mother who
was a human being. "Behold," he says, "you will
conceive in your womb and give birth to a son"—
acknowledge that this true human being assumed
the true substance of flesh from the flesh of the
Virgin! "He will be great and will be called the
Son of the Most High"—confess too that this
same Son is true God of true God, coeternal Son
forever of the eternal Father! HOMILIES ON THE
GOSPELS 1.3.[22]

JESUS WILL SAVE HIS PEOPLE FROM SIN.
EPHREM THE SYRIAN: The words "in the sixth
month" are reckoned in relation to Elizabeth's
pregnancy. "The angel was sent to a virgin," and
he said to her, "Behold, in your virginity you will
conceive in your womb and bear a son, and you
shall call his name Jesus." He was speaking about
him who was to appear in the body. He did not
say to her, "that name which is called Jesus," but
"you shall call his name." This shows that this
name is of the economy which is through the
body, since Jesus in Hebrew means "Savior." For
the angel said, "You shall call his name Jesus," that
is, Savior, "for he shall save his people from sins."
This name therefore refers not to his nature but
to his deeds. COMMENTARY ON TATIAN'S DIATES-
SARON 25.[23]

**MARY'S CONCEPTION OF JESUS HERALDS THE
RE-CREATION OF THE WORLD.** ANONYMOUS:
The captain of the angelic hosts was sent by God
Almighty to the pure Virgin to announce the
good tidings of a strange and secret wonder: that
God as man would be born a child of her without
seed, fashioning again the whole human race!
Proclaim, people, the good tidings of the re-cre-
ation of the world! EXAPOSTEILARION OF THE
ANNUNCIATION.[24]

**MARY CONCEIVES THE CREATOR OF ALL
THINGS.** ANONYMOUS: Gabriel flew down from
the vault of heaven and came to Nazareth; standing before the virgin Mary, he cried to her, "Rejoice! You shall conceive a son more ancient than
Adam, the Creator of all things and Savior of
those who cry to you. Rejoice, pure virgin!"

Gabriel brought from heaven good tidings to
the Virgin, and he cried out to her, "Rejoice! You
shall conceive him whom the world cannot contain; he shall be contained within your womb.
You shall bear him who shone forth from the
Father before the morning star!"[25]

The coeternal Word of the Father who has no
beginning, not being parted from the things on
high, has now descended here below, in his
boundless love taking pity on fallen humankind.
He has assumed the poverty of Adam, clothing
himself in a form strange to him. STICHERA OF
THE ANNUNCIATION.[26]

**MARY'S GENEALOGY: HOUSE OF DAVID AND
LEVI.** EPHREM THE SYRIAN: From what the angel
said to Mary, namely, "Elizabeth, your kinswoman," it could be supposed that Mary was from the
house of Levi. Nevertheless up to this, the prophecy was established within the framework of the
husbands. The family of David continued as far
as Joseph, who had espoused her, and the birth of
her child was reckoned through the framework of
the men, for the sake of the family of David. It is

---

[21]FC 52:24. [22]CS 110:22. [23]ECTD 52*. [24]FM 458-59**.
[25]Ps 110:3 (109:3 LXX). [26]FM 459**.

in Christ that the seed and family of David are brought to completion. Scripture is silent about Mary's genealogy since it is the generations of men that it numbers and reckons. If Scripture had been accustomed to indicate the family line through the mothers, it would be in order for one to seek the family of Mary. But, lest the words "Elizabeth, your kinswoman" were to show that Mary was also from the house of Levi, take note that the Evangelist has said elsewhere, concerning Joseph and Mary, that "they were both of the house of David."[27] The angel did not say to Mary that Elizabeth was her sister but "Elizabeth, your kinswoman." COMMENTARY ON TATIAN'S DIATESSARON 1.25.[28]

THE MYSTERY OF THE TIMELESS ENTERING TIME. JOHN THE MONK: Wonder! God is come among humanity; he who cannot be contained is contained in a womb; the timeless enters time, and great mystery: his conception is without seed, his emptying past telling! So great is this mystery! For God empties himself, takes flesh and is fashioned as a creature, when the angel tells the pure Virgin of her conception: "Rejoice, you who are full of grace; the Lord who has great mercy is with you!" STICHERA OF ANNUNCIATION.[29]

THE HOUSE OF DAVID AND JACOB IS THE UNIVERSAL CHURCH. BEDE: The time had come when, having redeemed the world through his blood, he was to be acknowledged as king not of the house of David alone but also of the whole church; moreover, that he was maker and governor of all generations. Hence the angel properly said afterwards, "and the Lord God will give him the seat of David his father," and he immediately added, "and he will reign in the house of Jacob forever." Now the house of Jacob refers to the universal church, which through its faith in and confession of Christ pertains to the heritage of the patriarchs—either among those who took their physical origin from the stock of the patriarchs or among those who, though brought forth

with respect to the flesh from other countries, were reborn in Christ by the spiritual washing. HOMILIES ON THE GOSPELS 1.3.[30]

1:34-35 The Conception of Jesus and More Designations of the Messiah

EXCEEDING ALL UNDERSTANDING. LEO THE GREAT: But the birth of our Lord Jesus Christ exceeds all understanding and goes beyond any precedent. SERMON 30.4.2.[31]

MARY'S VOW OF VIRGINITY. AUGUSTINE: Indeed, her virginity was itself more beautiful and more pleasing, because Christ, in his conception, did not himself take away that which he was preserving from violation by humanity; but, before he was conceived he chose one already consecrated to God of whom he would be born. HOLY VIRGINITY 4.[32]

THE VIRGIN BIRTH A DIVINE MYSTERY. AMBROSE: Here Mary seems to have disbelieved, unless you pay close attention, for it is not right that she who was chosen to bear the only-begotten Son of God should seem to have been without faith. And how could this be? Although the prerogative of the Mother, on whom a greater prerogative is straightway to be conferred, is intact, how could it be that Zechariah who had not believed was condemned to silence, but Mary, if she had not believed, would be exalted by the infusion of the Holy Spirit? But with a greater prerogative, also a greater faith must be reserved for her. But Mary must both believe, and not so heedlessly usurp. She must believe the angel and not usurp divine things. Nor is it easy to know "the mystery which has been hidden from eternity in God,"[33] which the higher powers could not know either. Nevertheless she did not deny the faith, she did not refuse the duty, but she conformed her will, she promised obedience. For

---

[27]See Lk 1:27; 2:4. [28]ECTD 53-54*. [29]FM 443-44*. [30]CS 110:23*. [31]FC 93:128-29*. [32]FC 27:146*. [33]Eph 3:9; cf. Col 1:26.

truly when she said, "How shall this be?" she did not doubt concerning the outcome but sought the nature of this same outcome. EXPOSITION OF THE GOSPEL OF LUKE 2.14.[34]

GABRIEL SHOULD FEAR MARY, NOT MARY GABRIEL. THEOPHANES: *Theotokos*: Make plain to me, how I, a virgin, shall bear him?

The angel: You seek to know from me the manner of your conceiving, Virgin, but this is beyond all interpretation! The Holy Spirit will overshadow you in his creative power and shall make this come to pass!

Theotokos: When she accepted the suggestion of the serpent, my mother Eve was banished from divine delight. Therefore I fear your strange greeting, for I take care that I not slip.

The angel: I am sent as God's messenger to disclose the divine will to you. Why are you afraid of me, undefiled one? I rather am afraid of you! Why do you stand in awe of me, O lady, who stand in reverent awe of you? CANON OF ANNUNCIATION.[35]

THE IMPREGNATING SPIRIT. PRUDENTIUS:
He had to be redeemed: my Spirit came down
And impregnated flesh made from the dust
With the divine nature; God has assumed
Humanity, joining it with divinity,
And kindled in men's hearts new love of me.
AGAINST SYMMACHUS 2.265-69.[36]

JESUS' BIRTH PREFIGURES OUR BIRTH TO NEW LIFE. PETER CHRYSOLOGUS: "Who was born from the Holy Spirit." Precisely thus is Christ born for you, in such a way that he may change your own manner of birth. . . . Formerly, death awaited you as the setting sun of your life; he wants you to have a new birth of life.

"Who was born from the Holy Spirit of the Virgin Mary." Where the Spirit is begetting, and a virgin giving birth, everything carried on is divine; nothing of it is merely human. SERMON 57.[37]

THE WATER OF BAPTISM IS LIKE THE VIR-
GIN'S WOMB. LEO THE GREAT: Each one is a partaker of this spiritual origin in regeneration. To every one, when he is reborn, the water of baptism is like the Virgin's womb, for the same Holy Spirit fills the font, who filled the Virgin, that the sin, which that sacred conception overthrew, may be taken away by this mystical washing. SERMON 24.3.[38]

FREEDOM THROUGH THE VIRGIN BIRTH.
AUGUSTINE: The first sinner, the first transgressor, begot sinners liable to death. To heal them, the Savior came from the Virgin; because he didn't come to you the way you came, seeing that he did not originate from the sexual appetite of male and female, not from that chain of lust. The Holy Spirit, it says, will come upon you. That was said to the Virgin glowing with faith, not seething with carnal lust. The Holy Spirit will come upon you, and the power of the Most High will overshadow you. Being overshadowed like that, how could she be seething with the heat of sexual desire? So, because he didn't come to you the way you came, he sets you free. SERMON 153.14.[39]

FRUITFUL BY THE HOLY SPIRIT. PRUDENTIUS:
When God's coming draws near, the angel
   Gabriel advances
From the Father's high throne and enters the
   house of the Virgin.
"Mary," he says, "the Holy Spirit will render
   you fruitful,
And you shall give birth to the Christ,
   O glorious Virgin."
SCENES FROM SACRED HISTORY 25.[40]

HOVERING SPIRIT SANCTIFIES FALLEN CRE-
ATION. EPHREM THE SYRIAN: It was fitting that the Architect of the works of creation should come and raise up the house that had fallen and that the hovering Spirit should sanctify the build-

---

[34]EHG 40*. [35]FM 450**. [36]FC 52:149. [37]FC 17:107. [38]NPNF 2 12:135*. [39]WSA 3 5:65. [40]FC 52:187.

ings that were unclean. Thus, if the Progenitor entrusted the judgment that is to come to his Son, it is clear that he accomplished the creation of humanity and its restoration through him as well. He was the live coal, which had come to kindle the briars and thorns.[41] He dwelt in the womb and cleansed it and sanctified the place of the birth pangs and the curses.[42] The flame, which Moses saw, was moistening the bush[43] and distilling the fat lest it be inflamed. The likeness of refined gold could be seen in the bush, entering into the fire but without being consumed. This happened so that it might make known that living fire which was to come at the end, watering and moistening the womb of the Virgin and clothing it like the fire that enveloped the bush. COMMENTARY ON TATIAN'S DIATESSARON 1.25.[44]

MARY NOW REPRESENTS TEMPLE, TABERNACLE AND ARK. THEOPHANES: *The angel:* Rejoice, lady; rejoice, most pure virgin! Rejoice, God-containing vessel! Rejoice, candlestick of the light, the restoration of Adam and the deliverance of Eve! Rejoice, holy mountain, shining sanctuary! Rejoice, bridal chamber of immortality!

Theotokos: The descent of the Holy Spirit has purified my soul; it has sanctified my body; it has made me a temple containing God, a divinely adorned tabernacle, a living sanctuary and the pure mother of life.

The angel: I see you as a lamp with many lights; a bridal chamber made by God! Spotless maiden, as an ark of gold, receive now the giver of the law, who through you has been pleased to deliver humankind's corrupted nature! CANON OF ANNUNCIATION.[45]

THE HOLY SPIRIT BRINGS A NEW CREATION. JOHN OF DAMASCUS: And through the invocation the overshadowing power of the Holy Ghost becomes a rainfall for this new cultivation. For just as all things whatsoever God made he made by the operation of the Holy Ghost, so also it is by the operation of the Spirit that these things are done which surpass nature and cannot be discerned except by faith alone. "How shall this be done to me," asked the blessed Virgin, "because I know not a man?" The archangel Gabriel answered, "The Holy Ghost shall come upon you, and the power of the Most High shall overshadow you." And now you ask how the bread becomes the body of Christ and the wine and water the blood of Christ. And I tell you that the Holy Ghost comes down and works these things which are beyond description and understanding. ORTHODOX FAITH 4.13.[46]

1:36-38 The Sign to Mary and Her Response of Faith

JESUS FROM PRIESTLY AND ROYAL TRIBES. BEDE: Now when the mediator between God and human beings[47] appeared in the world, it was fitting that he had his physical origin from both tribes because, in the humanity which he assumed, he would possess the roles of both priest and king. HOMILY ON THE GOSPELS 1.3.[48]

MARY'S OBEDIENCE REVERSES EVE'S DISOBEDIENCE. IRENAEUS: So the Lord now manifestly came to his own. Born by his own created order that he himself bears, he by his obedience on the tree renewed and reversed what was done by disobedience in connection with a tree. The power of that seduction by which the virgin Eve, already betrothed to a man, had been wickedly seduced was broken when the angel in truth brought good tidings to the Virgin Mary, who already by her betrothal belonged to a man. For as Eve was seduced by the word of an angel to flee from God, having rebelled against his Word, so Mary by the word of an angel received the glad tidings that she would bear God by obeying his Word. The former was seduced to disobey God and so fell, but the latter was persuaded to obey God, so that the Virgin Mary might become the advocate of Eve. As the human race

---

[41]See Gen 3:18; Is 9:18. [42]See Gen 3:16. [43]Ex 3:2-3. [44]ECTD 53*. [45]FM 455**. [46]FC 37:357. [47]1 Tim 2:5. [48]CS 110:26-27.

was subjected to death through the act of a virgin, so was it saved by a virgin was precisely balanced by the obedience of another. Then indeed the sin of the first formed man was amended by the chastisement of the First Begotten, the wisdom of the serpent was conquered by the sim-

plicity of the dove, and the chains were broken by which we were in bondage to death. AGAINST HERESIES 5.19-20.[49]

---

[49]LCC 1:389-90*.

1:39-45 THE VISITATION

[39]*In those days Mary arose and went with haste into the hill country, to a city of Judah,* [40]*and she entered the house of Zechariah and greeted Elizabeth.* [41]*And when Elizabeth heard the greeting of Mary, the babe leaped in her womb; and Elizabeth was filled with the Holy Spirit* [42]*and she exclaimed with a loud cry, "Blessed are you among women, and blessed is the fruit of your womb!* [43]*And why is this granted me, that the mother of my Lord should come to me?* [44]*For behold, when the voice of your greeting came to my ears, the babe in my womb leaped for joy.* [45]*And blessed is she who believed that there would be*[e] *a fulfilment of what was spoken to her from the Lord."*

e Or believed, for there will be

OVERVIEW: Mary visits Elizabeth so that the child in her womb might bless John and make him a forerunner (ORIGEN). Mary's humility leads her into the hill country of Judea to congratulate Elizabeth on the miraculous conception of John and to serve her cousin of advanced age in the final months of her pregnancy (BEDE).

John leaps in the womb as a miraculous sign of faith (AUGUSTINE). Already in the womb, John perceives the advent of the Christ and prophesies as the forerunner of the Messiah (MAXIMUS OF TURIN). The fleshly presence of the Messiah, the agent of creation, first causes Elizabeth's womb to be vivified, and then through the fruit of Mary's womb all of creation is vivified (EPHREM THE SYRIAN).

The incarnate presence of the Messiah evokes from Elizabeth a worshipful response in a psalmlike liturgical style. Her great voice is a sign of her devotion (BEDE). The aged Elizabeth cries out that Jesus is the Christ of God (PRUDENTIUS). Elizabeth, filled with the Holy Spirit, exclaims

the blessedness of Mary because of the fruit of her womb (ORIGEN). Elizabeth's question to Mary concerning the mother of her Lord coming to her shows Elizabeth's humility (BEDE). Mary's faith in God's promise leads the church to magnify the Lord as it now responds to Christ, the fruit of all the faithful (AMBROSE).

1:39-40 Mary Journeys to Greet Elizabeth

MARY VISITS ELIZABETH SO THAT JESUS COULD BLESS JOHN. ORIGEN: Better men go to weaker men to give them some advantage by their visits. Thus the Savior came to John to sanctify John's baptism. . . . Jesus was in her womb, and he hastened to sanctify John, who was still in his own mother's womb. Before Mary came and greeted Elizabeth, the infant did not rejoice in her womb. But as soon as Mary spoke the word that the Son of God, in his mother's womb, had supplied, "the infant [John] leaped in joy." At that moment Jesus made his forerunner a prophet for the first time. HOMILIES ON THE GOSPEL OF LUKE 7.1.[1]

MARY'S HUMILITY. BEDE: She went so that she could offer her congratulations concerning the gift which she had learned her fellow servant had received. This was not in order to prove the word of the angel by the attestation of a woman. Rather it was so that as an attentive young virgin she might commit herself to ministry to a woman of advanced age. HOMILIES ON THE GOSPELS 1.4.[2]

1:41 The Baby John Leaps in Elizabeth's Womb

JOHN'S LEAP A MIRACULOUS SIGN OF FAITH. AUGUSTINE: We see instances of leaping not only in children but even in animals, although certainly not for any faith or religion or rational recognition of someone coming. But this case stands out as utterly uncommon and new, because it took place in a womb, and at the coming of her who was to bring forth the Savior of humankind. Therefore this leaping, this greeting, so to speak, offered to the mother of the Lord is miraculous. It is to be reckoned among the great signs. It was not effected by human means by the infant, but by divine means in the infant, as miracles are usually wrought. LETTER 187.23.[3]

JOHN PROPHESIES FROM THE WOMB. MAXIMUS OF TURIN: Not yet born, already John prophesies and, while still in the enclosure of his mother's womb, confesses the coming of Christ with movements of joy—since he could not do so with his voice. As Elizabeth says to holy Mary, "As soon as you greeted me, the child in my womb exulted for joy." John exults, then, before he is born. Before his eyes can see what the world looks like, he can recognize the Lord of the world with his spirit. In this regard, I think that the prophetic phrase is appropriate: "Before I formed you in the womb I knew you, and before you came forth from the womb I sanctified you."[4] Thus we ought not to marvel that after Herod put him in prison,

he continued to announce Christ to his disciples from his confinement, when even confined in the womb he preached the same Lord by his movements. SERMON 5.4.[5]

THE VIVIFIED WOMB OF ELIZABETH. EPHREM THE SYRIAN: John jumped for joy to make an announcement concerning his future preaching. The infant of the barren woman exulted before the infant of the virgin. He sought out his mother's tongue and desired to pronounce a prophecy concerning the Lord. Therefore Elizabeth's conception was kept hidden from Mary for six months, until the infant would have limbs sufficiently formed to exult before the Lord with his jumping and become a witness to Mary through his exultation. Moreover, that he exulted in the womb of his mother was not of himself, nor because of his five months, but so that the divine gifts might show themselves in the barren womb that was now carrying him. It was also so that the other womb, that of the Virgin, would know the great gifts given to Elizabeth, and that the two soils might believe in the seeds they had received through the word of Gabriel, cultivator of both grounds. Since John could not cry out in his exultation and render witness to his Lord, his mother began to say, "You are blessed among women, and blessed is the fruit of your womb." Our Lord prepared his herald in a dead womb, to show that he came after a dead Adam. He vivified Elizabeth's womb first, and then vivified the soil of Adam through his body. COMMENTARY ON TATIAN'S DIATESSARON 1.30.[6]

1:42 Elizabeth's Liturgical Response

ELIZABETH'S VOICE OF DEVOTION. BEDE: [Elizabeth is attributed] properly with a great voice because she recognized the great gifts of God . . . [and] she sensed that he whom she knew to be present everywhere was also present bodily there. Indeed, by a "great" voice is not to be un-

---

[1]FC 94:28-29*. [2]CS 110:31-32**. [3]FC 30:239**. [4]Jer 1:5. [5]ACW 50:24**. [6]ECTD 57-58**.

derstood so much a loud voice as a devoted one. She was not capable of praising the Lord with the devotion of a moderate voice. Being full of the Holy Spirit, she was on fire, harboring in her womb the one than whom no one of those born of woman would be greater.[7] She rejoiced that he had come there—he who, conceived from the flesh of a virgin mother, would be called, and would be, the Son of the Most High. HOMILIES ON THE GOSPELS 1.4.[8]

ELIZABETH HERALDS CHRIST AS GOD. PRU-DENTIUS:

Believe what says the angel who was sent
From the Father's throne, or if your stolid ear
Catch not the voice from heaven, be wise
    and hear
The cry of aged woman, now with child.
O wondrous faith! The babe in senile womb
Greets through his mother's lips the Virgin's
    Son,
Our Lord; the child unborn makes known the
    cry
Of the Child bestowed on us,[9] for speechless
    yet,
He caused that mouth to herald Christ as
    God.
THE DIVINITY OF CHRIST 585-93.[10]

THE PRESENCE OF THE HOLY SPIRIT IN JOHN, ELIZABETH AND MARY. ORIGEN: Elizabeth, who was filled with the Holy Spirit at that moment, received the Spirit on account of her son. The mother did not inherit the Holy Spirit first. First John, still enclosed in her womb, received the Holy Spirit. Then she too, after her son was sanctified, was filled with the Holy Spirit. You will be able to believe this if you also learn something similar about the Savior. (In a certain number of manuscripts, we have discovered that blessed Mary is said to prophesy. We are not unaware of the fact that, according to other copies of the Gospel, Elizabeth speaks these words in prophecy.) Mary also was filled with the Holy Spirit when she began to carry the Savior in her womb. As soon as

she received the Holy Spirit, who was the creator of the Lord's body, and the Son of God began to exist in her womb, she too was filled with the Holy Spirit. HOMILIES ON THE GOSPEL OF LUKE 7.3.[11]

THE FRUIT OF MARY'S WOMB. BEDE: "Blessed is the fruit of your womb"—since through you we have recovered both the seed of incorruption and the fruit of our heavenly inheritance, which we lost in Adam. HOMILIES ON THE GOSPELS 1.4.[12]

1:43-45 Elizabeth's Wonder at Mary's Greeting

ELIZABETH'S HUMILITY. BEDE: "And whence does this happen to me, that the mother of my Lord should come to me?" Oh! What great humility in the mind of the prophet! How true the utterance of the Lord, in which he said, "Upon whom does my spirit rest if not upon one who is humble and quiet and who trembles at my words?"[13] As soon as Elizabeth saw the one who had come to her, she recognized that she was the mother of the Lord. But she discovered in herself no such merit by which she might have become worthy to be visited by such a guest. "Whence does this happen to me," she asked, "that the mother of my Lord should come to me?" Undoubtedly the very Spirit who conferred upon her the gift of prophecy at the same time endowed her with the favor of humility. Filled with the prophetic spirit, she understood that the mother of the Savior had drawn near to her. But being discreet in the spirit of humility, she understood that she herself was less than worthy of Mary's coming. HOMILIES ON THE GOSPELS 1.4.[14]

CHRIST THE FRUIT OF THE FAITHFUL. AMBROSE: You see that Mary did not doubt but believed and therefore obtained the fruit of faith. "Blessed . . . are you who have believed." But you also are blessed who have heard and believed. For

---

[7]Lk 7:28. [8]CS 110:32**. [9]Is 9:6. [10]FC 52:24-25. [11]FC 94:29. [12]CS 110:33*. [13]Is 66:2 LXX. [14]CS 110:34*.

a soul that has believed has both conceived and bears the Word of God and declares his works. Let the soul of Mary be in each of you, so that it magnifies the Lord. Let the spirit of Mary be in each of you, so that it rejoices in God.[15] She is the one mother of Christ according to the flesh, yet Christ is the Fruit of all according to faith. Every soul receives the Word of God, provided that, undefiled and unstained by vices, it guards its purity with inviolate modesty. EXPOSITION OF THE GOSPEL OF LUKE 2.26.[16]

---

[15]Lk 1:46-47. [16]EHG 45**.

1:46-56 THE MAGNIFICAT

[46]And Mary said,
  "My soul magnifies the Lord,
  [47]and my spirit rejoices in God my Savior,
  [48]for he has regarded the low estate of his handmaiden.
  For behold, henceforth all generations will call me blessed;
  [49]for he who is mighty has done great things for me,
  and holy is his name.
  [50]And his mercy is on those who fear him
  from generation to generation.
  [51]He has shown strength with his arm,
  he has scattered the proud in the imagination of their hearts,
  [52]he has put down the mighty from their thrones,
  and exalted those of low degree;
  [53]he has filled the hungry with good things,
  and the rich he has sent empty away.
  [54]He has helped his servant Israel,
  in remembrance of his mercy,
  [55]as he spoke to our fathers,
  to Abraham and to his posterity for ever."
[56]And Mary remained with her about three months, and returned to her home.

OVERVIEW: "The Magnificat is like an aria in opera; the action almost stops so that the situation may be savored more deeply."[1] The visitation marks the physical coming together of the mothers of these two final salvation figures (ORIGEN), but the Magnificat provides the theological significance of this meeting as Mary sums up her place in salvation history as she proclaims the new kingdom (EPHREM THE SYRIAN).

---

[1]R. Tannehill, The Narrative Unity of Luke-Acts, vol. 1, The Gospel According to Luke (Philadelphia: Fortress, 1986), p. 31.

Mary does not add anything to God by her song, but through the Magnificat, Christ is magnified in us through our image of him in our soul (ORIGEN). Mary is struck with a desire to sing a hymn of praise because she believes these things will happen despite the lowliness of her condition, "because he has regarded [literally, "looked upon"] with favor the low estate of his servant" (BEDE). In the Scriptures, humility is one of the virtues (ORIGEN).

Lowliness or the great reversal is accented by the theme of mercy for the generations and generations of those who fear the Holy One (ORIGEN) because he is not a respecter of persons. There are two general descriptions of how that mercy has been shown to Israel: the mighty arm of God scatters the proud and arrogant (BEDE), a clear reference to the exodus of the Israelites from Egypt[2] and to the scribes and Pharisees of Jesus' day (CYRIL OF ALEXANDRIA). God's "mighty ones" receive their strength from him, and their humility is a grace given (BEDE). Jesus gives a wonderful example of the rich and the hungry, the proud and the humble in the parable of the Pharisee and tax collector (AUGUSTINE).

By calling Israel a servant, Mary recalls the meaning of the name Israel—a man seeing God (BEDE). God comes in the suffering Servant to rescue his servant Israel, thereby remembering his promises to be merciful to his creation by giving the seed of Abraham a Savior (CYRIL OF ALEXANDRIA). The Seed of Abraham now rests in Mary's womb, the fulfillment of the covenant God promised, and through Mary's Son, God will give birth to the church—Abraham's eternal seed (BEDE).

1:46-49 *Mary's Hymn of Praise*

SALVATION BEGINS WITH WOMEN. ORIGEN: Elizabeth prophesies before John. Before the birth of the Lord and Savior, Mary prophesies. Sin began from the woman and then spread to the man. In the same way, salvation had its first beginnings from women. Thus the rest of women can also lay aside the weakness of their sex and imitate as closely as possible the lives and conduct of these holy women whom the Gospel now describes. HOMILIES ON THE GOSPEL OF LUKE 8.1.[3]

MARY PREACHES THE NEW KINGDOM. EPHREM THE SYRIAN: [Mary] revealed to Elizabeth what the angel spoke to her in secret, and that he called her blessed because she believed in the realization of the prophecy and the teaching that she heard. Then Mary gently brought forth the fruit of what she heard from the angel and Elizabeth: "My soul bless the Lord." Elizabeth had said, "Blessed is she who has believed," and Mary replied, "From henceforth all generations will call me blessed." It was then that Mary began to preach the new kingdom. "She returned home after three months," so that the Lord whom she was carrying would not begin service before his servant. She returned to her husband to clarify the matter, for if she had become pregnant through human fruit, it would have been appropriate for her to flee from her husband. COMMENTARY ON TATIAN'S DIATESSARON 1.28.[4]

THE LORD IS MAGNIFIED IN OUR IMAGE OF HIM. ORIGEN: Let us consider the Virgin's prophecy. She says, "My soul magnifies the Lord, and my spirit has rejoiced in God my Savior." Two subjects, "soul" and "spirit," carry out a double praise. The soul praises the Lord, the Spirit praises God—not because the praise of the Lord differs from the praise of God but because he who is God is also Lord, and he who is Lord is also God.

We ask how a soul can magnify the Lord. The Lord can undergo neither increase nor loss. He is what he is. Thus, why does Mary now say, "My soul magnifies the Lord?"... My soul is not directly an image of God. It was created as the image of an Image that already existed.... Each one of us shapes his soul into the image of Christ and makes either a larger or a smaller image of him. The image is either dingy and dirty, or it is clean and bright and corresponds to the form of

---

[2]See Ex 6:1-6; 15:6, 12, 16-17. [3]FC 94:33. [4]ECTD 56-57*.

the original. Therefore, when I make the image of the Image—that is, my soul—large and magnify it by work, thought and speech, then the Lord himself is magnified in my soul, because it is an image of him. Just as the Lord is thus magnified in our image of him, so too, if we are sinners, he diminishes and decreases.

But surely the Lord is not diminished, nor does he decrease. Rather, we create other images in ourselves instead of the Savior's image. Instead of being the image of the Word, or of wisdom, justice and the rest of the virtues, we assume the form of the devil. HOMILIES ON THE GOSPEL OF LUKE 8.1-3.[5]

MARY PROCLAIMS HER HUMILITY AND GOD'S HOLINESS. BEDE: In the following words she teaches us how worthless she felt of herself and that she received by the heavenly grace that was lavished on her every sort of good merit that she had. She says, "For he has considered the humility of his handmaid. For behold from this time on all generations will call me blessed." She demonstrates that in her own judgment she was indeed Christ's humble handmaid, but with respect to heavenly grace she pronounces herself all at once lifted up and glorified to such a degree that rightly her preeminent blessedness would be marveled at by the voices of all nations. HOMILIES ON THE GOSPELS 1.4.[6]

GOD DOES POWERFUL THINGS FOR THE HUMBLE. ORIGEN: "For behold, from now on all generations will call me blessed." If I take "all generations" literally, I apply it to believers. But, if I search for something more profound, I will notice how valuable it is to join to it, "because he who is powerful has done great things for me." For "everyone who humbles himself will be exalted." God looked upon the blessed Mary's humility, and on account of it "he who is powerful did great things for her, and holy is his name." HOMILIES ON THE GOSPEL OF LUKE 8.6.[7]

1:50-53 God's Mighty Acts of Mercy

MERCY FOR ALL BELIEVERS WHO FEAR GOD. ORIGEN: "And his mercy extends to generations of generations." God's mercy is not for one generation, nor for two, nor for three. It is not for five. It stretches "from generation to generation." "To those who fear him he has shown strength in his arm." You may approach the Lord as a weak man. If you fear him, you will be able to hear the promise the Lord makes to you on account of your fear of him. . . .

So, if you fear the Lord, he gives you courage or authority. He gives you the kingdom, so that you might be placed under the "king of kings" and possess the kingdom of heaven in Christ Jesus, to whom is glory and power for ages of ages. Amen. HOMILIES ON THE GOSPEL OF LUKE 8.6-7.[8]

GOD'S MERCY IS NOT A RESPECTER OF PERSONS. BEDE: She adds, more clearly, "And his mercy is for generations and generations to those who fear him." She names "generations and generations," referring either to both of the two peoples, namely, the Jews and the Gentiles, or alternatively to all the countries throughout the world which she foresaw would believe in Christ. For, as Peter said, "God is not a respecter of persons, but in every nation one who fears him and works justice is acceptable to him."[9] HOMILIES ON THE GOSPELS 1.4.[10]

GOD'S STRENGTH DESTROYS HUMAN PRIDE. BEDE: Because the venerable mother of God taught that his mercy would come to be present for all those who feared him throughout the world, it remained for her to also suggest what those who were proud and who despised the warnings of truth would deserve. "He has shown . . . might in his arm. He has scattered the proud in the imagination of their heart." "In his arm" signifies "under the control of his own strength." For he did not stand in need of any outside help, since, as was written with reference to him, the

---

[5]FC 94:33-34*. [6]CS 110:36-37**. [7]FC 94:36*. [8]FC 94:36. [9]Acts 10:34-35. [10]CS 110:37*.

strength is at hand when he wishes to do something.[11] This is said in contrast to our working of good, since we perform deeds of virtue not by the power of our own freedom to act, but in God.[12] And as it is written in another place, "And their arm did not save them, but your right hand and your arm, and the illumination of your countenance."[13] HOMILIES ON THE GOSPELS 1.4.[14]

MARY FORESEES THE PRIDE OF THE SCRIBES AND PHARISEES. CYRIL OF ALEXANDRIA: The arm enigmatically signifies the Word that was born of her. By the proud, Mary means the wicked demons who with their prince fell through pride; the Greek sages, who refused to receive the folly, as it seemed, of what was preached; and the Jews who would not believe and were scattered for their unworthy imaginations about the Word of God. By the mighty she means the scribes and Pharisees, who sought the chief seats. It is nearer the sense, however, to refer it to the wicked demons. When openly claiming mastery over the world, the Lord by his coming scattered them and transferred those whom they had made captive unto his own dominion. COMMENTARY ON LUKE.[15]

GOD'S MIGHTY ONES ARE HUMBLE. BEDE: Those whom he earlier calls "the proud" he here names "the mighty." Undoubtedly they are called proud because they extol themselves beyond measure as mighty with regard to their condition—not, however, because they are truly mighty, but because they trust in their own strength and scorn to seek their Maker's assistance. They, however, are truly mighty who know how to say with the apostle, "We can do all things in him who strengthens us, the Lord Jesus Christ."[16] Concerning them it is written, God does not cast off the mighty since he himself is mighty.[17] . . . However, this can also be properly understood to mean that sometimes those who had been rightly cast down by the Lord because of their self-glorification may in turn return to the grace of humili-

ty when he has mercy on them. HOMILIES ON THE GOSPELS 1.4.[18]

RICH AND HUNGRY—PHARISEE AND TAX COLLECTOR. AUGUSTINE: Who are the hungry? The humble, the needy. Who are the rich? Proud and self-important people. I will not send you far to find them. I will show you now, in one and the same temple, one of those rich who are sent away empty, and one of those poor who are filled with good things.

"Two men went up into the temple to pray. One a Pharisee and the other a tax collector."[19] . . . Observe the rich man burping his undigested food, breathing out the fumes of his intoxication —with pride, though, not with justice. "God," he says, "I thank you because I am not like other men, robbers, unjust, adulterers, like this tax collector here." . . .

Come, poor men—come along, hungry tax collector. Rather, stand there, where you are standing. The tax collector, you see, "was standing a long way off," but the Lord was drawing near to the humble. He did not dare to raise his eyes to heaven; yet where he did not raise his eyes, that is where he had his heart. SERMON 290.6.[20]

1:54 Mercy and Aid for Israel

MERCY FOR ISRAEL, A MAN SEEING GOD. BEDE: Through all the time of this transitory age, the just and merciful Creator is willing to oppose the proud and give grace to the humble.

After her general commemoration of the divine benevolence and justice, she did well to turn the words of her confession to the special divinely arranged plan of the unheard-of incarnation, by which God deigned to redeem the world, as she said, "He has taken his child Israel under his protection, being mindful of his mercy." Indeed, Israel means "a man seeing God," by

---

[11]Wis 12:18. [12]Ps 60:12 (59:14 LXX). [13]Ps 44:3 (43:4 LXX). [14]CS 110:38*. [15]CGSL 39**. [16]Phil 4:13. [17]Job 36:5. [18]CS 110:39*. [19]Lk 18:10. [20]WSA 3 8:128**.

which name is designated every society of redeemed human beings. On their account, God himself appeared in visible form among human beings, so that they might be capable of seeing God. He took Israel under his protection as a physician takes a sick person for whom he is caring. Or as a king, he defends the people from the invasion of enemies. Moreover, he returns them to liberty when the enemy has been overthrown and allows them to reign with him perpetually. HOMILIES ON THE GOSPELS 1.4.[21]

1:55-56 Abraham's Eternal Seed

GOD FULFILLS HIS PROMISE TO ISRAEL AND ABRAHAM. CYRIL OF ALEXANDRIA: He has taken hold of Israel—not of the Israel according to the flesh, who prides himself on the bare name, but of him who is so after the Spirit, in accordance with the true meaning of the appellation. The latter comprises those who look to God, believe in him and obtain through the Son the adoption of sons, according to the Word that was spoken and the promise made to the prophets and patriarchs of old. It has, however, a true application also to the carnal Israel, for many thousands and ten thousands of them believed. But he has remembered his mercy as he promised to Abraham and has accomplished what he said to him: that in his seed shall all the tribes of the earth be blessed.[22] This promise was not in the act of fulfillment by the impending birth of our common Savior Christ—who is the seed of Abraham,[23] in whom the Gentiles are blessed. For he took on him the seed of Abraham, according to the apostles' words, and fulfilled the promise made unto the fathers. COMMENTARY ON LUKE.[24]

THE CHURCH IS ABRAHAM'S ETERNAL SEED. BEDE: When blessed Mary was making mention of the memory of the fathers, she properly represented them by naming Abraham in particular. Although many of the fathers and holy ones mystically brought forward testimony of the Lord's incarnation, it was to Abraham that the hidden mysteries of this same Lord's incarnation and of our redemption were first clearly predicted. Also, to him it was specifically said, "And in you all the tribes of the earth will be blessed."[25] None of the faithful doubts that this pertains to the Lord and Savior, who in order to give us an everlasting blessing deigned to come to us from the stock of Abraham. However, "the seed of Abraham" does not refer only to those chosen ones who were brought forth physically from Abraham's lineage, but also to us. . . . Having been gathered together to Christ from the nations, we are connected by the fellowship of faith to the fathers, from whom we are far separated by the origin of our fleshly bloodline. We too are the seed and children of Abraham since we are reborn by the sacraments of our Redeemer, who assumed his flesh from the race of Abraham. HOMILIES ON THE GOSPELS 1.4.[26]

---

[21]CS 110:40**. [22]Gen 22:18. [23]Heb 2:16. [24]CGSL 40-41**. [25]Gen 12:3. [26]CS 110:41*.

1:57-66 THE BIRTH AND CIRCUMCISION OF JOHN

[57]Now the time came for Elizabeth to be delivered, and she gave birth to a son. [58]And her neighbors and kinsfolk heard that the Lord had shown great mercy to her, and they rejoiced with her. [59]And on the eighth day they came to circumcise the child; and they would have named him Zecha-

riah after his father, [60]but his mother said, "Not so; he shall be called John." [61]And they said to her, "None of your kindred is called by this name." [62]And they made signs to his father, inquiring what he would have him called. [63]And he asked for a writing tablet, and wrote, "His name is John." And they all marveled. [64]And immediately his mouth was opened and his tongue loosed, and he spoke, blessing God. [65]And fear came on all their neighbors. And all these things were talked about through all the hill country of Judea; [66]and all who heard them laid them up in their hearts, saying, "What then will this child be?" For the hand of the Lord was with him.

OVERVIEW: That this is the final Old Testament prophet who prepares for the Messiah is highlighted by the parallels between John and Jesus, a theme of the infancy narrative of Luke (EPHREM THE SYRIAN). John is born of the seed of man, but Jesus is born from a virgin without seed (SYNAXIS).

Circumcision on the eighth day is a foreshadowing of the release from death of all creation on the day of Jesus' resurrection. The child of Zechariah and Elizabeth receives the name John because it means "the grace of God" (BEDE). The manner of John's miraculous birth by the Spirit that enlivens a barren womb anticipates his preaching of repentance that awakens a dead world with the light of Christ (SYNAXIS).

What the angel bound up, this infant child and the power of his name now sets free so that this priest might prophesy concerning John's role in salvation history (MAXIMUS OF TURIN). This extraordinary reversal of the expectations of the people as to his name results in fear at the extraordinary miracle of John's birth that will draw people to him from every place to repent in preparation to receive God's sacramental mysteries (BEDE).

1:57-58 Elizabeth Bears a Son

THE PARALLELS BETWEEN JOHN AND JESUS.
EPHREM THE SYRIAN: The elderly Elizabeth gave birth to the last of the prophets, and Mary, a young girl, to the Lord of the angels. The daughter of Aaron gave birth to the voice in the desert,[1] but the daughter of David to the strong God of

the earth. The barren one gave birth to him who remits sins, but the Virgin gave birth to him who takes them away.[2] Elizabeth gave birth to him who reconciled people through repentance, but Mary gave birth to him who purified the lands of uncleanness. The elder one lit a lamp in the house of Jacob, his father, for this lamp itself was John,[3] while the younger one lit the Sun of Justice[4] for all the nations. The angel announced to Zechariah, so that the slain one would proclaim the crucified one and that the hated one would proclaim the envied one. He who was to baptize with water would proclaim him who would baptize with fire and with the Holy Spirit.[5] The light, which was not obscure, would proclaim the Sun of Justice. The one filled with the Spirit would proclaim concerning him who gives the Spirit. The priest calling with the trumpet would proclaim concerning the one who is to come at the sound of the trumpet at the end. The voice would proclaim concerning the Word, and the one who saw the dove would proclaim concerning him upon whom the dove rested, like the lightning before the thunder. COMMENTARY ON TATIAN'S DIATESSARON 1.31.[6]

JOHN THE FORERUNNER OF CHRIST. ANONYMOUS: Joyfully we honor you, O John most blessed, who have appeared on earth as equal of the angels in your unaccustomed way of life, and high above all humankind....

Unto you was revealed, O prophet, the mys-

---

[1]Is 63:9. [2]Jn 1:29. [3]Jn 5:35. [4]Mal 4:2 (3:20 LXX). [5]Mt 3:11. [6]ECTD 58-59*.

tery of the one essence of the Godhead in three consubstantial persons. For through the voice of the Father and the coming of the Spirit you have known him who was baptized to be the everlasting Word of God.

Child of a barren mother, O most venerable John, you were the spiritual dawn announcing the sun who shone forth from the virgin; and you have proclaimed the lamb who in his love for humankind takes away the sin of the world. SYNAXIS OF JOHN THE BAPTIST.[7]

1:59-63 The Circumcision and Naming of John

CIRCUMCISION ON THE EIGHTH DAY AN IMAGE OF THE RESURRECTION. BEDE: John's circumcision clearly set forth an image of the Lord's resurrection because it too occurred on the eighth day, that is, on the day after the sabbath. And just as the former was wont to release people from the punishable state of everlasting death, so the latter displayed the perfect newness of immortal life in our Creator, and revealed that it is to be hoped for in us. HOMILIES ON THE GOSPELS 2.20.[8]

JOHN'S NAME MEANS "GRACE OF GOD." BEDE: John means "the grace of God" or "in whom there is grace." By this name are expressed the entire extent of the grace of the gospel dispensation which he was to proclaim, and especially the Lord himself, through whom this grace was to be granted to the world. . . .

As to his subsequent declaration and confirmation of the name of John, and the opening of Zechariah's mouth and his speaking, blessing God, it is surely evident that once the grace of the new covenant was manifested by the apostles, a large number of priests also became obedient to the faith. HOMILIES ON THE GOSPELS 2.20.[9]

JOHN'S BIRTH ANTICIPATES CHRIST'S ADVENT. ANONYMOUS: O forerunner of Christ! . . . O Baptist inspired by God! We glorify Christ

who bowed his head before you in the Jordan and sanctified the nature of mortal humankind. . . .

O wise John the forerunner, you have looked down from the bank of the river upon the glory of the Father's Word, even the Son as he stood in the waters; and you have seen the Spirit descend as a dove, cleansing and enlightening the ends of the earth. To you the mystery of the Trinity was revealed; and to you we sing, honoring your divine festival.

O Baptist and forerunner, strengthened by the divine grace of Christ you have shown us the lamb that takes away all the sins of the world,[10] and with joy you have this day brought two disciples to him.[11] Entreat him that peace and great mercy may be given to our souls. SYNAXIS OF JOHN THE BAPTIST.[12]

1:64-66 Zechariah's Tongue Loosed

JOHN GAVE HIS FATHER BACK HIS VOICE. MAXIMUS OF TURIN: When John his son was born, among his neighbors there was concern about what name he should be given. Writing tablets were offered to his father so that he himself could put down the name that he had decided upon, so that he might express in writing what he could not in speech. Then, in a wonderful manner, when he had taken the tablets in order to begin writing, his tongue was loosened, the written word gave way to speech, and he did not write "John" but spoke it. Consider, then, the merit of the holy Baptist: he gave his father back his voice, he restored the faculty of speech to the priest. Consider, I say, his merit: John unloosed the mouth that the angel had bound. What Gabriel had closed the little child unlocked. . . . When John is born the father suddenly becomes a prophet or priest, speech attains its use, love receives an offspring, the office recognizes the priest. SERMON 6.1.[13]

---

[7]FM 400**. [8]CS 111:208*. [9]CS 111:206-7. [10]Jn 1:29, 35-36 [11]Jn 1:35-42. [12]FM 388-89**. [13]ACW 50:25*.

A SALUTARY FEAR DRAWS PEOPLE. BEDE: On the day of John's circumcision, when he also received his name, "fear came upon all their neighbors, and all these words were spread abroad throughout the mountain country of Judea." Furthermore, at the time of our Lord's resurrection, when the Spirit had been sent down from above and the glory of his name was made known to the world by the apostles, a most salutary fear immediately struck the hearts. Not only of the Jews, who were of the neighborhood either by their physical location or by their knowledge of the law, but also those of foreign nations, even to the ends of the earth. And John's reputation for virtue exceeded not only the whole mountain country of Judea, but also all the heights of worldly kingdoms and worldly wisdom, so that everywhere people left behind their former way of life and flocked together to attain the sacramental mysteries of his faith. HOMILIES ON THE GOSPELS 2.20.[14]

---

[14]CS 111:207-8*.

1:67-80 THE BENEDICTUS

[67]*And his father Zechariah was filled with the Holy Spirit, and prophesied, saying,*
[68]*"Blessed be the Lord God of Israel,*
for he has visited and redeemed his people,
[69]*and has raised up a horn of salvation for us*
in the house of his servant David,
[70]*as he spoke by the mouth of his holy prophets from of old,*
[71]*that we should be saved from our enemies,*
and from the hand of all who hate us;
[72]*to perform the mercy promised to our fathers,*
and to remember his holy covenant,
[73]*the oath which he swore to our father Abraham,* [74]*to grant us·*
that we, being delivered from the hand of our enemies,
might serve him without fear,
[75]*in holiness and righteousness before him all the days of our life.*
[76]*And you, child, will be called the prophet of the Most High;*
for you will go before the Lord to prepare his ways,
[77]*to give knowledge of salvation to his people*
in the forgiveness of their sins,
[78]*through the tender mercy of our God,*
when the day shall dawn upon us from on high
[79]*to give light to those who sit in darkness and in the shadow of death,*
to guide our feet into the way of peace."

^{80}*And the child grew and became strong in spirit, and he was in the wilderness till the day of his manifestation to Israel.*

f Or *whereby the dayspring will visit*. Other ancient authorities read *since the dayspring has visited*

OVERVIEW: The Benedictus hymn embraces the Old Testament and the New Testament by describing God's mighty acts of salvation in the past and how John and Jesus will bring these mighty acts to fulfillment (NICETA OF REMESIANA). The Holy Spirit now fills Zechariah so that his prophecy breaks the nine-month silence as he speaks to John's opened ears on the day of his circumcision (AMBROSE). Zechariah acknowledges at the beginning of this canticle the incarnation and atonement of Christ for which John will prepare (BEDE). The symbol of the horn in the house of David indicates power and royalty (JEROME). David's seed will produce a horn of salvation planted in the vineyard of Israel, whose vine is Christ (ORIGEN).[1] Central to this hymn is God's remembrance of his holy covenant and the oath he swore to Abraham, an oath that assures Israel of the certainty of God's promise (CYRIL OF ALEXANDRIA). Thus the motive is God's faithfulness to his promise to visit his people and redeem them from all their enemies, corporeal and spiritual (ORIGEN).

Just as John leapt in the womb when he heard the voice of Mary who bore his Savior, so now he hears the voice of his father, Zechariah, who instructs him before he goes forth into the wilderness like Moses (ORIGEN). John is called "prophet of the Most High" because his office is from God like all the prophets before him (CYRIL OF ALEXANDRIA).

John is that lamp that lights the way for Christ's coming, typified by the law, which preceded the coming of the Messiah (CYRIL OF ALEXANDRIA). God's goal of incarnation and atonement is to bring peace to his creation that now sits in darkness and the shadow of death and to guide his people to peace (BEDE). The dayspring from on high is the Son of the Highest (GREGORY OF NAZIANZUS). This is the Christ who is the Light and Sun that brings this peace to the creation (CYRIL OF ALEXANDRIA). The Evangelist concludes the Benedictus by giving the hearer a glimpse of the mystery of how John grew in the Spirit (ORIGEN).

1:67 Zechariah, Filled with the Holy Spirit, Prophesied

ZECHARIAH'S PROPHECY IS A HYMN. NICETA OF REMESIANA: That which was spiritual in the Old Testament, for example, faith, piety, prayer, fasting, patience, chastity and psalm singing— all this has been increased in the New Testament rather than diminished. Therefore you will find in the Gospel Zechariah, the father of John, who uttered a prophecy in the form of a hymn after his long silence. LITURGICAL SINGING 9.[2]

THE HOLY SPIRIT OPENS JOHN'S EARS. AMBROSE: Some might consider it ridiculous that [Zechariah] spoke to an eight-day-old infant.[3] But if we hold the truth, we will understand that the child who heard the salutation of Mary before his birth could hear the voice of his father. The prophet knew that a prophet has other ears that are opened by the Spirit of God despite bodily age. He who had the disposition to rejoice had the perception of understanding. EXPOSITION OF THE GOSPEL OF LUKE 2.34.[4]

1:68-70 God's Visitation and Redemption as Foretold

BLESSED FOR INCARNATION AND ATONEMENT. BEDE: Hear what Zechariah, prophesying and blessing God, said: "Blessed be the Lord God of

---

[1]See FC 94:10n. [2]FC 7:72*. [3]Lk 1:59. [4]EHG 49**; CSEL 32 4:59.

Israel, for he has visited and redeemed his people." Notice in these words that Zechariah was telling by way of prophecy, as if it had already come to pass, what he had foreseen in spirit had begun and would soon come to pass. By his appearance in the flesh our Lord visited us when we were distancing ourselves from him, and he chose to seek out and justify us when we were sinners. He visited us as a doctor visits an ill patient, and, in order to cure the ingrained sickness of our pride, he gave us the example of his own humility. He redeemed his people by giving us freedom, at the price of his own blood—we who had been sold into the slavery of sin and were committed to serving the ancient enemy. Therefore the apostle exhorts us, saying, "For you have been purchased at a great price. Glorify and carry God in your bodies."[5] HOMILIES ON THE GOSPELS 2.20.[6]

THE HORN IS FOR POWER AND ROYALTY. JEROME: The sound of the horn represents the man of God in all his sovereignty. In Scripture, the horn properly signifies kingship and power, just as it is written: "He has raised up a horn of salvation for us." HOMILIES ON THE PSALMS 25.[7]

REDEMPTION THROUGH DAVID'S SEED. ORIGEN: Over the course of three months Zechariah kept receiving spiritual nourishment from the Holy Spirit. Although he did not realize it, he was being instructed. Then he prophesied about Christ and said, "He redeemed his people and has raised up a horn of salvation for us in the house of his servant David," because Christ was "descended from David according to the flesh."[8] He was truly "a horn of salvation in the house of David," since the following passage reinforces it: "For a vineyard was planted on the horn-shaped ridge."[9] Which horn was it planted on? On Christ Jesus, of whom Scripture now says, "He raised up a horn of salvation for us in the house of his servant David, as he spoke by the mouth of his holy prophets from of old." HOMILIES ON THE GOSPEL OF LUKE 10.2.[10]

1:71-75 Remembering God's Covenant of Deliverance and Mercy

CHRIST IS MERCY AND JUSTICE. CYRIL OF ALEXANDRIA: Christ is mercy and justice. We have obtained mercy through him and been justified, having washed away the stains of wickedness through faith that is in him. COMMENTARY ON LUKE.[11]

GOD'S OATH DEMONSTRATES CERTAINTY. CYRIL OF ALEXANDRIA: No one should swear just because God swore to Abraham. For just as God's anger is not anger, nor does anger imply passion but signifies power exercised in punishment or some similar motion. So neither is an oath an act of swearing. For God does not swear but indicates the certainty of the event—so that which he says will necessarily come to pass. For God's oath is his own word, fully persuading those that hear and giving each one the conviction that what he has promised and said will certainly come to pass. COMMENTARY ON LUKE.[12]

DELIVERANCE IN HEAVEN AND ON EARTH. ORIGEN: "Deliverance from our enemies." We should not think that this means corporeal enemies, but rather spiritual ones. For the Lord Jesus came, "mighty in battle,"[13] to destroy all our enemies and free us from their snares, namely, from the hand of all our enemies "and from the hand of all who hate us." "To bring about mercy for our fathers." I believe that, when our Lord came, Abraham, Isaac and Jacob were blessed with God's mercy. Previously they had seen his day and rejoiced.[14] It is not believable that they did not profit from the later, when he came and was born of a virgin. And why do I speak of the patriarchs? I will boldly follow the authority of the Scriptures to higher planes, for the presence of the Lord Jesus and his work benefited not only what is earthly but also what is heavenly. There-

---

[5]1 Cor 6:20. [6]CS 111:208-9*. [7]FC 48:201. [8]Rom 1:3. [9]Is 5:1 LXX. [10]FC 94:40-41**. [11]CGSL 41*. [12]CGSL 41. [13]Ps 24:8. [14]See Jn 8:56.

fore the apostle too says, "Making peace by the blood of his cross, whether on earth or in heaven."[15] But if the Lord's presence was beneficial in heaven and on earth, why do you hesitate to say that his coming also benefited our ancestors? What Scripture said is fulfilled, "To perform the mercy promised to our fathers, and to remember his holy covenant, the oath which he swore to our father Abraham," to grant us deliverance "without fear from the hand of our enemies." Homilies on the Gospel of Luke 10.3.[16]

1:76-77 John to Prepare the Way of the Lord

Zechariah Teaches John as an Infant.
Origen: So John heard Jesus while he was still in his mother's womb, and he leaped up and rejoiced when he heard him. Why might you not believe that John could understand his father's prophecy once he was born, as Zechariah said to him: "And you, child, will be called the prophet of the Most High, for you will go before the Lord to prepare his ways." So I suppose that Zechariah hastily spoke to the infant because he knew John would soon be living in the desert, and therefore he would no longer enjoy John's presence. "For the boy was in the wilderness up to the day of his revelation to Israel."

Moses also lived in the desert. After turning forty years old, he fled from Egypt and pastured Jethro's herds for another forty years.[17] But John went out to the wilderness as soon as he was born. Homilies on the Gospel of Luke 10.6-7.[18]

Prophet of the Highest Comes from God.
Cyril of Alexandria: Know that Christ is the Most High.... What do those who neglect his divinity have to say? And why will they not understand that when Zechariah said "And you, child, will be called the prophet of the Most High, he meant "of God," of whom the rest of the prophets also belonged. Commentary on Luke.[19]

1:78-79 The Visitation of Peace on Those in Darkness

John as the Lamp Preceding Christ.
Cyril of Alexandria: For those under the law and dwelling in Judea, John the Baptist was a lamp preceding Christ. God also spoke of him in a similar way: "I have prepared a lamp for my anointed."[20] And the law also typified him in the lamp. In the first tabernacle it was necessary for the lamp to always remain lit. But the Jews, after being pleased with him for a short time, flocking to his baptism and admiring his mode of life, quickly made him sleep in death, doing their best to extinguish the ever-burning lamp. Therefore the Savior also spoke of him as "a burning and shining lamp, and you were willing to rejoice for a while in his light."[21] Commentary on Luke.[22]

God Enters the Darkness of Our World and Brings Light.
Bede: When Zechariah says, "for his people," he certainly does not mean that he found them his people upon his arrival but that he made them his by visiting and redeeming them. Do you want to hear about the condition in which he found this people and what he made of them? The end of this canticle clearly makes this evident by saying "the day shall dawn upon us from on high to give light to those who sit in darkness and in the shadow of death, to guide our feet into the way of peace." He found us sitting in darkness and in the shadow of death, weighed down by the ancient blindness of sins and ignorance, overcome by the deception and the errors of the ancient enemy. He is rightly called death and a lie,[23] just as on the contrary our Lord is called truth and life.[24] Our Lord brought us the true light of recognition of himself and, having taken away the darkness of errors, opened up for us a sure way to heaven. He guided our works so that we may be able to pursue the way of truth that he showed us and enter into the dwelling of everlasting

---

[15]Col 1:20. [16]FC 94:41*. [17]Ex 2:15; Acts 7:23, 30. [18]FC 94:42-43**. [19]CGSL 41**. [20]Ps 132:17 (131:17 LXX). [21]Jn 5:35. [22]CGSL 42**. [23]Jn 8:44. [24]Jn 14:6.

peace, which he promised us. HOMILIES ON THE GOSPELS 2.20.[25]

THE DAYSPRING IS THE SON OF THE MOST HIGH. GREGORY OF NAZIANZUS: What greater destiny can befall man's humility than that he should be intermingled with God, and by this intermingling should be deified, and that we should be so visited by the "dayspring from on high"? Further, that even the holy thing that should be born should be called the Son of the Most High and that he should be given "a name that is above every name"? And what else can this be but God? That every knee should bow to him that was made of no reputation for us, that mingled the form of God with the form of a servant, and that all the house of Israel should know that God has made him both Lord and Christ? For all this was done by the action of the begotten One, and by the good pleasure of him that begot him. ORATION 30.3, ON THE SON.[26]

CHRIST BRINGS PEACE. CYRIL OF ALEXANDRIA: For the world was wandering in error, serving the creation in the place of the Creator and was darkened over by the blackness of ignorance. Night, as it were, that had fallen upon the minds of all, permitted them not to see him, who is truly and by nature God. But the Lord of all rose for the Israelites, like a light and a sun. COMMENTARY ON LUKE.[27]

1:80 *John Grows Strong in Spirit*

HOW JOHN BECAME STRONG IN THE SPIRIT. ORIGEN: John, while still a little boy, grew and became stronger. But it is exceedingly difficult, and very rare among mortals, for one who is still a little child to grow in spirit. "But the boy grew and was strengthened in spirit." It is one thing to "grow," another to "be strengthened." Human nature is weak. It needs divine help to become stronger. We read, "The flesh is weak." What forces can strengthen it? The Spirit, of course, "for the spirit is quick to respond, but the flesh is weak." Someone who wants to become stronger should be strengthened only in spirit. Many are strengthened in the flesh, and their bodies become more powerful, but an athlete of God should become more powerful in spirit. Thus strengthened, he will crush the wisdom of the flesh. Spiritual activity will subject the body to the soul's command. We should not think that, when Scripture says, "he grew and was strengthened in spirit," what was written about John was just a narrative that does not pertain to us in any way. It is written for our imitation. We should take "growth" in the sense we have explained and be multiplied spiritually. HOMILIES ON THE GOSPEL OF LUKE 11.3.[28]

---

[25]CS 111:209. [26]LCC 3:178-79*. [27]CGSL 42*. [28]FC 94:45*.

2:1-20 THE BIRTH OF JESUS

[1]*In those days a decree went out from Caesar Augustus that all the world should be enrolled.* [2]*This was the first enrollment, when Quirinius was governor of Syria.* [3]*And all went to be enrolled, each to his own city.* [4]*And Joseph also went up from Galilee, from the city of Nazareth, to Judea, to the city of David, which is called Bethlehem, because he was of the house and lineage of*

David, [5]to be enrolled with Mary, his betrothed, who was with child. [6]And while they were there, the time came for her to be delivered. [7]And she gave birth to her first-born son and wrapped him in swaddling cloths, and laid him in a manger, because there was no place for them in the inn.

[8]And in that region there were shepherds out in the field, keeping watch over their flock by night. [9]And an angel of the Lord appeared to them, and the glory of the Lord shone around them, and they were filled with fear. [10]And the angel said to them, "Be not afraid; for behold, I bring you good news of a great joy which will come to all the people; [11]for to you is born this day in the city of David a Savior, who is Christ the Lord. [12]And this will be a sign for you: you will find a babe wrapped in swaddling cloths and lying in a manger." [13]And suddenly there was with the angel a multitude of the heavenly host praising God and saying,

[14]"Glory to God in the highest,
and on earth peace among men with whom he is pleased!"[g]

[15]When the angels went away from them into heaven, the shepherds said to one another, "Let us go over to Bethlehem and see this thing that has happened, which the Lord has made known to us." [16]And they went with haste, and found Mary and Joseph, and the babe lying in a manger. [17]And when they saw it they made known the saying which had been told them concerning this child; [18]and all who heard it wondered at what the shepherds told them. [19]But Mary kept all these things, pondering them in her heart. [20]And the shepherds returned, glorifying and praising God for all they had heard and seen, as it had been told them.

g Other ancient authorities read *peace, good will among men*

OVERVIEW: As the hearer comes to the birth of Jesus, he sees in the nativity of Jesus the source for all the great feasts in the church catholic: Easter, the ascension and Pentecost (CHRYSOSTOM). The first scene sets the historical context for the birth of Jesus with time designations for the census and the birth of the child (EUSEBIUS). The triumph of Augustus prefigures that of Christ, through whom all the faithful were enrolled in the name of the Godhead (CASSIA). By his birth during a census, Jesus pays tribute to Caesar so that his presence in the world might bring an eternal peace (BEDE).

Although Jesus was conceived in Nazareth, the census causes Mary to journey to Bethlehem so that he might be born in the city of David, for Bethlehem means "house of bread" (BEDE). Mary is betrothed to Joseph, but the babe in her womb was conceived without a man's seed (CYRIL OF ALEXANDRIA).

Bethlehem has now become the new Eden, for paradise will now be opened with the birth of Christ (IKOS OF THE NATIVITY). The Virgin Mary provides a temple for Jesus' flesh (CYRIL OF ALEXANDRIA). He is clearly God and man, the firstborn of Mary and the firstborn of all humanity, firstborn in grace (BEDE), who humbled himself so that we may become perfect humans (AMBROSE). Wrapped in swaddling clothes and not Tyrian purple, Jesus is lying in a manger (BEDE). Through swaddling clothes Jesus releases us from the bands of sin that bind us (JOHN THE MONK). He shows how he assumes our weak human nature so that he might restore to us our original robe of immortality (CHRYSOSTOM). And he is laid in a manger like fodder for people who act like beasts, so even now he is for us the bread from heaven (CYRIL OF ALEXANDRIA). The stable where he is born is also filled with dung, reflecting the humility of his birth (JEROME). The Lord of creation has no place to be born except a manger among beasts of burden (AMBROSE, JEROME). There is no room in the inn by the wayside because Jesus by his incarnation now becomes our way home (BEDE).

As angels catechized Mary and Joseph, so now they catechize the shepherds (AMBROSE). Like all shepherds of the flock who follow them, these shepherds need the presence of Christ. The angels announce in Jesus the healer of the nations (ORIGEN). When the angel announces that "today" a "Savior" is born, he signals the dawn of a new day that will scatter the darkness because of the presence of the kingdom of God in the person and ministry of Jesus (BEDE). The Savior has two miraculous births: born of the Father always, he is now born of a virgin once (AUGUSTINE). Beginning with the strips of cloth for the infant Jesus as a sign of the Messiah's birth and concluding with his dead body wrapped in a shroud at his burial,[1] Luke connects Jesus' birth, death and resurrection (GREGORY OF NAZIANZUS).

The *Gloria in Excelsis* states the earthly consequences of peace and goodwill through Jesus' birth (CYRIL OF ALEXANDRIA). In heaven, the result is glory to God; on earth, Jesus' birth brings peace to those upon whom God's favor rests (JEROME). Heaven is on earth in the person of Jesus, for they are joined together in his birth (JOHN THE MONK). In the birth of Jesus, God's glory is manifested on earth as peace and good will between God and humanity, between angels and men (GREGORY THE GREAT). Jesus is the man of peace who is the embodiment of consummate and perfect wisdom (AUGUSTINE). In the birth and death of Jesus of Nazareth, heaven and earth are joined together in peace (EPHREM THE SYRIAN).

Shepherds, the first proclaimers of the gospel, set the pattern for preaching of the church's shepherds. She ponders in her heart what she had heard, and she compares this with what she had read in the Old Testament and what she is now perceiving in the birth of Jesus (BEDE).

2:1-5 *The Roman Census*

ALL GREAT FEASTS HAVE THEIR ORIGIN IN JESUS' NATIVITY. CHRYSOSTOM: A feast day is about to arrive, and it is the most holy and awesome of all feasts. It would be no mistake to call it the chief and mother of all holy days. What feast is that? It is the day of Christ's birth in the flesh.

It is from this day that the feasts of the theophany, the sacred Pasch [Passover], the ascension and Pentecost had their source and foundation. Had Christ not been born in the flesh, he would not have been baptized, which is the theophany or manifestation. Nor would he have been crucified, which is the Pasch. Nor would he have sent down the Spirit, which is Pentecost. Therefore, just as different rivers arise from a single source, these other feasts have their beginnings in the birth of Christ. ON THE INCOMPREHENSIBLE NATURE OF GOD 6.23-24.[2]

THE HISTORICAL CONTEXT OF THE CENSUS. EUSEBIUS: It was the forty second year of the reign of Augustus and twenty-eight years after the oppression of Egypt and the death of Antony and Cleopatra when Jesus was born in Bethlehem according to the prophecies concerning him. Flavius Josephus mentions this census in the time of Quirinius, adding another account about the sect of Galileans that arose at about the same time. Luke, among our writers, mentions this sect in Acts, saying, "After him Judas the Galilean arose in the days of the census and drew some people after him. He also perished, and all who followed him were scattered."[3] ECCLESIASTICAL HISTORY 1.5.[4]

AUGUSTUS'S TRIUMPH PREFIGURES CHRIST'S TRIUMPH. CASSIA: When Augustus reigned alone upon earth, the many kingdoms of humankind came to end; and when you were made man of the pure Virgin, the many gods of idolatry were destroyed. The cities of the world passed under

---

[1]Lk 23:53. [2]FC 72:174-75*. [3]Acts 5:37. [4]FC 19:54-55*.

one single rule; and the nations came to believe in one sovereign Godhead. The peoples were enrolled by the decree of Caesar; and we, the faithful, were enrolled in the name of the Godhead, when you, our God, were made man. Great is your mercy: glory to you! STICHERA OF THE NATIVITY OF THE LORD.[5]

A TIME OF PEACE FOR JESUS, WHO IS OUR PEACE. BEDE: He chose a time of utmost peace as the time when he would be born because this was the reason for his being born in the world, that he might lead the human race back to the gifts of heavenly peace. And, indeed it is written: "For he is our peace, who has made us both one,"[6] that is, he who as a kind mediator and reconciler has made one house of God of angels and humanity. Jesus was born in a time of peace, so that even by the circumstance of the time he might teach that he was the very one of whom the prophecy sent before him spoke: "His sovereignty will be multiplied, and there will be no end of peace."[7] HOMILIES ON THE GOSPELS 1.6.[8]

BETHLEHEM MEANS "HOUSE OF BREAD." BEDE: And even to the end of the world the Lord would not cease to be conceived in Nazareth and born in Bethlehem, as often as any one of those who hear him, taking the flour of his Word, make for themselves a house of eternal bread. Daily in the virginal womb, that is, in the souls of the faithful, is he conceived by faith and brought forth by baptism. EXPOSITION OF THE GOSPEL OF LUKE 2.6.[9]

CHRIST CONCEIVED WITHOUT MAN'S SEED. CYRIL OF ALEXANDRIA: The Evangelist says that Mary was engaged to be married to Joseph, to show that the conception had taken place only upon her engagement, and that the birth of the Emmanuel was miraculous, and not in accordance with the laws of nature. For the Virgin did not bear from the emission of man's seed. And why was this so? Christ, who is the first fruits of all, the second Adam according to the Scriptures, was born of the Spirit, that he might transmit the

grace (of the spiritual birth) to us also. For we too were intended no longer to bear the name of sons of men, but rather of God. We have obtained the new birth of the Spirit in Christ first, that he might be "foremost among all,"[10] as Paul declares.

And the occasion of the census conveniently caused the virgin to go to Bethlehem, so that we might see another prophecy fulfilled. For it is written, "But you, Bethlehem Ephratha, who are little to be among the clans of Judah, from you shall come forth for me one who is to be ruler in Israel!"[11] Some argue that if he were brought forth in the flesh, the Virgin was corrupted. If she were not corrupted, then he was brought forth only in appearance. We reply, "the Lord, the God of Israel, has entered in and gone out, and the gate remains closed."[12] If, moreover, the Word was made flesh without sexual intercourse, being conceived altogether without seed, then he was born without injury to her virginity. COMMENTARY ON LUKE, HOMILY 1.[13]

2:6-7 The Birth of Jesus

BETHLEHEM HAS OPENED EDEN. ANONYMOUS: Bethlehem has opened Eden: Come, let us see! We have found joy hidden! Come, let us take possession of the paradise within the cave. There the unwatered stem has appeared, from which forgiveness blossoms forth! There the undug well is found from which David longed to drink of old![14] There the Virgin has borne a child, and at once the thirst of Adam and David is made to cease. Therefore let us hasten to this place where for our sake the eternal God was born as a little child! IKOS OF THE NATIVITY OF THE LORD.[15]

MARY IS THE TEMPLE FOR JESUS' FLESH. CYRIL OF ALEXANDRIA: The book of the sacred Gospels referring the genealogy to Joseph, who

---

[5]FM 172. [6]Eph 2:14. [7]Is 9:7. [8]CS 110:52-54. [9]SSGF 1:102-3*. [10]Col 1:15. [11]Mic 5:2. [12]Ezek 44:2 [13]CGSL 48**. [14]2 Sam 23:15. [15]FM 278**.

was descended from David's house, has proved through him that the Virgin also was of the same tribe as David, inasmuch as the divine law commanded that marriages should be confined to those of the same tribe. And Paul, the interpreter of the heavenly doctrines, clearly declares the truth, bearing witness that the Lord arose out of Judah.[16] The natures, however, which combined unto this real union were different, but from the two together is one God the Son, without the diversity of the natures being destroyed by the union. For a union of two natures was made, and therefore we confess one Christ, one Son, one Lord. And it is with this notion of a union that we proclaim the Virgin to be the mother of God, because God the Word was made flesh and became man, and by the act of conception united to himself the temple that he received from her. For we perceive that two natures, by an inseparable union, met together in him without confusion, and indivisibly. For the flesh is flesh and not deity, even though it became the flesh of God. In like manner also the Word is God and not flesh, though for the dispensation's sake he made the flesh his own. But although the natures which came together to form the union are both different and unequal to one another, yet he who is formed from them both is only one. We may not separate the one Lord Jesus Christ into man and God, but we affirm that Christ Jesus is one and the same, acknowledging the distinction of the natures, and preserving them free from confusion with one another. COMMENTARY ON LUKE, HOMILY 1.[17]

FIRSTBORN OF ALL HUMANITY. BEDE: He calls the Lord "firstborn," not because we should believe that Mary gave birth to other sons after him, since it is true that she was memorable for her unique perpetual chastity with Joseph her husband. But he properly names him "firstborn" because, as John says, "But to as many as received him he gave them the power to become sons of God."[18] Among these sons he rightfully holds the primacy who, before he was born in the flesh, was

Son of God, born without beginning. However, he descended to earth. He shared in our nature and lavished upon us a sharing in his grace, so that "he should be the firstborn of many brothers."[19] HOMILIES ON THE GOSPELS 1.6.[20]

FIRSTBORN IN GRACE. BEDE: He is the only-begotten of the substance of the divinity, firstborn in the assuming of humanity; firstborn in grace, only-begotten in nature. EXPOSITION OF THE GOSPEL OF LUKE 2.7.[21]

CHRIST BECAME A HUMBLE CHILD. AMBROSE: He was a baby and a child, so that you may be a perfect human. He was wrapped in swaddling clothes, so that you may be freed from the snares of death.[22] He was in a manger, so that you may be in the altar. He was on earth that you may be in the stars. He had no other place in the inn, so that you may have many mansions in the heavens.[23] "He, being rich, became poor for your sakes, that through his poverty you might be rich."[24] Therefore his poverty is our inheritance, and the Lord's weakness is our virtue. He chose to lack for himself, that he may abound for all. The sobs of that appalling infancy cleanse me, those tears wash away my sins. Therefore, Lord Jesus, I owe more to your sufferings because I was redeemed than I do to works for which I was created. . . .

You see that he is in swaddling clothes. You do not see that he is in heaven. You hear the cries of an infant, but you do not hear the lowing of an ox recognizing its Master, for the ox knows his Owner and the donkey his Master's crib.[25] EXPOSITION OF THE GOSPEL OF LUKE 2.41-42.[26]

SWADDLING CLOTHES, NOT TYRIAN PURPLE. BEDE: "He was wounded for our transgressions, he was bruised for our iniquities."[27] It should be noted that the sign given of the Savior's birth is not a

---

[16]Heb 7:14. [17]*CGSL* 47**. [18]Jn 1:12. [19]Rom 8:29. [20]CS 110:57. [21]*SSGF* 1:103. [22]See Ps 18:4 (17:5 LXX). [23]See Jn 14:2; Eph 2:6. [24]2 Cor 8:9. [25]Is 1:3. [26]*EHG* 52-53**. [27]Is 53:5.

child enfolded in Tyrian purple, but one wrapped with rough pieces of cloth. He is not to be found in an ornate golden bed, but in a manger. The meaning of this is that he did not merely take upon himself our lowly mortality, but for our sakes took upon himself the clothing of the poor. Though he was rich, yet for our sake he became poor, so that by his poverty we might become rich.[28] Though he was Lord of heaven, he became a poor man on earth, to teach those who lived on earth that by poverty of spirit they might win the kingdom of heaven. EXPOSITION OF THE GOSPEL OF LUKE 1.[29]

THROUGH SWADDLING CLOTHES JESUS LOOSES THE BANDS OF SIN. JOHN THE MONK: Rejoice, O Jerusalem, and celebrate, all who love Zion! Today the ancient bond of the condemnation of Adam is loosed. Paradise is opened to us: the serpent is laid low. Of old he deceived the woman in Paradise, but now he sees a woman become mother of the Creator. Oh, the depth of the riches of the wisdom and knowledge of God![30] The sinful vessel that brought death upon all flesh has become the first fruits of salvation through the Theotokos for all the world. For from her the all-perfect God is born a child, and by his birth he sets the seal on her virginity. Through his swaddling clothes he looses the bands of sin. And through becoming a child he heals Eve's pangs in travail. Therefore let all creation sing and dance for joy, for Christ has come to restore it and to save our souls! STICHERA OF THE NATIVITY OF THE LORD.[31]

SWADDLING CLOTHES AND MANGER SIGNAL A HUMAN BIRTH. CHRYSOSTOM: To prevent you from thinking that his coming to earth was merely an accommodation, and to give you solid grounds for truly believing that his was real flesh, he was conceived, born and nurtured. That his birth might be made manifest and become common knowledge, he was laid in a manger, not in some small room but in a lodging place before numerous people. This was the reason for the swaddling clothes and also for the

prophecies spoken long before. The prophecies showed not only that he was going to be a man but that he would be conceived, born and nurtured as any child would be. AGAINST THE ANOMOEANS 7.49.[32]

LIKE FODDER IN A MANGER. CYRIL OF ALEXANDRIA: He found humanity reduced to the level of the beasts. Therefore he is placed like feed in a manger, that we, having left behind our carnal desires, might rise up to that degree of intelligence which befits human nature. Whereas we were brutish in soul, by now approaching the manger, yes, his table, we find no longer feed, but the bread from heaven, which is the body of life. COMMENTARY ON LUKE, HOMILY 1.[33]

JESUS WAS BORN IN A STABLE OF DUNG. JEROME: He found no room in the Holy of Holies that shone with gold, precious stones, pure silk and silver. He is not born in the midst of gold and riches, but in the midst of dung, in a stable where our sins were filthier than the dung. He is born on a dunghill in order to lift up those who come from it: "From the dunghill he lifts up the poor."[34] ON THE NATIVITY OF THE LORD.[35]

HEAVENLY LIGHT IN AN EARTHLY INN. AMBROSE: He is brought forth from the womb but flashes from heaven. He lies in an earthly inn but is alive with heavenly light. EXPOSITION OF THE GOSPEL OF LUKE 2.42-43.[36]

THE LORD OF CREATION HAS NO PLACE TO BE BORN. JEROME: The Lord is born on earth, and he does not have even a cell in which to be born, for there was no room for him in the inn. The entire human race had a place, and the Lord about to be born on earth had none. He found no room among men. He found no room in Plato, none in Aristotle, but in a manger, among beasts

---

[28]2 Cor 8:9. [29]CCL 120:51-52. [30]Rom 11:33. [31]FM 265-66**. [32]FC 72:205*. [33]CGSL 50**. [34]Ps 113:7 (112:7 LXX). [35]FC 57:221**. [36]EHG 54**.

of burden and brute animals, and among the simple, too, and the innocent. For that reason the Lord says in the Gospel: "The foxes have dens, and the birds of the air have nests, but the Son of Man has nowhere to lay his head."[37] HOMILIES ON THE PSALMS 44.[38]

THE INCARNATION GUIDES US TO OUR HOME. BEDE: He who sits at the right hand of the Father goes without shelter from the inn, that he may for us get ready many mansions[39] in the house of his heavenly Father. Hence we have "because there was no room for him in the inn." He was born not in the house of his parents but at the inn, by the wayside, because through the mystery of the incarnation he is become the Way by which he guides us to our home, where we shall also enjoy the Truth and the Life. EXPOSITION OF THE GOSPEL OF LUKE 2.7.[40]

2:8-15 The Shepherds Hear the Announcement and Receive a Sign

CATECHETICAL LECTURES OF ANGELS. AMBROSE: See how divine care adds faith. An angel tells Mary, an Angel tells Joseph, an angel tells the shepherds. It does not suffice that a messenger is sent once. For every word stands with two or three witnesses. EXPOSITION OF THE GOSPEL OF LUKE 2.51.[41]

SHEPHERDS NEED THE PRESENCE OF CHRIST. ORIGEN: Listen, shepherds of the churches! Listen, God's shepherds! His angel always comes down from heaven and proclaims to you, "Today a Savior is born for you, who is Christ the Lord." For, unless that Shepherd comes, the shepherds of the churches will be unable to guard the flock well. Their custody is weak, unless Christ pastures and guards along with them. We read in the apostle: "We are coworkers with God."[42] A good shepherd, who imitates the good Shepherd, is a coworker with God and Christ. He is a good shepherd precisely because he has the best Shepherd with him, pasturing his sheep along with

him. For "God established in his church apostles, prophets, evangelists, shepherds and teachers. He established everything for the perfection of the saints."[43] HOMILIES ON THE GOSPEL OF LUKE 12.2.[44]

ANGELS ANNOUNCE THE BIRTH OF THE HEALER OF NATIONS. ORIGEN: After the Lord came to the earth, "He established peace through the blood of his cross, both for those upon the earth and those who are in heaven."[45] And the angels wanted people to remember their Creator. They had done everything in their power to cure them, but they were unwilling to be cured. Then the angels behold him who could effect a cure. They give glory and say, "Glory to God on high, and peace on earth." HOMILIES ON THE GOSPEL OF LUKE 13.3.[46]

BORN "TODAY" TO SIGNAL THE DAWN OF A NEW DAY. BEDE: It is good that the angel said "has been born today" and did not say "this night." He appeared with heavenly light to those who were conducting the watch by night and brought the good news that day was born. . . . He who appeared temporally in the city of David as a human being from a virgin mother was, in truth, himself born before all time and without spatial limitation, light from light, true God from true God. Because, therefore, the light of life rose for those of us dwelling in the region of the shadow of death,[47] the herald of this rising says, "A savior has been born to you today." So that being always advised by this word we may remember that the night of ancient blindness is past and the day of eternal salvation has arrived. Let us cast off the works of darkness.[48] And let us walk as children of light,[49] "for the fruit of the light is in all justice and holiness."[50] HOMILIES ON THE GOSPELS 1.6.[51]

---

[37]Lk 9:58. [38]FC 48:331-32*. [39]Jn 14:2. [40]SSGF 1:103-4. [41]EHG 57. [42]1 Cor 3:9. [43]Eph 4:11-12; 1 Cor 12:28. [44]FC 94:48-49**. [45]Col 1:20. [46]FC 94: 53*. [47]Is 9:2 (9:1 LXX). [48]Rom 13:12. [49]Eph 5:8. [50]Eph 5:9. [51]CS 110:61**.

Born of the Father Always, Born of the Virgin Once. Augustine: Your faith, which has gathered you all here in this large crowd, is well aware that a Savior was born for us today. He was born of the Father always, of his mother once; of the Father without reference to sex, of his mother without the use of it. With the Father, of course, there was no womb to conceive him in; with his mother there was no male embrace to beget him. By the first nativity from the Father nature was preserved. By the second nativity from his mother the seeds of grace were sown. In the former he retained the majesty of the divine substance. In the latter he took on fellowship with us in our human mortality. And the reason he was prepared to come through this latter birth was so that he might become obedient to the death[52] and by dying might conquer death. Sermon 372.1.[53]

Swaddling Bands. Gregory of Nazianzus: He was wrapped in swaddling bands, but at the resurrection he released the swaddling bands of the grave. He was laid in a manger but was praised by angels, disclosed by a star and adored by magi. Oration 29.19, On the Son.[54]

The Christ Child Makes for Us Peace and Goodwill. Cyril of Alexandria: Look not upon him who was laid in the manger as a babe merely, but in our poverty see him who as God is rich, and in the measure of our humanity him who prospers those in heaven, and who therefore is glorified even by the angels. And how noble was the hymn, "Glory to God in the highest, and on earth peace, and among men good will!" The angels and archangels, thrones and lordships, and the seraphim are at peace with God. Never in any way do they oppose his good pleasure but are firmly established in righteousness and holiness. But we wretched beings, by having set up our own lusts in opposition to the will of our Lord, had put ourselves into the position of his enemies. Christ has abolished this. "For he is our peace"[55] and has united us by himself to God the Father. He has taken away from

the middle the cause of the enmity and so justifies us by faith, makes us holy and without blame, and calls near to him those who were far off. Besides this, he has created the two people into one new man, so making peace and reconciling both in one body to the Father.[56] For it pleased God the Father to form into one new whole all things in him, and to bind together things below and things above, and to make those in heaven and those on earth into one flock. Christ therefore has been made for us both peace and goodwill. Commentary on Luke, Homily 2.[57]

Glory in Heaven, Peace on Earth. Jerome: In heaven, where there is no discord, glory rules. On earth, where every day is warfare, peace prevails. Peace among whom? Among men. Why are the Gentiles without peace? Why, too, the Jews? That is exactly the reason for the qualification: Peace among men of good will, among those who acknowledge the birth of Christ. On the Nativity of the Lord.[58]

Heaven and Earth Are Joined in the Birth of Christ. John the Monk: Heaven and earth are united today, for Christ is born! Today God has come upon earth, and humankind gone up to heaven. Today, for the sake of humankind, the invisible one is seen in the flesh. Therefore let us glorify him and cry aloud: glory to God in the highest, and on earth peace bestowed by your coming, Savior: glory to you!

Today in Bethlehem, I hear the angels: glory to God in the highest! Glory to him whose good pleasure it was that there be peace on earth! The Virgin is now more spacious than the heavens. Light has shone on those in darkness, exalting the lowly who sing like the angels: Glory to God in the highest!

Beholding him [Adam] who was in God's image and likeness fallen through transgression, Jesus bowed the heavens and came down, without

---

[52]Phil 2:8. [53]*WSA* 3 10:316**. [54]*FGFR* 258*. [55]Eph 2:14. [56]Eph 2:15-16. [57]*CGSL* 54**. [58]FC 57:223-24*.

change taking up his dwelling in a virgin womb, that he might refashion Adam fallen in corruption, and crying out: glory to your epiphany, my Savior and my God! STICHERA OF THE NATIVITY OF THE LORD.[59]

PEACE BETWEEN HUMANITY AND ANGELS. GREGORY THE GREAT: Before the Redeemer was born in the flesh, there was discord between us and the angels, from whose brightness and holy perfection we were separated, in punishment first of original sin and then because of our daily offences. Because through sin we had become strangers to God, the angels as God's subjects cut us off from their fellowship. But since we have now acknowledged our King, the angels receive us as fellow citizens. Because the King of heaven has taken unto himself the flesh of our earth, the angels from their heavenly heights no longer look down upon our infirmity. Now they are at peace with us, putting away the remembrance of the ancient discord. Now they honor us as friends, whom before they considered to be weak and despised. HOMILIES ON THE GOSPELS 8.2.[60]

A MAN OF CONSUMMATE AND PERFECT WISDOM. AUGUSTINE: Man is unable to rule over the lower things unless he in turn submits to the rule of a higher being. And this is the peace that is promised "on earth to men of good will." This is the life of a man of consummate and perfect wisdom. The prince of this world, who rules over the perverse and disorderly, has been cast out of a thoroughly pacified and orderly kingdom of this kind. When this peace has been established and strengthened within a man, then he who has been cast out—no matter what persecutions he may stir up from without increases the glory that is according to God. SERMON ON THE MOUNT 1.2.9.[61]

PEACE IN HEAVEN AND GLORY ON EARTH. EPHREM THE SYRIAN: As peace began to be established, the angels proclaimed: "Glory in the highest and peace on earth." When lower beings received peace from superior beings, "they cried, Glory on earth and peace in the heavens."[62] At that time when the divinity came down and was clothed in humanity, the angels cried, "Peace on earth." And at the time when that humanity ascended in order to be absorbed into the divinity and sit on the right, "Peace in heaven," the infants were crying forth before him, "Hosanna in the highest."[63] Hence the apostle also learned that one should say, "He made peace by the blood of his cross for that which is in heaven and on earth."[64]

A further interpretation is that the angels cried forth: "Glory in the highest and peace on earth," and that the children cried out, "Peace in heaven and glory on earth."[65] This is to show that just as the grace of his mercy gave joy to sinners on earth, so too their repentance gave joy to the angels in heaven.[66] "Glory to God!" came from free will. Peace and reconciliation were for those against whom he was angry, and hope and remission were for the guilty. COMMENTARY ON TATIAN'S DIATESSARON 2.14-15.[67]

2:16-20 The Response of the Shepherds, the People and Mary

SHEPHERDS FIRST PROCLAIMERS OF THE GOSPEL. BEDE: The shepherds did not keep silent about the hidden mysteries that they had come to know by divine influence. They told whomever they could. Spiritual shepherds in the church are appointed especially for this, that they may proclaim the mysteries of the Word of God and that they may show to their listeners that the marvels which they have learned in the Scriptures are to be marveled at. HOMILIES ON THE GOSPELS 1.7.[68]

MARY PONDERS THE FULFILLMENT OF OLD TESTAMENT PROPHECIES. BEDE: Abiding by the

---

[59]FM 263-64**. [60]SSGF 1:121**. [61]FC 11:24*; ACW 5:16. [62]Lk 19:38. [63]Mt 21:9. [64]Col 1:20. [65]Lk 19:38. [66]Lk 15:7-10. [67]ECTD 66-67*. [68]CS 110:68-69*.

rules of virginal modesty, Mary wished to divulge to no one the secret things which she knew about Christ. She reverently waited for the time and place when he would wish to divulge them. However, though her mouth was silent, in her careful, watchful heart she weighed these secret things. And this is what the Evangelist says, pondering in her heart—indeed, she weighed those acts which she saw in relation to those things which she had read were to be done. Now she saw that she herself, who had arisen from the stock of Jesse, had conceived God's Son of the Holy Spirit. She had read in the prophet, "A shoot will sprout from the root of Jesse, and a 'nazareus' will ascend from his root, and the Spirit of the Lord shall rest upon him."[69] She had read, "And you, Bethlehem Ephratha, are a little one among the thousands of Judah. Out of you will come forth for me the one who is ruler in Israel, and his coming forth is from the beginning, from the days of eternity."[70] She saw that she had given birth in Bethlehem to the Ruler of Israel, who was born eternal from the Father, God before the ages. She saw that she had conceived as a virgin, and given birth to a son, and called his name Jesus. She had read in the prophets, "Behold, a virgin will conceive and give birth to a son, and his name will be called Immanuel."[71] She had read, "An ox recognizes its owner and an ass its master's manger."[72] She saw the Lord lying in a manger, where an ox and an ass used to come to be nourished. She remembered that it had been said to her by the angel, "The Holy Spirit will come upon you, and the power of the Most High will overshadow you, and so the holy one who will be born from you will be called the Son of God."[73] She had read that the manner of his nativity could be recognized only by the revelation of an angel, in accordance with Isaiah's saying, "Who will tell of his generation?"[74] She had read, "And you, tower of the flock, misty daughter of Zion, to you shall it come, the former power shall come, the kingdom of the daughter of Jerusalem."[75] She heard that angelic powers, who are daughters of the city on high, had appeared to shepherds in a place which was in former times called "tower of the flock" from the gathering of cattle—and this is one mile to the east of Bethlehem. There, even now, the three tombs of these shepherds are pointed out in a church. She then knew that the Lord had come in the flesh, whose power is one and eternal with the Father, and he would give to his daughter the church the kingdom of the heavenly Jerusalem. Mary was comparing these things which she had read were to occur with those which she recognized as already having occurred. Nevertheless she did not bring these things forth from her mouth but kept them closed up in her heart. HOMILIES ON THE GOSPELS 1.7.[76]

---

[69]Is 11:1-2; Heb. *nezer* is "branch, shoot, sprout"; cf. Mt 2:23. [70]Mic 5:2. [71]Is 7:14. [72]Is 1:3. [73]Lk 1:35. [74]See Is 53:8. [75]Mic 4:8. [76]CS 110:69-70*.

2:21 THE CIRCUMCISION AND NAMING OF JESUS

[21]*And at the end of eight days, when he was circumcised, he was called Jesus, the name given by the angel before he was conceived in the womb.*

OVERVIEW: Jesus' circumcision is a one-time event availing for all. The name Jesus has the power to defeat Satan and the spirits of darkness (ORIGEN). Already on the eighth day of Jesus' life, his destiny of atonement and resurrection is revealed in his name, his circumcision and his baptism as the eschaton is inaugurated (BEDE, CYRIL OF ALEXANDRIA).

2:21 Circumcised on the Eighth Day

ALL HUMANITY IS CIRCUMCISED IN JESUS' CIRCUMCISION. ORIGEN: So, when he died, we died with him, and when he rose, we rose with him. Likewise, we were also circumcised along with him. After his circumcision, we were cleansed by a solemn purification. Hence we have no need at all for a circumcision of the flesh. You should know that he was circumcised for our sake. Listen to Paul's clear proclamation. He says, "For in him the whole fullness of deity dwells bodily, and you have come to fullness of life in him, who is the head of all rule and authority. In him also you were circumcised with a circumcision made without hands, by putting off the body of flesh in the circumcision of Christ. And you were buried with him in baptism, in which you were also raised with him through faith in the working of God, who raised him from the dead."[1] Therefore his death, his resurrection and his circumcision took place for our sake. HOMILIES ON THE GOSPEL OF LUKE 14.1.[2]

THE POWER IN THE NAME OF JESUS. ORIGEN: Christians are seen to draw their courage not from incantations but from the name of Jesus and from the commemoration of what he has done. For by his name it has happened very often that demons are put to flight from people, especially whenever they, who invoke them, pronounce them with the right disposition and with all trust. So great indeed is the power of the name of Jesus that sometimes it is efficacious even when spoken by the wicked. The name of Jesus heals the afflicted in mind, puts to flight the spirits of darkness, and to the sick is an ever present remedy. AGAINST CELSUS 1.6.[3]

THE LAST DAYS ARE INAUGURATED. BEDE: He therefore received in the flesh the circumcision decreed by the law, although he appeared in the flesh absolutely without any blemish of pollution. He who came in the likeness of sinful flesh[4]—not in sinful flesh—did not turn away from the remedy by which sinful flesh was ordinarily made clean. Similarly, not because of necessity but for the sake of example, he also submitted to the water of baptism, by which he wanted the people of the new law of grace to be washed from the stain of sins. . . .

The reason "the child who was born to us, the son who was given to us,"[5] received the name Jesus (that is, "Savior") does not need explanation in order to be understood by us, but we need eager and vigilant zeal so that we too may be saved by sharing in his name. Indeed, we read how the angel interprets the name of Jesus: "He will save his people from their sins."[6] And without a doubt we believe and hope that the one who saves us from sins is not failing to save us also from the corruptions which happen because of sins, and from death itself, as the psalmist testifies when he says, "Who forgives all your iniquity, who heals all your diseases."[7] Indeed, with the pardoning of all of our iniquities, all our diseases will be completely healed when, with the appearance of the glory of the resurrection, our last enemy, death, will be destroyed. . . . We read that circumcision was done with knives made of rock,[8] and the rock was Christ.[9] And by Christ's faith, hope and love the hearts of the good are purified not only in baptism but furthermore in every devout action. This daily circumcision of ours (that is, the continual cleansing of our heart) does not cease from always celebrating the sacrament of the eighth day. HOMILIES ON THE GOSPELS 1.11.[10]

THE EIGHTH DAY: CIRCUMCISION, BAPTISM AND RESURRECTION. CYRIL OF ALEXANDRIA: St. Paul says that "neither circumcision counts for anything nor uncircumcision."[11] On the eighth day Christ rose from the dead and gave us the

---

[1]Col 2:9-12. [2]FC 94:56*. [3]SSGF 1:188. [4]Rom 8:3. [5]Is 9:6. [6]Mt 1:21. [7]Ps 103:3 (102:3 LXX). [8]Josh 5:2. [9]1 Cor 10:4. [10]CS 110:103, 107-8**. [11]1 Cor 7:19.

spiritual circumcision. He then commanded the holy apostles, "Go therefore and make disciples of all nations, baptizing them in the name of the Father and of the Son and of the Holy Spirit."[12] And we affirm that the spiritual circumcision takes place chiefly in holy baptism, when Christ makes us partakers of the Holy Spirit too. Of this Joshua, that Jesus of old, who became the leader of the Israelites after Moses, was also a type. He led the children of Israel across the Jordan, then made them stop and immediately circumcised them with knives of stone. So when we have crossed the Jordan, Christ circumcises us with the power of the Holy Spirit, not by purifying the flesh but rather by cutting off the defilement that is in our souls. On the eighth day, therefore, Christ was circumcised and, as I said, received his name. We were saved by him and through him, because "in him also you were circumcised with a circumcision made without hands, by putting off the body of flesh in the circumcision of Christ. And you were buried with him in baptism, in which you were also raised with him."[13] His death, therefore, was for our sake, as were also his resurrection and his circumcision. For he died, so that we who have died together with him in his dying to sin, would no longer live for sin. Thus if we have died together with him, we shall also live together with him.[14] He is said to have died to sin, not because he had sinned, for he was without sin, neither was guile found on his lips,[15] but because of our sin. Therefore, just as we died together with him when he died, so will we also rise together with him. . . .

After Jesus' circumcision, the rite was abolished by the introduction of baptism, of which circumcision was a type. For this reason we are no longer circumcised. It seems to me that circumcision achieved three distinct ends. In the first place, it separated the descendants of Abraham by a sort of sign and seal and distinguished them from all other nations. Second, it prefigured in itself the grace and efficacy of divine baptism. Formerly a male who was circumcised was included among the people of God by virtue of that seal; nowadays, a person who is baptized and has formed in himself Christ the seal, becomes a member of God's adopted family. Third, circumcision is the symbol of the faithful when they are established in grace, as they cut away and mortify the tumultuous rising of carnal pleasures and passions by the sharp surgery of faith and by ascetic labors. They do this not by cutting the body but by purifying the heart. They do this by being circumcised in the spirit and not in the letter. Their praise, as St. Paul testifies, needs not the sentence of any human tribunal, but depends upon the decree from above.[16] Commentary on Luke, Homily 3.[17]

---

[12]Mt 28:19. [13]Col 2:11-12. [14]2 Tim 2:11. [15]1 Pet 2:22. [16]See Rom 2:29. [17]CGSL 57-58**.

2:22-40 THE INFANT LORD COMES TO HIS TEMPLE

[22]*And when the time came for their purification according to the law of Moses, they brought him up to Jerusalem to present him to the Lord* [23]*(as it is written in the law of the Lord, "Every male that opens the womb shall be called holy to the Lord")* [24]*and to offer a sacrifice according to what is said in the law of the Lord, "a pair of turtledoves, or two young pigeons."* [25]*Now there was*

a man in Jerusalem, whose name was Simeon, and this man was righteous and devout, looking for the consolation of Israel, and the Holy Spirit was upon him. ²⁶*And it had been revealed to him by the Holy Spirit that he should not see death before he had seen the Lord's Christ.* ²⁷*And inspired by the Spirit*^h *he came into the temple; and when the parents brought in the child Jesus, to do for him according to the custom of the law,* ²⁸*he took him up in his arms and blessed God and said,*

²⁹*"Lord, now lettest thou thy servant depart in peace,*

according to thy word;

³⁰*for mine eyes have seen thy salvation*

³¹*which thou hast prepared in the presence of all peoples,*

³²*a light for revelation to the Gentiles,*

and for glory to thy people Israel."

³³*And his father and his mother marveled at what was said about him;* ³⁴*and Simeon blessed them and said to Mary his mother,*

"Behold, this child is set for the fall and rising of many in Israel,

and for a sign that is spoken against

³⁵*(and a sword will pierce through your own soul also),*

that thoughts out of many hearts may be revealed."

³⁶*And there was a prophetess, Anna, the daughter of Phanuel, of the tribe of Asher; she was of a great age, having lived with her husband seven years from her virginity,* ³⁷*and as a widow till she was eighty-four. She did not depart from the temple, worshiping with fasting and prayer night and day.* ³⁸*And coming up at that very hour she gave thanks to God, and spoke of him to all who were looking for the redemption of Jerusalem.*

³⁹*And when they had performed everything according to the law of the Lord, they returned into Galilee, to their own city, Nazareth.* ⁴⁰*And the child grew and became strong, filled with wisdom; and the favor of God was upon him.*

h Or *in the Spirit*

Overview: Seventy weeks after the announcement of John's birth to Zechariah by the angel Gabriel and forty days after his birth, Jesus comes to his temple to fulfill the Torah for the second time. He comes from his circumcision to the altar just as we, after baptism, come to the sacrament of his body and blood (Bede). The closed womb of virginity that Jesus opens is signified by the east door of the temple, through which only the high priest may enter (Jerome). Joseph and Mary were of a "humble state," that is, too poor to be able to afford a lamb. Their offering was marked by poverty, simplicity and chastity (Origen). The true sacrifice of Christ was the chastity of his body and the grace of his spirit (Ambrose).

Simeon is portrayed like the other Old Testament saints in the infancy narrative (Zechariah, Elizabeth, Mary and Joseph). He and Anna are portrayed here as representatives of the synagogue (Bede). Simeon is privileged to see Jesus in the flesh, but this is the same way everyone sees Jesus when they grasp him with the eyes of faith (Augustine). Simeon is now set free to depart in peace according to the Lord's word, for he sees in Jesus release from the bondage of a fallen world (Origen). Simeon embodies in himself priesthood and prophecy, and what he presents to Jesus are the keys of the priestly and prophetic offices that unlock the sins that bind humanity (EPHREM THE SYRIAN). Simeon has seen salvation in this infant Jesus, because Jesus is salvation (BASIL THE GREAT). The mystery of Christ is revealed: he is a light to the Gentiles and glory to Israel (CYRIL OF ALEXANDRIA). Jesus is the occasion for the fall of the Jews and the resurrection of the Gentiles (AMPHILOCHIUS). Jesus' words and actions will be spoken against because he will not meet human expectations; everything about him is a sign to be contradicted (ORIGEN).

There are a number of interpretations of the sword passing through Mary's soul. One accents Mary's sorrow at the crucifixion of her son (JOHN OF DAMASCUS). Another suggests that it is Mary as the mother of God who removes the sword protecting paradise because of the sin of Eve (EPHREM THE SYRIAN). Another brings out the idea that she, like the other disciples, has misunderstood Jesus' destiny. An additional possibility, corresponding with Luke's earlier portrayal of Mary as the personification of Israel, sees the sword as God's revelation in Jesus' words and deeds throughout his ministry (AMBROSE, BASIL THE GREAT), that is, the sword of the Spirit. The revealing of many hearts refers to the swift healing that will take place for those who have fallen into doubt and rejection because of the crucifixion (BASIL THE GREAT).

Simeon's words confirm that women too can be saved (ORIGEN). Even in widowhood, Anna bears witness, and through her, so also does her father and her tribe (THEOPHYLACT). Anna represents the church, and the number of her years—eighty-four—is sacred (BEDE, AMBROSE). The scene closes with a shift from the temple in Jerusalem to the village of Nazareth in Galilee. Jesus is filled with wisdom, even from the time he was an infant (ORIGEN). His increase is according to his human nature, which remains for us a mystery (CYRIL OF ALEXANDRIA). Why Luke leaves out the flight to Egypt is explained by reading his Gospel and discerning its purpose (BEDE).

2:22-24 The Presentation in the Temple

MARY AND JESUS PLACE THEMSELVES UNDER THE LAW. BEDE: Mary, God's blessed mother and a perpetual virgin, was, along with the Son she bore, most free from all subjection to the law. The law says that a woman who "had received seed"[1] and given birth was to be judged unclean and that after a long period she, along with the offspring she had borne, were to be cleansed by victims offered to God. So it is evident that the law does not describe as unclean that woman who, without receiving man's seed, gave birth as a virgin. Nor does it so describe the son who was born to her. Nor does it teach that she had to be cleansed by saving sacrificial offerings. But as our Lord and Savior, who in his divinity was the one who gave the law, when he appeared as a human being, willed to be under the law. . . . So too his blessed mother, who by a singular privilege was above the law, nevertheless did not shun being made subject to the principles of the law for the sake of showing us an example of humility. HOMILIES ON THE GOSPELS 1.18.[2]

THE CLOSED WOMB JESUS OPENS IS THE EAST DOOR OF THE TEMPLE. JEROME: All heretics have gone astray by not understanding the mystery of his nativity. The statement "he who opens the womb shall be called holy to the Lord" is more applicable to the special nativity of the Savior than to that of all men, for Christ alone opened the closed doors of the womb of virginity, which nevertheless remained permanently closed. This is the closed east door, through which only the high priest enters and leaves, and nevertheless it is always closed. AGAINST THE PELAGIANS 2.4.[3]

SACRIFICES SHOW THE POVERTY OF MARY AND JOSEPH. ORIGEN: For this reason it seems wonderful that the sacrifice of Mary was not the first offering, that is, "a lamb a year old," but the second, since "she could not afford"[4] the first. For as it was written about her, Jesus' parents came "to offer a sacrifice" for him, "according to what is

---

[1]Lev 12:2 LXX. [2]CS 110:180*. [3]FC 53:299. [4]See Lev 5:7.

said in the law of the Lord, 'a pair of turtledoves, or two young pigeons.' " But this also shows the truth of what was written, that Jesus Christ "although he was rich, became a poor man."[5] Therefore, for this reason, he chose both a poor mother, from whom he was born, and a poor homeland, about which it is said, "But you, O Bethlehem Ephratha, who are little to be among the clans of Judah,"[6] and the rest. Homilies on Leviticus 8.4.3.[7]

Chastity of Body and Grace of the Spirit. Ambrose: Let us come now to the turtledove, chosen as a chaste victim by the law of God. Hence, when the Lord was circumcised, the dove was offered, because it is written in the law that there should be a presentation of "a pair of turtledoves or two young pigeons."[8] For this is the true sacrifice of Christ: chastity of body and grace of the spirit. Chastity belongs to the turtledove; grace, to the pigeon. Six Days of Creation 5.19.62.[9]

2:25-27 Simeon Waits for the Consolation of Israel

Simeon and Anna Represent Both Sexes Awaiting Redemption. Bede: Simeon and Anna, a man and a woman of advanced age, greeted the Lord with the devoted services of their professions of faith. As they saw him, he was small in body, but they understood him to be great in his divinity. Figuratively speaking, this denotes the synagogue, the Jewish people, who, wearied by the long awaiting of his incarnation, were ready with both their arms (their pious actions) and their voices (their unfeigned faith) to exalt and magnify him as soon as he came. They were ready to acclaim him and say, "Direct me in your truth and teach me, for you are my saving God, and for you I have waited all the day."[10] What needs to be mentioned, too, is that deservedly both sexes hurried to meet him, offering congratulations, since he appeared as the Redeemer of both. Homilies on the Gospels 1.18.[11]

Simeon Sees Christ in the Flesh. Augustine: The just Simeon saw him with his heart, because he recognized the infant. He saw him with his eyes, because he took the infant in his arms. Seeing him in both ways, recognizing the Son of God, and cuddling the one begotten of the Virgin, he said, "Now, Lord, you are letting your servant go in peace, since my eyes have seen your salvation." Notice what he said. You see, he was being kept until he should see with his eyes what he already perceived with faith. He took the baby body, he cradled the body in his arms. On seeing the body, that is, on perceiving the Lord in the flesh, he said, "My eyes have seen your salvation." How do you know this is not the way in which all flesh is going to see the salvation of God? Sermon 277.17.[12]

2:28-32 Simeon's Song: The Nunc Dimittis

Simeon Sees in Jesus Release from Bondage. Origen: Simeon knew that no one could release a man from the prison of the body with hope of life to come, except the anointed One whom he enfolded in his arms.

Hence he also says to him, "Now you dismiss your servant, Lord, in peace. For, as long as I did not hold Christ, as long as my arms did not enfold him, I was imprisoned and unable to escape from my bonds." This is true not only of Simeon but of the whole human race. Anyone who departs from this world, anyone who is released from prison and the house of those in chains, to go forth and reign, should take Jesus in his hands. He should enfold him with his arms and fully grasp him in his bosom. Then he will be able to go in joy where he longs to go....

Then he entered the temple—but not by chance or naively. He came to the temple in the Spirit of God.... If you wish to hold Jesus, and to embrace him with your hands, and to be made worthy of leaving prison, you too must struggle

[5]2 Cor 8:9. [6]Mic 5:2. [7]FC 83:159-60**. [8]Lev 12:8. [9]FC 42:210. [10]Ps 25:5 (24:5 LXX). [11]CS 110:183. [12]WSA 3 8:44.

with every effort to possess the guiding Spirit. Just come to God's temple. See, you stand now already in the temple of the Lord Jesus, his church. This is the temple built from living stones.[13] HOMILIES ON THE GOSPEL OF LUKE 15.1-3.[14]

SIMEON EMBODIES PROPHECY AND PRIESTHOOD. EPHREM THE SYRIAN: The Son came to the servant not to be presented by the servant, but so that, through the Son, the servant might present to his Lord the priesthood and prophecy that had been entrusted to his keeping. Prophecy and priesthood, which had been given through Moses, were both passed down, and came to rest on Simeon. He was a pure vessel who consecrated himself, so that, like Moses, he too could contain them both. These were feeble vessels that accommodated great gifts—gifts that one might contain because of their goodness but that many cannot accept, because of their greatness. Simeon presented our Lord, and in him he presented the two gifts he had, so that what had been given Moses in the desert was passed on by Simeon in the temple. Because our Lord is the vessel in which all fullness dwells,[15] when Simeon presented him to God, he poured out both of these upon him: the priesthood from his hands and prophecy from his lips. The priesthood had always been on Simeon's hands, because of ritual purifications. Prophecy, in fact, dwelt on his lips because of revelations. When both of these saw the Lord of both of these, they were combined and were poured into the vessel that could accommodate them both, in order to contain priesthood, kingship and prophecy.

That infant who was wrapped in swaddling clothes by virtue of his goodness was also dressed in priesthood and prophecy by virtue of his majesty. Simeon dressed him in these and presented him to the one who had dressed him in swaddling clothes. Then, as the old man returned him to his mother, he returned the priesthood with him. And when he prophesied to her about him: "This child is destined for the downfall and rising," he gave her prophecy with him as well.

So Mary took her firstborn and left. Although he was visibly wrapped in swaddling clothes, he was invisibly clothed with prophecy and priesthood. Thus, what Moses had been given was received from Simeon, and it remained and continued with the Lord of these two gifts. The former steward and the final treasurer handed over the keys of priesthood and prophecy to the one in authority over the treasury of both of these. This is why his Father gave him the Spirit without measure,[16] because all measures of the Spirit are under his hand. And to indicate that he received the keys from the former stewards, our Lord said to Simon, "I will give you the keys of the kingdom of heaven."[17] Now how could he give them to someone unless he had received them from someone else? So the keys he had received from Simeon the priest, he gave to another Simeon, the apostle. So even though the Jewish nation did not listen to the first Simeon, the Gentile nations would listen to the other Simeon. HOMILY ON OUR LORD 53.1-54.1.[18]

CHRIST IS SALVATION. BASIL THE GREAT: Now, it is a custom in Scripture to call the Christ of God, salvation, as Simeon says: "Now let your servant depart in peace, O Lord, because my eyes have seen your salvation." Therefore let us subject ourselves to God, because from him is salvation. He explains what salvation is. It is not some mere active force, which provides us with a certain grace for deliverance from weakness and for the good health of our body. What then is salvation?

"For he is my God and my Savior: he is my protector, I shall be moved no more."[19] The Son, who is from God, is our God. He himself is also Savior of the human race, who supports our weakness, who corrects the disturbance that springs up in our souls from temptations. HOMILY ON PSALM 61.2.[20]

THE MYSTERY OF CHRIST: LIGHT TO GEN-

---

[13]1 Pet 2:5. [14]FC 94:62-63*. [15]Col 2:9. [16]Jn 3:34. [17]Mt 16:19. [18]FC 91:328-30*. [19]Ps 61:3 LXX. [20]FC 46:343*.

tiles, Glory to Israel. Cyril of Alexandria: The mystery of Christ had been prepared even before the very foundation of the world but was manifested in the last ages of time. It became a light for those who in darkness and error had fallen under the devil's hand. These were they "who serve the creature instead of the Creator,"[21] worshiping moreover the dragon, the author of evil, and the impure throng of devils, to whom they attach the honor due God. Yet God the Father called them to the acknowledgment of the Son who is the true Light. . . .

Christ therefore became the Gentiles' light for revelation, but also for the glory of Israel. For even granting that some of them proved insolent and disobedient, and with minds that did not understand, yet there is a remnant there, saved and admitted to glory through Christ. The first fruits of these were the divine disciples, the brightness of whose renown lightens the whole world.

In another sense, Christ is the glory of Israel, for he came out of Israel according to the flesh, though he is God over all, and blessed for evermore. Amen.[22] Commentary on Luke, Homily 4.[23]

2:33-35 Simeon's Prophecy

For the Fall of the Jews, the Resurrection of the Gentiles. Amphilochius: He is set for the fall of the unbelieving Jews, but for the resurrection of the believing Gentiles. "And for a sign that is spoken against." The cross is a sign that is spoken against. Why? Because many who did not believe denied him at the cross. They ridiculed it both by deeds and words. They gave him vinegar to drink, offered him gall for his thirst, twisted a wreath of thorns to put on his brow, pierced his side with a spear, struck him with their hands, and shouted at him with offensive clamor: "He saved others, but cannot save himself."[24] Oration 2.8, On the Presentation of the Lord.[25]

Everything About Jesus Is a Sign That Is

Spoken Against. Origen: Everything that the plain narrative recounts about the Savior is spoken against. The Virgin is a mother. This is "a sign that is spoken against." "The Marcionites speak against this sign and insist that he was not born of a woman." The Ebionites speak against this sign and say that he was born of a man and a woman in the same way as we are born. He had a human body.

There is still another "sign that is spoken against." Some say that he came down from heaven. Others say that he had a body like ours, so that he could also redeem our bodies from sin by the likeness of his body to ours and give us hope of the resurrection. He rose from the dead. This is also "a sign that is spoken against." How did he rise? Was he just as he was when he died, or did he surely rise into a body of a better substance? . . .

I myself think that even the fact that the mouths of the prophets foretold him is a sign that is spoken against. . . . It does not mean that those who believe in him speak against these signs. We know indeed that everything that Scripture records is true. But, for unbelievers, all things that are written about him are "a sign that is spoken against." Homilies on the Gospel of Luke 17.4-5.[26]

The Sword That Passes Through Mary Is Her Grief. John of Damascus: However, this blessed one, who had been found worthy of gifts surpassing nature, did at the time of the passion suffer the pangs which she had escaped at childbirth. When she saw him put to death as a criminal—the man she knew to be God when she gave birth to him—her heart was torn from maternal compassion and she was rent by her thoughts as by a sword. This is the meaning of "and a sword will pierce through your own soul." But her grief gave way to the joy of the resurrection, the resurrection which proclaimed him to be God who had

---

[21]Rom 1:25. [22]Rom 9:5. [23]CGSL 60-61**. [24]Mt 27:42. [25]SSGF 1:175-79; CPG 3:64-67. [26]FC 94.72-73**.

died in the flesh. ORTHODOX FAITH 4.14.[27]

MARY REMOVES THE SWORD PROTECTING PARADISE BECAUSE OF EVE. EPHREM THE SYRIAN: Simeon said likewise, "You will remove the sword." Mary removed the sword that protected Paradise because of Eve.[28] Alternatively, "you will remove the sword," that is, a denial. For the Greek says clearly, the inner thoughts of a great number will be revealed, that is, the thoughts of those who had doubted. For he said, "You will remove the sword." Indeed, you too will doubt, because she thought that he was the gardener.[29] Mary wondered at his birth, it is said, and at his conception. She recounted to others how she had conceived, and indeed how she had given birth. Those who had doubted it were comforted by the wonderment of her word. COMMENTARY ON TATIAN'S DIATESSARON 2.17.[30]

THE SWORD THAT PIERCES MARY IS THE WORD OF GOD. AMBROSE: "And a sword will pierce through your own soul." Neither Scripture nor history tells us that Mary departed this life by a violent death. For it is not the soul but the body that can be pierced by a material sword. This, therefore, proves that Mary was not unaware of the heavenly mystery: "For the word of God is living and active, sharper than any two-edged sword, piercing to the division of soul and spirit, of joints and marrow, and discerning the thoughts and intentions of the heart."[31] God's Word exposes the thoughts and intents of the heart, because all things are open and naked to the eyes of Mary's Son, to whom the secrets of our conscience are visible. EXPOSITION OF THE GOSPEL OF LUKE 2.61.[32]

SWIFT HEALING REVEALS THE HEARTS OF THOSE WHO WERE SCANDALIZED. BASIL THE GREAT: "That the thoughts of many hearts may be revealed" means that after the scandal which happened at the cross of Christ to both the disciples and to Mary herself, some swift healing will follow from the Lord, confirming their hearts in their faith in him. Thus we see that even Peter, after having stumbled, clung more firmly to his faith in Christ. What was human, therefore, was proven unsound in order that the power of the Lord might be manifested. LETTER 260.[33]

2:36-38 Anna Waits for the Redemption of Jerusalem

ANNA'S PROPHECY SHOWS THAT WOMEN WILL BE SAVED. ORIGEN: Because it was necessary that women too should be saved, after Simeon there came a woman who was a prophet. Scripture says of her, "And Anna was a prophetess, a daughter of Phanuel, from the tribe of Asher." How beautiful the order is! The woman did not come before the man. First came Simeon, who took the child and held him in his arms. Then came the woman. Her exact words are not recorded. But the account says in general terms that "she gave praise to the Lord and spoke about him to everyone who was awaiting the redemption of Jerusalem." HOMILIES ON THE GOSPEL OF LUKE 17.9.[34]

ANNA'S FATHER AND TRIBE BEAR WITNESS. THEOPHYLACT: The Evangelist continues with this account of Anna. He lists both her father and her tribe, so that we might be convinced he is speaking the truth. He is summoning, as it were, many witnesses who knew her father and her tribe. THE EXPLANATION OF THE HOLY GOSPEL ACCORDING TO ST. LUKE 2.[35]

ANNA REPRESENTS THE CHURCH WIDOWED BY THE DEATH OF HER SPOUSE. BEDE: In a mystical sense Anna stands for the church, which in this present world is as it were widowed by the death of her Spouse. Even the number of the years of her widowhood designates the time in which the church, continuing on in the body, so-

---

[27]FC 37:366. [28]Gen 3:24. [29]Jn 20:15. [30]ECTD 67-68*. [31]Heb 4:12. [32]SSGF 1:180; CSEL 32 4:74; EHG 60**. [33]FC 28:231-32. [34]FC 94:74*. [35]EBT 37.

journs afar from her Lord. Seven times twelve make eighty-four. And seven relates to the full course of this world, which was wrought in seven days. But twelve belongs to the completeness of the apostolic teachings. Whoever, therefore, whether the universal church or anyone of the faithful, devotes the whole course of life to apostolic labors, is praised as serving the Lord for eighty-four years.

The period of seven years during which she lived with her husband is in accord with the time of the Lord's incarnation. For as I have said, the completeness of time is to be expressed by the number seven. Here because of the special quality of the Lord's majesty, the simple number of seven years expresses, in sign of its perfection, the time in which he taught while clothed in the flesh. It also favors the mysteries of the church that Anna is interpreted as the Lord's grace, that she is the daughter of Phanuel, who is called the face of the Lord, and descended from the tribe of Ashur, that is, blessed with children.[36] EXPOSITION OF THE GOSPEL OF LUKE 2.38.[37]

ANNA'S AGE IS SACRED. AMBROSE: Anna, who, by reason of her years of widowhood and her virtues, is set before us as wholly worthy of belief, announces that the Redeemer of all people has come.... Not without purpose, however, does he make mention of the eighty-four years of her widowhood, because both the seven twelves and the two forties seemed to imply a number that is sacred. EXPOSITION OF THE GOSPEL OF LUKE 2.62.[38]

2:39-40 The Child's Physical and Spiritual Growth

JESUS IS FILLED WITH WISDOM. ORIGEN: In the Gospel of Luke, the Holy Spirit writes this of him before he reached the age of twelve: "But the boy grew and was strengthened, and he was filled with wisdom." Human nature itself does not permit this, that wisdom is perfected before the twelfth year of life. It is one thing to participate in wisdom, another thing to be filled with wisdom. . . .

The Son of God "had emptied himself,"[39] and, for that reason, again he is filled with wisdom. "And the grace of God was upon him." He possessed the grace of God not when he reached young manhood, not when he taught openly, but already when he was a small child. HOMILIES ON THE GOSPEL OF LUKE 19.1-2.[40]

THE WORD MANIFESTED WISDOM PROPORTIONAL TO THE AGE THE BODY ATTAINED. CYRIL OF ALEXANDRIA: Do not think to yourself, "How can God grow?" "How can he who gives grace to angels and to men receive fresh wisdom?" Rather reflect upon the great skill with which we are initiated into his mystery. For the wise Evangelist did not introduce the Word in his abstract and incorporeal nature. He says of him that "he increased in stature and wisdom and grace," but after having shown that he was born in the flesh of a woman and took our likeness, he then assigns to him these human attributes. Only then does he call him a child and say that he grew in stature, as his body grew little by little, in obedience to corporeal laws. So he is said also to have increased in wisdom, not as receiving fresh supplies of wisdom. God is perceived by the understanding to be entirely perfect in all things and altogether incapable of being destitute of any attribute suitable to the Godhead. So God the Word gradually manifested his wisdom proportionally to the age which the body had attained.

The body then advances in stature, and the soul, in wisdom. The divine nature is capable of increase in neither one nor the other, seeing that the Word of God is all perfect. With good reason be connected the increase of wisdom with the growth of the bodily stature, because the divine nature revealed its own wisdom in proportion to the measure of the bodily growth. COMMENTARY ON LUKE, HOMILY 5.[41]

---

[36]Deut 33:24. [37]SSGF 1:168-69*. [38]SSGF 1:180*; CSEL 32 4:74. [39]Phil 2:7. [40]FC 94:80-81. [41]CGSL 63-64**.

WHY LUKE OMITS THE FLIGHT TO EGYPT.
BEDE: Luke here omits that which he knew was already sufficiently recorded by Matthew. After this the Lord, lest he be discovered and slaughtered by Herod, was taken into Egypt by his parents. When Herod was dead, he returned finally to Galilee, and began to live in his own village of Nazareth. Individual Evangelists are prone to omit certain things, which they see were recorded by others, or which they foresee in the Spirit will be recorded by others, so that in the continuous thread of their narration nothing seems omitted. What has thus been passed over, the diligent reader will discover by carefully going through each of the Gospels in turn. EXPOSITION OF THE GOSPEL OF LUKE 2.39.[42]

---

[42]*SSGF* 1:168-69.

2:41-52 THE YOUNG JESUS RETURNS TO HIS TEMPLE

[41]*Now his parents went to Jerusalem every year at the feast of the Passover.* [42]*And when he was twelve years old, they went up according to custom;* [43]*and when the feast was ended, as they were returning, the boy Jesus stayed behind in Jerusalem. His parents did not know it,* [44]*but supposing him to be in the company they went a day's journey, and they sought him among their kinsfolk and acquaintances;* [45]*and when they did not find him, they returned to Jerusalem, seeking him.* [46]*After three days they found him in the temple, sitting among the teachers, listening to them and asking them questions;* [47]*and all who heard him were amazed at his understanding and his answers.* [48]*And when they saw him they were astonished; and his mother said to him, "Son, why have you treated us so? Behold, your father and I have been looking for you anxiously."* [49]*And he said to them, "How is it that you sought me? Did you not know that I must be in my Father's house?"* [50]*And they did not understand the saying which he spoke to them.* [51]*And he went down with them and came to Nazareth, and was obedient to them; and his mother kept all these things in her heart.*

[52]*And Jesus increased in wisdom and in stature,[i] and in favor with God and man.*

---

i Or *years*

OVERVIEW: The story of Jesus in the temple at twelve years old teaches us about his humanity so that we might ascend into an understanding of his divinity. By beginning at twelve years old, Jesus is affirming his perfection (BEDE). The time notice of "three days" anticipates the resurrection narrative (AMBROSE). Jesus teaches by asking questions, showing the humility appropriate to a twelve-year-old (ORIGEN).

Although this passage is about Jesus doing the Father's business, it is first stated by Mary that Joseph is Jesus' father (EPHREM THE SYRIAN). Jesus must be present in the house of his Father, where the Father's business is transacted, among those to whom this business has been entrusted (ORIGEN). To be about the Father's business is to be coeternal with the Father's power and glory (BEDE).

Jesus is subject to Joseph, the greater subject to the lesser, although Joseph must have known that Jesus was greater than he (ORIGEN). Mary learns from her twelve-year-old son not as her child, but as her God (BEDE). Jesus advances in wisdom and grace, as his humanity is taught by his divinity (JEROME), an advance in body and soul as a result of the personal union of Godhead and humanity (JOHN OF DAMASCUS).

2:41-45 Jesus Is Lost in Jerusalem During the Passover

JESUS' HUMILITY SHOWS US HIS DIVINITY. BEDE: The Lord's coming every year to Jerusalem for the Passover with his parents is an indication of his human humility. It is characteristic of human beings to gather to offer God the votive offerings of spiritual sacrifices, and by plentiful prayers and tears to dispose their Maker toward them. Therefore the Lord, born a human being among human beings, did what God, by divine inspiration through his angels, prescribed for human beings to do. He himself kept the law which he gave in order to show us, who are human beings pure and simple, that whatever God orders is to be observed in everything. Let us follow the path of his human way of life. If we take delight in looking upon the glory of his divinity, if we want to dwell in his eternal home in heaven all the days of our lives,[1] it delights us to see the Lord's will and to be shielded by his holy temple. And lest we be forever buffeted by the wind of wickedness, let us remember to frequent the house, the church of the present time, with the requisite offerings of pure petitions. HOMILIES ON THE GOSPELS 1.19.[2]

A SIGN OF JESUS' PERFECTION. BEDE: This we may here affirm: By the number seven, as by the number twelve (which is made up from the parts of the number seven multiplied by each other), the whole universe of things, events and their

perfection is signified. Accordingly, that he may teach in what manner all places and times are to be employed, the divine Light of Christ rightly makes a beginning from the number twelve. EXPOSITION OF THE GOSPEL OF LUKE 2.42.[3]

2:46-50 Jesus Found in the Temple

THE THREE DAYS REFER TO THE RESURRECTION. AMBROSE: The beginning of the Lord's disputation is taken from his twelfth year. This number of the evangelists was intended for the preaching of the faith.[4] Nor is it idly that, forgetful of his parents according to the flesh, he who according to the flesh assuredly was filled with the wisdom and grace of God is found after three days in the temple. It is a sign that he who was believed dead for our faith would rise again after three days from his triumphal passion[5] and appear on his heavenly throne with divine honor. EXPOSITION OF THE GOSPEL OF LUKE 2.63.[6]

JESUS TEACHES THROUGH QUESTIONS. ORIGEN: Because he was a small child, he is found "in the midst of teachers," sanctifying and instructing them. Because he was a small child, he is found "in their midst," not teaching them but "asking questions." He did this because it is appropriate to his age, to teach us what befits boys, even if they are wise and learned. They should rather hear their teachers than want to teach them and not show off with a display of knowledge. He interrogated the teachers not to learn anything but to teach them by his questions. From one fountain of doctrine, there flow both wise questions and answers. It is part of the same wisdom to know what you should ask and what you should answer. It was right for the Savior first to become a master of learned interrogation. Later he would answer questions according to God's reason and Word. HOMILIES ON THE GOSPEL OF LUKE 19.6.[7]

---

[1]Ps 27:4 (26:4 LXX). [2]CS 110:188-89*. [3]SSGF 1:236*. [4]See Mt 10:1-2, 7. [5]See Mt 26:61; 27:63. [6]EHG 61**. [7]FC 94:82-83**.

MARY CALLS JOSEPH JESUS' FATHER. EPHREM THE SYRIAN: If, from the fact that some are called brothers of our Lord, people think that these are sons of Mary, take note that he was called son of Joseph. Not only did Jews call him the son of Joseph, but also Mary called him Joseph's son. For "I and your father have been seeking you with much anxiety." If the angel commanded Joseph to take Mary into his care,[8] this was to eliminate any suspicion from her slanderers, and especially so that he might protect her in case those who were scandalized in thinking that it was from the angel that she was pregnant might kill her. It was a great source of scandal to them that a virgin should give birth, because they were convinced that through her giving birth their city would be destroyed and that their kingdom, priesthood and prophecy would be abolished. It was for this reason too that they also killed the prophet Isaiah who announced these things, that a virgin would give birth to a child.[9] COMMENTARY ON TATIAN'S DIATESSARON 2.7.[10]

IN THE TEMPLE OF HIS FATHER. ORIGEN: Surely Jesus was in the temple that Solomon had built. He confesses that it is the temple of his Father, whom he revealed to us, and whose Son he said he was. HOMILIES ON THE GOSPEL OF LUKE 18.5.[11]

COETERNAL WITH THE FATHER. BEDE: Clearly the abode in the hearts of the elect of the holy Trinity, the nature of whose divinity is one and indivisible, cannot be disparate. Therefore, when he was sitting in the temple, the Lord said, "I must be about my Father's business," and this is a declaration of his power and glory which are coeternal with God the Father's. However, when he returned to Nazareth, he was subject to his parents, and this is an indication of his true humanity as well as an example of humility. He was subject to human beings in that human nature in which he is less than the Father. Hence he himself said, "I go to the Father because the Father is greater than I."[12] In that human nature, he was

made a little less than the angels.[13] In that other nature, however, in which he and the Father are one,[14] and in virtue of which he does not go to the Father only now and then but is always in him,[15] all things were made through him,[16] and he is before all things.[17] HOMILIES ON THE GOSPELS 1.19.[18]

2:51-52 Jesus Obeys His Parents and Is Faithful to His Heavenly Father

JESUS AND JOSEPH SHOW HOW THE GREATER IS SUBJECT TO THE LESSER. ORIGEN: Children, we should learn to be subject to our parents. The greater is subject to the lesser. Jesus understood that Joseph was greater than he in age, and therefore he gave him the honor due a parent. He gave an example to every son. . . . I think Joseph understood that Jesus, who was subject to him, was greater than he. He knew that the one subject to him was greater than he and, out of reverence, restrained his authority. So each one should realize that often a lesser man is put in charge of better men. HOMILIES ON THE GOSPEL OF LUKE 20.5.[19]

MARY LEARNS FROM JESUS AS FROM GOD. BEDE: Consider the most prudent woman Mary, mother of true Wisdom, as the pupil of her Son. For she learned from him, not as from a child or man but as from God. Yes, she dwelt in meditation on his words and actions. Nothing of what was said or done by him fell idly on her mind. As before, when she conceived the Word itself in her womb, so now does she hold within her his ways and words, cherishing them as it were in her heart. That which she now beholds in the present, she waits to have revealed with greater clarity in the future. This practice she followed as a rule and law through all her life. EXPOSITION OF THE GOSPEL OF LUKE 2.51.[20]

---

[8]Mt 1:20. [9]Is 7:14. [10]ECTD 63-64**. [11]FC 94:78-79. [12]Jn 14:28. [13]Ps 8:5 (8:6 LXX); Heb 2:9. [14]Jn 10:30. [15]Jn 14:10-11. [16]Jn 1:3. [17]Col 1:17. [18]CS 110:191**. [19]FC 94:86**. [20]SSGF 1:240.

JESUS' HUMAN NATURE INSTRUCTED BY HIS DIVINITY. JEROME: How does he who is Wisdom receive understanding? "Jesus advanced in wisdom and age and grace before God and men." This means not so much that the Son was instructed by the Father but that his human nature was instructed by his own divinity. There is the seer's prophecy of him who blossomed from the root of Jesse, "The spirit of the Lord shall rest upon him: a spirit of wisdom and of understanding."[21] HOMILY ON PSALM 15 (16).[22]

HYPOSTATIC UNION ASSURES PROPER GROWTH IN WISDOM. JOHN OF DAMASCUS: He is said to have progressed in wisdom and age and grace, because he did increase in age and by this increase in age brought more into evidence the wisdom inherent in him further. By making what is ours altogether his own, he made his own the progress of people in wisdom and grace, as well as the fulfillment of the Father's will, which is to say, people's knowledge of God and their salvation. Now, those who say that he progressed in wisdom and grace in the sense of receiving an increase in these are saying that the union was not made from the first instant of the flesh's existence. Neither are they holding the hypostatic union, but, misled by the empty-headed Nestorius, they are talking falsely of a relative union and simple indwelling, "understanding neither the things they say, nor whereof they affirm."[23] For, if from the first instant of its existence the flesh was truly united to God the Word—rather, had existence in him and identity of person with him—how did it not enjoy perfectly all wisdom and grace? It did not share the grace, and neither did it participate by grace in the things of the Word. Rather, because the human and divine things had become proper to the one Christ by the hypostatic union, then, since the same was at once God and man, it gushed forth with the grace and the wisdom and the fullness of all good things for the world. ORTHODOX FAITH 3.22.[24]

---

[21]Is 11:2. [22]FC 57:26**. [23]1 Tim 1:7. [24]FC 37:326-27**.

3:1-20 THE MINISTRY OF JOHN THE BAPTIST

[1]*In the fifteenth year of the reign of Tiberius Caesar, Pontius Pilate being governor of Judea, and Herod being tetrarch of Galilee, and his brother Philip tetrarch of the region of Ituraea and Trachonitis, and Lysanias tetrarch of Abilene,* [2]*in the high-priesthood of Annas and Caiaphas, the word of God came to John the son of Zechariah in the wilderness;* [3]*and he went into all the region about the Jordan, preaching a baptism of repentance for the forgiveness of sins.* [4]*As it is written in the book of the words of Isaiah the prophet,*

"The voice of one crying in the wilderness:
Prepare the way of the Lord,
make his paths straight.
[5]*Every valley shall be filled,*
and every mountain and hill shall be brought low,
and the crooked shall be made straight,

and the rough ways shall be made smooth;

⁶*and all flesh shall see the salvation of God."*

⁷*He said therefore to the multitudes that came out to be baptized by him, "You brood of vipers! Who warned you to flee from the wrath to come?* ⁸*Bear fruits that befit repentance, and do not begin to say to yourselves, 'We have Abraham as our father'; for I tell you, God is able from these stones to raise up children to Abraham.* ⁹*Even now the axe is laid to the root of the trees; every tree therefore that does not bear good fruit is cut down and thrown into the fire."*

¹⁰*And the multitudes asked him, "What then shall we do?"* ¹¹*And he answered them, "He who has two coats, let him share with him who has none; and he who has food, let him do likewise."* ¹²*Tax collectors also came to be baptized, and said to him, "Teacher, what shall we do?"* ¹³*And he said to them, "Collect no more than is appointed you."* ¹⁴*Soldiers also asked him, "And we, what shall we do?" And he said to them, "Rob no one by violence or by false accusation, and be content with your wages."*

¹⁵*As the people were in expectation, and all men questioned in their hearts concerning John, whether perhaps he were the Christ,* ¹⁶*John answered them all, "I baptize you with water; but he who is mightier than I is coming, the thong of whose sandals I am not worthy to untie; he will baptize you with the Holy Spirit and with fire.* ¹⁷*His winnowing fork is in his hand, to clear his threshing floor, and to gather the wheat into his granary, but the chaff he will burn with unquenchable fire."*

¹⁸*So, with many other exhortations, he preached good news to the people.* ¹⁹*But Herod the tetrarch, who had been reproved by him for Herodias, his brother's wife, and for all the evil things that Herod had done,* ²⁰*added this to them all, that he shut up John in prison.*

OVERVIEW: By placing this narrative in a historical context that is Roman and Jewish, Luke shows that the word of God that comes to John among kings and priests is a significant event in world history and salvation history (GREGORY THE GREAT). The church is gathered by the Word in the desert (AMBROSE). Jordan means "descent," as God's river descends from Christ for baptizing (ORIGEN). John comes to the Jordan preaching a baptism of repentance that leads to the forgiveness of sins (GREGORY THE GREAT). Faith in Christ is the highest form of repentance (CYRIL OF ALEXANDRIA). John's baptism enrolled the people in preparatory catechetical lectures (ORIGEN). To prepare the way of the Lord is equivalent to producing fruits worthy of repentance (CHRYSOSTOM) and thus make ready the reception of Christ (CYRIL OF ALEXANDRIA). The way of the Lord is a catechetical road, the way of

life in the person and works of the Messiah, Jesus, a way that is not a literal road but one that is in the heart (ORIGEN).

The vivid language of Isaiah 40 proclaims that the preparation for this road means dramatic changes in the topography of Israel signaling a reversal in the fallen creation because all will now see salvation in the coming of Jesus (CHRYSOSTOM). No barriers, even physical ones, are to prevent the inbreaking of God's truth (PRUDENTIUS). John's work of preparation of hearts for the coming of Christ is ongoing (ORIGEN). To see the salvation of God is to see Christ, as Simeon said in the Nunc Dimittis when he held Jesus in his arms (AUGUSTINE). Although John addresses the Jews for their wickedness that was expressed in disbelief, he calls everyone to repentance—catechumens, Jews and Gentiles (ORIGEN). And repentance always requires almsgiving, for we have been changed for the better and now produce works of mercy (AUGUSTINE). By faith, Gentiles become true descendents of Abraham as living stones, fulfilling the promise given to him by God (CYRIL OF ALEXANDRIA).

God's wrath is beginning to be poured out already now in the ministry of John (GREGORY THE GREAT). God's wrath is against the Jews, but a remnant of Israel will be saved (CYRIL OF ALEXANDRIA). Each instruction has to do with attachment to things of this world, and the teaching of good works must precede baptism. Luke the physician through John's preaching applies remedies to each ailment presented by the crowds, the tax collectors and the soldiers (CYRIL OF ALEXANDRIA). Giving up one of our two tunics prevents us from serving two masters. For the tax collectors this means not taking more than their allotted share, for if they take more than the law demands, they transgress the Holy Spirit (ORIGEN). For the soldiers it means not using the power of their office for extortion or violence, although by including them here John is commending military service (AUGUSTINE). The premier expression of the Old Testament law is to be merciful as the Father is merciful[1] by showing works of compassion required of everyone (AMBROSE).

Luke tells us that the people were wondering if John was "the Christ." John is not the bridegroom but the friend of the bridegroom (GREGORY THE GREAT). John, representing the Jews, is not worthy to untie Jesus' sandals because he prepares the way for Jesus who is the Christ; he baptizes in water while Jesus baptizes in the Holy Spirit and fire (CYRIL OF ALEXANDRIA) as fulfilled at Pentecost (CYRIL OF JERUSALEM). Christ is the Baptizer, for it is he who, through others, baptizes us with water, spirit and fire (CHRYSOSTOM).

John's call to repentance concludes by alerting his listeners that God will return as judge to separate those who bear true fruits from those who are unfruitful (AMBROSE). Luke says that John taught many other things, and his Gospel records many of these teachings. Herod may

imprison John, but he continues to teach, sending his disciples to Jesus to see if he is the coming one (ORIGEN). As John goes to prison, Jesus takes center stage in his baptism, making a clear break between the end of the ministry of John and the beginning of Jesus' public ministry (EUSEBIUS).

3:1-2 *The Historical Context of John's Ministry*

THE GATHERING OF THE GENTILES AND THE DISPERSION OF THE JEWS. GREGORY THE GREAT: Luke recalls the rulers of the Roman republic and the rulers of Judea to indicate the time when our Redeemer's forerunner received his mission to preach. . . .

Since John was coming to preach one who was to redeem some from Judea and many from among the Gentiles, the period of his preaching is indicated by naming the Gentiles' ruler and those of the Jews. But because the Gentiles were to be gathered together and Judea dispersed on account of the error of its faithlessness, this description of earthly rule also shows us that in the Roman republic one person presided. FORTY GOSPEL HOMILIES 6.[2]

SETTING THE STAGE FOR SALVATION HISTORY. GREGORY THE GREAT: It is apparent, then, that Judea, which lay divided among so many kings, had reached the end of its sovereignty. It was also appropriate to indicate not only under which kings but also under which high priests this occurred. Since John the Baptist preached one who was at once both king and priest, the evangelist Luke indicated the time of his preaching by referring to both the kingship and the high priesthood. FORTY GOSPEL HOMILIES 6.[3]

THE WORD GATHERS THE CHURCH IN THE DESERT. AMBROSE: The Son of God, who is to gather the church, first works in a servant. Thus

---

[1]Lk 6:36. [2]CS 123:35-36*. [3]CS 123:36.

St. Luke fittingly says that the Word of the Lord came to John, the son of Zechariah, in the wilderness, so that the church would not begin from a man but from the Word. For she is a wilderness, because children of depravity outnumber hers, though she has a husband. Then it is said to her, "Sing, O barren one,"[4] and, "Break forth together into singing, you waste places,"[5] because the desert had not yet been cultivated by any work of a flock of people, nor had those trees which could bear fruit displayed the crown of their merits. The one who said, "I am like a green olive tree in the house of the Lord,"[6] had not yet come, nor had that heavenly Vine borne fruit with its shoots of words on the trained branch of its own people.[7] So the Word came that the desolate earth would bring forth fruit for us. The Word came, and the voice followed, for the Word first works within before the voice follows. Hence David too says, "I believed, and then I spoke."[8] EXPOSITION OF THE GOSPEL OF LUKE 2.67.[9]

3:3-6 A Summary of John's Preaching

JORDAN MEANS "DESCENT." ORIGEN: "Jordan" means "descending." It is the "descending" river of God, one running with a vigorous force. It is the Lord our Savior. Into him we are baptized with true, saving water. Baptism is also preached "for the remission of sins." HOMILIES ON THE GOSPEL OF LUKE 21.4.[10]

FORGIVENESS COMES FROM CHRIST'S BAPTISM. GREGORY THE GREAT: "And he came into all the region of the Jordan, preaching a baptism of repentance for the forgiveness of sins." It is apparent to all who read that John not only preached a baptism of repentance but also bestowed it on some. Yet he was not able to bestow a baptism for the forgiveness of sins. Forgiveness of sins is granted us only in the baptism of Christ. We must note the words "preaching a baptism of repentance for the forgiveness of sins." He preached a baptism that would take away sins, but he was unable to give it himself. By his word

of preaching he was the forerunner of the Father's Word incarnate. By his baptism, which could not of itself take away sin, he was to be the forerunner of that baptism of repentance by which sins are taken away. His words prepared the way for the Redeemer's actual presence, and his preaching of baptism was a foreshadowing of the truth. FORTY GOSPEL HOMILIES 6.[11]

FAITH IN CHRIST THE HIGHEST FORM OF REPENTANCE. CYRIL OF ALEXANDRIA: Moreover, the fruit of repentance is, in the highest degree, faith in Christ. Next to it is the evangelic mode of life, and in general terms the works of righteousness as opposed to sin, which the penitent must bring forth as fruits worthy of repentance. COMMENTARY ON LUKE, HOMILY 7.[12]

REPENT TO PREPARE FOR JOHN'S BAPTISM. ORIGEN: The precursor of Christ—the voice of one crying in the wilderness—preaches in the desert of the soul that has known no peace. Not only then, but even now, a bright and burning lamp first comes and preaches the baptism of repentance for the forgiveness of sins. Then the true Light follows, as John himself said: "He must increase, but I must decrease."[13] The word came in the desert and spread in all the countryside around the Jordan. HOMILIES ON THE GOSPEL OF LUKE 21.3.[14]

TO PREPARE THE WAY IS TO CALL FOR FRUITS OF REPENTANCE. CHRYSOSTOM: Thus the prophet wrote that he shall come saying, "Prepare the way of the Lord, make his paths straight."[15] And John himself said when he came, "Bring forth fruits consistent with repentance," which corresponds with "prepare the way of the Lord." See that both by the words of the prophet and by his own preaching, this one thing is manifested alone. John was to come, making a way and pre-

---

[4]Is 54:1. [5]Is 52:9. [6]Ps 52:8. [7]See Jn 15:1. [8]Ps 115:1 LXX. [9]EHG 63**. [10]FC 94:89*. [11]CS 123:36-37*. [12]CGSL 71. [13]Jn 3:30. [14]FC 94:89**. [15]Is 40:3.

paring beforehand, not bestowing the gift, which was the remission, but ordering in good time the souls of such as should receive the God of all. HOMILIES ON THE GOSPEL OF MATTHEW 10.3.[16]

PREPARE BY MAKING READY TO RECEIVE CHRIST. CYRIL OF ALEXANDRIA: John, being chosen for the apostleship, was also the last of the holy prophets. For this reason, as the Lord has not come yet, he says, "Prepare the way of the Lord." What is the meaning of "Prepare the way of the Lord"? It means, Make ready for the reception of whatever Christ may wish to do. Withdraw your hearts from the shadow of the law, discard vague figures and no longer think perversely. Make the paths of our God straight. For every path that leads to good is straight and smooth and easy, but the one that is crooked leads down to wickedness those that walk in it. COMMENTARY ON LUKE, HOMILY 6.[17]

THE WAY JOHN PREPARES IS IN THE HEART. ORIGEN: "Prepare a way for the Lord." What way are we to prepare for the Lord? Surely not a material way. Can the Word of God go on such a journey? Should not the way be prepared for the Lord within? Should not straight and level paths be built in our hearts? This is the way by which the Word of God has entered. That Word dwells in the spaces of the human heart. HOMILIES ON THE GOSPEL OF LUKE 21.5.[18]

ISAIAH FORETELLS A REVERSAL IN NATURE TO SIGNAL THE COMING OF SALVATION. CHRYSOSTOM: Do you perceive how the prophet anticipated all by his words—the concourse of the people? Thus, when he says, "Every valley shall be filled, and every mountain and hill shall be brought low, and the rough ways shall be made smooth," he is signifying the exaltation of the lowly, the humiliation of the self-willed, the hardness of the law changed into easiness of faith. For it is no longer toils and labors, says he, but grace and forgiveness of sins, affording the way to salvation. Next he states the cause of these things,

saying, "All flesh shall see the salvation of God." No longer Jews and proselytes only, but also all earth and sea and the whole race of people may be saved. By "the crooked things" he signified our whole corrupt life, publicans, harlots, robbers and magicians, as many as having been perverted before, afterward walk in the right way. As Jesus himself likewise said, "Tax collectors and harlots go into the kingdom of God before you,"[19] because they believed. HOMILIES ON THE GOSPEL OF MATTHEW 10.3.[20]

NO BARRIERS TO THE COMING OF TRUTH. PRUDENTIUS:

As messenger of God, who was about to come,
He faithfully observed this law, constructing well,
That every hill might low become and tough ways plain,
Lest when the truth should glide from heaven down to earth
It then would find a barrier to its swift approach.

HYMNS FOR EVERY DAY 7.51-55.[21]

JOHN'S WORK OF PREPARATION IS ONGOING. ORIGEN: I believe that the mystery of John is still being achieved in the world today. If anyone is going to believe in Christ Jesus, John's spirit and power first come to his soul and "prepare a perfect people for the Lord." It makes the ways in the heart's rough places smooth and straightens out its paths. HOMILIES ON THE GOSPEL OF LUKE 4.6.[22]

THE SALVATION OF GOD IS THE CHRIST OF GOD. AUGUSTINE: Consider the text "And all flesh shall see the salvation of God." There is no difficulty at all in taking this to mean "And all flesh shall see the Christ of God." After all, Christ was seen in the body and will be seen in the body when he comes again to judge the living

---

[16]NPNF 1 10:63*. [17]CGSL 69**. [18]FC 94:90*. [19]Mt 21:31. [20]NPNF 1 10:64*. [21]FC 43:48. [22]FC 94:19.

and the dead. Scripture has many texts showing that he is the "salvation of God," particularly the words of the venerable old man, Simeon, who took the child in his arms and said, "Now let your servant go in peace, O Lord, according to your word, because my eyes have seen your salvation."[23] CITY OF GOD 22.29.[24]

3:7-9 John's Warning to the Crowds

JOHN'S CALL TO REPENT IS FOR EVERYONE.
ORIGEN: To you who are coming to baptism, Scripture says, "Bear fruits that befit repentance." Do you want to know what fruits befit repentance? Love is a fruit of the Spirit. Joy is a fruit of the Spirit. So are peace, patience, kindness, goodness, faith, gentleness, self-control,[25] and the others of this sort. If we have all of these virtues, we have produced "fruits that befit repentance." . . . John, the last of the prophets, prophesies the expulsion of the first nation and the call of the Gentiles. To those who were boasting about Abraham he says, "Do not begin to say to yourselves, 'We have Abraham for a father.'" And again he speaks about the Gentiles, "For I tell you, God is able from these stones to raise up children to Abraham."

From what stones? Surely he was not pointing to irrational, material stones but to people who were uncomprehending and sometimes hard. HOMILIES ON THE GOSPEL OF LUKE 22.6, 8-9.[26]

REPENTANCE REQUIRES ALMSGIVING. AUGUSTINE: In a word, therefore, let us all listen, and seriously reflect what great merit there is in having fed Christ when he was hungry—and what sort of a crime it is to have ignored Christ when he was hungry. Repentance for our sins does indeed change us for the better. But even repentance will not appear to be of much use to us if works of mercy do not accompany it. Truth bears witness to this through John, who said to those who came to him, "Bear fruits that befit repentance." And so those who haven't produced such fruits have no reason to suppose that by a barren repentance

they will earn pardon for their sins. SERMON 389.6.[27]

THE BAPTISM OF GENTILE STONES FULFILLS THE PROMISE TO ABRAHAM. CYRIL OF ALEXANDRIA: Can you see how most skillfully he humbles their foolish pride and shows that their being born of Abraham according to the flesh brings them no profit? Of what benefit is nobility of birth, if people's deeds are not accordingly earnest and they fail to imitate the virtue of their ancestors? The Savior says to them, "If you were Abraham's children, you would do what Abraham did."[28] The relationship that God requires is one of character and manners. Thus it is useless to boast of holy and good parents, while we fall short of their virtue.

But, says the Jew, if it is so, how is the seed of Abraham still to be multiplied? How can God's promise to him hold true, according to which he will multiply his seed as the stars of heaven? By the calling of the Gentiles, O Jew! God said to Abraham himself, "Through Isaac shall your descendants be named,"[29] adding that he has set Abraham as a father of many nations. But the phrase "through Isaac" means "according to promise." He is set, therefore, as a father of many nations by faith, that is to say, in Christ.

As can be seen, the blessed Baptist called them stones, because they as yet did not know the one who is by nature God. They were in error and in their great folly worshiped the creation instead of the Creator. But they were called and became the sons of Abraham and, by believing in Christ, acknowledged him who is by nature God. COMMENTARY ON LUKE, HOMILY 7.[30]

GEHENNA FOR ALL WHO DO NOT PRODUCE GOOD WORKS. GREGORY THE GREAT: The tree is the entire human race in this world. The axe is our Redeemer. His humanity is like the axe's handle and iron head. It is his divinity that cuts. The

---

[23]Lk 2:29-30. [24]FC 24:501. [25]Gal 5:22. [26]FC 94:95-96*. [27]WSA 3 10:411**. [28]Jn 8:39. [29]Gen 21:12 [30]CGSL 71-72**.

axe is now laid at the root of the tree because, although he is waiting patiently, what he will do is nonetheless apparent.

Every tree that does not bear good fruit will be cut down and thrown into the fire. Every wicked person, refusing to bear the fruit of good works in this life, will find the conflagration of Gehenna all the more swiftly prepared for him or her. We must note that he says that the axe is laid not at the branches but at the root. When the children of evil persons are destroyed, what else does this mean but that the branches of the tree that bears no fruit are being cut off? When an entire progeny is destroyed, as well as its parents, the tree that bears no fruit is being cut down from its root. Then nothing will be left from which descendants might sprout again. FORTY GOSPEL HOMILIES 6.[31]

THE AXE IS GOD'S WRATH, BUT A REMNANT IS SAVED. CYRIL OF ALEXANDRIA: What he means by the axe in this passage is the sharp wrath which God the Father brought on the Jews for their wickedness towards Christ and brazen violence. The wrath was brought on them like an axe. To this you may also add the parable in the Gospels about the fig tree. As an unfruitful plant, no longer of the generous kind, it was cut down by God. John does not say, however, that the axe was laid into the root, but at the root, that is, near the root. The branches were cut off, but the plant was not dug up by its root. Thus the remnant of Israel was saved and did not perish utterly. COMMENTARY ON LUKE, HOMILY 7.[32]

3:10-14 John's Response to Questions

LUKE THE PHYSICIAN APPLIES REMEDIES THROUGH JOHN. CYRIL OF ALEXANDRIA: St. Luke has introduced three groups of people that ask John questions—the multitudes, the tax collectors and the soldiers. Just as a skillful physician applies to each sickness a suitable and fitting remedy, so also the Baptist gave to each group, representing a mode of life, useful and appropriate ad-

vice. He told the multitudes to practice mutual kindness as they strive for repentance. In the case of the tax collectors, he put an end to unrestrained taxation. Then, very wisely, he told the soldiers to oppress no one but be content with their wages. COMMENTARY ON LUKE, HOMILIES 8-9.[33]

NOT SERVING TWO MASTERS. ORIGEN: To say that the person who has two coats should give one to someone who has none fits the apostles better than the crowd. To understand that this command fits the apostles more than the people, listen to what the Savior says to the apostles, "Do not take two coats on a journey."[34] Therefore, there are two garments with which each one is clothed. The command is to "share with him who has none." This denotes an alternate meaning: just as we may not "serve two masters," the Savior does not want us to have two coats, or to be clothed with a double garment. Otherwise, one would be the garment of the old man, the other of the new man. On the contrary, he desires that we strip ourselves of the old man and put on the new man.[35] Up to this point, the explanation is easy. HOMILIES ON THE GOSPEL OF LUKE 23.2-3.[36]

TAX COLLECTORS WHO EXACT MORE TRANSGRESS THE HOLY SPIRIT. ORIGEN: "Tax collectors also came to be baptized." According to the simple interpretation, he teaches the tax collectors to seek "no more" than the law commands. Those who exact more transgress not John's commandment but that of the Holy Spirit, who spoke through John. . . .

We said all this to show that John taught the tax collectors. Among them there were not only those who collected revenue for the state, but also those who were coming for repentance and were not literally tax collectors. And others were soldiers who were going out to the baptism of repentance. HOMILIES ON THE GOSPEL OF LUKE 23.5, 9.[37]

---

[31]CS 123:42. [32]CGSL 72**. [33]CGSL 73**. [34]Mt 10:10. [35]Eph 4:22-24. [36]FC 94:98*. [37]FC 94:99, 101-2*.

MILITARY SERVICE COMMENDED BY JOHN.
AUGUSTINE: If Christian practice condemned war in general, then the soldiers in the Gospel who asked how they were to be saved should have been given the advice to throw down their arms and give up military service entirely. Instead, they were told, "Rob no one by violence or by false accusation, and be content with your wages." LETTER 138.[38]

FRUITS WORTHY OF REPENTANCE. AMBROSE: The Baptist gave a fitting response to each kind of people. To the tax collectors he said that they should not exact payment beyond what was appointed. To the soldiers, that they should not make false accusations or rob anyone, by which he meant that their pay was fixed, so that wanting to have more, they could not resort to plunder. These and other precepts are appropriate for all occupations, and the practice of compassion is shared. Thus it is a common precept that the basic necessities of life must be provided for all occupations, all ages and all people. Neither the tax collector nor the soldier is exempted, neither the farmer nor the townsman, neither the rich man nor the pauper—all are commanded in common to give to the one who does not have. Compassion is the fullness of the virtues and therefore the form of the perfect virtue is placed before all. Neither should they spare their own food and clothing. Yet the measure of compassion is maintained in relation to the capacity of the human condition, so that each does not take all for himself but shares what he has with the poor. EXPOSITION OF THE GOSPEL OF LUKE 2.77.[39]

3:15 The People Think John Might Be the Christ

JOHN IS THE FRIEND OF THE BRIDEGROOM.
GREGORY THE GREAT: Because people had seen that John the Baptist was endowed with astonishing holiness, they believed . . . that he was the Christ, as is said in the Gospel. The people were deliberating, all questioning in their hearts concerning John, whether perhaps he might be the Christ, and they asked him, "Are you the Christ?" If John had not been a valley in his own eyes, he would not have been full of the grace of the Spirit. To make clear what he was, he answered, "There comes after me one who is stronger than I, the strap of whose sandal I am not worthy to untie."[40] Again he said, "He who has the bride is the bridegroom. The friend of the bridegroom, who stands and hears him, rejoices greatly at the bridegroom's voice. This joy of mine is now full. He must increase, but I must decrease."[41] FORTY GOSPEL HOMILIES 6.[42]

3:16 John Baptizes with Water; Jesus Baptizes with the Holy Spirit and Fire

REASONS WHY JESUS BAPTIZES WITH THE HOLY SPIRIT. CYRIL OF ALEXANDRIA: After this, John brings forward a second argument, saying, "I indeed baptize you in water. He shall baptize you in the Holy Spirit and in fire." This too is of great importance for the proof and demonstration that Jesus is God and Lord. For it is the sole and peculiar property of the Substance that transcends all, to be able to bestow on people the indwelling of the Holy Spirit and make those that draw near unto it partakers of the divine nature. But this exists in Christ, not as a thing received, nor by communication from another, but as his own and as belonging to his substance. He baptizes in the Holy Spirit. COMMENTARY ON LUKE, HOMILY 10.[43]

FIRE REFERS TO THE FIERY TONGUES AT PENTECOST. CYRIL OF JERUSALEM: John, filled with the Holy Spirit from his mother's womb, was sanctified for the purpose of baptizing the Lord. John himself did not impart the Spirit but preached the glad tidings of him who does. He says, "I indeed baptize you with water, for repentance. But he who is coming after me, he will bap-

---

[38]FC 20:47. [39]EHG 68**. [40]Mk 1:7. [41]Jn 3:29-30. [42]CS 123:38*. [43]CGSL 75**.

tize you with the Holy Spirit and with fire."[44] Why fire? Because the descent of the Holy Spirit was in fiery tongues. Concerning this the Lord says with joy, "I have come to cast fire upon the earth, and how I wish that it would be kindled!"[45] Catechetical Lectures 17.8.[46]

Jesus Baptizes Christians with the Holy Spirit and Fire. Chrysostom: What happened in the case of our Master's body also happens in the case of your own. Although John appeared to be holding his body by the head, it was the divine Word that led his body down into the streams of Jordan and baptized him. The Master's body was baptized by the Word, by the voice of his Father from heaven which said, "This is my beloved Son," and by the manifestation of the Holy Spirit which descended upon him. This also happens in the case of your body. The baptism is given in the name of the Father, the Son and the Holy Spirit. Therefore John the Baptist told us, for our instruction, that man does not baptize us but God: "There comes after me one who is mightier than I, and I am not worthy to loose the strap of his sandal. He will baptize you with the Holy Spirit and with fire."

For this reason, when the priest is baptizing he does not say, "I baptize so-and-so," but "So-and-so is baptized in the name of the Father and of the Son and of the Holy Spirit." In this way he shows that it is not he who baptizes but those whose names have been invoked, the Father, the Son and the Holy Spirit. Baptismal Instructions 11.13.[47]

3:17 The Coming Wrath of God

Judgment Will Separate the Fruitful from the Unfruitful. Ambrose: Through the sign of the fan, the Lord is said to have the right to distinguish merits. When the grain is winnowed on the threshing floor, the full grain is separated from the empty, the fruitful is separated from the worthless, as if by a weighing of a blowing breeze. So through this comparison, the Lord

is manifest, because on the day of judgment, he separates the merits and fruits of solid virtue from the unfruitful shallowness of worthless ostentation and inadequate deeds, before he establishes the people of perfect merit in a heavenly home. For he who has deserved to be like him is the perfect fruit. The Lord is like the grain of wheat that has died.[48] So he confers very many fruits on us, hated by chaff and no friend to worthless merits. And therefore, a fire that is not harmful by its nature will burn before him.[49] For he who burns up the evils of wickedness adds to the radiance of goodness. Exposition of the Gospel of Luke 2.82.[50]

3:18 A Summary of John's Proclamation

The Many Things John Taught. Origen: One who teaches the word of the gospel proclaims not just one thing but many. . . . Therefore John also preached "other things" to the people, which have not been recorded. But consider how many things there are that have been recorded. He proclaimed Christ. He pointed him out. He preached the baptism of the Holy Spirit. He taught the tax collectors salvation and the soldiers discipline. He taught that the threshing floor was being cleansed, trees cut down, and the rest, which the account in the Gospel narrates. Hence, apart from these things that have been written down, he is shown to have proclaimed other things which are not written down. For the Scripture says, "He also proclaimed many other things to the people and encouraged them." Homilies on the Gospel of Luke 27.1.[51]

3:19-20 John the Baptist Imprisoned

Herod Imprisons John, but He Keeps Teaching. Origen: Notice that even while in prison he is teaching. For he also had his disciples in that place. Why did they stay there, unless

---

[44]Mt 3:11. [45]Lk 12:49. [46]FC 64:100D**. [47]ACW 31:164-65*. [48]See Jn 12:24. [49]See Ps 96:3 LXX. [50]EHG 70-71**. [51]FC 94:112*.

John exercised the office of teacher even in prison and taught them with divine words? In the course of these words, a question about Jesus arose. John sends some of his disciples and asks, "Are you he who is to come, or do we wait for another?" The disciples return and announce to the teacher what the Savior had bidden them to say. With Jesus' words, John was armed for battle. He died confidently and was beheaded without resistance, strengthened by the words of the Lord himself and believing that he in whom he believed was truly the Son of God. This is what we have to say about John, and his freedom, and about Herod's madness. To his many other crimes he also added this one: he first shut John in prison and afterward beheaded him. HOMILIES ON THE GOSPEL OF LUKE 27.4.[52]

LUKE RECORDS JOHN'S IMPRISONMENT. EUSE-BIUS: Luke too, before beginning the acts of Jesus, makes a similar observation, saying that Herod added one more offense to his other crimes by shutting up John in jail. ECCLESIASTICAL HISTORY 3.24.[53]

---

[52]FC 94:113*. [53]HCCC 132.

3:21-22 THE BAPTISM OF JESUS

[21]*Now when all the people were baptized, and when Jesus also had been baptized and was praying, the heaven was opened,* [22]*and the Holy Spirit descended upon him in bodily form, as a dove, and a voice came from heaven, "Thou art my beloved Son;[j] with thee I am well pleased."[k]*

j Or *my Son, my (or the) Beloved*   k Other ancient authorities read *today I have begotten thee*

OVERVIEW: In the church year, the feast of the nativity is closely followed by the celebration of Jesus' baptism because of the parallels between these two great events (MAXIMUS OF TURIN). The opening of heaven is a programmatic theme for the rest of the Gospel, for the opened heaven signals the coming of the forgiveness of sins (ORIGEN). The mystery of the Trinity is present—Father, Son and Spirit are eternally three in one (AMBROSE). The great mystery is that Christ, true God and true man, anointed with the Holy Spirit and acknowledged by the Father, opens the way for fallen human beings to be incorporated into Christ through baptism and likewise to receive the Spirit and to be adopted as children of God (CYRIL OF ALEXANDRIA). From now on the Holy Spirit will accompany Jesus in his public ministry, for the Spirit is always the Spirit of Jesus (GREG-ory OF NAZIANZUS). As "the Anointed One," "the Messiah," "the Christ," Jesus stands in the waters of the Jordan both in solidarity with us and in substitution for us (CYPRIAN). By entering the waters of the Jordon on our behalf, he sanctifies water for our baptism (MAXIMUS OF TURIN). The appearance of the Holy Spirit as a dove recalls Noah after the flood,[1] pointing to the ark of Noah as the church where the dove was a symbol of peace, and pointing to Christ whose church is his body. The declaration that Jesus is the beloved Son is the high point of Jesus' baptism and shows the unity of Father and Son (AMBROSE).

THE PARALLELS BETWEEN JESUS' BIRTH AND BAPTISM. MAXIMUS OF TURIN: Today, then, is

---

[1]Gen 8:8.

another kind of birth of the Savior. We see him born with the same sort of signs, the same sort of wonders, but with greater mystery. The Holy Spirit, who was present to him then in the womb, now pours out upon him in the torrent. He who then purified Mary for him now sanctifies the running waters for him. The Father who then overshadowed in power now cries out with his voice. He who then, as if choosing the more prudent course, manifested himself as a cloud at the nativity now bears witness to the truth. So God says, "This is my beloved Son, in whom I am well pleased. Hear him." Clearly the second birth is more excellent than the first. The one brought forth Christ in silence and without a witness. The other baptized the Lord gloriously with a profession of divinity. From the one, Joseph, thought to be the father, absents himself. At the other, God the Father, not believed in, manifests himself. In the one the mother labors under suspicion because in her condition she lacked a father. In the other she is honored because God attests to his Son. SERMON 13A.[2]

HEAVEN OPENED SO THAT SIN COULD BE FORGIVEN. ORIGEN: The Lord was baptized. The heavens were opened, and the Holy Spirit came down upon him. A voice from the heavens thundered and said, "This is my beloved Son, in whom I am pleased." We should say that heaven was opened at the baptism of Jesus and for the plan of forgiving sins. These are not the sins of him "who had committed no sin, nor was deceit found in his mouth."[3] The heavens were opened and the Holy Spirit came down for the forgiveness of the whole world's sins. After the Lord "ascended on high, leading captivity captive,"[4] he gave them the Spirit. The Spirit had come to him, and he gave the Spirit at the time of his resurrection, when he said, "Receive the Holy Spirit. If you forgive anyone's sins, they will be forgiven him. If you retain them for anyone, they will be retained."[5] But "the Holy Spirit came down upon the Savior in the form of a dove." The dove is a gentle bird, innocent and simple. Hence we too are commanded to imitate the innocence of doves.[6] Such is the Holy Spirit: pure, swift, and rising up to the heights. HOMILIES ON THE GOSPEL OF LUKE 27.5.[7]

THE MYSTERY OF THE TRINITY PRESENT AT JESUS' BAPTISM. AMBROSE: Now let us consider the mystery of the Trinity. We say, "one God," but we confess the Father, and we confess the Son. For although it is written, "You shall love the Lord thy God and serve him alone,"[8] the Son denied that he is alone, saying, "I am not alone, for the Father is with me."[9] Nor is he alone now, for the Father bears witness that he is present. The Holy Spirit is present, because the Trinity can never be separated from Itself. Then "heaven was opened, the Holy Spirit descended in bodily shape like a dove." EXPOSITION OF THE GOSPEL OF LUKE 2.92.[10]

THE MYSTERY OF JESUS' BAPTISM. CYRIL OF ALEXANDRIA: But how then, they object, was he baptized and received the Spirit? We reply that he had no need of holy baptism. He was wholly pure and spotless, and the holiest of the holy. He did not need the Holy Spirit, for the Spirit that proceeds from God the Father is from him and equal to him in substance. Now, at last, we must explain God's plan of salvation. God, in his love of humankind, provided for us a way of salvation and of life. Believing in the Father, Son and Holy Spirit, and making this confession before many witnesses, we wash away all the filth of sin. The communication of the Holy Spirit enriched us, made us partakers of the divine nature and gained for us the grace of adoption as God's children. It was necessary, therefore, that the Word of the Father become for our sakes the pattern and way of every good work when he humbled himself to emptiness and deigned to assume our likeness. For it follows that he who is first in everything must set the example in this too. He commences the work himself in order that we may learn

---

[2]ACW 50:34*. [3]1 Pet 2:22. [4]Ps 68:18; Eph 4:8. [5]Jn 20:22-23. [6]See Mt 10:16. [7]FC 94:114. [8]Deut 10:20. [9]Jn 16:32. [10]EHG 77*.

about the power of holy baptism and learn how much we gain by approaching so great a grace. Having been baptized, he prays that you, my beloved, may learn that never-ceasing prayer is a thing most fitting for those who have once been counted worthy of holy baptism. COMMENTARY ON LUKE, HOMILY 11.[11]

THE HOLY SPIRIT VITAL TO JESUS' MINISTRY.

GREGORY OF NAZIANZUS: Christ is born; the Spirit is his forerunner.[12] Christ is baptized; the Spirit bears him witness. Christ is tempted. The Spirit leads him up.[13] Christ performs miracles. The Spirit accompanies him.[14] Christ ascends. The Spirit fills his place.[15] ORATION 31.29, ON THE HOLY SPIRIT.[16]

JESUS IS BAPTIZED FOR OUR SIN, NOT HIS.

CYPRIAN: From the first moment of his descent from the glories of heaven to earthly things, he did not disdain to put on man's flesh although he was the Son of God. Although he himself was not a sinner, he did not disdain to bear the sins of others. Having put aside his immortality for a time, he suffered himself to become mortal, in order that though innocent he might be slain for the salvation of the guilty. The Lord was baptized by his servant, and he, although destined to grant the remission of sins, did not disdain to have his body cleansed with the water of regeneration. THE GOOD OF PATIENCE 6.[17]

JESUS SACTIFIES ALL WATER WITH HIS BAPTISM.

MAXIMUS OF TURIN: Today, then, he is baptized in the Jordan. What sort of baptism is this, when the one who is dipped is purer than the font, and where the water that soaks the one whom it has received is not dirtied but honored with blessings? What sort of baptism is this of the Savior, I ask, in which the streams are made pure more than they purify? For by a new kind of consecration the water does not so much wash Christ as submit to being washed. Since the Savior plunged into the waters, he sanctified the outpouring of every flood and the course of every

stream by the mystery of his baptism. When someone wishes to be baptized in the name of the Lord, it is not so much the water of this world that covers him but the water of Christ that purifies him. Yet the Savior willed to be baptized for this reason—not that he might cleanse himself but that he might cleanse the waters for our sake. SERMON 13A.3.[18]

THE DOVE POINTS TO THE ARK AND TO CHRIST.

AMBROSE: Why like a dove? For the grace of the washing requires simplicity, so that we may be innocent like doves.[19] The grace of the washing requires peace, as in an earlier image the dove brought to the ark that which alone was inviolable by the flood.[20] He of whom the dove was the image, who now deigned to descend in the form of a dove, taught me that in that branch, in that ark, was the image of peace and of the church. In the midst of the floods of the world the Holy Spirit brings its fruitful peace to its church. David too taught, he who perceived the sacrament of baptism and said with the Spirit of prophecy, "Who will give me wings like a dove?"[21] EXPOSITION OF THE GOSPEL OF LUKE 2.92.[22]

THE VOICE OF THE FATHER AFFIRMS THE UNITY OF FATHER AND SON.

AMBROSE: We saw the Spirit, but in bodily form, let us also see the Father.[23] Because we cannot see, let us hear. Our merciful God is present. He will not forsake his temple. He wishes to build up every soul, he wishes to mold it for salvation, he wishes to convey living stones from earth to heaven.[24] He loves his temple. Let us love him. If we love God, let us keep his commandments.[25] If we love him, we shall know him. He who says that he knows him and keeps not his commandments is a liar.[26] For how can he who does not love Truth love God, for God is Truth?[27] Therefore let us hear the Fa-

---

[11]CGSL 80-81**. [12]Lk 1:31, 35. [13]Lk 4:2. [14]Mt 12:22. [15]Acts 1:9. [16]FGFR 295*. [17]FC 36:268*. [18]ACW 50:35*. [19]See Mt 10:16. [20]See Gen 8:10-11. [21]Ps 54:6 LXX. [22]EHG 77**. [23]See Jn 1:18. [24]1 Pet 2:5. [25]Jn 14:15. [26]1 Jn 2:4. [27]1 Jn 4:6-7.

ther, for the Father is invisible.[28] Yet the Son is invisible according to his divinity, for no one has seen God at any time.[29] So, while the Son is God, he is not seen as the Son, insofar as he is God. Yet he wished to show himself in the body. Because the Father did not wear a body, therefore the Father wished to prove to us that he is present in the Son, saying, "You are my beloved Son. In you I am well pleased." If you wish to learn that the Son is always present with the Father, read the voice of the Son saying, "If I go up into heaven, you are there. If I go down into the grave, you are present there."[30] If you seek evidence of the Father, you have heard it from John. Believe him by whom Christ believed he must be baptized, to whom the Father entrusted his Son, saying with a heavenly voice, "This is my beloved Son, in whom I am well pleased."[31] Exposition of the Gospel of Luke 2.94.[32]

---

[28]Col 1:15; 1 Tim 1:17. [29]Jn 1:18. [30]Ps 139:8 (138:8 LXX); cf. Amos 9:2. [31]Mt 3:17. [32]EHG 77-78*.

3:23-38 THE GENEALOGY OF JESUS

[23]*Jesus, when he began his ministry, was about thirty years of age, being the son (as was supposed) of Joseph, the son of Heli,* [24]*the son of Matthat, the son of Levi, the son of Melchi, the son of Jannai, the son of Joseph,* [25]*the son of Mattathias, the son of Amos, the son of Nahum, the son of Esli, the son of Naggai,* [26]*the son of Maath, the son of Mattathias, the son of Semein, the son of Josech, the son of Joda,* [27]*the son of Joanan, the son of Rhesa, the son of Zerubbabel, the son of Shealtiel,[1] the son of Neri,* [28]*the son of Melchi, the son of Addi, the son of Cosam, the son of Elmadam, the son of Er,* [29]*the son of Joshua, the son of Eliezer, the son of Jorim, the son of Matthat, the son of Levi,* [30]*the son of Simeon, the son of Judah, the son of Joseph, the son of Jonam, the son of Eliakim,* [31]*the son of Melea, the son of Menna, the son of Mattatha, the son of Nathan, the son of David,* [32]*the son of Jesse, the son of Obed, the son of Boaz, the son of Sala, the son of Nahshon,* [33]*the son of Amminadab, the son of Admin, the son of Arni, the son of Hezron, the son of Perez, the son of Judah,* [34]*the son of Jacob, the son of Isaac, the son of Abraham, the son of Terah, the son of Nahor,* [35]*the son of Serug, the son of Reu, the son of Peleg, the son of Eber, the son of Shelah,* [36]*the son of Cainan, the son of Arphaxad, the son of Shem, the son of Noah, the son of Lamech,* [37]*the son of Methuselah, the son of Enoch, the son of Jared, the son of Mahalaleel, the son of Cainan,* [38]*the son of Enos, the son of Seth, the son of Adam, the son of God.*

1 Greek *Salathiel*

Overview: Thirty was the age of David when he began his reign as king of Israel,[1] so Jesus' age suggests that he is the son of David, who will inherit "the throne of his father David."[2] Joseph was thirty years old when he began his service to the pharaoh[3] (Origen). The qualifying statement "being a son, as was supposed" affirms the virgin birth of Jesus in the genealogy and articulates one

---

[1]2 Sam 5:4. [2]Lk 1:33. [3]Gen 41:46.

of its themes: that Jesus is not Joseph's son but the Son of God (AMBROSE). The genealogy teaches us the fleshly line of Jesus Christ, son of Adam and Son of God (PRUDENTIUS). The genealogy is that of Joseph, since for the Jews the generations of a family are always listed through the husband. Some commentators suggest that Matthew gives the royal line of descent from David, while Luke names the priestly descent, for Jesus is King and Priest, and Luke's Gospel is represented by a calf. Luke's placement of the genealogy right after Jesus' baptism suggests that henceforth baptism into Christ will be the new birth into the new family of God (AMBROSE).

Significant names begin some of the lists, that is, David, Abraham and Enoch, and the final, seventy-eighth name is God. Luke includes other significant Old Testament saints, particularly those who were known for their righteousness before God. Matthew, unlike Luke, begins Jesus' genealogy with Abraham (AMBROSE) and includes in it women (Tamar, Ruth, Rahab and Uriah's wife), some of whom were known for their sinful behavior (ORIGEN).

3:23-38 Jesus—Son of Adam, Son of God

THE NUMBER THIRTY HAS GREAT THEOLOGICAL SIGNIFICANCE. ORIGEN: But also if you who hear these words direct your thoughts to the holy Scriptures in your leisure, you will discover many great events to be comprised under the number thirty or fifty. Joseph was thirty years old when he was led out of prison and received the rule of all Egypt that he might divert the calamity of an imminent famine by divine provision.[4] Jesus is reported to have been thirty years old when he came to baptism. HOMILIES ON GENESIS 2.5.[5]

JOSEPH WAS THOUGHT TO BE JESUS' FATHER. AMBROSE: It benefits no one to change what is written: "Who was thought to be the son of Joseph." For it was right that he was "thought" so, because he was not the Joseph's son by nature but was thought to be his Son, because he was born of

Mary, who was engaged to Joseph, her husband. So you have: "Is not this Joseph the carpenter's son?"[6] EXPOSITION OF THE GOSPEL OF LUKE 3.2.[7]

THE FLESHLY LINE OF SON OF ADAM, SON OF GOD. PRUDENTIUS:

What do you say about the sacred words of
    Luke
When he the genealogy repeats,
The fleshly line retracing through old sires?
Up generations seventy-two
Christ mounts—so many teachers into the
    world
He sent—and by the steps down to his birth
Goes back to Adam, head of earthly flesh.
The Father then receives his Son and us,
And Adam son of God becomes through
    Christ.
Nothing now remains but that you deem this
    race
Unreal, Levi, Judah, Simeon,
King David, other mighty kings, unreal,
The virgin's swelling womb itself grown big
With lying vapor, flimsy clouds and mist.
That airy blood dissolves, the bones grow soft
And melt, the trembling muscles disappear.
That every deed the idle wind dispels,
The breezes scatter, all an empty tale.
THE DIVINITY OF CHRIST 1001-18.[8]

WHY THIS IS JOSEPH'S GENEALOGY. AMBROSE: You see that the description of descent is connected by the old custom from the fathers to the sons and from the sons to the fathers. You see that the family is everywhere listed through the generations of the husband. Do not marvel if Matthew reports the order of the generations from Abraham to Joseph, and Luke from Joseph to Adam and to God. Do not marvel that Joseph's lineage is described. Indeed, being born according to the flesh, he must follow the usage of the flesh, and he who came into the world must be described in the cus-

---

[4]See Gen 41:46. [5]FC 71:83-84. [6]Mt 13:55. [7]EHG 81**. [8]FC 52:37-38.

tom of the world, particularly as the lineage of Mary is also in the lineage of Joseph. For since Joseph was a righteous man, he took a wife from his own tribe and his own country, nor could a righteous man contravene what is prescribed in the law.[9] "The inheritance of the people of Israel shall not be transferred from one tribe to another. For every one of the people of Israel shall cleave to the inheritance of the tribe of his fathers. Every daughter who possesses an inheritance in any tribe of the people of Israel shall be wife to one of the family of the tribe of her father, so that every one of the people of Israel may possess the inheritance of his fathers."[10] Therefore, also at the time of the enrollment, Joseph went up from his house and the country of David to be enrolled with Mary his wife.[11] She who enrolls from the same house and the same country surely signifies that she is of this same tribe and this same country. EXPOSITION OF THE GOSPEL OF LUKE 3.4.[12]

MATTHEW SHOWS A ROYAL LINE, LUKE A PRIESTLY ONE. AMBROSE: Here too some . . . raise issues: that Matthew counted forty-two generations from Abraham to Christ,[13] but Luke fifty, and that Matthew reported that the generation descended through some persons, and Luke mentioned others. In this matter, you can test what we said. Although Matthew wove some forefathers of the divine lineage, but Luke others, into the order of generation, nevertheless each indicated that the remaining ancestors were from the race of Abraham and David. Matthew thought the generation should be derived through Solomon,[14] but Luke through Nathan. This fact seems to show both a royal and a priestly family of Christ. We should not consider one account truer than the other, but that the one agrees with the other in equal faith and truth. According to the flesh, Jesus was truly of a royal and priestly family, King from kings, Priest from priests. Although the prophecy pertains not to the carnal but the celestial, since a King exults in the power of God,[15] to whom judgment is committed by the King, his Father,[16] and a Priest is

forever. Accordingly it is written, "You are a priest forever after the order of Melchizedek."[17] Then, each fittingly kept faith, so that Matthew established his origin led through kings, and Luke, by deriving the lineage of his race transmitted through priests from God to Christ, declared his very descent the more holy. At the same time, the image of a calf is indicated, in so much as he thinks the priestly mystery must be preserved. EXPOSITION OF THE GOSPEL OF LUKE 3.12-13.[18]

LUKE ECHOES JESUS' BAPTISM. AMBROSE: Therefore Luke also thought that his origin should be traced back to God. Because God is the true Father of Christ, either the Father according to the true generation or the Author of the mystical gift—according to the regeneration of baptism. Furthermore, he did not start by describing his generation but first set forth his baptism. He desired to show him as God, the Author of all, weaving everything together through baptism. He also stated that Christ derived from God in the order of succession, in order to prove him the Son of God according to nature, according to grace and according to the flesh. Then what clearer evidence is there of divine generation than that before speaking of Jesus' generation, Luke has the Father himself saying, "This is my beloved Son, in whom I am well pleased"?[19] EXPOSITION OF THE GOSPEL OF LUKE 3.11.[20]

LUKE INCLUDES SIGNIFICANT OLD TESTAMENT FIGURES IN HIS GENEALOGY. AMBROSE: He could not include more sons of Jacob, lest he seem to digress outside the generations in an irrelevant series. Of course, in the case of other, that is, distant, descendants of the patriarchs, Luke did not think the names should be omitted, but that those of Joseph, Judah, Simeon and Levi should be preferred beyond the rest. We know that there were four kinds of virtues in those

---

[9]See Num 4:1. [10]Num 36:6-8. [11]Lk 2:4-5. [12]EHG 82-83**. [13]Mt 1:2-17. [14]Mt 1:6-7. [15]Ps 21:1 (20:1 LXX). [16]See Jn 5:22. [17]Ps 110:4 (109:4 LXX). [18]EHG 87-88**. [19]Cf. Mt 3:17. [20]EHG 87*.

from whom they were descended. In Judah, the mystery of the Lord's passion was prefigured.[21] In Joseph, an example of chastity went before.[22] In Simeon, the payment for violated virginity was represented.[23] In Levi, the office of a priest was symbolized.[24] We observe the dignity of prophecy manifested also through Nathan so that because Christ Jesus is one and all,[25] diverse kinds of virtues went before also in individual forefathers. EXPOSITION OF THE GOSPEL OF LUKE 3.47.[26]

UNLIKE LUKE, MATTHEW LISTS WOMEN WHO ARE SINNERS IN HIS GENEALOGY. ORIGEN: Matthew, who makes him descend from the heavenly regions, mentions women—not any women at all, but sinners, and those whom Scripture had reproved. But Luke, who tells of Jesus at his baptism, mentions no woman. Matthew, as we said, names Tamar, who by deception lay with her father-in-law. Ruth was not from the race of Israel. I cannot discover where Rahab was taken from. The wife of Uriah violated her husband's bed. For our Lord and Savior had come for this end, to take upon himself humankind's sins. God "made him who had committed no sin to be sin for our sake."[27] For this reason, he came down into the world and took on the person of sinners and depraved people. He willed to be born from the stock of Solomon, whose sins have been recorded,[28] and from Rehoboam, whose transgressions are reported,[29] and from the rest of them, many of whom "did evil in the sight of the Lord."[30] HOMILIES ON THE GOSPEL OF LUKE 28.2.[31]

WHY LUKE'S ENUMERATION DIFFERS FROM MATTHEW'S. AMBROSE: Yet it seems needful to explain why St. Matthew began to enumerate the descent of Christ from Abraham but St. Luke led it from Christ up to God. But first I think we should not set aside by any means the question why St. Matthew, when he began the order of descent from Abraham, did not say, "The Book of the Generation of Abraham," but "The Book of the Generation of Jesus Christ, the Son of David, the Son of Abraham."[32] Why he named these two in particular. . . .

The Evangelist selected those two authors of the race, the one who received the promise concerning the congregation of the nations, the other who obtained the prophecy of the generation of Christ. Although he is later in the order of the succession, yet he is described before Abraham in the generation of the Lord, because it is more to have received the promise concerning Christ than that concerning the church, since the church itself is through Christ. Then there is one prince of the race according to the flesh, and another according to the spirit. The one is a prince by grace of children, the other through the faith of the peoples. For greater is he who saves than he who is saved. Hence he is called "the Son of David," "the Book of the Generation of Jesus Christ, the Son of David."[33] EXPOSITION OF THE GOSPEL OF LUKE 3.6, 10.[34]

---

[21]See Gen 49:10-12. [22]See Gen 39:7-15. [23]See Gen 34:25-31; cf. Jdt 9:2-4. [24]See Num 3:6. [25]Col 3:11. [26]EHG 108-9*. [27]2 Cor 5:21. [28]1 Kings 11:6-8. [29]1 Kings 14:21-31. [30]1 Kings 15:26, 34. [31]FC 94:115-16*. [32]Mt 1:1. [33]Mt 1:1. [34]EHG 83-84, 86-87**.

4:1-13 THE TEMPTATION OF JESUS IN THE DESERT

[1]*And Jesus, full of the Holy Spirit, returned from the Jordan, and was led by the Spirit* [2]*for forty days in the wilderness, tempted by the devil. And he ate nothing in those days; and when they were*

ended, he was hungry. [3]The devil said to him, "If you are the Son of God, command this stone to become bread." [4]And Jesus answered him, "It is written, 'Man shall not live by bread alone.'" [5]And the devil took him up, and showed him all the kingdoms of the world in a moment of time, [6]and said to him, "To you I will give all this authority and their glory; for it has been delivered to me, and I give it to whom I will. [7]If you, then, will worship me, it shall all be yours." [8]And Jesus answered him, "It is written,

'You shall worship the Lord your God,
and him only shall you serve.'"

[9]And he took him to Jerusalem, and set him on the pinnacle of the temple, and said to him, "If you are the Son of God, throw yourself down from here; [10]for it is written,

'He will give his angels charge of you, to guard you,'

[11]and

'On their hands they will bear you up,
lest you strike your foot against a stone.'"

[12]And Jesus answered him, "It is said, 'You shall not tempt the Lord your God.'" [13]And when the devil had ended every temptation, he departed from him until an opportune time.

OVERVIEW: Satan waits until Jesus is thirty to tempt him because it is only then that Jesus shows himself to be the Messiah at his baptism (EPHREM THE SYRIAN). The introduction deals with Jesus and his movements as he is led by the Spirit into the wilderness for fasting (CYRIL OF ALEXANDRIA). There is an Adam typology[1] and a Genesis background to this story as Adam is cast out of Paradise into the desert, whereas Christ the new Adam goes into the desert on our behalf to come forth from that wilderness of temptation to lead us back to Paradise (AMBROSE).

The first temptation tempts Jesus to the sin of gluttony that cursed the first Adam (ORIGEN). Adam fell by eating food that was not his to eat; Jesus conquers by not eating food that Satan tempts him with at a moment of great hunger after forty days of fasting (CYRIL OF ALEXANDRIA). Jesus the Son of God incarnate, the Word of God, is the bread of life from heaven[2] who shall feed the people bread—himself—and he defeats Satan with this heavenly bread, the Word of God (AMBROSE).

In the second temptation, the kingdoms Satan shows Jesus in a moment of time are not king-doms like Rome or Persia but his, Satan's, rule in the world (ORIGEN). The devil has taken this world by fraud, but now that Christ has come, he will restore this world back to its proper authority through his obedient suffering and death (CYRIL OF ALEXANDRIA).

In the final temptation Satan changes his tactics, but Jesus remains true to his person and unchanging nature (EPHREM THE SYRIAN). Adam was enticed by food, but here Israel repeats the sin of Eve, who longed to worship another besides the Lord (AMBROSE). The psalm addresses any just person who is given the power in Christ to tread upon the snakes and scorpions as the Lord promised to the seventy[-two][3] (ORIGEN). Though the temple may be destroyed, the pinnacle of the temple—Jesus—endures forever (PRUDENTIUS). Although Jesus will continue to confront Satan through his ministry, the devil becomes a roaring lion again at the crucifixion (AUGUSTINE). The temptation of Jesus by the devil foreshadows the conflict of the passion and Jesus' victory on the cross.

---

[1]Rom 5:12-21. [2]Jn 6:32, 35. [3]Lk 10:19.

4:1-2 Led by the Spirit into the Wilderness for Forty Days

WHY SATAN WAITS TO TEMPT JESUS. EPHREM THE SYRIAN: Why didn't Satan tempt him before his thirtieth year? He tempted Jesus because a definite sign of Christ's divinity had not yet been given from heaven. He appeared modest like others, and he had not received any obvious homage in the presence of his people. Satan refrained from tempting him until the beginning of this event. When he heard, "Now, behold the Lamb of God is coming," and "This is he who takes away the sins of the world,"[4] Satan was astonished. Yet he waited until Jesus was baptized to see if he would be baptized as if he needed to be baptized.

Then he saw the splendor of the light that appeared on the water, the voice that came from heaven. Then Satan knew that he who fulfills every need had gone down into the water and that he had not come to baptism as if he needed to be baptized. Satan reflected and said to himself, "As long as I have not tested him by combat through temptation I will not be able to identify him." But it was not fitting that the Benefactor should resist the will of him who had come to tempt him. For, not knowing how to tempt him, Satan did not dare approach him. COMMENTARY ON TATIAN'S DIATESSARON 4.4-5.[5]

LED BY THE SPIRIT INTO THE WILDERNESS FOR FASTING. CYRIL OF ALEXANDRIA: "He was led, therefore," it says, "in the Spirit in the wilderness forty days, being tempted of the devil." What is the meaning of the word *led*? It signifies not so much that he was led there as that he dwelt and continued there. . . .

He dwelt therefore in the wilderness in the Spirit, that is, spiritually. He fasted, granting no food whatsoever to the necessities of the body. I imagine someone may immediately object to this: And what harm, then, did it do Jesus to dwell in cities constantly? And in what way could it benefit him to choose to inhabit the wilderness? He did not lack one good thing. And why, too, did he

fast also? Why was it necessary for him to labor? He does not know what it means to have a depraved desire. For we adopt the practice of fasting as a very useful expedient, by which we kill pleasure and attack the law of sin that is in our bodies[6] and completely destroy those emotions which lead on to fleshly lust. But why did Christ need to fast? The Father slays the sin in the flesh by his body. He kills the motions of the flesh in us. He has abolished sin in miserable beings—in us. What kind of fasting could he need in anything that concerns himself? He is holy, undefiled by nature, wholly pure and without blemish. He cannot experience even the shadow of a change. COMMENTARY ON LUKE, HOMILY 12.[7]

ADAM GOES FROM PARADISE TO THE DESERT; CHRIST FROM THE DESERT TO PARADISE. AMBROSE: It is fitting that it be recorded that the first Adam was cast out of Paradise into the desert,[8] that you may observe how the second Adam returned from the desert to Paradise. . . . Adam brought death through the tree. Christ brought life through the cross. Adam, naked of spiritual things, covered himself with the foliage of a tree.[9] Christ, naked of worldly things, did not desire the trappings of the body. Adam lived in the desert. Christ lived in the desert, for he knew where he could find the lost. With their error canceled, he could recall them to Paradise. . . .

So Jesus, full of the Holy Spirit, is led into the desert for a purpose, in order to challenge the devil. If he had not fought, he would not have conquered him for me. EXPOSITION OF THE GOSPEL OF LUKE 4.7, 14.[10]

4:3-4 The First Temptation: Stones into Bread

GLUTTONY CAPTURED THE FIRST ADAM. ORIGEN: Mark and Luke say that Jesus "was tempted

---

[4]Jn 1:29. [5]ECTD 85-86**. [6]1 Cor 9:27. [7]CGSL 85-88**. [8]Gen 3:23-24; 1 Cor 15:45. [9]Gen 3:7. [10]EHG 115-16, 119**; CSEL 32 4:142-43, 146.

for forty days." It is clear that during those days the devil first tempted him from a distance to sleep, apathy, cowardice, and other such sins. Then, since he knew that Christ was hungry, the devil came closer to him and attacked him openly. Notice what he does. He had heard, both from John and from the voice that came from above, that "this man is a son of God."[11] He did not know that "the Son of God" had become man, for God concealed the inexpressible incarnation from him. So he assumed that Christ was a man who was pleasing to God because of his virtues. He was also jealous of him because of this honor just as he had been jealous of the old Adam. He was eager to cast this man down, just as he had cast Adam down. So he approaches Jesus and introduces the first temptation, that of gluttony, through which he had also captured the first Adam. Since there was no food anywhere, because the whole region was a desert, he knew that bread would satisfy Christ's hunger. He himself does not produce bread, because Christ was not going to take it from the enemy. But he commands him to make bread from the stones that he points to. Look at Satan's wiles and great wickedness—he tried to keep Christ from knowing his plot. He did not simply say, "Turn the stones into loaves of bread," but he prefixed it with, "If you are a son of God." He did this to show that he wanted this act done to prove that Christ is a son of God. For he was thinking that Christ would be provoked by his words and offended by the suggestion that he was not a "son of God." He thought that Christ would not recognize the deception and, as a man who has power from God, turn the stones into bread. Then, when he saw the bread, he would yield to his stomach, since he was very hungry. But the devil did not escape the notice of him who "catches the wise in their craftiness."[12] Christ answered him and said, "It is written, 'Man shall not live by bread alone,'" and the rest, because he knew the devil's villainy. He did not perform the sign that the devil sought, because he worked his signs to help those who saw them. FRAGMENTS ON LUKE 96.[13]

JESUS SAYS NEITHER "I CAN" NOR "I CANNOT." CYRIL OF ALEXANDRIA: Satan said, "If you are the Son of God, bid this stone become bread." He approaches him, therefore, as an ordinary man and as one of the saints, yet he had a suspicion that possibly he might be the Christ. How, then, did he hope to learn if this was the case? He reasoned that to change the nature of any thing into that which it was not would be the act and deed of a divine power. For it is God who makes these things and transforms them. "If he does this," said the devil, "certainly it is he who is expected to subvert my power. But if he refuses to work this change, I am dealing with a man. I will set aside my fear. I am delivered from danger." Therefore it was that Christ, knowing the monster's plan, neither made the change nor said that he was either unable or unwilling to make it. Rather, the Lord shakes him off as annoying and meddlesome, saying, "Man shall not live by bread alone." He means this: If God grants a man the ability, he can survive without eating and live as Moses and Elijah, who by the Word of the Lord passed forty days without taking food. If, therefore, it is possible to live without bread, why should I make the stone bread? He purposely does not say, "I cannot," that he may not deny his own power. Nor does he say, "I can," lest the devil, knowing that he is God, for whom alone such things are possible, should depart from him. Observe, I beg you, how the nature of man in Christ casts off the faults of Adam's gluttony. By eating we were conquered in Adam, by abstinence we conquered in Christ. COMMENTARY ON LUKE, HOMILY 12.[14]

JESUS DEFEATS SATAN WITH THE WORD OF GOD. AMBROSE: So, look at the arms of Christ with which he conquered for you, not for himself. For he who showed that stones could, through his majesty, be changed into bread by the transformation into a different nature, teaches that you must do nothing at the devil's behest nor for the pur-

---

[11]See Jn 1:34. [12]1 Cor 3:19. [13]FC 94:165-67. [14]CGSL 88**.

pose of manifesting virtue. At the same time, learn from the temptation itself the ingenious cunning of the devil. The devil tempts that he may test. He tests that he may tempt. In contrast, the Lord deceives that he may conquer. He conquers that he may deceive. For if he had changed nature, he would have betrayed its Creator. Thus he responded neutrally, saying, "It is written, 'That man lives not by bread alone, but by every word of God.' " You see what kind of arms he wields, to defend humanity, surrounded and protected against the inducements of appetite, against the assault of spiritual wickedness.[15] For he does not wield power as God—for what good would that be to me? So, as man, he summons common help for himself, so that eager for the food of the divine Word, he neglects the body's hunger and obtains the nourishment of the heavenly Word. Eager for this, Moses did not desire bread.[16] Eager for this, Elijah did not feel the hunger of a long fast.[17] For he who follows the Word cannot desire earthly bread when he receives the essence of the heavenly Bread.[18] There is no doubt that the divine surpasses the human, as the spiritual the physical. Therefore he who desires true life awaits that Bread which through its intangible substance strengthens human hearts.[19] At the same time, when he says, "Man lives not by bread alone," he shows that the man is tempted, that is, his acceptance of our flesh, not his divinity. EXPOSITION OF THE GOSPEL OF LUKE 4.19-20.[20]

4:5-8 The Second Temptation: Kingdoms of the Earth

SATAN SHOWED HOW HE RULED THE WORLD. ORIGEN: We should not think that when the devil showed Jesus the kingdoms of the world, he showed him, for example, the kingdom of the Persians and of the Indians. "He showed him all the kingdoms of the world," that is, his own kingdom, how he reigned in the world. HOMILIES ON THE GOSPEL OF LUKE 30.1.[21]

JESUS RESTORES KINGDOMS SEIZED BY

FRAUD. CYRIL OF ALEXANDRIA: Did you think to have him as your worshiper at whom all things tremble, while the seraphim and all the angelic powers sing hymns to his glory? It is written, "You shall worship the Lord your God, and him only shall you serve."[22] It is fitting that he made mention of this commandment, striking as it were at his very heart. Before his advent, Satan had deceived all under heaven and was himself worshiped everywhere. But the law of God, ejecting him from the dominion he had usurped by fraud, has commanded people to worship him only who by nature and in truth is God and to offer service to him alone. COMMENTARY ON LUKE, HOMILY 12.[23]

4:9-12 The Third Temptation: Pinnacle of the Temple

SATAN USES SCRIPTURE SELECTIVELY BY CONVENIENCE. EPHREM THE SYRIAN: [Satan] set [Jesus] up on the pinnacle of the temple. Satan wanted him to suppose that he who was a man could become God, by means of the godly house, just as Satan had once made Adam suppose that he could become God by means of that tree.[24] He brought him up to the mountain,[25] as though he were in need. "To you will I give the kingdoms, if you will adore me."[26] When he changed his mode of cunning, he did not change the true One with it. In the beginning God made him, and, when complete, he was in need and a worshiper.[27] But Satan became blind in the arrogance of his worship, because of all that he had acquired, and for this reason he was punished even more. Because Satan did not recognize the One who knew him intimately, our Lord addressed him by his name, Satan.[28] But he did not know how he should address our Lord.

Therefore he said to him, "Fall down from here, for it is written, 'They will guard you lest

---

[15]See Eph 6:12. [16]Ex 24:18. [17]1 Kings 19:4. [18]Jn 6:32, 50. [19]Ps 103:17. [20]EHG 121-22**; CSEL 32 4:148-49. [21]FC 94:123*. [22]Deut 6:13. [23]CGSL 89**. [24]Gen 3:5. [25]Mt 4:8. [26]Mt 4:9. [27]Heb 1:6. [28]Mt 4:10.

you stumble.'" Tempter, if it is concerning him that the psalm is fulfilled, is it not also written there, "With his wings, that he may deliver you"?[29] It is not possible for a bird to fall, for the air beneath its wings is like the earth. Is it not also written, "You will tread on the serpent and the lion"?[30] Satan studied only those passages from Scriptures that were convenient to him and omitted those which were harmful to him. The heretics are like this too. They appropriate from Scripture those passages that suit their erroneous teaching and omit those that refute their errors, thereby demonstrating that they are disciples of this master. COMMENTARY ON TATIAN'S DIATESSARON 4.8B-C.[31]

Eve Enticed by the Desire to Worship Another. AMBROSE: You see, ancient errors are undone in Christ's footprints, and the snares, first of the stomach, second of sexual sin, and third of ambition, are loosed. For Adam was enticed by food. Because he willingly transgressed in the matter of the forbidden tree, he also was charged with heedless ambition, for he desired to be like the Godhead.[32] Therefore the Lord first remitted the debt of the ancient wrong, in order that, having shaken off the yoke of captivity, we may learn to overcome our faults with the help of the Scriptures. . . . The devil shakes the whole world with cunning deceit, in order to corrupt people, and fights with all the enticements of this age. You must beware of his flattery all the more. Food had not persuaded Eve, nor had the forgetfulness of the commands deprived her. If she had been willing to worship the Lord alone, she would not have sought what was not due to her. So a remedy is given, which blunts the dart of ambition, so that we serve the Lord alone. Pious devotion lacks ambition. EXPOSITION OF THE GOSPEL OF LUKE 4.33-34.[33]

Jesus Did Not Need the Help of Angels. ORIGEN: Therefore let us see what the devil says to the Lord from the Scriptures. "Scripture says, 'He gave his angels a command concerning you that

they should raise you up in their hands, lest perhaps you strike your foot against a stone.'" See how crafty he is, even in the texts he quotes. For he wishes to diminish the Savior's glory, as if the Savior needed the help of angels. It is as if he would strike his foot unless he were supported by their hands. The devil takes his verse from Scripture and applies it to Christ. Yet it is written not of Christ but about the saints in general. Freely and in total confidence I contradict the devil. This passage cannot be applied to the person of Christ, for Christ does not need the help of angels. He is greater than the angels and obtained a better name than they by inheritance. "God never said to any of the angels, 'You are my Son; today I have begotten you.'"[34] HOMILIES ON THE GOSPEL OF LUKE 31.4.[35]

The Pinnacle of the Temple Is Christ. PRUDENTIUS:

> Still the pinnacle stands, outlasting the temple's destruction,
> For the corner raised up from that stone which the builders rejected[36]
> Will remain throughout all ages forever and ever.
> Now it is head of the temple and holds the new stones together.

SCENES FROM SACRED HISTORY 31.[37]

4:13 Until an Opportune Time

The Devil Returns as Roaring Lion at Crucifixion. AUGUSTINE: When the Lord had been tempted with this triple temptation—because in all the allurements of the world these three are to be found, either pleasure or curiosity or pride—what did the Evangelist say? After the devil had concluded every temptation—every kind, but of the alluring sort—there remained the other sort of temptation, by harsh and hard treatment, savage treatment, atrocious and fero-

---

[29]Ps 91:12. [30]Ps 91:13. [31]ECTD 87-88**. [32]Gen 3:5. [33]EHG 126-27**; CSEL 32 4:155-56. [34]Ps 2:7; Heb 1:5. [35]FC 94:127*. [36]Lk 20:17. [37]FC 52:189.

cious treatment. Yes, there remained the other sort of temptation. The Evangelist knew this, knew what had been carried out, what remained, and so he said, "After the devil had completed every temptation, he departed from him until the time." He departed from him in the form, that is, of the insidious serpent.[38] He is going to come in the form of the roaring lion.[39] The one who will trample on the lion and the cobra[40] will conquer him. Satan will return. He will enter Judas and will make him betray his master. He will bring along the Jews, not flattering now, but raging. Taking possession of his own instruments, he will cry out with the tongues of all of them, "Crucify him, crucify him!"[41] That Christ was the conqueror there, why should we be surprised? He was almighty God. SERMON 284.5.[42]

---

[38]Gen 3:1. [39]1 Pet 5:8. [40]Ps 91:13. [41]Lk 23:21. [42]WSA 3 8:91*.

4:14-15 THE BEGINNING OF JESUS' MINISTRY

[14]*And Jesus returned in the power of the Spirit into Galilee, and a report concerning him went out through all the surrounding country.* [15]*And he taught in their synagogues, being glorified by all.*

OVERVIEW: Luke records that Jesus "returned in the power of the Spirit" to indicate that the Spirit's power is manifest in Jesus' teaching in the synagogue (ORIGEN). There is a weekly rhythm to Jesus' teaching as he goes from sabbath meal to sabbath meal, from synagogue to synagogue, from one liturgical context to the next (EPHREM THE SYRIAN). The people were impressed with his teaching as reports about him spread throughout Galilee, but his fame must also come from the miracles he performed by his nature as the Son of God (CYRIL OF ALEXANDRIA).

4:14-15 Jesus Begins His Teaching in Galilee

THE POWER OF THE SPIRIT MANIFESTED.
ORIGEN: First of all, "Jesus, full of the Holy Spirit, returned from the Jordan and was led by the Spirit into the desert for forty days." When Jesus was being tempted by the devil, the word *spirit* is put down twice without any qualification since the Lord still had to struggle against him. See what is written about the Spirit emphatically and carefully, after he had fought and had overcame the three temptations that Scripture mentions. The passage says, "Jesus returned in the power of the Spirit." "Power" has been added, because he had trodden down the dragon and conquered the tempter in hand-to-hand combat. So "Jesus returned in the power of the Spirit to the land of Galilee, and reports about him went out to the whole surrounding region. He was teaching in their synagogues, and was glorified by all." HOMILIES ON THE GOSPEL OF LUKE 32.1.[1]

TEACHING IN THE SYNAGOGUE.
EPHREM THE SYRIAN: What was the custom of him who had come just now? He had come to Galilee and had begun to teach, not outside of the synagogue but within it. Since the matter was known through their worship service, he came to talk to them about their God. Otherwise it would have been

---

[1]FC 94:130*.

in order for him to proclaim to them outside their synagogue. COMMENTARY ON TATIAN'S DIATESSARON II.23.[2]

FAME COMES FROM HIS MIRACLES AS SON OF GOD. CYRIL OF ALEXANDRIA: After he mightily defeated Satan—after he crowned human nature in his own person with the spoils won by the victory over Satan—he returned to Galilee in the power of the Spirit, both exercising might and authority. He performed very many miracles and greatly astonished his people. He performed mir-

acles, because he is by nature and in truth the Son of God the Father, not because he received the grace of the Spirit from the outside as a gift, as the company of the saints do. He took what was his as his own proper inheritance. Yes, he said to the Father, "All that is mine is yours, and yours mine, and I am glorified in them."[3] He is glorified therefore by exercising as his own might and power the power of the Spirit who shares his substance. COMMENTARY ON LUKE, HOMILY 12.[4]

---

[2]ECTD 186. [3]Jn 17:10. [4]CGSL 91**.

4:16-30 JESUS' SERMON IN NAZARETH; LUKE'S PROPHET CHRISTOLOGY

[16]*And he came to Nazareth, where he had been brought up; and he went to the synagogue, as his custom was, on the sabbath day. And he stood up to read;* [17]*and there was given to him the book of the prophet Isaiah. He opened the book and found the place where it was written,*

[18]*"The Spirit of the Lord is upon me,*

because he has anointed me to preach good news to the poor.

He has sent me to proclaim release to the captives

and recovering of sight to the blind,

to set at liberty those who are oppressed,

[19]*to proclaim the acceptable year of the Lord."*

[20]*And he closed the book, and gave it back to the attendant, and sat down; and the eyes of all in the synagogue were fixed on him.* [21]*And he began to say to them, "Today this scripture has been fulfilled in your hearing."* [22]*And all spoke well of him, and wondered at the gracious words which proceeded out of his mouth; and they said, "Is not this Joseph's son?"* [23]*And he said to them, "Doubtless you will quote to me this proverb, 'Physician, heal yourself; what we have heard you did at Capernaum, do here also in your own country.'"* [24]*And he said, "Truly, I say to you, no prophet is acceptable in his own country.* [25]*But in truth, I tell you, there were many widows in Israel in the days of Elijah, when the heaven was shut up three years and six months, when there came a great famine over all the land;* [26]*and Elijah was sent to none of them but only to Zarephath, in the land of Sidon, to a woman who was a widow.* [27]*And there were many lepers in Israel in the time of the prophet Elisha; and none of them was cleansed, but only Naaman the Syrian."* [28]*When they heard this, all in the synagogue were filled with wrath.* [29]*And they rose up and put him out of the city,*

and led him to the brow of the hill on which their city was built, that they might throw him down headlong. [30]But passing through the midst of them he went away.

OVERVIEW: Jesus came to the synagogue of Nazareth in order to read Isaiah 61, a text chosen for this day by the providence of God to declare that the messianic era of salvation now begins in him (ORIGEN). This text and this episode reveal that Jesus is God and man. Jesus' baptism was an anointing by the Spirit, not because the Spirit was not already in Jesus, but to anoint him for us, so that he might reunite us with Spirit through our communion with his flesh (CYRIL OF ALEXANDRIA). The first words of Jesus' public ministry, from Isaiah, are a reference to the trinitarian plan of salvation (AMBROSE).

The application of Isaiah 61 as good news to the poor is that he is now present in the world to "release" the captives (EUSEBIUS). It was a prophecy of the Messiah's eschatological salvation, which now breaks into the world through Jesus' ministry in "the year of the Lord's favor" (ORIGEN). This acceptable year of the Lord refers to his ministry of miracles, when he releases creation from bondage, and to his crucifixion, when that release becomes a cosmic reality (CYRIL OF ALEXANDRIA).

After the reading from Isaiah was over, "the eyes of all in the synagogue" were fixed on Jesus, the Word made flesh (ORIGEN). With his first word, "today," Jesus announces in Galilee that the Jubilee year is now present in him and his ministry. The people are moved from bewilderment to intense anger by Jesus' message (CYRIL OF ALEXANDRIA). They reject Jesus out of envy and not out of charity (AMBROSE).

Jesus' first sermon proclaimed Luke's prophet Christology of teaching, miracles and then rejection. The people of Nazareth fulfill his prophecy by rejecting him (CYRIL OF ALEXANDRIA). How ironic that he escapes from their murderous grasp by a miracle! Not yet is it his hour (AMBROSE).

4:16-21 Jesus Reads the Scripture and

Announces Its Fulfillment

THE CHOICE OF ISAIAH. ORIGEN: It was no accident that he opens the scroll and finds the chapter of the reading that prophesies about him. This too was an act of God's providence. . . . Precisely the book of Isaiah was found, and the reading was no other but this one, which spoke about the mystery of Christ. HOMILIES ON THE GOSPEL OF LUKE 32.4.[1]

BY READING ISAIAH, JESUS SHOWS HE IS GOD AND MAN. CYRIL OF ALEXANDRIA: Now it was necessary that he should manifest himself to the Israelites and that the mystery of his incarnation should now shine forth to those who did not know him. Now that God the Father had anointed him to save the world, he very wisely orders this also [that his fame should now spread widely]. This favor he grants first to the people of Nazareth, because, humanly speaking, he had grown up among them. Having entered the synagogue, therefore, he takes the book to read. Having opened it, he selects a passage in the Prophets which declares the mystery concerning him. By these words he himself tells us very clearly by the voice of the prophet that he would both be made man and come to save the world. For we affirm that the Son was anointed in no other way than by having become like us according to the flesh and taking our nature. Being at once God and man, he both gives the Spirit to the creation in his divine nature and receives it from God the Father in his human nature. It is he who sanctifies the whole creation, both by shining forth from the Holy Father and by bestowing the Spirit. He himself pours forth his own Spirit on the powers above and on those who recognized his appearing. COMMENTARY ON LUKE, HOMILY 12.[2]

---

[1]FC 94:132*. [2]CGSL 91-92**.

JESUS ANOINTED BY THE SPIRIT FOR US.
CYRIL OF ALEXANDRIA: Jesus plainly shows by
these words that he took upon himself both the
very name of Christ and its reality for our sakes.
He humbled himself and submitted to the emptying of his glory for our sakes. "For the Spirit," he
says, "which by nature is in me by the sameness of
our substance and deity, also descended upon me
from outside of me. In the Jordan it came upon me
in the form of a dove, not because it was not in me
but in order to anoint me." Why did he choose to
be anointed? Because an ancient denunciation
made us destitute of the Spirit. It said, "My Spirit
shall not remain in these men, because they are
flesh."[3] COMMENTARY ON LUKE, HOMILY 12.[4]

**JESUS BEGINS HIS MINISTRY WITH A REFER-
ENCE TO THE TRINITY.** AMBROSE: Scripture
speaks of Jesus himself as God and man, perfect
in both natures. It speaks of the Father and the
Holy Spirit. For the Holy Spirit is shown as
Christ's partner when he descends in bodily
shape as a dove on Christ, when the Son of God
was baptized in the river, and when the Father
spoke from heaven.[5] So what greater testimony to
us who are weak than that Christ signified with
his own voice that he himself spoke by the prophets?[6] EXPOSITION ON THE GOSPEL OF LUKE 4.44-
45.[7]

GOOD NEWS TO THE POOR. EUSEBIUS: Our
Savior, after reading this prophecy through in the
synagogue one day to a multitude of Jews, shut
the book and said, "This day is this Scripture fulfilled in your ears." He began his own teaching
from that point. He began to preach the gospel to
the poor, putting in the forefront of his blessings:
"Blessed are the poor in spirit, for theirs is the
kingdom of heaven."[8] Yes, he proclaimed forgiveness to those who were hampered by evil spirits
and bound for a long time like slaves by demons.
He invited all to be free and to escape from the
bonds of sin, when he said, "Come to me, all you
that labor, and are heavy laden, and I will refresh
you."[9]

To the blind he gave sight, giving the power of
seeing to those whose bodily vision was
destroyed. He showered those in ancient times
who were blind in their minds to the truth with
the vision of the light of true religion. The prophecy before us shows it to be essential that Christ
himself should be the originator and leader of the
gospel activity. The same prophet foretells that
after him his own disciples should be ministers of
the same system: "How beautiful are the feet of
them that bring good tidings of good things, and
of those that bring good tidings of peace."[10]

Here he says very particularly that it is the feet
of those who publish the good news of Christ
that are beautiful. For how could they not be
beautiful, which in so small, so short a time have
run over the whole earth and filled every place
with the holy teaching about the Savior of the
world? PROOF OF THE GOSPEL 3.1.88C-89A.[11]

**FREEDOM FOR THE CAPTIVES IN THE YEAR OF
JUBILEE.** ORIGEN: He says, "He sent me to
preach the gospel to the poor." The "poor" stand
for the Gentiles, for they are indeed poor. They
possess nothing at all: neither God, nor the law,
nor the prophets, nor justice and the rest of the
virtues. For what reason did God send him to
preach to the poor? "To preach release to captives." We were the captives. For many years
Satan had bound us and held us captive and subject to himself. Jesus has come "to proclaim
release to captives and sight to the blind." By his
word and the proclamation of his teaching the
blind see. Therefore his "proclamation" should be
understood not only of the "captives" but also of
the "blind."

"To send broken men forth into freedom . . ."
What being was so broken and crushed as man,
whom Jesus healed and sent away? "To preach an
acceptable year to the Lord." . . . But all of this has
been proclaimed so that we may come to "the ac-

---

[3]Gen 6:3. [4]CGSL 92**. [5]Lk 3:22. [6]2 Pet 1:21. [7]EHG 131**; CSEL
32 4:161. [8]Mt 5:3. [9]Mt 11:28. [10]Is 52:7; Rom 10:15. [11]POG 1:102**.

ceptable year of the Lord," when we see after blindness, when we are free from our chains, and when we have been healed of our wounds. HOMILIES ON THE GOSPEL OF LUKE 32.4-5.[12]

ACCEPTABLE YEAR OF THE LORD EMBRACES JESUS' MIRACLES AND DEATH.

CYRIL OF ALEXANDRIA: What does preaching the acceptable year of the Lord mean? It signifies the joyful tidings of his own advent, that the time of the Lord—yes, the Son—had arrived. For that was the acceptable year in which Christ was crucified on our behalf, because we then were made acceptable to God the Father as the fruit borne by him. That is why the Lord said, "When I am lifted up from the earth, I will draw all men to myself."[13] Truly he returned to life the third day, having trampled on the power of death. After that resurrection he said to his disciples, "All power has been given to me."[14] That too is in every respect an acceptable year. In it we were received into his family and were admitted to him, having washed away sin by holy baptism, and been made partakers of his divine nature by the communion of the Holy Spirit. That too is an acceptable year, in which he manifested his glory by inexpressible miracles. COMMENTARY ON LUKE, HOMILY 12.[15]

LET EVERY CONGREGATION FIX ITS EYES ON JESUS, THE WORD OF GOD.

ORIGEN: When Jesus had read this passage, he rolled up "the scroll, gave it to the servant, and sat down. And the eyes of all in the synagogue were fixed on him." Now too, if you want it, your eyes can be fixed on the Savior in this synagogue, here in this assembly. When you direct the principal power of seeing in your heart to wisdom and truth and to contemplating God's Only-Begotten, your eyes gaze on Jesus. Blessed is that congregation of which Scripture testifies that "the eyes of all were fixed on him!" How much would I wish that this assembly gave such testimony. I wish that the eyes of all (of catechumens and faithful, of women, men and children)—not the eyes of the body, but the eyes of the soul—would gaze upon Jesus.

When you look to him, your faces will be shining from the light of his gaze. You will be able to say, "The light of your face, Lord, has made its mark upon us."[16] HOMILIES ON THE GOSPEL OF LUKE 32.6.[17]

THE WORD OF ISAIAH FULFILLED IN NAZARETH'S EARS.

CYRIL OF ALEXANDRIA: These words having been read to the assembled people, all eyes focused on Jesus, wondering perhaps how he could read without having been taught. The Israelites used to say that the prophecies concerning Christ were fulfilled, either in the persons of some of their more glorious kings or at least in the holy prophets. They did not correctly understand what was written about him, so they missed the true direction and traveled down another path. He carefully guards against error by saying, "This day is this prophecy fulfilled in your ears," that they might not again misinterpret the present prophecy. He expressly set himself before them in these words, as the person spoken of in the prophecy. It was he who preached the kingdom of heaven to the heathen. They were poor, having nothing—not God, not law, not prophets. Rather, he preached it to all who were without spiritual riches. He set the captives free; having overthrown the apostate tyrant Satan, he shed the divine and spiritual light on those whose heart was darkened. This is why he said, "I come as a light in this world."[18] It was he who took the chains of sin off of those whose heart was crushed by them. He clearly showed that there is a life to come, and sinners denounced in just judgment. Finally, it was he who preached the acceptable year of the Lord, the year in which the Savior's proclamation was made. By the acceptable year I think is meant his first coming, and by the day of restitution the day of judgment. COMMENTARY ON LUKE, HOMILY 12.[19]

4:22 The People Reject Jesus

[12]FC 94:131-32**. [13]Jn 12:32. [14]Mt 28:18. [15]CGSL 93**. [16]Ps 4:6. [17]FC 94:132-33**. [18]Jn 12:46. [19]CGSL 94-95**; PG 72:542.

Nazareth Rejects Jesus as the Son of Joseph. Cyril of Alexandria: Since they did not understand Christ who had been anointed and sent by God, who was the Author of such wonderful works, they returned to their usual ways and said foolish and useless things about him. They wondered at the words of grace that he spoke. Yet they treated these words as worthless. They said, "Isn't this Joseph's son?" But how does this diminish the glory of the Worker of the miracles? What prevents him from being both venerated and admired, even had he been, as was supposed, Joseph's son? Don't you see the miracles? Satan is fallen, the herds of devils are vanquished, and multitudes are set free from various kinds of sicknesses. You praise the grace that was present in his teachings. Do you, then, in Jewish fashion, think lightly of him, because you thought Joseph was his father? How absurd! Truly is it said about them, "See! They are a foolish people. They are without understanding! They have eyes and don't see, ears, and do not hear."[20] Commentary on Luke, Homily 12.[21]

4:23-27 Jesus Speaks of His Rejection by His People

Nazareth Rejects Jesus Out of Envy. Ambrose: The Savior deliberately explains why he performed no miracles of virtue in his own country, to prevent someone from thinking that we should value affection for our country very little. He who loved all could not but love his fellow citizens. But those who envy his country deprive themselves of love, for "love does not envy, it is not puffed up."[22] Yet his country does not lack divine blessings. Isn't it a greater miracle that Christ was born there? So, you see what measure of evil envy brings. His country is found unworthy because of envy, the country in which he toiled as a citizen, which was worthy that the Son of God be born there. Exposition of the Gospel of Luke 4.47.[23]

In His Rejection, Jesus Fulfills the Prophetic Pattern. Cyril of Alexandria: Jesus rebuked them, therefore, for asking so foolishly, "Isn't this Joseph's son?" Keeping to the goal of his teaching, he says, "Truly, I tell you, that no prophet is acceptable in his country." As I have mentioned, certain Jews affirmed that the prophecies relating to Christ had been fulfilled in the holy prophets or in certain of their own more distinguished men. For their good, he draws them away from such a supposition. He said that Elijah had been sent to a single widow and that the prophet Elisha had healed but one leper, Naaman the Syrian. By these he refers to the church of the heathen, who were about to accept him and be healed of their leprosy, by reason of Israel's remaining impenitent. Commentary on Luke, Homily 12.[24]

4:28-29 The Angry Reaction

An Attempt to Kill Jesus. Cyril of Alexandria: So they threw him out of their city, pronouncing by their action their own condemnation. So they confirmed what the Savior had said. They themselves were banished from the city that is above, for not having received Christ. That he might not convict them only of impiety in words, he permitted their disrespect of him to proceed to deeds. Their violence was irrational and their envy untamed. Leading him to the brow of the hill, they sought to throw him from the cliff. But he went through the midst of them without taking any notice, so to say, of their attempt. He did not refuse to suffer—he had come to do that very thing—but to wait for a suitable time. Now at the beginning of his preaching, it would have been the wrong time to have suffered before he had proclaimed the word of truth. Commentary on Luke, Homily 12.[25]

4:30 Jesus Went on His Way

The Time of Jesus' Passion Had Not Yet

---

[20]Jer 5:21. [21]CGSL 95**; PG 72:443. [22]1 Cor 13:4. [23]EHG 132**; CSEL 32 4:161-62. [24]CGSL 95-96**; PG 72:543. [25]CGSL 96**; PG 72:543-546.

COME. AMBROSE: Jesus speaks about the sacrileges of the Jews, which the Lord had foretold long ago through the prophet. These sacrileges were predicted in the verse of a psalm which declares that he would suffer when in the body. It says, "They repaid me with evil things for good."[26] These are fulfilled in the Gospel. For when he himself spread blessings among the peoples, they inflicted injuries. No wonder they who threw the Savior out of their nation lost salvation.[27]

At the same time, understand that he was not forced to suffer the passion of his body. It was voluntary. He was not taken by the Jews but given by himself. Indeed, he is taken when he wants to be. He glides away when he wants to.[28] He is hung when he wants to be. He is not held when he does not wish it. Here he goes up to the summit of the hill to be thrown down. But, behold, the minds of the furious men were suddenly changed or confused. He descended through their midst, for the hour of his passion had not yet come.[29] Indeed, he still preferred to heal the Jews, rather than destroy them, so that through the unsuccessful outcome of their frenzy, they would cease to want what they could not attain. EXPOSITION OF THE GOSPEL OF LUKE 4.55-56.[30]

---

[26]Ps 35:12 (34:12 LXX). [27]See Mt 8:34. [28]See Jn 18:7-8. [29]Jn 8:20. [30]EHG 135-36**; CSEL 32 4:166-67.

4:31-44 TEACHING AND HEALING IN CAPERNAUM

[31]*And he went down to Capernaum, a city of Galilee. And he was teaching them on the sabbath;* [32]*and they were astonished at his teaching, for his word was with authority.* [33]*And in the synagogue there was a man who had the spirit of an unclean demon; and he cried out with a loud voice,* [34]*"Ah!" What have you to do with us, Jesus of Nazareth? Have you come to destroy us? I know who you are, the Holy One of God."* [35]*But Jesus rebuked him, saying, "Be silent, and come out of him!" And when the demon had thrown him down in the midst, he came out of him, having done him no harm.* [36]*And they were all amazed and said to one another, "What is this word? For with authority and power he commands the unclean spirits, and they come out."* [37]*And reports of him went out into every place in the surrounding region.*

[38]*And he arose and left the synagogue, and entered Simon's house. Now Simon's mother-in-law was ill with a high fever, and they besought him for her.* [39]*And he stood over her and rebuked the fever, and it left her; and immediately she rose and served them.*

[40]*Now when the sun was setting, all those who had any that were sick with various diseases brought them to him; and he laid his hands on every one of them and healed them.* [41]*And demons also came out of many, crying, "You are the Son of God!" But he rebuked them, and would not allow them to speak, because they knew that he was the Christ.*

[42]*And when it was day he departed and went into a lonely place. And the people sought him and came to him, and would have kept him from leaving them;* [43]*but he said to them, "I must preach*

the good news of the kingdom of God to the other cities also; for I was sent for this purpose." [44]*And he was preaching in the synagogues of Judea.*[n]

m Or *Let us alone*   n Other ancient authorities read *Galilee*

OVERVIEW: Immediately following the sermon at Nazareth, Jesus appears in the synagogue at Capernaum to affirm his teaching in Nazareth through miracles of healing that show that he is the great Physician of his creation (CYRIL OF ALEXANDRIA). The new creation begins where the old creation ceases—on the sabbath. Jesus shows that he is present to release men and women from bondage (AMBROSE). Thus the teaching, exorcisms and healings of Jesus all testify to this new "authority" in "his word," especially as the power of his word is shown in his power over the demons. Jesus makes no distinction between body and soul: he rebukes the demon, and it comes out after a violent struggle; he rebukes the fever of Peter's mother-in-law, and it leaves her (CYRIL OF ALEXANDRIA).

Jesus rebukes demons who call him "the Son of God" because they know him to be the Christ, and those demons come out (CYRIL OF ALEXANDRIA). But under no circumstances are we to listen to demons, even when they speak the truth (ATHANASIUS). Jesus encourages his disciples to rebuke those who sin, and if they repent, to forgive them. For Jesus is the chief Physician who has come to heal us from the fever of our sins (JEROME). The messianic signs of the new era of salvation are present in the anointed One (ATHANASIUS). The healing of the creation comes from the holy flesh of Jesus (CYRIL OF ALEXANDRIA). This kingdom of God is none other than the kingdom of the Creator of all things, Jesus Christ, who has come to recreate (TERTULLIAN).

4:31-41 *Casting Out Demons and Healing Diseases*

MIRACLES TESTIFY THAT JESUS THE PHYSICIAN HEALS CREATION. CYRIL OF ALEXANDRIA: People who cannot be brought by argument to the sure knowledge of him who by nature and in truth is God and Lord may perhaps be won by miracles to a quiet obedience. Therefore helpfully, or rather necessarily, he often completes his lessons by going on to perform some mighty work. For the people of Judea were not ready to believe. They snubbed the words of those who called them to salvation. The people of Capernaum had this character especially. For this reason the Savior reproved them. He said, "And you, Capernaum, who are exalted to heaven, shall be brought down to hell."[1] Although he knows them to be both disobedient and hard of heart, nevertheless he visits them as a most excellent physician would visit those who were suffering from a very dangerous disease and endeavors to rid them of their illness. He himself says, "Those who are healthy have no need of a physician, only those who are sick."[2] He taught, therefore, in their synagogues with great freedom of speech. For he had foretold this by the voice of Isaiah: "I have not spoken in secret, nor in a dark place of the earth."[3] COMMENTARY ON LUKE, HOMILY 12.[4]

NEW CREATION BEGINS ON THE SABBATH. AMBROSE: He describes the works of divine healing begun on the sabbath day, to show from the outset that the new creation began where the old creation ceased. He showed us that the Son of God is not under the law but above the law, and that the law will not be destroyed but fulfilled.[5] For the world was not made through the law but by the Word, as we read: "By the Word of the Lord were the heavens established."[6] Thus the law is not destroyed but fulfilled, so that the renewal of humankind, already in error, may occur. The apostle too says, "Stripping yourselves of the

---

[1]Lk 10:15. [2]Lk 5:31. [3]Is 45:19. [4]CGSL 96-97**. [5]Mt 5:17. [6]Ps 33:6 (32:6 LXX).

old man, put on the new, who was created according to Christ."[7] He fittingly began on the sabbath, that he may show himself as Creator. He completed the work that he had already begun by weaving together works with works. Exposition of the Gospel of Luke 4.58.[8]

Jesus Heals Men and Women. Ambrose: St. Luke did well to first set before us the man freed from a spirit of wickedness, then substituted the healing of a woman. The Lord had come to heal both sexes, and man must first be cured because he was created first. But woman, who had sinned by an uncertain mind rather than depravity, must not be overlooked. Exposition of the Gospel of Luke 4.57.[9]

The Power of Jesus' Word. Cyril of Alexandria: The bystanders, witnesses of such great deeds, were astonished at the power of his word. He performed his miracles, without offering up a prayer, asking no one else at all for the power to accomplish them. Since he is the living and active Word of God the Father, by whom all things exist, and in whom all things are, in his own person he crushed Satan and closed the profane mouth of impure demons. Commentary on Luke, Homily 12.[10]

Jesus Rebukes Fever Possessing Peter's Mother-in-Law. Cyril of Alexandria: Jesus arrived at Simon's house and found Simon's mother-in-law sick of a fever. He stood and rebuked the fever, and it left her. Matthew and Mark say that the fever left her.[11] There is no hint of any living thing as the active cause of the fever. But Luke's phrase says that he stood over her, and rebuked the fever, and it left her. I do not know whether we are not compelled to say that that which was rebuked was some living thing unable to sustain the influence of him who rebuked it. It is not reasonable to rebuke a thing without life, and unconscious of the rebuke. Commentary on Luke, Homily 12.[12]

Unclean Demons Know Jesus Is the

Christ. Cyril of Alexandria: He would not permit the unclean demons to confess him. It was not right for them to usurp the glory of the apostolic office or to talk of the mystery of Christ with polluted tongues. Yes, nothing they say is true. Let no one trust them. Light cannot be recognized with the help of darkness, as the disciple of Christ teaches us, where he says, "What accord has Christ with Belial? Or what has a believer in common with an unbeliever?"[13] Commentary on Luke, Homily 12.[14]

We Are Never to Listen to Demons. Athanasius: Even when the demons spoke the truth, for they spoke the truth when they said, "Thou are the Son of God," the Lord himself silenced them and forbade them to speak. He did this to keep them from sowing their own wickedness in the midst of the truth. He also wished us to get used to never listening to them even though they seem to speak the truth. Life of St. Anthony 26.[15]

Jesus the Chief Physician. Jerome: "Now Simon's mother-in-law was kept in her bed sick with a fever." May Christ come to our house and enter in and by his command cure the fever of our sins. Each one of us is sick with a fever. Whenever I give way to anger, I have a fever. There are as many fevers as there are faults and vices. Let us beg the apostles to intercede for us with Jesus, that he may come to us and touch our hand. If he does so, at once our fever is gone. He is an excellent physician and truly the chief Physician. Moses is a physician. Isaiah is a physician. All the saints are physicians, but he is the chief Physician. Homilies on the Gospel of Mark 75.[16]

Jesus Has Power over Death. Athanasius: What irreverent men do not believe, the spirits

[7]Col 3:9-10; Eph 4:22, 24. [8]EHG 137**; CSEL 32 4:168. [9]EHG 136-37**; CSEL 32 4:167-68. [10]PG 72:547-50; CGSL 98**. [11]Mt 8:15. [12]CGSL 99**. [13]2 Cor 6:15. [14]CGSL 101**. [15]FC 15:159**. [16]FC 57:144*.

see—that he is God. So they flee and fall down at his feet, saying just what they uttered when he was in the body. ON THE INCARNATION 5.32.[17]

THE HOLY FLESH OF JESUS HEALS HIS CRE-ATION. CYRIL OF ALEXANDRIA: Jesus laid his hands upon the sick one by one and freed them from their malady. He demonstrated that the holy flesh, which he had made his own and endowed with godlike power, possessed the active presence of the might of the Word. He intended us to learn that, although the only-begotten Word of God became like us, yet he is nonetheless God. He wants us to know that he is easily able, even by his own flesh, to accomplish all things. His body was the instrument by which he performed miracles. . . .

Jesus, then, entered Peter's house, where a woman was lying stretched upon a bed, exhausted with a violent fever. As God, he might have said, "Put away the disease, arise," but he adopted a different course of action. As a proof that his own flesh possessed the power of healing, because it is the flesh of God, he touched her hand. "Immediately," it says, "the fever left her." Let us therefore also receive Jesus. When he has entered into us and we have received him into mind and heart, then he will quench the fever of unbefitting pleasures. He will raise us up and make us strong, even in spiritual things, so that we might serve him by performing those things that please him. But observe again, I ask, how great is the usefulness of the touch of his holy

flesh. For it both drives away diseases of various kinds, and a crowd of demons, and overthrows the power of the devil. It heals a very great multitude of people in one moment of time. Although he was able to perform these miracles by a word and the preference of his will, yet to teach us something useful for us, he also lays his hands upon the sick. For it was necessary, most necessary, for us to learn that the holy flesh which he had made his own was endowed with the activity of the power of the Word by his having implanted in it a godlike might. Let it then take hold of us, or rather let us take hold of it by the mystical "giving of thanks." May we do this so that it might free us also from the sicknesses of the soul, and from the assault and violence of demons. COMMENTARY ON LUKE, HOMILY 12.[18]

4:42-44 Jesus Proclaims the Kingdom of God

HE DEPARTED TO A DESERT PLACE. TERTULLIAN: "He departed, and went into a desert place." This was, indeed, the Creator's customary region. It was proper that the Word should there appear in body, where before he had appeared in a cloud. To the gospel also was suitable that condition of place which had once been prophesied for the law. "Let the wilderness and the solitary place, therefore, be glad and rejoice"; so had Isaiah promised. AGAINST MARCION 4.8.[19]

---

[17]NPNF 2 4:53**; LCC 3:86. [18]CGSL 99-101**. [19]ANF 3:355.

5:1-11 PETER'S CALL BY JESUS TO FOLLOW HIM

[1]*While the people pressed upon him to hear the word of God, he was standing by the lake of Gennesaret.* [2]*And he saw two boats by the lake; but the fishermen had gone out of them and were washing their nets.* [3]*Getting into one of the boats, which was Simon's, he asked him to put out a little from the*

land. And he sat down and taught the people from the boat. [4]And when he had ceased speaking, he said to Simon, "Put out into the deep and let down your nets for a catch." [5]And Simon answered, "Master, we toiled all night and took nothing! But at your word I will let down the nets." [6]And when they had done this, [7]they enclosed a great shoal of fish; and as their nets were breaking, they beckoned to their partners in the other boat to come and help them. And they came and filled both the boats, so that they began to sink. [8]But when Simon Peter saw it, he fell down at Jesus' knees, saying, "Depart from me, for I am a sinful man, O Lord." [9]For he was astonished, and all that were with him, at the catch of fish which they had taken; [10]and so also were James and John, sons of Zebedee, who were partners with Simon. And Jesus said to Simon, "Do not be afraid; henceforth you will be catching men." [11]And when they had brought their boats to land, they left everything and followed him.

OVERVIEW: The technical vocabulary of fishing is scattered throughout this passage, suggesting that the hearer take seriously the image of fishing as a metaphor for the work of Jesus and a picture of the church in the present time (AUGUSTINE). Because Christ is present in the boat, it becomes a symbol of the church (MAXIMUS OF TURIN). The miracle *is* about "catching men alive"—through the ministry of the means of grace, which establishes the church and keeps the church growing even today as Jesus draws people into his church through the preaching of the gospel (CYRIL OF ALEXANDRIA). This church is called out into the deep as was Noah (MAXIMUS OF TURIN).

As the prophets toiled all night, so did the apostles. One boat represents the Jews and the other overloaded boat the Gentiles (EPHREM THE SYRIAN). Peter, like the demons, recognizes that Jesus is "the holy One of God," and his fear comes from being in the presence of this holiness as a sinner (CYRIL OF ALEXANDRIA). To capture people alive is to declare to them the kingdom of God in Jesus and bring them into that kingdom through the sacraments of the church (MAXIMUS OF TURIN).

5:1-3 Teaching the Crowds

FIRST CATCH OF FISH THE CHURCH IN THE PRESENT TIME. AUGUSTINE: So let me recall with you those two catches of fish made by the disciples at the command of the Lord Jesus Christ: one before his passion, the other after his resurrection. These two catches of fish stand for the whole church, both as it is now and as it will be at the resurrection of the dead. Now, as you can see, it contains countless numbers, both good and bad. After the resurrection it will contain only the good, and a definite number of them.

So call to mind that first catch, where we may see the church as it is in this present time. The Lord Jesus found his disciples fishing, when he first called them to follow him. They had caught nothing all night. But when they saw him, they heard him telling them, "Let down your nets." "Master," they said, "we toiled all night and took nothing! But at your word I will let down the nets." They cast them at the command of the Almighty. What else could happen, but that which he intended? But all the same, he was pleased, as I said, to indicate something to us that he knew would be to our advantage.

The nets were cast. The Lord had not yet suffered, not yet risen again. The nets were cast. They caught so many fish that two boats were filled, and the very nets were torn by that vast quantity of fish. Then he said to them, "Follow me, and I will make you fishers of men."[1] They received from him the nets of the Word of God, they cast them into the world as into a deep sea, and they caught the vast multitude of Christians that we can see and marvel at. Those two boats,

---

[1]Mt 4:19.

though, stood for the two peoples, Jews and Gentiles, synagogue and church, those circumcised and those uncircumcised. SERMON 248.2.[2]

5:4-7 The Miraculous Catch of Fish

JESUS CHOOSES PETER'S BOAT INSTEAD OF MOSES'. MAXIMUS OF TURIN: He chooses Peter's boat and forsakes Moses'—that is to say, he spurns the faithless synagogue and takes the faithful church. For God appointed the two as boats, so to speak, which would fish for the salvation of humankind in this world as in a sea. As the Lord says to the apostles, "Follow me, and I will make you fishers of men."[3] . . .

The church is called out into the deep, delving, as it were, into the profound mysteries of the heavens, into that depth concerning which the apostle says, "O the depth of the riches and wisdom and knowledge of God!"[4] For this reason he says to Peter, "Put out into the deep,"—that is to say, into the depths of reflection upon the divine generation. For what is more profound than what Peter says to the Lord, "You are the Christ, the Son of the living God?"[5] . . .

This boat sails upon the deeps of this world, so that, when the earth is destroyed, it will preserve unharmed all those it has taken in. Its foreshadowing can be seen already in the Old Testament. For as Noah's ark preserved alive everyone whom it had taken in when the world was going under,[6] so also Peter's church will bring back unhurt everyone whom it embraces when the world goes up in flames.[7] And as a dove brought the sign of peace to Noah's ark when the flood was over,[8] so also Christ will bring the joy of peace to Peter's church when the judgment is over. SERMON 49.1-3.[9]

CHRIST CONTINUES TO CATCH PEOPLE IN THE NETS OF PREACHING. CYRIL OF ALEXANDRIA: He told Simon and his companions to sail off a little from the land and to let down the net for a draught. But they replied that they had been toiling the whole night and had caught nothing.

However, in the name of Christ, they let down the net, and immediately it was full of fish. By a visible sign and by a miraculous type and representation, they were fully convinced that their labor would be rewarded, and the zeal displayed in spreading out the net of the gospel teaching would be fruitful. Within this net they should most certainly catch the shoals of the heathen. But note that neither Simon nor his companions could draw the net to land. Speechless from fright and astonishment—for their wonder had made them mute—they beckoned to their partners, to those who shared their labors in fishing, to come and help them in securing their prey. For many have taken part with the holy apostles in their labors, and still do so, especially those who inquire into the meaning of what is written in the holy Gospels. Yet besides them there are also others: the pastors and teachers and rulers of the people, who are skilled in the doctrines of truth. For the net is still being drawn, while Christ fills it, and calls to conversion those who, according to the Scripture phrase, are in the depths of the sea, that is to say, those who live in the surge and waves of worldly things. COMMENTARY ON LUKE, HOMILY 12.[10]

BY FAITH PETER CASTS THE NETS OF CHRIST'S TEACHING. MAXIMUS OF TURIN: That you may understand that the Lord was speaking of spiritual fishing, however, Peter says, "Master, we toiled all night and took nothing! But at your word I will let down the nets." It is as if he were saying, "Through the whole night our fishing has brought us nothing, and we have been laboring in vain. Now I will not fish with fishing gear but with grace, not with diligence acquired by skill but with the perseverance acquired by devotion." When Peter lets down the nets at the word, therefore, he is in fact letting down the teachings in Christ. When he unfolds the tightly

---

[2]WSA 3 7:112-13*. [3]Mt 4:19. [4]Rom 11:33. [5]Mt 16:16. [6]Gen 7:1—8:22. [7]1 Pet 3:20-21. [8]Gen 8:10-11. [9]ACW 50:115-16**. [10]CGSL 105**.

woven and well-ordered nets at the command of the Master, he is really laying out words in the name of the Savior in a fitting and clear fashion. By these words he is able to save not creatures but souls. "We toiled all night," he says, "and took nothing." Peter, who beforehand was unable to see in order to make a catch, enduring darkness without Christ, had indeed toiled through the whole night. But when the Savior's light shone upon him the darkness scattered, and by faith he began to discern in the deep what he could not see with his eyes. SERMON 110.2.[11]

THE TWO BOATS REPRESENT THE JEWS AND GENTILES. EPHREM THE SYRIAN: We have been toiling all night. This refers symbolically to the prophets. His teaching came down from on high on the world, which stands by way of parable for the sea. The two boats represent the circumcised and the uncircumcised. They made a sign to their companions. This refers symbolically to the seventy-two, for these disciples were too few in number for the catch and the harvest. COMMENTARY ON TATIAN'S DIATESSARON 5.18.[12]

5:8-11 Peter's Confession and Jesus' Absolution

PETER'S FEAR COMES FROM THE PRESENCE OF

HOLINESS. CYRIL OF ALEXANDRIA: For this reason also Peter, carried back to the memory of his former sins, trembles and is afraid. As an impure man, he does not dare to receive the one who is pure. His fear was praiseworthy, because he had been taught by the law to distinguish between the holy and the profane.[13] COMMENTARY ON LUKE, HOMILY 12.[14]

THIS BOAT IS THE CHURCH THAT GIVES LIFE. MAXIMUS OF TURIN: Ordinarily people are not given life on a boat but transported. Nor are they comforted on a vessel but anxious about its journey. Notice also that this boat is not a boat that is given to Peter to be piloted—rather, it is the church, which is committed to the apostle to be governed. For this is the vessel that does not kill but gives life to those borne along by the storms of this world as if by waves. Just as a little boat holds the dying fish that have been brought up from the deep, so also the vessel of the church gives life to human beings who have been freed from turmoil. Within itself, I say, the church gives life to those who are half-dead, as it were. SERMON 110.[15]

---

[11]ACW 50:239-40**. [12]ECTD 103*. [13]Ezek 22:16. [14]CGSL 105**. [15]ACW 50:238-39*.

5:12-16 THE CLEANSING OF A LEPER

[12]While he was in one of the cities, there came a man full of leprosy; and when he saw Jesus, he fell on his face and besought him, "Lord, if you will, you can make me clean." [13]And he stretched out his hand, and touched him, saying, "I will; be clean." And immediately the leprosy left him. [14]And he charged him to tell no one; but "go and show yourself to the priest, and make an offering for your cleansing, as Moses commanded, for a proof to the people."° [15]But so much the more the

report went abroad concerning him; and great multitudes gathered to hear and to be healed of their infirmities. ¹⁶*But he withdrew to the wilderness and prayed.*

o Greek *to them*

OVERVIEW: The healing of the leper is part of Jesus' preaching of the kingdom of God, showing clearly Jesus' divinity in his power over sickness and his humanity as he stretches out his hand to touch the leper (CYRIL OF ALEXANDRIA). Jesus breaks with Israel's purity code because he touches the leper, and instead of Jesus becoming unclean, Jesus remains clean and cleanses the leper too, showing that he cannot be defiled by the leper's unclean leprosy (EPHREM THE SYRIAN). But it also may be that Jesus understands the leper's confession to be pious and faithful, and at his word the healing happens because of the power of that word. The significance of Jesus' action is more striking when considered in light of Old Testament theology, for in sending the leper to the priests Jesus shows that this healing came not through the law but through grace (AMBROSE). By sending the leper to the priest, these levitical sacrifices on his behalf foreshadow Jesus' baptism in his blood on the cross. (CYRIL OF ALEXANDRIA).[1] Jesus regularly retreats from the cities into the desert and thereby shows us how to pray (CYPRIAN).

5:12-13 Jesus' Healing

JESUS DEMONSTRATES HIS DIVINITY AND HUMANITY. CYRIL OF ALEXANDRIA: He accepts his petition and confesses that he is able and says, "I will; be cleansed." He grants him also the touch of his holy and all-powerful hand. Immediately the leprosy departed from him, and his affliction was ended. Join with me, therefore, in adoring Christ, thus exercising at the same time both a divine and a bodily power. For it was a divine act so to will as for all that he willed to be present unto him. To stretch out the hand, however, was a human act. Christ, therefore, is perceived to be One of both, if, as is the case, the Word was made

flesh. COMMENTARY ON LUKE, HOMILY 12.[2]

JESUS CANNOT BE DEFILED. EPHREM THE SYRIAN: Go, show yourself.[3] This was for the sake of the priests. For the leper was afraid to touch him lest he defile him. But the Lord touched him to show him that he would not be defiled, he, at whose rebuke the defilement fled from the defiled one. COMMENTARY ON TATIAN'S DIATESSARON 12.21.[4]

5:14-15 Jesus' Instructions

JESUS RESPONDS TO THE LEPER'S PIOUS CONFESSION. AMBROSE: The authority of power in the Lord is here compared with the steadfastness of faith manifest in the leper. He fell on his face because it is a mark of humility and modesty that each feel shame for the sins of his life, but shyness did not restrict his confession. He showed the wound, he begged for the remedy, and the very confession is full of piety and faith. "If you will," it says, "you can make me clean." He conceded the power to the Lord's will. But he doubted concerning the Lord's will, not as if unbelieving in piety, but as if aware of his own impurity, he did not presume. The Lord replies to him with a certain holiness. "I will: be clean. And immediately the leprosy departed from him." For there is nothing between God's command and his work, because the work is in the command. Thus he spoke, and they came into being.[5] You see that it cannot be doubted that the will of God is power. If, therefore, his will is power, those who affirm that the Trinity is of One will affirm that it is of one power. Thus the leprosy departed immediately. In order that you may understand the effect of healing,

---

[1]Lk 12:49-50; Heb 13:10-16. [2]*CGSL* 106**. [3]Mt 8:4. [4]*ECTD* 201**. [5]Ps 33:9 (32:9 LXX); cf. Jdt 16:14.

he added truth to the work. EXPOSITION OF THE GOSPEL OF LUKE 5.2-3.[6]

HEALED BY GRACE AND NOT BY LAW.

AMBROSE: He is commanded to show himself to the priest and sacrifice for his cleansing. In offering himself to the priest, the priest may understand that he was cured not by the ordinance of the law but by the grace of God above the law. When the sacrifice is performed according to Moses' precept,[7] the Lord shows that he did not destroy the law but fulfilled it.[8] Furthermore, by proceeding according to the law, he was seen to heal above the law those whom the remedies of the law had not healed. "For the law is spiritual,"[9] and therefore it is seen that a spiritual sacrifice is commanded. EXPOSITION OF THE GOSPEL OF LUKE 5.8.[10]

CHRIST'S BAPTISM IN BLOOD FORESHADOWED IN THE LEVITICAL SACRIFICES.

CYRIL OF ALEXANDRIA: Anyone can see the profound and mighty mystery of Christ written for our benefit in Leviticus.[11] For the law of Moses declares the leper defiled and gives orders for him to be put out of the camp as unclean. What if the malady is relieved? It commands that he should then be capable of readmission. Moreover, it clearly specifies the manner in which he is to be pronounced clean. . . .

We may see, then, in the birds (offered at the cleansing of the leper) Christ suffering in the flesh according to the Scriptures[12] but remaining also beyond the power of suffering. . . . That the one bird then was slain, and that the other was baptized indeed in its blood, while itself exempt from slaughter, typified what was really to happen. For Christ died in our place, and we, who have been baptized into his death, he has saved by his own blood. COMMENTARY ON LUKE, HOMILY 12.[13]

5:16 Jesus Withdraws to Pray

JESUS SHOWS US HOW TO PRAY.

CYPRIAN: Not by words alone, but also by deeds has God taught us to pray. He himself prayed frequently and demonstrated what we ought to do by the testimony of his own example. As it is written: "But he himself was in retirement in the desert, and in prayer," and again, "He went out into the mountain to pray and continued all night in prayer to God." But if he who was without sin prayed, how much more ought sinners to pray, and if he prayed continually, watching through the whole night with uninterrupted petitions, how much more ought we to lie awake at night in continuing prayer! THE LORD'S PRAYER 29.[14]

---

[6]EHG 147-48**. [7]Lev 14:1-32. [8]Mt 5:17. [9]Rom 7:14. [10]EHG 149**. [11]Lev 13:8. [12]1 Pet 4:1. [13]CGSL 107-8**. [14]FC 36:152**.

5:17-26 JESUS HEALS AND FORGIVES A PARALYTIC

[17]On one of those days, as he was teaching, there were Pharisees and teachers of the law sitting by, who had come from every village of Galilee and Judea and from Jerusalem; and the power of the Lord was with him to heal.[p] [18]And behold, men were bringing on a bed a man who was paralyzed, and they sought to bring him in and lay him before Jesus;[q] [19]but finding no way to bring him in, because of the crowd, they went up on the roof and let him down with his bed through the tiles

into the midst before Jesus. ²⁰And when he saw their faith he said, "Man, your sins are forgiven you." ²¹And the scribes and the Pharisees began to question, saying, "Who is this that speaks blasphemies? Who can forgive sins but God only?" ²²When Jesus perceived their questionings, he answered them, "Why do you question in your hearts? ²³Which is easier, to say, 'Your sins are forgiven you,' or to say, 'Rise and walk'? ²⁴But that you may know that the Son of man has authority on earth to forgive sins"—he said to the man who was paralyzed—"I say to you, rise, take up your bed and go home." ²⁵And immediately he rose before them, and took up that on which he lay, and went home, glorifying God. ²⁶And amazement seized them all, and they glorified God and were filled with awe, saying, "We have seen strange things today."

p Other ancient authorities read *was present to heal them*   q Greek *him*

OVERVIEW: When the paralytic's friends carry him to the roof, remove the roof and let him down before Jesus, it shows their seriousness and persistence and affirms that every sick person and every sinner needs intercessors before the Lord (AMBROSE) as did this paralytic whose friends place him in the presence of Jesus.

Jesus the Physician will show that he is present in his creation to heal spiritually through forgiveness and physically by healing the paralytic (CYRIL OF ALEXANDRIA). Jesus shows that he is able to heal the whole person (AMBROSE). Jesus' forgiveness leads to a discussion as to whether his absolution is blasphemy and whether he is the Son of God (EPHREM THE SYRIAN). Jesus, who is able to know their hearts and minds, is certainly also able to forgive sins. The main point Jesus makes is to declare that he, the Son of Man, has authority on earth to forgive sins, and this authority will be given to his church (CYRIL OF ALEXANDRIA). The command to return home is a command to return to Paradise (AMBROSE).

5:17-19 *The Paralytic and His Friends*

SICK PEOPLE AND SINNERS NEED INTERCESSORS. AMBROSE: You who judge, learn to excuse! You who are sick, learn to accomplish. If you do not trust in the forgiveness of grave sinners, call intercessors, call the church who will pray for you. Because of his regard for the church, the Lord forgives what he may refuse you. And al-

though we must not neglect the faith in the narrative, so that we may indeed believe that the body of the paralytic was healed, we must also acknowledge the healing of the inner man whose sins are forgiven. EXPOSITION OF THE GOSPEL OF LUKE 5.11-12.[1]

5:20 *The Miracle of Forgiveness*

JESUS HEALS SPIRITUALLY AND PHYSICALLY. CYRIL OF ALEXANDRIA: When the Savior says to him, "Man, your sins are forgiven you," he addresses this to humankind in general. For those who believe in him, being healed of the diseases of the soul, will receive forgiveness of the sins which they formerly committed. He may also mean this: "I must heal your soul before I heal your body. If this is not done, by obtaining strength to walk, you will only sin more. Even though you have not asked for this, I as God see the maladies of the soul which brought on you this disease." COMMENTARY ON LUKE, HOMILY 12.[2]

JESUS CURES THE WHOLE PERSON. AMBROSE: But the Lord, wanting to save sinners,[3] shows himself to be God both by his knowledge of secrets and by the wonder of his actions. He adds, "Which is easier, to say, 'Your sins are forgiven you,' or to say, 'Rise and walk?'" In this passage he shows the full likeness of the resurrection. Along-

---

[1]EHG 150-51**. [2]CGSL 110-11**. [3]1 Tim 1:15.

side of healing the wounds of body and mind, he also forgives the sins of the spirits, removes the weakness of the flesh, and thus heals the whole person. It is a great thing to forgive people's sins—who can forgive sins, but God alone? For God also forgives through those to whom he has given the power of forgiveness. Yet it is far more divine to give resurrection to bodies, since the Lord himself is the resurrection.[4] EXPOSITION OF THE GOSPEL OF LUKE 5.12-13.[5]

5:21-24 The Dispute

PHARISEES DOUBT JESUS IS GOD. EPHREM THE SYRIAN: While the Pharisee doubted that our Lord was a prophet, he was unwittingly pledging himself to the truth by thinking, "If this man were a prophet, he would know that this woman is a sinner."[6] Therefore, if our Lord indeed knows that she is a sinner, then, Pharisee, by your own reasoning he indeed is a prophet. And so our Lord did not hesitate to point out not only that she was a sinner but also that she had sinned very much, so that the testimony of his own mouth would trap the accuser. [The Pharisee] was one of those who had said, "Who can forgive sins but God alone?" Our Lord took this testimony from them, that whoever is able to forgive sin is God. From this point on, the struggle was for our Lord to show them whether or not he was able to forgive sin. And so he quickly healed the parts [of the body] that were visible, to confirm that he had forgiven the sins which were not visible. HOMILY ON OUR LORD 21.1.[7]

JESUS WHO KNOWS THE HEARTS AND MINDS ALSO FORGIVES SINS. CYRIL OF ALEXANDRIA: He then, as was said, announced forgiveness of sins, since he is endowed with a most godlike authority. But the declaration disturbed again the ignorant and envious gang of the Pharisees. They said one to another, "Who is this that speaks blasphemies?" But would you have said this about him, Pharisee, if you had known the divine Scriptures, and borne in mind the words of prophecy,

and understood the adorable and mighty mystery of the incarnation? Instead, they now involve him in a charge of blasphemy, bringing against him the uttermost penalty and condemning him to death. The law of Moses commanded that whoever spoke blasphemies against God should be put to death.[8] But no sooner have they arrived at this height of daring, than he immediately shows that he is God, to convict them once more of intolerable impiety, "Why do you question in your hearts?" If you, therefore, Pharisee, say, "Who can forgive sins but God only?" I will also say to you, "Who can know hearts, and see the thoughts hidden in the depth of the understanding, but God only?" For he himself says somewhere by the voice of the prophets, "I, the Lord, search the minds and try the heart."[9] David also said somewhere concerning both him and us, "He who fashions the hearts of them all."[10] Therefore he who as God knows both the hearts and minds, as God also forgives sins. COMMENTARY ON LUKE, HOMILY 12.[11]

5:25-26 The Miracle of Healing

JESUS GIVES TO HIS CHURCH POWER TO HEAL AND FORGIVE. CYRIL OF ALEXANDRIA: A place still remains open for disbelief when it is said, "Your sins are forgiven you"—for people cannot see the forgiven sins with the eyes of the body. By contrast, the putting off of the disease and the paralytic's rising up and walking carries with it a clear demonstration of a godlike power. Jesus adds, "Rise, take up your bed and go home." And he returned to his house, delivered from the infirmity from which he had so long suffered. This very fact proves that the Son of man has power on earth to forgive sins. But to whom does he refer when he says this? Himself only, or us too? Both the one and the other are true. For he forgives sins as the incarnate God, the Lord of the law. We too have received from him this

---

[4]Jn 11:25. [5]EHG 151*. [6]Lk 7:39. [7]FC 91:295**. [8]Lev 24:16. [9]Jer 17:10. [10]Ps 33:15 (32:15 LXX). [11]CGSL 111-12**.

splendid and most admirable grace. He has crowned human nature with this great honor also, having even said to the holy apostles, "Truly, I say to you, whatever you bind on earth shall be bound in heaven, and whatever you loose on earth shall be loosed in heaven."[12] And again, "If you forgive the sins of any, they are forgiven; if you retain the sins of any, they are retained."[13] And what is the occasion on which we find him speaking this to them? It was after he had trampled on the power of death and risen from the grave, when he breathed on them and said, "Receive the Holy Spirit."[14] After he had made them partakers of his nature and bestowed upon them the indwelling of the Holy Spirit, he also made them sharers of his glory, by giving them power both to remit and to bind sins. And as we have been commanded to perform this very act, how much more must he himself remit sins, when he gives to others authority to enable them to do so? COMMENTARY ON LUKE, HOMILY 12.[15]

To Return Home Is to Return to Paradise. AMBROSE: What is this bed which he is commanded to take up, as he is told to rise? It is the same bed which was washed by David every night,[16] the bed of pain on which our soul lay sick with the cruel torment of conscience. But if anyone has acted according to Christ's teaching, it is already not a bed of pain but of repose. Indeed, through the compassion of the Lord, who turns for us the sleep of death into the grace of delight, that which was death begins to be repose. Not only is he ordered to take up his bed, but also to go home to his house, that is, to return to Paradise. That is our true home which first fostered man, lost not lawfully, but by deceit. Therefore, rightfully is the home restored, since he who would abolish the obligation of deceit and reform the law has come. EXPOSITION OF THE GOSPEL OF LUKE 5.14.[17]

---

[12]Mt 18:18. [13]Jn 20:23. [14]Jn 20:22. [15]CGSL 112**. [16]Ps 6:6 (6:7 LXX). [17]EHG 151-52**.

5:27-39 LEVI'S CALL AND BANQUET

[27]*After this he went out, and saw a tax collector, named Levi, sitting at the tax office; and he said to him, "Follow me."* [28]*And he left everything, and rose and followed him.*

[29]*And Levi made him a great feast in his house; and there was a large company of tax collectors and others sitting at table^r with them.* [30]*And the Pharisees and their scribes murmured against his disciples, saying, "Why do you eat and drink with tax collectors and sinners?"* [31]*And Jesus answered them, "Those who are well have no need of a physician, but those who are sick;* [32]*I have not come to call the righteous, but sinners to repentance."*

[33]*And they said to him, "The disciples of John fast often and offer prayers, and so do the disciples of the Pharisees, but yours eat and drink."* [34]*And Jesus said to them, "Can you make wedding guests fast while the bridegroom is with them?* [35]*The days will come, when the bridegroom is taken away from them, and then they will fast in those days."* [36]*He told them a parable also: "No one tears a piece from a new garment and puts it upon an old garment; if he does, he will tear the new, and the piece from the new will not match the old.* [37]*And no one puts new wine into old wineskins; if he does, the new wine will burst the skins and it will be spilled, and the skins will be destroyed.*

38But new wine must be put into fresh wineskins. 39And no one after drinking old wine desires new; for he says, 'The old is good.'"s

r Greek *reclining* s Other ancient authorities read *better*

OVERVIEW: Only Luke describes Levi as a tax collector, emphasizing that Levi was part of the group considered to consist of the worst of sinners (CYRIL OF ALEXANDRIA). The table fellowship with sinners characterized the essence of Jesus' ministry and was at the center of his controversy with the religious establishment, particularly the Pharisees, for whom this feast with Levi awakens their unbelief (AMBROSE). They are envious of Jesus because they do not understand that he is present as physician and not as judge (CYRIL OF ALEXANDRIA). His healing is also forgiveness, for his mission is to sinners, not to the hypocrites or self-righteous (BEDE). To receive Christ into our homes at our table is to prepare for him, the Bridegroom, a banquet of good works (AMBROSE).

This imagery of Christ as the bridegroom anticipates the presence of Christ at the Lord's Supper (AMBROSE) and the messianic feast when Christ takes his bride, the heavenly Jerusalem. The disciples are therefore worthy of the title "wedding guests" as members of the church who will also become ministers of the feast (EPHREM THE SYRIAN). The disciples will fast after Jesus ascends, for they will continually be putting off the old garment of the old man that was first stripped off in baptism (AMBROSE). For the days are coming when the bridegroom will be taken away, a reference to his death and his departure out of this world, including his ascension. The parables of the new garment and the new wine have the same point: those who insist on adhering to the old covenant will have no share in the new creation (CYRIL OF ALEXANDRIA).

5:27-28 Levi's Call to Discipleship

LEVI THE PUBLICAN CALLED TO FOLLOW JESUS. CYRIL OF ALEXANDRIA: Levi was a publican, a man greedy for dirty money, filled with an uncontrolled desire to possess, careless of justice in his eagerness to have what did not belong to him. Such was the character of the publicans. Yet he was snatched from the workshop of sin itself and saved when there was no hope for him, at the call of Christ the Savior of us all. For Jesus said to him, " 'Follow me.' And he left all and followed him." What most wise Paul says is true: "that Christ came to save sinners."[1] Do you see how the only-begotten Word of God, having taken upon him the flesh, transferred to himself the devil's goods? COMMENTARY ON LUKE, HOMILY 12.[2]

5:29-32 Levi's Feast and Jesus' First Response to Pharisees and Scribes

THE FEAST WITH LEVI AWAKENS HIS FAITH. AMBROSE: Then follows the spiritual calling of the tax collector, whom he orders to follow him not by steps of the body but by character of the mind. Matthew once greedily embezzled from fishermen the profits they earned from hard labor and dangers. When he was called, he abandoned his office, which was to rob others of their money. Yes, he left that shameful seat, to walk totally in the footsteps of the Lord with his mind. He also prepared a great feast, because he who receives Christ in the house inside him eats the finest foods—plentiful pleasures. So the Lord enters willingly and reclines in the character of one who has believed. EXPOSITION OF THE GOSPEL OF LUKE 5.16.[3]

ENVY AND FAULT FINDING MOTIVATE THE PHARISEES. CYRIL OF ALEXANDRIA: But for what reason do the Pharisees blame the Savior for eating with sinners? Because it was the law to distinguish between the holy and the pro-

---

[1]1 Tim 1:15. [2]CGSL 113**. [3]EHG 152**; CSEL 32 4:185.

fane,[4] that is, holy things were not to be brought into contact with things profane. They made the accusation therefore as if they were vindicating the law. Yet it really was envy against the Lord and readiness to find fault. But he shows them that he is present now, not as a judge but as a physician. He performs a proper function of the physician's office, being in the company of those in need to be healed. But no sooner had they received an explanation of their first accusation than they bring forward another, finding fault because his disciples did not fast. They wished to use this charge as an opportunity to accuse Christ. COMMENTARY ON LUKE, HOMILIES 21-22.[5]

JESUS CALLS SINNERS TO REPENTANCE. BEDE: "I have not come to call the just but sinners" can also be properly understood in this way. He has not called those who, wishing to establish their own justice, have not been made subject to the justice of God.[6] He calls those who, being conscious of their weakness, are not ashamed to confess that we have all offended in many things.[7] In them too is fulfilled his saying that he had not come to call the just but sinners. That is, he does not call the exalted but the humble. He does not call those puffed up about their own justice but those showing themselves devotedly subject to the one who justifies the wicked. Such people, when they are converted, bear witness with a sincere heart that they must not be regarded as just, but sinners.

It is a pleasure to remember, beloved, . . . to what a height of justice the Lord fetched Matthew, whom he chose out of his tax collecting activities in order to increase for sinners their hope of forgiveness. The apostolic band into which he was incorporated teaches what kind of person he became. HOMILIES ON THE GOSPELS 1.21.[8]

TO RECEIVE CHRIST IS TO PREPARE A BANQUET OF GOOD WORKS. AMBROSE: People are hungry when Christ is absent and they lack the abundance of good desserts. Truly, one for whom his own virtue suffices for pleasure, who receives

Christ in his own home, prepares a great feast. It is a spiritual banquet of good works, at which the rich people go without and the poor one feasts. It says, "The sons of the Bridegroom cannot fast while the Bridegroom is with them." EXPOSITION OF THE GOSPEL OF LUKE 5.19.[9]

5:33-35 Jesus' Second Response to Pharisees and Scribes

THE BRIDEGROOM IS ALWAYS WITH US AT THE LORD'S SUPPER. AMBROSE: "But the days will come when the Bridegroom shall be taken from them." Which are these days in which Christ is taken from us, especially when he himself has said, "I shall be with you, even to the end of the world,"[10] when he has said, "I will not leave you orphans"?[11] For it is certain that if he were to leave us, we could not be saved. None can take Christ from you, unless you take yourself away. Your boasting will not take you away, nor arrogance, nor may you presume on the law for yourself. "For he came not to call the righteous, but sinners."[12] . . . The righteous are those who do not strike him who strikes them,[13] who love their enemy.[14] If we do not endure thus, the opposite is found. "I came not to call the righteous." Christ does not call those who say they are righteous, for not knowing God and seeking to establish their own righteousness, they have not submitted themselves to the righteousness of God.[15] Therefore the usurpers of righteousness are not called to grace. For if grace comes from penitence, surely one who scorns penitence renounces grace. Those who make themselves out to be holy will be wounded. The Bridegroom is taken from them.[16] Neither Caiaphas nor Pilate took Christ from us. We cannot fast, because we have Christ, and we feast on the body and blood of Christ.[17] For how does he who does not hunger seem to fast? How

---

[4]Lev 10:10. [5]*CGSL* 115**. [6]Rom 10:3. [7]Jas 3:2. [8]CS 110:212-13. [9]*EHG* 153**. [10]Mt 28:20. [11]Jn 14:18. [12]Mt 9:13. [13]See Mt 5:39; Lk 6:29; 1 Pet 2:23. [14]See Mt 5:44; Lk 6:27. [15]Rom 10:3. [16]Mt 9:15. [17]Jn 6:53.

does he who does not thirst seem to fast? Then, how can he who drinks Christ thirst when he himself said, "Whosoever shall drink of the water that I will give him shall be thirsty no more"?[18] Then what follows will declare the saying to concern the fasting of the spirit. Exposition of the Gospel of Luke 5.20-22.[19]

Why the Disciples Are Called Bridal Guests. Ephrem the Syrian: During the entire period that our Lord was in the midst of the world, he compared it with a bridal chamber and himself with the bridegroom. For the bridal guests cannot fast while the bridegroom is with them.[20] . . .

He called his disciples bridal guests because they are members of the church, and ministers of the feast, and heralds who invite those who sit at table. Commentary on Tatian's Diatessaron 5.22a-22b.[21]

Fasting Refers to the Old Garment Put Off in Baptism. Ambrose: Then in this passage, fasting represents the old garment that the apostle thought should be taken off. He said, "Strip yourselves of the old man with his deeds,"[22] so that we may put on the new man, which is renewed by the sanctification of baptism. Then the series of teachings is suited to the same garment, lest we mix the deeds of the old and the new man, when the physical exterior performs the works of the flesh. The inner man,[23] which is reborn, should not have the varied appearance of old and new actions but be the same color as Christ. With zeal of mind, it should imitate him for whom he was cleansed by baptism. So let the discolored coverings of the mind, which are displeas-

ing to the Bridegroom, be absent, for one who has not a wedding garment is displeasing to him.[24] What can please the Bridegroom, except peace of spirit, purity of heart and clarity of mind? Exposition of the Gospel of Luke 5.23.[25]

To Be Taken Away Is to Ascend into Heaven. Cyril of Alexandria: For all things are good in their season, but what is the meaning of the Bridegroom being taken away from them? It is his being taken up into heaven. Commentary on Luke, Homiies 21-22.[26]

5:36-39 Jesus' Summary Parables Epitomize the Scene

No Share in the New Creation. Cyril of Alexandria: Those who live according to the law cannot receive the institutions of Christ. These institutions cannot be admitted into the hearts of such as have not as yet received the renewing by the Holy Spirit. The Lord shows this by saying that a tattered patch cannot be put upon a new garment, nor can old skins hold new wine. The first covenant has grown old, nor was it free from fault. Those, therefore, who adhere to it and keep at heart the antiquated commandment have no share in the new order of things in Christ. In him all things are become new,[27] but their mind being decayed, they have no harmony or point of mutual agreement with the ministers of the new covenant. Commentary on Luke, Homilies 21-22.[28]

---

[18]Jn 4:13. [19]EHG 153-55**. [20]Mk 2:19. [21]ECTD 105*. [22]Col 3:9. [23]See Rom 7:22. [24]See Mt 22:12. [25]EHG 155-56**. [26]CGSL 116. [27]2 Cor 5:17. [28]CGSL 116-17**.

6:1-11 THE FIRST SABBATH CONTROVERSY

[1]On a sabbath,[t] while he was going through the grainfields, his disciples plucked and ate some heads of grain, rubbing them in their hands. [2]But some of the Pharisees said, "Why are you doing what is not lawful to do on the sabbath?" [3]And Jesus answered, "Have you not read what David did when he was hungry, he and those who were with him: [4]how he entered the house of God, and took and ate the bread of the Presence, which it is not lawful for any but the priests to eat, and also gave it to those with him?" [5]And he said to them, "The Son of man is lord of the sabbath."

[6]On another sabbath, when he entered the synagogue and taught, a man was there whose right hand was withered. [7]And the scribes and the Pharisees watched him, to see whether he would heal on the sabbath, so that they might find an accusation against him. [8]But he knew their thoughts, and he said to the man who had the withered hand, "Come and stand here." And he rose and stood there. [9]And Jesus said to them, "I ask you, is it lawful on the sabbath to do good or to do harm, to save life or to destroy it?" [10]And he looked around on them all, and said to him, "Stretch out your hand." And he did so, and his hand was restored. [11]But they were filled with fury and discussed with one another what they might do to Jesus.

t Other ancient authorities read *On the second first sabbath* (on the second sabbath after the first)

OVERVIEW: The sabbath is of the Father's making, so Jesus the Physician may dispense from it for healing from head to toe (EPHREM THE SYRIAN). This Son of man brings the sabbath of grace not of law, the sabbath of the eternal resurrection. Jesus makes it clear to the scribes and Pharisees that they have misunderstood the sabbath. By entering the cornfields on the sabbath, Jesus has the disciples enter the world (the field) and the abundant fruitfulness of the saints as humanity multiplies (the corn) and as they participate in the fruits of the church in the apostolic work (AMBROSE). What David did with the bread of presence in the tabernacle, Christ now does with grain that is not yet bread on the sabbath, for the showbread is the bread of heaven that is now the Eucharist in our churches (CYRIL OF ALEXANDRIA).

The second part of the sabbath controversy is linked to the first, as Jesus heals the man with a withered hand in order to show the Pharisees the kind of mercy God requires (CYRIL OF ALEXAN-

DRIA). Jesus' healing rebukes the evil interpretation of the sabbath by the Pharisees. Stretching forth the hand is the common remedy for any ailment, especially as the hand stretches forth in works of charity (AMBROSE).

6:1-5 Jesus' Theology of the Sabbath

THE SABBATH IS OF THE FATHER'S MAKING.
EPHREM THE SYRIAN: "Behold, your disciples are doing what is not lawful to do on the sabbath."[1] Our Lord had instructed them in advance and trained them in the truth of the just, so that whenever he dispensed from the law fully, they would not be alarmed. His Father had also dispensed from sabbaths to show that the sabbath was of his own making. He was also continuing to dispense from it that he might show that these were discerning remedies, proposed by the skilled

---

[1]Mt 12:2.

physician for the pain which stretches from the sole of the foot to the head.[2] COMMENTARY ON TATIAN'S DIATESSARON 5.23.[3]

THE ALLEGORICAL MEANING OF THE FIELD, THE CORN AND THE FRUIT. AMBROSE: The

Lord Jesus begins to divest man [people] of the observation of the old law and clothes him with the new covering of grace not only through the understanding of words but also through the very usage and appearance of actions. Already on the sabbath, he leads him through the corn-fields, that is, he brings him to what abounds in fruit. What the sabbath, the standing corn, and the ears mean to him is no small mystery. The field is this whole world, and the standing corn of the field is an abundant fruitfulness of saints in the sowing of the human race. The ears of the field are the fruits of the church that the apostles scattered with their works and on which they fed, sustaining themselves on our progress. The corn was already standing rich in abundant ears of virtues. The fruits of our merit are compared with these, because they also wither in a shower or are parched by the sun or soaked by the rain or shattered by storms or hoarded by the reapers in the storehouses of the blessed granaries. The earth has already received the Word of God, and the nourishing field sown with heavenly seed has brought forth abundant fruit. The disciples hungered for the salvation of humankind, and by the splendid miracles of their works they plucked as if from the husks of their bodies fruits of their minds to the light of faith. The Jews thought that this was not permitted on the sabbath, but Christ through the gift of new grace designated the idleness of the law as a work of grace. EXPOSITION OF THE GOSPEL OF LUKE 5.28-29.[4]

THE SHOWBREAD IS THE BREAD FROM HEAVEN. CYRIL OF ALEXANDRIA: Now although

David acted contrary to what the law approves, he is rightly and justly esteemed by us as worthy of all admiration because he was truly a saint and prophet. Since the law of Moses expressly commands justice and does not consider the person being judged,[5] "how," he says, "do you condemn my disciples while you still admire as a saint and prophet the blessed David, although he did not keep Moses' command?"

There is clearly indicated to us by the loaves of the showbread the bread that comes down from heaven to be set upon the holy tables of the churches and all the furniture of the table. Bread used for the performance of its mystical service was a plain type of the divine treasures. Spiritually the bread signifies the twelve apostles, of whom we shall speak in due order when our comments reach the disciples themselves. COMMENTARY ON LUKE, HOMILIES 21-22.[6]

6:6-11 Jesus' Healing on the Sabbath

JESUS HEALS ON THE SABBATH TO TEACH THE PHARISEES MERCY. CYRIL OF ALEXANDRIA:

The miracle sometimes converts to faith those who had disbelieved the word, but the Pharisees watched him to see if he would heal on the sabbath. The nature of an envious person is such that he makes the praises of others food for his own disease and is wickedly maddened by their reputation. Once more he spoke to this; "he reveals deep and mysterious things; he knows what is in the darkness, and the light dwells with him."[7] And why did he do this? Perhaps it might be to move the cruel and unpitying Pharisee to compassion. The man's malady [his withered hand] perhaps might shame them and persuade them to dispel the flames of their envy.

This question is most wise indeed and a most suitable statement to meet their folly. If it is lawful to do good on the sabbath and nothing prevents the sick being pitied by God, cease picking up opportunities for fault-finding against Christ and bringing down on your own head the sentence which the Father has decreed against those

---

[2]See Is 1:5-6. [3]ECTD 106*. [4]EHG 158**. [5]Deut 1:16. [6]CGSL 121**. [7]Dan 2:22.

who dishonor the Son. You have heard the Father where he says of the Son by the voice of David, "I will crush his foes before him and strike down those who hate him."[8] But if it is not lawful to do good on the sabbath and the law forbids the saving of life, you have made yourself an accuser of the law. COMMENTARY ON LUKE, Homily 23.[9]

JESUS REBUKES THE PHARISEES' INTERPRETATION. AMBROSE: "Are you angry at me because I have healed the whole man on the sabbath day?"[10] In this place he revivified with the salutary strength of good works the hand which Adam stretched out to pluck the fruit of the forbidden tree.[11] The hand which had withered through a crime was healed by good deeds. Christ thereby rebuked the Jews who violated the precepts of the law with evil interpretations. They thought that they should rest even from good works on the sabbath, since the law prefigured in the present the form of the future in which indeed the days of rest from evils, not from blessings, would come. EXPOSITION OF THE GOSPEL OF LUKE 5.39.[12]

STRETCH OUT YOUR HAND FOR OTHERS. AMBROSE: Then you heard the words of the Lord, saying, "Stretch forth your hand." That is the common and universal remedy. You who think that you have a healthy hand beware lest it is withered by greed or by sacrilege. Hold it out often. Hold it out to the poor person who begs you. Hold it out to help your neighbor, to give protection to a widow, to snatch from harm one whom you see subjected to unjust insult. Hold it out to God for your sins.[13] The hand is stretched forth; then it is healed. Jeroboam's hand withered when he sacrificed to idols; then it stretched out when he entreated God.[14] EXPOSITION OF THE GOSPEL OF LUKE 5.40.[15]

---

[8]Ps 89:23. [9]CGSL 122*. [10]Jn 7:23. [11]Gen 3:6. [12]EHG 161*. [13]See Is 1:15, 17. [14]1 Kings 13:4-6. [15]EHG 162*.

6:12-16 THE CALLING OF THE TWELVE

[12]*In these days he went out to the mountain to pray; and all night he continued in prayer to God. [13]And when it was day, he called his disciples, and chose from them twelve, whom he named apostles; [14]Simon, whom he named Peter, and Andrew his brother, and James and John, and Philip, and Bartholomew, [15]and Matthew, and Thomas, and James the son of Alphaeus, and Simon who was called the Zealot, [16]and Judas the son of James, and Judas Iscariot, who became a traitor.*

OVERVIEW: To prepare for the selection and naming of the Twelve, who will form the apostolic foundation of the church, Jesus withdraws alone to uninhabited places to pray, not for himself but for us, since he is our advocate on account of our sins (AMBROSE). The twelve apostles are named so that none may add themselves to this select group (CYRIL OF ALEXANDRIA). The name *apostle* bestows on them a special honor (EUSEBIUS). Jesus appointed simple people like fishermen and tax collectors to proclaim the good news of salvation to the world in order that triumph of his truth over human wisdom may be revealed (AMBROSE). Jesus chose the Twelve so that through them we who are earthly may share in the heavenly gifts (JOHN OF DAMASCUS). Luke honors Matthew by placing him before Thomas, something Matthew does not do in his list of the Twelve (EUSEBIUS). Only Luke concludes the list of the Twelve with the word *betrayer*, for even Judas is called by Jesus (AMBROSE).

6:12 Jesus Prays Alone on the Mountain

JESUS INTERCEDES AND PRAYS FOR US.
AMBROSE: So the Lord prays, not to entreat for himself but to intercede for me. Although the Father placed all things in the power of his Son,[1] yet the Son, in order to fulfill the form of a man, thinks that the Father must be entreated for us, because he is our Advocate.... If he is an Advocate, he must intercede on account of my sins....

It says, "He passed the whole night in prayer." A model is given to you. A form is prescribed which you must imitate.... Unless I am mistaken, it is nowhere found that he prayed with the apostles. Everywhere he entreats alone, for human prayers do not grasp the counsels of God,[2] nor can anyone share with Christ in the inward mysteries. EXPOSITION OF THE GOSPEL OF LUKE 5.42-43.[3]

6:13-16 Jesus Chooses the Twelve Apostles

THE APOSTLES ARE ONLY THESE TWELVE.
CYRIL OF ALEXANDRIA: Note the extreme moderation of the Evangelist. He does not simply say that the holy apostles were appointed, but rather, by introducing the record of these chief ones each by name, takes care that no other one should venture to enroll himself in the company of those that were chosen. COMMENTARY ON LUKE, HOMILY 23.[4]

THE NAME APOSTLE BESTOWS A SPECIAL HONOR.
EUSEBIUS: But our Lord and Savior, not very long after the beginning of his preaching, called the twelve apostles and to them alone of all his disciples he gave the name of apostles as a special honor.[5] Later he proclaimed seventy others,

and them also he sent out two by two in advance of himself into every place and city where he himself was to come. ECCLESIASTICAL HISTORY 1.10.[6]

JESUS CHOOSES FISHERMEN AND TAX COLLECTORS.
AMBROSE: It says, "He called unto him his disciples, and he chose twelve of them," whom he appointed sowers of the faith, to spread the help of human salvation throughout the world. At the same time, observe the heavenly counsel. He chose not wise men, nor rich men, nor nobles, but fishermen[7] and tax collectors,[8] whom he would direct, lest they seem to have seduced some by wisdom, or bought them with riches, or attracted them to their own grace with the authority of power and nobility. He did this so that the reasoning of truth, not the grace of disputation, should prevail. EXPOSITION OF THE GOSPEL OF LUKE 5.44.[9]

JESUS CALLED THE TWELVE TO MAKE US HEAVENLY.
JOHN OF DAMASCUS: He also chose twelve disciples, whom he called apostles, and commanded them to preach the kingdom of heaven which he came upon earth to declare, and to make heavenly us who are low and earthly, by virtue of his incarnation. BARLAAM AND JOSEPH 7.52.[10]

LUKE HONORS MATTHEW BY PLACING HIM BEFORE THOMAS.
EUSEBIUS: If you listen to Luke, you will not hear him calling Matthew a publican nor subordinating him to Thomas, for he knows him to be the greater, and puts him first and Thomas second. Mark has done the same.... So Luke honored Matthew, according to what they delivered, who from the beginning were eyewitnesses and ministers of the Word. PROOF OF THE GOSPEL 3.5.120.[11]

JESUS EVEN CHOSE JUDAS.
AMBROSE: Judas too

---

[1]Jn 17:2. [2]See Wis 9:13; Is 40:13. [3]EHG 162-63**. [4]CGSL 125*. [5]Mt 10:1-4; Mk 3:14-19. [6]FC 19:72. [7]Mt 4:18. [8]Mt 10:3. [9]EHG 163*. [10]LCL 34:93*. [11]POG 1:138.

is chosen, not through inadvertence but through Providence. How great is the truth that not even a hostile minister weakens! How great is the integrity of the Lord, who preferred to endanger his judgment among us, rather than his compassion! For he had assumed the frailty of man, and therefore [he did not] refuse those aspects of human weakness. He was willing to be forsaken, he was willing to be betrayed, he was willing to be surrendered by his own apostles, so that you, when abandoned by an ally, betrayed by an ally, may bear it in good order. EXPOSITION OF THE GOSPEL OF LUKE 5.45.[12]

---

[12]*EHG* 163-64.

6:17-19 THE PEOPLE HEAR JESUS AND ARE HEALED

[17]*And he came down with them and stood on a level place, with a great crowd of his disciples and a great multitude of people from all Judea and Jerusalem and the seacoast of Tyre and Sidon, who came to hear him and to be healed of their diseases;* [18]*and those who were troubled with unclean spirits were cured.* [19]*And all the crowd sought to touch him, for power came forth from him and healed them all.*

OVERVIEW: Jesus heals the sick after electing the Twelve to show that he is the Christ and that they have been chosen by God (CYRIL OF ALEXANDRIA). These crowds came from everywhere, from all of Judea, from the holy city of Jerusalem and from the coastal towns of Tyre and Sidon to be healed by Jesus (AMBROSE).

6:17-19 Hearing and Healing

JESUS HEALS TO SHOW HE IS THE CHRIST.
CYRIL OF ALEXANDRIA: When he had appointed the holy apostles, he performed very many wonderful miracles, rebuking demons, delivering from incurable diseases whoever drew near to him, and displaying his own most divine power. He did these works so that both the Jews, who had run together to him, and those from the country of the Greeks might know that Christ was not some ordinary man of those in our degree but, on the contrary, God. He honored these chosen disciples with the dignity of the apostolate. He was the Word that was made man but retained nevertheless his own glory. "For power went forth from him and healed all." Christ did not borrow strength from some other person, but being himself God by nature, even though he had become flesh, he healed them all, by the demonstration of power over the sick. COMMENTARY ON LUKE, HOMILY 25.[1]

JESUS DESCENDED TO HEAL THE LOWLY.
AMBROSE: Note all things carefully. He ascends with the apostles and descends to the crowds. How would a crowd see Christ, except at a low level? It does not follow him to the heights; it does not climb to majestic places. So when he descends, he finds the weak, for the weak cannot be

---

[1]*CGSL* 127**.

high up. Thus also Matthew teaches that the weak were healed down below.[2] First each was healed, so that little by little, with increasing virtue, he could ascend to the mountain. On the plain he heals each, that is, he calls them back from recklessness. He turns away the harm of blindness. He descends to heal our wounds, so that in an effective and abundant manner he makes us partakers in his heavenly nature. EXPOSITION OF THE GOSPEL OF LUKE 5.46.[3]

---

[2]Mt 8:1-4. [3]EHG 164**.

6:20-26 CATECHETICAL LECTURES: A WAY OF LIFE AND A WAY OF DEATH

[20]*And he lifted up his eyes on his disciples, and said:*
"Blessed are you poor, for yours is the kingdom of God.
[21]*"Blessed are you that hunger now, for you shall be satisfied.*
"Blessed are you that weep now, for you shall laugh.
[22]*"Blessed are you when men hate you, and when they exclude you and revile you, and cast out your name as evil, on account of the Son of man!* [23]*Rejoice in that day, and leap for joy, for behold, your reward is great in heaven; for so their fathers did to the prophets.*
[24]*"But woe to you that are rich, for you have received your consolation.*
[25]*"Woe to you that are full now, for you shall hunger.*
"Woe to you that laugh now, for you shall mourn and weep.
[26]*"Woe to you, when all men speak well of you, for so their fathers did to the false prophets.*

OVERVIEW: By lifting up his eyes to heaven, Jesus calls his hearers' thoughts to be uplifted (ORIGEN). Luke's Gospel continues the Old Testament catechetical tradition of the two ways: the way of life and the way of death (DIDACHE). Luke subsumes the eight beatitudes into four. Luke's hearers then and now should see beyond themselves to the One who was made poor for them (AMBROSE), who hungered in the wilderness for them, who wept for them as he entered Jerusalem, who received hate, insults and exclusion for them, and who was cast out and crucified outside Jerusalem as evil—the Son of man.

Christ's rebuke of the rich is addressed to those who do not know how to use their possessions properly. Those who weep for their sins are those who are hungering for righteousness (AMBROSE). Weeping is a requirement and laughter a benefit of wisdom (AUGUSTINE).

The final beatitude has similar themes: rejection or acceptance by the religious establishment as those who preach the gospel are persecuted for Jesus' sake (CYRIL OF ALEXANDRIA). Christians suffer because Jesus Christ suffered. The Lord describes the disciples' rejoicing in the midst of afflictions, for persecution is pleasure and enjoyment and certainty of heavenly treasures (GREGORY OF NYSSA). Jesus also calls to memory those prophets who have undergone and endured similar sufferings for the sake of the kingdom and the apostles who rejoice over their suffering for the sake of Christ (ORIGEN). Virtuous living that flows from Christ will not ever bring praise from all people, for human impulses resist such a life (Chrysostom).

6:20-26 Blessings and Woes

To Lift the Eyes. Origen: The phrase "lift up your eyes" occurs in many places in Scripture. By this expression, the divine Word admonishes us to exalt and lift up our thoughts. It invites us to elevate the insight that lies below in a rather sickly condition and is stooped and completely incapable of looking up.[1] For instance, it is written in Isaiah, "Lift up your eyes on high and see. Who has made all these things known?"[2]

The Savior too, when he is about to deliver the Beatitudes, lifts up his eyes to the disciples and says "blessed" are such and such. Commentary on the Gospel of John 13.274-77.[3]

The Way of Life. Anonymous: There are two ways, one of life, and one of death. Between the two ways there is a great difference.

Now, this is the way of life: "First, you must love God who made you, and second, your neighbor as yourself."[4] Whatever you want people to refrain from doing to you, you must not do to them.[5]

What these proverbs teach is this: "Bless those who curse you" and "pray for your enemies." Moreover, "fast for those who persecute you." For "what credit is it to you if you love those who love you? Is that not the way the heathen act?" But "you must love those who hate you,"[6] and then you will make no enemies. "Abstain from physical passions."[7] If someone strikes you "on the right cheek, turn to him the other too, and you will be perfect."[8] If someone "forces you to go one mile with him, go along with him for two." If someone robs you "of your overcoat, give him your suit as well."[9] If someone deprives you of "your property, do not ask for it back." (You could not get it back anyway!) "Give to everybody who begs from you, and ask for no return." Didache 1.1-5.[10]

Four Beatitudes; Four Cardinal Virtues. Ambrose: Let us see how St. Luke encompassed the eight blessings in the four. We know that there are four cardinal virtues: temperance, justice, prudence and fortitude. One who is poor in spirit is not greedy. One who weeps is not proud but is submissive and tranquil. One who mourns is humble. One who is just does not deny what he knows is given jointly to all for us. One who is merciful gives away his own goods. One who bestows his own goods does not seek another's, nor does he contrive a trap for his neighbor. These virtues are interwoven and interlinked, so that one who has one may be seen to have several, and a single virtue befits the saints. Where virtue abounds, the reward too abounds. . . . Thus temperance has purity of heart and spirit, justice has compassion, patience has peace, and endurance has gentleness. Exposition of the Gospel of Luke 5.62-63, 68.[11]

Jesus, Though Rich, Became Poor for Us. Ambrose: "Blessed," it says, "are the poor." Not all the poor are blessed, for poverty is neutral. The poor can be either good or evil, unless, perhaps, the blessed pauper is to be understood as he whom the prophet described, saying, "A righteous poor man is better than a rich liar."[12] Blessed is the poor man who cried and whom the Lord heard.[13] Blessed is the man poor in offense. Blessed is the man poor in vices. Blessed is the poor man in whom the prince of this world finds nothing.[14] Blessed is the poor man who is like that poor Man who, although he was rich, became poor for our sake.[15] Matthew fully revealed this when he said, "Blessed are the poor in spirit."[16] One poor in spirit is not puffed up, is not exalted in the mind of his own flesh. This beatitude is first, when I have laid aside every sin, and I

---

[1]See Lk 13:11. [2]Is 40:26. [3]FC 89:125**. [4]Mt 22:37-39; Lev 19:18. [5]Mt 7:12. [6]Mt 5:44, 46-47; Lk 6:27-28, 32-33. [7]1 Pet 2:11. [8]Mt 5:39, 48; Lk 6:29. [9]Mt 5:40-41. [10]LCC 1:171*. [11]EHG 170-71**. [12]Prov 19:22 LXX. [13]Cf. Ps 34:6 (33:7 LXX). [14]See Jn 14:30. [15]See 2 Cor 8:9. [16]Mt 5:3.

have taken off all malice, and I am content with simplicity, destitute of evils. All that remains is that I regulate my conduct. For what good does it do me to lack worldly goods, unless I am meek and gentle? EXPOSITION OF THE GOSPEL OF LUKE 5.53-54.[17]

WOE TO THOSE WHO MISUSE THEIR POSSESSIONS.

AMBROSE: Although there are many charms of delights in riches, yet there are more incentives to practice virtues. Although virtue does not require assistance and the contribution of the poor person is more commended than the generosity of the rich, yet with the authority of the heavenly saying, he condemns not those who have riches but those who do not know how to use them. The pauper is more praiseworthy who gives with eager compassion and is not restrained by the bolts of looming scarcity. He thinks that he who has enough for nature does not lack. So the rich person is the more guilty who does not give thanks to God for what he has received, but vainly hides wealth given for the common use and conceals it in buried treasures.[18] Then the offense consists not in the wealth but in the attitude. EXPOSITION OF THE GOSPEL OF LUKE 5.69.[19]

REPENTANCE INVOLVES A BENEFICIAL SORROW.

AMBROSE: Purify yourself with your tears. Wash yourselves with mourning. If you weep for yourself, another will not weep for you. . . . One who is a sinner weeps for himself and rebukes himself, that he may become righteous, for just people accuse themselves of sin.[20] Let us pursue order, because it is written, "Set in order love in me."[21] I have laid down sin. I have tempered my conduct. I have wept for my transgressions. I begin to hunger. I hunger for righteousness. The sick, when he is seriously ill, does not hunger, because the pain of the illness excludes hunger. What is the hunger for righteousness?[22] What is the bread of which it is said, "I have been young and am old, and I have not seen the righteous man forsaken, nor his seed begging bread"?[23] Surely one who is hungry seeks increase of

strength. What greater increase of virtue is there than the rule of righteousness? EXPOSITION OF THE GOSPEL OF LUKE 5.55-56.[24]

WEEPING IS A REQUIREMENT, LAUGHTER A REWARD OF WISDOM.

AUGUSTINE: If you propose a choice between these two things, which is better, to laugh or to cry? Is there anybody who wouldn't prefer to laugh? Because repentance involves a beneficial sorrow, the Lord presented tears as a requirement and laughter as the resulting benefit. How? When he says in the Gospel, "Blessed are those who cry, because they shall laugh." So crying is a requirement, laughter the reward, of wisdom. He wrote laughter to mean joy. He did not mean howling with laughter but jumping for joy. SERMON 175.2.[25]

PATIENT SUFFERING OF PERSECUTION.

CYRIL OF ALEXANDRIA: The Lord mentioned persecution already, even before the apostles had been sent on their mission. The Gospel anticipated what would happen. So he forewarns them for their benefit, that even the assault of things grievous to bear will bring its reward and advantage to them. They shall scold you, he says, as deceivers do, and try to mislead you. They shall separate you from them, even from their friendship and society. Let none of these things trouble you, he says. What harm will their intemperate tongue do a well-established mind? The patient suffering of these things will not be without fruit, he says, to those who know how to endure piously. It is the pledge of the highest happiness. Besides, he points out for their benefit, nothing strange will happen to them, even when suffering these things. On the contrary, they will resemble those who before their time were the bearers to the Israelites of the words that came from God above. These prophets were persecuted. They were sawn in two. They perished slain by the sword. They

---

[17]EHG 166-67**. [18]Mt 25:18. [19]EHG 171-72**. [20]Prov 18:17. [21]Song 2:4. [22]See Mt 5:6. [23]Ps 37:25 (36:25 LXX). [24]EHG 167-68**. [25]WSA 3 5:266**.

endured blame unjustly cast on them. He would have them also understand that they shall be partakers with those whose deeds they have imitated. They shall not fail in winning the prophet's crown, after having traveled by the same road. COMMENTARY ON LUKE, HOMILY 27.[26]

PERSECUTION IS CERTAINTY OF HEAVENLY TREASURES. GREGORY OF NYSSA: The Christian who has advanced by means of good discipline and the gift of the Spirit to the measure of the age of reason experiences glory and pleasure and enjoyment that is greater than any human pleasure. These come to one after grace is given to him, after being hated because of Christ, being driven, and enduring every insult and shame in behalf of his faith in God. For such a person, whose entire life centers on the resurrection and future blessings, every insult and scourging and persecution and the other sufferings leading up to the cross are all pleasure and refreshment and surety of heavenly treasures. For Jesus says, "Blessed are you when men reproach you and persecute you and, speaking falsely, say all manner of evil against you; for my sake rejoice and exult because your reward is great in heaven."[27] ON THE CHRISTIAN MODE OF LIFE.[28]

THE APOSTLES WORTHY OF SUFFERING DIS-

HONOR. ORIGEN: I beg you to remember in your entire present contest the great reward laid up in heaven for those who are persecuted and reviled for righteousness' sake. Be glad and leap for joy on account of the Son of man,[29] just as the apostles once rejoiced when they were counted worthy to suffer dishonor for his name.[30] EXHORTATION TO MARTYRDOM 4.[31]

VIRTUOUS LIVING WILL NOT BRING PRAISE FROM ALL PEOPLE. CHRYSOSTOM: "Woe to you when all people speak well of you." Notice how by the word *woe* he revealed to us the extent of the punishment awaiting such people. This word *woe*, after all, is an exclamation of lament, so that it is as if he is lamenting their fate when he says, "Woe to you when all people speak well of you." Notice too the precision in the expression: he didn't simply say "people" but "all people." You see, it is not possible for a virtuous person who travels by the straight and narrow path and follows Christ's commands to enjoy the praise and admiration of all people—so strong is the impulse of evil and the resistance to virtue. HOMILIES ON GENESIS 23.8.[32]

---

[26]CGSL 130-31**. [27]Mt 5:11-12; Lk 6:22-23. [28]FC 58:156*. [29]See Mt 5:10-12. [30]Acts 5:41. [31]OSW 43*. [32]FC 82:93-94**.

6:27-38 CATECHETICAL LECTURES: LOVE YOUR ENEMIES

[27]"But I say to you that hear, Love your enemies, do good to those who hate you, [28]bless those who curse you, pray for those who abuse you. [29]To him who strikes you on the cheek, offer the other also; and from him who takes away your coat do not withhold even your shirt. [30]Give to every one who begs from you; and of him who takes away your goods do not ask them again. [31]And as you wish that men would do to you, do so to them.

[32]"If you love those who love you, what credit is that to you? For even sinners love those who love

them. *³³And if you do good to those who do good to you, what credit is that to you? For even sinners do the same. ³⁴And if you lend to those from whom you hope to receive, what credit is that to you? Even sinners lend to sinners, to receive as much again. ³⁵But love your enemies, and do good, and lend, expecting nothing in return;ᵛ and your reward will be great, and you will be sons of the Most High; for he is kind to the ungrateful and the selfish. ³⁶Be merciful, even as your Father is merciful.*

³⁷"Judge not, and you will not be judged; condemn not, and you will not be condemned; forgive, and you will be forgiven; ³⁸give, and it will be given to you; good measure, pressed down, shaken together, running over, will be put into your lap. For the measure you give will be the measure you get back."

v Other ancient authorities read *despairing of no man*

OVERVIEW: The world loves its faults and hates its nature, while the Christian attitude to the world should be the opposite (AUGUSTINE). To love one's enemies requires a counterintuitive act of the will, an act that Christians alone are capable of doing (TERTULLIAN). Love for one's enemies is an expression of the charity that flows directly from the love of God. Christ prays for those slandering him while he suffered on the cross (AMBROSE). Jesus implies that the violence of being struck on the cheek is not punishment for a criminal act but comes from persecution.[1] To accomplish the unnatural act of nonresistance requires patience (AUGUSTINE). Disciples must be prepared to be treated violently and stripped of their clothes and their material goods. The merciful person suffers injustice (ISAAC OF NINEVEH). If people have the mind of Christ, as taught in the Beatitudes, then they will accept such persecution as to be expected because Christ is the fulfillment of the law and through his blood he has transformed the law (EPHREM THE SYRIAN). Stephen, the first Christian martyr, shows how he follows Christ's example by loving his enemies (CYPRIAN). The hearer cannot help but think of Jesus' passion, when he willingly was beaten and stripped. Jesus wants them to go beyond mere reciprocity into gift giving. But it is a gift and a loan, a gift from us but a loan because what we lend has been given to us by the Lord (BASIL THE GREAT).

God has left the deposit of his divine image and likeness in us, and this divine image is seen in those who are merciful as the Father in heaven is merciful (ORIGEN). Mercy is an attribute of God (CYRIL OF ALEXANDRIA). All these verses characterize God as merciful to the just and the unjust (JUSTIN MARTYR).

After a great climax in the sermon, "Become merciful, just as your Father is merciful,"[2] there come practical examples of how this mercy is to be shown to others, namely, sacrificing the desire for vengeance and seeking compassion for the neighbor (AUGUSTINE). Sinners cannot judge sinners. Instead of judging others, one must consider his own misdoings (CYRIL OF ALEXANDRIA). Jesus' disciples are to portray God's character to the world and are to judge with justice and forgive with grace (EPHREM THE SYRIAN).

The mercy of Jesus expresses itself in two ways: forgiveness and generosity, the two forms of almsgiving and the two wings of prayer. Forgiveness is expressed through acts of mercy because of the mercy, charity and forgiveness that come from the Lord. This forgiveness spills over into generosity that overflows in abundance because it comes from God—the kind of generosity whereby Christians become granaries for the poor (AUGUSTINE). God's bounty is a paradox, especially as he uses human standards to describe his own gift-giving (CYRIL OF ALEXANDRIA).

6:27-34 Eight Imperatives: Love Your Enemies

[1]See 1 Pet 4:13-16. [2]Lk 6:36.

To Love Your Enemies Is to Love the World.

AUGUSTINE: We are also prohibited both from loving that world and, if we understand rightly, are commanded to love it. We are prohibited, of course, where it is said to us, "Do not love the world."[3] But we are commanded when it is said to us, "Love your enemies." They are the world, which hates us. Therefore we are both prohibited from loving in it what the world itself loves, and we are commanded to love in it what the world hates, namely, the handiwork of God and the various comforts of his goodness. We are prohibited from loving the fault in it and are commanded to love its nature. The world loves the fault in itself and hates its nature. So we rightly love and hate it, although it perversely loves and hates itself. TRACTATES ON THE GOSPEL OF JOHN 87.4.[4]

The Custom of Christians Only.

TERTULLIAN: To love friends is the custom for all people, but to love enemies is customary only for Christians. To SCAPULA 1.[5]

The Virtue of Charity.

AMBROSE: Love is commanded when it is said, "Love your enemies," so that the saying which was uttered already before the church may be fulfilled: "Set in order love in me."[6] For love is set in order when the precepts of love are formed. See how it began from the heights and cast the law undeneath the backs of the gospel's blessing. The law commands the revenge of punishment.[7] The gospel bestows love for hostility, benevolence for hatred, prayer for curses, help for the persecuted, patience for the hungry and grace of reward. How much more perfect the athlete who does not feel injury! EXPOSITION OF THE GOSPEL OF LUKE 5.73.[8]

On the Cross, Christ Prays for His Slanderers.

AMBROSE: What Christ said in word, he proved also by example. Indeed, when he was on the cross, he said in reference to his persecutors who were slandering him, "Father, forgive them, for they do not know what they are doing," so that he might pray for his slanderers, although he could have forgiven them himself. THE PRAYER OF JOB AND DAVID 2.2.6.[9]

To Turn the Other Cheek Requires Patience.

AUGUSTINE: Temporal goods are to be despised in favor of eternal ones, as things on the left are to be despised in favor of those on the right. This has always been the aim of the holy martyrs. A final just vengeance is looked for, that is, the last supreme judgment, only when no chance of correction remains. But now we must be on our guard, more than anything else, not to lose patience in our eagerness to be justified, for patience is to be more highly prized than anything an enemy can take from us against our will. LETTER 138.[10]

The Merciful Person Suffers Injustice.

ISAAC OF NINEVEH: When a man overcomes justice by mercy, he is crowned, though not with crowns awarded under the Law to the righteous, but with the crowns of the perfect who are under the Gospel. For, the ancient Law also dictates that a man must give to the poor from his own means, and clothe the naked, and love his neighbour as himself, and forbids injustice and lying. But the perfection of the Gospel's dispensation commands the following: "Give to every man that asketh of thee, and of him that taketh away thy goods ask them not again." And further, a man must not merely with joy suffer injustice as regards his possessions and the rest of the external things which come upon him, but he must also lay down his life for his brother. This is the merciful man. ASCETICAL HOMILIES 4.[11]

Old Testament Law Transformed.

EPHREM THE SYRIAN: "An eye for an eye" is the perfection of justice. "Whoever strikes you on the cheek, turn the other to him" is the consummation of grace. While both continually have their criteria, he proposed them to us through the two successive Testaments. The first Testament had the killing of animals for compensation, because

---

[3]1 Jn 2:15. [4]FC 90:149-50*. [5]FC 10:151. [6]Song 2:4. [7]See Ex 21:23-36. [8]*EHG 173**. [9]FC 65:356*. [10]FC 20:45*. [11]AHSIS 30.

justice did not permit that one should die in place of another. The second Testament was established through the blood of a man, who through his grace gave himself on behalf of all.[12] One therefore was the beginning, and the other the completion. He in whom are both the end and the beginning is perfect. In the case of those who do not understand, the beginning and end are estranged one from the other. In the study of them, however, they are one.

Therefore this principle of a blow for a blow[13] has indeed been transformed. If you strive for perfection, whoever strikes you, turn to him the other [cheek]. COMMENTARY ON TATIAN'S DIATESSARON 6.11B-12.[14]

STEPHEN IS AN EXAMPLE OF LOVE FOR ENEMIES. CYPRIAN: How will you love your enemies and pray for your adversaries and persecutors?[15] We see what happened in the case of Stephen. When he was being killed by the violence and stones of the Jews, he did not ask for vengeance but forgiveness for his murderers, saying: "O Lord, do not lay this sin against them."[16] So it was most fitting that the first martyr for Christ who, in preceding by his glorious death the martyrs that were to come, was not only a preacher of the Lord's suffering but also an imitator of his most patient gentleness. THE GOOD OF PATIENCE 16.[17]

LEND WITHOUT HOPE OF RECEIVING. BASIL THE GREAT: "Lend to those from whom you do not hope to receive in return." "And what sort of a loan is this," he says, "to which there is no hope of a return attached?" Consider the force of the statement, and you will admire the kindness of the Lawmaker. When you have the intention of providing for a poor person for the Lord's sake, it is at the same time both a gift and a loan. It is a gift because of the expectation of no repayment, but a loan because of the great gift of the Master who pays in his place and who, receiving trifling things through a poor person, will give great things in return for them. HOMILY ON PSALM 14.[18]

6:35-36 Imitate God

THE DIVINE IMAGE SEEN IN HUMAN MERCY. ORIGEN: The traces of the divine image are clearly recognized not through the likeness of the body, which undergoes corruption, but through the intelligence of the soul. We see the divine image in its righteousness, temperance, courage, wisdom, discipline, and through the entire chorus of virtues that are present essentially in God. These can be in people through effort and the imitation of God, as also the Lord points out in the Gospel when he says, "Be merciful, even as your Father is merciful" and "Be perfect, as your Father is perfect."[19] ON FIRST PRINCIPLES 4.10.[20]

MERCY AN ATTRIBUTE OF GOD. CYRIL OF ALEXANDRIA: Closely neighboring, so to speak, upon the virtues which we have just mentioned is compassion, of which he next makes mention. For it is a most excelling thing, and very pleasing to God, and in the highest degree proper for pious souls. It may suffice for us to imprint upon our mind that compassion is an attribute of the divine nature. "Be merciful," he says, "as your heavenly Father is merciful." COMMENTARY ON LUKE, HOMILY 29.[21]

MERCY ON THE JUST AND THE UNJUST. JUSTIN MARTYR: We pray for you that you might experience the mercy of Christ. He instructed us to pray for our enemies, when he said, "Be kind and merciful, even as your heavenly Father is merciful." We can observe that almighty God is kind and merciful, causing his sun to shine on the ungrateful and on the just and sending rain to both the holy and the evil. All of them, he has told us, he will judge.[22] DIALOGUE WITH TRYPHO 96.[23]

6:37-38 Four Imperatives: Do Not Judge

---

[12]See Heb 9:11-14. [13]See Ex 21:24; Lev 24:20. [14]ECTD 115-16**. [15]Mt 5:44. [16]Acts 7:58-60. [17]FC 36:278. [18]FC 46:190**. [19]Mt 5:48. [20]OSW 216*. [21]CGSL 133**. [22]See Mt 5:45. [23]FC 6:299-300**.

THE PRACTICE OF MERCY. AUGUSTINE: The practice of mercy is twofold: when vengeance is sacrificed and when compassion is shown. The Lord included both of these in his brief sentence: "Forgive, and you shall be forgiven; give, and it shall be given to you." This work has the effect of purifying the heart, so that, even under the limitations of this life, we are enabled with pure mind to see the immutable reality of God. There is something holding us back, which has to be loosed so that our sight may break through to the light. In connection with this the Lord said, "Give alms, and behold, all things are clean to you."[24] Therefore the next and sixth step is that cleansing of the heart. LETTER 171A.[25]

DO NOT JUDGE, BUT CONSIDER YOUR OWN MISDOINGS. CYRIL OF ALEXANDRIA: He cuts away from our minds a very unmanageable passion, the commencement and begetter of pride. While it is people's duty to examine themselves and to order their conduct according to God's will, they leave this alone to busy themselves with the affairs of others. He that judges the brother, as the disciple of Christ says, speaks against the law and judges the law.[26] The lawgiver and judge are One. The judge of the sinning soul must be higher than that soul. Since you are not, the sinner will object to you as judge. Why judge your neighbor? But if you venture to condemn him, having no authority to do it, it is yourself rather that will be condemned, because the law does not permit you to judge others.

Whoever therefore is guided by good sense, does not look at the sins of others, does not busy himself about the faults of his neighbor, but closely reviews his own misdoings. Such was the blessed psalmist, falling down before God and saying on account of his own offenses, "If you, Lord, closely regard iniquities, who can endure?"[27] Once again, putting forward the infirmity of human nature as an excuse, he prays for a reasonable pardon, saying, "Remember that we are dirt."[28] COMMENTARY ON LUKE, HOMILY 29.[29]

JUDGE FROM JUSTICE, FORGIVE FROM GRACE. EPHREM THE SYRIAN: Do not judge, that is, unjustly, so that you may not be judged, with regard to injustice. With the judgment that you judge shall you be judged.[30] This is like the phrase "Forgive, and it will be forgiven you." For once someone has judged in accordance with justice, he should forgive in accordance with grace, so that when he himself is judged in accordance with justice, he may be worthy of forgiveness through grace. Alternatively, it was on account of the judges, those who seek vengeance for themselves, that he said, "Do not condemn." That is, do not seek vengeance for yourselves. Or, do not judge, from appearances and opinion and then condemn, but admonish and advise. COMMENTARY ON TATIAN'S DIATESSARON 6.18B.[31]

TWO KINDS OF ALMSGIVING: GIVING AND FORGIVING. AUGUSTINE: The Christian soul understands how far removed he should be from theft of another's goods when he realizes that failure to share his surplus with the needy is like to theft. The Lord says, "Give, and it shall be given to you. Forgive, and you shall be forgiven." Let us graciously and fervently perform these two types of almsgiving, that is, giving and forgiving, for we in turn pray the Lord to give us good things and not to repay our evil deeds. SERMON 206.2.[32]

TWO WINGS OF PRAYER. AUGUSTINE: "Forgive, and you will be forgiven." "Give, and it will be given you." These are the two wings of prayer, on which it flies to God. Pardon the offender what has been committed, and give to the person in need. SERMON 205.3.[33]

MERCY, CHARITY AND FORGIVENESS. AUGUSTINE: So there is hope in God's mercy, if our misery is not so barren as to yield no work of mercy. What do you want from the Lord? Mercy.

---

[24]Lk 11:41. [25]FC 30:70*. [26]Jas 4:11. [27]Ps 129:3. [28]Ps 102:14. [29]CGSL 137-38**. [30]Mt 7:2. [31]JSSS 2:122*. [32]FC 38:87. [33]WSA 3 6:105.

Give, and it shall be given to you. What do you want from the Lord? Pardon. Forgive, and you will be forgiven. SERMON 179A.1.[34]

CHRISTIANS ARE THE GRANARIES OF THE POOR. AUGUSTINE:

You give alms. You receive alms. You pardon. You are pardoned. You are generous. You are treated generously. Listen to God saying, "Forgive, and you will be forgiven. Give, and things will be given to you."

Keep the poor in mind. I say this to all of you. Give alms, my brothers and sisters, and you won't lose what you give. Trust God. I'm not only telling you you won't lose what you do for the poor, but I'm telling you plainly, this is all that you won't lose. . . . Come now, let's see if you can cheer the poor up today. You be their granaries, so that God may give to you what you can give to them, and so that he may forgive whatever sins

you have committed. SERMON 376A.3.[35]

THE PARADOX OF GOD'S BOUNTY. CYRIL OF ALEXANDRIA:

He has given us full assurance that God, who gives all things abundantly to those who love him, shall reward us with bountiful hand. He said, "Good measure, and squeezed down, and running over shall they give into your bosom." He added this too, "For with what measure you give, it shall be measured to you." There is, however, an apparent incompatibility between the two declarations. If we are to receive good measure, and squeezed down, and running over, how shall we be paid back the same measure we give? For this implies an equal reward, and not one of far-surpassing abundance. COMMENTARY ON LUKE, HOMILY 29.[36]

---

[34]WSA 3 5:306. [35]WSA 3 10:350*. [36]CGSL 133-34**.

6:39-46 THE GOAL OF CATECHETICAL LECTURES

[39]He also told them a parable: "Can a blind man lead a blind man? Will they not both fall into a pit? [40]A disciple is not above his teacher, but every one when he is fully taught will be like his teacher. [41]Why do you see the speck that is in your brother's eye, but do not notice the log that is in your own eye? [42]Or how can you say to your brother, 'Brother, let me take out the speck that is in your eye,' when you yourself do not see the log that is in your own eye? You hypocrite, first take the log out of your own eye, and then you will see clearly to take out the speck that is in your brother's eye.

[43]"For no good tree bears bad fruit, nor again does a bad tree bear good fruit; [44]for each tree is known by its own fruit. For figs are not gathered from thorns, nor are grapes picked from a bramble bush. [45]The good man out of the good treasure of his heart produces good, and the evil man out of his evil treasure produces evil; for out of the abundance of the heart his mouth speaks.

[46]"Why do you call me 'Lord, Lord,' and not do what I tell you?"

OVERVIEW: There is a natural transition between the prohibition against judging and the parables that follow, since they illustrate what Jesus has been saying. Undue judgment and criticism lead to hypocrisy and are not to be tolerated (CYRIL OF ALEXANDRIA).

The good tree is the Holy Spirit, and the bad tree is the devil and his angels (ORIGEN). One's fruits, that is, deeds and words, reveal that person's character and state of heart (CYRIL OF ALEXANDRIA).

The tabernacle and the temple illustrate how a firm foundation is necessary for a solid building, for both these structures serve as an image of the universal church that produces Jews and Gentiles, who in turn are characterized by works and faith. It is difficult to judge one's thought and intentions, for they are determined by the disposition of the heart. A lesser deed produces a great reward and a more significant act a lesser reward, as the widow's mite illustrates, as well as the example of those hypocrites who cry out "Lord, Lord" (BEDE).

6:39-42 Sight Instead of Blindness

PARABLES ILLUSTRATE JESUS' TEACHING.
CYRIL OF ALEXANDRIA: This parable he added as a most necessary attachment to what had been said. The blessed disciples were about to be the initiators and teachers of the world. It was necessary for them therefore to prove themselves possessed of everything piety requires. They must know the pathway of the evangelic mode of life and be workmen ready for every good work. They must be able to bestow upon well-instructed hearers such correct and saving teaching as exactly represents the truth. This they must do, as having already first received their sight and a mind illuminated with the divine light, lest they should be blind leaders of the blind. It is not possible for those enveloped in the darkness of ignorance to guide those who are afflicted in the same way into the knowledge of the truth. Should they attempt it, they will both roll into the ditch of carelessness.

He overthrew the bragging passion of boastfulness, which most give way, that they may not enviously strive to surpass their teachers in honor. He added, "The disciple is not above his teacher." Even if some make such progress, as to attain to a virtue that rivals that of their teachers,

they will range themselves no higher than their level and be their imitators. Paul shall again support us. He says, "Imitate me, as I also imitate Christ."[1] COMMENTARY ON LUKE, HOMILY 29.[2]

HYPOCRITES DO NOT SEE THE MOTE IN THEIR OWN EYES.
CYRIL OF ALEXANDRIA: He had previously shown us that judging others is utterly wicked and dangerous. It causes final condemnation. "Do not judge," he said, "and you shall not be judged." Do not condemn, and you shall not be condemned. By conclusive arguments, he persuades us to avoid the very wish of judging others. Deliver yourself first from your great crimes and your rebellious passions, and then you may set him right who is guilty of only minor offenses COMMENTARY ON LUKE, HOMILY 33.[3]

6:43-46 Transformation: Good Fruit Instead of Bad Fruit

THE GOOD AND BAD TREES.
ORIGEN: "The good tree" is the Holy Spirit. The "bad tree" is the devil and his underlings. The person who has the Holy Spirit manifests the fruits of the Spirit, which the apostle describes when he says, "The fruit of the Spirit is love, joy, peace, patience, kindness, goodness, faith, gentleness, self-control."[4] The one who has the opposing power brings forth briars and thistles, the passions of dishonor. FRAGMENTS ON LUKE 112.[5]

CHARACTER IS SHOWN BY THE DEEDS IN ONE'S LIFE.
CYRIL OF ALEXANDRIA: See again, Christ commands that those who come to us must be distinguished not by their clothing but by what they really are. "By its fruit," he says, "the tree is known." It is ignorance and folly for us to expect to find the choicer kinds of fruits on thorns, grapes for instance, and figs. So it is ridiculous for us to imagine that we can find in hypocrites and the profane anything that is admirable,

---

[1] 1 Cor 11:1. [2] CGSL 138**. [3] CGSL 139*. [4] Gal 5:22-23. [5] FC 94:172-73*.

such as the nobleness of virtue. . . .

This is also made clear by another declaration of our Lord. "The good man," he says, "as out of a good treasure, pours forth from the heart, good things." One who is differently disposed, and whose mind is the prey of fraud and wickedness, necessarily brings forth what is concealed deep within. The things that are in the mind and heart boil over and are vomited forth by the stream of speech that flows out of it. The virtuous person therefore speaks such things as become his character, while one who is worthless and wicked vomits forth his secret impurity. COMMENTARY ON LUKE, HOMILY 33.[6]

HUMAN BEINGS ARE TREES; THEIR WORKS ARE THE FRUIT. BEDE: "Every tree which does not bear fruit will be cut down and cast into the fire."[7] He is referring to human beings as trees and to their works as the fruit. Do you want to know which are the bad trees and what are the bad fruits? The apostle teaches us this. He says, "The works of the flesh are manifest: they are fornication, impurity, self-indulgence, idolatry, sorcery, malice, strife, jealousy, anger, quarrels, conflict, factions, envy, murder, drunkenness, carousing, and things of this sort."[8] Do you want to hear whether trees which bring forth fruits such as these belong in the heavenly temple of the eternal King? The apostle continues: "I warn you, as I warned you before, that those who do such things will not attain the kingdom of God."[9] He subsequently lists the fruits of a good tree. He says, "The fruit, however,

of the Spirit is charity, joy, peace, patience, goodness, kindness, faith, gentleness, self-control."[10] HOMILIES ON THE GOSPELS 2.25.[11]

THE DISPOSITION OF THE HEART DETERMINES THE NATURE OF THE FRUIT. BEDE: "The good man produces good from the good treasure in his heart, and the evil man produces evil from the evil treasure." The treasure in one's heart is the intention of the thought, from which the Searcher of hearts judges the outcome. . . . Christ subsequently adds force to his pronouncement by clearly showing that good speech without the additional attestation of deeds is of no advantage at all. He asks, "And why do you call me, 'Lord, Lord,' and not do what I say?" To call upon the Lord seems to be the gift of a good treasure, the fruit of a good tree. "For everyone who calls upon the name of the Lord will be saved."[12] If anyone who calls upon the name of the Lord resists the Lord's commands by living perversely, it is evident that the good that the tongue has spoken has not been brought out of the good treasure in his heart. It was not the root of a fig tree but that of a thorn bush that produced the fruit of such a confession—a conscience, that is, bristling with vices, and not one filled with the sweetness of the love of the Lord. HOMILIES ON THE GOSPELS 2.25.[13]

---

[6]CGSL 140-41**. [7]Mt 3:10. [8]Gal 5:19-21. [9]Gal 5:19. [10]Gal 5:22-23. [11]CS 111:257**. [12]Joel 2:32; Acts 2:21; Rom 10:13. [13]CS 111:259-60*.

6:47-49 A FIRM FOUNDATION

[47]*Every one who comes to me and hears my words and does them, I will show you what he is like:* [48]*he is like a man building a house, who dug deep, and laid the foundation upon rock; and when a flood arose, the stream broke against that house, and could not shake it, because it had been well built."* [49]*But he who hears and does not do them is like a man who built a house on the ground*

without a foundation; against which the stream broke, and immediately it fell, and the ruin of that house was great."

w Other ancient authorities read *founded upon the rock*

OVERVIEW: The builder of the house on a rock is Christ, and the house that he builds is the church. The firm foundation that is deep and on a rock is the catechetical teaching of Jesus, the patriarchs and prophets and the apostolic church (BEDE), for Scripture is the field in which we build the house on the rock of Christ (AUGUSTINE). Christians build on the foundation of virtues Christ won for us with his life, death and resurrection (AMBROSE).

6:47-49 *The House Built on a Rock*

CHRIST IS THE BUILDER; THE FOUNDATION IS SOLID. BEDE: The Lord indicates what the true distinction between good and bad fruits is by continuing under another figure of speech. He says, "Everyone who comes to me and listens to my words and does them, I will show you who he is like. He is like a man building a house." Now this man building a house is the mediator between God and humankind, the man Christ Jesus,[1] who deigned to build and consecrate a beloved and holy house for himself, namely, the church, in which to remain forever.

"He dug deep, and laid the foundation upon rock," for he strove to root out completely whatever base drives he found in the hearts of his faithful. When the traces of earlier habits and unnecessary thoughts had been cast out, he could have a firm and unshakable dwelling place in them. He himself is the rock upon which he laid the foundation for a house of this sort. Just as in building a house nothing is to be preferred to the rock on which the foundation is laid, so holy church has its rock, namely, Christ, concealed in the depths of its heart. . . .

"When a flood came, the stream was dashed against that house and could not shake it, for it had been founded upon the rock." The explanation is obvious: the church is often struck by distressful situations but is not overthrown. If any believers are overcome by evils, if they yield, they surely did not belong to this house. If they had taken a stand founded on the rock of faith instead of on the sand of faithlessness, they would have been absolutely incapable of ever being shaken. HOMILIES ON THE GOSPELS 2.25.[2]

SCRIPTURE IS THE FIELD WHERE WE BUILD THE HOUSE. AUGUSTINE: In a certain place in the Gospel, the Lord says that the wise hearer of his word ought to be like a man who, wishing to build, digs rather deeply until he comes to bedrock. There without anxiety he establishes what he builds against the onrush of a flood, so that when it comes, rather it may be pushed back by the solidity of the building than that house collapse by the impact. Let us consider the Scripture of God as being a field where we want to build something. Let us not be lazy or content with the surface. Let us dig more deeply until we come to rock: "Now the rock was Christ."[3] TRACTATES ON THE GOSPEL OF JOHN 23.1.[4]

BUILT ON THE FOUNDATION OF VIRTUES. AMBROSE: He teaches that the foundation of the virtues is obedience of heavenly instructions, whereby this house of ours cannot be shaken by the flow of desires, by the assault of spiritual wickedness,[5] by the rain of the world or the dark arguments of heretics. EXPOSITION OF THE GOSPEL OF LUKE 5.82.[6]

---

[1] 1 Tim 2:5. [2] CS 111:260-61*. [3] Cf. 1 Cor 10:4. [4] FC 79:212**. [5] See Eph 6:12. [6] EHG 177*.

7:1-10 THE HEALING
OF THE CENTURION'S SLAVE

¹*After he had ended all his sayings in the hearing of the people he entered Capernaum.* ²*Now a centurion had a slave who was dear^x to him, who was sick and at the point of death.* ³*When he heard of Jesus, he sent to him elders of the Jews, asking him to come and heal his slave.* ⁴*And when they came to Jesus, they besought him earnestly, saying, "He is worthy to have you do this for him,* ⁵*for he loves our nation, and he built us our synagogue."* ⁶*And Jesus went with them. When he was not far from the house, the centurion sent friends to him, saying to him, "Lord, do not trouble yourself, for I am not worthy to have you come under my roof;* ⁷*therefore I did not presume to come to you. But say the word, and let my servant be healed.* ⁸*For I am a man set under authority, with soldiers under me: and I say to one, 'Go,' and he goes; and to another, 'Come,' and he comes; and to my slave, 'Do this,' and he does it."* ⁹*When Jesus heard this he marveled at him, and turned and said to the multitude that followed him, "I tell you, not even in Israel have I found such faith."* ¹⁰*And when those who had been sent returned to the house, they found the slave well.*

x Or *valuable*

OVERVIEW: Jesus shows love for enemies by healing the slave of a Gentile centurion (AMBROSE). The Jewish elders, representing Israel, commend the centurion to Jesus because he built a synagogue where God was present in his Word (MAXIMUS OF TURIN). Soldiers are capable of being faithful followers of Jesus, as this centurion and Cornelius[1] clearly show (AUGUSTINE). Unworthy, he becomes worthy (EPHREM THE SYRIAN). Instead of being a soldier for the emperor, he now becomes a soldier of peace for Jesus (MAXIMUS OF TURIN). At the same time, however, Jesus shows his humility in healing the centurion's slave (AMBROSE).

7:1-2 A Valued Slave

JESUS DEMONSTRATES LOVE FOR ENEMIES.
AMBROSE: The servant of a Gentile centurion is immediately brought to the Lord for healing; this represented the people of the nations who were held in the bonds of worldly slavery, sick with deadly passions, to be cleansed by the Lord's blessing. The Evangelist did not err in saying that he was at the point of death, for he would have died if Christ would not have healed him. He fulfilled the rule with heavenly love, he who so loved his enemies that he snatched them from death and admitted them to the hope of eternal salvation. EXPOSITION OF THE GOSPEL OF LUKE 5.83.[2]

7:3-5 The Jewish Elders

THE CENTURION BUILT A SYNAGOGUE FOR GOD'S PRESENCE. MAXIMUS OF TURIN: In order to praise the centurion more, the Jews said to the Lord, "It is right that you should help him, for he is a lover of our nation, and he himself has built us a synagogue." If one who has constructed a place where Christ is always denied is visited with heavenly mercy, how much more to be visited is one who has built a tabernacle where Christ is daily preached! The Lord did not approve the

---

[1]Acts 10:1—11:30. [2]EHG 177*.

work that the centurion had done but the spirit in which he accomplished it. If he eagerly built a synagogue at a time when there were as yet no Christians, it is understood that he would all the more eagerly have built a church had there been Christians. He still preaches Christ even though he builds a synagogue. SERMON 87.1.[3]

7:6-9 The Centurion

AN EXAMPLE OF A FAITHFUL SOLDIER. AUGUSTINE: Do not imagine that someone cannot please God while he is engaged in military service. Take as an example holy David to whom the Lord gave such high testimony. Many just men of that time were soldiers. The centurion was the soldier who said to the Lord, "I am not worthy that you should enter under my roof, but only say the word and my servant shall be healed." LETTER 189.[4]

THE FIRST GENTILE TO HAVE FAITH. EPHREM THE SYRIAN: "I am not worthy that you should enter my house. I am not capable of receiving the Sun of Righteousness in its entirety; a little radiance from it is sufficient for me to remove sickness, as it does for the darkness." When our Lord heard this, he marveled at him. God marveled at a human being. He said to those who were near him, "Truly, I say to you, not even in anyone among the house of Israel have I found this kind of faith." . . . The centurion had brought them, and he came so that they would be advocates on his behalf. He rebuked them because they did not possess his faith. To show that the centurion's faith was the first of the faith of the Gentiles, he said, "Do not imagine that this faith can be limited to the centurion." For he saw and believed.[5] "Many will believe who have not seen."[6] "Many

will come from the east and from the west and will sit at table with Abraham, Isaac and Jacob in the kingdom of heaven, etc."[7] COMMENTARY ON TATIAN'S DIATESSARON 6.22B.[8]

A SOLDIER OF PEACE FOR THE SAVIOR. MAXIMUS OF TURIN: See how the devout centurion becomes worthier to receive health as he confesses that he is unworthy. In considering his dwelling unacceptable, he has made it the more honorable and acceptable. . . . The Lord does not go to his house, but the Lord's healing goes. The Savior does not visit the sick man, but the Savior's health visits him. SERMON 87.[9]

7:10 The Slave Is Healed

HEALING THE CENTURION'S SLAVE A SIGN OF HUMILITY. AMBROSE: How great is the sign of divine humility, that the Lord of heaven by no means disdained to visit the centurion's servant! Faith is revealed in deeds, but humanity is more active in compassion. Surely he did not act this way because he could not cure in his absence, but in order to give you a form of humility for imitation he taught the need to defer to the small and the great alike. In another place he says to the ruler, "Go, your son lives,"[10] that you may know both the power of Divinity and the grace of humility. In that case he refused to go to the ruler's son, lest he seem to have had regard for riches. In this case he went himself lest he seem to have despised the humble rank of the centurion's servant. All of us, slave and free, are one in Christ.[11] EXPOSITION OF THE GOSPEL OF LUKE 5.84.[12]

---

[3]ACW 50:255-56**. [4]FC 30:268*. [5]Jn 20:8. [6]Jn 20:29. [7]Mt 8:11. [8]ECTD 125-26*. [9]ACW 50:256-57**. [10]Jn 4:50. [11]See Gal 3:28, Col 3:11. [12]EHG 177*.

7:11-17 THE RAISING OF THE WIDOW'S SON

¹¹*Soon afterward*^y *he went to a city called Nain, and his disciples and a great crowd went with him.* ¹²*As he drew near to the gate of the city, behold, a man who had died was being carried out, the only son of his mother, and she was a widow; and a large crowd from the city was with her.* ¹³*And when the Lord saw her, he had compassion on her and said to her, "Do not weep."* ¹⁴*And he came and touched the bier, and the bearers stood still. And he said, "Young man, I say to you, arise."* ¹⁵*And the dead man sat up, and began to speak. And he gave him to his mother.* ¹⁶*Fear seized them all; and they glorified God, saying, "A great prophet has arisen among us!" and "God has visited his people!"* ¹⁷*And this report concerning him spread through the whole of Judea and all the surrounding country.*

y Other ancient authorities read *Next day*

OVERVIEW: Luke connects this resurrection from the dead with the previous healing to show that the raising of the dead is the miracle that demonstrates that Jesus is the fulfillment of the Old Testament prophetic hope and that with him the messianic age has dawned (CYRIL OF ALEXANDRIA). The one who died was the only son of the woman, and she is a widow, drawing the hearer into emotional involvement in the story. Jesus, the Virgin's son, meets the widow's son (EPHREM THE SYRIAN). The dead man meets Jesus, the life and the resurrection (CYRIL OF ALEXANDRIA). The weeping of the woman moves Jesus to compassion, just as the mother of the church now intercedes for us in our grief (AMBROSE). The power of holiness and of life is in him, for it is the holy body of Jesus, the Word made flesh, that brings salvation to this dead man and to all of humanity. At this point, the miracle causes Jesus' fame to spread throughout Judea and the surrounding territory (CYRIL OF ALEXANDRIA).

7:11-12 The Setting

THE DEAD RESTORED TO LIFE. CYRIL OF ALEXANDRIA: Observe how he joins miracle to miracle. In the former instance, the healing of the centurion's servant, he was present by invitation, but here he draws near without being invited. No one summoned him to restore the dead man to life, but he comes to do so of his own accord. He seems to me to have purposely made this miracle also follow upon the former. COMMENTARY ON LUKE, HOMILY 36.[1]

THE VIRGIN'S SON MEETS THE WIDOW'S SON. EPHREM THE SYRIAN: The Virgin's son met the widow's son. He became like a sponge for her tears and as life for the death of her son. Death turned about in its den and turned its back on the victorious one. COMMENTARY ON TATIAN'S DIATESSARON 6.23.[2]

THE DEAD MAN MEETS THE LIFE AND THE RESURRECTION. CYRIL OF ALEXANDRIA: The dead man was being buried, and many friends were conducting him to his tomb. Christ, the life and resurrection, meets him there. He is the Destroyer of death and of corruption. He is the One in whom we live and move and are.[3] He is who has restored the nature of man to that which it originally was and has set free our death-fraught flesh from the bonds of death. He had mercy upon the woman, and that her tears might be

---

[1]*CGSL* 153*. [2]*ECTD* 126. [3]Acts 17:28.

stopped, he commanded saying, "Weep not." Immediately the cause of her weeping was done away. COMMENTARY ON LUKE, HOMILY 36.[4]

7:13-15 The Compassion and the Miracle

THE CHURCH, THE SORROWING MOTHER. AMBROSE: Although there is grave sin that you cannot wash away yourself with the tears of your penitence, let the mother of the church weep for you. She who intercedes for all as a widowed mother for only sons is she who suffers with the spiritual grief of nature when she perceives her children urged on to death by mortal sins. We are heart of her heart, for there is also a spiritual heart that Paul has, saying, "Yes, brother, I want some benefit from you in the Lord. Refresh my heart in Christ."[5] We are the heart of the church, since we are members of his Body, of his flesh and of his bones.[6] Let the pious mother grieve, let the crowd, too, help. Let not only the crowd but also a multitude feel pity for a good parent. Already at the funeral you will arise, already will you be released from the sepulcher; the attendants at your funeral will stand still, you will begin to speak words of life, all will be afraid; for very many are corrected by the example of one. They will praise God, who has bestowed upon us such great help for the avoidance of death. EXPOSITION OF THE GOSPEL OF LUKE 5.92.[7]

THE HOLY BODY OF JESUS BRINGS SALVATION. CYRIL OF ALEXANDRIA: Christ raised him who was descending to his grave. The manner of his rising is plain to see. "He touched," it says, "the bier and said, 'Young man, I say unto thee, arise.'" How was not a word enough for raising him who was lying there? What is so difficult to it or past accomplishment? What is more powerful than the Word of God? Why then did he not work the miracle by only a word but also touched the bier? It was, my beloved, that you might learn that the holy body of Christ is productive for the salvation of man. The flesh of the almighty Word is the body of life and was clothed with his might. Consider that iron when brought into contact with fire produces the effects of fire and fulfills its functions. The flesh of Christ also has the power of giving life and annihilates the influence of death and corruption because it is the flesh of the Word, who gives life to all. May our Lord Jesus Christ also touch us that delivering us from evil works, even from fleshly lusts, he may unite us to the assemblies of the saints. COMMENTARY ON LUKE, HOMILY 36.[8]

7:16-17 The Response of the People

THE NEWS SPREAD EVERYWHERE. CYRIL OF ALEXANDRIA: Let it be known to people everywhere that the Lord is God, and even though he appeared in a form like us, yet has he given us the indications of a godlike power and majesty on many occasions and in a multitude of ways. He drove away diseases and rebuked unclean spirits. He gave the blind their sight. Finally, he even expelled death itself from the bodies of men, death that cruelly and mercilessly had tyrannized humankind from Adam even to Moses, according to the expression of the divine Paul.[9] That widow's son at Nain arose unexpectedly and wonderfully. The miracle did not remain unknown to everyone throughout Judea but was announced abroad as a divine sign, and admiration was upon every tongue. COMMENTARY ON LUKE, HOMILY 37.[10]

---

[4]CGSL 153*. [5]Philem 20. [6]Eph 5:30; cf. 1 Cor 12:12. [7]EHG 180. [8]CGSL 155**. [9]Rom 5:14. [10]CGSL 156**.

7:18-35 JOHN THE BAPTIST AND JESUS

[18]The disciples of John told him of all these things. [19]And John, calling to him two of his disciples, sent them to the Lord, saying, "Are you he who is to come, or shall we look for another?" [20]And when the men had come to him, they said, "John the Baptist has sent us to you, saying, 'Are you he who is to come, or shall we look for another?'" [21]In that hour he cured many of diseases and plagues and evil spirits, and on many that were blind he bestowed sight. [22]And he answered them, "Go and tell John what you have seen and heard: the blind receive their sight, the lame walk, lepers are cleansed, and the deaf hear, the dead are raised up, the poor have good news preached to them. [23]And blessed is he who takes no offense at me."

[24]When the messengers of John had gone, he began to speak to the crowds concerning John: "What did you go out into the wilderness to behold? A reed shaken by the wind? [25]What then did you go out to see? A man clothed in soft clothing? Behold, those who are gorgeously appareled and live in luxury are in kings' courts. [26]What then did you go out to see? A prophet? Yes, I tell you, and more than a prophet. [27]This is he of whom it is written,

'Behold, I send my messenger before thy face,

who shall prepare thy way before thee.'

[28]I tell you, among those born of women none is greater than John; yet he who is least in the kingdom of God is greater than he." [29](When they heard this all the people and the tax collectors justified God, having been baptized with the baptism of John; [30]but the Pharisees and the lawyers rejected the purpose of God for themselves, not having been baptized by him.)

[31]"To what then shall I compare the men of this generation, and what are they like? [32]They are like children sitting in the market place and calling to one another,

'We piped to you, and you did not dance;

we wailed, and you did not weep.'

[33]For John the Baptist has come eating no bread and drinking no wine; and you say, 'He has a demon.' [34]The Son of man has come eating and drinking; and you say, 'Behold, a glutton and a drunkard, a friend of tax collectors and sinners!' [35]Yet wisdom is justified by all her children."

OVERVIEW: John sends his disciples to confirm his own preaching about Jesus, so that before he died, his disciples would be strengthened and not be scattered like sheep without a shepherd (EPHREM THE SYRIAN). The progress or manner of Jesus' ministry has not been what John expected, for John is a type of the law who confines hearts in prison as the world awaits the coming of the Messiah who is the fullness of the law (AMBROSE).

Instead of responding to the question of John's disciples by saying "I am the Messiah," Jesus performs miracles that testify that he is "the coming One" (CYRIL OF ALEXANDRIA). By highlighting the miracles, Luke affirms that the Old Testament is being fulfilled as Isaiah had foretold (CHRYSOSTOM). The stumbling block that could cause observers to be scandalized is Jesus' humility in fulfillment of the prophecies of the Old Testament (CYRIL OF ALEXANDRIA).

John's role as the precursor of Jesus in God's plan of salvation is described as subordinate. Jesus speaks his words about John against the scribes and Pharisees so that they might see that greatness in the kingdom of heaven comes by faith and not by legal righteousness (CYRIL OF ALEXANDRIA). In preparing the way for Jesus, John eschews the trappings of the world, for he is unlike those who are swayed like a reed that has no deep roots and loves the fleeting waters. The reed makes a pen, which may flow with the Spirit because it has been dipped in the blood of Christ (AMBROSE).

John is the greatest prophet born of a woman, but Jesus is the greatest prophet born of a virgin, fulfilling the prophecy of Moses in Deuteronomy (AMBROSE).[1] John announces the new era, but as a historical figure (born of a woman) he is not part of the new era, and therefore those in the new era (born of God) are greater than he is (CYRIL OF ALEXANDRIA).

To receive Jesus as the Messiah is to declare God to be just or righteous. It means to receive his plan of salvation as it is manifested in the baptism of John, a baptism of repentance (AMBROSE). "This generation" includes Pharisees, Sadducees, elders, lawyers, and the foremost men (CYRIL OF ALEXANDRIA). Playing the flute and dancing are activities characteristic of a wedding, where there is rejoicing over the presence of the bridegroom and his bride,[2] as Jesus is the Bridegroom who comes forth from Mary's womb (MAXIMUS OF TURIN). Dirges and mourning are appropriate at a funeral, where one weeps over the fatal result of sin. The songs and dances recall the canticles of the prophets like Moses and Ezekiel (AMBROSE). The people of this generation reveal the childish characteristic of insisting on their own way, and they will not be won for the faith by either dancing or mourning (CYRIL OF ALEXANDRIA). The children of Wisdom turn out to be the most unlikely folk and the most unpopular members of Palestinian society: tax collectors and sinners who make up the church of the just (AUGUSTINE).

7:18-23 John's Question and Jesus' Answer

JOHN SENT HIS DISCIPLES. EPHREM THE SYRIAN: John sent them to him not to interrogate him, but rather that the Lord might confirm those former things that John had proclaimed to them. John was directing the minds of his disciples toward the Lord. . . . He sent them out in such a way that, having seen Jesus' miracles, they might be confirmed in their faith in him. COMMENTARY ON TATIAN'S DIATESSARON 9.2.[3]

JOHN IS A TYPE OF THE LAW. AMBROSE: John is the type of the law which was the foreteller of Christ, the law which was held confined in the hearts of the unbelievers as if in prisons[4] devoid of eternal light. The fruitful inner workings of punishment and the doors of malice restrained their hearts. The law rightly cannot achieve an outcome full of evidence of the divine dispensation without the assent of the gospel. EXPOSITION OF THE GOSPEL OF LUKE 5.94.[5]

MIRACLES TESTIFY THAT JESUS IS THE COMING ONE. CYRIL OF ALEXANDRIA: "In that same hour he healed many of sicknesses and of scourges, and of evil spirits; and gave sight to many that were blind." He made them spectators and eyewitnesses of his greatness and gathered into them a great admiration of his power and ability. They then bring forward the question and beg in John's name to be informed whether he is "he who comes." Here see, I ask, the beautiful art of the Savior's management. He does not simply say, "I am." If he had spoken this, it would have been true. He leads them to the proof given by the works themselves. In order that having accepted faith in him on good grounds and being furnished with knowledge from what had been done, they may return to him who sent them. "Go," he says, "tell John the things that you have seen and heard." "For you have heard indeed," he says, "that

---

[1]Deut 18:15, 19; cf. Acts 3:23. [2]See Lk 5:34. [3]ECTD 154-55*. [4]Cf. Mt 11:2. [5]EHG 181**.

I have raised the dead by the all-powerful word and by the touch of the hand. While you stood by, you have also seen that those things that were spoken of old time by the holy prophets are accomplished: the blind see, the lame walk, the lepers are cleansed, the dumb hear, the dead rise, and the poor are preached to. The blessed prophets had announced all these things before, as about in due time to be accomplish by my hands. I bring to pass those things that were prophesied long before, and you are yourselves spectators of them. Return and tell those things that you have seen with your own eyes accomplished by my might and ability, and which at various times the blessed prophets foretold." COMMENTARY ON LUKE, HOMILY 37.[6]

ISAIAH FORETOLD THE HEALING MIRACLES OF JESUS. CHRYSOSTOM: Christ would work miracles and teach as soon as he came to well-known sections of his own country, and this had been foretold.

Isaiah went on to tell of other marvels and showed how Christ cured the lame, and how he made the blind to see and the mute to speak. "Then the eyes of the blind shall be opened, and the ears of the deaf unstopped."[7] After that he spoke of the other marvels: "Then shall the lame man leap like a hart, and the tongue of the dumb sing for joy."[8] This did not happen until his coming. DEMONSTRATION AGAINST THE PAGANS 8-9.[9]

JESUS' HUMILITY IN FULFILLMENT OF THE OLD TESTAMENT. CYRIL OF ALEXANDRIA: "And blessed is he who is not offended in me!" The Jews were indeed offended, either as not knowing the depth of the mystery or because they did not seek to know the mystery. Every part of the inspired Scripture announced beforehand that the Word of God would humble himself to emptiness and be seen on earth. This plainly refers to when he was as we are and would justify by faith every thing under heaven. Although Scripture prophesied all this, they stumbled against him, struck

against the rock of offense,[10] fell, and were ground to powder.[11] Although they plainly saw him clothed with unspeakable dignity and surpassing glory, by means of the wondrous deeds he performed, they threw stones at him and said, "Why do you, being a man, make yourself God?"[12] In answer to these things Christ rebuked the immeasurable infirmity of their intellect and said, "If I do not the works of my Father, believe me not; but if I do, then though you believe not me, believe my works."[13] Blessed is he who does not stumble against Christ, that is, he who believes him. COMMENTARY ON LUKE, HOMILY 37.[14]

7:24-28 The Witness of Jesus About John

GREATNESS IN THE KINGDOM BY FAITH. CYRIL OF ALEXANDRIA: There were certain people who prided themselves upon their performance of what was required by the law, namely, the scribes, Pharisees, and others of their party. He proves that those who believe in him are superior to them and that the glories of the followers of the law are small in comparison with the evangelical way of life. He uses as an example him who was the best of their whole class yet born of woman, the blessed Baptizer. He affirmed that he is a prophet, or rather above the measure of the prophets. Christ also says that among those born of women no one had arisen greater than him in the righteousness that is by the law. He declares that he who is small, who falls short of his measure, and is inferior to him in the righteousness that is by the law, is greater than he. He is not greater in legal righteousness but in the kingdom of God, in faith and the glories which result from faith. Faith crowns those that receive it with glories that surpass the law. . . .

For this reason, Jesus brings the blessed Baptizer to our attention as one who had attained the foremost place in legal righteousness and to incomparable praise. Still he is ranked as less than

---

[6]CGSL 159**. [7]Is 35:5. [8]Is 35:6. [9]FC 73:199-200**. [10]Is 8:14; Rom 9:33. [11]Lk 20:18. [12]Jn 10:33. [13]Jn 10:37. [14]CGSL 159**.

one who is least. He says, "The least is greater than he in the kingdom of God." The kingdom of God signifies, as we affirm, the grace that is by faith, by means of which we are accounted worthy of every blessing and of the possession of the rich gifts which come from above from God. It frees us from all blame and makes us to be the children of God, partakers of the Holy Spirit and heirs of a heavenly inheritance. COMMENTARY ON LUKE, HOMILY 38.[15]

JOHN ESCHEWS THE TRAPPINGS OF THIS WORLD. AMBROSE: "What did you go out into the desert to see? A reed shaken with the wind?" When he admonished John's disciples to believe in the cross of the Lord, as they departed he turned to the crowds and began to call the poor to virtue. He did this for fear that they would be exalted in heart, fickle in mind and weak in foresight, and might prefer the showy to the useful and the fleeting to the eternal. "What did you go out into the desert to see?" The world here seems to be compared with a desert, still uncultivated, barren and infertile, which the Lord said could not yield increase. We think that people, swollen in the physical mind, devoid of inner virtue and boasting with the brittle loftiness of worldly glory are to be imitated as the example and image. Dangerous people, whom an inconstant way of life disquiets with the storms of this world, are rightly to be compared with a reed.[16] We are reeds founded on no root of a more robust nature. . . . Reeds love rivers and the fleeting. Perishing things of the earth delight us. EXPOSITION OF THE GOSPEL OF LUKE 5.103-4.[17]

HOW THE BELIEVER IS LIKE A FLOWING PEN. AMBROSE: If someone plucks this reed from the nursery garden of the earth, divests it of what is unnecessary, strips off the old man with his deeds,[18] and fits it to the hand of a swiftly writing scribe,[19] it begins to be not a reed but a pen. This pen imprints the precepts of Holy Writ in the inner mind and inscribes them on the tables of the heart.[20] . . . Imitate this pen in the moderation of your flesh. Do not dip your pen, your flesh, in ink but in the Spirit of the living God so that what you write may be eternal. Paul wrote the epistle with such a pen, of which he says, "You are the epistle of Christ, written not with ink but with the Spirit of the living God."[21] Dip your flesh in the blood of Christ, as it is written, "that your foot may be dipped in blood."[22] Moisten the footprint of your spirit and the steps of your mind with the sure confession of the Lord's cross. You dip your flesh in Christ's blood as you wash away vices, purge sins and bear the death of Christ in your flesh, as the apostle taught us, saying, "bearing about in our body the dying of Jesus Christ."[23] EXPOSITION OF THE GOSPEL OF LUKE 5.105-6.[24]

JOHN THE GREATEST PROPHET BORN OF A WOMAN; JESUS THE GREATEST BORN OF A VIRGIN. AMBROSE: He is even greater than he of whom Moses said, "The Lord our God will stir up a prophet among you,"[25] and "For the time will come that every soul that shall not hear that same prophet shall be destroyed from among the people."[26] If Christ is a prophet, then how is John greater than all prophets? Surely we do not deny that Christ is a prophet? On the contrary, I maintain both that the Lord is the Prophet of prophets and that John is greater than all, but of those born of a woman, not of a virgin. He was greater than those to whom he could be equal in the condition of birth. Another nature is not to be compared with human generations. There can be no comparison between man and God, for each is preferred to his own. There could be no comparison of John with the Son of God, so that he is thought to be below the angels.[27] EXPOSITION OF THE GOSPEL OF LUKE 5.110.[28]

BORN OF WOMAN OR BORN OF GOD. CYRIL OF ALEXANDRIA: "What then did you go out to see?"

---

[15]*CGSL* 161-62**. [16]Cf. 3 Macc 2:22. [17]*EHG* 184-85**. [18]Col 3:9. [19]Ps 44:1 LXX. [20]2 Cor 3:2. [21]2 Cor 3:3. [22]Ps 68:23 (67:24 LXX). [23]2 Cor 4:10. [24]*EHG* 185-86**. [25]Deut 18:15, 18. [26]Acts 3:23. [27]Cf. Ps 8:5; Heb 2:7, 9. [28]*EHG* 188*.

Perhaps you say, "A prophet." Yes, I agree. He is a saint and a prophet. He even surpasses the dignity of a prophet. Not only did he announce before that I am coming but pointed me out close at hand, saying, "Behold the Lamb of God that bears the sin of the world."[29] The prophet's voice testified of him as the one who was sent before my face to prepare the way before me.[30] I witness that there has not arisen among those born of women one greater than he. He that is least, in the life according to the law, in the kingdom of God is greater than he. How and in what manner is he greater? In that the blessed John, together with as many as preceded him, was born of woman, but they who have received the faith are no longer called the sons of women, but as the wise Evangelist said, "are born of God."[31] Commentary on Luke, Homily 38.[32]

7:29-30 The People Who Accept and Reject God's Plan of Salvation

God Is Justified Through Baptism. Ambrose: God himself is justified through baptism, but people justify themselves by confessing their sins, as it is written, "First confess your transgressions, that you may be justified."[33] One is justified because the gift of God is not rejected through stubbornness but acknowledged through righteousness. "The Lord is righteous and has loved righteousness."[34] The justification of God is in those who see him to have bestowed his gifts not on the unworthy and the guilty but on the righteous and those made guiltless by baptism. Let us then justify the Lord that we may be justified by the Lord. Exposition of the Gospel of Luke 6.2.[35]

7:31-35 Judgment on Those Who Reject God's Plan

Jewish Leaders the Men of This Generation. Cyril of Alexandria: The prophet's words will apply to us, "Woe to them that call evil good, and good evil. Who call bitter sweet and

sweet bitter. Who put light for darkness, and darkness for light."[36] This was the character of the Israelites and especially of those who were their chiefs, the scribes, namely, and Pharisees. Christ said about them, "To what shall I liken the men of this generation?" Commentary on Luke, Homily 39.[37]

A Wedding Where Christ Is the Bridegroom. Maximus of Turin: People are in the habit of dancing or singing as the custom is with vows, particularly at marriages, and so we have marriages to which a vow is attached and at which we are expected to dance or sing. Our vows are celebrated when the church is united to Christ. John says, "The one who has the bride is the bridegroom."[38] It is good for us to dance because of this marriage, for David, both king and prophet, danced before the ark of the covenant "with much singing."[39] He broke into dancing in high rejoicing, for in the Spirit he foresaw Mary, born of his own line, brought into Christ's chamber. He says, "And he, like a bridegroom, will come forth from his chamber."[40] He sang more than the other prophetic authors did because he was gladder than the rest of them. By these joys, he united those coming after him in marriage. By inviting us to his own vows in a more charming way than usual, having danced with such joy in front of the ark before his marriage, he taught us what we ought to do at those other vows. The prophet David danced. Sermon 42.5.[41]

The Songs and Dances of the Prophets. Ambrose: "Therefore, wisdom is justified by all her children." He fittingly says "by all," because justice is preserved around all. In order that an acceptance of the faithful may happen, a rejection of the unbelieving must occur. Very many Greeks say this, "Wisdom is justified by all her works," because the duty of justice is to preserve the mea-

---

[29]Jn 1:29. [30]Mal 3:1. [31]Jn 1:12. [32]CGSL 163**. [33]Is 43:26. [34]Ps 11:7 (10:7 LXX). [35]EHG 193*. [36]Is 5:20. [37]CGSL 165*. [38]Jn 3:29. [39]2 Sam 6:14. [40]Ps 19:5. [41]ACW 50:106-7**.

sure around the merit of each. It aptly says, "We have piped to you, and you have not danced." Moses sang a song when he stopped the flow in the Red Sea for the crossing of the Jews,[42] and the same waves encircled the horses of the Egyptians and, falling back, drowned their riders. Isaiah sang a song of his beloved's vineyard,[43] signifying that the people who before had been fruitful with abundant virtues would be desolate through shameful acts. The Hebrews sang a song when the soles of their feet grew moist at the touch of the bedewing flame, and while all burned within and without, the harmless fire caressed them alone and did not scorch.[44] Habakkuk also learned to assuage universal grief with a song and prophesied that the sweet passion of the Lord would happen for the faithful.[45] The prophets sang songs with spiritual measures, resounding with prophecies of universal salvation. The prophets wept, softening the hard hearts of the Jews with sorrowful lamentations.[46] Exposition of the Gospel of Luke 6.6-7.[47]

A Child's Game. Cyril of Alexandria: There may have been perchance a sort of game among the Jewish children, something of this kind. A group of youths was divided into two parts. One made fun of the confusion in the world, the uneven course of its affairs, and the painful and rapid change from one extreme to the other, by playing some of them on instruments of music. The other group wailed. Neither did the mourners share the merriment of those who were playing music and rejoicing, nor did those with the instruments of music join in the sorrow of those who were weeping. Finally, they rebuked one another with their lack of sympathy, so to speak, and absence of affection. The one party would say, "We have played unto you, and you have not danced." The others would respond, "We have wailed to you, and you have not wept." Commentary on Luke, Homily 39.[48]

Wisdom Is Justified by All Her Children. Augustine: The Lord made a truly necessary addition to these words when he said, "And wisdom is justified by her children." If you ask who those children are, read what is written, "The sons of wisdom are the church of the just."[49] Letter 36.[50]

---

[42]Ex 15:1-18. [43]Is 5:1-7. [44]See 1 Macc 2:59; 3 Macc 6:6; Dan 3:19-25. [45]Hab 3:13. [46]Is 46:12. [47]EHG 195*. [48]CGSL 165-66**. [49]Sir 3:1. [50]FC 12:161*.

7:36-50 JESUS EATS WITH A PHARISEE AND FORGIVES A SINFUL WOMAN

[36]*One of the Pharisees asked him to eat with him, and he went into the Pharisee's house, and took his place at table.* [37]*And behold, a woman of the city, who was a sinner, when she learned that he was at table in the Pharisee's house, brought an alabaster flask of ointment,* [38]*and standing behind him at his feet, weeping, she began to wet his feet with her tears, and wiped them with the hair of her head, and kissed his feet, and anointed them with the ointment.* [39]*Now when the Pharisee who had invited him saw it, he said to himself, "If this man were a prophet, he would have known who and what sort of woman this is who is touching him, for she is a sinner."* [40]*And Jesus answering said to him, "Simon, I have something to say to you." And he answered, "What is it,*

Teacher?" [41]*"A certain creditor had two debtors; one owed five hundred denarii, and the other fifty.* [42]*When they could not pay, he forgave them both. Now which of them will love him more?"* [43]*Simon answered, "The one, I suppose, to whom he forgave more." And he said to him, "You have judged rightly."* [44]*Then turning toward the woman he said to Simon, "Do you see this woman? I entered your house, you gave me no water for my feet, but she has wet my feet with her tears and wiped them with her hair.* [45]*You gave me no kiss, but from the time I came in she has not ceased to kiss my feet.* [46]*You did not anoint my head with oil, but she has anointed my feet with ointment.* [47]*Therefore I tell you, her sins, which are many, are forgiven, for she loved much; but he who is forgiven little, loves little."* [48]*And he said to her, "Your sins are forgiven."* [49]*Then those who were at table with him began to say among themselves, "Who is this, who even forgives sins?"* [50]*And he said to the woman, "Your faith has saved you; go in peace."*

OVERVIEW: Jesus enters into the house of a Pharisee to carry on in the flesh the business of heaven (PETER CHRYSOLOGUS). Another version of an anointing appears in Matthew's Gospel, but the Simon in Matthew is not a Pharisee but a leper[1] (AMBROSE). The woman who anointed Jesus' feet represents the church, coming to Simon the Pharisee, whose house represents the synagogue (PETER CHRYSOLOGUS).

Only someone who had been forgiven much and therefore loved much could anoint Jesus' feet as the sinful woman did (AMBROSE). The acts of love by the woman toward Jesus are symbols of the Lord's teaching (CLEMENT OF ALEXANDRIA), indicating that she welcomes him as a prophet from God who has come to forgive even the worst of sinners. Like the woman, the church responds to Jesus in faith, for he is the Judge who will separate the sheep from the goats (PETER CHRYSOLOGUS). This sinful woman understands that Jesus is the Prophet, not the Pharisee; she is the believer, not the Pharisee (AMBROSE). The woman's humility secures her forgiveness of sins (AUGUSTINE). Simon the Pharisee is humiliated by the woman, whose lips are made holy by kissing Jesus' feet, and she is forgiven her sin (EPHREM THE SYRIAN).

This issue of love is mentioned first in the parable of the two debtors who represent the two peoples, Jews and Gentiles (AMBROSE). Jesus tells this parable to Simon as an act of reconciliation. What the woman receives from Jesus the Physician in the forgiveness of her sins is miraculous healing that is equivalent to the miracles of healing Jesus did throughout Galilee; these miracles prompted the invitation to Simon's house for a meal (EPHREM THE SYRIAN). She kisses him on his feet because she believes in him, just as the church today exchanges a kiss at the communion so as to show publicly its faith and its confession by kissing Christ in kissing one another. Christ continues to be anointed with oil as the church anoints the least and the lowly with the oil of charity (AMBROSE).

It is the woman who confesses Jesus as God, and not Simon the Pharisee, who sees him only as a man (EPHREM THE SYRIAN). Jesus shows him that he is the final, eschatological prophet by forgiving the sins of the woman who anointed his feet (CYRIL OF ALEXANDRIA). In contrast to Simon and the other Pharisees, who do not understand that Jesus is the Messiah who forgives sins, she, who owed the great debt and was forgiven, showed great love (ORIGEN). She loves more because she has been forgiven more (JOHN CASSIAN). Behind it all are God's gracious plan and her faith in Jesus, who is the center of the plan because he is love, and it is his love that forgives sins (AMBROSE).

7:36 The Lukan Framework of Persons, Place and Time

---

[1]Mt 26:6-16..

THE BUSINESS OF HEAVEN. PETER CHRYSOLO-
GUS: You perceive that Christ came to the Pharisee's table not to be filled with food for the body
but to carry on the business of heaven while he
was in the flesh. SERMON 93.[2]

LUKE'S VERSION COMPARED WITH MAT-
THEW'S. AMBROSE: Matthew depicts this
woman pouring ointment upon Christ's head,[3]
and perhaps therefore was reluctant to call her a
sinner. According to Luke, a sinner poured ointment on Christ's feet. She cannot be the same
woman, lest the Evangelists seem to have contradicted each other. . . . If you understand this,
you will see this woman, and you will certainly
see her blessed wherever this gospel is preached.
Her memory will never pass away, since she
poured the fragrances of good conduct and the
ointment of righteous deeds on the head of
Christ.[4] EXPOSITION OF THE GOSPEL OF LUKE
6.14-15.[5]

7:37-38 The Woman Washes, Dries, Kisses and Anoints Jesus' Feet

THE WOMAN AS CHURCH AND THE PHARISEE
AS SYNAGOGUE. PETER CHRYSOLOGUS: "And behold," it says, "a woman in the town who was a
sinner." Who is this woman? Beyond any doubt,
she is the church. . . .

She heard that Christ had come to the house
of the Pharisee, that is, to the synagogue. She
heard that there, that is, at the Jewish Passover,
he had instituted the mysteries of his passion,
disclosed the sacrament of his body and blood,
and revealed the secret of our redemption. She ignored the scribes like contemptible doorkeepers.
"Woe to you lawyers! You who have taken away
the key of knowledge."[6] She broke open the doors
of quarrels and despised the very superiority of
the Pharisaical group. Ardent, panting and per-
spiring, she made her way to the large inner
chamber of the banquet of the law. There she
learned that Christ was betrayed amid sweet
cups and a banquet of love. SERMON 95.[7]

ANOINTING SHOWS GREAT LOVE. AMBROSE:
Blessed is one who can anoint the feet of Christ
even with oil. Simon had still not anointed him,
but more blessed is she who anoints with ointment. The grace of many flowers gathered into a
bouquet scatters different sweetness of fragrance.
Perhaps none but the church alone can produce
that ointment. The church has innumerable flowers of different fragrance. She fittingly assumes
the likeness of a prostitute, because Christ also
took upon himself the form of a sinner.
EXPOSITION OF THE GOSPEL OF LUKE 6.21.[8]

SYMBOLS OF THE LORD'S TEACHING. CLEMENT
OF ALEXANDRIA: That woman had not yet entered communion with the Word, because she
was still a sinner. She paid the Master honor with
what she considered the most precious thing she
had, her perfume. She wiped off the remainder of
the perfume with the garland of her head, her
hair. She poured out upon the Lord her tears of
repentance. Therefore her sins were forgiven her.

This is a symbol of the Lord's teachings and of
his sufferings. The anointing of his feet with
sweet-smelling myrrh suggests the divine teaching whose good smell and fame has spread to the
ends of the earth. "Their sound has gone forth to
the ends of the earth."[9] Moreover, those anointed
feet of the Lord (not to be too subtle) are the
apostles. The sweet odor of the myrrh prefigures
their reception of the Holy Spirit. I mean that the
figure of the Lord's feet is to be understood of the
apostles, who journeyed about the whole world
preaching the gospel. CHRIST THE EDUCATOR
2.8.[10]

LIKE THE WOMAN, THE CHURCH RESPONDS
TO JESUS IN FAITH. PETER CHRYSOLOGUS:
With her hands of good works, she holds the feet
of those who preach his kingdom. She washes
them with tears of charity, kisses them with

---

[2]FC 17:143*. [3]Mt 26:7. [4]Mt 26:13. [5]EHG 197-98**. [6]Lk 11:52.
[7]FC 17:149-50*. [8]EHG 200*. [9]Ps 19:4 (18:5 LXX); Rom 10:18. [10]FC
23:146-47*.

praising lips, and pours out the whole ointment of mercy, until he will turn her. This means that he will come back to her and say to Simon, to the Pharisees, to those who deny, to the nation of the Jews, "I came into your house. You gave me no water for my feet."

When will he speak these words? He will speak them when he will come in the majesty of his Father and separate the righteous from the unrighteous like a shepherd who separates the sheep from the goats. He will say, "I was hungry, and you did not give me to eat. I was thirsty, and you gave me no drink. I was a stranger, and you did not take me in."[11] This is equivalent to saying, "But this woman, while she was bathing my feet, anointing them and kissing them, did to the servants what you did not do for the Master." She did for the feet what you refused to the Head. She expended upon the lowliest members what you refused to your Creator. Then he will say to the church, "Your sins, many as they are, are forgiven you because you have loved much." SERMON 95.[12]

7:39-40 The Pharisee Misjudges the Woman's Actions

THE WOMAN, NOT THE PHARISEE, WAS THE BELIEVER. AMBROSE: See the organization of the house. The sinful woman is glorified in the house of the Pharisee. The church is justified in the house of the law and the prophet, not the Pharisee. The Pharisee did not believe, but the woman believed. Then he said, "If he were a prophet, he would know surely who and what manner of woman this is that touches him." Judea is the house of the law that is written not on stones but on the tablets of the heart.[13] The church is justified in this as already greater than the law, because the law does not know of the forgiveness of offences. The law does not possess the mystery in which secret sins are cleansed; therefore, what is lacking in the law is perfected in the gospel. EXPOSITION OF THE GOSPEL OF LUKE 6.23.[14]

SUBMISSIVE TO THE JUSTICE OF GOD. AUGUSTINE: She will not think that she has been forgiven little and so love little, and, ignorant of the justice of God and seeking to establish her own, not submit to the justice of God.[15] Simon was ensnared in this vice, and the woman, to whom many sins were forgiven because she loved much, surpassed him. She will more safely and more truly consider that all the sins that God preserved her from committing should be accounted as though they are forgiven. HOLY VIRGINITY 41.[16]

IMPURE LIPS MADE HOLY BY KISSING JESUS' FEET. EPHREM THE SYRIAN: Our Lord worked wonders with common things so that we would know the things those who scorn wonders are deprived of knowing. If such healing as this was snatched from his hem in secret, he was most certainly capable of the healing that his word worked in public. If impure lips became holy by kissing his feet, how much holier would pure lips become by kissing his mouth? With her kisses, the sinful woman received the favor of blessed feet that had worked to bring her the forgiveness of sins. She was graciously comforting with oil the feet of her Physician, who had graciously brought the treasury of healing to her suffering. The One who fills the hungry was not invited because of his stomach. The One who justifies sinners invited himself because of the sinful woman's repentance. HOMILY ON OUR LORD 13-19.[17]

7:41-43 The Parable of the Two Debtors

TWO DEBTORS REPRESENT THE JEWS AND THE GENTILES. AMBROSE: Who are those two debtors if not the two peoples, the one from the Jews, the other from the Gentiles, in debt to the Creditor of the heavenly treasure? . . . We do not owe this Creditor material wealth but standards of merits, accounts of virtues. The weight of seriousness, the likeness of righteousness, and the sound

---

[11]Mt 25:42. [12]FC 17:150-51*. [13]2 Cor 3:3. [14]EHG 200-201**. [15]Rom 10:3. [16]FC 27:195**. [17]FC 91:289**.

of confession measure the worth of this wealth. Woe is me if I do not have what I have received. One can pay off the whole debt to this Creditor only with difficulty. Woe is me if I do not ask, "Remit my debt." The Lord would not have taught us to pray for the forgiveness of our sins[18] if he had not known that some would be worthy debtors, only with difficulty.[19] . . . There is nothing that we can worthily repay to God for the harm to the flesh he assumed, for the blows, the cross, the death and the burial. Woe is me if I have not loved! I dare to say that Peter did not repay and thereby loved more. Paul did not repay. He certainly repaid death for death, but he did not repay other debts, because he owed much. I hear him saying, because he did not repay, "Or who has given a gift to him that he might be repaid?"[20] Even if we were to repay cross for cross, death for death, do we repay that we possess all things from him, by him, and in him?[21] Let us repay love for our debt, charity for the gift, and grace for wealth. He to whom more is given loves more. EXPOSITION OF THE GOSPEL OF LUKE 6.24, 26.[22]

JESUS TELLS THE PARABLE TO BRING ABOUT RECONCILIATION WITH SIMON. EPHREM THE SYRIAN:

Our Lord devised a statement that was like an arrow. He put conciliation at its tip and anointed it with love to soothe the parts of the body. He no sooner shot it at the one who was filled with conflict, than conflict turned to harmony. Directly following the humble statement of our Lord, who said, "Simon, I have something to say to you," he who had secretly withdrawn responded, "Speak, my Lord." A sweet saying penetrated a bitter mind and brought out fragrant fruit. He who was a secret detractor before the saying gave public praise after the saying. Humility with a sweet tongue subdues even its enemies to do it honor. Humility does not put its power to the test among its friends but among those who hate its display of its trophies. HOMILY ON OUR LORD 24.2.[23]

7:44-48 Jesus Forgives the Woman's Sins

JESUS THE PHYSICIAN BRINGS MIRACULOUS HEALING TO THE WOMAN'S SINS. EPHREM THE SYRIAN:

Healing the sick is a physician's glory. Our Lord did this to increase the disgrace of the Pharisee, who discredited the glory of our Physician. He worked signs in the streets, worked even greater signs once he entered the Pharisee's house than those that he had worked outside. In the streets, he healed sick bodies, but inside, he healed sick souls. Outside, he had given life to the death of Lazarus. Inside, he gave life to the death of the sinful woman. He restored the living soul to a dead body that it had left, and he drove off the deadly sin from a sinful woman in whom it dwelt. That blind Pharisee, for whom wonders were not enough, discredited the common things he saw because of the wondrous things he failed to see. HOMILY ON OUR LORD 42.2.[24]

TO KISS CHRIST. AMBROSE:

A kiss is a mark of love. . . .

He truly kisses Christ's feet who, in reading the Gospel, recognizes the acts of the Lord Jesus and admires them with holy affection. With a reverent kiss, he caresses the footprints of the Lord as he walks. We kiss Christ, therefore, in the kiss of Communion: "Let him who reads understand."[25] . . .

The church does not cease to kiss Christ's feet and demands not one but many kisses in the Song of Songs.[26] Since like blessed Mary she listens to his every saying, she receives his every word when the Gospel or the Prophets are read, and she keeps all these words in her heart.[27] The church alone has kisses, like a bride. A kiss is a pledge of nuptials and the privilege of wedlock. LETTER 62.[28]

CHRIST ANOINTED WITH OIL AS THE CHURCH ANOINTS THE LOWLY AND THE LEAST. AMBROSE:

The church washes the feet of

---

[18]See Mt 6:12. [19]Cf. Lk 11:4. [20]Rom 11:35. [21]Rom 11:36. [22]EHG 201-2**. [23]FC 91:299-300**. [24]FC 91:317**. [25]Mt 24:15. [26]Song 1:2. [27]Lk 2:51. [28]FC 26:390-92**.

Christ, wipes them with her hair, anoints them with oil, and pours ointment on them. She not only cares for the wounded and caresses the weary, but she also moistens them with the sweet perfume of grace. She pours this grace not only on the rich and powerful but also on those of lowly birth. She weighs all in an equal balance. She receives all into the same bosom. She caresses all in the same embrace.

Christ died once. He was buried once. Nevertheless he wants ointment to be poured on his feet each day. What are the feet of Christ on which we pour ointment? They are the feet of Christ of whom he himself says, "What you have done for one of the least of these, you have done to me."[29] The woman in the Gospel refreshes these feet. She moistens them with her tears when sin is forgiven of the lowest of persons, guilt is washed away, and pardon is granted. The one who loves even the least of God's people kisses these feet. The one who makes known the favor of his gentleness to those who are frail anoints these feet with ointment. The Lord Jesus himself declares that he is honored in these martyrs and apostles. LETTER 62.[30]

THE WOMAN SEES JESUS AS GOD; THE PHARISEE SEES HIM AS A MAN. EPHREM THE SYRIAN: She, through her love, brought into the open the tears that were hidden in the depths of her eyes, and the Lord, because of her courage, brought into the open the thoughts that were hidden in the Pharisee.... Our Lord, standing in the middle, worked out a parable between the two of them, so that the sinful woman might be encouraged through his pronouncing the parable and the Pharisee may be denounced through the explanation of the parable. COMMENTARY ON TATIAN'S DIATESSARON 7.18.[31]

7:49-50 Go in Peace

JESUS SHOWS HE IS THE PROPHET BY FORGIVING HER SINS. CYRIL OF ALEXANDRIA: He came that he might forgive the debtors much and

little and show mercy upon small and great, that there might be no one whatsoever who did not participate in his goodness. As a pledge and plain example of his grace, he freed that unchaste woman from her many iniquities by saying, "Your sins are forgiven you." A declaration such as this is truly worthy of God! It is a word joined with supreme authority. Since the law condemned those that were in sin, who, I ask, was able to declare things above the law, except the One who ordained it? He immediately both set the woman free and directed the attention of that Pharisee and those who were dining with him to more excellent things. They learned that the Word being God was not like one of the prophets, but rather far beyond the measure of humanity although he became man. COMMENTARY ON LUKE, HOMILY 40.[32]

HE FORGIVES REPEATEDLY. ORIGEN: A first forgiveness is the one by which we are baptized "for the remission of sins."[33] A second remission is in the suffering of martyrdom. The third is the one that is given through alms. The Savior says, "But nevertheless, give what you have and, behold, all things are clean for you." A fourth forgiveness of sins is given for us through the fact that we also forgive the sins of our brothers. The Lord and Savior says, "If you will forgive from the heart your brothers' sins, your Father will also forgive you your sins. But if you will not forgive your brothers from the heart, neither will your Father forgive you."[34] He taught us to say in prayer, "Forgive us our debts as we forgive our debtors."[35] A fifth forgiveness of sins is when "someone will convert a sinner from the error of his way." Divine Scripture says, "Whoever will make a sinner turn from the error of his way will save a soul from death and cover a multitude of sins." A sixth forgiveness comes through the abundance of love. The Lord himself says, "Truly I say to you, her many sins are forgiven because she loved much." The apostle says, "Because love

[29]Mt 25:40. [30]FC 26:393-94**. [31]ECTD 137*. [32]CGSL 171-72*. [33]Lk 11:41. [34]Mt 6:14-15. [35]Mt 6:12.

will cover a multitude of sins."[36] There is still a seventh forgiveness of sins through penance, although admittedly it is difficult and toilsome. The sinner washes "his couch in tears,"[37] and his "tears" become his "bread day and night."[38] HOMILIES ON LEVITICUS 2.4.5.[39]

ONE LOVES MORE WHO HAS BEEN FORGIVEN MORE. JOHN CASSIAN: It happens that, whatever state of life a man has reached, he sometimes can offer pure and devout prayer. Even in the lowliest place, where a man is repenting from fear of punishment and the judgment to come, his petitions can enrich him with the same fervor of spirit as the man, who attained to purity of heart, gazes upon God's blessing and is filled with an overwhelming happiness. As the Lord said, "The one who knows he has been forgiven more begins to love more." CONFERENCES 2.9.[40]

CHRIST IS OUR LOVE WHO FORGIVES SINS. AMBROSE: Christ is our love. Love is good, since it offered itself to death for transgressions. Love

is good, which forgave sins. Let our soul clothe herself with love of a kind that is "strong as death."[41] Just as death is the end of sins, so also is love, because the one who loves the Lord ceases to commit sin. For "charity thinks no evil and does not rejoice over wickedness, but endures all things."[42] If someone does not seek his own goods, how will he seek the goods of another?[43] That death through the bath of baptism,[44] through which every sin is buried, is strong and forgives every fault. The woman in the Gospel brought this kind of love. The Lord says, "Her many sins have been forgiven her, because she has loved much." The death of the holy martyrs is also strong. It destroys previous faults. Since it involves a love not less than theirs, death that is equal to the martyrs' suffering is just as strong for taking away the punishment of sins. ISAAC, OR THE SOUL 8.75-76.[45]

---

[36]1 Pet 4:8. [37]Ps 6:6 (6:7 LXX). [38]Ps 42:3 (41:4 LXX). [39]FC 83:47**. [40]LCC 12:221*. [41]Song 8:6. [42]1 Cor 13:5-7. [43]1 Cor 13:5. [44]Tit 3:5. [45]FC 65:59-60*.

8:1-18 THE PARABLE OF THE SOWER AND THE MYSTERIES OF THE KINGDOM

[1]*Soon afterward he went on through cities and villages, preaching and bringing the good news of the kingdom of God. And the twelve were with him,* [2]*and also some women who had been healed of evil spirits and infirmities: Mary, called Magdalene, from whom seven demons had gone out,* [3]*and Joanna, the wife of Chuza, Herod's steward, and Susanna, and many others, who provided for them[z] out of their means.*

[4]*And when a great crowd came together and people from town after town came to him, he said in a parable:* [5]*"A sower went out to sow his seed; and as he sowed, some fell along the path, and was trodden under foot, and the birds of the air devoured it.* [6]*And some fell on the rock; and as it grew up, it withered away, because it had no moisture.* [7]*And some fell among thorns; and the thorns grew with it and choked it.* [8]*And some fell into good soil and grew, and yielded a hundredfold."* *As he said this, he called out, "He who has ears to hear, let him hear."*

⁹*And when his disciples asked him what this parable meant, ¹⁰he said, "To you it has been given to know the secrets of the kingdom of God; but for others they are in parables, so that seeing they may not see, and hearing they may not understand. ¹¹Now the parable is this: The seed is the word of God. ¹²The ones along the path are those who have heard; then the devil comes and takes away the word from their hearts, that they may not believe and be saved. ¹³And the ones on the rock are those who, when they hear the word, receive it with joy; but these have no root, they believe for a while and in time of temptation fall away. ¹⁴And as for what fell among the thorns, they are those who hear, but as they go on their way they are choked by the cares and riches and pleasures of life, and their fruit does not mature. ¹⁵And as for that in the good soil, they are those who, hearing the word, hold it fast in an honest and good heart, and bring forth fruit with patience.*

¹⁶*"No one after lighting a lamp covers it with a vessel, or puts it under a bed, but puts it on a stand, that those who enter may see the light. ¹⁷For nothing is hid that shall not be made manifest, nor anything secret that shall not be known and come to light. ¹⁸Take heed then how you hear; for to him who has will more be given, and from him who has not, even what he thinks that he has will be taken away."*

z Other ancient authorities read *him*

OVERVIEW: Luke reports here the news that some women put their possessions at the disposal of Jesus and the Twelve. The apostles will follow Jesus' example by having women provide for them as they preach the gospel (AUGUSTINE). Jesus is the sower who sows the seed (CYRIL OF ALEXANDRIA), and he is the only cultivator of the soil from the foundation of the universe (CLEMENT OF ALEXANDRIA). The seed must first decay and die before it rises and brings forth fruit (CLEMENT OF ROME). Seed should not be sown beside the way but in the way itself, which is Jesus, who is the Way (ORIGEN).

"The one who has ears to hear, let him hear"—the ear gives access to the heart and the inner person (BASIL THE GREAT). Jesus clearly divides people into two categories: those who have been given by God knowledge of the mysteries of the kingdom, and the rest, who do not know the mysteries (CYRIL OF ALEXANDRIA).

In addition to identifying the seed as the Word of God (i.e., the gospel), Jesus also implies that the birds are the devil, who snatches the good seed on the path (CYRIL OF ALEXANDRIA) by

removing from the memory the words of catechetical lectures (SYMEON THE NEW THEOLOGIAN). The ungrateful soul is like a pathway for evil (EPHREM THE SYRIAN). The sprouts on the rocks that wither away stand for those who succumb in the time of temptation and trial (CYRIL OF ALEXANDRIA), for the hard Word of God finds hard soil during times of persecution (EPHREM THE SYRIAN). The thorns represent the anxieties, riches and pleasures of life that choke the seed (CYRIL OF ALEXANDRIA, PASCHASIUS OF DUMIUM). There are degrees to the success of the good fruit (CYRIL OF ALEXANDRIA). The illuminating Word that is in the baptized should light up the house church and shine from it, like a beacon, to others journeying toward it (ORIGEN). To those who have, that is, to those who have the faith and life and perseverance—all gifts of God through his Word—more will be given to them by God: salvation on the last day (EPHREM THE SYRIAN).

8:1-3 Women Support Jesus

THE APOSTLES FOLLOW JESUS' EXAMPLE.

AUGUSTINE: If anyone does not believe that wherever they preached the gospel the apostles brought women of holy life with them, so that these women might minister the necessities of life to them from their abundance, let him hear the Gospel and realize that the apostles did this by the example of our Lord himself. THE WORK OF MONKS 5.6.[1]

8:4-8 The Parable of the Sower

THE SOWER IS JESUS. CYRIL OF ALEXANDRIA: He is truly the Sower of all that is good, and we are his farm. The whole harvest of spiritual fruits is by him and from him. He taught us this when he said, "Without me you can do nothing."[2] COMMENTARY ON LUKE, HOMILY 41.[3]

ONE CULTIVATOR OF THE SOIL. CLEMENT OF ALEXANDRIA: It is clear that the Greek preliminary education combined with philosophy itself has come from God to human beings not as an ultimate goal but rather as rainstorms bursting on fertile soil, manure heaps, and houses alike. Grass and wheat sprout alike. Fig trees and other, less respectable trees grow on top of graves. These growths emerge in the pattern of the genuine articles, because they enjoy the same power of the rain, but they do not have the same charm as those that grow in rich soil. They either wither or are torn up. Yes, the parable of the seed as explained by the Lord has its place here too. There is only one cultivator of the soil within human beings. It is the One who from the first, from the foundation of the universe, has been sowing the seeds with potential growth, who has produced rain on every appropriate occasion in the form of his sovereign Word. Differences arise from the times and places that receive the Word. STROMATEIS 1.7.1-2.[4]

SEED THAT GROWS MUST DECAY FIRST. CLEMENT OF ROME: Let us consider, beloved, the resurrection: the night sleeps, and the day arises; the day departs, and night returns. Let us look at the crops to see how and in what manner the planting takes place. "The sower went forth" and cast each of the seeds into the ground, and they, falling on the ground dry and bare, decay. Then from their decay, the greatness of the Lord's providence raises them up, and from one seed many grow up and bring forth fruit. 1 CLEMENT 24.[5]

SOWED ON JESUS THE WAY. ORIGEN: If we hear "the word" and from this hearing our earth "immediately" produces vegetation that "withers" before it comes to maturity or fruit, our earth will be called "rocky." Those things that are said should press forward in our ears with deeper roots so that they both "bear fruit" of works and contain the seeds of future works. Then each one on our earth will truly bear fruit in accordance with its potential, "some a hundred fold," some "sixty," others "thirty." We also considered it is necessary to admonish you that our fruit does not have "darnel" or "tares." This is so that it is not "beside the way" but sown in the way that says, "I am the way,"[6] so that the birds of heaven may not eat our fruits or our vine. HOMILIES ON GENESIS 1.4.[7]

EARS REFER TO THE INNER PERSON. BASIL THE GREAT: What should we say concerning this: "He who has ears to hear, let him hear"? It is evident that some possess ears better able to hear the words of God. What does he say to those who do not have those ears? "Hear, you deaf, and, you blind, behold."[8] All such expressions are used in reference to the inner man. HOMILY ON PSALM 33.13.[9]

8:9-10 The Meaning of Parables

MYSTERIES REVEALED TO THE FAITHFUL. CYRIL OF ALEXANDRIA: The word of the Savior, so to speak, is constantly hidden. The blessed psalmist has also brought him before us saying, "I

---

[1]FC 16:338**. [2]Jn 15:5. [3]CGSL 178**. [4]FC 85:48-49*. [5]FC 1:29-30. [6]Jn 14:6. [7]FC 71:53**. [8]Is 42:18. [9]FC 46:272*.

will open my mouth in parables."[10] See what he spoke in olden times happened. "A large multitude was assembled round him of people from all Judea, and he spoke to them in parables." Since they were not worthy to learn the mysteries of the kingdom of heaven, he wrapped the word for them in darkness. . . .

It was not granted to them to know the mysteries of the kingdom of heaven, but rather to us, who are more ready to embrace the faith. He has given us, since he is perfect wisdom, the ability to understand parables and the dark saying, the words of the wise and their riddles.[11] Parables, we may say, are the images not of visible objects but rather spiritual and understandable by the intellect. The parable points out to the eyes of the mind what is impossible to see with the eyes of the body. It beautifully shapes out the subtlety of intellectual things by means of the things of sense and palpable to the touch. COMMENTARY ON LUKE, HOMILY 41.[12]

8:11-15 *The Parable of the Sower Explained*

THE DEVIL SNATCHES GOOD SEED OFF THE PATH. CYRIL OF ALEXANDRIA: The seed is the Word of God. Those on the way are they who have heard. Afterwards, the devil comes and takes away the Word from their heart, that they may not believe and be saved. We see in a moment that the hardness of the ground causes the seed on the pathways to be snatched away. A pathway always is hard and untilled, because it is exposed to every one's feet. It does not admit any seed into it, but it lies rather upon the surface, ready for any birds that will to snatch it away. All whose minds are hard and unyielding, and so to speak, pressed together, do not receive the divine seed. The divine and sacred admonition does not find an entrance into them. They do not accept the words that would produce in them the fear of God and by means of which they could bring forth as fruits the glories of virtue. They have made themselves a beaten and trampled pathway for unclean demons, yes, for Satan himself, such

as never can bear holy fruit. Let those who are awake, whose heart is sterile and unfruitful, open your mind, receive the sacred seed, be like productive and well-tilled soil, bring forth to God the fruits that will raise you to an incorruptible life. COMMENTARY ON LUKE, HOMILY 41.[13]

THE DEVIL REMOVES THE WORD OF CATECHESIS. SYMEON THE NEW THEOLOGIAN: When you come out of the church, do not begin to be distracted toward empty and useless matters, lest the devil come and find you occupied with them. It is like when a crow finds on the plain a grain of wheat, before it has been covered with earth, and picks it up and flies off. The devil removes the memory of these words of catechetical lectures from your hearts,[14] and you find yourselves empty and deprived of beneficial teaching. DISCOURSE 30.1.[15]

THE UNGRATEFUL SOUL A PUBLIC HIGHWAY FOR EVIL. EPHREM THE SYRIAN: "For it fell on the edge of the path."[16] This is an image of the ungrateful soul, like the one who received one talent despised the goodness of him who gave it.[17] Because this ground was tardy in receiving its seed, it became a public highway for all evil. Consequently there was no place in its ground for the Teacher to penetrate into it like a laborer, break up its hardness and sow his seed there. The Lord described the evil one in the imagery of a bird who snatches it away.[18] He made known that the evil one does not forcefully snatch away from the heart the teaching entrusted to it. In the parable's imagery, he revealed the voice of the gospel standing at the door of the ears like the grain of wheat on the surface of the ground that has not hidden in its womb the seed which fell upon it. The birds were not permitted to penetrate the earth in search of the seed that the earth hid under its wings. COMMENTARY ON TATIAN'S DIATESSARON 11.13.[19]

---

[10]Ps 78:2 (77:2 LXX). [11]Prov 1:6. [12]CGSL 177-78**. [13]CGSL 178**. [14]Cf. Mt 13:19. [15]SNTD 318*. [16]Mt 13:19. [17]Mt 25:24-30. [18]Mk 4:4, 15. [19]ECTD 182*.

PERSECUTION CAUSES CONFUSION AND LOSS OF FAITH. CYRIL OF ALEXANDRIA: Let us consider those others of whom Christ said, "And those upon the rock are they who, when they hear, receive the word with joy, and they have no root. These believe for a while and in time of temptation depart away." There are men whose faith has not been proved. They depend simply on words and do not apply their minds to examining the mystery. Their piety is sapless and without root. When they enter the churches, they feel pleasure often in seeing so many assembled. They joyfully receive instruction in the mysteries from him whose business it is to teach and laud him with praises. They do this without discretion or judgment, but with unpurified wills. When they go out of the churches, at once they forget the sacred doctrines and go about in their customary course, not having stored up within themselves any thing for their future benefit. If the affairs of Christians go on peacefully and no trial disturbs them, even then they scarcely maintain the faith, and that, so to speak, in a confused and tottering state. When persecution troubles them and the enemies of the truth attack the churches of the Savior, their heart does not love the battle, and their mind throws away the shield and flees. COMMENTARY ON LUKE, HOMILY 41.[20]

A HARD WORD FINDS NO PLACE ON HARD GROUND. EPHREM THE SYRIAN: "That which fell on the rock . . ."[21] The good Lord revealed his mercy. Although the hardness of the ground was not cultivated, he did not withhold its seed from it. This ground represents those who turn away from his teaching like those who said, "This word is hard; who can listen to it?"[22] It is like Judas, who heard his word and flourished through his signs but was without fruit in the moment of testing. COMMENTARY ON TATIAN'S DIATESSARON 11.14.[23]

WORLDLY CARES CHOKE THE SEED. CYRIL OF ALEXANDRIA: "Those that fell among the thorns are they who have heard, and go, and are choked by cares and wealth and pleasures of the world, and yield no fruit." The Savior scatters the seed that acquired a firm hold in the souls that received it. It already shot up and just began to be visible when worldly cares choke it and it dries up, being overgrown by empty occupations. The prophet Jeremiah said, "It becomes a handful, that can produce no meal."[24] In these things, we must be like skillful farmers who patiently cleared away the thorns and uprooted whatever is hurtful, and then we scatter the seed in clean furrows. One can say with confidence that doubtless "they will come with joy, bearing their sheaves."[25] If a person scatters seed in ground that is fertile in thorns, fruitful in briars and densely covered with useless stubble, he sustains a double loss. First, he loses his seed, and second, his work. In order that the divine seed may blossom well in us, let us first cast out of the mind worldly cares and the unprofitable anxiety which makes us seek to be rich. COMMENTARY ON LUKE, HOMILY 41.[26]

ALMS AND FAITH INSTEAD OF RICHES. PASCHASIUS OF DUMIUM: Alms and faith must not leave you. Remember that every day death is near and act as if the tomb already enclosed you. Do not care for this world, since anxiety for the world and the desire for riches are thorns that choke the good seed. QUESTIONS AND ANSWERS OF THE GREEK FATHERS 43.2.[27]

GOOD SEED YIELDS GOOD FRUIT IN DEGREES. CYRIL OF ALEXANDRIA: This good seed is worthy of admiration. Rich and well-productive land brings forth fruit a hundredfold. They say that the best soils sometimes under cultivation produce a hundredfold, so this is a mark of every fertile and productive spot. One of the holy prophets said from the mouth of God, "And all nations shall congratulate you, because you are a desirable land."[28] When the divine word falls upon a pure mind skillful in

---

[20]CGSL 178-79**. [21]Mt 13:20. [22]Jn 6:60. [23]ECTD 182**. [24]Hos 8:7. [25]Ps 126:6 (125:6 LXX). [26]CGSL 80**. [27]FC 62:165-66**. [28]Mal 3:12.

cleansing itself from things hurtful, it fixes its root deeply and shoots up like an ear of corn. It brings its fruit to perfection being strong in blade and beautifully flowered. COMMENTARY ON LUKE, HOMILY 41.[29]

8:16-18 Admonition About Catechetical Lectures and Hearing

THE WORD OF GOD IS LIKE A LAMP. ORIGEN: Scripture does not say this about a tangible lamp but about a comprehensible one. One does not "light" the lamp and conceal it "with a vessel" or put it "under a bed, but on the lamp stand" within himself. The vessels of the house are the powers of the soul. The bed is the body. "Those who go in" are those who hear the teacher. . . .

He calls the holy church a "lamp stand." By its

proclamation, the Word of God gives light to all who are in this world and illuminates those in the house with the rays of the truth, filling the minds of all with divine knowledge. FRAGMENTS ON LUKE 120, 122.[30]

FAITH AND FORGIVENESS. EPHREM THE SYRIAN: "To the one who has, it will be given, and from him who has not, even what he has will be taken from him." This is like, "Let the one who has ears listen."[31] This is for those who have spiritual ears within the bodily ears, so that they may listen to his spiritual words. He was increasing his teaching over and above what they already possessed. COMMENTARY ON TATIAN'S DIATESSARON 6.19.[32]

---

[29]CGSL 180**. [30]FC 94:174-75**. [31]Mt 11:15. [32]ECTD 123**.

8:19-21 THE NEW KINSHIP

[19]Then his mother and his brothers came to him, but they could not reach him for the crowd. [20]And he was told, "Your mother and your brothers are standing outside, desiring to see you." [21]But he said to them, "My mother and my brothers are those who hear the word of God and do it."

OVERVIEW: The Word of God, heard in faith, creates this new family of God, which will be the Christian church and which already now is the heavenly community where Jesus reigns as the Ancient of Days (CYRIL OF ALEXANDRIA). Jesus consciously overturns the Old Testament kinship laws that defined one's identity as a member of Israel through genealogy and family relationships, for the family of God now consists of those who do his will (BASIL THE GREAT).

8:19-21 Jesus' Family Are Hearers of the Word

THE NEW FAMILY OF JESUS HEAR THE WORD

AND DO IT. CYRIL OF ALEXANDRIA: The present lesson teaches us that obedience and listening to God are the causes of every blessing. Some entered and spoke respectfully about Christ's holy mother and his brothers. He answered in these words, "My mother and my brothers are they who hear the word of God and do it."

Now do not let any one imagine that Christ scorned the honor due to his mother or contemptuously disregarded the love owed to his brothers. He spoke the law by Moses and clearly said, "Honor your father and your mother, that it may be well with you."[1] How, I ask, could he have re-

---

[1]Deut 5:16.

135

jected the love due to brothers, who even commanded us to love not merely our brothers but also those who are enemies to us? He says, "Love your enemies."[2] What does Christ want to teach? His object is to exalt highly his love toward those who are willing to bow the neck to his commands. I will explain the way he does this. The greatest honors and the most complete affection are what we all owe to our mothers and brothers. If he says that they who hear his word and do it are his mother and brothers, is it not plain to every one that he bestows on those who follow him a love thorough and worthy of their acceptance?

He would make them readily embrace the desire of yielding themselves to his words and of submitting their mind to his yoke, by means of a complete obedience. COMMENTARY ON LUKE, HOMILY 42.[3]

KINSHIP BY DOING GOD'S WILL. BASIL THE GREAT: Intimacy with the Lord is not explained in terms of kinship according to the flesh, but it is achieved by cheerful willingness in doing the will of God. THE MORALS 22.[4]

---

[2]Mt 5:44. [3]CGSL 182**. [4]FC 9:104*.

8:22-25 THE CALMING OF THE STORM

[22]One day he got into a boat with his disciples, and he said to them, "Let us go across to the other side of the lake." So they set out, [23]and as they sailed he fell asleep. And a storm of wind came down on the lake, and they were filling with water, and were in danger. [24]And they went and woke him, saying, "Master, Master, we are perishing!" And he awoke and rebuked the wind and the raging waves; and they ceased, and there was a calm. [25]He said to them, "Where is your faith?" And they were afraid, and they marveled, saying to one another, "Who then is this, that he commands even wind and water, and they obey him?"

OVERVIEW: The disciples' faith was tested by the storm (CYRIL OF ALEXANDRIA). Jesus must be Lord over creation and the one who has come to defeat Satan, as shown also by his exorcism where the demons are associated with the lake[1] (EPHREM THE SYRIAN). Creation is obedient to Jesus' command (CYRIL OF ALEXANDRIA). When Jesus calms the wind and waves, he transforms turmoil into tranquility and chaos into paradise (CHRYSOSTOM).

8:22-25 Even the Wind and Water Obey Him

LITTLENESS OF FAITH TESTED. CYRIL OF ALEXANDRIA: When Christ calmed the storm, he

also changed the faith of the holy disciples that was shaken along with the ship into confidence. He no longer permitted it to be in doubt. He worked a calm in them, smoothing the waves of their weak faith. He said, "Where is your faith?" Another Evangelist, however, affirms that he said, "Why are you fearful, O you of little faith?"[2] When the fear of death unexpectedly befalls people, it sometimes troubles even a well-established mind and exposes it to the blame of smallness of faith. This is also the effect of any other trouble

---

[1]Lk 8:26-39. [2]Mt 8:26.

too great to bear upon those it tries. COMMENTARY ON LUKE, HOMILY 43.[3]

JESUS SHOWS THAT HE IS THE SON OF THE CREATOR. EPHREM THE SYRIAN: He who was sleeping was awakened and cast the sea into a sleep. He reveals the wakefulness of his divinity that never sleeps by the wakefulness of the sea that was now sleeping. He rebuked the wind and it became still. What is this power, or what is this goodness of Jesus? See, he subjected by force that which was not his. Our Lord showed that he was the Son of the Creator by means of the wind of the sea and by the spirits and demons that he silenced. COMMENTARY ON TATIAN'S DIATESSARON 6.25.[4]

ALL CREATION OBEDIENT TO CHRIST'S COMMAND. CYRIL OF ALEXANDRIA: There is also much in this for the admiration and improvement of those who hear. Creation is obedient to whatever Christ chooses to command. What excuse can help us if we do not submit to do the same? What excuse can deliver from the fire and condemnation one who is disobedient and not easily led? He sets up, so to speak, the neck of his haughty mind against Christ's commands, and his heart is impossible to soften. Understanding that all those things that have been brought into existence by God entirely agree with his will, it is our duty to become like the rest of creation and avoid disobedience as a thing that leads to perdition. Let us rather submit to him who summons us to salvation and to the desire of living uprightly and lawfully, that is, evangelically. Christ will fill us with the gifts that come from above and from him. COMMENTARY ON LUKE, HOMILY 43.[5]

SHELTER IN THE STORM. CHRYSOSTOM: We are also sailing on a voyage, not from one land to another but from earth to heaven. Let us prepare our power of reasoning as a pilot able to conduct us on high, and let us gather a crew obedient to it. Let us prepare a strong ship, the kind that the buffeting and discouragements of this life will not submerge, or the wind of false pretense raise up, but will be sleek and swift. If we prepare the ship, pilot and the crew in this way, we will sail with a favoring wind and draw to ourselves the Son of God, the true Pilot. He will not permit our ship to be overwhelmed, even if countless winds blow. He will rebuke the winds and the sea and will bring about a great calm in place of the tempest. COMMENTARY ON ST. JOHN 1.[6]

---

[3]CGSL 187-88**. [4]ECTD127**. [5]CGSL 189**. [6]FC 33:10*.

8:26-39 DEMON POSSESSION AMONG THE GERASENES

[26]*Then they arrived at the country of the Gerasenes,[a] which is opposite Galilee.* [27]*And as he stepped out on land, there met him a man from the city who had demons; for a long time he had worn no clothes, and he lived not in a house but among the tombs.* [28]*When he saw Jesus, he cried out and fell down before him, and said with a loud voice, "What have you to do with me, Jesus, Son of the Most High God? I beseech you, do not torment me."* [29]*For he had commanded the unclean spirit to come out of the man. (For many a time it had seized him; he was kept under*

guard, and bound with chains and fetters, but he broke the bonds and was driven by the demon into the desert.) ³⁰Jesus then asked him, "What is your name?" And he said, "Legion"; for many demons had entered him. ³¹And they begged him not to command them to depart into the abyss. ³²Now a large herd of swine was feeding there on the hillside; and they begged him to let them enter these. So he gave them leave. ³³Then the demons came out of the man and entered the swine, and the herd rushed down the steep bank into the lake and were drowned.

³⁴When the herdsmen saw what had happened, they fled, and told it in the city and in the country. ³⁵Then people went out to see what had happened, and they came to Jesus, and found the man from whom the demons had gone, sitting at the feet of Jesus, clothed and in his right mind; and they were afraid. ³⁶And those who had seen it told them how he who had been possessed with demons was healed. ³⁷Then all the people of the surrounding country of the Gerasenes^a *asked him to depart from them; for they were seized with great fear; so he got into the boat and returned. ³⁸The man from whom the demons had gone begged that he might be with him; but he sent him away, saying, ³⁹"Return to your home, and declare how much God has done for you." And he went away, proclaiming throughout the whole city how much Jesus had done for him.*

a Other ancient authorities read *Gadarenes*, others *Gergesenes*

OVERVIEW: There are details in the miracle that may sound strange to the ears of one who has never encountered a person possessed by demons: the nakedness, the chains, the madness, the abyss and the destruction of the pigs. But the details clearly show the cruelty of demons when they possess a person. Jesus releases those who are in bondage to the demonic forces and therefore is feared by them. They show haughtiness and pride in the way they address Jesus (CYRIL OF ALEXANDRIA). How ironic that the demon possessed who confess Jesus as the Son of God the Most High know better who Jesus is than the heretics (HILARY OF POITIERS).

Jesus asks the name of the demon for the sake of the plan of salvation, since he wants to release this man from the many demons possessing him (CYRIL OF ALEXANDRIA). This demoniac was an unclean Gentile from outside Israel, the epitome of Gentiles doomed to death who are caught in the futility of their pagan worship (AMBROSE), which really is the worship of demons.[1]

A change takes place in the demoniac through his conversion as he is freed from his sepulchral prison (PRUDENTIUS). The demons drop out of sight and are not mentioned again. The hearer may wonder what happened to them after the swine drowned. While the narrative provides no answer to that question, several observations may be offered. First, and most striking, is the mercy of Jesus (EPHREM THE SYRIAN). The unclean spirits are now in unclean animals. Swine are a natural abode for demons (AMBROSE). Jesus allows the demons to enter the swine to show that they have no power over them, who are of lower value in God's creation, and therefore have no power over human beings who are ranked highest in God's created order (CYRIL OF ALEXANDRIA). The presence of Jesus, who is identified by the demon as "Son of God the Most High," is met with faith by some and with rejection by others—the two reactions explained by the parable of the sower—the two reactions represented by the synagogue and the church (AMBROSE).

8:26-27 The Demoniac Naked and Living in Tombs

---

[1]1 Cor 10:20.

DEMON POSSESSION SHOWS THE CRUELTY OF DEMONS. CYRIL OF ALEXANDRIA: In great misery and nakedness, he wandered among the graves of the dead. He was in utter wretchedness, leading a disgraceful life. He was a proof of the cruelty of the demons and a plain demonstration of their impurity.... Whoever they possess and subject to their power, at once they make him an example of great misery, deprived of every blessing, destitute of all sobriety, and entirely deprived even of reason.

Some say, "Why do they possess people?" I answer those who wish to have this explained that the reason of these things is very deep. Somewhere one of his saints addressed God by saying, "Your judgments are a vast abyss."[2] As long as we bear this in mind, we will perhaps not miss the mark. The God of all purposely permits some to fall into their power. He does not do this so that they may suffer but that we may learn by their example how the demons treat us and may avoid the desire of being subject to them. The suffering of one edifies many. COMMENTARY ON LUKE, HOMILY 44.[3]

8:28-31 The Demons Fear Jesus as Son of God Most High

THE DEMONS' RESPONSE FEARFUL YET PRIDEFUL. CYRIL OF ALEXANDRIA: The Gerasene, or rather the herd of demons lying concealed within him, fell down before Christ's feet, saying, "What is there between me and you, Jesus, Son of God Most High? I beseech you, do not torment me." I ask you to observe here the mixture of fear with great audacity and conceited pride. The words which he is forced to shout are coupled with inflated haughtiness! It is a proof of the pride of the enemy that he ventures to say, "What is there between me and you, Jesus, Son of God Most High?" You certainly know that he is the Son of God Most High....

I beseech you to again observe the incomparable majesty of Christ who transcends all. With irresistible might and unequalled authority he crushes Satan by simply willing that it should be. COMMENTARY ON LUKE, HOMILY 44.[4]

DEMONS KNOW BETTER THAN HERETICS WHO JESUS IS. HILARY OF POITIERS: Did not the devils know the real nature of this name? It is fitting that the heretics should be found guilty, not by the teachings of the apostles but by the mouth of demons. The latter often exclaim, "What have I to do with you, Jesus, Son of the Most High God?" The truth drew out this reluctant confession, and being forced to obey, their grief testifies to the strength of this nature. This power overcomes them, since they abandon bodies that they have possessed for a long time. They pay their tribute of honor when they acknowledge the nature of Christ. In the meantime, Christ testifies that he is the Son by his miracles as well as by his name. O heretic, where do you find the name of a creature or the favor of an adoption among those words by which the demons admit who he is? ON THE TRINITY 6.49.[5]

JESUS ASKS THE DEMON'S NAME FOR THE SAKE OF THE PLAN OF SALVATION. CYRIL OF ALEXANDRIA: Christ asked him and commanded him to tell what his name was. He said, "Legion," because many devils had entered him. Did Christ ask this because he did not know it, and like one of us, wished to learn something that had escaped him? Is it not perfectly absurd for us to say or imagine any thing like this? Being God, he knows all things and searches the hearts and inner parts.[6] He asked for the plan of salvation's sake, that we might learn that a great crowd of devils shared the one soul of the man, giving birth a wretched and impure madness in him. He was their work. They certainly are wise to do evil, as the Scripture says, but they have no knowledge to do good.[7] COMMENTARY ON LUKE, HOMILY 44.[8]

THE NAKED DEMONIAC REPRESENTS THE GENTILES. AMBROSE: We know that in the Gospel according to Matthew, two men attacked by

---

[2]Ps 36:6 (35:7 LXX). [3]CGSL 191**. [4]CGSL 191-92**. [5]FC 25:218-19**. [6]Ps 7:8 (7:9 LXX). [7]Jer 4:22. [8]CGSL 192**.

demons met Christ in the country of the Gerasenes.[9] Here St. Luke introduces one such man as naked. Whoever has lost the covering of his nature and virtue is naked. I think that we should not idly disregard but seek the reason why the Evangelists seem to disagree about the number. Although the number disagrees, the mystery agrees. A man who has an evil spirit is a figure of the Gentile people, covered in vices, naked to error, vulnerable to sin. EXPOSITION OF THE GOSPEL OF LUKE 6.44.[10]

FREED FROM HIS SEPULCHRAL PRISON. PRUDENTIUS:

> In his sepulchral prison the savage demon had broken
> Fetters of iron that bound him; he darts forth and kneels before Jesus.
> But the Lord sets the man free and orders the devil to madden
> Herds of the swine and to plunge with them into the depths of the vast sea.

SCENES FROM SACRED HISTORY 36.[11]

8:32-33 The Exorcism of the Demons

THE DEMONS ENTERED THE SWINE. EPHREM THE SYRIAN: The Gadarenes established a ruling for themselves that they would not come out or view the signs of our Lord. Consequently he drowned their swine so that they would have to come out against their will. "Legion," which had been chastened, is a symbol of the world. He commanded the demons to enter the swine and not the man. He, concerning whom they had said, "It is by Beelzebub that he casts out,"[12] engaged in battle against Satan on the mountain and against Legion, the chief of his force.[13] When they entered the swine, he drowned them at that very moment. The force of the merciful One who was keeping watch over this man was known by this. They were begging him not to send them out of that region and not to send them to Gehenna. COMMENTARY ON TATIAN'S DIATESSARON 6.26.[14]

THE DEMONIAC LIVES LIKE A SWINE, SO SWINE RECEIVE HIS DEVILS. AMBROSE: People are the authors of their own tribulation. If someone did not live like a swine, the devil would never have received power over him. If he did receive power, it would be power not to destroy but to test him. After the Lord's coming, the devil could already not corrupt the good, so perhaps he now does not seek the destruction of all people but only of the fickle. A mugger does not lie in wait for armed men but for the defenseless. He who understands that the strong will despise him or the powerful destroy him troubles only the weak with wrongs. Someone says, "Why does God permit this to the devil?" I say, "So that good people may be tested and the wicked punished, for this is the punishment of sin." This is also according to the law, because the Lord sends fever, trembling, evil spirits, blindness, and all scourges according to the punishment of sinners.[15] EXPOSITION OF THE GOSPEL OF LUKE 6.48-49.[16]

8:34-37 The Response of the Herdsmen and the Townspeople

DEMONS HAVE NO POWER OVER SWINE OR US. CYRIL OF ALEXANDRIA: We may also learn this from what befell the herd of swine. Wicked demons are cruel, mischievous, hurtful and treacherous to those who are in their power. The fact clearly proves this, because they hurried the swine over a precipice and drowned them in the waters. Christ granted their request that we might learn from what happened that their disposition is ruthless, bestial, incapable of being softened, and solely intent on doing evil to those whom they can get into their power.

If there is anyone among us who is wanton, swinish, filth loving, impure and willingly contaminated with the abominations of sin, God permits such a one to fall into their power and sink into the abyss of damnation. It will never happen

---

[9]Mt 8:28. [10]EHG 208**. [11]FC 52:190. [12]Lk 11:15. [13]Cf. Mk 5:13. [14]ECTD 127-28*. [15]See Deut 28:59. [16]EHG 210**.

that those who love Christ will become subject to them. It will never happen to us as long as we walk in his footsteps, avoid negligence in the performance of what is right, desire those things which are honorable, and belong to that virtuous and praiseworthy lifestyle that Christ has marked out for us by the precepts of the gospel. COMMENTARY ON LUKE, HOMILY 44.[17]

8:38-39 The Response of the Demoniac

THE DEMONIAC GOES FROM SYNAGOGUE TO CHURCH. AMBROSE: It says, "The herdsmen saw this and fled."[18] Neither professors of philosophy nor leaders of the synagogue can offer any cure when people perish. Christ alone takes away the sins of the people, provided they do not refuse to submit to healing. He does not want to cure the unwilling and soon abandon the weak for whom it seems that his presence is a burden, like the peoples of the Gerasenes. They went out from that country, which appears to be an image of the synagogue, and begged him to depart from them, because they were very afraid.... Why does Christ not accept the healed man but advise him to return home? Perhaps this occurs to avoid a cause of boasting and give an example to unbelievers, although that home may be an inn by nature. Since he received the healing of his mind, Christ commanded him to depart from the tombs and the graves[19] and to return to that spiritual home. He who had in him the grave of the mind became a temple of God. EXPOSITION OF THE GOSPEL OF LUKE 6.50, 53.[20]

---

[17]CGSL 193-94**. [18]Mt 8:33. [19]Mt 8:28. [20]EHG 210-11**.

8:40-56 THE RAISING OF JAIRUS'S DAUGHTER AND THE HEALING OF THE WOMAN WITH A HEMORRHAGE

[40]Now when Jesus returned, the crowd welcomed him, for they were all waiting for him. [41]And there came a man named Jairus, who was a ruler of the synagogue; and falling at Jesus' feet he besought him to come to his house, [42]for he had an only daughter, about twelve years of age, and she was dying.

As he went, the people pressed round him. [43]And a woman who had had a flow of blood for twelve years[b] and could not be healed by any one, [44]came up behind him, and touched the fringe of his garment; and immediately her flow of blood ceased. [45]And Jesus said, "Who was it that touched me?" When all denied it, Peter[c] said, "Master, the multitudes surround you and press upon you!" [46]But Jesus said, "Some one touched me; for I perceive that power has gone forth from me." [47]And when the woman saw that she was not hidden, she came trembling, and falling down before him declared in the presence of all the people why she had touched him, and how she had been immediately healed. [48]And he said to her, "Daughter, your faith has made you well; go in peace."

[49]While he was still speaking, a man from the ruler's house came and said, "Your daughter is dead; do not trouble the Teacher any more." [50]But Jesus on hearing this answered him, "Do not

fear; only believe, and she shall be well." [51] *And when he came to the house, he permitted no one to enter with him, except Peter and John and James, and the father and mother of the child.* [52] *And all were weeping and bewailing her; but he said, "Do not weep; for she is not dead but sleeping."* [53] *And they laughed at him, knowing that she was dead.* [54] *But taking her by the hand he called, saying, "Child, arise."* [55] *And her spirit returned, and she got up at once; and he directed that something should be given her to eat.* [56] *And her parents were amazed; but he charged them to tell no one what had happened.*

b Other ancient authorities add *and had spent all her living upon physicians*   c Other ancient authorities add *and those who were with him*

OVERVIEW: His power over the death of a twelve-year old girl and over the twelve-year sickness of a hemorrhaging woman demonstrates that Jesus is the resurrection and the life (CYRIL OF ALEXANDRIA). The accounts bring out several parallels and similarities: the girl at twelve years old is about to die at an age when she would have entered womanhood, and a woman has been hemorrhaging for twelve years, as long as the little girl had been alive. Jesus vivifies the one and heals the other (EPHREM THE SYRIAN).

The dying daughter represents the synagogue and the woman with the flow of blood the church as it reaches out in faith to touch the hem of Jesus' garment (AMBROSE). The woman with the flow of blood is also unclean, which is why she stays hidden and steals the healing from the hem of Jesus' garment (CYRIL OF ALEXANDRIA). Yet in her hiddenness, Jesus' divinity is revealed, and he sees in her a hidden faith that is proclaimed to the crowds (EPHREM THE SYRIAN).

Jesus has shown his power over nature, demon possession and sickness. These three miracles lead up to the final miracle: the passion of Jesus and his resurrection from the dead (AMBROSE). The woman touches the tassel of Jesus' garment, his sacred hem, and she is healed (PRUDENTIUS). The power to heal is inherent in Jesus' very nature as God, and flows out of him to heal this woman (CYRIL OF ALEXANDRIA). The reason Jesus heals her womb is to show that clothed in our humanity he might reveal his divinity through the art of healing. Jesus says to the woman healed of a twelve-year flow of blood, "Daughter, your faith has saved you. Go in peace." Faith is the means by which anyone now may enter the family of Jesus,[1] and peace is the crown of victory she receives because of her faith (EPHREM THE SYRIAN). These words of Jesus are spoken to the girl's father to give him comfort. To believe in the possibility of resurrection for his daughter requires faith that in Jesus there is the cause of life (CYRIL OF ALEXANDRIA).

The people laugh at Jesus when he says that the girl is not dead but sleeping, but Jesus does not lie, for those who die in Christ will arise from the dead (CYRIL OF ALEXANDRIA). So when Jesus awakens her he orders that food be given to her to show that she is fully alive and well (EPHREM THE SYRIAN). Jesus' command to silence, before his resurrection, alerts catechumens to the significance of Jesus' resurrection as central to the mystery of the faith and to those mysteries—the sacraments—through which their bodies as well as their souls are fed holy food and touched with Christ's resurrection power (AMBROSE).

8:40-42 Jairus's Daughter Near Death

TWO MIRACLES TESTIFY THAT JESUS IS THE RESURRECTION AND THE LIFE. CYRIL OF ALEXANDRIA: Christ foreknew his mystery, even before the foundations of the world. It was in the last ages of the world that he arose for the inhabitants of earth. Having borne the sin of the world,

[1]Lk 8:19-21.

he abolished both it and death, which is its consequence and was brought upon us by its means. He plainly said, "I am the resurrection and the life,"[2] and "he that believes on me has everlasting life, and shall not come into judgment, but has passed from death unto life."[3] We will see this fulfilled in facts. The ruler of the synagogue of the Jews came near and, embracing the Savior's knees, begged him to deliver his daughter from the bonds of death. Look, she already was brought down to this and was in extreme danger! The Savior consented and set out with him. He was even hurrying on to the house of the one who invited him and was aware that what was being done would profit many of those who followed him and would also be for his own glory. On the way, he saved the woman who was the victim of a severe and incurable malady. No one could stop her issue of blood that ruined the art of physicians. No sooner had she touched the hem in faith, than he immediately healed her. A miracle so glorious and revealed was, so to speak, the work merely of Christ's journey. COMMENTARY ON LUKE, HOMILY 46.[4]

TWELVE YEARS. EPHREM THE SYRIAN: When the woman with a hemorrhage learned that the Lord said to the leader of the synagogue, "Believe, and your daughter will live," she thought to herself that he who could bring back the soul of a little girl of twelve into her body would also be able to take away an illness of twelve years and expel it from the body. When she heard him say, "Believe firmly and your daughter will live," this woman reflected, "I can give the faith he requires as the price." The healing came forth from his mouth, and he negotiated as its price the faith expressed by the woman's mouth. He gave a clear healing and demanded a clear price. The healing that came out from his lips could be heard publicly, and he required from the lips a faith openly professed. Although the woman professed before everyone, they did not believe her, especially since her pains were hidden. When the Lord opened the eyes of the blind man, they called him a mad-

man,[5] and when he restored Lazarus to life, certain people, even among those who had seen for themselves, did not believe. This is why he restored the little girl of twelve years to life. He who was able to put the continued vitality of twelve years in the body back into its place was also able to arrest and banish from its place a flow of blood that continued for twelve years. He who was able to alleviate one illness was also able to banish another. He who was able to vivify all the dead members of this little girl was also able to heal the woman's womb. COMMENTARY ON TATIAN'S DIATESSARON 7.26.[6]

8:43-48 Healing the Woman with the Flow of Blood

THE DAUGHTER REPRESENTS THE SYNAGOGUE, THE WOMAN THE CHURCH. AMBROSE: The assembly of the nations is like the woman who spent all her money on physicians. The assembly of nations also lost all the gifts of nature and squandered the inheritance of life. It was holy, shy, pious, ready in faith, and hesitant in modesty, because it is a sign of modesty to recognize the weakness of faith and not to despair of pardon. The shy woman touched the hem, the faithful approached, the pious believed, the wise knew she was healed. The holy people of the nations that believed in God were so ashamed of their sin that they abandoned it. Brought faith, they believed. They showed devotion, so that they entreated. They put on wisdom, so that they perceived their own health. They took confidence, so that they confessed the alien truth that they snatched.[7]

Why is Christ touched from behind? Is it because it is written, "You shall follow the Lord your God"?[8] Why is it that the twelve-year-old daughter of the ruler was dying and the woman with a flow of blood was afflicted for twelve years, except that it is understood that as long as the synagogue flourished, the church suffered? The

---

[2]Jn 11:25. [3]Jn 5:24. [4]CGSL 200**. [5]Jn 10:20. [6]ECTD 141-42**. [7]Eph 2:12. [8]Deut 13:4.

weakness of the one is the virtue of the other, because by their offense salvation has come to the Gentiles.[9] The consummation of the one is the beginning of the other, the beginning not of nature but of salvation. Exposition of the Gospel of Luke 6.56-57.[10]

The Woman Remains Hidden. Cyril of Alexandria: What made that sick woman wish to remain hidden? The law of wise Moses imputed impurity to any woman who was suffering from a flow of blood and everywhere called her unclean. Whoever was unclean could not touch any thing that was holy or approach a holy man. For this reason the woman was careful to remain concealed, for fear that having transgressed the law she should have to bear the punishment which it imposed. When she touched, she was healed immediately and without delay. Commentary on Luke, Homily 45.[11]

The Woman Testifies to Jesus' Divinity, and Jesus to Her Faith. Ephrem the Syrian: Glory to you, hidden offspring of Being, because the hidden suffering of her that was afflicted proclaimed your healing. Using a woman whom they could see, he enabled them to see the divinity that cannot be seen. The Son's divinity became known through his healing, and the afflicted woman's faith was revealed through her being healed. She caused him to be proclaimed, and she was proclaimed with him. Truth was being proclaimed together with its heralds. If she was a witness to his divinity, he in turn was a witness to her faith.

She poured faith on him by way of reward, and he bestowed healing on her as the outcome of her reward. Since the woman's faith had become public, her healing also was proclaimed in public. The physicians were put to shame about their remedies because his power became resplendent and magnified the Son. It became evident how great faith surpasses the healing art and how hidden power surpasses visible remedies. Commentary on Tatian's Diatessaron 7.1-2.[12]

Signs of Jesus' Passion and Resurrection. Ambrose: It says, "Servants came to the ruler, saying, 'Do not trouble him.'" Still they were without faith in the resurrection, which Jesus foretold in the law[13] and fulfilled in the gospel. When he came into the house, he approved a few eyewitnesses to the imminent resurrection, because many did not immediately believe the resurrection.[14] Then, as the Lord said, "'The girl is not dead but sleeps,' they laughed him to scorn." Whoever does not believe, jeers. Those who think they are dead will weep for their dead, but when there is faith in resurrection, there is the appearance not of death but of sleep. Exposition of the Gospel of Luke 6.61-62.[15]

His Sacred Hem. Prudentius:
Then a woman, weak and timid, touched
    his sacred garment's hem:
Instant was his blessed healing, and
    the pallor left her cheek,
As the hemorrhage she had suffered
Through so many years was stopped.
Hymn for Every Day 9.33-44.[16]

The Power to Heal Is Inherent in Jesus' Nature as God. Cyril of Alexandria: "For I know," he said, "that power has gone out from me." It transcends our order, or probably that even of the angels, to send out any power of their own nature, as something that is of themselves. Such an act is an attribute appropriate only to the nature that is above everything and supreme. Every created being God endows with power, whether of healing or something similar, does not possess it of itself but as a thing given it by God. All things are given and worked in the creature, and it can do nothing of itself. As God he said, "I know that power has gone forth from me." Commentary on Luke, Homily 45.[17]

---

[9]Rom 11:11. [10]EHG 212**. [11]CGSL 198**. [12]ECTD 129**. [13]See Ps 15:10 LXX. [14]See Acts 17:32. [15]EHG 214**. [16]FC 43:62. [17]CGSL 199**.

THE REASON JESUS HEALS HER WOMB.
EPHREM THE SYRIAN: "Who touched me? For a power has gone forth from me." A detail such as this is not reported about our Physician in any other place. This is because in no other place did our Physician encounter an affliction such as this. This affliction was presented to many physicians, yet only one Physician encountered this affliction to heal it. Many physicians encountered and wearied her. Only one encountered her who was able to give her rest from the toil of many physicians. The art of healing encountered a shameful affliction but added pain after pain to it. The more they came, the worse the affliction got.[18] The fringe of the Lord's cloak touched her[19] and uprooted this suffering from its root. She perceived within herself that he healed her affliction.[20]

Since the art of healing clothed with all our practical wisdom was reduced to silence, the divinity clothed with garments was proclaimed. He clothed himself in the body and came down to humanity, so that humanity might loot him. He revealed his divinity through signs, so that faith in his humanity alone could not be explained. He revealed his humanity that the higher beings might believe that he was a lower being, and he revealed his divinity so that the lower beings would accept that he was a higher being. He took on a human body so that humanity might be able to attain to divinity, and he revealed his divinity so that his humanity might not be trampled under foot. COMMENTARY ON TATIAN'S DIATESSARON 7.16-17.[21]

DECLARATION OF PEACE A CROWN OF HER VICTORY. EPHREM THE SYRIAN: If the woman once cured had withdrawn from him in secret, our Lord would have deprived her of a crown of victory. It was fitting that the faith that shined out brightly in hidden agony was publicly crowned. He wove an eloquent crown for her, because he said to her, "Go in peace."[22] The peace he gave was the crown of her victory. When he said, "Go in peace," he did not end here but also added, "Your faith has saved you,"[23] so that they would

know who was this crown's Lord. This would make known that the peace his mouth wove was the crown that crowned her faith. "Your faith has saved you." If it was faith that restored her to life, it is clear that he crowned her faith with a crown. This is why he cried out, "Who touched my garments?"[24] He said this so all the people might know who touched more than anyone else did. She chose to honor him more than others do, first, by approaching from behind, and second, in that she touched the fringe of his cloak. It was also fitting that he would honor her before all of these, she who chose to honor him more than all these. COMMENTARY ON TATIAN'S DIATESSARON 7.10.[25]

8:49-56 *The Raising of Jairus's Daughter*

A WORD OF COMFORT TO THE FATHER. CYRIL OF ALEXANDRIA: A messenger from the synagogue ruler's house met them saying, "Your daughter is dead; do not trouble the Teacher." What was Christ's answer, seeing that he possesses universal sovereignty? He is Lord of life and death. By the all-powerful determination of his will, he accomplishes whatever he desires. He saw the man oppressed with the weight of sorrow, fainting, stunned, and all but despairing of the possibility of his daughter being rescued from death. Misfortunes are able to disturb even an apparently well constituted mind and to estrange it from its settled convictions. To help him, he gives him a kind and saving word that is able to sustain him in his fainting state and work in him an unwavering faith: "Fear not, only believe, and she shall live." COMMENTARY ON LUKE, HOMILY 46.[26]

DEATH IS SLEEP FOR THOSE WHO WILL ARISE IN CHRIST. CYRIL OF ALEXANDRIA: Coming to the house of his supplicant, he quiets their funeral songs, silences the musicians, and stops the tears of the weepers, saying, "The girl

---

[18]Cf. Mk 5:26. [19]Mt 9:20. [20]See Mk 5:29. [21]ECTD 136-37*. [22]Mk 5:34. [23]Mt 9:22. [24]Mk 5:30. [25]ECTD 133**. [26]CGSL 200-201**.

is not dead but rather sleeps." "And they," it says, "laughed at him." I ask you to observe here the great skill of the management. Although he well knew that the girl was dead, he said, "She is not dead but rather sleeps." What is his reason? By their laughing at him, they might give a clear and manifest acknowledgment that the daughter was dead. There would probably be some of that group who always resist his glory who would reject the divine miracle and say that the damsel was not yet dead. Delivering from sickness was nothing very extraordinary for Christ. To have the acknowledgment of many that the girl was dead, he said that she was rather sleeping. Let no one affirm that Christ spoke falsely. To him, as being life by nature, there is nothing dead. Having a firm hope of the resurrection of the dead, we call the dead "those that sleep" for this reason. They will arise in Christ, and as the blessed Paul says, "They live to him,"[27] because they are about to live. COMMENTARY ON LUKE, HOMILY 46.[28]

CHRIST RAISES THE YOUNG GIRL. CYRIL OF ALEXANDRIA: When he came to the house in which the girl was lying dead, he took with him only three of the holy apostles and the father and the mother of the girl. The manner in which he performed the miracle was worthy of God. "Having taken her," it says, "by the hand, he said, 'Girl, arise'; and she arose immediately." O the power of a word and the might of commands that nothing can resist! O the life producing touch of the hand that abolishes death and corruption! These are the fruits of faith, for the sake of which the hand of Moses also gave the law to those of old time. COMMENTARY ON LUKE, HOMILY 46.[29]

THE GIRL IS GIVEN FOOD. EPHREM THE SYRIAN: When the woman was healed, our Lord said, "Who touched me?" so that she could profess her healing before everyone. Also in the case of the little girl, he said, "She is sleeping"[30] so that the spectators might testify that she was dead, and

then seeing her restored to life, these who scorned would be converted into believers. The witness given by them concerning the death of the little girl and her restoration to life performed by the Lord was a witness in anticipation of his death. Those who would see that he was alive again would not deny it. COMMENTARY ON TATIAN'S DIATESSARON 7.27A.[31]

TAKING FOOD PROVES SHE IS ALIVE. AMBROSE: What shall I say about the daughter of the ruler of the synagogue, at whose death the people were mourning and the flute players were playing their music? In the belief that she was indeed dead, solemn funeral services were being performed. The spirit returned immediately at the voice of the Lord, she arose with revived body, and she partook of food to furnish proof that she was alive. ON HIS BROTHER SATYRUS 2.82.[32]

LIKE THE DAUGHTER, THE CHURCH RISES TO EAT HOLY FOOD. AMBROSE: Jesus took the girl's hand, healed her, and ordered that she should be given something to eat. This is evidence of life, so that not an apparition[33] but the truth may be believed. Blessed is he whose hand Wisdom holds. I wish that righteousness held my acts and my hands. I want the Word of God to hold me, bring me into his closet,[34] turn away the spirit of error,[35] replace it with that of salvation, and order that I be given something to eat! The Word of God is the Bread of heaven.[36] The Wisdom that filled the holy altar with the nourishment of the divine body and blood says, "Come, eat of my bread, and drink wine that I have mixed for you."[37] What is the reason for such diversity? Above, Christ raised the son of the widow in public.[38] Here, he dismissed several eyewitnesses. I think that the Lord's compassion is also revealed since the widowed mother of an only son

---

[27]Rom 6:8. [28]CGSL 201**. [29]CGSL 201*. [30]Mt 9:24. [31]ECTD 142**. [32]FC 22:233. [33]Cf. Mt 14:26; Lk 24:37-43. [34]See Song 1:4. [35]1 Jn 4:6. [36]Jn 6:51. [37]Prov 9:5. [38]Lk 7:12.

did not suffer delay. He is prompt; for fear that she would be further afflicted. It is also wise that the church would immediately believe through the widow's son, but the Jews, albeit a few, would believe through the daughter of the ruler of the synagogue. EXPOSITION OF THE GOSPEL OF LUKE 6.63-64.[39]

---

[39]EHG 214-15**.

9:1-6 THE SENDING OF THE TWELVE

[1]*And he called the twelve together and gave them power and authority over all demons and to cure diseases, [2]and he sent them out to preach the kingdom of God and to heal. [3]And he said to them, "Take nothing for your journey, no staff, nor bag, nor bread, nor money; and do not have two tunics. [4]And whatever house you enter, stay there, and from there depart. [5]And wherever they do not receive you, when you leave that town shake off the dust from your feet as a testimony against them."[6]And they departed and went through the villages, preaching the gospel and healing everywhere.*

OVERVIEW: In commissioning the Twelve, Jesus gives the disciples the privilege of participating in his prophetic pattern of preaching and miracles of healing, a special honor to the Twelve and the seventy (EUSEBIUS). He glorifies his disciples by giving them power and authority over demons and the ability to heal diseases. Jesus sends them into a ministry that will leave them dependent on the Lord of the harvest without provisions so that they may be free from the anxiety of the body (CYRIL OF ALEXANDRIA). Their feet, without sandals, are the beautiful feet of those who preach the good news (AMBROSE). The mission of the Twelve (and of the others) is to the house, where they are to be dependent on the hospitality of others to provide for their needs (CYRIL OF ALEXANDRIA). The dust from any place that does not receive their preaching is profane, to be shaken off lest it stain God's people and be brought into God's house as they enter the presence of the "new temple" (AMBROSE). Through these undistinguished and ill-equipped men, Jesus is able to conquer the world with the gospel (CHRYSOSTOM).

9:1-2 The Twelve Preach and Heal

TWELVE AND SEVENTY GIVEN SPECIAL HONOR. EUSEBIUS: The Lord and Savior, not very long after the beginning of his preaching, called the twelve apostles. He gave the name of apostles to them alone of all his disciples as a special honor.[1] Later he proclaimed seventy others and sent them also out two by two in advance of himself into every place and city where he himself was to come. ECCLESIASTICAL HISTORY 1.10.[2]

JESUS GIVING THEM POWER TO HEAL AND EXORCISE. CYRIL OF ALEXANDRIA: The grace bestowed upon the holy apostles is worthy of all admiration. But the bountifulness of the Giver

---

[1]Cf. Mt 10:1-4. [2]FC 19:72*.

147

surpasses all praise and admiration. He gives them, as I said, his own glory. They receive authority over the evil spirits. They reduce to nothing the pride of the devil that was so highly exalted and arrogant. They render ineffectual the demon's wickedness. By the might and efficacy of the Holy Spirit, burning them as if they were on fire, they make the devil come forth with groans and weeping from those whom he had possessed.
. . .

He glorified his disciples, therefore, by giving them authority and power over the evil spirits and over sicknesses. Did he honor them without reason and make them famous without any logical cause? How can this be true? It was necessary, most necessary, that they should be able to work miracles, having been publicly appointed ministers of sacred proclamations. By means of their works, they then could convince men that they were the ministers of God and mediators of all beneath the heaven. The apostles then could invite them all to reconciliation and justification by faith and point out the way of salvation and of life that is this justification. COMMENTARY ON LUKE, HOMILY 47.[3]

9:3-5 Instructions for the Mission of the Twelve

FREE FROM ANXIETY ABOUT THE BODY. CYRIL OF ALEXANDRIA: It was most appropriate for Jesus to instruct his disciples to take nothing with them. He wished them both to be free from all worldly care, and so entirely exempt from the labors that worldly things require, that they would not even worry about obtaining necessary and indispensable food for themselves. Manifestly, One who instructs them to abstain even from things such as these entirely cuts away the love of riches and the desire of gain. For their glory, he said, and, so to speak, their crown, is to possess nothing. He separates them even from such things as are necessary for their use, by commanding them to carry nothing whatsoever, neither staff, nor bag, nor bread, nor money nor two coats. Observe, therefore, as I said, that he takes

them away from worthless distractions and anxiety about the body. He commands them not to worry about food, repeating to them, as it were, that passage in the psalm: "Cast your care upon the Lord, and he shall feed you."[4] For what Christ says is also true: "You are not able to serve God and money." And, "For where your treasure is, there will your heart be also."[5] COMMENTARY ON LUKE, HOMILY 47.[6]

FEET THAT ARE BEAUTIFUL IN PREACHING THE GOOD NEWS. AMBROSE: This is a great vision. But if you wish to see it, remove the sandals from your feet.[7] Remove every chain of sin. Remove the chains of the world. Leave behind earthly sandals. Jesus sent the apostles without sandals, without money, gold and silver, so that they would not carry earthly things with them. The one who seeks to do good is praised not for his sandals but for the swiftness and grace of his feet. The Scripture says, "How beautiful are the feet of those who preach the gospel of peace, of those who bring glad tidings of good things!"[8] Therefore remove the sandals from your feet, that they may be beautiful for preaching the gospel. FLIGHT FROM THE WORLD 5.25.[9]

DEPENDENT ON THE HOSPITALITY OF OTHERS. CYRIL OF ALEXANDRIA: He commanded them both to remain in one house, and from it to take their departure. For it was right that those who had once received them should not be defrauded of the gift. It is also right that the holy apostles themselves should not place any impediment in the way of their own zeal and earnestness in preaching God's message. This would happen if they allowed themselves to be carried off to various houses by those whose object was not to learn some necessary lesson but to set before them a luxurious table, beyond what was moderate and necessary. COMMENTARY ON LUKE, HOMILY 47.[10]

---

[3]CGSL 207-9**. [4]Ps 55:22 (54:23 LXX). [5]Mt 6:21. [6]CGSL 210**. [7]Ex 3:5. [8]Is 52:7; Rom 10:15. [9]FC 65:300-301**. [10]CGSL 211**.

UNBELIEVING HOUSES THAT REJECT APOSTOLIC PREACHING ARE ABANDONED.

AMBROSE: So the faith of the church must be sought first and foremost. If Christ is to dwell in a house, it undoubtedly must be chosen. But lest an unbelieving people or a heretical teacher deface its home, the church is commanded that the fellowship of heretics be avoided and the synagogue shunned. The dust is to be shaken off your feet lest when the dryness of barren unbelief crumbles the sole of your mind it is stained as if by a dry and sandy soil. A preacher of the gospel must take on himself the bodily weaknesses of a faithful people, so to speak. He must lift up and remove from his own soles worthless actions as if they were dust. For it is written: "Who is weak, and I am not weak?"[11] Any church which rejects faith and does not possess the foundations of apostolic preaching is to be abandoned lest it be able to stain others with unbelief. The apostle also clearly affirmed this by saying "Reject a man that is a heretic after the first admonition."[12] EXPOSITION OF THE GOSPEL OF LUKE 6.68.[13]

9:6 The Twelve Depart

UNDISTINGUISHED AND ILL-EQUIPPED MEN.

CHRYSOSTOM: Christ had the power to set the human race free from all these evils—not only the Romans but also the Persians and simply every race of barbarians. He succeeded in doing this with no force of arms, nor expenditure of money, nor by starting wars of conquest, nor by inflaming men to battle. He had only eleven men to start with, men who were undistinguished, without learning, ill-informed, destitute, poorly clad, without weapons, or sandals, men who had but a single tunic to wear. DEMONSTRATION AGAINST THE PAGANS 1.7.[14]

---

[11]2 Cor 11:29. [12]Tit 3:10. [13]EHG 216-17**. [14]FC 73:189*.

9:7-17 HEROD QUESTIONS THE IDENTITY OF JESUS; THE FEEDING OF THE FIVE THOUSAND

[7]Now Herod the tetrarch heard of all that was done, and he was perplexed, because it was said by some that John had been raised from the dead, [8]by some that Elijah had appeared, and by others that one of the old prophets had risen. [9]Herod said, "John I beheaded; but who is this about whom I hear such things?" And he sought to see him.

[10]On their return the apostles told him what they had done. And he took them and withdrew apart to a city called Bethsaida. [11]When the crowds learned it, they followed him; and he welcomed them and spoke to them of the kingdom of God, and cured those who had need of healing. [12]Now the day began to wear away; and the twelve came and said to him, "Send the crowd away, to go into the villages and country round about, to lodge and get provisions; for we are here in a lonely place." [13]But he said to them, "You give them something to eat." They said, "We have no more than five loaves and two fish—unless we are to go and buy food for all these people." [14]For there were about five thousand men. And he said to his disciples, "Make them sit down in companies, about

fifty each." [15]*And they did so, and made them all sit down.* [16]*And taking the five loaves and the two fish he looked up to heaven, and blessed and broke them, and gave them to the disciples to set before the crowd.* [17]*And all ate and were satisfied. And they took up what was left over, twelve baskets of broken pieces.*

OVERVIEW: Luke alone stresses the teachings about the kingdom of God in the introduction to this miracle, namely, "to preach the kingdom of God and to heal the sick," and then concludes with the notice that Jesus spoke about the kingdom and healed the sick (BEDE). The kingdom of God comes as the Messiah teaches, heals and feeds his people, as was promised by the prophets of old (AMBROSE).

The feeding of the five thousand has Old Testament precedents. Jesus is the prophet like Moses, who feeds the people in the wilderness (CYRIL OF ALEXANDRIA). There are also some allegorical aspects to the feeding miracle that connect it to the Old Testament; for example, the five loaves represent the five books of Moses (AUGUSTINE). The five loaves may also represent the five senses, with the seven loaves in the feeding of the four thousand the sanctified bread of rest that anticipates the eight loaves of the resurrection (AMBROSE).

This bread is the Word of God that grows mystically in the way that the water becomes wine at the wedding of Cana. The miraculous food of loaves and fish multiplied for thousands will give way to the stronger food of Christ, his body and blood. This feeding miracle is a foretaste of the satisfaction of the church at the Lord's table and at the heavenly banquet (AMBROSE).

In the feeding of the five thousand, the Creator gives substantial food to his creation through the Messiah in abundance for lasting life (PRUDENTIUS). Such an abundance encourages those who have little to offer hospitality to strangers, for the Lord will provide what is needed (CYRIL OF ALEXANDRIA). This abundance comes from the heavenly table of the Lord (PRUDENTIUS). Table fellowship with Jesus is a foretaste of the future eschatological meal, which Jesus as the bread of life prepares for believers for the life of the world (CYRIL OF ALEXANDRIA).

9:7-11 Introduction to the Miracle

TEACHING AND HEALING PRECEDE THE MIRACLE. BEDE: You see, our Lord provided encouragement for the multitude that was following him as the Passover, the Jews' festival day, was drawing near. He did this by his words of salvation, together with the help of his cures. As another Evangelist wrote, he spoke to them about the kingdom of God and healed those who were in need of being cured. When his acts of teaching and healing were completed, he refreshed them most abundantly from a small amount of food. HOMILIES ON THE GOSPELS 2.2.[1]

THOSE WHO RECEIVE THE FOOD OF CHRIST ARE FIRST HEALED. AMBROSE: After the law has passed away, the food of the gospel begins to feed the hungry hearts of the people.... It was fitting that those whom he had healed from the pain of wounds he freed from hunger with spiritual nourishment. Thus none receives the food of Christ unless he was first healed, and the calling first heals those who are called to the feast.[2] If one was lame, he received the ability to walk, so that he came. If one lacked the sight of his eyes, he could indeed not enter the house of the Lord, unless his sight was restored. EXPOSITION OF THE GOSPEL OF LUKE 6.69-70.[3]

9:12-15 Preparation

MOSES' MIRACLE OF MANNA. CYRIL OF ALEX-

---

[1]CS 111:13*. [2]See Lk 14:21. [3]EHG 217**.

ANDRIA: The feeding of the multitudes in the desert by Christ is worthy of all admiration. But it is also profitable in another way. We can plainly see that these new miracles are in harmony with those of ancient times. They are the acts of one and the same power. He rained manna in the desert upon the Israelites. He gave them bread from heaven. "Man did eat angels' food,"[4] according to the words of praise in the Psalms. But look! He has again abundantly supplied food to those who needed food in the desert. He brought it down, as it were, from heaven. Multiplying that small amount of food many times and feeding so large a multitude, so to speak, with nothing, is like that first miracle. COMMENTARY ON LUKE, HOMILY 48.[5]

THE FIVE BOOKS OF MOSES. AUGUSTINE: The five loaves are understood as the five books of Moses. Rightly, they are not wheat but barley loaves because they belong to the Old Testament. You know that barley was created in such a way that one can scarcely get to its kernel. This kernel is clothed with a covering of husk, and this husk is tenacious and adhering, so that it is stripped off with effort. Such is the letter of the Old Testament, clothed with the coverings of carnal mysteries. If one gets to its kernel, it feeds and sat-isfies. TRACTATES ON THE GOSPEL OF JOHN 24.5.[6]

THE MYSTERY OF THE LOAVES EXPLAINED. AMBROSE: For we read that first five thousand are fed with five loaves, then four thousand with seven loaves.[7] So let us seek the mystery which the miracle represents. Those five thousand, like the body's five senses, seem to have received from Christ food similar to physical food. But the four thousand[8] are still in the body and in the world that is known to be of four elements. . . . Seven baskets of fragments remained from the four thousand.[9] This bread of sabbaths is no ordinary bread. It is sanctified bread. It is a bread of rest. Perhaps, if you will first eat the five loaves with the senses, I shall dare also to say you will not eat

bread on earth on the third day, after eating the five loaves and the seven.[10] You will eat eight loaves above the earth, like those who are in the heavens. As the seven loaves are loaves of rest, so the eight loaves are the loaves of the resurrection. Therefore those who are fed on the seven loaves will persevere to the third day and, perhaps, attain the whole faith and steadfastness of the future resurrection. Then there is the voice of the saints: "We will go a three days' journey, that we may feast with the Lord our God."[11] EXPOSITION OF THE GOSPEL OF LUKE 6.79-80.[12]

9:16 *The Miracle*

BREAD IS THE WORD OF GOD THAT GROWS MYSTICALLY. AMBROSE: This bread which Jesus breaks is truly the mystical Word of God and a discourse about Christ which is increased while it is distributed. From a few discourses, he ministered abundant nourishment to all peoples. He gave discourses to us like loaves that are doubled when they are poured forth from our mouths. That bread in an incomprehensible fashion is visibly increased when it is broken, when it is distributed, when it is eaten without any understanding of how it is provided. . . . Truly, Christ's gifts seem small but are very great. They are not bestowed on one person but on peoples, for the food grew in the mouth of those who ate it. This food seemed to be for bodily nourishment but was taken for eternal salvation. EXPOSITION OF THE GOSPEL OF LUKE 6.86, 88.[13]

CHRIST HAS YET TO FEED THEM WITH STRONGER FOOD. AMBROSE: The order of the mystery is preserved everywhere. The first healing is bestowed on wounds through the remission of sins. Then the nourishment of the heavenly table abounds, although this multitude

---

[4]Ps 78:25 (77:25 LXX). [5]CGSL 215**. [6]FC 79:234-35**. [7]Mt 15:34-38. [8]Mt 15:38. [9]Mt 15:37. [10]Mt 15:32. [11]Ex 5:3. [12]EHG 221-22**. [13]EHG 224-26**.

is not yet refreshed with stronger foods, nor do hearts hungry for more solid faith feed on the body and blood of Christ.[14] He says, "I gave you milk to drink, not meat. For you then were not strong, nor are you yet."[15] The five loaves are like milk, but the more solid meat is the body of Christ, and the stronger drink is the blood of the Lord.[16] Not immediately at first do we feast on all foods, nor do we drink all drinks. "First drink this," he says. Thus there is a first, then a second thing that you drink. There is also a first thing that you eat, then a second, and then a third. At first there are five loaves, then there are seven.[17] The third loaf is the true body of Christ. So, then, let us never abandon such a Lord. He agrees to bestow on us nourishment according to the strength of each, lest either too strong a food oppress the weak or too meager a nourishment not satisfy the strong. EXPOSITION OF THE GOSPEL OF LUKE 6.71-72.[18]

SATISFACTION FROM FEEDING MIRACLE FORESHADOWS THE LORD'S BODY AND BLOOD. AMBROSE: There is also a mystery in that the people who eat are satisfied. The apostles minister to them.[19] The sign is given of hunger satisfied forever because one who has received the food of Christ will never hunger again.[20] The future distribution of the Lord's body and blood is based in the ministry of the apostles. It is already there in the miracle in the way five loaves are multiplied for five thousand people. It is clear that the people were satisfied not with a little but with an abundance of food. EXPOSITION OF THE GOSPEL OF LUKE 6.84.[21]

9:17 The Meal

ABUNDANCE FOR LASTING LIFE. PRUDENTIUS:
"Place," he said, "in these twelve baskets all the
    fragments that remain."
Thousands at that feast reclining, with abun-
    dance had been fed
On the five loaves they had eaten and two
    fishes multiplied.[22]

You, our bread, our true refection, never-
    failing sweetness are.[23]
He can nevermore know hunger, who is at
    your banquet fed,[24]
Nourishing not our fleshly nature, but impart-
    ing lasting life.[25]
HYMNS FOR EVERY DAY 9.58-63.[26]

ABUNDANCE OF THE MIRACLE ENCOURAGES HOSPITALITY TO STRANGERS. CYRIL OF ALEXANDRIA: But what was the result of the miracle? It was the satisfying of a large multitude with food. There were as many as five thousand men besides women and children, according to what another of the holy Evangelists has added to the narrative.[27] Nor did the miracle end here. There were also gathered twelve baskets of fragments. And what do we infer from this? A plain assurance that hospitality receives a rich recompense from God. The disciples offered five loaves. After a multitude this large had been satisfied, there was gathered for each one of them a basketful of fragments. Let nothing, therefore, prevent willing people from receiving strangers, no matter what there may be likely to blunt the will and readiness of men. Let no one say, "I do not possess suitable means. What I can do is altogether trifling and insufficient for many." Receive strangers, my beloved. Overcome that reluctance which wins no reward. The Savior will multiply the little you have many times beyond expectation. Although you give but little, you will receive much. For he that sows blessings shall also reap blessings,[28] according to the blessed Paul's words. COMMENTARY ON LUKE, HOMILY 48.[29]

ABUNDANCE FROM THE HEAVENLY TABLE. PRUDENTIUS:
God has broken five loaves and two fishes and
    fed the five thousand

---

[14]Heb 5:12-14. [15]1 Cor 3:2. [16]Lk 22:19-20. [17]Mt 15:34. [18]*EHG* 218**. [19]Cf. Mt 14:19; 15:36; Mk 6:42. [20]Jn 6:35. [21]*EHG* 224**. [22]Mt 14:17-20; Mk 6:38-41; Jn 6:9-13. [23]See Jn 6:56. [24]See Jn 6:35. [25]See Jn 6:51-52. [26]FC 43:64. [27]Mt 14:21. [28]2 Cor 9:6. [29]*CGSL* 215**.

With these foods that satisfy to the fullest
their hunger.
Then twice six baskets are filled with the fragments that are left over:
Such is the bounty dispensed from the heavenly table forever.

Scenes from Sacred History 37.[30]

Jesus Offers Himself as Bread of Life.
Cyril of Alexandria: [Jesus] offers himself as
the bread of life to those who believe in him.[31] It
is he who came down from heaven and gave life to
the world. Commentary on Luke, Homily 48.[32]

---

[30]FC 52:191. [31]Jn 6:33. [32]CGSL 216*.

9:18-22 PETER'S CONFESSION AND THE FIRST PASSION PREDICTION

[18]Now it happened that as he was praying alone the disciples were with him; and he asked them,
"Who do the people say that I am?" [19]And they answered, "John the Baptist; but others say, Elijah;
and others, that one of the old prophets has risen." [20]And he said to them, "But who do you say
that I am?" And Peter answered, "The Christ of God." [21]But he charged and commanded them to
tell this to no one, [22]saying, "The Son of man must suffer many things, and be rejected by the elders
and chief priests and scribes, and be killed, and on the third day be raised."

Overview: Peter is the first disciple; in fact, he
is the first human being in the Gospel to make
the confession that Jesus is the Christ, the Son of
God. The Lord is forcing the disciples to sort out
the rumors that are floating among the crowds.
And the light finally dawns on Peter that he is
greater than all the prophets because he is "the
Christ of God," and he confesses that this Jesus is
the Christ who is Savior of all (Cyril of Alexandria). To confess Jesus as the Christ is to confess
the faith, for this is a confession of him as God,
the incarnate one, the crucified and resurrected
one (Ambrose). The great miracle of the feeding
of the five thousand elicits Peter's confession that
Jesus is "the Christ of God" (Cyril of Alexandria). The disciples are to keep secret the fact
that the Messiah must suffer and die, then rise
because of the scandal of the passion (Ambrose).
It is only after the resurrection that they are to
proclaim the passion and resurrection of Jesus as

Jesus' final words to his disciples command
(Cyril of Alexandria).

9:18-20 The Confession of Peter

**Jesus' Question Forces the Disciples to
Sort Out the Rumors.** Cyril of Alexandria: You see the skillfulness of the question. He
did not at once say, "Who do you say that I am?"
He refers to the rumor of those that were outside
their company. Then, having rejected it and
shown it unsound, he might bring them back to
the true opinion. It happened that way. When the
disciples had said, "Some, John the Baptist, and
others, Elijah, and others, that some prophet of
those in old time has risen up," he said to them,
"But you, who do you say that I am?" Oh! how
full of meaning is that word *you!* He separates
them from all others, that they may also avoid the
opinions of others. In this way, they will not con-

ceive an unworthy idea about him or entertain confused and wavering thoughts. Then they will not also imagine that John had risen again, or one of the prophets. "You," he says, "who have been chosen," who by my decree have been called to the apostleship, who are the witnesses of my miracles. Who do you say that I am?" COMMENTARY ON LUKE, HOMILY 49.[1]

PETER CONFESSES JESUS TO BE THE SAVIOR OF ALL. CYRIL OF ALEXANDRIA: There are many who have been called Christ, from having in various ways been anointed by God. Some have been anointed as kings. Some have been anointed as prophets. They have been so called because they have been anointed. But he who is God the Father's Christ is One, and One only. Not as though we are christs, and not God's christs, belonging to some other person. There is only one Christ, because he and he alone has as his Father God who is in heaven. Since, therefore, most wise Peter, confessing the faith correctly and without error, said, "the Christ of God," it is plain that Peter referred to Jesus as God. For Peter confessed Jesus to be God's sole Christ, distinguishing him from those to whom the appellation generally belongs. For though he be by nature God and shone forth inexpressibly from God the Father as his only-begotten Word, yet he became flesh according to the Scripture. COMMENTARY ON LUKE, HOMILY 49.[2]

TO CONFESS JESUS AS THE CHRIST IS TO CONFESS THE FAITH. AMBROSE: Although the other apostles know, yet Peter answers for them all, "You are the Christ, the Son of the living God."[3] Thus he who manifested both the nature and the name, in whom is the sum of the virtues, encompassed all things. Do we also ask questions about the generation of God, when Paul has judged that he knows nothing, save Christ Jesus and him crucified, and Peter thought nothing else should be confessed, save that he is the Son of God? We also scrutinize when and how he was born and how great he is in the contemplation of human weakness. Paul knew that therein was a

stumbling block of a question, rather than the increase of edification, and therefore he judged that he knew nothing but Christ Jesus. Peter knew that all things are in the Son of God, for the Father has given all things to the Son.[4] EXPOSITION OF THE GOSPEL OF LUKE 6.93.[5]

FEEDING OF FIVE THOUSAND PROMPTS PETER'S CONFESSION. CYRIL OF ALEXANDRIA: It came to pass that he was alone, praying. His disciples were with him. He asked them, "Whom do the multitudes say that I am?" Now the first thing we have to examine is what it was which led our Lord Jesus Christ to propose to the holy apostles this question or inquiry. No word or deed of his is either at an unseasonable time or without a fitting reason. Rather, he does all things wisely and in their season. What, therefore, do we say, or what suitable explanation do we find for his present acts? He had fed a vast multitude of five thousand men in the desert. How did he feed them? With five loaves! Breaking two small fish into morsels with them! These so multiplied out of nothing that twelve baskets of fragments even were taken up. The blessed disciples, therefore, were astonished as well as the multitudes, and saw by what had been wrought, that he is in truth God and the Son of God. COMMENTARY ON LUKE, HOMILY 49.[6]

9:21-22 The Prediction of the Passion and Resurrection

SILENCE COMMANDED OF THE DISCIPLES. AMBROSE: The Lord Jesus Christ was at first unwilling to be extolled, lest any murmuring arise. He rebuked his disciples, lest they say this to anyone, because the Son of man must suffer many things, and be rejected by the elders and the chief priests and the scribes, and be slain, and be raised the third day. Perhaps he added this because the Lord knew that even the disciples would believe

---

[1]CGSL 218**. [2]CGSL 218-19**. [3]Mt 16:16. [4]Jn 3:35. [5]EHG 227*. [6]CGSL 217*.

with difficulty in his passion and resurrection. Therefore he preferred to be the defender of his own passion and resurrection, so that faith would be born of action, and not discord of hearsay. Thus Christ refused to boast but preferred to seem unimportant in order to undergo his passion. Do you boast, who are low born? Must you walk the same path that Christ walked, which he himself walked? This is the recognition of him, this is the imitation of him through obscurity and a good reputation,[7] so that you may glory in the cross as he was glorified. Thus Paul walked and therefore glories, saying, "God forbid that I should glory, save in the cross of our Lord Jesus Christ."[8] EXPOSITION OF THE GOSPEL OF LUKE 6.99-100.[9]

SILENCE ABOUT JESUS' PASSION UNTIL AFTER THE RESURRECTION. CYRIL OF ALEXANDRIA: When the disciple Peter had professed his faith, Jesus charged them, it says, and commanded them to tell it to no one. "For the Son of man," he said, "is about to suffer many things, and be rejected, and killed, and the third day he shall rise again." Wasn't it the duty of disciples to proclaim him everywhere? This was the very business of those appointed by him to the apostleship. But, as the sacred Scripture says, "There is a time for everything."[10] There were things yet unfulfilled which must also be included in their preaching about him. They must also proclaim the cross, the passion, and the death in the flesh. They must preach the resurrection of the dead, that great and truly glorious sign by which testimony is borne him that the Emmanuel is truly God and by nature the Son of God the Father. He utterly abolished death and wiped out destruction. He robbed hell, and overthrew the tyranny of the enemy. He took away the sin of the world, opened the gates above to the dwellers upon earth, and united earth to heaven. These things proved him to be, as I said, in truth God. He commanded them, therefore, to guard the mystery by a seasonable silence until the whole plan of the dispensation should arrive at a suitable conclusion. COMMENTARY ON LUKE, HOMILY 49.[11]

---

[7]See 2 Cor 6:8. [8]Gal 6:14. [9]EHG 230-31**. [10]Eccles 3:1. [11]CGSL 221**.

9:23-27 THE CONSEQUENCES OF DISCIPLESHIP

[23]And he said to all, "If any man would come after me, let him deny himself and take up his cross daily and follow me. [24]For whoever would save his life will lose it; and whoever loses his life for my sake, he will save it. [25]For what does it profit a man if he gains the whole world and loses or forfeits himself? [26]For whoever is ashamed of me and of my words, of him will the Son of man be ashamed when he comes in his glory and the glory of the Father and of the holy angels. [27]But I tell you truly, there are some standing here who will not taste death before they see the kingdom of God."

OVERVIEW: The scandal of the cross is first mentioned in connection with disciples following Jesus. The cross embraces the entire passion of Jesus on our behalf (JEROME). To bear the cross is to be ready to die for Christ, although the habits of life present major obstacles to accomplishing this. Such is the condition of those who have been baptized into Christ's death and resurrection (BASIL THE GREAT). For the saints, what proves hard and difficult is not to be feared but to be experienced as joy. Pleasures and riches recede, but righteousness delivers one from death. One who attempts to save his life now because he loves the world will lose it eternally because he will show that he is ashamed of the Son of man; one who loses his life now will save it eternally for the Son of man will not be ashamed of him when he comes in glory at the second coming. Blessings and rewards await those who are unashamed of Jesus and his words (CYRIL OF ALEXANDRIA). Those who eat the bread from heaven—Jesus Christ—will not taste death (AMBROSE).

9:23 To Follow Jesus Requires Self-Denial

THE CROSS IS THE PASSION OF JESUS. JEROME: In truth, Christ came and made firm the human race that had been disturbed, so that it may not be moved for all eternity. His cross is the pillar of humankind; on this pillar he has built his house. When I say the cross, I am not thinking of the wood but of the passion. . . . Furthermore, what is the warning in the Gospel? "Unless you take up my cross, and daily follow me." Mark what it says: Unless your soul has been made as ready for the cross as mine was for you, you cannot be my disciples. HOMILY ON PSALM 95 (96).[1]

HABITS OF LIFE A MAJOR IMPEDIMENT. BASIL THE GREAT: For we must deny ourselves and take up the cross of Christ and thus follow him. Now self-denial involves the entire forgetfulness of the past and surrender of one's will—surrender which it is very difficult, not to say quite impossible, to achieve while living in the promiscuity customary in the world. And in addition, the social intercourse demanded by such a life is even an obstacle to taking up one's cross and following Christ. Readiness to die for Christ, the mortification of one's members on this earth, preparedness for every danger which might befall us on behalf

of Christ's name, detachment from this life—this it is to take up one's cross; and we regard the obstacles springing from the habits of life in society as major impediments thereto. THE LONG RULES.[2]

TO BEAR THE CROSS IS TO BE BAPTIZED. BASIL THE GREAT: It is necessary, therefore, to receive instruction before baptism, having first removed any impediment to learning and so making ourselves fit to receive the instruction. Our Lord Jesus Christ himself confirms this assertion by his example and also by the formal injunction: "So every one of you that does not renounce all that he possesses cannot be my disciple;"[3] and . . . by the definitive declaration: "He that takes not up his cross daily and follows me is not worthy of me." . . . And then we are ready for the baptism of water, which is a type of the cross and of death, burial and resurrection from the dead. . . .

Whoever, therefore, is worthy to be baptized in the name of the Holy Spirit and who has been born anew undergoes a change of abode, habits and associates, so that, walking by the Spirit we may merit to be baptized in the name of the Son and to put on Christ. CONCERNING BAPTISM.[4]

9:24-25 Saving and Losing Life

WHAT PROVES HARD GIVES JOY TO THE SAINTS. CYRIL OF ALEXANDRIA: What fear, therefore, can the saints now feel, if that which seemed to be hard proves rather joyous to them that bear it. COMMENTARY ON LUKE, HOMILY 50.[5]

RIGHTEOUSNESS DELIVERS FROM DEATH. CYRIL OF ALEXANDRIA: Even though one has wealth and abundance of possessions, yet what profit has he from them when he has lost himself? Treasures profit not the wicked, but the fashion of this world passes away; and like clouds those pleasures recede, and riches fly away from those that possess them. But righteousness delivers from

---

[1]FC 48:188. [2]FC 9:246-47. [3]Lk 14:33. [4]FC 9:383-85. [5]CGSL 224.

death. COMMENTARY ON LUKE, HOMILY 50.[6]

9:26 To Lose One's Life at the Second Coming

REWARD AND BLESSINGS FOR THOSE UNASHAMED. CYRIL OF ALEXANDRIA: Those who are ashamed at him and at his words will meet with the reward they merit. . . .

He also begets in them fear as well, in that he says that he shall descend from heaven, not in his former lowliness and humiliation, like unto us, but in the glory of his Father; even in godlike and transcendent glory, with the holy angels keeping guard around him. Most miserable, therefore, and ruinous would it be to be condemned of cowardice and indolence when the Judge has descended from above and the angelic ranks stand at his side. But great and most blessed and a foretaste of final blessedness it is to be able to rejoice in labors already accomplished and await the recompense of past toils. For such as these shall be praised, Christ himself saying unto them, "Come, you blessed of my Father, inherit the kingdom prepared for you from the foundation of the world."[7] May we also be deemed worthy of these rewards by the grace and lovingkindness of Christ the Savior of us all. COMMENTARY ON LUKE, HOMILY 50.[8]

9:27 Seeing the Kingdom of God

THOSE WHO EAT THE BREAD FROM HEAVEN. AMBROSE: Thus, if we wish not to fear death, let us stand where Christ is, so that he may say of us too, "There are some standing here that shall not taste death." It is not enough to stand unless the standing is where Christ is, for only those who can stand with Christ cannot taste death. It is therein lawful through the quality of the very word to ponder that those who are seen to have deserved the fellowship with Christ will not have even the perception of death. Surely the death of the body may be tasted by dedication; the life of the soul may be held by possession.

But what is it to taste death? Unless, perhaps, bread may be death, just as bread is life? For there are those who eat the bread of sorrow;[9] there are also the Ethiopian peoples who received the dragon as food.[10] May it be far from us to devour the dragon's poison, for we have the true Bread, that Bread which came down from heaven.[11] He who keeps what is written eats that Bread. Thus there are those who will not taste death until they see the kingdom of God. EXPOSITION OF THE GOSPEL OF LUKE 7.2-3.[12]

---

[6]CGSL 224. [7]Mt 25:34. [8]CGSL 224-25*. [9]Ps 126:3 LXX. [10]Ps 74:13-14 (73:13-14 LXX). [11]Jn 6:51. [12]EHG 237-38.

9:28-36 THE TRANSFIGURATION

[28]Now about eight days after these sayings he took with him Peter and John and James, and went up on the mountain to pray. [29]And as he was praying, the appearance of his countenance was altered, and his raiment became dazzling white. [30]And behold, two men talked with him, Moses and Elijah, [31]who appeared in glory and spoke of his departure, which he was to accomplish at Jerusalem. [32]Now Peter and those who were with him were heavy with sleep, and when they wakened they saw his glory and the two men who stood with him. [33]And as the men were parting from

him, Peter said to Jesus, "Master, it is well that we are here; let us make three booths, one for you and one for Moses and one for Elijah"—not knowing what he said. [34]As he said this, a cloud came and overshadowed them; and they were afraid as they entered the cloud. [35]And a voice came out of the cloud, saying, "This is my Son, my Chosen;[d] listen to him!" [36]And when the voice had spoken, Jesus was found alone. And they kept silence and told no one in those days anything of what they had seen.

d Other ancient authorities read *my Beloved*

OVERVIEW: Jesus' "exodus, which he was about to fulfill in Jerusalem" refers to his "departure," his death, resurrection and ascension. To this Jesus, Son and chosen Servant, all should listen (CYRIL OF ALEXANDRIA). The eighth day on which this event takes place foreshadows the resurrection, which also occurs on the eighth day. Peter, James and John, who go up the mountain with him, are sons of the church, for they will come to see God's triumph in the cross and behold the glory of the resurrection because of the purity of their faith (AMBROSE).

Moses and Elijah appear on the mount with Jesus and the disciples as pillars who were the two witnesses from Mount Sinai "in the hollow of the rock" (CYRIL OF JERUSALEM). They represent the Law and Prophets, and Jesus, the Word of God, appears with them to show that he is Lord of the prophets (EPHREM THE SYRIAN). Only Luke records the content of their heavenly conversation: Moses and Elijah are speaking about the mystery of Jesus' exodus in Jerusalem (BEDE).

Even though they are asleep, the disciples are able to perceive the glory of God. Peter's great devotion to Jesus, Moses and Elijah wanted to make three tabernacles, although in the ignorance of his humanity he did not realize that human beings cannot make a tabernacle for God (AMBROSE). For Peter, seeing the glory of Jesus and Moses and Elijah, the kingdom of God had come even now (CYRIL OF ALEXANDRIA).

The cloud that overshadows them does not sprinkle them with moisture but with faith to believe that Jesus is the Son of God (AMBROSE). The

voice of the Father assures them, just before Jesus turns toward his passion in Jerusalem, that the Father is coeternal with the Son (BEDE). The great theophany of Jesus' transfiguration gives us a glimpse of the mystery of the future resurrected life in Christ (GREGORY OF NAZIANZUS). The silence of the disciples confirms their misunderstanding, for if they were to speak of seeing Moses and Elijah, they would be thought of as fools. Some things are not yet fully in the open, but his hour will come, as will the new day when the disciples shall once again preach (EPHREM THE SYRIAN).

9:28-29 Description of Jesus' Transfiguration

THE ORDER OF THE KINGDOM: SUFFERING, THEN GLORY. CYRIL OF ALEXANDRIA: "I say to you, there are some of those standing here who shall not taste of death until they have seen the kingdom of God." . . . By the "kingdom of God" he means the sight of the glory in which he will appear at his revelation to the inhabitants of earth. He will come in the glory of God the Father and not in a humble condition like ours. How did he make those who received the promise spectators of a thing so wonderful? He goes up into the mountain taking three chosen disciples with him. He is transformed to such a surpassing and godlike brightness that his garments even glittered with rays of fire and seemed to flash like lightning. Besides, Moses and Elijah stood at Jesus' side and spoke with one another about his departure that he was about, it says, to accomplish at Jerusalem. This meant the mystery of the dispensation in the flesh and of his precious suffering upon the cross. It is also true that the law of Moses and the word of the holy prophets foreshadowed the mystery of Christ. The law of Moses foreshadowed it by types and shadows, painting it as in a picture. The holy prophets in different ways declared beforehand that in due time he would appear in our likeness and for the salvation and life of us all, agree to suffer death on the tree. Moses and Elijah standing before him and talking with one another was a sort of representation. It excellently displayed our Lord Jesus Christ as having the law and the prophets for his bodyguard. It displayed Christ as being the Lord of the Law and the Prophets, as foretold in them by those things that they proclaimed in mutual agreement beforehand. The words of the prophets are not different from the teachings of the law. I imagine this was what the most priestly Moses and the most distinguished of the prophets Elijah were talking about with one another. COMMENTARY ON LUKE, HOMILY 51.[1]

THE EIGHTH DAY FORESHADOWS THE RESURRECTION. AMBROSE: You may know that Peter, James and John did not taste death and were worthy to see the glory of the resurrection. It says "about eight days after these words, he took those three alone and led them onto the mountain." Why is it that he says "eight days after these words"? He that hears the words of Christ and believes will see the glory of Christ at the time of the resurrection. The resurrection happened on the eighth day, and most of the psalms were written "For the eighth."[2] It shows us that he said that he who because of the Word of God shall lose his own soul will save it,[3] since he renews his promises at the resurrection.[4] But Matthew and Mark say that they were taken after six days.[5] We may say this means after six thousand years, because a thousand years in God's sight are as one day.[6] We counted more than six thousand years. We prefer to understand six

days as a symbol, because God created the works of the world in six days,[7] so that we understand works through the time and the world through the works. EXPOSITION OF THE GOSPEL OF LUKE 7.6-7.[8]

PETER, JAMES AND JOHN ARE SONS OF THE CHURCH. AMBROSE: Only three, three chosen, were led to the mountain.... This perhaps means none can see the glory of the resurrection except he who has preserved the mystery of the Trinity intact with the undefiled purity of faith. Peter, who received the keys of the kingdom,[9] John, to whom his mother was entrusted,[10] and James, who was the first to mount a bishop's throne, ascended. EXPOSITION OF THE GOSPEL OF LUKE 7.9.[11]

9:30-31 Jesus' Conversation with Moses and Elijah

MOSES AND ELIJAH THE TWO WITNESSES FROM MOUNT SINAI. CYRIL OF JERUSALEM: What strange thing do we announce when we say that God became man and when you say that Abraham received the Lord as a guest? What strange thing do we announce when Jacob says, "I have seen a heavenly being face to face, yet my life has been spared"?[12] The same Lord who ate with Abraham also ate with us. What strange thing do we announce? We present two witnesses who stood before the Lord on Mount Sinai: Moses was "in the hollow of the rock,"[13] and Elijah was once in the hollow of the rock.[14] Being present at his transfiguration on Mount Tabor, they spoke to his disciples "of his death that he was about to fulfill in Jerusalem." CATECHETICAL LECTURES 12.16.[15]

LORD OF THE PROPHETS. EPHREM THE SYRIAN: Moses and Elijah appeared beside him so that

---

[1]CGSL 227**. [2]Ps 6:1; 12:1 LXX and Vulgate. [3]Lk 9:24. [4]See Mt 16:25-27. [5]See Mt 17:1; Mk 9:2. [6]Ps 89:4 LXX. [7]Gen 2:1. [8]EHG 239-40*. [9]Mt 16:19. [10]Jn 19:27. [11]EHG 240-41*. [12]Gen 32:30. [13]Ex 33:22. [14]1 Kings 19:13. [15]FC 61: 236-37**.

they might know that he was Lord of the prophets. He transformed his face on the mountain before he died, so that they would not be in doubt concerning the transformation of his face after his death. He changed the garments which he was wearing so that they might know that it is also he who will raise to life the body with which he was clothed. He, who gave his body a glory that no one can reach, is able to raise it to life from the death that everyone tastes. COMMENTARY ON TATIAN'S DIATESSARON 14.8.[16]

ONLY LUKE REFERS TO JESUS' EXODUS: BEDE: Luke writes more clearly of how they appeared and what they spoke about with him. Luke says that Moses and Elijah were seen in majesty, and they spoke of his passing away which he was about to fulfill in Jerusalem. Moses and Elijah, who talked with the Lord on the mountain and spoke about his passion and resurrection, represent the revelations of the law and prophets that were fulfilled in the Lord. . . .

It is appropriate that the Evangelist reported Moses and Elijah were "seen in majesty." The mark of the favor with which they are to be crowned is shown by the preeminence of their majesty. It is also appropriately recorded that they spoke about his passing away, which was to be fulfilled in Jerusalem. To his faithful, the Redeemer's passion has become a unique subject for praise. The more they remember that they could not have been saved apart from his grace, the more they should always ponder the greater memory of this grace in a faithful heart, and bear faithful witness to it. HOMILIES ON THE GOSPELS 1.24.[17]

9:32-35 Peter's Response and the Voice from Heaven

THE DISCIPLES BEHOLD HIS GLORY EVEN IN SLEEP. AMBROSE: Peter saw this grace, and so did those who were with him, although they were heavy with sleep. The incomprehensible magnificence of the Godhead overwhelms the perceptions of our body. If the sharpness of bodily vision cannot bear the ray of the sun directly into watching eyes, how may the corruption of human members endure the glory of God? The garment of the body, purer and finer after the removal of the materiality of vices, is made for the resurrection. Perhaps they were so heavy with sleep that they saw the radiance of the resurrection after their rest. Keeping vigil, they saw his majesty, because no one sees the glory of Christ unless he is vigilant.[18] EXPOSITION OF THE GOSPEL OF LUKE 7.17.[19]

PETER'S UNTIMELY ZEAL. AMBROSE: It says, "It is good for us to be here." "My desire is to depart and be with Christ, for that is far better."[20] The diligent workman is not content to praise. Even more admirable, not only in affection but also in pious deeds, he promises a ministry of common worship for the building of three tabernacles. Although he did not know what he said, he promised an observance that does not heap up the fruits of piety in indiscreet carelessness but in untimely zeal. His ignorance came from his condition, but his promise from his devotion. The human condition is corruptible in this. This mortal body is not capable of making a tabernacle for God. EXPOSITION OF THE GOSPEL OF LUKE 7.18.[21]

PETER THOUGHT THE KINGDOM HAD COME. CYRIL OF ALEXANDRIA: The dispensation was still at its beginning and not yet fulfilled. How would it have been fitting for Christ to abandon his love for the world and depart from his purpose of suffering on its behalf? By undergoing death in the flesh and by abolishing death by the resurrection from the dead, he redeemed all under heaven. Peter therefore knew not what he said. COMMENTARY ON LUKE, HOMILY 51.[22]

THE CLOUD SPRINKLES THE DISCIPLES. AMBROSE: "While he spoke, there came a cloud,

---

[16]ECTD 217*. [17]CS 110:239-40*. [18]See Lk 12:37. [19]EHG 243-44**. [20]Phil 1:23. [21]EHG 244**. [22]CGSL 227-28**.

and overshadowed them." That is the overshadowing of the divine Spirit, who is not dark with the emotions of humankind but unveils secrets. This is also revealed in another place when an angel says, "And the power of the Most High shall overshadow you."[23] The effect of this is shown when the voice of God is heard, saying, "This is my beloved Son; hear him." Elijah is not the Son, and Moses is not the Son. This is the Son whom only you see, because they had withdrawn when he began to be described as Lord. . . . It was a luminous cloud that does not soak us with rainwater or the downpour of storm, but from dew that sprinkles the minds of men with faith sent by the voice of almighty God. EXPOSITION OF THE GOSPEL OF LUKE 7.19-20.[24]

THE FATHER'S VOICE ASSURES THE DISCIPLES JESUS IS COETERNAL. BEDE: The Father's voice did not forbid them to listen to Moses and Elijah (that is, to the Law and the Prophets). It rather suggested to all of them that listening to his Son was to take precedence since he came to fulfill the Law and the Prophets.[25] It impressed on them that the light of gospel truth was to be put ahead of all the types and obscure signs of the Old Testament. By the benevolent, divinely arranged plan when the moment of the cross was drawing near, he strengthened them so that the disciples' faith might not falter when the Lord was crucified. He revealed to them how also his humanity was to be lifted up by heavenly light through his resurrection. The heavenly voice of the Father gave assurance that the Son was coeternal to the Father in his divinity so that when the hour of the passion approached, they would be less sorrowful at his dying. They remembered that after his death he would soon be glorified as

a human being, although in his divinity he had always been glorified by God his Father.

Since the disciples were fleshly and still fragile in substance, they were afraid and fell upon their faces when they heard God's voice. Since the Lord was a benevolent master in everything, he consoled them at the same time by his word and his touch, and he lifted them up. HOMILIES ON THE GOSPELS 1.24.[26]

JESUS INITIATES US INTO THE MYSTERY OF THE FUTURE. GREGORY OF NAZIANZUS: He was bright as the lightning on the mountain and became more luminous than the sun, initiating us into the mystery of the future. ORATION 3.19, ON THE SON.[27]

9:36 The Silence of the Three Disciples

SO AS NOT TO APPEAR AS FOOLS. EPHREM THE SYRIAN: As they came down from the mountain, he commanded them, "You must not speak openly of what you have seen to anyone."[28] Why did he command this? He said this because he knew that others would not believe them but would take them for fools. They would say, "Do you know where Elijah came from?" and "See, Moses is buried, and no one has succeeded in finding his grave." There would be blasphemy and scandal because of this. He said, "Wait until you have received the power,"[29] because when you will speak and they will not believe, you will raise the dead for their confusion and your own glory. COMMENTARY ON TATIAN'S DIATESSARON 14.10.[30]

---

[23]Lk 1:35. [24]EHG 244-45*. [25]Mt 5:17. [26]CS 110:242-43**. [27]LCC 3:174. [28]Mt 17:9; Mk 9:9. [29]Acts 1:4, 8. [30]ECTD 218**.

9:37-43 THE HEALING OF AN EPILEPTIC

[37]On the next day, when they had come down from the mountain, a great crowd met him. [38]And behold, a man from the crowd cried, "Teacher, I beg you to look upon my son, for he is my only child; [39]and behold, a spirit seizes him, and he suddenly cries out; it convulses him till he foams, and shatters him, and will hardly leave him. [40]And I begged your disciples to cast it out, but they could not." [41]Jesus answered, "O faithless and perverse generation, how long am I to be with you and bear with you? Bring your son here." [42]While he was coming, the demon tore him and convulsed him. But Jesus rebuked the unclean spirit, and healed the boy, and gave him back to his father. [43]And all were astonished at the majesty of God.

OVERVIEW: Jesus bestows gifts on those who are capable of receiving them in faith. The unbelief of the boy's father (not the disciples) led to the apostles' failure to cast out the demon. "Generation" refers to a kind of people: unbelieving, twisted, focusing here on the father, who did not believe in Christ's power as it was working through his holy apostles (CYRIL OF ALEXANDRIA).

9:37-43 Freeing the Captives

CHRIST BESTOWS GIFTS ON THOSE CAPABLE OF RECEIVING THEM. CYRIL OF ALEXANDRIA: This lesson proves that he delivered us from the power of unclean spirits. We heard read that a man ran toward him from among the crowd and related the intolerable illness of his son. He said that he was cruelly torn by an evil spirit and suffered violent convulsions. The manner of his approach was not free from fault, because he shouted loudly against the company of the holy apostles, saying that they could not rebuke Satan. It would have been more fitting for him to honor Jesus when asking his aid and imploring grace. He grants us our request when we honor and confide in him as being the Almighty, whose power nothing can withstand. COMMENTARY ON LUKE, HOMILY 52.[1]

UNBELIEF OF THE MAN HAS NO MIRACULOUS

OUTCOME. CYRIL OF ALEXANDRIA: The father of the demoniac was rude and not courteous. He did not simply ask for the healing of the child, and in so doing crown the healer with praises. On the contrary, he spoke disrespectfully of the disciples and found fault with the grace given them. "I brought him," he says, "to your disciples, and they could not cast it out." It was owing to your lack of faith that the grace did not help. Do you not understand that you were the cause that the child was not delivered from his severe illness? COMMENTARY ON LUKE, HOMILY 52.[2]

THE MAN FOUND FAULT WITH CHRIST'S POWER IN THE APOSTLES. CYRIL OF ALEXANDRIA: The man was thoroughly an unbeliever and perverse, refusing the straight paths, straying from the mark, and wandering from the right ways. Christ does not want to be with those who think this way and have fallen into this wickedness. If one may speak in the manner of people, Christ is tired and weary of them. He teaches us this saying, "How long am I to be with you and bear with you?" The father says that the disciples, who received at Christ's wish power to cast them out, were powerless to cast out evil spirits. He finds fault with the grace itself, rather than with those who received it. It

---

[1]*CGSL* 229**. [2]*CGSL* 230**.

was wicked blasphemy, because if grace is powerless, the fault and blame is not with those who received it but rather with the grace itself. Anyone who wishes may see that the grace that worked in them was Christ's grace. COMMENTARY ON LUKE, HOMILY 52.[3]

---

[3]CGSL 231**.

9:43-45 THE SECOND PASSION PREDICTION

But while they were all marveling at everything he did, he said to his disciples, [44]"Let these words sink into your ears; for the Son of man is to be delivered into the hands of men." [45]But they did not understand this saying, and it was concealed from them, that they should not perceive it; and they were afraid to ask him about this saying.

OVERVIEW: The second passion prediction follows quickly upon Jesus' first prediction and the transfiguration in order to prepare his disciples for his crucifixion and resurrection. Jesus' passion is also foreshadowed by the scapegoat in the desert, which is sacrificed for sins. The disciples, in a state of confusion and misunderstanding, did not understand this word about the passion (CYRIL OF ALEXANDRIA).

9:43-45 The Mystery of Christ's Passion

THE MYSTERY OF THE PASSION FOLLOWS THE TRANSFIGURATION. CYRIL OF ALEXANDRIA: In order that those who were going to teach the whole world might know exactly his mystery, he usefully and necessarily explains it clearly to them beforehand. He says, "Lay these words to your hearts; for the Son of man is about to be delivered into the hands of men." The reason that led Christ to speak this is, I think, a subject both useful and necessary for our consideration. He had then led Peter, James and John up into the mountain. He was transfigured before them, and his countenance shone as the sun. He showed them the glory, with which in due time he will arise upon the world. He will come, not in humiliation such as ours or in the lowliness of the human condition as such, but in the majesty and splendor of the Godhead, and in transcendent glory. Again, when he came down from the mountain, he delivered a man from a wicked and violent spirit. He certainly was ready to bear for our sakes his saving passion and endure the wickedness of the Jews. As the minister of his mysteries, he by the grace of God "tasted death for every man."[1] When this happened, there is nothing unlikely in supposing that the disciples would be troubled. Perhaps in their secret thoughts even they would say, "How is One so glorious, who raised the dead by his godlike power, rebuked the seas and winds, and by a word crushed Satan, now seized as a prisoner and caught in these murderers' traps? Were we mistaken in thinking that he is God? Have we fallen from the true opinion regarding him?" Those who did not know the mystery that our Lord Jesus Christ would endure the cross and death would find therein an occasion of stumbling. COMMENTARY ON LUKE, HOMILY 53.[2]

---

[1]Heb 2:9. [2]CGSL 232-33**.

THE SCAPEGOAT FORESHADOWED CHRIST'S PASSION. CYRIL OF ALEXANDRIA: The mystery of the passion may be seen also in another instance. According to the Mosaic law, two goats were offered. They were not different in any way from one another,[3] but they were alike in size and appearance. Of these, one was called "the lord," and the other was called "sent-away." When the lot was cast for the one called "lord," it was sacrificed. The other one was sent away from the sacrifice, and therefore had the name of "sent-away." Who was signified by this? The Word, though he was God, was in our likeness and took the form of us sinners, as far as the nature of the flesh was concerned. The male or female goat was sacrificed for sins. Death was our desert, for we had fallen under the divine curse because of sin. When the Savior of all undertook the responsibility, he transferred to himself what was due to us and laid down his life, that we might be sent away from death and destruction. COMMENTARY ON LUKE, HOMILY 53.[4]

---

[3]Lev 16:7-8. [4]CGSL 234**.

9:46-50 WHO IS THE GREATEST?

[46]*And an argument arose among them as to which of them was the greatest.* [47]*But when Jesus perceived the thought of their hearts, he took a child and put him by his side,* [48]*and said to them, "Whoever receives this child in my name receives me, and whoever receives me receives him who sent me; for he who is least among you all is the one who is great."*

[49]*John answered, "Master, we saw a man casting out demons in your name, and we forbade him, because he does not follow with us."* [50]*But Jesus said to him, "Do not forbid him; for he that is not against you is for you."*

OVERVIEW: Jesus as the Word of God made flesh knows their thoughts about their greatness. Like a good physician of souls, he amputates their passion for vainglory by bringing a little child before them as an illustration. The child represents a pattern of simplicity and innocence. To be least is to be like Christ. John's action of rebuke may be a sign of envy among the disciples. Like Moses and the seventy elders of Israel, the disciples need to learn that God's power over Satan extends beyond themselves (CYRIL OF ALEXANDRIA).

9:46-50 Receiving Jesus As a Child

JESUS THE PHYSICIAN OF SOULS AMPUTATES THE PASSION OF VAINGLORY. CYRIL OF ALEX-ANDRIA: The passion and lust of pride attacked some of the holy apostles. The mere argument about who of them was the greatest is the mark of an ambitious person, eager to stand at the head of the rest. Christ, who did not sleep, knows how to deliver. He saw this thought in the disciple's mind, springing up, in the words of Scripture,[1] like some bitter plant. He saw the weeds, the work of the wicked sower. Before it grew up tall, struck its root down deep, grew strong, and took possession of the heart, he tears up the evil by the very root. . . .

In what way does the Physician of souls amputate pride's passion? How does he deliver the be-

---

[1]See Heb 12:15.

loved disciple from being the prey of the enemy and from a thing hateful to God and man? "He took a child," it says, "and set it by him." He made the event a means of benefiting both the holy apostles themselves and us their successors. This illness, as a rule, preys upon all those who are in any respect superior to other people. COMMENTARY ON LUKE, HOMILY 54.[2]

A PATTERN OF SIMPLICITY AND INNOCENCE.

CYRIL OF ALEXANDRIA: What kind of type and representation did he make the child he had taken? He made the child a representation of an innocent and humble life. The mind of a child is empty of fraud, and his heart is sincere. His thoughts are simple. He does not covet rank and does not know what is meant by one man being higher than another is. . . .

Christ brought forward the child as a pattern of simplicity and innocence, and set him by him. He showed him as in an object lesson, that he accepts and loves those who are like the child. He thinks they are worthy of standing at his side, as being like-minded with him and anxious to walk in his steps. COMMENTARY ON LUKE, HOMILY 54.[3]

TO BE THE LEAST IS TO BE LIKE CHRIST.

CYRIL OF ALEXANDRIA: Christ calls him least whom lowly things please and who from modesty does not think highly of himself. This person pleases Christ. It is written that "every one that exalts himself shall be humbled, and he that humbles himself shall be exalted."[4] Christ himself somewhere says, "Blessed are the poor in spirit, for theirs is the kingdom of heaven."[5] The ornament of a sanctified soul is a poor and humble mind. . . . Let the illness of pride be far from those who love Christ. Let us rather consider our companions as better than we are and be anxious to decorate ourselves with the humility of mind that is well pleasing to God. Being simpleminded, as fits saints, we will be with Christ who honors simplicity. COMMENTARY ON LUKE, HOMILY 54.[6]

SIGNS OF ENVY AMONG THE DISCIPLES.

CYRIL OF ALEXANDRIA: "Teacher, we saw one casting out devils in your name, and we forbade him." Has the sting of envy troubled the holy disciples? Do they grudge those highly favored? Have even they taken within themselves a passion so abominable and hateful to God? "We saw one casting out devils in your name, and we forbade him." Tell me, do you forbid one who in Christ's name troubles Satan and crushes evil demons? Was it not your duty rather to think that he was not the doer of these wonders, but that the grace that was in him performed the miracle by the power of Christ? How do you forbid him who in Christ wins the victory? "Yes," he says, "for he follows not with us." O blind speech! "What if he is not numbered among the holy apostles, who are crowned with Christ's grace, yet he is equally with you adorned with apostolic powers?" There is great diversity in Christ's gifts. The blessed Paul teaches this, saying, "To one is given through the Spirit the utterance of wisdom, and to another the utterance of knowledge according to the same Spirit."[7] COMMENTARY ON LUKE, HOMILY 55.[8]

POWER OVER SATAN EXTENDS BEYOND THE APOSTLES.

CYRIL OF ALEXANDRIA: What is the meaning of his "not walking with us," or what is the force of the expression? Listen and I will tell you as well as I can. The Savior gave the holy apostles authority over unclean spirits, to cast them out and to heal all disease and all sickness among the people.[9] They did so, and the grace given them was effective. They returned with joy, saying, "Lord, even the devils are subject to us in your name."[10] They imagined that permission to be invested with the authority that he granted them was not given to anyone else but only to them. They came near for this reason. They wanted to learn whether others also might exercise it, although they were not appointed to the office of apostle or even to the office of teacher.

We find something like this also in the ancient,

---

[2]CGSL 237*. [3]CGSL 237-38**. [4]Lk 14:11. [5]Mt 5:3. [6]CGSL 238-39**. [7]1 Cor 12:8. [8]CGSL 240**. [9]Mt 10:1. [10]Lk 10:17.

sacred Scriptures. God once said to the priest Moses, "Choose seventy men from the elders of Israel, and I will take of the Spirit that is on you and give it to them."[11] When those who were chosen assembled at the first tabernacle, except for only two men who remained in the camp, the spirit of prophecy descended on them. Not only did those who assembled in the holy tabernacle prophesy but also those who remained in the camp. It says, "Joshua the son of Nun, the minister of Moses, one of his chosen men, said, 'My lord Moses, forbid them.' But Moses said to him, 'Are you jealous for my sake? Would that all the Lord's people were prophets, that the Lord would put his spirit upon them!'"[12] Christ at that time made the priest Moses speak by the Holy Spirit. Here also in per-

son he says to the holy apostles, "Do not forbid him who is crushing Satan." Christ crushes Satan in his name, for he is not against you. He says, "For he who is not against you is on your side." All who wish to act to his glory are on the side of us who love Christ and are crowned by his grace. This is a law to the churches continuing even to this day. We honor only those who lift up holy hands purely and without fault or blame. In Christ's name, they rebuke unclean spirits and deliver multitudes from various diseases. We know that it is Christ who works in them. COMMENTARY ON LUKE, HOMILY 55.[13]

---

[11]Num 11:16. [12]Num 11:28-29. [13]CGSL 240-41**.

9:51 THE TURNING POINT IN JESUS' MINISTRY: THE FIRST TRAVEL NOTICE

[51]*When the days drew near for him to be received up, he set his face to go to Jerusalem.*

OVERVIEW: At this turning point of Luke's Gospel, Jesus begins the journey toward his death in Jerusalem. His lifting up refers to all that he does for our redemption—his passion, resurrection and ascension (CYRIL OF ALEXANDRIA).

9:51 Jesus Turns His Face to Go to Jerusalem

LIFTING UP REFERS TO PASSION, RESURRECTION AND ASCENSION. CYRIL OF ALEXANDRIA: It says, "When the days drew near for him to be

received up, he set his face to go to Jerusalem." This means that after he would endure his saving passion for us, the time would come when he should ascend to heaven and dwell with God the Father, so he determined to go to Jerusalem. This is, I think, the meaning of his "set his face." COMMENTARY ON LUKE, HOMILY 56.[1]

---

[1]CGSL 243**.

9:52-56 JESUS IS REJECTED IN SAMARIA

^{52}*And he sent messengers ahead of him, who went and entered a village of the Samaritans, to make ready for him;* ^{53}*but the people would not receive him, because his face was set toward Jerusalem.* ^{54}*And when his disciples James and John saw it, they said, "Lord, do you want us to bid fire come down from heaven and consume them?"^{e}* ^{55}*But he turned and rebuked them.^{f}* ^{56}*And they went on to another village.*

e Other ancient authorities add *as Elijah did*   f Other ancient authorities add *and he said, "You do not know what manner of spirit you are of; for the Son of man came not to destroy men's lives but to save them"*

OVERVIEW: Sending the disciples ahead of him, their experience of rejection, and Jesus' rebuke of them are all for their benefit and part of their training for what they will face after Pentecost. The disciples are to benefit from preaching the gospel and experiencing rejection, learning how to accept this with longsuffering and gentleness and not with a vengeful spirit (CYRIL OF ALEXANDRIA).

9:52-56 The Journey to Jerusalem Begins

THE DISCIPLES SENT TO SAMARIA AS A PREPARATORY EXERCISE. CYRIL OF ALEXANDRIA: It would be false to affirm that our Savior did not know what was about to happen, because he knows all things. He knew, of course, that the Samaritans would not receive his messengers. There can be no doubt of this. Why then did he command them to go before him? It was his custom to benefit diligently the holy apostles in every possible way, and because of this, it was his practice sometimes to test them. . . . On this occasion, he also tested them. He knew that the Samaritans would not receive those who went forward to announce that he would stay with them. He still permitted them to go that this again might be a way of benefiting the holy apostles.

What was the purpose of this occurrence? He was going up to Jerusalem, as the time of his passion was already drawing near. He was about to endure the scorn of the Jews. He was about to be destroyed by the scribes and Pharisees and to suffer those things that they inflicted upon him when they went to accomplish all of violence and wicked boldness. He did not want them to be offended when they saw him suffering. He also wanted them to be patient and not to complain greatly, although people would treat them rudely. He, so to speak, made the Samaritans' hatred a preparatory exercise in the matter. They had not received the messengers. . . .

For their benefit, he rebuked the disciples and gently restrained the sharpness of their wrath, not permitting them to grumble violently against those who sinned. He rather persuaded them to be patient and to cherish a mind that is unmovable by anything like this. COMMENTARY ON LUKE, HOMILY 56.[1]

THE DISCIPLES BENEFIT FROM PREACHING THE GOSPEL AND EXPERIENCING REJECTION. CYRIL OF ALEXANDRIA: It also benefited them in another way. They were to be the instructors of the whole world and to travel through the cities and villages, proclaiming everywhere the good tidings of salvation. Of necessity, while seeking to fulfill their mission, they must fall in with wicked people who would reject the divine tidings and not receive Jesus to stay with them. . . . Christ rebuked them for their own good when they were enraged beyond measure at the hatred of the Sa-

[1]*CGSL* 243-44**.

maritans. He did this so they might learn that as ministers of the divine tidings, they must rather be full of longsuffering and gentleness, not revengeful. They must not be given to wrath or sav-

agely attack those who offend them. COMMENTARY ON LUKE, Homily 56.[2]

²CGSL 245**.

9:57-62 CONDITIONS ON A PILGRIMAGE

[57]*As they were going along the road, a man said to him, "I will follow you wherever you go."* [58]*And Jesus said to him, "Foxes have holes, and birds of the air have nests; but the Son of man has nowhere to lay his head."* [59]*To another he said, "Follow me." But he said, "Lord, let me first go and bury my father."* [60]*But he said to him, "Leave the dead to bury their own dead; but as for you, go and proclaim the kingdom of God."* [61]*Another said, "I will follow you, Lord; but let me first say farewell to those at my home."* [62]*Jesus said to him, "No one who puts his hand to the plow and looks back is fit for the kingdom of God."*

OVERVIEW: The would-be disciple who claims to be willing to follow Jesus wherever he goes is presumptuous in his declaration, thrusting himself into apostolic honor without realizing that to follow Jesus is to take up his cross. For the Son of man to have a place to lay his head, the devil must be cast out (CYRIL OF ALEXANDRIA).

Disciples must learn that the divine takes precedence over the human and that human obligation cannot stand in the way of Christian discipleship (BASIL THE GREAT). One is called to love God more than one's father or mother (CYRIL OF ALEXANDRIA). Why would anyone want to return to the devil or the world from which they have escaped (CYPRIAN)?

9:57-62 Fitness for Proclaiming the Kingdom

THE WOULD-BE DISCIPLE. CYRIL OF ALEXANDRIA: A certain man came near to Christ the Savior of us all, saying, "Teacher, I will follow you wherever you go." Christ rejected the man, saying

that the foxes have holes, and the birds of heaven a place to lodge in; but he had no place to lay his head. . . . It is easy for anyone that will examine such matters accurately to perceive that in the first place there was great ignorance in his manner of coming near. Second, it was full of excessive presumptuousness. His wish was not simply to follow Christ, as so many others of the Jewish multitude did, but rather to thrust himself into apostolic honors. This was the following that he was seeking, being self-called. The blessed Paul writes that no one takes the honor to himself unless he is called of God, as Aaron also was.[1] Aaron did not enter the priesthood through himself, but on the contrary, God called him. We find none of the holy apostles promoted himself to the office of apostle but rather received the honor from Christ. He said, "Come after me, and I will make you to become fishers of men."[2] This man, as I said, boldly took upon himself honorable gifts, and, although no one called him, thrust himself into what was

¹Heb 5.4. ²Mk 1:17.

above his rank. COMMENTARY ON LUKE 57.[3]

SATAN MUST BE CAST OUT. CYRIL OF ALEXANDRIA: He rebuked him not to reproach him but rather to correct him, so that he might of his own desire grow better and become eager in following the ways of virtue. . . . The simple meaning of the passage that is at hand follows. The beasts and birds have dens and dwellings, but I have nothing to offer of those things that are the objects of general pursuit. I do not have a place where to dwell, rest and lay my head. Profounder thoughts achieve the inner and secret symbolism of the passage. He seems to mean by the foxes and birds of heaven those wicked, cunning and impure powers, the herds of demons. . . . We affirm that he did not say this about the material and visible birds. He said this about those impure and wicked spirits that often remove the heavenly seed that fell on the hearts of people and carry it away, so that they may not bring forth any fruit. As long as the foxes and birds have holes and dens in us, how can Christ enter? Where can he rest? COMMENTARY ON LUKE, HOMILY 57.[4]

HUMAN OBLIGATION GIVES WAY TO CHRISTIAN DISCIPLESHIP. BASIL THE GREAT: The man said, "Allow me first to go and bury my father." The Lord replied, "Let the dead bury their dead; but go and preach the kingdom of God." Another man said, "Let me first arrange my affairs at home." He rebuked him with a stern threat, saying, "No man, putting his hand to the plow and looking back, is fit for the kingdom of God." A person who wishes to become the Lord's disciple must repudiate a human obligation, however honorable it may appear, if it slows us ever so slightly in giving the wholehearted obedience we owe to God. CONCERNING BAPTISM 1.1.[5]

LOVE GOD MORE THAN YOUR FATHER OR MOTHER. CYRIL OF ALEXANDRIA: "Leave the dead burying their dead, but go, preach the kingdom of God." There were, no doubt, other guardians and relatives of his father. I consider them dead, because they had not yet believed in Christ nor been able to receive the new birth by holy baptism to incorruptible life. "Let them," he says, "bury their dead, because they also have within them a dead mind and still have not been numbered among those who possess the life that is in Christ." We learn from this that the fear of God is to be set even above the reverence and love due to parents. The law of Moses, in the first place, commanded that you shall love the Lord God with all your soul, all your might and all your heart.[6] It put as second to it the honor due to parents, saying, "Honor your father and your mother." COMMENTARY ON LUKE, HOMILY 58.[7]

DO NOT RETURN TO THE WORLD. CYPRIAN: The Lord warns us of this in his gospel lest we return to the devil again and to the world, which we have renounced and from which we have escaped. He says, "No one, having put his hand to the plow and looking back, is fit for the kingdom of God." Again he says, "And let him who is in the field not turn back. Remember Lot's wife."[8] Lest anyone, either because of some desire for wealth or by his own charm be persuaded from following Christ, he added, "He that does not renounce all that he possesses, cannot be my disciple." EXHORTATION TO MARTYRDOM 5.13.7.[9]

---

[3]CGSL 246-47**. [4]CGSL 247-48**. [5]FC 9:345**. [6]Deut 6:5. [7]CGSL 250**. [8]Lk 17:31-32. [9]FC 36:325-26*.

10:1-16 JESUS SENDS THE SEVENTY

¹*After this the Lord appointed seventy*[g] *others, and sent them on ahead of him, two by two, into every town and place where he himself was about to come.* ²*And he said to them, "The harvest is plentiful, but the laborers are few; pray therefore the Lord of the harvest to send out laborers into his harvest.* ³*Go your way; behold, I send you out as lambs in the midst of wolves.* ⁴*Carry no purse, no bag, no sandals; and salute no one on the road.* ⁵*Whatever house you enter, first say, 'Peace be to this house!'* ⁶*And if a son of peace is there, your peace shall rest upon him; but if not, it shall return to you.* ⁷*And remain in the same house, eating and drinking what they provide, for the laborer deserves his wages; do not go from house to house.* ⁸*Whenever you enter a town and they receive you, eat what is set before you;* ⁹*heal the sick in it and say to them, 'The kingdom of God has come near to you.'* ¹⁰*But whenever you enter a town and they do not receive you, go into its streets and say,* ¹¹*'Even the dust of your town that clings to our feet, we wipe off against you; nevertheless know this, that the kingdom of God has come near.'* ¹²*I tell you, it shall be more tolerable on that day for Sodom than for that town.*

¹³*"Woe to you, Chorazin! woe to you, Bethsaida! for if the mighty works done in you had been done in Tyre and Sidon, they would have repented long ago, sitting in sackcloth and ashes.* ¹⁴*But it shall be more tolerable in the judgment for Tyre and Sidon than for you.* ¹⁵*And you, Capernaum, will you be exalted to heaven? You shall be brought down to Hades.*

¹⁶*"He who hears you hears me, and he who rejects you rejects me, and he who rejects me rejects him who sent me."*

g Other ancient authorities read *seventy-two*

OVERVIEW: Just as the Twelve foresee the episcopal ministry of the church, so the seventy represent the presbyterate (BEDE). Barnabas, for example, was thought to be among the seventy by some of the early Fathers, as well as Sosthenes, Matthias and Thaddaeus (EUSEBIUS). Jesus' sending out the seventy "as lambs in the midst of wolves" fulfills the saying from Isaiah that wolves and lambs will dwell together in peace in the eschaton as a little child leads them (AMBROSE).[1]

But they will be able to survive as sheep among wolves because Jesus is their Shepherd, and he will protect them from the wolves, even in the midst of persecution. The disciples are sent without provisions, for they are to be dependent on the Lord of the harvest (CYRIL OF ALEXAN-

DRIA). They are heralds of the gospel, not merchants (EPHREM THE SYRIAN).

The greeting of peace is to be given to all, without discrimination, even though it will be received only by those who are children of peace (AUGUSTINE), for this greeting of peace discloses the essence of the Father. The disciples are not to be diverted in their mission in any way, and so they are not even to greet anyone on the road lest this keep them from their appointed goal of proclaiming the kingdom of God (AMBROSE). When the disciples are rejected, they are to shake off the dust of their feet, the dust of the just as a sign of vengeance against the unrepentant who will be

---

[1]Is 11:6; 65:25.

worse off than the inhabitants of Sodom (EPHREM THE SYRIAN). For to reject the seventy is to receive a harsher punishment than Tyre and Sidon (AMBROSE).

The disciples are given the great honor of speaking for Christ. And when Christ speaks through his disciples, it is by his Spirit, and when the disciples are rejected for speaking this Word, it is Jesus and his Father who are also rejected (CYRIL OF ALEXANDRIA). To speak for Christ is the power of the gospel (IRENAEUS).

10:1-2 *The Sending of the Seventy(-Two)*

THE SEVENTY-TWO DISCIPLES SIGNIFY THE FUTURE PRESBYTERATE. BEDE: The number of the twelve apostles marked the beginning of the episcopal rank. It is also apparent that the seventy-two disciples, who were also sent out by the Lord to preach the word, signify in their selection the lesser rank of the priesthood that is now called the presbyterate. For the same reason, it is appropriate that these seventy-two figured in the last part of the priestly clothing, as those twelve had been in the first. It was fitting that the type of those who would occupy a higher rank in the body of the High Priest (that is, in the church of Christ) should have a higher place in the typical clothing of the Old Testament high priest. ON THE TABERNACLE 3.[2]

BARNABAS, SOSTHENES, MATTHIAS AND THADDAEUS PART OF THE SEVENTY. EUSEBIUS: The names of the apostles of the Savior are clear to everyone from the Gospels,[3] but no list of the seventy disciples is in circulation anywhere. Some have said, to be sure, that Barnabas was one of them, and the Acts of the Apostles[4] and Paul writing to the Galatians[5] have made special mention of him. They say Sosthenes was of these as well.[6] Together with Paul, he wrote to the Corinthians. Tradition also holds that Matthias, who was listed among the apostles in place of Judas,[7] and Joseph Justus,[8] who was honored with him at the same casting of lots, were considered

worthy of the same calling among the seventy. They say that Thaddaeus was also one of them, about whom I shall presently relate a story which has come down to us. On observation, you would find that the disciples of the Savior appear to have been more than the seventy. Paul says that after the resurrection from the dead Cephas saw him first, then the Twelve.[9] After these saw him, he was seen by more than five hundred brothers all at once, some of whom he says had fallen asleep, although the majority were still alive at the time that this account was being composed by him. ECCLESIASTICAL HISTORY 1.12.1-3.[10]

10:3 *As Lambs in the Midst of Wolves*

THE DISCIPLES FULFILL ISAIAH'S SAYING. AMBROSE: He says this to the seventy disciples whom he appointed and sent out in pairs before his face. Why did he send them two by two? Pairs of animals were sent into the ark, that is, the female with the male, according to number, unclean[11] but cleansed by the sacrament of the church.... Those animals are opposites, so that the one eats the other. A good shepherd does not know how to fear wolves for his flock, and therefore he sends those disciples not against a prey but to grace. The forethought of the good Shepherd prevents the wolves from harming the lambs.[12] He sends lambs among wolves in order that the saying may be fulfilled, "Then wolves and lambs shall feed together."[13] EXPOSITION OF THE GOSPEL OF LUKE 7.44, 46.[14]

DISCIPLES SURVIVE AMONG WOLVES WITH CHRIST AS THEIR SHEPHERD. CYRIL OF ALEXANDRIA: How then does he command the holy apostles, who are innocent men and "sheep," to seek the company of wolves, and go to them of their own will? Is not the danger apparent? Are

---

[2]TTH 18:128-29*. [3]Mt 10:2-4; Mk 3:14-19. [4]Acts 4:36; 13:1. [5]Gal 2:1, 9. [6]1 Cor 1:1; Acts 18:17. [7]Acts 1:23-26. [8]Joseph Barsabas, surnamed Justus, who also had been with Christ from the beginning and so may well have been one of the seventy. [9]1 Cor 15:5-7. [10]FC 19:75-76*. [11]Gen 7:2. [12]Jn 10:12-13. [13]Is 65:25. [14]EHG 252**.

they not set up as ready prey for their attacks? How can a sheep prevail over a wolf? How can one so peaceful conquer the savageness of beasts of prey? "Yes," he says, "for they all have me as their Shepherd: small and great, people and princes, teachers and students. I will be with you, help you, and deliver you from all evil. I will tame the savage beasts. I will change wolves into sheep, and I will make the persecutors become the helpers of the persecuted. I will make those who wrong my ministers to be sharers in their pious designs. I make and unmake all things, and nothing can resist my will." Commentary on Luke, Homily 61.[15]

10:4-12 Instructions for the Mission of Preaching the Kingdom

The Disciples Are to Be Dependent on the Lord of the Harvest. Cyril of Alexandria: When preaching to people everywhere the Word that he spoke and calling the inhabitants of the whole earth to salvation, he requires them to travel about without purse, bag or shoes. They are to travel rapidly from city to city and from place to place. Let no one say that the object of his teaching was to make the holy Apostles refuse the use of the ordinary articles of equipment. What good or what harm would it do them to have shoes on their feet or go without them? By this command, he does wish them to learn and to attempt to practice that they must lay all thought of their livelihood on him. They must call to mind the saint who said, "Cast your care on the Lord, and he will feed you."[16] He gives what is needful for life to the saints. Commentary on Luke, Homily 62.[17]

Heralds, Not Merchants. Ephrem the Syrian: He sent them two by two, in his likeness. He sent them preaching without a salary, as he had done. . . .

"Behold, I am sending you forth like lambs among the wolves," to show that as long as the Shepherd was with them they would not be harmed. To encourage them, he said, "He who re-

ceives you, receives me."[18] . . . He forbid them to take money for fear they would be considered businessmen and not announcers. Commentary on Tatian's Diatessaron 8.1a, 1c.[19]

A Greeting of Peace Is to Be Given to All. Augustine: Our Lord said to his disciples, "Whatever house you enter, first say, 'Peace to this house!' And if a son of peace is there, your peace will rest on him; but, if not, it will return to you." . . .

Since we do not know who is a son of peace, it is our part to leave no one out, to set no one aside, but to desire that all to whom we preach this peace be saved. We are not to fear that we lose our peace if he to whom we preach it is not a son of peace, and we are ignorant of the fact. Our peace will return to us. That means our preaching will profit us, not him. If the peace we preach rests upon him, it will profit both him and us. Admonition and Grace 15.46.[20]

No Greeting Lest Performance of Apostolic Duties Hindered. Ambrose: Consider it is not only "Salute no man," but "by the way" is not carelessly added. When Elisha sent his servant to lay his staff on the body of the dead child, he also commanded him not to salute any man he met.[21] He ordered him to hurry to go in order to perform the office of proclaiming the resurrection, lest he be turned from the duty laid upon him by conversation with someone along the way. The zeal of greeting is not taken away here, but an obstacle to the practice of piety is removed. When divine commands are given, human obligations are surrendered for a little while. Salutation is fine, but the performance of duties to God is finer because it is more fitting. Hindrance of these duties has often brought offenses. Even honorable acts are prohibited, for fear that the grace of ceremony deceive and hinder the ministry of the task, de-

---

[15]*CGSL* 263-64**. [16]Ps 55:22 (54:23 LXX). [17]*CGSL* 266-67**. [18]Jn 13:20. [19]*ECTD* 145-46**. [20]FC 2:301-2*. [21]2 Kings 4:29.

lay in which is sinful. EXPOSITION OF THE GOSPEL OF LUKE 7.63.[22]

A SIGN OF VENGEANCE FOR THE UNREPENTANT. EPHREM THE SYRIAN: "Shake off the dust of your feet"[23] shows that he will require vengeance on those who receive the disciples poorly. The disciples will throw back on these people that very dust which adhered to them from the path. They will return it back on them, so that these might learn that those who pass through their paths will return by them. Since these received the dust of the just, they will merit the vengeance of the just, unless they repent. Only their dust defiled them, not their mire. It will be easier for Sodom,[24] because the angels who went there did not perform a sign in Sodom but made Sodom itself a sign for creation.[25] . . .

Move to another city away from whatever town that does not receive you. If they persecute you in that one, flee to another. The Lord did not extend this word to everyone, but only to his disciples because it was the beginning of the new preaching, and these people were few. COMMENTARY ON TATIAN'S DIATESSARON 8.6-7.[26]

10:13-15 Woes to Chorazin and Bethsaida and Capernaum

REJECTION OF THE SEVENTY. AMBROSE: He also teaches that those who judged that the gospel should not be followed should be subjected to a harsher punishment than those who thought that the law should be dissolved. EXPOSITION OF THE GOSPEL OF LUKE 7.65.[27]

10:16 The Christological Principle of Representation

CHRIST ENTRUSTS DISCIPLES WITH THE GREAT HONOR OF SPEAKING HIS WORDS. CYRIL OF ALEXANDRIA: Consider the great authority he gave the holy apostles, how he declared them praiseworthy, and how he decorated them with the highest honors. . . . "He that hears you,"

he says, "hears me, and he that rejects you, rejects me; and he that rejects me, rejects him that sent me." O what great honor! What incomparable dignities! O what a gift worthy of God! Although men, the children of earth, he clothes them with a godlike glory. He entrusts his words to them that they who resist anything or venture to reject them may be condemned. When they are rejected, he assures them that he suffers this. Then again, he shows that the guilt of this wickedness, as being committed against him, rises up to God the Father. See with the eyes of the mind how vast a height he raises the sin committed by men in rejecting the saints! What a wall he builds around them! How great security he contrives for them! He makes them such as must be feared and in every way plainly provides for their being uninjured. COMMENTARY ON LUKE, HOMILY 63.[28]

CHRIST SPEAKS THROUGH THE DISCIPLES. CYRIL OF ALEXANDRIA: Christ gives those who love instruction the assurance that whatever is said concerning him by the holy apostles or evangelists is to be received necessarily without any doubt and to be crowned with the words of truth. He who hears them, hears Christ. For the blessed Paul also said, "You desire proof that Christ is speaking in me."[29] Christ himself somewhere also said to the holy disciples, "For it is not you that speak, but the Spirit of your Father that speaks in you."[30] Christ speaks in them by the consubstantial Spirit. If it is true, and plainly it is, that they speak by Christ, how can they err? He affirms that he who does not hear them, does not hear Christ, and that he who rejects them rejects Christ, and with him the Father. COMMENTARY ON LUKE, HOMILY 63.[31]

TO SPEAK FOR CHRIST. IRENEAUS: The Lord of all gave the power of the gospel to his apostles. By them, we also have learned the truth, that is, the

---

[22]EHG 258-59**. [23]Mt 10:14. [24]Mt 10:15. [25]Gen 19:1-29. [26]ECTD 148-49**. [27]EHG 259*. [28]CGSL 270*. [29]2 Cor 13:3. [30]Mt 10:20. [31]CGSL 270**.

teaching of the Son of God. The Lord said to them, "He who hears you hears me, and he who despises you despises me, and him who sent me."

AGAINST HERESIES 3, PREFACE.[32]

[32]LCC 1:369**.

10:17-24 THE RETURN OF THE SEVENTY

[17]*The seventy[g] returned with joy, saying, "Lord, even the demons are subject to us in your name!"* [18]*And he said to them, "I saw Satan fall like lightning from heaven.* [19]*Behold, I have given you authority to tread upon serpents and scorpions, and over all the power of the enemy; and nothing shall hurt you.* [20]*Nevertheless do not rejoice in this, that the spirits are subject to you; but rejoice that your names are written in heaven."*

[21]*In that same hour he rejoiced in the Holy Spirit and said, "I thank thee, Father, Lord of heaven and earth, that thou hast hidden these things from the wise and understanding and revealed them to babes; yea, Father, for such was thy gracious will.[h]* [22]*All things have been delivered to me by my Father; and no one knows who the Son is except the Father, or who the Father is except the Son and any one to whom the Son chooses to reveal him."*

[23]*Then turning to the disciples he said privately, "Blessed are the eyes which see what you see!* [24]*For I tell you that many prophets and kings desired to see what you see, and did not see it, and to hear what you hear, and did not hear it."*

g Other ancient authorities read *seventy-two*   h Or *so it was well-pleasing before thee*

OVERVIEW: This power over the devil confirms the Word that Christ has sent them to preach. Satan falls from heaven because Jesus has come from heaven to defeat him (CYRIL OF ALEXANDRIA). Like lightning that flashes for a moment and is gone, so also is Satan's power vanquished as he falls beneath the victory of the cross that crushes him as was foretold in Genesis (EPHREM THE SYRIAN). The power of the disciples to trample on serpents and scorpions comes from the reality that Christ has crushed the Serpent's head, for even when they are poisoned by scorpions and serpents, Christ heals them through the medicine of his wounds on the cross (MAXIMUS OF TURIN). Christ subdues Satan in his baptism in the Jordan and thereby gives us power

through our common baptism with him (CYRIL OF JERUSALEM).

They are to rejoice not in the apostolic honors they have been given, but that their names are written in God's book of life beside the names of Abraham, Isaac, Jacob, and all the chosen people of old. Jesus rejoices in the enlightenment of those in darkness (CYRIL OF ALEXANDRIA). Children are ready for salvation more than the worldly wise (CLEMENT OF ALEXANDRIA). The Son knows the Father perfectly because he is from God (CHRYSOSTOM). The power of the kingdom of God—casting out demons, cleansing lepers, raising the dead—has now been given to the disciples, a gift not even bestowed on kings and prophets (CYRIL OF ALEXANDRIA).

10:17-20 The Disciples' Joy over Triumph Against Demons

POWER CONFIRMS THE WORD THAT THEY PREACH. CYRIL OF ALEXANDRIA: According to Christ's declaration, the harvest indeed was great, but the laborers were few. In addition to those first chosen, he appointed seventy others and sent them to every village and city of Judea before his face to be his forerunners and to preach the things that belonged to him.

The authority that they carried to rebuke evil spirits and the power of crushing Satan was not given to them that they might be regarded with admiration. It was given to them so that Christ would be glorified by their means. Those whom they taught would believe that he was by nature God and the Son of God. He was invested with so great glory and supremacy and might, as to be even able to bestow upon others the power of trampling Satan under their feet. COMMENTARY ON LUKE, HOMILY 64.[1]

SATAN FALLS LIKE LIGHTNING FROM HEAVEN. CYRIL OF ALEXANDRIA: What is Christ's reply? "I saw Satan fall like lightning from heaven." That is, "I am aware of this, because as you set out on this journey by my will, you have conquered Satan. I saw him fall like lightning from heaven." This means that he was thrown down from on high to earth, from overweening pride to humiliation, from glory to contempt, from great power to utter weakness. The saying is true, because before the coming of the Savior, he possessed the world. All was subject to him, and there was no one able to escape the trap of his overwhelming might. Everyone worshiped him. He had temples and altars for sacrifice everywhere and had an innumerable multitude of worshipers. Since the only-begotten Word of God came down from heaven, he has fallen like lightning. COMMENTARY ON LUKE, HOMILY 64.[2]

THE VICTORY OF THE CROSS CRUSHES SATAN. EPHREM THE SYRIAN: "I was looking at Satan, who fell like lightning from the heavens." It was not that he was actually in the heavens. He was not in them when he said, "I will place my throne above the stars,"[3] but he fell from his greatness and his dominion. "I was looking at Satan, who fell like lightning from the heavens." He did not fall from heaven, because lightning does not fall from heaven, since the clouds create it. Why then did he say "from the heavens"? This was because it was as though it was from the heavens, as if lightning which comes suddenly. In one second, Satan fell beneath the victory of the cross. Ordinary people were anointed and sent out by reason of their mission and were highly successful in a second, through miracles of healing those in pain, sickness and evil spirits. It was affirmed that Satan suddenly fell from his dominion, like lightning from the clouds. Just as lightning goes out and does not return to its place, so too did Satan fall and did not again have control over his dominion. "Behold, I am giving you dominion." COMMENTARY ON TATIAN'S DIATESSARON 10.13.[4]

CHRIST HEALS US THROUGH THE CROSS. MAXIMUS OF TURIN: Since we possess the Lord Jesus who has freed us by his suffering, let us always look on him and hope for medicine for our wounds from his sign. That is to say, if perhaps the poison of greed spreads in us, we should look to him, and he will heal us. If the malicious desire of the scorpion stings us, we should beg him, and he will cure us. If bites of worldly thoughts tear us, we should ask him, and we will live. These are the spiritual serpents of our souls. The Lord was crucified in order to crush them. He says concerning them, "You will tread upon serpents and scorpions, and they will do no harm to you." SERMON 37.5.[5]

CHRIST'S BAPTISM GIVES THE BAPTIZED DIGNITY. CYRIL OF JERUSALEM: He [Jesus] was not baptized to receive the forgiveness of sins. He

---

[1]CGSL 273-74**. [2]CGSL 274**. [3]Is 14:13. [4]ECTD 172**. [5]ACW 50:92*.

was without sin. Being sinless, still he was baptized so that he might give grace and dignity to those who receive the sacrament. "Since the children share in flesh and blood, so he in like manner has shared in these,"[6] that we, sharing his incarnate life, might also share his divine grace. Jesus was baptized that we in turn also made here partakers with him, might receive not only salvation but also the dignity. CATECHETICAL LECTURES 3.11.[7]

DISCIPLES NOT TO REJOICE IN APOSTOLIC HONORS. CYRIL OF ALEXANDRIA: To rejoice only in the fact that they were able to work miracles and crush the herds of demons was possibly likely to produce in them the desire of arrogance. The neighbor and relative of this passion constantly is pride. Most usefully the Savior of all rebukes the first boasting and quickly cuts away the root that sprang up in them—the shameful love of glory. He was imitating good farmers who, when they see a thorn springing up in their parks or gardens, immediately tear it up with the blade of the pickax before it strikes its root deep. COMMENTARY ON LUKE, HOMILY 64.[8]

10:21-22 Jesus' Praise to the Father

JESUS REJOICES IN THE HOLY SPIRIT. CYRIL OF ALEXANDRIA: He sent them, decorated with apostolic dignity and distinguished by the work of the grace of the Holy Spirit. He gave them power over unclean spirits to cast them out. Having performed many miracles, they returned, saying, "Lord, even the devils are subject to us in your name." As I have already said, he was full of joy, or rather of exultation because he knew that those he sent had benefited many, and they, above all others, had learned his glory by experience. Being good and loving to humanity and wishing that all should be saved, he found his reason for rejoicing in the conversion of those who were in error, the enlightenment of those in darkness, and the acknowledgment of his glory by those who were without knowledge and instruction. COMMENTARY ON LUKE, HOMILY 65.[9]

CHILDREN READY FOR SALVATION MORE THAN WORLDLY WISE. CLEMENT OF ALEXANDRIA: After we have repented of our sins, renounced our wickedness, and have been purified by baptism, we turn back to the eternal light, as children to their Father. "Rejoicing in the spirit, Jesus said, 'I praise you, Father, God of heaven and earth, that you have hidden these things from the wise and prudent, and revealed them to little ones.'" The Educator and Teacher is naming us "little ones," meaning that we are more ready for salvation than the worldly wise who, believing themselves wise, have blinded their own eyes. He cries out in joy and in great delight, as if attuning himself to the spirit of the little ones, "Yes, Father, for such was your good pleasure." That is why he has revealed to little ones what has been hid from the wise and prudent of this world. CHRIST THE EDUCATOR 1.6.[10]

THE SON KNOWS THE FATHER PERFECTLY. CHRYSOSTOM: The proof that the Son knows the Father perfectly rests on the fact that he is "the one who is from God." The Son has clear knowledge of the Father, because he is from God. The fact that he is from God is a sign and indication that he knows him clearly. An inferior essence would not be able to have clear knowledge of a superior essence, even if the difference between them were slight. ON THE INCOMPREHENSIBLE NATURE OF GOD 5.25.[11]

10:23-24 Jesus' Beatitude on the Disciples

THE POWER OF THE KINGDOM OF GOD. CYRIL OF ALEXANDRIA: He also gave the holy apostles power and might even to raise the dead, cleanse lepers, heal the sick, and by the laying on of hands to call down from heaven the Holy Spirit on anyone they wanted. He gave them power to bind and to loose people's sins. His words are "I say to you, whatever you will bind on earth, will

---

[6]Heb 2:14. [7]FC 61:115**. [8]CGSL 275-76**. [9]CGSL 277-78**. [10]FC 23:31-32*. [11]FC 72:148*.

be bound in heaven.[12] Whatever you will loose on earth, will be loosed in heaven." These are the things we see ourselves possessing. Blessed are our eyes and the eyes of those of all who love him. We have heard his wonderful teaching. He has given us the knowledge of God the Father, and he has shown him to us in his own nature. The things that were by Moses were only types and symbols. Christ has revealed the truth to us. He has taught us that not by blood and smoke, but rather by spiritual sacrifices, we must honor him who is spiritual, immaterial and above all understanding. COMMENTARY ON LUKE, HOMILY 67.[13]

---

[12]Mt 18:18. [13]CGSL 286**.

10:25-37 THE STORY OF THE GOOD SAMARITAN

[25]And behold, a lawyer stood up to put him to the test, saying, "Teacher, what shall I do to inherit eternal life?" [26]He said to him, "What is written in the law? How do you read?" [27]And he answered, "You shall love the Lord your God with all your heart, and with all your soul, and with all your strength, and with all your mind; and your neighbor as yourself." [28]And he said to him, "You have answered right; do this, and you will live."

[29]But he, desiring to justify himself, said to Jesus, "And who is my neighbor?" [30]Jesus replied, "A man was going down from Jerusalem to Jericho, and he fell among robbers, who stripped him and beat him, and departed, leaving him half dead. [31]Now by chance a priest was going down that road; and when he saw him he passed by on the other side. [32]So likewise a Levite, when he came to the place and saw him, passed by on the other side. [33]But a Samaritan, as he journeyed, came to where he was; and when he saw him, he had compassion, [34]and went to him and bound up his wounds, pouring on oil and wine; then he set him on his own beast and brought him to an inn, and took care of him. [35]And the next day he took out two denarii[i] and gave them to the innkeeper, saying, 'Take care of him; and whatever more you spend, I will repay you when I come back.' [36]Which of these three, do you think, proved neighbor to the man who fell among the robbers?" [37]He said, "The one who showed mercy on him." And Jesus said to him, "Go and do likewise."

i The denarius was a day's wage for a laborer

OVERVIEW: The lawyer wants to entrap Jesus, but in doing so he shows that he does not understand the mystery of the incarnation, for this is not a mere man before him but the very Son of God (CYRIL OF ALEXANDRIA). The answer assumes that the way of Torah is the way of life. All the teaching of Jesus stays aloft on the two wings of these two commandments (EPHREM THE SYR-IAN). For to know the law is to know the sacrament of the divine incarnation, which is to know the truth (AMBROSE). Jesus' response to the lawyer's question about eternal life shows that the lawyer has missed his prey and that his interrogation of Jesus will bear no fruit (CYRIL OF ALEXANDRIA).

The good Samaritan is his neighbor because

he showed pity (ORIGEN). For all people are our neighbors, not only our brothers and relatives but also strangers (JEROME). Jericho is an image of the world to which Adam has been cast out from Paradise. It is a great surprise that the third traveler is a Samaritan—and he is portrayed as the hero in the story—for this Samaritan is none other than Christ (AMBROSE).

Most of the church fathers treat the parable of the Good Samaritan allegorically with a christological interpretation (ORIGEN). It identifies the good samaritan with Jesus, the oil and wine as the sacraments, and the inn as the church, showing that God's mercy may be found only in the sacraments of the church (AUGUSTINE). By binding up the wounds of the man, the Samaritan shows that he has many remedies for healing. The next day when he arrives is the Lord's day, the day of resurrection. The two pence he gives him are the two Testaments for preaching the gospel, for the innkeeper is a steward of the mysteries (AMBROSE). Legalists who cross-examine Jesus make no progress until they recognize that they are the man half dead and Jesus is the one who does mercy as neighbor, for he is the one who wishes to be called our neighbor (AUGUSTINE), and we now love him as we love our neighbor (AMBROSE).

10:25 Inheriting Eternal Life

THE MYSTERY OF THE INCARNATION. CYRIL OF ALEXANDRIA: Anyone who thoroughly understands the mystery of the incarnation may say to the lawyer, "If you were skillful in the law and in the meaning of its hidden teaching, you would not forget who he is you try to tempt. You thought that he was a mere man, only man, and not God who appeared in human likeness, knows what is secret, and can look into the hearts of those who approach him. In many ways Emmanuel is depicted to you by the shadowing of Moses. You saw him there sacrificed as a lamb, yet conquering the destroyer and abolishing death by his blood. You saw him in the arrangement of the ark, in which the divine law was deposited. In his holy flesh he was as in an ark, being the Word of the Father, the Son that was begotten of him by nature. You saw him as the mercy seat in the holy tabernacle, around which stood the seraphim."[1] He is our mercy seat for pardon of our sins. Yes, and even as man he is glorified by the seraphim, who are the intelligent and holy powers above. They stand around his divine and exalted throne. COMMENTARY ON LUKE, HOMILY 68.[2]

10:26-28 Love God and One's Neighbor

TWO WINGS HOLD TEACHING ALOFT. EPHREM THE SYRIAN: What is the greatest and first commandment of the law? He said to him, "You shall love the Lord your God, and your neighbor as yourself."[3] . . . All this teaching is held high through the two commandments, as though by means of two wings, that is, through the love of God and of humanity. COMMENTARY ON TATIAN'S DIATESSARON 16.23.[4]

TO KNOW THE LAW IS TO KNOW THE INCARNATION. AMBROSE: With these verses belongs the text that exposes those who seem to themselves to be experts on the law, who keep the letter of the law but disregard its spirit. He teaches that they are ignorant of the law from its very first chapter. He proves this immediately at the beginning of the law. Both the Father and the Son proclaimed and announced the sacrament of the divine incarnation, saying, "You shall love the Lord your God"[5] and "You shall love your neighbor as yourself."[6] The Lord said to the lawyer, "Do this, and you shall live." He who did not know his neighbor, because he did not believe in Christ, answered, "Who is my neighbor?" Whoever does not know Christ does not know the law either. How can he know the law when he is ignorant of the Truth, since the law proclaims the Truth? EXPOSITION OF THE GOSPEL OF LUKE 7.69-70.[7]

---

[1]Perhaps Cyril meant "cherubim." [2]CGSL 288**. [3]Mt 22:36-37, 39. [4]ECTD 254-55**. [5]Deut 6:5. [6]Lev 19:18. [7]EHG 261*.

THE LAWYER MISSES HIS PREY. CYRIL OF
ALEXANDRIA: He says, "What is written in the
law? How do you read?" The lawyer repeated
what is in the law. As if to punish his wickedness
and reprove his malicious purpose, Christ, knowing all things, says, "You have answered correctly;
do this, and you will live." The lawyer missed his
prey. He shot off the mark. His wickedness is unsuccessful. The sting of envy ceased. The net of
deceit is torn. His sowing bears no fruit, and his
toil gains no profit. As some ship overwhelmed
by misfortune, he has suffered a bitter shipwreck.
COMMENTARY ON LUKE, HOMILY 69.[8]

10:29 Who Is One's Neighbor?

**THE ONE WHO SHOWS PITY IS THE NEIGH-
BOR.** ORIGEN: He [the Lord] teaches that the man
going down was the neighbor of no one except of
him who wanted to keep the commandments and
prepare himself to be a neighbor to every one that
needs help. This is what is found after the end of
the parable, "Which of these three does it seem to
you is the neighbor of the man who fell among robbers?" Neither the priest nor the Levite was his
neighbor, but—as the teacher of the law himself
answered—"he who showed pity" was his neighbor. The Savior says, "Go, and do likewise." HOMI-
LIES ON THE GOSPEL OF LUKE 34.2.[9]

ALL PEOPLE ARE OUR NEIGHBORS. JEROME:
Some think that their neighbor is their brother,
family, relative or their kinsman. Our Lord teaches who our neighbor is in the Gospel parable of a
certain man going down from Jerusalem to Jericho. . . . Everyone is our neighbor, and we should
not harm anyone. If, on the contrary, we understand our fellow human beings to be only our
brother and relatives, is it then permissible to do
evil to strangers? God forbid such a belief! We are
neighbors, all people to all people, for we have
one Father. HOMILY ON PSALM 14 (15).[10]

10:30-35 The Parable of the Good Samaritan

JERICHO AN IMAGE OF THE WORLD. AMBROSE:
Jericho is an image of this world. Adam, cast out
from Paradise,[11] that heavenly Jerusalem,[12]
descended to it by the mistake of his transgression, that is, departing from the living to hell, for
whom change not of place but of conduct made
the exile of his nature. He was greatly changed
from that Adam who enjoyed eternal blessedness.
When he turned aside to worldly sins, Adam fell
among thieves, among whom he would not have
fallen if he had not strayed from the heavenly
command and made himself vulnerable to them.
Who are those thieves, if not the angels of night
and darkness, who sometimes transform themselves into angels of light[13] but cannot persevere?
These first steal the clothes of spiritual grace that
we have received and are then accustomed to in-
flict wounds. If we preserve unstained the garments that we have put on, we cannot feel the
robbers' blows. Beware, for fear that you are first
stripped as Adam was first stripped of the heavenly command, defrauded of protection, and divest-
ed of the garment of faith.[14] He received a mortal
wound by which the whole human race would
have fallen if that Samaritan, on his journey, had
not tended his serious injuries. EXPOSITION OF
THE GOSPEL OF LUKE 7.73.[15]

JESUS IS THE GOOD SAMARITAN. AMBROSE:
That extraordinary Samaritan did not himself
shun him whom the priest and the Levite had
shunned. In the name of a sect, you may not shun
him whom you will admire by interpretation of
the word. Indeed, "guard" is signified by the name
Samaritan. The interpretation means this. Who
is the Guard, if not, "The Lord preserves the infants"?[16] Thus, as there is one Jew in the letter
and another in the spirit,[17] so there is one Samaritan in public, another in secret. Here the Samaritan is going down. Who is he except he who
descended from heaven, who also ascended to

---

[8]CGSL 289**. [9]FC 94:138*. [10]FC 48:41*. [11]Gen 3:23. [12]Heb 12:22.
[13]2 Cor 11:14. [14]See Gen 3:7. [15]EHG 262-63**. [16]Ps 114:6 LXX.
[17]Rom 2:28-29.

heaven, the Son of man who is in heaven?[18] When he sees half-dead him whom none could cure before, like her with an issue of blood who had spent all her inheritance on physicians, he came near him.[19] He became a neighbor by acceptance of our common feeling and kin by the gift of mercy. EXPOSITION OF THE GOSPEL OF LUKE 7.74.[20]

AN ALLEGORICAL INTERPRETATION OF THE GOOD SAMARITAN. ORIGEN: One of the elders wanted to interpret the parable as follows. The man who was going down is Adam. Jerusalem is paradise, and Jericho is the world. The robbers are hostile powers. The priest is the law, the Levite is the prophets, and the Samaritan is Christ. The wounds are disobedience. The beast is the Lord's body. The *pandochium* (that is, the stable), which accepts all who wish to enter, is the church. The two denarii mean the Father and the Son. The manager of the stable is the head of the church, to whom its care has been entrusted. The fact that the Samaritan promises he will return represents the Savior's second coming. . . .

The Samaritan, "who took pity on the man who had fallen among thieves," is truly a "guardian," and a closer neighbor than the Law and the Prophets. He showed that he was the man's neighbor more by deed than by word. According to the passage that says, "Be imitators of me, as I too am of Christ,"[21] it is possible for us to imitate Christ and to pity those who "have fallen among thieves." We can go to them, bind their wounds, pour in oil and wine, put them on our own animals, and bear their burdens. The Son of God encourages us to do things like this. He is speaking not so much to the teacher of the law as to us and to everyone when he says, "Go and do likewise." If we do, we will receive eternal life in Christ Jesus, to whom is glory and power for ages of ages. Amen. HOMILIES ON THE GOSPEL OF LUKE 34.3, 9.[22]

GOD'S MERCY FOUND IN THE SACRAMENTS OF THE CHURCH. AUGUSTINE: Robbers left you half-dead on the road, but you have been found lying there by the passing and kindly Samaritan. Wine and oil have been poured on you. You have received the sacrament of the only-begotten Son. You have been lifted onto his mule. You have believed that Christ became flesh. You have been brought to the inn, and you are being cured in the church.

That is where and why I am speaking. This is what I too, what all of us are doing. We are performing the duties of the innkeeper. He was told, "If you spend any more, I will pay you when I return." If only we spent at least as much as we have received! However much we spend, brothers and sisters, it is the Lord's money. SERMON 179A.7-8.[23]

THE PHYSICIAN HAS MANY REMEDIES. AMBROSE: "And bound up his wounds, pouring in oil and wine." That Physician has many remedies with which he is accustomed to cure. His speech is a remedy. One of his sayings binds up wounds, another treats with oil, another pours in wine. He binds wounds with a stricter rule. He treats with the forgiveness of sins. He stings with the rebuke of judgment as if with wine. EXPOSITION OF THE GOSPEL OF LUKE 7.75.[24]

THE NEXT DAY IS THE DAY OF THE RESURRECTION. AMBROSE: "The next day," what is this next day, if not that day of the Lord's resurrection, of which it was said, "This is the day which the Lord has made"?[25] "He took out two coins, and gave them to the host, and said, 'Take care of him.'" EXPOSITION OF THE GOSPEL OF LUKE 7.79.[26]

THE TWO COINS ARE THE TWO TESTAMENTS. AMBROSE: What are those two coins, unless perhaps the two Testaments that contain revealed within them the image of the eternal King, at the price of whose wounds we are healed? Precious blood redeemed us, that we may avoid the sores

---

[18]Jn 3:13; cf. Jn 6:33. [19]Mt 9:20; Lk 8:43-44. [20]EHG 263**. [21]1 Cor 11:1. [22]FC 94:138, 141*. [23]WSA 3 5:312*. [24]EHG 263*. [25]Ps 118:24 (117:24 LXX). [26]EHG 264*.

of final death.[27] EXPOSITION OF THE GOSPEL OF LUKE 7.80.[28]

THE INNKEEPER IS A STEWARD OF THE MYSTERIES. AMBROSE: Blessed is that innkeeper who can care for another's wounds. Blessed is he to whom Jesus says, "Whatever you shall spend over and above, I will repay you." A good steward is one who also spends over and above. Paul is a good steward, whose sermons and epistles overflow with the knowledge that he received. He followed the moderate command of the Lord with almost immoderate effort of mind and body, so that he raised many from deep sorrow by the stewardship of spiritual exhortation. He was a good keeper of his inn, in which the ass knows his master's crib[29] and the flocks of lambs are enclosed. He feared that the way would be easy for ravening wolves howling outside the corrals to attack the sheepfolds. EXPOSITION OF THE GOSPEL OF LUKE 7.82.[30]

10:36-37 The One Who Showed Mercy

CHRIST DESIRES TO BE OUR NEIGHBOR. AUGUSTINE: God our Lord wished to be called our neighbor. The Lord Jesus Christ meant that he was the one who gave help to the man lying half-dead on the road, beaten and left by the robbers. The prophet said in prayer, "As a neighbor and as one's own brother, so did I please."[31] Since the divine nature is far superior and above our human nature, the command by which we are to love God is distinct from our love of our neighbor. He shows mercy to us because of his own goodness, while we show mercy to one another because of God's goodness. He has compassion on us so that we may enjoy him completely, while we have compassion on another that we may completely enjoy him. CHRISTIAN INSTRUCTION 33.[32]

LOVE FOR CHRIST AS NEIGHBOR. AMBROSE: Since no one is closer than he who tended to our wounds, let us love him as our Lord, and let us love him as our neighbor. Nothing is so close as the head to the members.[33] Let us also love him who is the follower of Christ, let us love him who in unity of body has compassion on another's need. EXPOSITION OF THE GOSPEL OF LUKE 7.84.[34]

---

[27]1 Pet 1:19. [28]EHG 264*. [29]Is 1:3. [30]EHG 264-65**. [31]Ps 34:14 LXX. [32]FC 2:51*. [33]See 1 Cor 6:15; Eph 5:30. [34]EHG 265*.

10:38-42 MARY AND MARTHA

[38]*Now as they went on their way, he entered a village; and a woman named Martha received him into her house.* [39]*And she had a sister called Mary, who sat at the Lord's feet and listened to his teaching.* [40]*But Martha was distracted with much serving; and she went to him and said, "Lord, do you not care that my sister has left me to serve alone? Tell her then to help me."* [41]*But the Lord answered her, "Martha, Martha, you are anxious and troubled about many things;* [42]*one thing is needful.*[j] *Mary has chosen the good portion, which shall not be taken away from her."*

j Other ancient authorities read *few things are needful, or only one*

OVERVIEW: Martha demonstrates generous hospitality as she receives Jesus into her home; this is a great work, for she is preparing food for the Holy of Holies and his saints. Mary feasted on the justice and truth of Jesus, who is the Bread of life (Augustine). The body of Christ needs hearers and doers of the Word of God, as the appointment of deacons in Acts points out (Ambrose). In fact, it could be argued that Martha's love was more fervent than Mary's, for she was prepared to serve him even before he came, and she was the first to run and meet him when he came to raise her brother, Lazarus, from the dead (Ephrem the Syrian). By praising Mary, Jesus is in no way criticizing Martha, but he is making clear that service to the body is transitory, whereas listening to the Word of God is eternal (John Cassian). Mary is fully engaged in the business of the journey, singing alleluias of praise as she receives from the Lord his teaching (Augustine).

10:38-42 One Thing Is Needful

Martha Prepares Food for the Holy of Holies and His Saints. Augustine: The Lord had a body. And just as he deigned to assume a physical body for our sake, so also did he deign to be hungry and thirsty. As a result of the fact that he deigned to be hungry and thirsty, he condescended to be fed by those he himself enriched. He condescended to be received as a guest, not from need but from favor.

Martha was busy satisfying the needs of those who were hungry and thirsty. With deep concern, she prepared what the Holy of Holies and his saints would eat and drink in her house. It was an important but transitory work. It will not always be necessary to eat and drink, will it? When we cling to the most pure and perfect Goodness, serving will not be a necessity. Sermons 255.2.[1]

Mary Feasted on the Bread of Life. Augustine: What was Mary enjoying while she was listening? What was she eating? What was she drinking? Do you know? Let's ask the Lord, who keeps such a splendid table for his own people, let's ask him. "Blessed," he says, "are those who are hungry and thirsty for justice, because they shall be satisfied."[2] It was from this well-

spring, from this storehouse of justice, that Mary, seated at the Lord's feet, was in her hunger receiving some crumbs. You see, the Lord was giving her then as much as she was able to take. But as for the whole amount, which he was going to give at his table of the future, not even the disciples, not even the apostles themselves, were able to take in at the time when he said to them, "I still have many things to say to you, but you are unable to hear them now."[3] . . .

What was Mary enjoying? What was she eating? I'm persistent on this point, because I'm enjoying it too. I will venture to say that she was eating the one she was listening to. I mean, if she was eating truth, didn't he say himself, "I am the truth"?[4] What more can I say? He was being eaten, because he was the Bread. "I," he said, "am the bread who came down from heaven."[5] This is the bread which nourishes and never diminishes. Sermon 179.5.[6]

The Body of Christ Needs Hearers and Doers of the Word. Ambrose: Virtue does not have a single form. In the example of Martha and Mary, there is added the busy devotion of the one and the pious attention of the other to the Word of God, which, if it agrees with faith, is preferred even to the very works, as it is written: "Mary has chosen the good portion, which shall not be taken away from her." So let us also strive to have what no one can take away from us, so that not careless but diligent hearing may be granted to us. For even the seeds of the heavenly Word itself are likely to be taken away if they are sowed by the wayside.[7] Let the desire for wisdom lead you as it did Mary. It is a greater and more perfect work. Do not let service divert the knowledge of the heavenly Word. . . . Nor is Martha rebuked in her good serving, but Mary is preferred because she has chosen the better part for herself, for Jesus abounds with many blessings and bestows many gifts. And therefore the wiser choos-

---

[1]FC 3 8:350**. [2]Mt 5:6. [3]Jn 16:12. [4]Jn 14:6. [5]Jn 6:41. [6]WSA 3 5:301**. [7]Lk 8:5, 12.

es what she perceives as foremost. EXPOSITION OF THE GOSPEL OF LUKE 7.85-86.[8]

MARTHA'S LOVE MORE FERVENT THAN MARY'S. EPHREM THE SYRIAN: Mary came and sat at his feet. This was as though she were sitting on firm ground at the feet of him who had forgiven the sinful woman her sins.[9] She had put on a crown in order to enter into the kingdom of the Firstborn. She had chosen the better portion, the Benefactor, the Messiah himself. This will never be taken away from her. Martha's love was more fervent than Mary's, for before he had arrived there, she was ready to serve him. "Do you not care that my sister has left me to serve alone?" When he came to raise Lazarus to life, she ran and came out first.[10] COMMENTARY ON TATIAN'S DIATESSARON 8.15.[11]

TO LISTEN TO THE WORD IS ETERNAL. JOHN CASSIAN: To cling always to God and to the things of God—this must be our major effort, this must be the road that the heart follows unswervingly. Any diversion, however impressive, must be regarded as secondary, low-grade and certainly dangerous. Martha and Mary provide a most beautiful scriptural paradigm of this outlook and of this mode of activity. In looking after the Lord and his disciples, Martha did a very holy service. Mary, however, was intent on the spiritual teaching of Jesus, and she stayed by his feet, which she kissed and anointed with the oil of her good faith. . . . In saying "Mary chose the good portion," he was saying nothing about Martha, and in no way was he giving the appearance of criticizing her. Still, by praising Mary he was saying that the other was a step below her. Again, by saying "it will not be taken away from her," he was showing that Martha's role could be taken away from her, since the service of the body can only last as long as the human being is there, whereas the zeal of Mary can never end. CONFERENCE 1.8.[12]

MARY SINGS ALLELUIAS. AUGUSTINE: At present alleluia is for us a traveler's song, but this tiresome journey brings us closer to home and rest where, all our busy activities over and done with, the only thing that will remain will be alleluia.

That is the delightful part that Mary chose for herself, as she sat doing nothing but learning and praising, while her sister, Martha, was busy with all sorts of things. Indeed, what she was doing was necessary, but it wasn't going to last. SERMON 255.1-2.[13]

---

[8]EHG 265-66**. [9]Lk 7:38. [10]Jn 11:20. [11]ECTD 153**. [12]JCC 42-43. [13]WSA 3 7:158**.

11:1-13 THE LORD'S PRAYER

[1]*He was praying in a certain place, and when he ceased, one of his disciples said to him, "Lord, teach us to pray, as John taught his disciples."* [2]*And he said to them, "When you pray, say:*

"Father, hallowed be thy name. Thy kingdom come. [3]*Give us each day our daily bread;*[k] [4]*and forgive us our sins, for we ourselves forgive every one who is indebted to us; and lead us not into temptation."*

[5]*And he said to them, "Which of you who has a friend will go to him at midnight and say to him, 'Friend, lend me three loaves;* [6]*for a friend of mine has arrived on a journey, and I have noth-*

ing to set before him'; ⁷and he will answer from within, 'Do not bother me; the door is now shut, and my children are with me in bed; I cannot get up and give you anything'? ⁸I tell you, though he will not get up and give him anything because he is his friend, yet because of his importunity he will rise and give him whatever he needs. ⁹And I tell you, Ask, and it will be given you; seek, and you will find; knock, and it will be opened to you. ¹⁰For every one who asks receives, and he who seeks finds, and to him who knocks it will be opened. ¹¹What father among you, if his son asks for[l] a fish, will instead of a fish give him a serpent, ¹²or if he asks for an egg, will give him a scorpion? ¹³If you then, who are evil, know how to give good gifts to your children, how much more will the heavenly Father give the Holy Spirit to those who ask him!"

k Or *our bread for the morrow* l Other ancient authorities insert *bread, will give him a stone; or if he asks for*

OVERVIEW: Jesus taught his disciples how to pray (ORIGEN). By instructing his disciples to address God as Father, Jesus places them by participation in prayer into the same relationship with God that he has, which is a privilege and a responsibility (CYRIL OF ALEXANDRIA). Throughout the Gospel, the disciples will observe Jesus' relationship to God the Father and come to realize that through the Son of God they are children of God and that all prayers to the Father are always through the Son (ORIGEN).

Jesus first petitions the Father regarding who God is—his name—and what God does—his reigning as King. Jesus instructs his disciples to treat God's name as holy by calling on God as Father so that his name may be kept holy among us, trusting that he will respond graciously for the sake of his Son. Only the saints can pray, "your kingdom come," for the wicked do not want the Lord's judgment while they are still in their sins. To pray that God's will be done on earth as it is in heaven is to pray for pure and blameless lives like the saints in heaven who dwell in the holiness of God's presence (CYRIL OF ALEXANDRIA). In fact, to pray for the kingdom is to pray for yourself as one of the saints who dwell in the kingdom (AUGUSTINE).

To pray for bread is to pray for saintlike poverty and not for wealth, for only those in need may pray this petition. It contains the enigmatic *epiousios*, leading to many different interpretations but focusing on bread that is necessary and suffi-

cient (EPHREM THE SYRIAN). The history of interpretation reflects two principal understandings: (1) physical bread needed for life in this world and (2) eschatological bread that provides the life of the age to come as spiritual sustenance even now. Rather than opposing those two possibilities, Luke's overall theology suggests that both may be in view (JOHN CASSIAN). In praying for bread, we are praying for Christ our bread, since Christ is life, life is bread, and did he not say, "I am the bread of life" (TERTULLIAN)?

The forgiveness of sins, next in the Lord's Prayer, balances the petition for bread. To forgive sins is to imitate God, who gives us absolution from all our iniquities (CYRIL OF ALEXANDRIA). To forgive sin is to serve God as he has served us by forgiving us our sins (ORIGEN). The tempter is the devil, not the Lord, as is demonstrated by Jesus' temptations by the devil in the wilderness (TERTULLIAN). Luke does not include the petition to deliver us from evil, for being led into temptation is the same as being delivered from evil (CYRIL OF ALEXANDRIA).

The rules of hospitality in the first century required that the entire community assist in entertaining a midnight guest. Jesus is speaking about the hospitality of God, who, no matter what the circumstances, is honorable and generous, supplying what we need, for God is much more gracious than any human being might be (AUGUSTINE). The three loaves represent the nourishment we receive from God in the heavenly mysteries (AMBROSE).

We are to ask in prayer, to seek by living properly, and knock by persevering in faith (BEDE). As the bestower of good and gracious gifts, God promises with an oath that he will answer our prayers if we ask, seek and knock, but always according to his timetable (CYRIL OF ALEXANDRIA). To knock on the Lord's door is to pray to him. What we are to seek is the kingdom of God and his justice that is reflected in a human father who gives good gifts to his children (BEDE). The fish, egg and bread represent the good and gracious gifts of faith, hope and love our Father in heaven gives to his children on earth (AUGUSTINE). When we ask the Father for living bread, he gives us the Son through the Holy Spirit (ORIGEN). When we pray, we are to ask for those gifts that come from the Spirit, not for things that will harm us in body or soul, for God our Father wishes to give us the good gifts that make us holy and blameless with the saints and the holy angels (CYRIL OF ALEXANDRIA).

11:1-4 Petitioning the Father

JESUS' DISCIPLE WANTS TO KNOW HOW JESUS PETITIONS THE FATHER. ORIGEN: I think that one of Jesus' disciples was conscious in himself of human weakness, which falls short of knowing how we ought to pray.... Are we then to conclude that a man who was brought up in the instruction of the law, who heard the words of the prophets and did not fail to attend the synagogue, did not know how to pray until he saw the Lord praying "in a certain place"? It would certainly be foolish to say this. The disciple prayed according to the customs of the Jews, but he saw that he needed better knowledge about the subject of prayer. ON PRAYER 2.4.[1]

THE PRIVILEGE AND RESPONSIBILITY OF CALLING GOD FATHER. CYRIL OF ALEXANDRIA: For the Savior said, "When you pray, say, 'Our Father.'" And another of the holy Evangelists adds, "who art in heaven."[2] ...

He gives his own glory to us. He raises slaves to the dignity of freedom. He crowns the human condition with such honor as surpasses the power of nature. He brings to pass what was spoken of old by the voice of the psalmist: "I said, you are gods, and all of you children of the Most High."[3] He rescues us from the measure of slavery, giving us by his grace what we did not possess by nature, and permits us to call God "Father," as being admitted to the rank of sons. We received this, together with all our other privileges, from him. One of these privileges is the dignity of freedom, a gift peculiarly befitting those who have been called to be sons.

He commands us, therefore, to take boldness and say in our prayers, "Our Father." We, who are children of earth and slaves and subject by the law of nature to him who created us, call him who is in heaven "Father." Most fittingly, he enables those who pray to understand this also. Since we call God "Father" and have been counted worthy of such a distinguished honor, we must lead holy and thoroughly blameless lives. We must behave as is pleasing to our Father and not think or say anything unworthy or unfit for the freedom that has been bestowed on us....

The Savior of all very wisely grants us to call God "Father," that we, knowing well that we are sons of God, may behave in a manner worthy of him who has honored us. He will then receive the supplications that we offer in Christ. COMMENTARY ON LUKE, HOMILY 71.[4]

PRAYERS TO THE FATHER ARE ALWAYS THROUGH THE SON. ORIGEN: Perhaps we should ... pray ... only to the God and Father of all, to whom even our Savior himself prayed, as we have explained, and to whom he taught us to pray. When he heard "teach us to pray," he did not teach us to pray to himself but to the Father by saying "Our Father in heaven and so forth." ...

When the saints give thanks to God in their prayers, they acknowledge through Christ Jesus

---

[1]OSW 85*. [2]Mt 6:9. [3]Ps 82:6 (81:6 LXX). [4]CGSL 300-302**.

the favors he has done. If it is true that one who is scrupulous about prayer should not pray to someone else who prays but rather to the Father whom our Lord Jesus taught us to address in prayers, it is especially true that no prayer should be addressed to the Father without him. ON PRAYER 15.1-2.[5]

WE PRAY THAT GOD'S NAME MAY BE HALLOWED AMONG US. CYRIL OF ALEXANDRIA:
What, therefore, is the meaning of "hallowed be your name"? . . .

When it is our settled conviction and belief that he who by nature is God over all is Holy of the Holies, we confess his glory and supreme majesty. We then receive his fear into our mind and lead upright and blameless lives. By this we become holy ourselves, and we may be able to be near unto the holy God. . . . The prayer is, therefore, "May your name be kept holy in us, in our minds and wills." This is the significance of the word *hallowed*. If a person says, "Our Father, hallowed be your name," he is not requesting any addition to be made to God's holiness. He rather asks that he may possess such a mind and faith to feel that his name is honorable and holy. The act is the source of life and the cause of every blessing. How must being this influenced by God be worthy of the highest estimation and useful for the salvation of the soul? COMMENTARY ON LUKE, HOMILY 72.[6]

ONLY THE SAINTS MAY PRAY "YOUR KINGDOM COME." CYRIL OF ALEXANDRIA: God is our King before the worlds.[7] Since God always reigns and is omnipotent, with what view do those who call God "Father" offer up to him their requests and say, "Your kingdom come"?

They seem to desire to behold Christ the Savior of all rising again upon the world. He will come. He will come and descend as judge, no longer in a lowly condition like us or in the humility of human nature. He will come in glory such as becomes God, as he dwells in the unapproachable light,[8] and with the angels as his guards. He somewhere said, "The Son of man shall come in the glory of his Father, with his holy angels."[9] . . .

That judgment seat is terrifying. The Judge is unbiased. It is a time of pleading, or rather of trial and of retribution. The fire, enduring punishment and eternal torments are prepared for the wicked. How can men pray to behold that time? . . . The wicked and impure lead low and lewd lives and are guilty of every vice. In no way is it fitting for them in their prayers to say, "your kingdom come." . . .

The saints ask that the time of the Savior's perfect reign may come, because they have labored dutifully, have a pure conscience and look for the reward of what they have already done. Just as those who, expecting a festival and merriment about ready to come and shortly to appear, thirst for its arrival, so also do they. They trust that they will stand glorious in the presence of the Judge and hear him say, "Come, you blessed of my Father, inherit the kingdom prepared for you from the foundations of the world."[10] . . . They fully believed what he said about the consummation of the world.

When he will appear to them again from heaven, they will shine like the sun in the kingdom of their Father.[11] They correctly say in their prayers, "your kingdom come." For they feel confident that they will receive a reward for their bravery and attain to the consummation of the hope set before them. COMMENTARY ON LUKE, HOMILY 73.[12]

TO DO THE WILL OF GOD. CYRIL OF ALEXANDRIA: Why then did he command the saints to say to God the Father in heaven, "Your will be done; as in heaven, so on earth?" . . . This petition is worthy of the saints and full of all praise. . . .

We request that power may be given to those on earth to do the will of God and imitate the conduct practiced above in heaven by the holy angels. . . .

The saints request that both Israel as well as

---

[5]*OSW* 112-13*. [6]*CGSL* 303-4**. [7]Ps 73:12 LXX. [8]1 Tim 6:16. [9]Mt 16:27. [10]Mt 25:34. [11]Mt 13:43. [12]*CGSL* 306-8**.

the Gentiles may be counted worthy of peace from on high and be comforted since they were in misery and caught in the net of sin without possibility of escape. Having received the righteousness that is in Christ by faith, they may become pure and skillful in every good work. They pray, "Your will be done, as in heaven, so on earth for this reason." As I said, the will of God over all is that those on earth should live in holiness, piously, without blame, being washed from all impurity, and diligent in imitating the spiritual beauty of the spirits above in heaven. The church on earth, since it was the visible likeness and image of the church of the firstborn[13] that is above, may please Christ. COMMENTARY ON LUKE, HOMILY 74.[14]

TO PRAY FOR THE KINGDOM. AUGUSTINE: "Your kingdom come." To whom do we address this petition? Will the kingdom of God not come unless we ask for it? That kingdom will exist after the end of the world. God has a kingdom forever. He is never without a kingdom, for all creation is subject to him. Then for what kingdom do we wish? It is written in the Gospel, "Father, take possession of the kingdom prepared for you from the foundation of the world." See, that is the kingdom of which we speak when we say, "Thy kingdom come." May that kingdom come within us and may we be found within that kingdom. That is our petition. Of course it will come. How will that benefit you if it finds you at the left hand? In this petition, you also wish a blessing on yourself. It is on your own behalf that you pray. In this petition, this is what you desire and long for, namely, that you may so live as to have a share in the kingdom that will be given to all the saints. When you say, "Thy kingdom come," you pray for yourself, because you pray that you may lead a good life. May we partake of your kingdom. May the kingdom that is to come to your saints and your righteous ones also come to us. SERMON 56.6.[15]

THE BREAD OF THE DAY IS THE BREAD OF NECESSITY. EPHREM THE SYRIAN: "Give us our constant bread of the day." Look, he has said,

"Seek the kingdom of God, and these things over and above will be given to you as well."[16] He said "of the day" to teach us poverty in relation to the things of the world. It is sufficient for only our need, or else when we are anxious for a time, we might withdraw from intimacy with God. This bread of the day indicates necessity. He does not just give us only bread but also clothing and other things, as he said, "Your Father knows what your needs are before you ask him."[17] COMMENTARY ON TATIAN'S DIATESSARON 6.16A.[18]

DAILY BREAD IS SPIRITUAL AND PHYSICAL. JOHN CASSIAN: "Give us this day our supersubstantial bread."[19] Another Evangelist uses the term *daily*.

The first expression indicates that this bread has a noble and substantial character by which its exalted splendor and holiness surpass all substances and all creatures.

With "daily" the Evangelist shows that without this bread we cannot live a spiritual life for even a day. When he says "this day," he shows that the bread must be eaten each day. It will not be enough to have eaten yesterday unless we eat similarly today. May our daily poverty encourage us to pour out this prayer at all times, for there is no day on which it is unnecessary for us to eat this bread to strengthen the heart of the person within us.

"Daily" can also be understood as referring to our present life. That is, "give us this bread while we linger in this present world." We know that in the time to come you will give it to whoever deserves it, but we ask that you give it to us today. He who has not received it in this life will not be able to partake of it in that next life. CONFERENCE 9.21.[20]

CHRIST IS OUR BREAD. TERTULLIAN: Divine Wisdom arranged the order of this prayer with exquisite choice. After the matters that pertain to heaven—that is, after the name of God, the will

---

[13]Heb 12:23. [14]CGSL 309-11**. [15]FC 11:243-44*. [16]Mt 6:33. [17]Mt 6:8, 33. [18]ECTD 118*. [19]Mt 6:11. [20]JCC 114*.

of God and the kingdom of God—it should make a place for a petition for our earthly needs too! Our Lord taught us, "Seek first the kingdom, and then these things shall be given you besides."[21] We should rather understand "give us this day our daily bread" in a spiritual sense. For Christ is "our bread," because Christ is life, and the life is bread. "I am," he said, "the bread of life."[22] Shortly before this he said, "The bread is the word of the living God who has come down from heaven."[23] Then, because his body is considered to be in the bread, he said, "This is my body."[24] When we ask for our daily bread, we are asking to live forever in Christ and to be inseparably united with his body. ON PRAYER 6.[25]

To Forgive Sins Is to Imitate God.

CYRIL OF ALEXANDRIA: He requires his disciples to be gentle and slow to anger, so that they may be able to say blamelessly in their prayers, "Forgive us our sins, for we also forgive every one that is indebted unto us." . . . He first commands them to ask forgiveness of the sins they commit and then to confess that they entirely forgive others. If I may say so, they ask God to imitate the patience that they practice. The same gentleness that they show to their fellow servants, they pray that they may receive in equal measure from God, who gives justly, and knows how to show mercy to everyone. . . .

The Savior of all and Lord with good reason did not conclude this clause of the prayer at this point but commanded us to add, "For we also ourselves have forgiven every one who is indebted to us." This is fitting to say only for those who have chosen a virtuous life and are practicing without carelessness "the will of God" that, as Scripture says, "is good and acceptable and perfect."[26] . . .

We must ask God for the forgiveness of the sins that we have committed. First, we must have forgiven whoever has offended us in anything. This is if their sin is against us and not against the glory of the supreme God. We are not masters over such actions but only over those that have been committed against ourselves. By forgiving the brothers what they do to us, we will then certainly find

Christ, the Savior of all, gentle and ready to show us mercy. COMMENTARY ON LUKE, HOMILY 76.[27]

To Forgive Sins Is to Serve God.

ORIGEN: Luke says, "Forgive us our sins," since sins are associated with our debts if we have not paid them. He says the same thing as Matthew but does not seem to leave room for the person who wishes to forgive debtors only if they repent. He says that our Savior has given the law that we should add to our prayer, "For we ourselves forgive every one who is indebted to us." Surely we all have authority to forgive sins against ourselves. This is clear from "as we forgive our debtors"[28] and from "for we ourselves forgive every one who is indebted to us." The person inspired by Jesus and known by his fruits,[29] as the apostles were, has received the Holy Spirit. He has become spiritual by being led by the Spirit to do everything by reason as a child of God.[30] This person forgives whatever God forgives and retains sins that cannot be healed, serving God as the prophets by not speaking his own words but those of the divine will.[31] He also serves God who alone has authority to forgive. ON PRAYER 28.7-8.[32]

The Devil Is the Tempter.

TERTULLIAN: To complete the prayer which was so well arranged, Christ added that we should pray not only that our sins be forgiven but also that we should completely shun them. "Lead us not into temptation," that is, do not allow us to be led by the tempter. God forbid that our Lord should seem to be the tempter, as if he were not aware of one's faith or were eager to upset it! That weakness and spitefulness belongs to the devil. Even in the case of Abraham, God ordered the sacrifice of his son not to tempt his faith but to prove it. He did this to set an example for his commandment that he was later to teach that no one should hold his loved ones dearer than God.[33] Christ himself was

---

[21]Lk 12:31. [22]Jn 6:35. [23]Jn 6:33. [24]Mt 26:26; Mk 14:22; Lk 22:19. [25]FC 40:164-65*. [26]Rom 12:2. [27]CGSL 315-17**. [28]Mt 6:12. [29]Mt 7:16, 20; Lk 6:44. [30]Rom 8:14. [31]Jn 20:23. [32]OSW 150*. [33]Lk 14:26.

tempted by the devil and pointed out the subtle director of the temptation. He confirms this passage by his words to his apostles later when he says, "Pray that you may not enter into temptation."[34] They were tempted to desert their Lord because they had indulged in sleep instead of prayer. The phrase that balances and interprets "lead us not into temptation" is "but deliver us from evil." ON PRAYER 8.[35]

BEING DELIVERED FROM EVIL. CYRIL OF ALEXANDRIA: When we are intent in prayer, he commands us to say, "Lead us not into temptation." Luke concludes the prayer with these words, but Matthew adds, "but deliver us from the evil one."[36] There is a certain close connection in the clauses, because when people are not being led into temptation, they are also delivered from the evil one. If anyone were perhaps to say that not being led into is the same as being delivered from it, he would not err from the truth. COMMENTARY ON LUKE, HOMILY 77.[37]

11:5-8 The Friend at Midnight: How the Father Answers Our Petitions

GOD GIVES GRACIOUSLY. AUGUSTINE: A man whose friend came to him from a journey had nothing to set before him. He wished to borrow three loaves from a friend. Perhaps this number symbolizes the Trinity of one substance. The man woke him as he slept in the middle of his servants. He begged insistently and importunately, so that he gave him as many as he wished. If a man awakened from sleep is forced to give unwillingly in answer to a request, God, who does not know sleep and who wakens us from sleep that we may ask, gives much more graciously. LETTER 130.[38]

THE NOURISHMENT OF THE HEAVENLY MYSTERY. AMBROSE: You see that he who woke his friend at midnight demanding three loaves of bread and, persisting in his intention to receive, finds that his requests are not denied. What are those three loaves if not the nourishment of the

heavenly mystery? If you love the Lord your God, you will be able to deserve this not only for yourself but also for others. Then who is a greater friend to us than he who surrendered his own body for us?[39] EXPOSITION OF THE GOSPEL OF LUKE 7.87.[40]

11:9-13 Ask, Seek, Knock: How the Father Gives His Spirit

ASK BY PRAYING, SEEK BY PROPER LIVING, KNOCK BY PERSEVERING. BEDE: Desiring that we arrive at the joys of the heavenly kingdom, our Lord and Savior taught us to ask these joys of him and promised that he would give them to us if we asked for them. "Ask," he said, "and it will be given to you, seek and you will find, knock and it will be opened to you." Dearly beloved . . . , we earnestly and with our whole heart must ponder these words of our Lord. He bears witness that the kingdom of heaven is not given to, found by and opened to those who are idle and unoccupied but to those who ask for it, seek after it and knock at its gates. The gate of the kingdom must be asked for by praying. It must be sought after by living properly. It must be knocked at by persevering. HOMILIES ON THE GOSPELS 2.14.[41]

THE BESTOWER OF DIVINE GIFTS. CYRIL OF ALEXANDRIA: The Bestower of divine gifts enters himself and speaks: "I also say to you, 'Seek, and you shall find; knock, and it shall be opened to you; for every one that asks receives; and he who seeks finds: and whosoever knocks, it shall be opened to him.'" These words have the full force of an oath, not that God is false, although the promise is not accompanied with an oath. To show that the smallness of their faith was groundless, he sometimes confirms his hearers by an oath. The Savior is also found in many places prefacing his words by saying, "Truly, truly, I say to you." He makes this very promise on oath. You

---

[34]Lk 22:46. [35]FC 40:166-67*. [36]Mt 6:13. [37]CGSL 318**. [38]FC 18:388**. [39]Jn 15:13. [40]EHG 266-67**. [41]CS 111:124**.

will not be free from guilt if you disbelieve it. COMMENTARY ON LUKE, HOMILY 78.[42]

SEEK THE KINGDOM OF GOD AND HIS JUSTICE. BEDE: If we look into the words of our Lord and Savior that he encourages us to ask God our Father after the example of an earthly parent, we quickly recognize what is the righteousness that can open for us the way to the heavenly kingdom. "Which one of you," he says, "if his son asks his father for bread, will give him a stone? Or if he asks for a fish, will give him a serpent in place of the fish? Or if he asks for an egg, will hand him a scorpion?" This is truly a clear comparison, easy for all hearers to understand. Any human, mortal, weak and still burdened with sinful flesh, does not refuse to give the good things which he possesses, although they are earthly and weak, to the children whom he loves. Our heavenly Father, even more than this man, lavishes the good things of heaven, which do not perish, on those who ask of him and are endowed with fear and love of him. HOMILIES ON THE GOSPELS 2.14.[43]

FAITH, HOPE AND CHARITY SYMBOLIZED BY THE FISH, EGG AND BREAD. AUGUSTINE: Of those three things that the apostle commends, faith is either signified by the fish, because of the water of baptism, or because it remains unharmed by the waves of this world. The Serpent is opposed to it, because it craftily and deceitfully persuaded man not to believe in God. The egg symbolizes hope, because the chick is not yet alive but will be; it is not yet seen but is hoped. "Hope that is seen is not hope."[44] The scorpion is opposed to hope, because whoever hopes for eternal life forgets the things that are behind and reaches out to those that are before.[45] It is dangerous for him to look backward, and he is on guard against the rear of the scorpion, which has a poisoned dart in its tail. Bread symbolizes love, because "the greatest of these is love,"[46] and among foods, bread certainly surpasses all others in value. The stone is opposed

to it because the stonehearted cast out love. It may be that these gifts signify something more appropriate, yet he who knows how to give good gifts to his children urges us to ask, seek and knock. LETTER 130.[47]

SONSHIP IN JESUS. ORIGEN: He who believes that the mouth of Jesus cannot lie would hesitate a moment to be persuaded to pray, when he says, "Ask, and it will be given you . . . for everyone who asks, receives." When we ask for the living bread, the good Father certainly gives him (and not the stone that his adversary wishes to give to Jesus and his disciples for food) to those who have received the Spirit of sonship from the Father.[48] The Father gives a good gift, raining it down from heaven for those who ask him. ON PRAYER 10.2.[49]

WHAT TO PRAY FOR, AND WHAT NOT TO PRAY FOR. CYRIL OF ALEXANDRIA: We sometimes come near to our bounteous God offering him petitions for various objects according to each one's pleasure. Sometimes we pray without discernment or any careful examination of what truly is to our advantage, and if granted by God would prove a blessing or would be to our injury if we received it. Rather, by the inconsiderate impulse of our fancy, we fall into desires full of ruin that thrust the souls of those that entertain them into the snare of death and the meshes of hell. When we ask of God anything of this kind, we will by no means receive it. On the contrary, we offer a petition suitable only for ridicule. Why will we not receive it? Is the God of all weary of bestowing gifts on us? By no means. "Why then," someone may say, "will he not give, since he is bounteous in giving?" . . .

When he says, "You who are evil," he means "you whose mind is capable of being influenced by evil and not uniformly inclined to good like the God of all." "You know how to give good gifts

---

[42]CGSL 322. [43]CS 111:128-29, 130-31*. [44]Rom 8:24. [45]Phil 3:13. [46]1 Cor 13:13. [47]FC 18:388-89**. [48]Rom 8:15. [49]OSW 101*.

to your children; how much more shall your heavenly Father give a good spirit to them that ask him?" By a "good spirit" he means "spiritual grace." This is good in every way. If a person receives it,

he will become most blessed and worthy of admiration. COMMENTARY ON LUKE, HOMILY 79.[50]

[50]CGSL 324-25**.

11:14-36 OPPOSITION TO JESUS

[14]*Now he was casting out a demon that was dumb; when the demon had gone out, the dumb man spoke, and the people marveled.* [15]*But some of them said, "He casts out demons by Beelzebul, the prince of demons";* [16]*while others, to test him, sought from him a sign from heaven.* [17]*But he, knowing their thoughts, said to them, "Every kingdom divided against itself is laid waste, and a divided household falls.* [18]*And if Satan also is divided against himself, how will his kingdom stand? For you say that I cast out demons by Beelzebul.* [19]*And if I cast out demons by Beelzebul, by whom do your sons cast them out? Therefore they shall be your judges.* [20]*But if it is by the finger of God that I cast out demons, then the kingdom of God has come upon you.* [21]*When a strong man, fully armed, guards his own palace, his goods are in peace;* [22]*but when one stronger than he assails him and overcomes him, he takes away his armor in which he trusted, and divides his spoil.* [23]*He who is not with me is against me, and he who does not gather with me scatters.*

[24]*"When the unclean spirit has gone out of a man, he passes through waterless places seeking rest; and finding none he says, 'I will return to my house from which I came.'* [25]*And when he comes he finds it swept and put in order.* [26]*Then he goes and brings seven other spirits more evil than himself, and they enter and dwell there; and the last state of that man becomes worse than the first."*

[27]*As he said this, a woman in the crowd raised her voice and said to him, "Blessed is the womb that bore you, and the breasts that you sucked!"* [28]*But he said, "Blessed rather are those who hear the word of God and keep it!"*

[29]*When the crowds were increasing, he began to say, "This generation is an evil generation; it seeks a sign, but no sign shall be given to it except the sign of Jonah.* [30]*For as Jonah became a sign to the men of Nineveh, so will the Son of man be to this generation.* [31]*The queen of the South will arise at the judgment with the men of this generation and condemn them; for she came from the ends of the earth to hear the wisdom of Solomon, and behold, something greater than Solomon is here.* [32]*The men of Nineveh will arise at the judgment with this generation and condemn it; for they repented at the preaching of Jonah, and behold, something greater than Jonah is here.*

[33]*"No one after lighting a lamp puts it in a cellar or under a bushel, but on a stand, that those who enter may see the light.* [34]*Your eye is the lamp of your body; when your eye is sound, your*

whole body is full of light; but when it is not sound, your body is full of darkness. [35]*Therefore be careful lest the light in you be darkness.* [36]*If then your whole body is full of light, having no part dark, it will be wholly bright, as when a lamp with its rays gives you light."*

OVERVIEW: The Lord's Prayer was given in a private conversation between Jesus and his disciples. Now the audience switches to the crowds, who at first are amazed at Jesus' exorcism of a man who is deaf and dumb. Then some of the crowd, accusing him of driving out demons by Beelzebul, test him by asking for a sign (CYRIL OF ALEXANDRIA). Opposition against Jesus arises after his exorcism of a deaf-mute; the first challenge concerns whether his ability to cast out demons is from God or Beelzebul. The reality of God's kingdom in Christ is that it is eternal and undivided. Jesus' common sense response is clear: if he were in league with Satan, he would not be attacking Satan's emissaries (CYRIL OF ALEXANDRIA).

Jesus casts out demons by the finger of God, which is the Holy Spirit, for he is the new and greater prophet like Moses who brings with him the kingdom of God. Jesus' statement that "the kingdom of God has come upon you" means he is the final, eschatological prophet promised by Moses[1] (CYRIL OF ALEXANDRIA).

Jesus has already demonstrated his power over Satan when, with the Word of God, he overcame the devil's suggestions that he bypass the cross. Jesus will complete his mission and achieve the final victory over Satan. Satan is not with Jesus but stands against him. When Satan is cast out, the void must be filled with the Messiah, the stronger one, or else Satan will return with even more force and vehemence (CYRIL OF ALEXANDRIA). The human soul is pictured as a house that needs an occupant—and if it is left empty, an undesirable tenant will take up residence. Once a house has been swept clean by baptism and furnished by the Lord's Supper, it must remain holy and pure by a life of grace (ORIGEN). This picture supports Augustine's view that all people have a God-shaped void within that only God can fill satisfactorily.

Jesus does not deny the truth of the beatitude spoken by the woman from the crowd; he adds to her words. Mary is blessed more for believing the words of Jesus than she is for conceiving his flesh in her body (AUGUSTINE). Those who are blessed are those who worship Jesus as the Son of God by hearing his word (EPHREM THE SYRIAN).

The sign of Jonah is the passion and resurrection fulfilled in Jesus (CYRIL OF ALEXANDRIA). The sign of Jonah functioned in two ways: for those who believe, it was for their rising; for those who did not, it was their destruction.[2] The Queen of the South is a type of the church because like the church, she will condemn an unbelieving generation by coming to the Lord (EPHREM THE SYRIAN). The mystery of Christ and his church is that it extends even to Gentiles and barbarians like the Ninevites and the Queen of the South (AMBROSE).

The lamp represents the light of the gospel, which shines through Jesus and his preaching, and the lampstand is Christ's church, upon which he stands (CYRIL OF ALEXANDRIA). Those who have been catechized and baptized are not to hide this light, for faith must not be hidden under the law but must shine forth through Christ (AMBROSE). Jesus expands the metaphor to the eye. The eye is the mind that receives the simple light of Christ so that it might have the mind of Christ (SYMEON THE NEW THEOLOGIAN).

11:14 *Jesus Casts Out a Demon from a Deaf-Mute*

CHRIST'S POWER CASTS OUT A MUTE DEMON. CYRIL OF ALEXANDRIA: They were even grinding their teeth at Christ, the Savior of all,

---

[1]Deut 18:15. [2]See Lk 2:34.

because he made the multitudes wonder by his many divine and astonishing miracles. The very devils cried out at his overwhelming and godlike power and authority. . . .

"There was brought to him one who was possessed with a mute devil." Now mute devils are difficult for any one of the saints to rebuke. They are more obstinate than any other kind and excessively bold. There was nothing difficult to the all-powerful will of Christ, the Savior of us all. . . . Upon the accomplishment of this wonderful act, the multitude extolled him with praises and hastened to crown the worker of the miracle with godlike honor. COMMENTARY ON LUKE, HOMILY 80.[3]

11:15-16 Seeking a Sign from Jesus

THE SCRIBES AND PHARISEES DEMAND A SIGN. CYRIL OF ALEXANDRIA: "But certain of them," it says, "being scribes and Pharisees," with hearts intoxicated with pride and envy, found in the miracle fuel for their illness. They did not praise him but even went to the very opposite extreme. Having stripped him of the godlike deeds he did, they assigned to the devil almighty power and made Beelzebub the source of Christ's strength. They said, "He casts out devils by him." Others who were afflicted with a similar wickedness ran without discernment into a disgraceful forwardness of speech. Being stung by envy, they required seeing him work a sign from heaven. They called out, as it were, and said, "Even if you have expelled from a man a bitter and malicious demon, that as yet is no such great matter, nor worthy of admiration. What is done up to now is no proof of divine ability." . . . Such were their forward fault findings. The fact of their wishing to ask a sign from heaven proves nothing else than that they entertained such thoughts as these concerning him. COMMENTARY ON LUKE, HOMILY 80.[4]

11:17-20 The Kingdom Has Come in Jesus' Ministry

JESUS' COMMONSENSE RESPONSE. CYRIL OF ALEXANDRIA: He proceeds to arguments drawn from common things but which have the force of truth in them. . . .

Kingdoms are established by the fidelity of subjects and the obedience of those under the royal scepter. Houses are established when those who belong to them in no way whatsoever thwart one another but, on the contrary, agree in will and deed. I suppose it would establish the kingdom too of Beelzebub, had he determined to abstain from everything contrary to himself. How then does Satan cast out Satan? It follows then that devils do not depart from people on their own accord but retire unwillingly. "Satan," he says, "does not fight with himself." He does not rebuke his own servants. He does not permit himself to injure his own armorbearers. On the contrary, he helps his kingdom. "It remains for you to understand that I crush Satan by divine power." COMMENTARY ON LUKE, HOMILY 80.[5]

THE FINGER OF GOD IS THE HOLY SPIRIT. CYRIL OF ALEXANDRIA: By the finger of God, he means the Holy Spirit. The Son is called the hand and arm of God the Father because he does all things by the Son, and the Son in a similar way works by the Spirit. Just as the finger is attached to the hand as something not foreign from it but belonging to it by nature, so also the Holy Spirit, by reason of his being equal in substance, is joined in oneness to the Son, although he proceeds from God the Father. The Son does every thing by the consubstantial Spirit. Here he purposely says that by the finger of God he casts out devils, speaking as a man. The Jews in the infirmity and folly of their mind would not have endured it if he said, "by my own Spirit I cast out devils." COMMENTARY ON LUKE, HOMILY 81.[6]

IN JESUS, WE SEE THE KINGDOM OF GOD. CYRIL OF ALEXANDRIA: Although he is by nature

---

[3]CGSL 327**. [4]CGSL 327-28**. [5]CGSL 328-29**. [6]CGSL 331**.

God and the Giver of the Spirit from God the Father to those who are worthy and employs as his own that power which is from him, he spoke as a man. He is consubstantial with him, and whatever is said to be done by God the Father, this necessarily is by the Son in the Spirit. He says, "If I, being a man, and having become like you, cast out devils in the Spirit of God, human nature has in me first attained to a godlike kingdom." For it has become glorious by breaking the power of Satan and rebuking the impure and abominable spirits. This is the meaning of the words "the kingdom of God has come upon you." Commentary on Luke, Homily 81.[7]

11:21-22 Jesus Has Conquered Satan

The Stronger One Prevails over Satan. Cyril of Alexandria: He has conquered the ruler of this world. Having, so to speak, hamstrung him and stripped him of the power he possessed, he has given him over for a prey to his followers. He says, "The strong man, being armed, guards his house; all his goods are in peace. But when one who is stronger than he shall come on him and overcome him, he takes away all his armor wherein he trusted and divides his spoil." This is a plain demonstration and type of the matter depicted after the manner of human affairs. . . . Before the coming of the Savior, he was in great power, driving and shutting up in his own stall flocks that were not his own but belonging to God over all. He was like some voracious and most insolent robber. Since the Word of God who is above all, the Giver of all might and Lord of powers attacked him, having become man, all his goods have been plundered and his spoil divided. Those of old who had been ensnared by him into ungodliness and error have been called by the holy apostles to the acknowledgment of the truth and been brought near to God the Father by faith in his Son. Commentary on Luke, Homily 81.[8]

11:23 Those Who Reject Jesus

Satan Is Not with Jesus. Cyril of Alexandria: "He that is not with me," he says, "is against me, and he that gathers not with me, scatters." "For I," he says, "have come to save every man from the hands of the devil and to deliver from his deceit those whom he had ensnared. I came to set the prisoners free, to give light to those in darkness, to raise up them that had fallen, to heal the brokenspirited, and to gather together the children of God who were scattered abroad. This was the object of my coming. Satan is not with me; on the contrary he is against me. He ventures to scatter those whom I have gathered and saved. How then can he, who wars against me and sets his wickedness in array against my purposes, give me power against himself? How is it not foolish even barely to imagine the possibility of such a thing as this?" Commentary on Luke, Homily 81.[9]

11:24-26 Satan's Conqueror, Jesus

The Void Left by Satan's Absence. Cyril of Alexandria: That the Jewish crowds fall into such thoughts concerning Christ he makes plain by saying, "When the wicked spirit has gone out from the man, it returns with seven other spirits more bitter than itself, and the last state of that man is worse than the first." As long as they were in bondage in Egypt and lived according to the customs and laws of the Egyptians that were full of all impurity, they led polluted lives. An evil spirit dwelled in them, because it dwells in the hearts of the wicked. When in the mercy of God they had been delivered by Moses and received the law as a schoolmaster calling them to the light of the true knowledge of God, the impure and polluted spirit was driven out. Since they did not believe in Christ but rejected the Savior, the impure spirit again attacked them. He found their heart empty and devoid of all fear of God, swept and took up his dwelling in them. Commentary on Luke, Homily 81.[10]

---

[7]CGSL 331**. [8]CGSL 331-32**. [9]CGSL 332**. [10]CGSL 332**.

THE HOUSE SWEPT CLEAN MUST REMAIN HOLY. ORIGEN: The unclean spirit dwelt in us before we believed, before we came to Christ when our soul was still committing fornication against God and was with its lovers, the demons. Afterward it said, "I will return to my first husband," and came to Christ, who "created" it from the beginning "in his image." Necessarily the adulterous spirit gave up his place when it saw the legitimate husband. Christ received us, and our house has been "cleansed" from its former sins. It has been "furnished" with the furnishing of the sacraments of the faithful that they who have been initiated know. This house does not deserve to have Christ as its resident immediately unless its life and conduct are so holy, pure and incapable of being defiled that it deserves to be the "temple of God." It should not still be a house, but a temple in which God dwells. If it neglects the grace that was received and entangles itself in secular affairs, immediately that unclean spirit returns and claims the vacant house for itself. "It brings with it seven other spirits more wicked," so that it may not be able again to be expelled, "and the last state of that kind of person is worse than the first." It would be more tolerable that the soul would not have returned to its first husband once it became a prostitute than having gone back after confession to her husband, to have become an adulteress again. There is no "fellowship," as the apostle says, "between the temple of God and idols," no "agreement between Christ and Belial." HOMILIES ON EXODUS 8.4.[11]

11:27-28 Blessings for Hearing and Keeping the Word

MARY BLESSED BY FAITH. AUGUSTINE: Mary was more blessed in accepting the faith of Christ than in conceiving the flesh of Christ. To someone who said, "Blessed is the womb that bore you," he replied, "Rather, blessed are they who hear the word of God and keep it."

Finally, for his brothers, his relatives according to the flesh who did not believe in him, of what advantage was that relationship? Even her mater-

nal relationship would have done Mary no good unless she had borne Christ more happily in her heart than in her flesh. HOLY VIRGINITY 3.[12]

THOSE WHO WORSHIP JESUS ARE BLESSED. EPHREM THE SYRIAN: "Blessed is the womb that bore you." He took blessedness from the one who bore him and gave it to those who were worshiping him. It was with Mary for a certain time, but it would be with those who worshiped him for eternity. "Blessed are those who hear the word of God and keep it." COMMENTARY ON TATIAN'S DIATESSARON 11.10.[13]

11:29-32 Like Jonah, Jesus Is a Sign

THE SIGN OF JONAH. CYRIL OF ALEXANDRIA: He will not grant you another sign, so that he may give holy things to dogs or throw pearls before swine....

He said only the sign of Jonah will be given to them. This means the passion on the cross and the resurrection from the dead. COMMENTARY ON LUKE, HOMILY 82.[14]

A SIGN FOR THE FALL AND RISING OF MANY IN ISRAEL. EPHREM THE SYRIAN: The sign of Jonah served the Ninevites in two ways. If they would have rejected it, they would have gone down to Sheol alive like Jonah, but they were raised from the dead like him because they repented. Just as in the case of our Lord, who was set for the fall and the rising of many,[15] people either lived through his being killed or died through his death.... They were asking him for a sign from heaven[16] like thunder.... Jonah, after he went up from within the fish, was a negative sign to the Ninevites, because he proclaimed the destruction of their city. The disciples were also this way after the resurrection of our Lord. COMMENTARY ON TATIAN'S DIATESSARON 11.2.[17]

---

[11]FC 71:324-25*. [12]FC 27:146*. [13]ECTD 180. [14]CGSL 335**. [15]Lk 2:34. [16]Mk 8:11. [17]ECTD 175-76*.

THE QUEEN OF THE SOUTH IS A TYPE OF THE CHURCH. EPHREM THE SYRIAN: The Queen of the South will condemn it[18] because she is a type of the church. Just as she came to Solomon, so too the church came to our Lord, and just as she condemned this generation, so also will the church. If she, who wished to see wisdom that passes away and a king who was mortal, was judging the synagogue, how much more the church, which desires to see a king who does not pass away and wisdom which does not go astray, will judge? If we suffer with him, we will also be glorified with him.[19] COMMENTARY ON TATIAN'S DIATESSARON 11.4.[20]

THE MYSTERY OF CHRIST AND HIS CHURCH. AMBROSE: The mystery of the church is clearly expressed. Her flocks stretch from the boundaries of the whole world. They stretch to Nineveh through penitence[21] and to the Queen of the South through zeal to obtain wisdom. Thus it may know the words of the peaceable Solomon.[22] The queen's kingdom is undivided and rises from diverse and distant peoples to one body. That great sacrament is concerning Christ and the church,[23] but this is nevertheless greater because of what prefigured it. The mystery is now fulfilled in truth. There was the image of Solomon, but here is Christ in his own body. EXPOSITION OF THE GOSPEL OF LUKE 7.96.[24]

11:33-36 The Eye Illuminates the Body

CHRIST IS THE LAMP AND HIS CHURCH THE LAMPSTAND. CYRIL OF ALEXANDRIA: He says that a lamp is always elevated and put on a stand to be of use to those who see. Let us consider the inference that follows from this. Before the coming of our Savior, the father of darkness, Satan, made the world dark and blackened all things with an intellectual gloom. In this state of affairs, the Father gave us the Son to be a lamp to the world, to illumine us with divine light and to rescue us from satanic darkness. Since you blame the lamp because it is not hid-den but on the contrary is being set high on a stand and gives its light to those who see, then blame Christ for not wishing to be concealed. On the contrary, he wishes to be seen by all, illuminating those in darkness and shedding on them the light of the true knowledge of God. He did not fulfill his miracles so much in order to be wondered at or to become famous. He did miracles so we might believe that although he is God by nature, yet he became man for our sakes, but without ceasing to be what he was. The holy church is like a lampstand, shining by the doctrine he proclaims. He gives light to the minds of all by filling them with divine knowledge. COMMENTARY ON LUKE, HOMILY 82.[25]

FAITH MUST NOT BE HIDDEN UNDER THE LAW. AMBROSE: The Word of God is our faith. The Word of God is the light, and faith is the lamp. "That was the true Light, that enlightens everyone that comes into this world."[26] The lamp cannot shine unless it has received light from elsewhere. The lamp that is lit is the virtue and perception of our mind, so that the woman can find the coin that she lost.[27] No one finds faith beneath the law, for the law is within a bushel basket. Grace is outside. The law overshadows, but faith illumines. No one conceals his faith within the bushel basket of the law but brings it to the church in which shines the sevenfold grace of the Spirit.[28] . . . The church standing on the highest mountain of all, that is, on Christ, cannot be hidden in the darkness and ruins of this world.[29] Shining with the splendor of the eternal Sun, it enlightens us with the light of spiritual grace. EXPOSITION OF THE GOSPEL OF LUKE 7.98-99.[30]

THE MIND OF CHRIST THAT ILLUMINES THE WHOLE BODY. SYMEON THE NEW THEOLOGIAN: What else does he mean by "the eye" than simply the mind, which will never become simple un-

---

[18]Mt 12:42. [19]Rom 8:17. [20]ECTD 176*. [21]Jonah 3:5. [22]See 1 Kings 10:1; 2 Chron 9:1. [23]Eph 5:32. [24]EHG 271**. [25]CGSL 336**. [26]Jn 1:9. [27]Lk 15:8. [28]Is 11:2. [29]Mt 5:14. [30]EHG 272-73**.

less it contemplates the simple light? The simple light is Christ. He who has his light shining in his mind is said to have the mind of Christ.[31] When your light is this simple, then the whole immaterial body of your soul will be full of light. If the mind is evil, that is, darkened and extinguished, then this body of yours will be full of darkness. . . .

We say, "See to it, brothers, that while we seem to be in God and think that we have communion with him[32] we should not be found excluded and separated from him, since we do not now see his light." If that light had kindled our lamps, that is, our souls, it would shine brightly in us. Our God and Lord Jesus Christ said, "If your whole body is full of life, having no dark part, it will be wholly bright, as when a lamp with its rays gives you light." What other witness greater than this shall we adduce to make the matter clear to you? If you disbelieve the Master, how will you, tell me, believe your fellow servant? DISCOURSES 33.2.[33]

---

[31]1 Cor 2:16. [32]1 Jn 1:6. [33]SNTD 340-41*.

11:37-54 JESUS TEACHES AND EATS AT THE HOME OF A PHARISEE

[37]While he was speaking, a Pharisee asked him to dine with him; so he went in and sat at table. [38]The Pharisee was astonished to see that he did not first wash before dinner. [39]And the Lord said to him, "Now you Pharisees cleanse the outside of the cup and of the dish, but inside you are full of extortion and wickedness. [40]You fools! Did not he who made the outside make the inside also? [41]But give for alms those things which are within; and behold, everything is clean for you.

[42]"But woe to you Pharisees! for you tithe mint and rue and every herb, and neglect justice and the love of God; these you ought to have done, without neglecting the others. [43]Woe to you Pharisees! for you love the best seat in the synagogues and salutations in the market places. [44]Woe to you! for you are like graves which are not seen, and men walk over them without knowing it."

[45]One of the lawyers answered him, "Teacher, in saying this you reproach us also." [46]And he said, "Woe to you lawyers also! for you load men with burdens hard to bear, and you yourselves do not touch the burdens with one of your fingers. [47]Woe to you! for you build the tombs of the prophets whom your fathers killed. [48]So you are witnesses and consent to the deeds of your fathers; for they killed them, and you build their tombs. [49]Therefore also the Wisdom of God said, 'I will send them prophets and apostles, some of whom they will kill and persecute,' [50]that the blood of all the prophets, shed from the foundation of the world, may be required of this generation, [51]from the blood of Abel to the blood of Zechariah, who perished between the altar and the sanctuary. Yes, I tell you, it shall be required of this generation. [52]Woe to you lawyers! for you have taken away the key of knowledge; you did not enter yourselves, and you hindered those who were entering."

[53]As he went away from there, the scribes and the Pharisees began to press him hard, and to provoke him to speak of many things, [54]lying in wait for him, to catch at something he might say.

Overview: At this his second meal with Pharisees, the controversy between Jesus and these religious authorities continues, this time over purification laws and the Old Testament precedents for the practice of the Pharisees. Jesus uses the metaphor of washing the inside and outside of a cup or dish to show that the Pharisees may appear clean on the outside, when in reality they are full of covetousness and wickedness on the inside (Cyril of Alexandria).

The God who created "the inside" and "the outside" requires both to be cleansed. The cup represents the suffering of our body and shows that for the outer body to be cleansed, the contents of the cup must be pure, and this happens through almsgiving, compassion and the Word of God (Ambrose). Almsgiving includes all acts of mercy, including the forgiveness of sins (Augustine). The Pharisees pay attention to outward shows of piety, such as tithing, first seats in the synagogue and greetings in the marketplaces, but they neglect to show true justice and love to others and love for God (Cyril of Alexandria). Thus Jesus compares them with "unmarked tombs" that deceive those who follow them (Ambrose). These beautifully adorned but unmarked graves are a sign of hypocrisy that keeps them from receiving what Jesus has come to bring and that leads others to follow the path of wickedness (Cyril of Alexandria).

Jesus' teaching against the Pharisees, in general, is perceived also by one of the lawyers as an insult (Cyril of Alexandria). They follow the pattern of their ancestors, who killed the prophets who prepared for Jesus because these prophets pointed out their wickedness. By building their tombs, they emulate them (Ambrose), for the tomb that they are building is the tomb of Jesus, the Prince of life and the Savior and Deliverer of all (Cyril of Alexandria). What Jesus is offering the lawyers and Pharisees is an opportunity to repent of what they will do to him, the final eschatological prophet (Ephrem the Syrian).

The "key of knowledge" is the Messiah proclaimed in the Old Testament Scriptures, the door into the prophets (Ephrem the Syrian). He is "the key of David"[1] that opens the kingdom to all who interpret the Old Testament by the Spirit (Jerome). The key that unlocks the door into the law interprets the law through Christ (Cyril of Alexandria). The key of knowledge lost by the Pharisees is found by the apostles (Maximus of Turin).

11:37-38 The Teaching and the Meal

Controversy over Purification Laws.
Cyril of Alexandria: The Pharisee invites him to an entertainment for his own purpose. The Savior of all submits to this for providence's sake. He made the matter an opportunity of giving instruction, not consuming the time of their meeting in the enjoyment of food and delicacies but in the task of making those who were assembled there more virtuous. The dull Pharisee himself supplied an occasion for his speech, "because he wondered," it says, "that he did not wash before dinner." Did he wonder at him as having done something of which he approved, as being especially worthy of the saints? This was not his view. How could it be? On the contrary, he was offended because although he had the reputation of a righteous man and a prophet, he did not conform himself to their unreasonable customs. . . .

Our argument is this. "O foolish Pharisee, you boast much of your knowledge of the sacred Scriptures. You are always quoting the law of Moses. Tell us where Moses gave you this commandment? What commandment ordained by God requires people to wash before eating? The waters of sprinkling were indeed given by the command of Moses for the cleansing of bodily uncleanness, as being a type of the baptism which really is holy and cleansing, even that in Christ. Those who were called to the priesthood were also bathed in water. The divine Moses bathed Aaron and the Levites. The law thereby declared by means of the baptism enacted in type and

---

[1]Is 22:22; Rev 3:7.

shadow that even its priesthood did not have what is sufficient for sanctification. On the contrary, it needs divine and holy baptism for the true cleansing. COMMENTARY ON LUKE, HOMILY 83.[2]

11:39-41 The Hypocrisy of the Pharisees

JESUS TEACHES ABOUT TRUE PURIFICATION. CYRIL OF ALEXANDRIA: What did the Savior say? He appropriately rebuked them, saying, "Now you Pharisees clean the outside of the cup and the dish, but what is in you is full of looting and wickedness." It would have been easy for the Lord to use other words with the view of instructing the foolish Pharisee, but he has found an opportunity. He connects his teaching with what was before their eyes. Since it was the time for eating and sitting at the table, he takes as a plain comparison the cup and the dish. He shows that those who sincerely serve God must be pure and clean, not only from bodily impurity but from what is hidden within in the mind. Utensils that serve the table must be cleansed from those impurities that are on the outside as well from those that are within. He says that he who made that which is on the outside also made that which is on the inside. This means that he who created the body also made the soul. Since they are both the works of one virtue-loving God, their purification must be uniform. COMMENTARY ON LUKE, HOMILY 83.[3]

THE CUP OF OUR BODY. AMBROSE: In what follows there is no doubt that the suffering of the body is shown by the name of cup,[4] when the Lord says, "Should I not drink the cup that my Father has given me?"[5] Whoever swallows bodily frailty in spiritual love and pours it into the mind and spirit so that the interior drains the weakness of the exterior drinks his body. You perceive that the inside, not the outside, of this cup or platter defiles us. A good teacher taught us how we should cleanse the pollution of our body, saying, "Give alms, and behold, all things are clean to you."[6] Do you see how many remedies there are? Compassion cleanses us. The Word of God

cleanses us, according to what is written: "Now you are clean by reason of the word that I have spoken to you."[7] Not only in this passage but also in others you have revealed how great grace is. "Alms delivers from death."[8] "Store up alms in the heart of the poor, and it shall obtain help for you on the evil day."[9] EXPOSITION OF THE GOSPEL OF LUKE 7.100-101.[10]

ACTS OF MERCY ARE EXAMPLES OF ALMSGIVING. AUGUSTINE: What our Lord says, "Give alms, and behold, all things are clean to you," applies to all useful acts of mercy. It does not apply just to the one who gives food to the hungry, drink to the thirsty, clothing to the naked, hospitality to the wayfarer or refuge to the fugitive. It also applies to one who visits the sick and the prisoner, redeems the captive, bears the burdens of the weak, leads the blind, comforts the sorrowful, heals the sick, shows the erring the right way, gives advice to the perplexed, and does whatever is needful for the needy. Not only does this person give alms, but the person who forgives the trespasser also gives alms as well. He is also a giver of alms who, by blows or other discipline, corrects and restrains those under his command. At the same time he forgives from the heart the sin by which he has been wronged or offended or prays that it be forgiven the offender. Such a person gives alms not only because he forgives and prays but also because he rebukes and administers corrective punishment, since in this he shows mercy. . . .

There are many kinds of alms. When we do them, we are helped in receiving forgiveness of our own sins. ENCHIRIDION 19.72.[11]

11:42-44 Three Woes Against the Pharisees

PHARISEES PASS OVER JUDGMENT AND LOVE OF GOD. CYRIL OF ALEXANDRIA: The transgres-

---

[2]CGSL 337-38**. [3]CGSL 338**. [4]See Lk 22:42. [5]Jn 18:11. [6]Cf. Acts 10:14-15. [7]Jn 15:3. [8]Tob 12:9. [9]Sir 29:12. [10]EHG 273**. [11]LCC 7:382**.

sion of one commandment transgresses the law. It proves the man to be without the law. When anyone disregards those commandments, which especially are important above the rest, what words will he find able to save him from deserved punishment? The Lord proved that the Pharisees merited these severe censures, saying, "Woe to you, Pharisees, who tithe mint, rue and all herbs and pass over judgment and the love of God!" You should have done these things and not passed by the others, that is, to leave them undone. They omitted as of no importance those duties which they were especially bound to practice, like justice and the love of God. They carefully and scrupulously observed, or rather commanded the people subject to their authority to observe, only those commandments that were means of great revenues for themselves. COMMENTARY ON LUKE, HOMILY 84.[12]

THE PHARISEES DECEIVE THEIR FOLLOWERS. AMBROSE: He also rebukes the arrogance and showy display of the Jews when they seek the first places at feasts.[13] The sentence of condemnation is also pronounced on those who, skilled in law, are as "sepulchers that are not seen." They cheat with their show and deceive with their practice, so that when they speak fair words outwardly, they are full of foulness within.[14] Very many teachers do this when they demand from others what they themselves cannot imitate. They are tombs, as elsewhere it says, "Their throat is an open sepulcher."[15] EXPOSITION OF THE GOSPEL OF LUKE 7.103.[16]

BEAUTIFULLY ADORNED UNMARKED GRAVES A SIGN OF HYPOCRISY. CYRIL OF ALEXANDRIA: Those who desire to be greeted by everyone in the marketplace and anxiously consider it a great matter to have the foremost seats in the synagogue do not differ in any way from graves that do not appear as graves. On the outside, they are beautifully decorated but are full of all impurity. See here, I pray that hypocrisy is utterly blamed. It is a hateful malady toward God and humanity. The hypocrite is not whatever he

seems to be and is thought to be. He borrows the reputation of goodness and conceals his real shame. He will not practice the very thing that he praises and admires. It is impossible for you to hide your hypocrisy for long. Just as the figures painted in pictures fall off as time dries up the colors, so also hypocrisies, after escaping observation for a very little time, are soon convicted of being really nothing. COMMENTARY ON LUKE, HOMILY 84.[17]

11:45-54 Jesus' Teaching Against the Lawyers

THE LAWYERS WORTHY OF THE SAME REBUKE AS THE PHARISEES. CYRIL OF ALEXANDRIA: The Savior of all was rebuking the Pharisees as men who were wandering far from the right way and fallen into unbecoming practices. . . . The band of wicked lawyers was indignant at these things, and one of them stood up to contradict the Savior's declarations. He said, "Teacher, in saying these things, you reproach us also." . . . These men subject themselves to blame. Rather, the force of truth showed that they were liable to the same accusations as the Pharisees and were of one mind with them. They are partners of their evil deeds if they consider that what Christ said to the others was spoken also against them. COMMENTARY ON LUKE, HOMILY 85.[18]

THE PHARISEES EMULATE THEIR ANCESTORS. AMBROSE: It is also a good argument against the vainest superstition of the Jews, who by building the tombs of the prophets condemned the actions of their ancestors. Then, by imitating their ancestors' actions, they turned the judgment back on themselves. By building the tombs of the prophets, they accused those who had killed them of their crime. By the imitation of similar acts, they declared themselves heirs of their ancestors' iniquity. Not the building but the imitation is an of-

---

[12]CGSL 340-41. [13]See Mt 23:6; Mk 12:39; Lk 20:46. [14]Mt 23:27. [15]Ps 5:9 LXX. [16]EHG 274**. [17]CGSL 342**. [18]CGSL 343**.

fense. Those who by crucifying the Son of God added a crime worse than their ancestors' wrong-doing cannot be absolved of their hereditary wickedness. He fittingly added elsewhere, "Fill up then the measure of your fathers,"[19] because there is no worse sin that they can commit than the assault on God. Wisdom sends the apostles and the prophets to them. Who is Wisdom if not Christ? EXPOSITION OF THE GOSPEL OF LUKE 7.106-7.[20]

THE PHARISEES AND LAWYERS BUILD THE TOMB OF CHRIST. CYRIL OF ALEXANDRIA:
What wicked act were they guilty of in building the tombs of the saints? Were they not rather doing them a distinguished honor? What doubt can there be of this? It is necessary to see what Christ teaches us. From time to time, the ancestors of the Jews put to death the holy prophets who were bringing them the word of God and leading them into the right way. Their descendants, acknowledging that the prophets were holy and venerable men, built tombs over them, as bestowing on them an honor suitable to the saints. Their ancestors murdered them, but they, believing that they were prophets and holy men, became the judges of those who murdered them. By determining to pay honor to those who were killed, they accused the others of doing wrong. They, who condemned their ancestors for such cruel murders, were about to become guilty of equal crimes and commit the same, or rather more abominable, offenses. They murdered the Prince of life, the Savior and Deliverer of all. They also added to their wickedness toward him other abominable murders. They put Stephen to death, not for being accused of anything shameful but rather for admonishing them and speaking to them what is contained in the inspired Scriptures. Besides this, they committed other crimes against every saint who preached the gospel message of salvation to them. COMMENTARY ON LUKE, HOMILY 85.[21]

JESUS OFFERS AN OPPORTUNITY FOR REPENTANCE. EPHREM THE SYRIAN: He said, "That all the blood of the just may come on you,"[22] because

they killed the Avenger of the righteous ones' deaths. The vengeance for their deaths is sought from their hands. One who kills the judge is indeed a friend of murderers, because in killing the judge, he has suppressed vengeance and opened the way for murderers. The Lord also said, "From the blood of Abel, the righteous one, to the blood of Zechariah,"[23] and not only until then but even until this day. Although still among them, he did not avenge his own blood until after they killed him, lest they say that it had been predetermined that he do this. He pronounced the sentence of judgment in relation to the righteous who had gone before, so that they might respect the righteous who were to follow. He gave them an opportunity to do penance for having put him to death, although according to the law, there could be no opportunity for repentance for one who murders the prophets. The law says, "Let the one who kills die,"[24] and not, "See if he does penance, and then pardon him." He gave them an opportunity to do penance, if they had wished, for having put him to death. COMMENTARY ON TATIAN'S DIATESSARON 18.9.[25]

JESUS AS THE DOOR INTO THE PROPHETS.
EPHREM THE SYRIAN: Woe to you, lawyers, because you have hidden the keys! That is, because they had hidden the knowledge of our Lord's manifestation which was in the prophecies. If our Lord is the door, as he has said,[26] it is clear that the keys of knowledge belong to him. The scribes and Pharisees did not want to enter through this door of life, in keeping with what he had said, "See, the kingdom is among you."[27] [He was referring to] himself, for he was standing in their midst. COMMENTARY ON TATIAN'S DIATESSARON 18.8.[28]

THE KEY OF KNOWLEDGE THAT OPENS THE KINGDOM. JEROME: John says in the book of Rev-

---

[19]Mt 23:32. [20]EHG 274-75**. [21]CGSL 345**. [22]Mt 23:35. [23]Mt 23:35. [24]Ex 21:12. [25]ECTD 274-75**. [26]Jn 10:7-9. [27]Lk 17:21. [28]ECTD 274.

elation, "He who has the key of David, he who opens and no one shuts, and who shuts and no one opens."[29] The scribes and Pharisees held this key in the law. The Lord warns them in the Gospel, "Woe to you lawyers, who hold the key of the kingdom of heaven." O you Pharisees, who hold the keys of the kingdom and do not believe in Christ who is the gate of the kingdom and the door. The promise is made to you, but it is granted to us. You have the flesh, but we have the spirit. Since you deny the spirit, you have lost the flesh with the spirit. HOMILY ON PSALM 88 (89).[30]

THE KEY OF KNOWLEDGE IS TO INTERPRET THE LAW IN CHRIST. CYRIL OF ALEXANDRIA: We consider that the key of knowledge means the law itself, and by faith in him, I mean justification in Christ. Although the law was in shadow and type, yet those types show to us the truth, and those shadows depict to us in many ways the mystery of Christ. A lamb was sacrificed according to the law of Moses. They ate its flesh. They anointed the lintels with its blood and overcame the destroyer. The blood of a mere sheep could not turn away death. Christ was typified under the form of a lamb. He endures to be the victim for the life of the world and saves by his blood those who are partakers of him. One might mention many other instances as well, by means of which we can discern the mystery of Christ sketched out in the shadows of the law. When speaking to the Jews,

he once said, "There is one that accuses you, even Moses, whom you trusted. For if you had believed Moses, you should have also believed me, because he wrote of me."[31] "You search the Scriptures, because you think that in them you have eternal life; and it is they that bear witness to me."[32] Every word of divinely inspired Scripture looks to him and refers to him. As it has been shown, if Moses speaks, he typified Christ. If the holy prophets that you name speak, they also proclaimed to us in many ways the mystery of Christ, preaching beforehand the salvation that is by him. COMMENTARY ON LUKE, HOMILY 86.[33]

KEY OF KNOWLEDGE LOST BY THE PHARISEES BUT FOUND BY THE APOSTLES. MAXIMUS OF TURIN: This key is Christ the Lord, by whom the hidden places of our hearts are unlocked to believing faith. The Pharisees lost this key, and the apostles found it. The Lord says to Peter, "I will give you the keys of the kingdom of heaven." The hand of the synagogue, abandoning Christ, withered up among the leaders of the Jews. The hand of the synagogue grew unhealthy, for whoever deserts the source, which is Christ, immediately gets sick and is found sicker than all the other members. SERMON 43.2.[34]

---

[29]Rev 3:7. [30]FC 57:66-67*. [31]Jn 5:45-46. [32]Jn 5:39. [33]CGSL 349-50**. [34]ACW 50:108*.

12:1-12 CONFESSING JESUS

[1]*In the meantime, when so many thousands of the multitude had gathered together that they trod upon one another, he began to say to his disciples first, "Beware of the leaven of the Pharisees, which is hypocrisy. [2]Nothing is covered up that will not be revealed, or hidden that will not be known. [3]Therefore whatever you have said in the dark shall be heard in the light, and what you have whispered in private rooms shall be proclaimed upon the housetops.*

⁴"I tell you, my friends, do not fear those who kill the body, and after that have no more that they can do. ⁵But I will warn you whom to fear: fear him who, after he has killed, has power to cast into hell;ᵐ yes, I tell you, fear him! ⁶Are not five sparrows sold for two pennies? And not one of them is forgotten before God. ⁷Why, even the hairs of your head are all numbered. Fear not; you are of more value than many sparrows.

⁸"And I tell you, every one who acknowledges me before men, the Son of man also will acknowledge before the angels of God; ⁹but he who denies me before men will be denied before the angels of God. ¹⁰And every one who speaks a word against the Son of man will be forgiven; but he who blasphemes against the Holy Spirit will not be forgiven. ¹¹And when they bring you before the synagogues and the rulers and the authorities, do not be anxious how or what you are to answer or what you are to say; ¹²for the Holy Spirit will teach you in that very hour what you ought to say."

m Greek Gehenna

OVERVIEW: The beginning of this discourse could be a fitting summary of Jesus' criticism of the Pharisees and lawyers,[1] now labeled as hypocrisy, which, as Jesus just told them, takes away the key of knowledge. To love Christ is to be like-minded with him and imitate the faith of the ancestors like Abraham, who feared neither life nor death (CYRIL OF ALEXANDRIA). Those who fear people who can kill the body are the ones who will be cast into hell, for they were ashamed to confess Jesus in the face of persecution; Jesus will not confess them before the Father in heaven (ORIGEN). In the world to come, nothing that is part of the natural body will be lost, for all will be restored, even ugly outgrowths, even all our hair (AUGUSTINE). God's care for sparrows and his knowledge of the number of hairs on our head give comfort to those who doubt his providential care (CYRIL OF ALEXANDRIA).

Jesus describes here the strength of an uncorrupted faith. The gospel cannot be firm in part and waver in part (CYPRIAN). Eternal life is given to those who acknowledge Christ, through whom they have been saved (PSEUDO-CLEMENT OF ROME). To blaspheme against the Spirit is to blaspheme against the holy Trinity (CYRIL OF ALEXANDRIA). The Holy Spirit will be their catechist, giving them the teaching they will need at the critical hour, as he inspires the martyrs in the face of death (CYRIL OF JERUSALEM). They are warned

not to resist the Spirit, and they have Jesus' promise that they will be taught by the Spirit (BASIL THE GREAT).

12:1-3 Beware the Hypocrisy of the Pharisees

HYPOCRISY TAKES AWAY THE KEY OF KNOWLEDGE. CYRIL OF ALEXANDRIA: Being angry at this reproof, it says they began to urge him vehemently. This means to attack him with cunning, oppose him and show their hatred of him. They also tried, it says, to silence him about many things. What again is the meaning of their silencing him? It is that they required him to answer immediately and without consideration their wicked questions, expecting that he would fall and say something objectionable. They did not know that he was God. They despised him, were proud and disrespectful. Christ told his friends, that is, his disciples, to beware of the leaven of the Pharisees and scribes, meaning by leaven their false pretense. Hypocrisy is hateful to God and humanity. It does not bring a reward, and it is utterly useless for the salvation of the soul. It is rather the cause of its damnation. Although sometimes it may escape detection for a little while, before long, it is sure to be uncovered

---

[1] Lk 11:37-54.

and bring disgrace on them. It is like an unattractive woman when she is stripped of that external embellishment which she produced by artificial means. COMMENTARY ON LUKE, HOMILY 86.[2]

12:4-7 Whom to Fear and Not Fear

IMITATING THE FAITH OF THE ANCESTORS.
CYRIL OF ALEXANDRIA: To put it in another light, as being his friends, we should not fear death but rather imitate the faith of the holy ancestors. When he was tempted, the patriarch Abraham offered his only-begotten son Isaac, considering that God was able to raise him up even from the dead.[3] What terror of death can assail us, now that life has abolished death?[4] Christ is the resurrection and the life.[5] COMMENTARY ON LUKE, HOMILY 87.[6]

FEAR THE ONE WHO CAN KILL THE BODY.
ORIGEN: Notice that this commandment is not given to Jesus' servants but to his friends.[7] "Do not fear those who kill the body, and after that have no more that they can do." The One to fear is he "who can destroy both soul and body in hell."[8] He alone, "after he has killed," has "power to throw into hell." He throws into hell those who fear those who kill the body and do not fear "him who, after he has killed, has power to cast into hell." We may suppose that no matter who else has the hair of his head numbered, the verse is obviously true of those who are cut off for Jesus. We will confess the Son of God before people and not before gods, that he who is confessed may confess us in turn before God and his Father, and confess in heaven the one who confessed him on earth. EXHORTATION TO MARTYRDOM 34.[9]

NO HAIR LOSS IN THE WORLD TO COME.
AUGUSTINE: When our Lord said, "not a hair," he was not thinking of length but of the number of hairs, as we see from these words, "The hairs of your head are numbered." I still think that nothing that was a natural part of the body should be

lost. Ugly outgrowths, which have the purpose of reminding us of the penal condition of mortal life, will be integrated into the substance as a whole so that no deformity will appear in any one part. After all, a human artist can make a botch of a statue and then reshape it into beauty without a loss of any of his material. It is not a matter of chiseling away some paticular part that was ugly or out of proportion. He can break down and remold the same mass of material so that nothing but the blemish disappears. Of course, the omnipotent Artist can do this even better. There is no deformity of any human body, whether normal, exceptional or even monstrous, which he cannot so eliminate as to leave the total substance intact, while the ugliness disappears. Such outgrowths are not out of place among the other miseries of temporal existence, but they are incompatible with the happiness of the saints in the life to come. CITY OF GOD 22.19.[10]

COMFORT FOR THOSE WHO DOUBT GOD'S PROVIDENCE IN CHRIST. CYRIL OF ALEXANDRIA: To bestow yet another means of comfort on our minds, he forcibly added that five sparrows are scarcely perhaps worth a penny, and yet God does not forget even one of them. He also said that the separate hairs of your head are all numbered. Consider how great care he takes of those that love him. The Preserver of the universe extends his aid to things so worthless and descends to the smallest animals. How can he forget those who love him, especially when he takes so great care of them? He condescends to visit them, to know exactly each particular of their state, and even how many are the hairs of their heads. . . .

Let us not doubt that with a rich hand he will give his grace to those who love him. He will not permit us to fall into temptation. If, by his wise purpose he permits us to be taken in the snare in order that we may gain glory by suffering, he will

---

[2]CGSL 351**. [3]Heb 11:19. [4]2 Tim 1:10. [5]Jn 11:25. [6]CGSL 353**. [7]Jn 15:15. [8]Mt 10:28. [9]OSW 64:66*. [10]FC 24:468-69*.

most assuredly grant us the power to bear it. COMMENTARY ON LUKE, HOMILY 87.[11]

12:8-10 *Confessing and Denying Now and in the Eschaton*

THE STRENGTH OF AN UNCORRUPTED FAITH. CYPRIAN: In the Gospel, the Lord speaks saying, "Everyone who acknowledges me before men, I will also acknowledge him before my Father who is in heaven; but whoever denies me, even I will deny him." He does not deny him who denies or acknowledge him who acknowledges. The gospel cannot be firm in part and waver in part. Either both must be strong or both must lose the force of truth. If those who deny will not be guilty of a crime, those who acknowledge him will not receive the reward of virtue. If he crowns the faith that has conquered, he must punish the treachery that has been conquered. If the gospel can be broken, the martyrs can be of no benefit. If the gospel cannot be broken, they who become martyrs, according to the gospel, cannot act contrary to the gospel. Most beloved brothers and sisters, let no one defame the dignity of the martyrs. Let no one destroy their glories and crowns. The strength of an uncorrupted faith is sound. No one can say or do anything against Christ whose hope, faith, virtue and glory are entirely in Christ. They who have performed the commands of God cannot be the authors of anything done by the bishops contrary to the command of God. THE LAPSED 20.[12]

ACKNOWLEDGE HIM THROUGH WHOM WE ARE SAVED. PSEUDO-CLEMENT OF ROME: "He who acknowledges me before men, I will acknowledge before my Father." This is our reward, if we acknowledge him who saves us. How do we acknowledge him? We acknowledge him by doing what he says and by obeying his commands, and by honoring him not only with our lips but with all our heart and mind.[13] He says in Isaiah as well, "This people honors me with their lips, but their heart is far from me."[14] 2 CLEMENT 3.1-5.[15]

BLASPHEMY AGAINST THE HOLY SPIRIT IS AGAINST THE TRINITY. CYRIL OF ALEXANDRIA: He has taught us that blasphemy is the most wicked crime for people to commit. He said that whoever speaks a word against the Son of man will be forgiven, but whoever blasphemes against the Holy Spirit will not be forgiven. In what way is this to be understood? If the Savior means that if any one of us uses any scornful word toward some mere man, he will receive forgiveness if he repents, the matter is free from all difficulty. Since God is by nature good, he will free from blame all those who repent. If the declaration has reference to Christ, the Savior of all, how can he who has spoken against him be innocent or secure from condemnation? Some one who has not learned the meaning of his mystery or understood that being by nature God he humbled himself to our estate and became man may say something blasphemous to a certain extent against him. If this is not so wicked as to pass forgiveness, God will pardon those who have sinned from ignorance. . . .

On another hand, condemnation and the eternal punishment both in this world and in that which is to come is inevitable for those who have blasphemed the Godhead itself.

By "the Spirit," he means not only the Holy Spirit but also the whole nature of the Godhead, as understood [to consist] in the Father, the Son and the Holy Spirit. The Savior also somewhere said, "God is a Spirit."[16] Blasphemy against the Spirit is against the whole supreme substance. The nature of the Deity, as offered for our understanding in the holy and adorable Trinity, is one. COMMENTARY ON LUKE, HOMILY 88.[17]

12:11-12 *The Spirit Will Teach Believers*

THE HOLY SPIRIT INSPIRES THE MARTYRS. CYRIL OF JERUSALEM: You must also know that the Holy Spirit empowers the martyrs to bear

---

[11]CGSL 353-54**. [12]FC 36:75**; ACW 25:29-30**. [13]Cf. Mk 12:30. [14]Is 29:13; cf. Mt 15:8; Mk 7:6. [15]LCC 1:194*. [16]Jn 4:24. [17]CGSL 357-58**.

witness. . . . A person cannot testify as a martyr for Christ's sake except through the Holy Spirit. If "no man can say 'Jesus is Lord,' except in the Holy Spirit,"[18] will any man give his life for Jesus' sake except through the Holy Spirit? CATECHETICAL LECTURES 16.21.[19]

THE HOLY SPIRIT'S INSTRUCTION. BASIL THE GREAT: The Christian should not fear or be distressed in difficult circumstances and thus be distracted from trust in God. He should take courage as if the Lord were at hand directing his affairs and strengthening him against all his adversaries. It is as if the Holy Spirit were instructing him even as to the very replies he should make to his enemies. THE MORALS 63.[20]

[18]1 Cor 12:3. [19]FC 64:89*. [20]FC 9:150*

12:13-21 THE PARABLE OF THE RICH FOOL

[13]*One of the multitude said to him, "Teacher, bid my brother divide the inheritance with me."* [14]*But he said to him, "Man, who made me a judge or divider over you?"* [15]*And he said to them, "Take heed, and beware of all covetousness; for a man's life does not consist in the abundance of his possessions."* [16]*And he told them a parable, saying, "The land of a rich man brought forth plentifully;* [17]*and he thought to himself, 'What shall I do, for I have nowhere to store my crops?'* [18]*And he said, 'I will do this: I will pull down my barns, and build larger ones; and there I will store all my grain and my goods.* [19]*And I will say to my soul, Soul, you have ample goods laid up for many years; take your ease, eat, drink, be merry.'* [20]*But God said to him, 'Fool! This night your soul is required of you; and the things you have prepared, whose will they be?'* [21]*So is he who lays up treasure for himself, and is not rich toward God."*

OVERVIEW: What one should seek is an inheritance of immortality, not one of money, and one should never call Jesus to be divider of the latter (AMBROSE). Covetousness divides, but charity gathers people together (AUGUSTINE). Covetousness is nothing more than a form of idolatry. This general principle leads to a parable that revolves around the concept of gift. Is he going to hoard the gift, as a proud and fearful Pharisee might do and thus be guilty of greed (CYRIL OF ALEXANDRIA)? The bellies of the poor are safer storehouses than one's barns (AUGUSTINE).

He had not seen that the love of God creates a habit of good works that are the only preparation necessary for the life to come. Those who know they are mortal should not come to the end unprepared (LEO THE GREAT). Only virtue and compassion follow us after death (AMBROSE). To be rich toward God is to love virtue instead of wealth and to believe that God is the giver of all things, including life and salvation (CYRIL OF ALEXANDRIA).

12:13-14 *The Question of Inheritance*

AN INHERITANCE OF IMMORTALITY SHOULD BE SOUGHT. AMBROSE: This whole passage is provided so that suffering may be endured for confession of the Lord. . . . Since greed is often accustomed to tempt virtue, the Lord adds the precept to remove this sin by stating the precedent, "Who has appointed me judge or divider over you?" He who descended for a divine purpose fittingly declines earthly tasks and does not allow himself to be a judge of lawsuits and an arbitrator of riches. He is to judge the living and the dead and apportion deserts.[1] You must not consider what you seek but from whom you request it. You must also not think that you must shout against big or little things. This brother is fittingly rebuked. He eagerly desired to trouble the steward of the heavenly with the corruptible. Not a neutral judge but piety as mediator should divide an inheritance among brothers, although people should seek an inheritance of immortality, not of money. EXPOSITION OF THE GOSPEL OF LUKE 7.122.[2]

COVETOUSNESS DIVIDES; CHARITY GATHERS TOGETHER. AUGUSTINE: He was correct when he did not listen to the man who, in disagreement with his brother, said, "Master, tell my brother to divide the inheritance with me." He said, "Master, tell my brother." Tell him what? He said, "To divide the inheritance with me." The Lord said, "Speak, man." Why do you want to divide it except because you are human? Whenever someone says, "I am of Paul," but another, "I am of Apollos," are you not merely human?[3] "Tell me, man, who has appointed me a judge of the inheritance among you? I have come to gather, not to scatter." He said, "I say to you, guard against all greed." Greed wants to divide, just as love desires to gather. What is the significance of "guard against all greed," unless it is "fill yourselves with love"? We, possessing love for our portion, inconvenience the Lord because of our brother just as that man did against his brother, but we do not use the same plea. He said, "Master, tell my brother to divide the inheritance with me." We say, "Master, tell my brother that he may have my inheritance." SERMON 265.9.[4]

12:15 The First Principle: A Person's Life Does Not Consist in the Abundance of Possessions

COVETOUSNESS IS EQUIVALENT TO IDOLATRY. CYRIL OF ALEXANDRIA: Jesus does not leave us without instruction. Having found a good opportunity, he makes a profitable and saving speech. Protesting against them, he declares, "Take heed, and keep yourselves from all greed." He showed us that covetousness is a pitfall of the devil and hateful to God. The wise Paul even calls it idolatry,[5] perhaps as being suitable for only those who do not know God or as being equal in the balance with the defilement of those people who choose to serve sticks and stones. It is a snare of evil spirits, by which they drag down a person's soul to the nets of hell. For this reason, he says very correctly, as setting them on their guard, "Take heed and keep yourselves from all greed," from great and small and from defrauding anyone whoever he may be. Greed is hateful to God and humankind. COMMENTARY ON LUKE, HOMILY 89.[6]

12:16-20 The Parable of the Rich Fool

SURROUNDED BY WEALTH, BLIND TO CHARITY. CYRIL OF ALEXANDRIA: What does the rich man do, surrounded by a great supply of many blessings beyond all numbering? In distress and anxiety, he speaks the words of poverty. He says, "What should I do?" . . . He does not look to the future. He does not raise his eyes to God. He does not count it worth his while to gain for the mind those treasures that are above in heaven. He does not cherish love for the poor or desire the esteem it gains. He does not sympathize with suffering. It gives him no pain nor awakens his pity. Still more irrational, he settles for himself the length of his life, as if he would also reap this from the ground. He says, "I will say to myself, 'Self, you have goods laid up for many years. Eat, drink, and enjoy yourself.'" "O rich man," one may say, 'You have storehouses for your fruits, but where will you receive your many years? By the decree of God, your life is shortened.'"

---

[1]Acts 10:42; 2 Tim 4:1. [2]EHG 279-80**. [3]1 Cor 3:4. [4]FC 38:418-19*. [5]Col 3:5. [6]CGSL 360**.

"God," it tells us, "said to him, 'You fool, this night they will require of you your soul. Whose will these things be that you have prepared?'" COMMENTARY ON LUKE, HOMILY 89.[7]

THE BELLIES OF THE POOR ARE SAFER STOREHOUSES THAN OUR BARNS. AUGUSTINE: "The redemption of a man's soul is his riches."[8] This silly fool of a man did not have that kind of riches. Obviously he was not redeeming his soul by giving relief to the poor. He was hoarding perishable crops. I repeat, he was hoarding perishable crops, while he was on the point of perishing because he had handed out nothing to the Lord before whom he was due to appear. How will he know where to look, when at that trial he starts hearing the words "I was hungry and you did not give me to eat"?[9] He was planning to fill his soul with excessive and unnecessary feasting and was proudly disregarding all those empty bellies of the poor. He did not realize that the bellies of the poor were much safer storerooms than his barns. What he was stowing away in those barns was perhaps even then being stolen away by thieves. But if he stowed it away in the bellies of the poor, it would of course be digested on earth, but in heaven it would be kept all the more safely. The redemption of a man's soul is his riches.[10] SERMON 36.9.[11]

THE HABIT OF GOOD WORKS. LEO THE GREAT: The devil, even in the midst of our efforts, does not relax his schemes. At certain periods of time, we must take care of the reenergizing of our strength. The mind, concerned with the goods of the present, can rejoice in the temperate weather and the fertile fields. When the fruits are gathered into great barns, it can say to its soul, "You have many good things; eat." It may receive a kind of rebuke from the divine voice and may hear it saying, "Fool, this very night they demand your soul from you. The things you have prepared, whose will they be?"

This should be the careful consideration of wise people, that since the days of this life are short and the time uncertain, death should never be unexpected for those who are to die. Those who know that they are mortal should not come to an unprepared end. SERMON 90.4.1.[12]

THE COMPANIONS OF THE DEAD. AMBROSE: He uselessly accumulates wealth when he does not know how he will use it. He is like him who, when his full barns were bursting from the new harvest, prepared storehouses for his abundant fruits, not knowing for whom he gathered them.[13] The things that are of the world remain in the world, and whatever riches we gather are bequeathed to our heirs. The things that we cannot take away with us are not ours either. Only virtue is the companion of the dead. Compassion alone follows us. It is the guide to the heavens and the first of the mansions. Through the use of worthless money, it acquires eternal dwellings for the dead. The Lord's commands testify when he says, "Make friends for yourselves by means of unrighteous mammon, so that when it fails they may receive you into the eternal habitations."[14] EXPOSITION OF THE GOSPEL OF LUKE, HOMILY 7.122.[15]

12:21 The Second Principle: One Who Is Not Rich Toward God Is Such a Fool

TO BE RICH TOWARD GOD. CYRIL OF ALEXANDRIA: It is true that a person's life is not from one's possessions or because of having an overabundance. He who is rich toward God is very blessed and has glorious hope. Who is he? Evidently, one who does not love wealth but rather loves virtue, and to whom few things are sufficient.[16] It is one whose hand is open to the needs of the poor, comforting the sorrows of those in poverty according to his means and the utmost of his power. He gathers in the storehouses that are above and lays up treasures in heaven. Such a one shall find the interest of his virtue and the reward of his right and blameless life. COMMENTARY ON LUKE, HOMILY 89.[17]

[7]CGSL 361**. [8]Prov 13:8. [9]Mt 25:42. [10]Prov 13:8. [11]WSA 3 2:180*. [12]FC 93:382*. [13]Ps 38:7 LXX. [14]Lk 16:9. [15]EHG 280-81**. [16]Cf. Lk 10:42. [17]CGSL 362**. [17]FC 17:67*.

12:22-34 DO NOT BE ANXIOUS

[22]And he said to his disciples, "Therefore I tell you, do not be anxious about your life, what you shall eat, nor about your body, what you shall put on. [23]For life is more than food, and the body more than clothing. [24]Consider the ravens: they neither sow nor reap, they have neither storehouse nor barn, and yet God feeds them. Of how much more value are you than the birds! [25]And which of you by being anxious can add a cubit to his span of life?" [26]If then you are not able to do as small a thing as that, why are you anxious about the rest? [27]Consider the lilies, how they grow; they neither toil nor spin;[o] yet I tell you, even Solomon in all his glory was not arrayed like one of these. [28]But if God so clothes the grass which is alive in the field today and tomorrow is thrown into the oven, how much more will he clothe you, O men of little faith! [29]And do not seek what you are to eat and what you are to drink, nor be of anxious mind. [30]For all the nations of the world seek these things; and your Father knows that you need them. [31]Instead, seek his[p] kingdom, and these things shall be yours as well.

[32]"Fear not, little flock, for it is your Father's good pleasure to give you the kingdom. [33]Sell your possessions, and give alms; provide yourselves with purses that do not grow old, with a treasure in the heavens that does not fail, where no thief approaches and no moth destroys. [34]For where your treasure is, there will your heart be also."

n Or to his stature   o Other ancient authorities read Consider the lilies; they neither spin nor weave   p Other ancient authorities read God's

---

OVERVIEW: Jesus teaches his disciples not to be anxious about food and clothing, for this anxiety will lead to apostasy. The disciples are to study and ponder how God cares for the ravens and the lilies as a means for comforting us with knowledge of his loving care for us (CYRIL OF ALEXANDRIA). If God's providence cares for irrational creatures, how much more for rational creatures? For with the angels, believers are the flowers of the world whose fragrance is the smell of sanctification (AMBROSE).

Get rid of earthly possessions; serve the kingdom by giving to others as a response of faith (CYRIL OF ALEXANDRIA). By selling your possessions you are freed from their bondage (PETER CHRYSOLOGUS). Almsgiving produces the true riches which are heavenly (CYRIL OF ALEXANDRIA). There are two alternatives: fleeting treasure on earth or eternal treasure in heaven. Avarice gives us treasure on earth while almsgiving lifts our

hearts into heaven (PETER CHRYSOLOGUS). So to lift up your hearts to heaven is to do good works, for such works show where our treasure truly is (AUGUSTINE).

12:22-28 Three Imperatives About Food and Clothing

A CALL TO ABANDON ANXIETY. CYRIL OF ALEXANDRIA: How carefully and with what great skill he brings the lives of the holy apostles to spiritual excellence. And with them he benefits us too, because he desires all humankind to be saved and to choose the wise and more excellent life. For this reason he makes them abandon unnecessary anxiety and does not allow a careworn and frenetic diligence that would make them wish to gather what exceeds their necessities. In these matters excess adds nothing to our benefit. "Do not be anxious," therefore, he says, "about your life, what you shall eat, nor about your body, what you shall put on. For life is more than food, and the body more than clothing." He did not simply say, "Do not be anxious," but added "about your life," that is, do not give much attention to these things, but devote your earnestness to things of far greater importance. For life indeed is of more importance than food, and the body is more important than clothing. Since, therefore, we are at risk concerning both life and body, and pain and punishment are decreed against those who will not live uprightly, let all anxiety be laid aside with regard to clothing and food. . . .

These things, in turn, are followed immediately by a savage crowd of other desires, the result being apostasy from God. . . . It is our duty, therefore, to stay away from all worldly desires, and rather to take delight in those things which please God. Commentary on Luke, Homily 90.[1]

God's Care for Birds and Flowers. Cyril of Alexandria: But perhaps you will reply to this, "Who then will give us the necessities of life?" Our answer to this is as follows: The Lord is worthy to be trusted, and he clearly promises it to you and through little things gives you full assurance that he will be true also in that which is great. "Consider," he says, "the ravens: they neither sow nor reap, they have neither storehouse nor barn, and yet God feeds them." . . . Through the birds and the flowers of the field, he produces in you a firm and unwavering faith. Nor does he permit us at all to doubt, but rather he gives us the certainty that he will grant us his mercy and stretch out his comforting hand, that we may have sufficiency in all things. It is, moreover, a very wicked thing that while those who are placed under the yoke of bodily slavery depend on their masters as sufficient to supply them with food and clothing, we will not consent to put our trust in almighty God, when he promises us the necessities of life. Commentary on Luke, Homily 90.[2]

Flowers and Grass Illustrate Divine Mercy. Ambrose: It is indeed a good and moral saying. By the comparison with flowers and grass, the Lord's words provoke us to faith in the gift of divine mercy, either literally, because we are unable to add to our body's stature, or spiritually, because we cannot exceed the measure of our stature without the favor of God. For what is so moral for persuasion as when you see that even the nonrational things are so clothed by God's providence that they lack no use for grace or for ornament? Then you believe the more that rational man, if he places all his usefulness in God and does not dishonor the faith with intent to waver, can never lack, inasmuch as he has rightly trusted in the favor of God? Exposition of the Gospel of Luke 7.125.[3]

Angels, Martyrs and Saints Are the Flowers of the World. Ambrose: It is pleasing to note that lilies spring not from the barrenness of mountains and the wildness of forests but from the loveliness of gardens. These are the fruit-bearing gardens of diverse virtues, as it is written, "A garden locked is my sister, my bride, a garden locked, a fountain sealed."[4] Where there is integrity, chastity, piety, faithful silence of secrets, the radiance of angels, there are the violets of confessors, the lilies of virgins, the roses of martyrs. And let no one think it is inappropriate to compare lilies with angels, when Christ called himself a lily, saying, "I am a rose of Sharon, a lily of the valleys."[5] Christ is fittingly a lily, because where there is the blood of martyrs, there is the Christ, who is a flower exalted, undefiled and blameless, in which the roughness of thorns does not offend but enveloping grace begins to shine. Roses have thorns which are the torments of the martyrs. The indivisible Godhead, which did not feel torments, has no thorns. Therefore, if lilies, like angels, are clothed beyond the glory of men,[6] we should not despair of the mercy of God toward us—we to whom through the grace of the resurrection the Lord promises the likeness of angels.[7]

---

[1]*CGSL* 363-64**. [2]*CGSL* 364**. [3]*EHG* 281-82*. [4]Song 4:12. [5]Song 2:1. [6]See Mt 6:29. [7]Mt 22:30.

In this passage, Jesus also seems to touch on the question which the apostle did not overlook, either—the question that the nations of this world would ask, namely, how will the dead rise and with what manner of body will they come?[8] By saying, "Seek the kingdom, and these things shall be yours as well," Jesus indicates that grace will not be lacking for the faithful in the present or in the future, if only those who desire the heavenly do not seek the earthly. It is unseemly for the soldiers of the kingdom[9] to worry about food. The King knows how to feed, cherish and clothe his household, and therefore he said, "Cast your burden on the Lord, and he will sustain you."[10] EXPOSITION OF THE GOSPEL OF LUKE 8.128-30.[11]

12:29-33 Imperatives About the Kingdom

SEEK THE KINGDOM. CYRIL OF ALEXANDRIA: He announced as a general law, useful and necessary for salvation, not only to the holy apostles but to all living on the earth, that people must seek his kingdom. He announced this, being sure that what he gives will be sufficient for them to be in need of nothing else. What, then, does he say? Fear not, little flock. And by "do not fear," he means that they must believe that certainly and without doubt their heavenly Father will give the means of life to those who love him. He will not neglect his own. Rather he will open his hand to them—the hand which ever fills the universe with goodness.[12] COMMENTARY ON LUKE, HOMILY 91.[13]

NO FEAR FOR THOSE WHO WILL BE GIVEN A KINGDOM. PETER CHRYSOLOGUS: The flock is little in the eyes of the world, but great in the eyes of God. It is little—because he calls glorious those whom he has trained to the innocence of sheep and to Christian meekness. The flock is little, not as the remnant of a big one, but as one which has grown from small beginnings. This little flock denotes the infancy of his newborn church, and immediately he promises that through the blessings of heaven this church will

soon have the dignity of his kingdom. SERMON 22.[14]

REAL RICHES COME THROUGH ALMSGIVING.
CYRIL OF ALEXANDRIA: Give away these earthly things, and win that which is in heaven. Give that which you must leave, even against your will, that you may not lose things later. Lend your wealth to God, that you may be really rich.

Concerning the way in which to lend it, Jesus next teaches us saying, "Sell your possessions, and give alms; provide yourselves with purses that do not grow old, with a treasure in the heavens that does not fail." The blessed David teaches us exactly the same in the psalms, where by inspiration he says of every merciful and good man, "He has distributed freely, he has given to the poor; his righteousness endures forever."[15] Worldly wealth has many foes. There are numerous thieves, and this world of ours is full of oppressors. Some plunder by secret means, while others use violence and tear it away even from those who resist. But no one can do damage to the wealth that is laid up above in heaven. God is its keeper, and he does not sleep. COMMENTARY ON LUKE, HOMILY 91.[16]

12:34 Where Your Treasure Is

ALMSGIVING RAISES OUR HEARTS INTO HEAVEN. PETER CHRYSOLOGUS: All this is what that treasure brings about. Either through almsgiving it raises the heart of a man into heaven, or through greed it buries it in the earth. That is why he said, "For where your treasure is, there your heart will be also." O man, send your treasure on, send it ahead into heaven, or else your God-given soul will be buried in the earth. Gold comes from the depth of the earth—the soul, from the highest heaven. Clearly it is better to carry the gold to where the soul resides than to bury the soul in the mine of the gold. That is why

---

[8]1 Cor 15:35. [9]See 2 Cor 10:3. [10]Ps 55:22 (54:23 LXX). [11]EHG 283-84*. [12]Ps 104:28 (103:28 LXX). [13]CGSL 366**. [14]FC 17:65**. [15]Ps 112:9 (111:9 LXX). [16]CGSL 368**.

God orders those who will serve in his army here below to fight as men stripped of concern for riches and unencumbered by anything. To these he has granted the privilege of reigning in heaven. SERMON 22.[17]

LIFT YOUR HEARTS TO HEAVEN. AUGUSTINE: If you lack earthly riches, do not seek them in the world by evil deeds. If they fall to your lot, let them be stored up in heaven by good works. A manly Christian soul should neither be overjoyed at acquiring them nor cast down when they are gone. Let us instead reflect on what the Lord says: "Where thy treasure is, there your heart will be also." Surely when we hear that we should lift up our hearts, the familiar answer that we make should not be a lie. LETTER 189.[18]

---

[17]FC 17:67*. [18]FC 30:270**.

12:35-48 WATCH FOR THE COMING OF THE SON OF MAN

[35]"Let your loins be girded and your lamps burning, [36]and be like men who are waiting for their master to come home from the marriage feast, so that they may open to him at once when he comes and knocks. [37]Blessed are those servants whom the master finds awake when he comes; truly, I say to you, he will gird himself and have them sit at table, and he will come and serve them. [38]If he comes in the second watch, or in the third, and finds them so, blessed are those servants! [39]But know this, that if the householder had known at what hour the thief was coming, he[q] would not have left his house to be broken into. [40]You also must be ready; for the Son of man is coming at an unexpected hour."

[41]Peter said, "Lord, are you telling this parable for us or for all?" [42]And the Lord said, "Who then is the faithful and wise steward, whom his master will set over his household, to give them their portion of food at the proper time? [43]Blessed is that servant whom his master when he comes will find so doing. [44]Truly, I say to you, he will set him over all his possessions. [45]But if that servant says to himself, 'My master is delayed in coming,' and begins to beat the menservants and the maidservants, and to eat and drink and get drunk, [46]the master of that servant will come on a day when he does not expect him and at an hour he does not know, and will punish[r] him, and put him with the unfaithful. [47]And that servant who knew his master's will, but did not make ready or act according to his will, shall receive a severe beating. [48]But he who did not know, and did what deserved a beating, shall receive a light beating. Every one to whom much is given, of him will much be required; and of him to whom men commit much they will demand the more."

q Other ancient authorities add *would have watched and*   r Or *cut him in pieces*

OVERVIEW: "Let your loins be girded" echoes the careful instructions given to Moses and Aaron on how to eat the Passover: "your loins girded, your sandals on your feet, and your staff in your hand; and you shall eat it in haste."[1] We are not to take Jesus' command literally but to recognize that these instructions are for a physical, mental and spiritual alertness (CYRIL OF ALEXANDRIA). Having loins girded with continence and lamps burning with good works (AUGUSTINE) is absolutely necessary, for we do not know when the Lord is coming (DIDACHE).

The first parable mentions the Lord's return from the feast of heaven, for there is always joy at a festival, and he returns in order to serve us by girding his loins. The three hours of watch represent the three ages of a person—childhood, adulthood and old age—through which one is to remain watchful through repentance and faith. While the slaves girded themselves, the Lord girds himself (CYRIL OF ALEXANDRIA). Jesus' table fellowship is marked by humble service. The mark of a Christian is to be prepared for the Lord's coming at any time (BASIL THE GREAT).

Are the previous two parables directed toward the apostles or to all of Jesus' followers? What is true for every Christian is true for the Twelve as disciples—and it is directed in a heightened sense to the Twelve as stewards and apostles, and to those who are called to be teachers of the church (CYRIL OF ALEXANDRIA).

Jesus describes the Lord's unexpected return "on a day on which [the steward] does not expect and at an hour at which he does not know" to divide between the faithful and unfaithful steward (AUGUSTINE). Unfaithful stewards, neglectful of their duties, are worthy of utter wretchedness (CYRIL OF ALEXANDRIA). Feigned ignorance, however, is the greatest offense of all, for there is no refuge in the darkness of ignorance (AUGUSTINE). The danger is always greater for confessors than for those who live in ignorance; even confessors of the faith find it hard to be ready (CYPRIAN). Deliberate sins are worse than sins of ignorance. Make no mistake, these warnings are for disci-

ples-apostles-ministers, and the severity of judgment on them is great (BASIL THE GREAT).

12:35 Serve and Watch

THE TRUE MEANING OF LOINS GIRDED AND LAMPS BURNING. CYRIL OF ALEXANDRIA: The girding of our loins signifies the readiness of the mind to work hard in every thing praiseworthy. Those who apply themselves to bodily labors and are engaged in strenuous toil have their loins girded. The lamp apparently represents the wakefulness of the mind and intellectual cheerfulness. We say that the human mind is awake when it repels any tendency to slumber off into that carelessness that often is the means of bringing it into subjection to every kind of wickedness. When sunk in stupor, the heavenly light within the mind is liable to be endangered, or even already is in danger from a violent and impetuous blast of wind. Christ commands us to be awake. To this, his disciple also arouses us by saying, "Be awake. Be watchful."[2] Further on, the very wise Paul also says, "Awake, O sleeper, and arise from the dead: and Christ shall give you light."[3] COMMENTARY ON LUKE, HOMILY 92.[4]

CONTINENCE AND GOOD WORKS. AUGUSTINE: What does it mean to gird the loins? It is to restrain lustful appetites. This is about self-control. To have lamps burning is to shine and glow with good works. This is about justice. He was not silent here as to why we should do these things, adding to his statement, "And you yourselves should be like men waiting for their master's return from the wedding." When he comes, he will repay us who have restrained ourselves from yielding to what lust has demanded and who have done what love has commanded, that we might reign in his perfect and everlasting peace, free from the struggle of evil and enjoying the supreme delight of good. ON CONTINENCE 7.[5]

---

[1]Ex 12:11. [2]1 Pet 5:8. [3]Eph 5:14. [4]CGSL 370**. [5]FC 16:208-9**.

Preparation for the Parousia. Didache: "Watch" over your life. Do not let "your lamps" go out, and do not keep "your loins unbelted," but "be ready," for "you do not know the hour when our Lord is coming." Meet together frequently in your search for what is good for your souls, since "a lifetime of faith will be of no advantage"[6] to you unless you prove to be fully responsive to the very end. In the final days, many false prophets and seducers will appear. Sheep will turn into wolves, and love into hatred. With the increase of iniquity, people will hate, persecute and betray each other. Then the world deceiver will appear in the guise of God's Son. Didache 16.1-4.[7]

12:36-40 The Readiness of Christian Slaves

Christ Returns to Serve Us. Cyril of Alexandria: We should look for Christ's coming again from heaven. He will come in the glory of the Father with the holy angels. He has taught us saying that we must be like those who wait for their lord to return from the banqueting house, so that when he comes and knocks, they may open the door to him immediately. For Christ will return as from a feast. This plainly shows that God always dwells in festivals that are fitting for him. In heaven above, there is no sadness whatsoever since nothing can occasion grief. That heavenly nature is incapable of passion and of being affected by anything whatsoever of this kind. Commentary on Luke, Homily 92.[8]

The Three Watches Correspond to the Three Ages. Cyril of Alexandria: We typically divide the night into three or four watches. The sentinels on the city walls, who watch the motions of the enemy, after being on guard three or four hours, deliver the watch and guard over to others. With us, there are three ages. The first is childhood. The second is youth. The third is old age. Now the first of these, in which we are still children, is not called to account by God but is deemed worthy of pardon, because of the innocence as yet of the mind and the weakness of the understanding. The second and the third—the periods of adulthood and old age—owe obedience and piety of life to God, according to his good pleasure. Whoever is found watching and well belted, whether by chance he is still young or has arrived at old age, shall be blessed. For he will be counted worthy of attaining to Christ's promises. Commentary on Luke, Homily 92.[9]

Jesus Reverses Our Expectations. Cyril of Alexandria: When he comes and finds us girded, awake and our hearts enlightened, then he immediately will make us blessed. "He will gird his loins and serve them." By this, we learn that he will reward us proportionately. Since we are weary with toil, he will comfort us, setting before us spiritual banquets and spreading the abundant table of his gifts. Commentary on Luke, Homily 92.[10]

Preparedness the Mark of a Christian. Basil the Great: What is the mark of a Christian? It is to watch daily and hourly and to stand prepared in that state of total responsiveness pleasing to God, knowing that the Lord will come at an hour that he does not expect. The Morals 22.[11]

12:41-48 The Readiness of the Apostle

Is the Parable for All Believers or Only the Apostles? Cyril of Alexandria: Blessed Peter, considering within himself the force of what Christ said, rightly asked which of the two was meant: the declaration referred to all believers, or only to them? That is, to those who had been called to the discipleship, and especially honored by the grant of apostolic powers? Commentary on Luke, Homily 93.[12]

Addressed to Apostles and Teachers of the Church. Cyril of Alexandria: What is

---

[6]*Epistle of Barnabas* 4:9. [7]LCC 1:178-79**. [8]CGSL 371**. [9]CGSL 372**. [10]CGSL 372**. [11]FC 9:205*. [12]CGSL 374**.

our Lord's reply? He makes use of a clear and very evident example to show that the commandment especially belongs to those who occupy a more influential position and have been admitted into the rank of teachers. "Who," he says, "is the faithful and wise servant, whom his lord will set over his household, to give the allowance of food at its season?" . . .

This is the simple and plain meaning of the passage. If we now fix our mind accurately upon it, we will see what it signifies and how useful it is for the benefit of those who have been called to the office of apostle, that is, to the office of teacher. The Savior has ordained faithful men of great understanding, and well instructed in the sacred doctrines, as stewards over his servants who have been won by faith to the acknowledgment of his glory. He has ordained them, commanding them to give their fellow servants their allowance of food. He does not do this simply and without distinction but rather at its proper season. I mean spiritual food, as is sufficient and fitting for each individual. COMMENTARY ON LUKE, HOMILY 93.[13]

THE MASTER WILL RETURN. AUGUSTINE:
Many people abuse for their own impious purposes his tardiness in coming. The bad slave says, "My master is taking his time." He starts beating his fellow slaves and getting drunk with the bad ones. His master will come on a day he does not know, and at an hour he is unaware of, and will cut him off. You see, it is the body of ministers and prelates who give their fellow slaves their food in due season. "He will separate him off," it says. He has good ones and bad ones. "He separates the good from the bad." "He will assign his portion with the hypocrites." He will not do this to the whole ministry, because in it too there are those who are longing for the Lord to come. In its ranks are also to be found the group of which it is said, "Blessed is that slave whom his master, when he comes, finds so doing." "He will come and separate him." SERMON 37.15.[14]

NEGLECTFUL STEWARDSHIP LEADS TO UTTER

WRETCHEDNESS WITH UNBELIEVERS. CYRIL OF ALEXANDRIA:
He says, "Neglecting the duty of being diligent and faithful, and despising watchfulness in these things as being superfluous, he lets his mind grow intoxicated with worldly cares. He is seduced into improper courses, dragging by force and oppressing those who are subject to him. If he is not giving them their portion, he will be in utter wretchedness." I think this and this only is the meaning of his being cut in two. "His portion," he says, "will be with the unbelievers." Whoever has done wrong to the glory of Christ or attempted to disregard the flock entrusted to his charge does not differ in any way from those who do not know him. These persons will be rightly counted among those who have no love for him. COMMENTARY ON LUKE, HOMILY 93.[15]

NO REFUGE IN THE DARKNESS OF IGNORANCE. AUGUSTINE:
Now if those ignorant of the law are in a worse condition than those who know the law, how can this saying of our Lord in the Gospel be true? "That servant who knew his master's will but did not make ready or act according to his will shall receive a severe beating. But he who did not know and did what deserved a beating shall receive a light beating." You see that this passage shows clearly a person who *knows* sins more seriously than one who does *not know*. Yet we must not on this account take refuge in the darkness of ignorance so as to find there an excuse for our conduct. Not to know is one thing; unwillingness to know is another. ON GRACE AND FREE WILL 3.[16]

EVEN CONFESSORS FIND IT DIFFICULT TO REMAIN FAITHFUL. CYPRIAN:
We must perceive and confess that the very frightful devastation of that affliction which has destroyed and is destroying our flock in great part has come about because of our sins. We do not keep the way of the Lord, nor do we observe the heavenly commands given to us for salvation. Our Lord did the

[13]CGSL 374**. [14]WSA 3 2:192-93**. [15]CGSL 375**. [16]FC 59:256*.

will of the Father. Eager for our inheritance and advantage, following after pride, giving way to envy and to neglecting simplicity and faith, renouncing the world in words only and not in deeds, each one pleasing himself and displeasing all,[17] we do not do the will of God.

We are beaten as we deserve. It is written, "But that servant who knows his master's will and did not obey his will, will be beaten with many stripes." But what blows and stripes do we not deserve, when even confessors, who should have been an example in good morals to the rest, do not keep discipline? LETTER 11.1.[18]

THE SEVERITY OF THE LORD'S JUDGMENT.
BASIL THE GREAT: When I consult the New Testament, I find that our Lord Jesus Christ does not absolve from punishment even sins committed in ignorance, although he attaches a harsher threat

to deliberate sins. "And that servant who knew his master's will but did not make ready or act according to his will shall receive a severe beating. But he who did not know and did what deserved a beating shall receive a light beating." I hear something like this from the lips of the only-begotten Son of God and consider the anger of the holy apostles against sinners. I observe that the sufferings of those who have transgressed in even one particular are not less serious but rather more serious than those cited from the Old Testament. I then comprehend the severity of the judgment. Our Lord says, "To whomever much is given, much will be required of him." PREFACE ON THE JUDGMENT OF GOD.[19]

---

[17]See 2 Pet 2:13-15. [18]FC 51:29*. [19]FC 9:47*.

12:49-53 THE BAPTISM JESUS MUST UNDERGO

[49]"I came to cast fire upon the earth; and would that it were already kindled! [50]I have a baptism to be baptized with; and how I am constrained until it is accomplished! [51]Do you think that I have come to give peace on earth? No, I tell you, but rather division; [52]for henceforth in one house there will be five divided, three against two and two against three; [53]they will be divided, father against son and son against father, mother against daughter and daughter against her mother, mother-in-law against her daughter-in-law and daughter-in-law against her mother-in-law."

OVERVIEW: Jesus speaks about his suffering and death as the kindling of eschatological fire and as an eschatological baptism that lead to his coming in judgment. This fire is the fire of the gospel that comes to us by the Holy Spirit in holy baptism (CYRIL OF ALEXANDRIA). This fire illumining the secrets of the hearts of the Emmaus disciples was the Word of God (AMBROSE). This fire is that of the Holy Spirit at Pentecost (CYRIL OF JERUSALEM). Fire that reveals the malice of sin and uncovers acts

of charity is part of catechetical lectures before baptism where Christ is put on through his cross and resurrection (BASIL THE GREAT).

Jesus began his ministry with a water baptism in the Jordan, where he placed himself under God's wrath on behalf of all humanity; Jesus completes his ministry with a bloody baptism on the cross, where the full wrath of God is placed upon him as he atones for the world's sin. Jesus' baptism on the cross is set in a series of baptisms in Scripture, the baptism to which all other baptisms point (JOHN OF DAMASCUS). Fire and baptism, therefore, refer to Jesus' death on the cross and his glorious resurrection (CYRIL OF ALEXANDRIA). Jesus is not telling us that we are not to love our families, but we are not to love them more than we love God. Although the number three against two and two against three adds up to five people, six are listed: father, son, mother, daughter, mother-in-law and daughter-in-law. But taken literally and mystically, the numbers reconcile when one considers that each person is either of the house of God or of the devil (AMBROSE).

12:49-50 Fire and Baptism

THE FIRE OF THE GOSPEL AND HOLY SPIRIT AT BAPTISM. CYRIL OF ALEXANDRIA: We affirm that the fire that Christ sent out is for humanity's salvation and profit. May God grant that all our hearts be full of this. The fire is the saving message of the gospel and the power of its commandments. We were cold and dead because of sin and in ignorance of him who by nature is truly God. The gospel ignites all of us on earth to a life of piety and makes us fervent in spirit, according to the expression of blessed Paul.[1] Besides this, we are also made partakers of the Holy Spirit, who is like fire within us. We have been baptized with fire and the Holy Spirit. We have learned the way from what Christ says to us. Listen to his words: "Truly I say to you, that except a man be born of water and spirit, he cannot see the kingdom of God."[2]

It is the divinely inspired Scripture's custom to give the name of fire sometimes to the divine and sacred words and to the efficacy and power which is by the Holy Spirit by which we are made fervent in spirit. COMMENTARY ON LUKE, HOMILY 94.[3]

THE FIRE OF SCRIPTURE. AMBROSE: Love is good, having wings of burning fire that flies through the saints' breasts and hearts and consumes whatever is material and earthly but tests whatever is pure. With its fire, love makes whatever it has touched better. The Lord Jesus sent this fire on earth. Faith shined brightly. Devotion was enkindled. Love was illuminated. Justice was resplendent. With this fire, he inflamed the heart of his apostles, as Cleophas bears witness, saying, "Was not our heart burning within is, while he was explaining the Scriptures?"[4] The wings of fire are the flames of the divine Scripture. ISAAC, OR THE SOUL 8.77.[5]

THE FIRE OF THE HOLY SPIRIT AT PENTECOST. CYRIL OF JERUSALEM: Why is it "fire"? It is because the descent of the Holy Spirit was in fiery tongues. Concerning this the Lord says with joy, "I came to cast fire upon the earth, and would that it were already kindled!" CATECHETICAL LECTURES 17.8.[6]

FIRE CATECHIZES. BASIL THE GREAT: He also said, "I came to cast fire upon the earth; and would that it were already kindled!" These flaming words from the lips of our Lord Jesus Christ reveal the malice of sin. He also reveals the excellence of good actions performed for the glory of God and his Christ.... Then we are ready for the baptism of water, which is a type of the cross, death, burial and resurrection from the dead....

One who is prepared to be baptized in the name of the Holy Spirit is one who has been born anew, who undergoes a change of residence, habits and associates so that, walking by the Spirit, he may be ready to be baptized in the name of the Son and to put on Christ. CONCERNING BAPTISM 1.2.[7]

12:51-53 Peace and Division

JESUS' BAPTISM IN BLOOD A CLIMAX OF BIBLICAL BAPTISMS. JOHN OF DAMASCUS: A first baptism was by the flood for the cutting away of sin. A second baptism was by the sea and the

---

[1]Rom 12:11. [2]Jn 3:5. [3]CGSL 377**. [4]Lk 24:32. [5]FC 65:60-61**. [6]FC 64:101*. [7]FC 9:384-85**.

cloud,[8] because the cloud is a symbol of the Spirit, while the sea is a symbol of the water. A third baptism is that of the law, because every unclean person washed himself with water and also washed his garments and then entered the camp.[9] A fourth is that of John, which was an introductory baptism leading those thus baptized into repentance so that they might believe in Christ. "I indeed," he says, "baptize you in water, but he that will come after me, he will baptize you in the Holy Spirit and fire."[10] John purified with water in advance to prepare for the Spirit. A fifth baptism is the Lord's baptism with which he was baptized. He was not baptized because he needed purification. He was baptized so that by making my purification his own, he might "crush the heads of the dragons in the waters,"[11] wash away the sin and bury all of the old Adam in the water, sanctify the baptizer, fulfill the law, reveal the mystery of the Trinity and become for us a model and example for the reception of baptism. We also are baptized with the perfect baptism of the Lord, which is by water and the Spirit. It is said that Christ baptizes in fire because he poured out the grace of the Spirit on the holy apostles in the form of tongues of fire. The Lord says, "John indeed baptized with water, but you will be baptized with the Holy Spirit and fire, not many days from now."[12] It may also be that he is said to baptize with fire because of the chastising baptism of the fire to come. A sixth baptism is that which is by repentance and tears, which is truly painful. A seventh baptism is that which is by blood and martyrdom. Christ was also baptized with this for our sake. This baptism is exceedingly sublime and blessed because second stains do not pollute it. An eighth baptism, which is the last, is not saving. While being destructive of evil, since evil and sin no longer hold power, it chastises endlessly. ORTHODOX FAITH 4.9.[13]

FIRE AND BAPTISM REFER TO JESUS' DEATH AND RESURRECTION. CYRIL OF ALEXANDRIA:

He teaches us this by saying, "I have a baptism to be baptized with; and how I am constrained until it is accomplished!" By his baptism, he means his death in the flesh. By being constrained because of it, he means that he was saddened and troubled until it was accomplished. What was to happen when it was accomplished? The saving message of the gospel would not be proclaimed only in Judea. Comparing it with fire, he said, "I have come to send fire upon earth—but that now it should be published even to the whole world." Before the precious cross and his resurrection from the dead, his commandments and the glory of his divine miracles were spoken of in Judea only. COMMENTARY ON LUKE, HOMILY 94.[14]

PARENTS ARE NOT TO BE LOVED MORE THAN GOD. AMBROSE:

Spiritual understanding is at work in every passage of the Gospels. In the present case, fearing that the rigidity of a simple explanation may offend someone, the sequence of the sense is to be qualified by spiritual depth. . . . We will believe that the Lord took care to advise reverence for the Godhead at the same time as the grace of piety. He said, "You will love the Lord your God, and you will love your neighbor."[15] Is the present so changed as to erase the names of close kin and set affections at variance? Are we to believe that he has commanded discord within families? How is he our peace, who has made both one?[16] How does he himself say, "My peace I give to you, my peace I leave with you,"[17] if he has come to separate fathers from sons and sons from fathers by the division of households? How is he cursed who dishonors his father[18] and devout who forsakes him? If we observe that the first is because of religion and the second through piety, we shall think this question is simple. It is necessary that we should esteem the human less than the divine. If honor is to be paid to parents, how much more to your parents' Creator, to whom you owe gratitude for your parents! If they by no means recognize their Father, how do you recognize them? He does not say children should reject a father but that

---

[8]1 Cor 10:2. [9]Lev 14:8. [10]Mt 3:11. [11]Ps 74:13 (73:13 LXX). [12]Acts 1:5. [13]FC 37:346-47**. [14]CGSL 379**. [15]Lk 10:27. [16]Eph 2:14. [17]Jn 14:27. [18]Deut 27:16.

God is to be set before all. Then you have in another book, "He that loves father or mother more than me is not worthy of me."[19] You are not forbidden to love your parents, but you are forbidden to prefer them to God. Natural children are true blessings from the Lord, and no one must love the blessing that he has received more than God by whom the blessing, once received, is preserved. EXPOSITION OF THE GOSPEL OF LUKE 7.134-36.[20]

A MYSTICAL MEANING: EACH IS THE HOUSE OF GOD OR THE DEVIL. AMBROSE: Even according to the letter, a religious explanation is not lacking for those with a devout understanding. We think a deeper meaning should also be explained. He added, "There will be from now on five in one house divided, three against two, and two against three." Who are these five, when the exposition given seems to be of six persons, father and son, mother and daughter, mother-in-law and daughter-in-law? The same woman can be understood as both mother and mother-in-law, because she who is the mother of the son is the mother-in-law of his wife. According to the letter, the reason for the number is not absurd. It is evident that bonds of nature do not bind faith, because children are obedient in faith because of the duty of piety.

It also seems suitable to explain this meaning with a mystical interpretation. One man is one house, because each is the house of either God or the devil. A spiritual man is a spiritual house, as we have in the epistle of Peter, "Be also as living stories built up, a spiritual house, a holy priesthood."[21] In this house, two are divided against three and three against two. EXPOSITION OF THE GOSPEL OF LUKE 7.136-38.[22]

---

[19]Mt 10:37. [20]EHG 286-87**. [21]1 Pet 2:5. [22]EHG 287-88**.

12:54-59 TWO EXHORTATIONS FOR THE PRESENT TIME

[54]*He also said to the multitudes, "When you see a cloud rising in the west, you say at once, 'A shower is coming'; and so it happens.* [55]*And when you see the south wind blowing, you say, 'There will be scorching heat'; and it happens.* [56]*You hypocrites! You know how to interpret the appearance of earth and sky; but why do you not know how to interpret the present time?*

[57]*"And why do you not judge for yourselves what is right?* [58]*As you go with your accuser before the magistrate, make an effort to settle with him on the way, lest he drag you to the judge, and the judge hand you over to the officer, and the officer put you in prison.* [59]*I tell you, you will never get out till you have paid the very last copper."*

OVERVIEW: What was foretold in the law has now dawned in the mystery of Christ's passion as the Lamb who is sacrificed for the salvation of all (CYRIL OF ALEXANDRIA). It is also a strong warning to act accordingly (BASIL THE GREAT). If one does not make peace on the way and become freed from one's adversary, then one will be judged and thrown into a prison out of which he will never gain release. What one does in this life determines the verdict of the judge, who is Christ

(ORIGEN), when life is over (CYRIL OF ALEXANDRIA). If we have debts, no matter how small or large, the judge delivers us over to the debt collectors who are now our masters, and we cannot be set free unless we have paid the debt that we owe. Only Jesus has the power to forgive us our debts, no matter how large or small, for without his forgiveness we are powerless to be released from our debts (ORIGEN). The Word of God is our opponent if we commit a sin (AUGUSTINE).

12:54-56 Signs of the Times

SIGNS FROM THE LAW POINT TO THE DAWN OF THE MYSTERY OF CHRIST. CYRIL OF ALEXANDRIA: People focus their attention on things of this kind. From long observation and practice they tell beforehand when rain will fall or violent winds will blow. One especially sees that sailors are very skillful in this matter. He says that it would be suitable for those who can calculate things of this sort and may foretell storms that are about to happen to focus the penetrating eyes of the mind also on important matters. What are these? The law showed beforehand the mystery of Christ, that he would shine out in the last ages of the world on the inhabitants of the earth and submit to be a sacrifice for the salvation of all. It even commanded a lamb to be sacrificed as a type of him who died towards evening and at lighting of lamps.[1] We might now understand that when, like the day, this world was declining to its close, the great, precious and truly saving passion would be fulfilled. The door of salvation would be thrown wide open to those who believe in him, and abundant happiness be their share. In the Song of Songs, we also find Christ calling to the bride described there. The bride personally represents the church, in these words, "Arise, come, my neighbor, my beautiful dove. Look, the winter is past, and the rain is gone. It has passed away. The flowers appear on the ground. The time of the pruning has come."[2] As I said, a certain springlike calm was about to arise for those who believe in him. COMMENTARY ON LUKE, HOMILY 95.[3]

12:57-59 Appearing Before the Judge

READ THE SIGNS. BASIL THE GREAT: Having recognized the nature of this present time from the signs revealed to us by the Scriptures, we should dispose our affairs accordingly. THE MORALS 17.[4]

THE JUDGE IS CHRIST. ORIGEN: Who do you think that judge is? I do not know any other judge besides our Lord Jesus Christ. Of him Scripture says elsewhere, "He will put the sheep on the right, but the goats on the left."[5] "Whoever confesses me before others, him will I also confess before my Father who is in heaven. Whoever denies me before others, I will deny him before my Father who is in heaven."[6] HOMILIES ON THE GOSPEL OF LUKE 35.10.[7]

THE JUDGE'S VERDICT DEPENDENT ON THIS LIFE. CYRIL OF ALEXANDRIA: He has shown that it is our duty to be watchful in seeking to be delivered quickly from our sins and to escape from blame before we arrive at the end of our natural lives. . . .

Without exception, all of us on earth are guilty of offenses. Wicked Satan has a lawsuit against us and accuses us, because he is the enemy and the exactor.[8] While we are on the way, before we have arrived at the end of our present life, let us deliver ourselves from him. Let us do away with the offenses of which we have been guilty. Let us close his mouth. Let us seize the grace that is by Christ that frees us from all debt and penalty and delivers us from fear and torment. Let us fear that if our impurity is not cleansed away, we will be carried before the judge and given over to the exactors, the tormentors, from whose cruelty no one can escape. They will exact vengeance for every fault, whether it is great or small. COMMENTARY ON LUKE, HOMILY 95.[9]

---

[1]Ex 12:6. [2]Song 2:10-12. [3]*CGSL* 381-82**. [4]FC 9:93*. [5]Mt 25:33. [6]Mt 10:32-33. [7]FC 94:147*. [8]Ps 8:2 (8:3 LXX). [9]*CGSL* 383**.

OUR DEBTS AND OUR DEBT COLLECTORS.

ORIGEN: Each one of us incurs a penalty for each single sin, and the size of the penalty is according to the quality and nature of the offense. I should show some testimony from the Scriptures about the penalty and monetary fines. One man incurs a debt of five hundred denarii and owes that much. Another is obliged to pay fifty denarii. The creditor cancels these debts for both debtors. "Another one," as the Scripture says, "is brought forward, who owed ten thousand talents."[10] He is obliged to pay ten thousand talents. . . .

The debt collector comes to claim his due. I resist him. I know that if I owe nothing, he has no power over me. If I am a debtor, the debt collector will send me to prison, fulfilling the order of which we have spoken. The enemy brings me to the ruler, and the ruler to the judge. The judge will hand me over to the debt collector, and the debt collector will put me in prison. What law governs that prison? I will not come out of it, nor will the debt collector allow me to go out, unless I have paid every debt. HOMILIES ON THE GOSPEL OF LUKE 35.10, 13.[11]

ONLY JESUS CAN FORGIVE US OUR DEBTS.

ORIGEN: The debt collector does not have the power to cancel for me even a penny of the debt or the smallest portion of it. Only one can cancel a debt when the debtors are unable to pity their debts. Scripture says, "One man came to him who owed five hundred denarii, and another who owed fifty. Since they did not have the money to pay him, he forgave both of them."[12] He who for-gave was the Lord. He who collects debts is not the Lord but one whom the Lord assigns to collect debts.

You were not worthy to have a debt of five hundred denarii, or fifty, canceled. You did not deserve to hear, "Your offenses are forgiven you."[13] You will be sent to prison, and there you will have payment exacted by labor and work or by punishments and torture. You will not get out unless you have paid the penny and the "last farthing," which in Greek means "meager amount." HOMILIES ON THE GOSPEL OF LUKE 35.13-14.[14]

IF YOU SIN, YOUR ADVERSARY IS THE WORD OF GOD.

AUGUSTINE: Let us try to find out who is the opponent with whom we should agree, fearing that he might deliver us to the judge, and the judge deliver us to the officer. Let us try to find him and be in agreement with him. If you are committing a sin, your adversary is the word of God. For instance, perhaps you may like to get drunk. It says to you, "Do not do that." You may like to frequent the circus and indulge in frivolities. It says to you, "Do not do that." You may like to commit adultery. The word of God says to you, "Do not do it." In whatever sins you wish to follow your own will, it says to you, "Do not do that." It is the enemy of your will until it becomes the assurance of your salvation. Oh, what an honest and helpful enemy! SERMON 109.3.[15]

---

[10]Lk 7:41-42. [11]FC 94:147-49**. [12]Lk 7:41-42. [13]Lk 7:48. [14]FC 94:149*. [15]FC 11:297-98**.

13:1-9 REPENTANCE AND THE PARABLE OF THE FIG TREE

[1]There were some present at that very time who told him of the Galileans whose blood Pilate had mingled with their sacrifices. [2]And he answered them, "Do you think that these Galileans

were worse sinners than all the other Galileans, because they suffered thus? [3]*I tell you, No; but unless you repent you will all likewise perish.* [4]*Or those eighteen upon whom the tower in Siloam fell and killed them, do you think that they were worse offenders than all the others who dwelt in Jerusalem?* [5]*I tell you, No; but unless you repent you will all likewise perish."*

[6]*And he told this parable: "A man had a fig tree planted in his vineyard; and he came seeking fruit on it and found none.* [7]*And he said to the vinedresser, 'Lo, these three years I have come seeking fruit on this fig tree, and I find none. Cut it down; why should it use up the ground?'* [8]*And he answered him, 'Let it alone, sir, this year also, till I dig about it and put on manure.* [9]*And if it bears fruit next year, well and good; but if not, you can cut it down.'"*

OVERVIEW: The report about the Galileans whose blood Pilate mingled with their sacrifices may have occurred on Herod's birthday, when John was beheaded as an attempt by Pilate to shame Herod, who was not yet his friend (EPHREM THE SYRIAN). These Galileans were no more sinners than the other Galileans, and their tragedy cannot be connected with any specific or exceptional sin, including the suggestion that they were killed because their sacrifice was impure (AMBROSE).

Jesus uses the parable as an allegory of Israel's history and his intervention into their world as their Savior (EPHREM THE SYRIAN). In his teaching, the fig tree represents the whole human race that God has come to save (AUGUSTINE). Both a vineyard and a fig tree are common Old Testament metaphors for Israel. In Jesus' parable the fig tree is planted in the vineyard, and this has led some interpreters to suggest that the tree might represent a group within Israel, such as the leadership of the synagogue (CYRIL OF ALEXANDRIA).

The clearing of the ground for others may be an allusion to the incorporation of Gentiles into the Israel of God. The vinedresser's intercession suggests that he may represent Jesus himself as well as the early apostolic mission to the Jews, but all who proclaim the gospel of God's merciful clemency in Jesus and who prayerfully intercede for the perishing are carrying out the role of the vinedresser. And so the fourth year is Jesus' incarnation, where he comes as husbandman to nour-

ish Israel (CYRIL OF ALEXANDRIA).

13:1-5 *The Blood of the Galileans and the Tower of Siloam*

PILATE KILLS THE GALILEANS ON HEROD'S BIRTHDAY. EPHREM THE SYRIAN: They came and informed Jesus concerning the men from Galilee, whose blood Pilate had mixed with their sacrifices, on the festival of Herod's birthday, when he cut off John's head.[1] Since Herod had illegally killed John, Pilate sent and killed those who were present at the feast. Since he was not able to injure Herod, he destroyed his accomplice to his shame, and he left him in anger until the day of the Lord's judgment. The two were reconciled through the pretext of the Lord.[2] Pilate mixed their blood with their sacrifices, because the Roman authorities forbid them to offer sacrifice. Pilate found them transgressing the law and offering sacrifices, and he destroyed them at that same place and time. COMMENTARY ON TATIAN'S DIATESSARON 14.25.[3]

THE SACRIFICES WERE IMPURE. AMBROSE: From those Galileans whose blood Pilate mingled with their sacrifices, the symbolic interpretation appears to refer to those who under the devil's power offer sacrifice impurely. Their prayer becomes sin,[4] just as it is written of Judas the traitor, who, amid the sacrifices, planned the betrayal

---

[1]Mt 14:10. [2]Lk 23:12. [3]ECTD 225-26*. [4]Ps 109:7 (108:7 LXX).

of the Lord's blood.[5] Exposition of the Gospel of Luke 7.159.[6]

13:6-9 The Parable of the Fig Tree

The Fig Tree Is the Synagogue. Ephrem the Syrian: He told another parable, "A certain man had planted a fig tree in his vineyard and he said to the vinedresser." This refers to the law, taking its point of view. "Behold, for three years I have come seeking fruit on this fig tree." This refers to the three captivities in which the Israelites were taken away, so that they might be chastened, but they were not chastened. . . . The fig tree is a figure of the synagogue. He sought the fruits of faith in it, but it did not have that which it could offer. . . .

During three years, he showed himself among them as Savior. When he wished that the fig tree be uprooted, the event was similar to that earlier one, when the Father said to Moses, "Permit me to destroy the people."[7] He gave Moses a reason to intercede with him. Here he also showed the vinedresser that he wished to uproot it. The vinedresser made known his plea, and the merciful One showed his pity, that if, in another year, the fig tree did not produce fruit, it would be uprooted. The vinedresser however did not condemn through vengeance like Moses, who, after having interceded and was heard, said, "For the day of their ruin is near and that which is about to happen to them is fast approaching."[8] . . . We are not saying that the Jews are tares, for they are capable of being chosen, but they are not pure wheat grains, for they can be rejected. Commentary on Tatian's Diatessaron 14.26-27.[9]

The Lord's Three Visits Through the Patriarchs, the Prophets and the Gospel. Augustine: The Lord also has something very fitting to say about a fruitless tree, "Look, it is now three years that I have been coming to it. Finding no fruit on it, I will cut it down, to stop it blocking up my field." The gardener intercedes. . . .

This tree is the human race. The Lord visited this tree in the time of the patriarchs, as if for the first year. He visited it in the time of the law and the prophets, as if for the second year. Here we are now; with the gospel the third year has dawned. Now it is as though it should have been cut down, but the merciful one intercedes with the merciful one. He wanted to show how merciful he was, and so he stood up to himself with a plea for mercy. "Let us leave it," he says, "this year too. Let us dig a ditch around it." Manure is a sign of humility. "Let us apply a load of manure; perhaps it may bear fruit."

Since it does bear fruit in one part, and in another part does not bear fruit, its Lord will come and divide it. What does that mean, "divide it"? There are good people and bad people now in one company, as though constituting one body. Sermon 254.3.[10]

The Fig Tree Represents the Synagogue. Cyril of Alexandria: Now the literal sense of this passage does not need a single word of explanation. When we search into its inward, secret and unseen meaning, we affirm it as follows. The Israelites, after our Savior's crucifixion, were doomed to fall into the miseries they deserved, Jerusalem being captured, and its inhabitants slaughtered by the enemy's sword. Their houses would be burned with fire, and even the temple of God demolished. It is probable that he compares the synagogue of the Jews with a fig tree. The sacred Scripture also compares them with various plants: the vine, the olive, and even to a forest.[11] Commentary on Luke, Homily 96.[12]

In the Gentiles Another Tree Is Planted. Cyril of Alexandria: He says, "Look, these three years I have come seeking fruit on this fig tree, and I find none. Cut it down; why should it use up the ground?" It is as if he would say, "Let the place of this barren fig tree be laid bare; then some other tree will come up or may be plant-

---

[5]Cf. Jn 13:18. [6]EHG 295**. [7]Ex 32:10. [8]See Ex 32:34. [9]ECTD 226-27**. [10]WSA 3 7:153**. [11]Hos 10:1; Jer 11:16; Zech 11:1. [12]CGSL 387-88**.

ed there." This was also done. The crowds of the Gentiles were called into its place and took possession of the inheritance of the Israelites. It became the people of God, the plant of paradise, a good and honorable seed. It knows how to produce fruit, not in shadows and types but rather by a pure and perfectly stainless service that is in spirit and truth, as being offered to God, who is an immaterial Being. COMMENTARY ON LUKE, HOMILY 96.[13]

WHETHER THE VINEDRESSER IS THE DOOR OR THE FATHER. CYRIL OF ALEXANDRIA: If any one should say that the vinedresser is the Son, this view also has a suitable reason on its side. He is our Advocate with the Father, our propitiation,[14] and the gardener of our souls. He constantly prunes away whatever is harmful and fills us with rational and holy seeds so we may produce fruits for him. He spoke of himself, "A sower went out to sow his seed."[15] It does not influence the glory of the Son to assume the character of the vinedresser. The Father assumes it himself, without being exposed to any blame for so doing. The Son said to the holy apostles, "I am the Vine; you are the branches; my Father is the Vinedresser."[16] COMMENTARY ON LUKE, HOMILY 96.[17]

---

[13]CGSL 388-89**. [14]1 Jn 2:1. [15]Lk 8:5. [16]Jn 15:1. [17]CGSL 389**.

13:10-17 THE SECOND SABBATH CONTROVERSY

[10]*Now he was teaching in one of the synagogues on the sabbath.* [11]*And there was a woman who had had a spirit of infirmity for eighteen years; she was bent over and could not fully straighten herself.* [12]*And when Jesus saw her, he called her and said to her, "Woman, you are freed from your infirmity."* [13]*And he laid his hands upon her, and immediately she was made straight, and she praised God.* [14]*But the ruler of the synagogue, indignant because Jesus had healed on the sabbath, said to the people, "There are six days on which work ought to be done; come on those days and be healed, and not on the sabbath day."* [15]*Then the Lord answered him, "You hypocrites! Does not each of you on the sabbath untie his ox or his ass from the manger, and lead it away to water it?* [16]*And ought not this woman, a daughter of Abraham whom Satan bound for eighteen years, be loosed from this bond on the sabbath day?"* [17]*As he said this, all his adversaries were put to shame; and all the people rejoiced at all the glorious things that were done by him.*

OVERVIEW: Jesus releases a woman who had a "spirit of weakness" for eighteen years from this chain of bondage to Satan and to sin, that she might change to a better course (CYRIL OF ALEXANDRIA). Here Jesus teaches about the release he brings by announcing absolution to her, for she is like a vine the Lord has cultivated and freed to bear fruit (AMBROSE). Here is Jesus, the Word made flesh, the agent of creation coming to God's creation and working on the sabbath his new creation (CYRIL OF ALEXANDRIA).

In the ensuing discussion, the chief of the synagogue stands as one who does not understand the meaning of the sabbath, for he takes it literally but not spiritually (AUGUSTINE). If the sabbath could be used to free animals from bondage, the sabbath could be used to free people from bondage of sin and sickness (AMBROSE). The chief of the synagogue is not able to read the signs of this present, critical time in light of the ministry of Jesus and is consumed with jealousy and envy that Jesus is honored and worshiped as God. He and those of his ilk were being put to shame by Jesus' words, whereas the multitudes rejoiced at the glorious things Jesus was doing (CYRIL OF ALEXANDRIA).

13:10-13 The Sabbath Miracle

GOD ALLOWS SATAN AND SIN TO BIND THIS WOMAN. CYRIL OF ALEXANDRIA: "There was in the synagogue a woman who for eighteen years was bowed down by infirmity." Her case may prove to be of great benefit to those who have understanding. We must gather what is to our advantage from every quarter. By what happened to her, we may see that Satan often receives authority over certain persons who fall into sin and have grown lax in their efforts toward piety. Whomever he gets into his power, he may involve in bodily diseases since he delights in punishment and is merciless. . . . The accursed Satan is the cause of disease to the human bodies, just we affirm that Adam's transgression was his doing, and by means of it our bodily frames have become liable to infirmity and decay. COMMENTARY ON LUKE, HOMILY 96.[1]

THE INFIRM WOMAN LIKE A VINE. AMBROSE: The members of the church are similar to this vine. They are planted with the root of faith and held in check by the shoots of humility. . . . He placed in the church a tower of apostles, prophets and doctors who are ready to defend the peace of the church. He dug around it when he had freed it from the burden of earthly anxieties. Nothing burdens the mind more than concern for the world and lust for either wealth or power.

An example of this is in the Gospel. We can read the story of the woman "who had sickness caused by a spirit, and she was bent over so that she was unable to look upwards." In fact, her soul was bent over. It inclined to earthly rewards and did not possess heavenly grace. Jesus saw her and addressed her. She immediately laid aside her earthly burdens. These people also were burdened with lusts. He addressed them in these words, "Come to me, all you who labor and are burdened, and I will give you rest."[2] The soul of that woman breathed once more and stood up like a vine around which the soil has been dug and cleared. SIX DAYS OF CREATION 3.50.[3]

JESUS OVERCOMES DEATH AND DESTRUCTION. CYRIL OF ALEXANDRIA: The incarnation of the Word and his assumption of human nature took place for the overthrow of death, destruction and the envy harbored against us by the wicked Serpent, who was the first cause of evil. This plainly is proved to us by facts themselves. He set free the daughter of Abraham from her protracted sickness, calling out and saying, "Woman, you are loosed from your infirmity." A speech most worthy of God, and full of supernatural power! With the royal inclination of his will, he drives away the disease. He also lays his hands upon her. It says that she immediately was made straight. It is now also possible to see that his holy flesh bore in it the power and activity of God. It was his own flesh, and not that of some other Son beside him, distinct and separate from him, as some most impiously imagine. COMMENTARY ON LUKE, HOMILY 96.[4]

13:14-17 The Discussion About Healing on the Sabbath

THE SYNAGOGUE LEADER TOOK THE SABBATH LITERALLY. AUGUSTINE: The whole human race, like this woman, was bent over and bowed down to the ground. Someone already understands these enemies. He cries out against them and says to God, "They have bowed my soul down."[5] The devil and his angels have bowed the souls of men and women down to the ground. He has bent them forward to be intent on temporary and

---

[1]CGSL 390**. [2]Mt 11:28. [3]FC 42:104-5*. [4]CGSL 391**. [5]Ps 57:6.

earthly things and has stopped them from seeking the things that are above.[6]

Since that is what the Lord says about the woman whom Satan had bound for eighteen years, it was now time for her to be released from her bondage on the sabbath day. Quite unjustly, they criticized him for straightening her up. Who were these, except people bent over themselves? Since they quite failed to understand the very things God had commanded,[7] they regarded them with earthbound hearts. They used to celebrate the sacrament of the sabbath[8] in a literal, material manner and did not notice its spiritual meaning. SERMON 162B.[9]

THE SABBATH IS FOR FREEDOM FROM SIN AND SICKNESS. AMBROSE: Not understanding this, the ruler of the synagogue commanded that no one should be healed on the sabbath since the sabbath is an image of a future day of rest, days of rest from evil deeds, not from good works. It is commanded that, neither bearing the burden of offenses nor being devoid of good works, we shall celebrate future sabbaths after death. The Lord then is seen to reply spiritually when he says, "You hypocrites, does not every one of you on the sabbath day untie his ox or his donkey and lead them to water?" Why did Jesus mention another creature? He showed the future to his opponents, the rulers of the synagogue. The Jewish and the Gentile peoples would lay aside the thirst of the body and the world's heat through the abundance of the Lord's fountain. "The ox knows his owner, and the ass his master's feeding trough."[10] The people who were fed on the food of common hay, which before it is plucked up is withered away,[11] received the Bread that came down from heaven.[12] EXPOSITION OF THE GOSPEL OF LUKE 7.174-75.[13]

CHOKED WITH RAGE. CYRIL OF ALEXANDRIA: "But he says that you are loosed from your infirmity, and she is loosed." Well, do you not also unloose your belt on the sabbath? . . . Did she that very day begin weaving or working at the loom? No, he says that she was made straight. The healing was a labor. No, you are not angry because of the sabbath. Since you see Christ honored and worshiped as God, you are frantic, choked with rage, and waste away with envy. You have one thing concealed in your heart and profess and make pretext of another. For this reason you are most excellently convicted by the Lord, who knows your vain reasoning. You receive the title that fits you, being called hypocrite, pretender, and insincere. COMMENTARY ON LUKE, HOMILY 96.[14]

13:17 The Reaction of Jesus' Opponents and the Crowds

SHAME AND GLADNESS. CYRIL OF ALEXANDRIA: Shame fell then on those who had uttered these corrupt opinions, stumbled against the chief cornerstone, and had been broken. When busied in straightening his crooked vessels, they clashed against the wise Potter and resisted the Physician. They could make no reply. They had unanswerably convicted themselves. They were put to silence, doubting what they should say. The Lord closed their bold mouths. The crowds who reaped the benefit of the miracles were glad. The glory and splendor of his works solved all inquiry and doubt in those who sought him without ill will. COMMENTARY ON LUKE, HOMILY 96.[15]

---

[6]See Col 3:1. [7]Ex 20:8-11. [8]The text says "baptism," but the editors reasonably suggest that it is a mistake for "sabbath." [9]WSA 3 5:167**. [10]Is 1:3. [11]Ps 128:6 LXX. [12]Jn 6:33. [13]EHG 302**. [14]CGSL 392-93**. [15]CGSL 393**.

13:18-21 PARABLES ABOUT THE KINGDOM

[18]*He said therefore, "What is the kingdom of God like? And to what shall I compare it?* [19]*It is like a grain of mustard seed which a man took and sowed in his garden; and it grew and became a tree, and the birds of the air made nests in its branches."*

[20]*And again he said, "To what shall I compare the kingdom of God?* [21]*It is like leaven which a woman took and hid in three measures of flour, till it was all leavened."*

OVERVIEW: The kingdom of God is compared with a mustard seed because the agricultural imagery of a seed that is sown and grows is a perfect description of how faith grows (PETER CHRYSOLOGUS). In Matthew, the mustard seed is compared with faith that can move mountains, and if the kingdom of heaven is like a mustard seed, then faith is as a grain of mustard seed (AMBROSE). Like the humble seed planted in the ground, Christ's humility is expressed in his birth of a woman and his burial into the bosom of the earth. Like the mighty tree that ascends into the heavens, Christ's exaltation comes from his resurrection and ascension (MAXIMUS OF TURIN).

The disciples were warned not to succumb to the evil leaven of the Pharisees, which is hypocrisy,[1] but instead the crowds are to perceive the divine leaven of Jesus that works in us through the Word of God (CYRIL OF ALEXANDRIA). His teaching and miracles are signs that the kingdom of God is already a present reality, although they may seem small, insignificant and hidden. The doctrine of Christ is leaven because the bread is Christ (AMBROSE). This yeast of Christ the church spreads throughout the world, announcing that the great victory of liberation over Satan is already present in Jesus and that the scope of that victory one day will be fully revealed (BEDE).

13:18-19 The Kingdom of God Is Like a Mustard Seed

HOW THE KINGDOM IS LIKE A MUSTARD

SEED. PETER CHRYSOLOGUS: As the text says, the kingdom of God is like a grain of mustard seed, because the kingdom is brought by a word from heaven. It is received through hearing and sown by faith. It takes root through belief and grows by hope. It is diffused by profession, and it expands through virtue. It is spread out into branches. To these branches, it invites the birds of heaven, the powers of spiritual insight. In those branches, it receives them in a peaceful abode. SERMON 98.[2]

THE MUSTARD SEED IS COMPARED WITH FAITH AND THE KINGDOM OF HEAVEN.

AMBROSE: If the kingdom of heaven is as a grain of mustard seed, and faith is as a grain of mustard seed, surely faith is the kingdom of heaven and the kingdom of heaven is faith. One who has faith has the kingdom. The kingdom and faith is among us. We read, "The kingdom of heaven is within you,"[3] and "Have faith in yourselves."[4] Peter, who had all faith, received the keys of the kingdom of heaven to unlock it also for others.[5] EXPOSITION OF THE GOSPEL OF LUKE 7.177.[6]

CHRIST IS LIKE THE MUSTARD SEED. MAXIMUS OF TURIN: There is written in these words of the Lord, "Someone took and threw it into his garden. It grew and became a tree, and the birds of heaven roosted in its branches." Let us look more

---

[1]Lk 12:1. [2]FC 17:158*. [3]Lk 17:21. [4]Mk 11:12. [5]See Mt 16:9. [6]EHG 303**.

closely to find out to whom all these things pertain. We said before that the nature of mustard might resemble the holy martyrs because they are rubbed by different sufferings. Since Scripture says, "And it grew and became a tree, and the birds of heaven roosted in its branches," I think that this is more properly compared to the Lord Christ himself. Born a man, he was humbled like a seed and in ascending to heaven was exalted like a tree. It is clear that Christ is a seed when he suffers and a tree when he rises. He is a seed when he endures hunger and a tree when he satisfies five thousand men with five loaves. In the one case, he endures barrenness in his human condition, in the other he bestows fullness by his divinity. I would say that the Lord is a seed when he is beaten, scorned and cursed, but a tree when he enlightens the blind, raises the dead and forgives sins. In the Gospel, he says that he is a seed: "Unless the grain of wheat, falling upon the earth, dies."[7] SERMON 25.2.[8]

13:20-21 The Kingdom of God Is Like Leaven

THE WORD OPERATES IN US LIKE LEAVEN.
CYRIL OF ALEXANDRIA: The leaven is small in quantity, yet it immediately seizes the whole mass and quickly communicates its own properties to it. The Word of God operates in us in a similar manner. When it is admitted within us, it makes us holy and without blame. By pervading our mind and heart, it makes us spiritual. Paul says, "Our whole body and spirit and soul may be kept blameless in the day of our Lord Jesus Christ."[9] The God of all clearly shows that the divine Word is poured out even into the depth of our understanding. . . .

We receive the rational and divine leaven in our mind. We understand that by this precious, holy and pure leaven, we may be found spiritually unleavened and have none of the wickedness of the world, but rather be pure, holy partakers of Christ. COMMENTARY ON LUKE, HOMILY 96.[10]

CHRIST IS HIDDEN IN THE CHURCH.
AMBROSE: The grain of wheat is Christ, because he was spiritual leaven for us, and many think that Christ is the leaven that enlivens the virtue which we have received. Since the leaven in the flour surpassed its own kind in strength and not in appearance, Christ was preeminent among the fathers, equal in body, incomparable in divinity. The holy church is prefigured in the woman in the Gospel. We are her flour, and she hides the Lord Jesus in the inner parts of our mind until the radiance of heavenly wisdom envelopes the secret places of our spirit. EXPOSITION OF THE GOSPEL OF LUKE 7.187.[11]

THE DOCTRINE OF CHRIST IS LEAVEN.
AMBROSE: There are three measures: of the flesh, of the soul and of the spirit. This is truer of the spirit in which we all live. . . . The woman, who prefigures the church, mixes with them the virtue of spiritual doctrine, until the whole hidden inner person of the heart[12] is leavened and the heavenly bread arises to grace.[13] The doctrine of Christ is fittingly called leaven, because the bread is Christ. The apostle said, "For we, being many, are one bread, one body."[14] Leavening happens when the flesh does not lust against the Spirit, nor the Spirit against the flesh.[15] We mortify the deeds of the flesh,[16] and the soul, aware that through the breath of God it has received the breath of life, shuns the earthly germs of worldly needs. EXPOSITION OF THE GOSPEL OF LUKE 7.191-92.[17]

THE CHURCH SPREADS LEAVEN.
BEDE: A woman took some yeast when the church, by the Lord's generosity, secured the energy of love and faith from on high. She hid this in three measures of flour until the whole batch was leavened. She did this when she performed her ministry of imparting the word of life to parts of Asia Minor, Europe and Africa, until all the ends of the world were on fire with love for the heavenly kingdom. HOMILIES ON THE GOSPELS 2.13.[18]

---

[7]Jn 12:24. [8]ACW 50:61-62**. [9]1 Thess 5:23. [10]CGSL 395**. [11]EHG 307**. [12]See 1 Pet 3:4. [13]Jn 6:31. [14]1 Cor 10:17. [15]Gal 5:17. [16]See Rom 8:13. [17]EHG 309-10**. [18]CS 111:120.

13:22-30 THE SECOND TRAVEL NOTICE AND ENTERING THE KINGDOM BANQUET

[22]*He went on his way through towns and villages, teaching, and journeying toward Jerusalem.* [23]*And some one said to him, "Lord, will those who are saved be few?" And he said to them,* [24]*"Strive to enter by the narrow door; for many, I tell you, will seek to enter and will not be able.* [25]*When once the householder has risen up and shut the door, you will begin to stand outside and to knock at the door, saying, 'Lord, open to us.' He will answer you, 'I do not know where you come from.'* [26]*Then you will begin to say, 'We ate and drank in your presence, and you taught in our streets.'* [27]*But he will say, 'I tell you, I do not know where you come from; depart from me, all you workers of iniquity!'* [28]*There you will weep and gnash your teeth, when you see Abraham and Isaac and Jacob and all the prophets in the kingdom of God and you yourselves thrust out.* [29]*And men will come from east and west, and from north and south, and sit at table in the kingdom of God.* [30]*And behold, some are last who will be first, and some are first who will be last."*

OVERVIEW: The question raised about how many will be saved and Jesus' answer about the way of salvation shows what is important: not how many but how. To enter the narrow gate requires a steadfast faith and a spotless morality. The wide door is reserved for those who ignore the law and demonstrate this by their sinful behavior (CYRIL OF ALEXANDRIA). The food they ate in Jesus' presence was Christ, food that is even eaten by his enemies, who have rejected him (AUGUSTINE).

Table fellowship with Jesus during his earthly ministry does not guarantee a place at the eschatological banquet. Even some who partake of the Lord's Supper may do so to their own condemnation because they do not recognize the body and blood of the Lord[1] and therefore have not done the will of the Father (CYRIL OF ALEXANDRIA). The magi represent all those who come from every corner of the globe to sit at the eschatological wedding feast (AUGUSTINE). The irony is that those guests who will participate in this eschatological banquet are more likely to be the outcasts of Israel and Gentiles, fitting Luke's great reversal motif, in which the last will be first and the first will be last (CYRIL OF ALEXANDRIA).

13:22-29 *Warnings on the Journey*

NOT HOW MANY ARE SAVED. CYRIL OF ALEXANDRIA: "Strive to enter in by the narrow door." This reply may seem perhaps to wander from the scope of the question. The man wanted to learn whether there would be few who are saved, but he explained to him the way whereby he might be saved himself. He said, "Strive to enter in by the narrow door." What do we answer to this objection? . . . It was a necessary and valuable thing to know how a man may obtain salvation. He is purposely silent to the useless question. He proceeds to speak of what was essential, namely, of the knowledge necessary for the performance of those duties by which people can enter the narrow door. COMMENTARY ON LUKE, HOMILY 99.[2]

TO ENTER THE NARROW GATE. CYRIL OF ALEXANDRIA: I now consider it my duty to mention why the door to life is narrow. Whoever would enter must first before everything else pos-

---

[1] 1 Cor 11:27. [2] *CGSL* 396**.

sess an upright and uncorrupted faith and then a spotless morality, in which there is no possibility of blame, according to the measure of human righteousness. . . . One who has attained to this in mind and spiritual strength will enter easily by the narrow door and run along the narrow way. COMMENTARY ON LUKE, HOMILY 99.[3]

THOSE WHO IGNORE THE LAW. CYRIL OF ALEXANDRIA: "Wide is the door, and broad the way that brings down many to destruction." What are we to understand by its broadness? It means an unrestrained tendency toward carnal lust and a shameful and pleasure-loving life. It is luxurious feasts, parties, banquets and unrestricted inclinations to everything that is condemned by the law and displeasing to God. A stubborn mind will not bow to the yoke of the law. This life is cursed and relaxed in all carelessness. Thrusting from it the divine law and completely unmindful of the sacred commandments, wealth, vices, scorn, pride and the empty imagination of earthly pride spring from it. Those who would enter in by the narrow door must withdraw from all these things, be with Christ and keep the festival with him. COMMENTARY ON LUKE, HOMILY 99.[4]

THE FOOD THEY ATE IN THE STREETS. AUGUSTINE: Christ has hidden enemies. All those who live unjust and irreligious lives are Christ's enemies, even if they are signed with his name and are called Christians. I mean the ones to whom he is going to say, "I do not know you," and they say to him, "Lord, in your name we ate and drank. In your name, we performed many deeds of power. What did we eat and drink in your name?" You see that they did not value their food very highly, and yet it was with reference to it that they said they belonged to Christ. Christ is the food that is eaten and drunk. Even Christ's enemies eat and drink him. The faithful know the Lamb without spot on which they feed, if only they fed on it in such a way that they are not liable to punishment! The

apostle says, "Whoever eats and drinks unworthily is eating and drinking judgment upon himself."[5] SERMON 308A.6.[6]

ENTERING THE NARROW GATE. CYRIL OF ALEXANDRIA: You may count certain others among those able to say to the judge of all, "We have eaten and drunk in your presence, and you have taught in our streets." Who again are these? Many have believed in Christ and have celebrated the holy festivals in his honor. Frequenting the churches, they also hear the doctrines of the gospel, but they remember absolutely nothing of the truths of Scripture. With difficulty, they bring with them the practice of virtue, while their heart is quite bare of spiritual fruitfulness. These will also weep bitterly and grind their teeth, because the Lord will also deny them. He said, "Not everyone that says to me, 'Lord, Lord,' shall enter into the kingdom of heaven, but he that does the will of my Father who is in heaven."[7] COMMENTARY ON LUKE, HOMILY 99.[8]

FROM ALL CORNERS OF THE WORLD. AUGUSTINE: The shepherds came from nearby to see, and the magi came from far away to worship. This is the humility for which the wild olive deserved to be grafted into the olive tree and against nature to produce olives. It deserved to change nature through grace. They come from the farthest parts of the earth, saying according to Jeremiah, "Truly our fathers worshiped lies."[9] They come, not just from one part of the world, but as the Gospel according to Luke says, "from east and west, from north and south, to sit down with Abraham and Isaac and Jacob in the kingdom of heaven." SERMON 203.3.[10]

13:30 The Surprising Reversal

THE GENTILES FIRST IN THE KINGDOM. CYRIL OF ALEXANDRIA: He showed that the Jews

---

[3]CGSL 397**. [4]CGSL 397**. [5]1 Cor 11:29. [6]WSA 3 9:59**. [7]Mt 7:21. [8]CGSL 398**. [9]Jer 16:19. [10]WSA 3 6:96*.

were about to fall from their rank of being in a spiritual sense his household and that the multitude of the Gentiles should enter in their place. He said that many who received the call would come from the east, west, north and south. They

will rest with the saints. COMMENTARY ON LUKE, HOMILY 99.[11]

---

[11]CGSL 398-99*.

13:31-35 JESUS' PROPHETIC DESTINY IN JERUSALEM

[31]At that very hour some Pharisees came, and said to him, "Get away from here, for Herod wants to kill you." [32]And he said to them, "Go and tell that fox, 'Behold, I cast out demons and perform cures today and tomorrow, and the third day I finish my course. [33]Nevertheless I must go on my way today and tomorrow and the day following; for it cannot be that a prophet should perish away from Jerusalem.' [34]O Jerusalem, Jerusalem, killing the prophets and stoning those who are sent to you! How often would I have gathered your children together as a hen gathers her brood under her wings, and you would not! [35]Behold, your house is forsaken. And I tell you, you will not see me until you say, 'Blessed is he who comes in the name of the Lord!'"

OVERVIEW: On the surface, the Pharisees seem to be positively inclined toward Jesus when they warn him in strong words to "depart from here and continue on your journey, because Herod wants to kill you." Although they may sound favorably inclined toward Jesus, their heart is full of hate (CYRIL OF ALEXANDRIA). Herod the fox first attempted to thwart this plan with the slaughter of the holy innocents in Bethlehem (AUGUSTINE).

Jesus' ministry is that of releasing those captive in bondage to Satan, sickness and sin, testifying to the gracious presence of God, and pointing to his passion on the cross (CYRIL OF ALEXANDRIA). Jesus' prophetic destiny of rejection, suffering, death and resurrection must take place in Jerusalem, the holy city for whom Jesus patiently waits, the place where God dwells and atonement must take place (EPHREM THE SYRIAN). In Luke's Gospel, the day when Jesus is acclaimed as the blessed Coming One is Palm Sunday, when on

this triumphant day of entrance, Jesus is brought to the brink of reaching his goal (CYRIL OF ALEXANDRIA).

13:31 The Warning of the Pharisees

THE PHARISEES FULL OF HATRED. CYRIL OF ALEXANDRIA: What hour does he mean as that in which the Pharisees said these things to Jesus? He was occupied in teaching the Jewish multitudes, when someone asked him whether there were many that are saved. He, however, passed by the question as unprofitable and turned to what he saw as a suitable topic, namely, the way by which people must walk to become heirs of the kingdom of heaven. He said, "Strive to enter through the narrow gate,"[1] and told them that if they refuse so to do, they will see Abraham and

---

[1]Lk 13:24.

Isaac and Jacob and all the prophets in the kingdom of God, and themselves cast out. He also added that whereas they had been the first, they would be the last at the calling of the heathen. These remarks goaded the mind of the Pharisees to anger. They saw the multitudes already repenting and receiving with eagerness faith in him. They saw that now they needed only a little more instruction to learn his glory and the great and adorable mystery of the incarnation. Likely to lose their office of leaders of the people and already fallen and expelled from their authority over them and deprived of their profits—for they were fond of wealth, and covetous, and given to lucre—they made pretense of loving him, and even drew near, and said, "Get away from here, for Herod wants to kill you." COMMENTARY ON LUKE, HOMILY 100.[2]

13:32-33 Jesus' Response About His Destiny

HEROD THE FOX. AUGUSTINE: The Lord said of Herod, "Go and tell that fox." Because it [the fox] was troubled, what did it do? It slaughtered infants. What did it do? It slaughtered infants in place of the infant Word. They were made martyrs by the shedding of their blood, before they could confess the Lord with their mouths. And these are the first fruits that Christ sent to the Father. An infant came, and infants went. An infant came to us, infants went to God. From the mouths of infants and sucklings you have perfected praise.[3] SERMON 375.1.[4]

THE MIRACLES OF JESUS POINT TO HIS PASSION. CYRIL OF ALEXANDRIA: But what did he tell them to say? "Behold, I cast out demons and perform cures today and tomorrow, and the third day I finish my course." You see that he declares his intention of performing what he knew would grieve the troop of Pharisees. So they drive him from Jerusalem, fearing that by the display of miracles he will win many to faith in himself. But inasmuch as their purpose there did not escape him since he was God, he declares his intention of

performing what they hated and says that he shall also rebuke unclean spirits and deliver the sick from their sufferings and be perfected. This means that of his own will he will endure the passion on the cross for the salvation of the world. He knew, therefore, as it appears, both how and when he would endure death in the flesh. COMMENTARY ON LUKE, HOMILY 100.[5]

JESUS MUST DIE IN JERUSALEM. EPHREM THE SYRIAN: It was prophetic that Moses had given [the Israelites] the order to offer their sacrifices in one single place[6]—there to offer the lamb in sacrifice and [there] to accomplish an image of the redemption. Herod did not kill [the Lord] with the infants of Bethlehem,[7] nor did the Nazarenes when they hurled him down from the mountain,[8] since it was not possible for him to die outside of Jerusalem. For it cannot be that a prophet should perish outside of Jerusalem. Take note that although it was Jerusalem that killed him, nevertheless Herod and Nazareth were united with regard to his death, and vengeance will be required of both for his death. Learn also from this that not only will vengeance for his blood be required of the inhabitants of Jerusalem, but also everyone who saw and denied him will be convicted for having killed him. In saying "between the sanctuary and the altar,"[9] he has indeed shown their perversity, in that they did not respect even the place of atonement. The words, "How often would I have gathered your children together," are similar to these, "See, these three years I have come, seeking fruit on this fig tree, and I find none."[10] COMMENTARY ON TATIAN'S DIATESSARON 18.10.[11]

13:34-35 Jesus' Lament over Jerusalem

JERUSALEM REJECTED THOSE WHO SPEAK FOR GOD. CYRIL OF ALEXANDRIA: He shows that Jerusalem is guilty of the blood of many

---

[2]CGSL 401*. [3]Ps 8:2. [4]WSA 3 10:328. [5]CGSL 402. [6]Deut 12:2-18. [7]Mt 2:13-18. [8]Lk 4:29-30. [9]Mt 23:35. [10]Lk 13:7. [11]ECTD 275-76**.

saints, declaring that it is not possible for a prophet to perish away from it. From this it follows that its people were about to fall from being members of God's spiritual family, that they were about to be rejected from the hope of the saints and entirely deprived of the inheritance of those blessings which are in store for those who have been saved by faith. He showed them that they were forgetful of God's gifts, and stubborn, and slothful to everything that might have profited them, saying, "O Jerusalem, Jerusalem, killing the prophets and stoning those who are sent to you! How often would I have gathered your children together as a hen gathers her brood under her wings, and you would not! Behold, your house is forsaken." He taught them through the most wise Moses, and ordained for them the law to direct them in their conduct, and to be their ruler and guide in a life worthy of admiration. Though this law was but as yet in shadows, it nevertheless possessed the type of the true worship. He admonished them by the holy prophets. He would have had them under his wings, that is, under the protection of his power, but they lost the valuable blessings by being disposed to evil, ungrateful and scornful. COMMENTARY ON LUKE, Homily 100.[12]

JESUS FORESHADOWS HIS TRIUMPHANT ENTRANCE. CYRIL OF ALEXANDRIA: "And I tell you," he says, "you will not see me until you say, 'Blessed is he that comes in the name of the Lord.'" What does this mean? The Lord withdrew from Jerusalem and left as unworthy of his presence those who said, "Get away from here." And after he had walked about Judea and saved many and performed miracles which no words can adequately describe, he returned again to Jerusalem. It was then that he sat upon a colt of a donkey, while vast multitudes and young children, holding up branches of palm trees, went before him, praising him and saying, "Hosanna to the Son of David. Blessed is he who comes in the name of the Lord."[13] Having left them, therefore, as being unworthy, he says that when the time of his passion has arrived, he will then barely be seen by them. Then again he went up to Jerusalem and entered amidst praises, and at that very time endured his saving passion in our behalf, that by suffering he might save and renew to incorruption the inhabitants of the earth. God the Father has saved us by Christ. COMMENTARY ON LUKE, Homily 100.[14]

---

[12]CGSL 402-3**. [13]Mt 21:9. [14]CGSL 403**.

14:1-24 SABBATH HEALING, MEAL ETIQUETTE AND THE BANQUET PARABLE

[1]*One sabbath when he went to dine at the house of a ruler who belonged to the Pharisees, they were watching him.* [2]*And behold, there was a man before him who had dropsy.* [3]*And Jesus spoke to the lawyers and Pharisees, saying, "Is it lawful to heal on the sabbath, or not?"* [4]*But they were silent. Then he took him and healed him, and let him go.* [5]*And he said to them, "Which of you, having a son[s] or an ox that has fallen into a well, will not immediately pull him out on a sabbath day?"* [6]*And they could not reply to this.*

⁷*Now he told a parable to those who were invited, when he marked how they chose the places of honor, saying to them,* ⁸*"When you are invited by any one to a marriage feast, do not sit down in a place of honor, lest a more eminent man than you be invited by him;* ⁹*and he who invited you both will come and say to you, 'Give place to this man,' and then you will begin with shame to take the lowest place.* ¹⁰*But when you are invited, go and sit in the lowest place, so that when your host comes he may say to you, 'Friend, go up higher'; then you will be honored in the presence of all who sit at table with you.* ¹¹*For every one who exalts himself will be humbled, and he who humbles himself will be exalted."*

¹²*He said also to the man who had invited him, "When you give a dinner or a banquet, do not invite your friends or your brothers or your kinsmen or rich neighbors, lest they also invite you in return, and you be repaid.* ¹³*But when you give a feast, invite the poor, the maimed, the lame, the blind,* ¹⁴*and you will be blessed, because they cannot repay you. You will be repaid at the resurrection of the just."*

¹⁵*When one of those who sat at table with him heard this, he said to him, "Blessed is he who shall eat bread in the kingdom of God!"* ¹⁶*But he said to him, "A man once gave a great banquet, and invited many;* ¹⁷*and at the time for the banquet he sent his servant to say to those who had been invited, 'Come; for all is now ready.'* ¹⁸*But they all alike began to make excuses. The first said to him, 'I have bought a field, and I must go out and see it; I pray you, have me excused.'* ¹⁹*And another said, 'I have bought five yoke of oxen, and I go to examine them; I pray you, have me excused.'* ²⁰*And another said, 'I have married a wife, and therefore I cannot come.'* ²¹*So the servant came and reported this to his master. Then the householder in anger said to his servant, 'Go out quickly to the streets and lanes of the city, and bring in the poor and maimed and blind and lame.'* ²²*And the servant said, 'Sir, what you commanded has been done, and still there is room.'* ²³*And the master said to the servant, 'Go out to the highways and hedges, and compel people to come in, that my house may be filled.* ²⁴*For I tell you,ᵃ none of those men who were invited shall taste my banquet.'"*

s Other ancient authorities read *an ass*   a The Greek word for *you* here is plural

---

OVERVIEW: Jesus is invited by a local dignitary to "eat bread" at the festive sabbath evening Seder, where he performs a miracle and directs teaching for the benefit of the host and invited guests since they are Pharisees (AMBROSE). The sabbath is an occasion for controversy with the Pharisees or religious authorities, because they do not understand that to keep the sabbath is to offer oneself up to God in a holy and virtuous life that is a spiritual sacrifice pleasing to God. The controversy with the Pharisees and their careful observation of Jesus at the table during the sabbath accent the essence of the sabbath laws that never forbid showing mercy and kindness to those who were in need (CYRIL OF ALEXANDRIA).

Jesus' instructions to his guests at the table are about humility, a gift that he bestows on his followers. He is calling the Pharisees to imitate him in a life that is modest and praiseworthy, and not to be seekers of vainglory as they are demonstrating at this banquet (CYRIL OF ALEXANDRIA). Jesus is making a clear distinction between those who are humble and those who are proud (AUGUSTINE). Jacob's ladder of ascent and descent represents this way of life through which we are exalted or humbled (BENEDICT).

Jesus indicates that table fellowship with out-casts brings a state of blessedness now because they cannot repay and that one's reward will be at the end-time banquet when the poor will sit at table on the true sabbath of the just (IRENAEUS). Humility is a mark of the messianic age in the teaching of Jesus, a humility marked by the confession of sins (AUGUSTINE). Jesus responds to the statement of an unbaptized man by the parable that illustrates the nature of the kingdom of heaven (CYRIL OF ALEXANDRIA). Jesus is calling us to the *agape* feast of the heavenly food of his Word (CLEMENT OF ALEXANDRIA). Those invited to eat bread in the kingdom of God are the pure and spotless (ATHANASIUS).

In the banquet parable the man who gives the supper is God the Father, which he gives on behalf of his Son, Jesus Christ, who is sacrificed as the Lamb at evening. The slave who is sent is none other than Christ, who appears in the form of a slave, although he is the very Son of God. The invitation to come to the supper is a signal that in Christ the gifts of the kingdom have been prepared for everybody. After this glorious announcement, the parable deals with three different persons who offer excuses as to why they cannot attend the feast because they are focused on earthly matters and not on spiritual ones (CYRIL OF ALEXANDRIA).

When the slave reports this rejection by the invited guests, the Lord of the house commands his slave to go out into the highways and byways of the city to bring in the poor, disabled, blind and lame who represent the Jewish people apart from religious establishment (CYRIL OF ALEXANDRIA). When the slave reports to his Lord that there is room even after inviting these outcasts, his Lord sends him outside the city, that is, outside Israel to Gentiles (AMBROSE). Jesus' desire to reach all nations is fulfilled by this invitation to the Gentiles (CYRIL OF ALEXANDRIA).

14:1-6 Sabbath Healing

A HEALING, A MEAL AND TABLE HOSPITAL-

ITY. AMBROSE: First, Christ cures the man with dropsy. The abundant flow of the flesh had oppressed the functions of his soul and had quenched the glow of his spirit. Then, Christ teaches humility. At the feast, Christ gently opposes the longing for a better seat, so that the humanity of persuasion excludes the harshness of coercion, reason promotes the effect of persuasion, and correction chastises pride. He joins humanity to this, as if at the next threshold. The boundaries of the Lord's saying differentiated this, if it is conferred on the poor and the weak. There is a greedy disposition in those who would be rewarded for hospitality. EXPOSITION OF THE GOSPEL OF LUKE 7.195.[1]

FOR THE BENEFIT OF THE PHARISEES. CYRIL OF ALEXANDRIA: A Pharisee, of higher rank than usual, invited Jesus to a banquet. Although he knew their bad intentions, he went with him and ate in their company. He did not submit to this act of condescension to honor his host. He rather instructed his fellow guests by words and miraculous deeds that might lead them to the acknowledgment of the true service, even that taught us by the gospel. He knew that even against their will he would make them eyewitnesses of his power and his suprahuman glory. Perhaps they might believe that he is God and the Son of God, who took on our likeness but was unchanged and did not cease to be what he had been. COMMENTARY ON LUKE, HOMILY 101.[2]

PHARISEES DO NOT KNOW HOW TO KEEP THE SABBATH. CYRIL OF ALEXANDRIA: He became the guest of his host to fulfill a duty. It says, "They watched him." Why did they watch him? They watched to see if he would disregard the honor of the law and so do something forbidden on the sabbath day. O senseless Jew, understand that the law was a shadow and type, waiting for the truth. The truth was Christ and his commandments. Why then do you arm the type against the

---

[1]EHG 311-12**. [2]CGSL 407**.

truth? Why set the shadow in array against the spiritual interpretation? Keep your sabbath rationally.... Those who had the office to minister among you according to the law used to offer God the appointed sacrifices, even on the sabbath. They slaughtered the victims in the temple and performed the acts of service that were required of them. No one rebuked them, and the law itself was silent. It did not forbid people ministering on the sabbath. This was a type for us. As I said, it is our duty, keeping the sabbath in a rational manner, to please God by a sweet spiritual fragrance. As I have already said, we perform this when ceasing from sins, we offer God a life holy and worthy of admiration as a sacred oblation, steadily advancing to all virtue. This is the spiritual sacrifice well pleasing to God. COMMENTARY ON LUKE, HOMILY 101.[3]

THE LAW DOES NOT FORBID MERCY ON THE SABBATH. CYRIL OF ALEXANDRIA: As they were silent from ill will, Christ refutes their unrelenting shamelessness by the convincing arguments that he uses. "Whose son of you," he says, "or whose ox shall fall into a pit, and he will not immediately draw him out on the sabbath day?" If the law forbids showing mercy on the sabbath, why do you take compassion on that which has fallen into the pit? ... The God of all does not cease to be kind. He is good and loving to people. COMMENTARY ON LUKE, HOMILY 101.[4]

14:7-14 First and Last at the Banquet Table

JESUS CALLS US TO BE HUMBLE, MODEST AND PRAISEWORTHY. CYRIL OF ALEXANDRIA: "When," he says, "a man more honorable than you comes, he that invited you and him will say, 'Provide a place for this man.'" Oh, what great shame is there in having to do this! It is like a theft, so to speak, and the restitution of the stolen goods. He must restore what he has seized because he had no right to take it. The modest and praiseworthy person, who without fear of blame might have claimed the dignity of sitting among the foremost, does not seek it. He yields to others what might be called his own, that he may not even seem to be overcome by empty pride. Such a one shall receive honor as his due. He says, "He shall hear him who invited him say, 'Come up here.'" ...

If any one among you wants to be set above others, let him win it by the decree of heaven and be crowned by those honors that God bestows. Let him surpass the many by having the testimony of glorious virtues. The rule of virtue is a lowly mind that does not love boasting. It is humility. The blessed Paul also counted this worthy of all esteem. He writes to those who eagerly desire saintly pursuits, "Love humility." COMMENTARY ON LUKE, HOMILY 102.[5]

THE HUMBLE AND THE PROUD. AUGUSTINE: There are humble religious, and there are proud religious. The proud ones should not promise themselves the kingdom of God. The place to which dedicated chastity leads is certainly higher, but the one who exalts himself will be humbled. Why seek the higher place with an appetite for the heights, when you can make it simply by holding on to lowliness? If you exalt yourself, God throws you down. If you cast yourself down, God lifts you up. One may not add to or subtract from the Lord's pronouncement. SERMON 354.8.[6]

JACOB'S LADDER THE PLACE OF EXALTATION OR HUMILIATION. BENEDICT: The Scripture asserts that "everyone that exalts himself will be humbled, and he that humbles himself will be exalted." ...

If we want to attain to true humility and come quickly to the top of that heavenly ascent to which we can only mount by lowliness in this present life, we must ascend by good works. We must erect the mystical ladder of Jacob, where angels ascending and descending appeared to him. Ascent and descent mean that we go downward when we exalt ourselves and rise when we are humbled. The ladder represents our life in this

---

[3]CGSL 407-8**. [4]CGSL 408-9**. [5]CGSL 411**. [6]WSA 3 10:160-61*.

world, which our Lord erects to heaven when our heart is humbled. The sides of the ladder represent our soul and body, sides between which God has placed several rungs of humility and discipline, whereby we are to ascend if we would answer his call. RULE OF ST. BENEDICT 7.[7]

THE POOR INVITED TO THE TABLE. IRENAEUS: Where are the hundredfold rewards in this age for the dinners offered to the poor? These things will be during the times of the kingdom, on the seventh day that is sanctified when God rested from all his works that he made. This is the true sabbath of the just, in which they will have no earthly work to do, but will have a table prepared before them by God, who will feed them with all kinds of delicacies. AGAINST HERESIES 5.33.2.[8]

14:15-24 The Banquet Beatitude and Story

WHY JESUS TOLD THE PARABLE. CYRIL OF ALEXANDRIA: One of those who were sitting at the table with them said, "Blessed is he that shall eat bread in the kingdom of God." Probably this man was not yet spiritual but earthly, and not able to understand correctly what Christ spoke. He was not one of those who believed, nor had he been baptized. He supposed that the rewards of the saints for their mutual labors of love would be in things pertaining to the body. Since they were too dull in heart to comprehend a precise idea, Christ outlines for them a parable that explains the nature of the era about to be instituted for their sakes. COMMENTARY ON LUKE, HOMILY 104.[9]

THE HEAVENLY FOOD OF JESUS' WORD. CLEMENT OF ALEXANDRIA: The holy *agape* is the sublime and saving creation of the Lord. . . .

An *agape* is in reality heavenly food, a banquet of the Word. The *agape*, or love, "bears all things, endures all things, hopes all things. Love never fails."[10] "Blessed is he who eats bread in the kingdom of God." The most unlikely of all downfalls is charity that does not fail[11] to be thrown down

from heaven to earth among all these dainty seasonings. Do you still imagine that I refer to a meal that will be destroyed?[12] "If I distribute my goods to the poor and do not have love," Scripture says, "I am nothing."[13] The whole law and the word depend on this love.[14] If you love the Lord your God and your neighbor,[15] there will be a heavenly feast in heaven. The earthly feast, as we have proved from Scripture, is called a supper. It is permeated with love yet is not identified with it but is an expression of mutual and generous good will. CHRIST THE EDUCATOR 2.1.[16]

THE BREAD OF ETERNAL LIFE. ATHANASIUS: Oh, brothers and sisters, what a banquet that is! How great is the harmony and joy of those who eat at this heavenly table! They enjoy food that produces everlasting life, not that ordinary food which passes right on through the body. Who will be considered worthy to be in that group? Who is so blessed as to be called to and counted worthy of that divine feast? "Blessed is he who will eat bread in your kingdom." Although he has been washed, even a person who has been judged worthy of this heavenly calling and has been sanctified by it can become unclean. How can he become unclean? "Counting as unclean the blood of the covenant by which be was sanctified and despising the Spirit of grace,"[17] he hears the Lord say, "Friend, how did you get in here without wedding garments?"[18] FESTAL LETTER.[19]

GOD THE FATHER PROVIDES THE SUPPER. CYRIL OF ALEXANDRIA: We understand the man to be God the Father. For similes represent the truth but are not the truth itself. The Creator of the universe and the Father of glory made a great supper, a festival for the whole world, in honor of Christ. In the last times of the world and at our world's setting, the Son rose for us. At this time, he suffered death for our sakes and gave us to eat

---

[7]LCC 12:301*. [8]LCC 1:394*. [9]CGSL 418**. [10]1 Cor 13:8. [11]1 Cor 13:8. [12]See 1 Cor 6:13. [13]1 Cor 13:3. [14]Mt 22:40. [15]Mk 12:30-31. [16]FC 23:96-97**. [17]Heb 10:29. [18]Mt 22:12. [19]ARL 122-23*.

his flesh, the bread from heaven that gives life to the world. Toward evening and by the light of torches, the lamb was also sacrificed according to the law of Moses. With good reason, the invitation that is by Christ is called a supper. COMMENTARY ON LUKE, HOMILY 104.[20]

THE SLAVE WHO IS SENT IS CHRIST. CYRIL OF ALEXANDRIA: Next, who is he that was sent? It says he was a slave. Perhaps it is Christ. Although God the Word is by nature God and the very Son of God the Father from whom he was revealed, he emptied himself to take the form of a slave. Being God of God, he is Lord of all. One may justly apply the title of a slave to the limits of his humanity. Although he had taken the form of a slave, he was still Lord as being God. COMMENTARY ON LUKE, HOMILY 104.[21]

TO BESTOW GIFTS ON ALL THE WORLD. CYRIL OF ALEXANDRIA: What was the nature of the invitation? "Come, for look, all things are ready." God the Father has prepared in Christ gifts for the inhabitants of the earth. Through Christ, he bestowed the forgiveness of sins, cleansing away of all defilement, communion of the Holy Spirit, glorious adoption as children, and the kingdom of heaven. To these blessings, Christ invited Israel, before all others, by the commandments of the gospel. Somewhere he has even said by the voice of the psalmist, "But I have been sent as a king by him," that is, by God the Father, "on Zion his holy mountain to preach the commandment of the Lord."[22] COMMENTARY ON LUKE, HOMILY 104.[23]

THOSE MAKING EXCUSES. CYRIL OF ALEXANDRIA: "They began," it says, "all of them at once to make excuse," that is, as with one purpose, without any delay, they made excuse.... By senselessly giving themselves up to these earthly matters, they cannot see things spiritual. Conquered by the love of the flesh, they are far from holiness. They are covetous and greedy after wealth. They seek things that are below but make no account in the slightest degree of the

hopes that are stored up with God. It would be far better to gain the joys of paradise instead of earthly fields and temporary furrows. COMMENTARY ON LUKE, HOMILY 104.[24]

PHARISEES AND SCRIBES REJECT THE INVITATION. CYRIL OF ALEXANDRIA: It says that when the house owner heard their refusal, he was angry and commanded "to gather from the streets and marketplaces of the city the poor, the maimed, the blind, and the lame." Who are they who refused to come because of lands, farming and the physical procreation of children? It must be those who stood at the head of the Jewish synagogue. They were people with wealth, the slaves of covetousness with their mind set on profit on which they lavished all their seriousness. COMMENTARY ON LUKE, HOMILY 104.[25]

GENTILES AND OUTCASTS CALLED FROM THE HIGHWAYS. AMBROSE: He turned to the Gentiles from the careless scorn of the rich. He invites both good and evil to enter in order to strengthen the good and change the disposition of the wicked for the better. The saying that was read today is fulfilled, "Then wolves and lambs will feed together."[26] He summons the poor, the maimed and the blind. By this, he shows us either that handicaps do not exclude us from the kingdom of heaven and whoever lacks the enticements of sinning rarely offends, or that the Lord's mercy forgives the weakness of sinners. Whoever glories in the Lord[27] glories as one redeemed from reproach not by works but by faith.[28]

He sends them into the highways,[29] because wisdom sings aloud in passages.[30] He sends them to the streets, because he sent them to sinners, so that they should come from the broad paths to the narrow way that leads to life.[31] He sends them to the highways and hedges. They, who are not busied with any desires for present things, hurry

---

[20]CGSL 418**. [21]CGSL 418**. [22]Ps 2:6. [23]CGSL 418-19**. [24]CGSL 419**. [25]CGSL 419**. [26]Is 65:25. [27]See Jer 9:23-24; 1 Cor 1:31; 2 Cor 10:17. [28]See Rom 9:32. [29]Mt 22:9. [30]Prov 1:20. [31]Mt 7:13-14.

to the future on the path of good will. Like a hedge that separates the wild from the cultivated and wards off the attacks of wild beasts, they can distinguish between good and evil and extend a rampart of faith against the temptations of spiritual wickedness.[32] EXPOSITION OF THE GOSPEL OF LUKE 7.202-3.[33]

THE INVITATION TO THE GENTILES. CYRIL OF ALEXANDRIA: The leaders of the Israelites re-mained aloof from the supper, as being obstinate, proud and disobedient. They scorned a surpassing invitation, because they had turned aside to earthly things and focused their mind on the vain distractions of this world. The common crowd was invited, and immediately after them the Gentiles. COMMENTARY ON LUKE, HOMILY 104.[34]

---

[32]See Eph 6:12. [33]EHG 313-14**. [34]CGSL 420**.

14:25-35 THE CONDITIONS OF DISCIPLESHIP

[25]*Now great multitudes accompanied him; and he turned and said to them,* [26]*"If any one comes to me and does not hate his own father and mother and wife and children and brothers and sisters, yes, and even his own life, he cannot be my disciple.* [27]*Whoever does not bear his own cross and come after me, cannot be my disciple.* [28]*For which of you, desiring to build a tower, does not first sit down and count the cost, whether he has enough to complete it?* [29]*Otherwise, when he has laid a foundation, and is not able to finish, all who see it begin to mock him,* [30]*saying, 'This man began to build, and was not able to finish.'* [31]*Or what king, going to encounter another king in war, will not sit down first and take counsel whether he is able with ten thousand to meet him who comes against him with twenty thousand?* [32]*And if not, while the other is yet a great way off, he sends an embassy and asks terms of peace.* [33]*So therefore, whoever of you does not renounce all that he has cannot be my disciple.*

[34]*"Salt is good; but if salt has lost its taste, how shall its saltness be restored?* [35]*It is fit neither for the land nor for the dunghill; men throw it away. He who has ears to hear, let him hear."*

OVERVIEW: There is a great paradox here. On the one hand we are to love our enemies, but on the other, we are to hate our families insofar as they are an obstacle to eternal life (AUGUSTINE). Jesus is not saying that we cannot love our family, but we dare not love them more than we love him (CYRIL OF ALEXANDRIA). At the same time, we cannot let our natural mother and our affections for her supersede our love for holy mother church, which nourishes us with food that lasts for eternity (AUGUSTINE). What Jesus is calling us to is to be crucified, to die and be buried with him in baptism (BASIL THE GREAT).

The apostles serve as examples of those who have left everything behind to carry the cross (TERTULLIAN). The cross comes at the end of the list of the costs of discipleship. Death for Christ is the final trial to be endured by Jesus' disciples (SYMEON THE NEW THEOLOGIAN). Both parables teach that to be a disciple of Jesus requires invincible fortitude and unwavering zeal (CYRIL OF ALEXANDRIA). On Christ, the foundation of the tower, virtue is built and produced in the life of the Christian (GREGORY OF NYSSA).

This leads to the final requirement of discipleship and the other purpose of the parables: renouncing possessions. The citizenship of those who follow Christ is in heaven (BASIL THE GREAT). Like the savor of the Word of God, let there be salt in your life to bring salvation (CYRIL OF ALEXANDRIA). The seriousness of the discipleship requirements is summed up by Jesus' final words: "The one having ears to hear, let him hear" (ORIGEN).

14:25-27 Hating Family and Carrying the Cross

THE PARADOX OF LOVING ENEMIES AND HATING ONE'S OWN FAMILY. AUGUSTINE: On another occasion, the Lord says, "Whoever comes to me and does not hate his father and mother, and wife and children, and brothers and sisters, and even his own soul, cannot be my disciple." As a rule, this is more upsetting to the mind of new Christians who are eager to begin at once to live in accordance with the precepts of Christ. To those who do not fully grasp its meaning, it would seem contradictory. . . . He has condescended to call his disciples to the eternal kingdom. He also called them brothers. In the kingdom these relationships are transcended, because "there is neither Jew nor Greek, neither male nor female, neither slave nor freeman, but Christ is all things and in all."[1] The Lord says, "For in the resurrection they will neither be married nor marry, but will be as the angels of God in heaven."[2] Whoever wishes to prepare himself now for the life of that kingdom must not hate people but those earthly relationships through which the present life is sustained, the temporary life that begins at birth and ends with death. Whoever does not hate this necessity does not yet love that other life in which there will be no condition of birth and death, the condition that makes marriages natural on earth. SERMON ON THE MOUNT 15.[3]

JESUS PERMITS US TO LOVE FAMILY BUT NOT MORE THAN GOD. CYRIL OF ALEXANDRIA: He says, "He that loves father or mother more than me is not worthy of me. He that loves son or daughter more than me is not worthy of me."[4] By adding "more than me," it is plain that he permits us to love, but not more than we love him. He demands our highest affection for himself and that very correctly. The love of God in those who are perfect in mind has something in it superior both to the honor due to parents and to the natural affection felt for children. COMMENTARY ON LUKE, HOMILY 105.[5]

THE CHURCH IS THE HOLY MOTHER OF YOUR NATURAL MOTHER. AUGUSTINE: The Lord gives the signal for us to stand guard in camp and to build the tower from which we may recognize and ward off the enemy of our eternal life. The heavenly trumpet of Christ urges the soldier to battle, and his mother holds him back. . . .

What does she say or what argument does she give? Perhaps is it those ten months when you lay in her womb and the pangs of birth and the burden of rearing you? You must kill this with the sword of salvation. You must destroy this in your mother that you may find her in life eternal. Remember, you must hate this in her if you love her, if you are a recruit of Christ and have laid the foundations of the tower. Passers by may not say, "This man began to build and was not able to finish." That is earthly affection. It still has the ring of the "old man."[6] Christian warfare invites us to destroy this earthly affection both in ourselves and in our relatives. Of course, no one should be ungrateful to his parents or mock the list of their services to him, since by them he was brought into this life, cherished and fed. A man should always pay his family duty, but let these things keep their place where higher duties do not call.

Mother church is also the mother of your mother. She conceived you both in Christ. . . .

---

[1]Gal 3:28; Col 3:11 [2]Mt 22:30. [3]FC 11:60-61**. [4]Mt 10:37. [5]CGSL 421-22**. [6]Eph 4:22; Col 3:9; Rom 6:6.

Know that her Spouse took human flesh that you might not be attached to fleshly things. Know that all the things for which your mother scolds you were undertaken by the eternal Word that you might not be subject to the weakness of flesh. Ponder his humiliations, scourging and death, even the death of the cross.[7] LETTER 243.[8]

TO BE A DISCIPLE OF JESUS. BASIL THE GREAT: The Father did not send the only-begotten Son, the living God, to judge the world but to save the world.[9] True to himself and faithful to the will of the good God his Father, he points to a doctrine whereby we may be made worthy of becoming his disciples with his severe decree. He says, "If any man comes to me and does not hate his father and mother, and his wife and children and brothers and sisters, yes, and his own life also, he cannot be my disciple." This hatred teaches the virtue of piety by withdrawing us from distractions and does not lead us to devise hurtful schemes against one another. "Whoever," says the Lord, "does not carry his cross and come after me, cannot be my disciple." Receiving the baptism of water, we make this same agreement when we promise to be crucified and to die and to be buried with him.[10] CONCERNING BAPTISM 1.1.[11]

THE APOSTLES LEFT EVERYTHING. TERTULLIAN: If you want to be the Lord's disciple, you must take up your cross and follow the Lord. Take up your stress and your tortures or at least your body, which is like a cross. Parents, wives, children are all to be left for God's sake. Are you hesitating about crafts, businesses and professions for the sake of children or parents? The proof that family as well as crafts and business are to be left for the Lord's sake was given us when James and John were called by the Lord and left both father and ship. It was given when Matthew was roused from the seat of custom and when faith allowed no time even to bury a father. ON IDOLATRY 12.[12]

THE FORM OF MARTYRDOM AMID CIVIL

PEACE IS THE DEATH OF SELF-WILL. SYMEON THE NEW THEOLOGIAN: I heard his holy voice speaking to all without distinction. "He who does not leave father and mother and brothers and all that he possesses and take up his cross and follow me is not worthy of me." I learned from Scripture and from experience itself that the cross comes at the end for no other reason than that we must endure trials and tribulations and finally voluntary death itself. In times past, when heresies prevailed, many chose death through martyrdom and various tortures. Now, when we through the grace of Christ live in a time of profound and perfect peace, we learn for sure that cross and death consist in nothing else than the complete putting to death of self-will. He who pursues his own will, however slightly, will never be able to observe the law of Christ the Savior. DISCOURSES 20.1.[13]

14:28-32 The Parables of the Tower and the King Preparing for War

THE PARABLES TEACH FORTITUDE AND ZEAL. CYRIL OF ALEXANDRIA: Next he uses two examples to encourage his friends to an unconquerable strength and to establish those who want to attain to honors by patience and endurance in an unwavering zeal. If anyone wants to build a tower, he first counts if he has sufficient means to finish it. Otherwise when he has laid the foundation and is not able to finish it, people will laugh at him. Those who choose to lead a glorious and blameless life should store up beforehand in their mind a sufficient zeal. They should remember him who says, "My son, if you come close to serve the Lord, prepare yourself for every temptation. Make your heart straight and endure."[14] How will those who do not have this zeal be able to reach the goal that is set before them?

"Or what king," he says, "wishing to make war

---

[7]Mt 20:19; Mk 10:34; Lk 18:32-33; Jn 19:1-3; Phil 2:8. [8]FC 32:223-24**. [9]Jn 12:47. [10]Rom 6:4-11. [11]FC 9:346-47**. [12]LCC 5:96*. [13]SNTD 232**. [14]Sir 2:1.

with another king, does not consider with himself, whether with his ten thousand he can prevail over one who is more mighty than himself?" What does this mean? "We do not wrestle against blood and flesh, but against governments, empires, the world rulers of this present darkness, and wicked spirits in the heavenly regions."[15] We also have a crowd of other enemies. They are the fleshly mind, the law that rages in our members, passions of many kinds, the lust of pleasure, the lust of the flesh, the lust of wealth, and others. We must wrestle with these. This is our savage troop of enemies. How will we conquer? "We will conquer believing that in God we shall do courageously," as Scripture says, "and he will bring to nothing those that oppress us."[16] COMMENTARY ON LUKE, HOMILY 105.[17]

VIRTUE BUILT ON THE FOUNDATIONS OF THE TOWER. GREGORY OF NYSSA: The Gospel somewhere says that a person who begins to build a tower but stops with the foundations and never completes it is ridiculous. What do we learn from this parable? We learn that we should work to bring every aspiration to a conclusion, completing the work of God by an elaborate building up of his commandments. One stone does not make a complete tower, nor does one commandment bring the perfection of the soul to its desired measure. It is necessary to both erect the foundation and, as the apostle says, "to lay upon it a foundation of gold and precious stones."[18] That is what the products of the commandments are called by the prophet when he says, "I have loved your commandment more than gold and much precious stone."[19] ON VIRGINITY 18.[20]

14:33 Leaving Possessions Behind

OUR CITIZENSHIP IS IN HEAVEN. BASIL THE GREAT: Whoever would truly be a follower of God must break the bonds of attachment to this life. This is done through complete separation

from and forgetfulness of old habits. It is impossible for us to achieve our goal of pleasing God unless we snatch ourselves away from fleshly ties and worldly society. We are then transported to another world in our manner of living. The apostle said, "But our citizenship is in heaven."[21] The Lord specifically said, "Likewise every one of you that does not renounce all that he possesses cannot be my disciple." THE LONG RULES 5.[22]

14:34-35 The Parable of the Salt

THE TASTY SALT IS THE WORD OF GOD. CYRIL OF ALEXANDRIA: "Salt is good, but if the salt becomes tasteless, with what can it be seasoned? It is cast out," he says. He continues, "Let there be salt in you," that is, the divine words that bring salvation. If we despise these, we become tasteless, foolish and utterly useless. The congregation of the saints must throw out these things, by the gift of mercy and love to them from Christ, the Savior of us all. COMMENTARY ON LUKE, HOMILY 105.[23]

PEOPLE OF GOD ARE THE PRESERVATIVE OF THE WORLD. ORIGEN: People of God are truly the salt of the earth. They preserve the order of the world. Society is held together as long as the salt is uncorrupted. If the salt lost its savor, it is neither suitable for the land or the manure pile. It will be thrown out and trampled underfoot. "He that has ears, let him hear" the meaning of these words. When God gives to the tempter permission to persecute us, then we suffer persecution. When God wishes us to be free from suffering even in the middle of a world that hates us, we enjoy a wonderful peace. We trust in the protection of him who said, "Be of good cheer, I have overcome the world."[24] AGAINST CELSUS 8.70.[25]

[15]Eph 6:12. [16]Ps 59:12 LXX. [17]CGSL 423**. [18]1 Cor 3:12. [19]Ps 118:127 LXX. [20]FC 58:56*. [21]Phil 3:20. [22]FC 9:242-43*. [23]CGSL 423*. [24]Jn 16:33. [25]ANCL 23:553-54*.

15:1-10 THE LOST SHEEP AND THE LOST COIN

[1]Now the tax collectors and sinners were all drawing near to hear him. [2]And the Pharisees and the scribes murmured, saying, "This man receives sinners and eats with them."

[3]So he told them this parable: [4]"What man of you, having a hundred sheep, if he has lost one of them, does not leave the ninety-nine in the wilderness, and go after the one which is lost, until he finds it? [5]And when he has found it, he lays it on his shoulders, rejoicing. [6]And when he comes home, he calls together his friends and his neighbors, saying to them, 'Rejoice with me, for I have found my sheep which was lost.' [7]Just so, I tell you, there will be more joy in heaven over one sinner who repents than over ninety-nine righteous persons who need no repentance.

[8]"Or what woman, having ten silver coins,[t] if she loses one coin, does not light a lamp and sweep the house and seek diligently until she finds it? [9]And when she has found it, she calls together her friends and neighbors, saying, 'Rejoice with me, for I have found the coin which I had lost.' [10]Just so, I tell you, there is joy before the angels of God over one sinner who repents."

t The drachma, rendered here by *silver coin*, was about a day's wage for a laborer

OVERVIEW: The Pharisees and scribes were grumbling because they would not accept that Jesus became human so that he might save publicans and sinners (CYRIL OF ALEXANDRIA). They were imitating the behavior of the Israelites in the desert. The two parables are written to heal our wounds, for they represent the divine remedy that comes from the Trinity, the father representing God the Father, the shepherd Christ, and the woman the church (AMBROSE). The shepherd shows the virtue of patience by searching for the sheep, just as the father waits patiently for his prodigal son to come home (TERTULLIAN). He must carry it back to the village, yet he rejoices. The shoulders of the shepherd are the arms of the cross bearing the burden of restoration (AMBROSE). From the harsh realities of the wilderness the sheep is restored on the shoulders of the shepherd to lush meadows of living waters (PRUDENTIUS). The good Shepherd restores the sheep from his wandering, but it is the Father who receives him back with feasting (BASIL THE GREAT).

The parable of the lost coin emphasizes the same themes as the parable of the lost sheep. The lost coin that is found is faith restored and the redemption of the soul (AMBROSE). There is joy over the restoration of a fallen sinner who was made in God's image and is now returned to church that celebrates a feast (CYRIL OF ALEXANDRIA). All of heaven rejoices over the conversion of a sinner. The Father bestows upon all the baptized the gifts of the kingdom. We are the sheep of the shepherd, the precious coin with the imprint of the King, and the son for whom he has prepared his banquet (AMBROSE).

15:1-2 Jesus Welcomes Sinners

TO SAVE PUBLICANS AND SINNERS. CYRIL OF ALEXANDRIA: Tell me, O Pharisee, why do you grumble because Christ did not scorn to be with publicans and sinners, but purposely provided for them this means of salvation? To save people, he yielded himself to emptiness, became like us, and clothed himself in human poverty. COMMENTARY ON LUKE, HOMILY 106.[1]

---

[1]CGSL 427-28*.

15:3-10 *The Parables of the Lost Sheep and the Lost Coin*

Three Parables Represent the Trinity.
Ambrose: St. Luke did not idly present three parables in a row. By the parables of the sheep that strayed and was found, the coin which was lost and was found, and the son who was dead and came to life,[2] we may cure our wounds, being encouraged by a threefold remedy. "A threefold cord will not be broken."[3] Who are the father,[4] the shepherd and the woman? They are God the Father, Christ and the church. Christ carries you on his body, he who took your sins on himself. The church seeks, and the Father receives. The shepherd carries. The mother searches. The father clothes.[5] First mercy comes, then intercession, and third reconciliation. Each complements the other. The Savior rescues, the church intercedes, and the Creator reconciles. The mercy of the divine act is the same, but the grace differs according to our merits. The weary sheep is recalled by the shepherd, the coin which was lost is found, the son retraces his steps to his father and returns, guilty of error but totally repentant.[6] Exposition of the Gospel of Luke 7.207-8.[7]

The Lord's Patience for the Lost. Tertullian: There is a breadth of patience in our Lord's parables, the patience of the shepherd that makes him seek and find the straying sheep. Impatience would readily take no account of a single sheep, but patience undertakes the wearisome search. He carries it on his shoulders as a patient bearer of a forsaken sinner. In the case of the prodigal son, it is the patience of his father that welcomes, clothes, feeds and finds an excuse for him in the face of the impatience of his angry brother. The one who perished is rescued, because he embraced repentance. Repentance is not wasted because it meets up with patience! On Patience 12.[8]

Resting in the Arms of the Cross on the Shoulders of Christ. Ambrose: Let us rejoice that the sheep that had strayed in Adam is lifted on Christ. The shoulders of Christ are the arms of the cross. There, I laid down my sins. I rested on the neck of that noble yoke. The sheep is one in kind, not in appearance, because "we are all one body"[9] but many members. It is written, "You are the body of Christ, and members individually."[10] "The Son of man came to seek and save what was lost."[11] He sought all, because "as in Adam all men die, so also in Christ shall all be made alive."[12] Exposition of the Gospel of Luke 7.209.[13]

The Sheep Restored to Verdant Fields.
Prudentius:

When one ailing sheep lags behind the others
And loses itself in the sylvan mazes,
Tearing its white fleece on the thorns and
   briers,
   Sharp in the brambles,
Unwearied the Shepherd, that lost one
   seeking,
Drives away the wolves and on his strong
   shoulders
Brings it home again to the fold's safekeeping,
   Healed and unsullied.
He brings it back to the green fields and
   meadows,[14]
Where no thorn bush waves with its cruel
   prickles,
Where no shaggy thistle arms trembling
   branches
   With its tough briars.
But where palm trees grow in the open
   woodland,
Where the lush grass bends its green leaves,
   and laurels
Shade the glassy streamlet of living water
   Ceaselessly flowing.
Hymn for Every Day 8.33-45.[15]

---

[2]Lk 15:24. [3]Eccles 4:12. [4]Lk 15:11-12. [5]Lk 15:22. [6]Lk 15:20-21. [7]*EHG* 315-16**. [8]FC 40:214-15*. [9]1 Cor 10:17. [10]1 Cor 12:27. [11]Lk 19:10; cf. Ezek 34:16. [12]1 Cor 15:22. [13]*EHG* 316*. [14]Ps 23:2 (22:2 LXX). [15]FC 43:57.

THE GOOD SHEPHERD RESTORES THE SHEEP.
BASIL THE GREAT: Leaving those that have not strayed, the good Shepherd seeks you. If you will surrender yourself, he will not hold back. In his kindness, he will lift you up on his shoulders, rejoicing that he has found his sheep that was lost. The Father stands and awaits your return from your wandering. Only turn to him, and while you are still afar off, he will run and embrace your neck. With loving embraces, he will enfold you, now cleansed by your repentance. . . . He says, "Truly I say to you that there is joy in heaven before God over one sinner who repents." If any one of those who seem to stand will bring a charge that you have been quickly received, the good Father himself will answer for you. He will say, "It is fitting that we should celebrate and be glad, for this my daughter was dead and is come to life again. She was lost and is found." LETTER 46.[16]

THE LOST COIN IS FAITH. AMBROSE: The price of the soul is faith. Faith is the lost drachma that the woman in the Gospel seeks diligently. We read that she lit a candle and swept her house. After finding it, she calls together her friends and neighbors, inviting them to rejoice with her because she has found the drachma that she had lost. The damage to the soul is great if one has lost the faith or the grace that he has gained for himself at the price of faith. Light your lamp. "Your lamp is your eye,"[17] that is, the interior eye of the soul. Light the lamp that feeds on the oil of the spirit and shines throughout your whole house. Search for the drachma, the redemption of your soul. If a person loses this, he is troubled, and if he finds it, he rejoices. LETTER 20.[18]

JOY OVER THE FALLEN SINNER RESTORED IN GOD'S IMAGE. CYRIL OF ALEXANDRIA: This second parable compares what was lost to a drachma. It is as one out of ten, a perfect number and of a sum complete in the accounting. The number ten also is perfect, being the close of the series from the unit upwards. This parable clearly shows that we are in the royal likeness and image, even that

of God over all. I suppose the drachma is the denarius on which is stamped the royal likeness. We, who had fallen and had been lost, have been found by Christ and transformed by holiness and righteousness into his image. . . .

A search was made for that which had fallen, so the woman lighted a lamp. . . . By the light, what was lost is saved, and there is joy for the powers above. They rejoice even in one sinner that repents, as he who knows all things has taught us. They keep a festival over one who is saved, united with the divine purpose, and never cease to praise the Savior's gentleness. What great joy must fill them when all beneath heaven is saved and Christ calls them by faith to acknowledge the truth? They put off the pollution of sin and freed their necks from the bonds of death. They have escaped from the blame of their wandering and fall! We gain all these things in Christ. COMMENTARY ON LUKE, HOMILY 106.[19]

EACH CONVERSION BRINGS JOY IN HEAVEN.
AMBROSE: The shepherd is rich. We are his hundredth portion. He has innumerable flocks of angels, of archangels, of dominions, of powers, of thrones,[20] of the others whom he left on the mountains. Since these are rational, they fittingly rejoice in the salvation of people. Although this also may be of benefit as an incentive to honesty, if each believes that his conversion would be pleasing to the hosts of angels, whose protection is to be sought and whose displeasure feared. Be a source of joy to the angels. May they rejoice in your return. EXPOSITION OF THE GOSPEL OF LUKE 7.210.[21]

THE FATHER CONFERS ON US THE WEALTH OF THE KINGDOM. AMBROSE: The woman did not idly rejoice to find her coin. The coin, having the image of the emperor, is not ordinary.[22] The image of the King is the register of the church. We are sheep. Let us pray that he would be pleased to

---

[16]FC 13:127-28**. [17]Mt 6:22. [18]FC 26:106*. [19]CGSL 429-30**. [20]Col 1:16. [21]EHG 316-17*. [22]See Mt 22:19-21; Lk 20:24.

place us beside the water of rest.[23] We are sheep. Let us seek pastures. We are coins. Let us have a price. We are sons. Let us hurry to the Father.[24] Let us not fear because we have squandered the inheritance of spiritual dignity that we received on earthly pleasures.[25] Since the Father conferred on the Son the treasure that he had, the wealth of faith is never made void.[26] Although he has given all, he possesses all and does not lose what he has bestowed. Do not fear that perhaps he will not receive you, for the Lord has no pleasure in the destruction of the living.[27] Already meeting you on the way, he falls on your neck, "for the Lord

sets the fallen right."[28] He will give you a kiss, that is, the pledge of piety and love. He will order the robe, ring and the shoes to be brought.[29] You still dread harshness, but he has restored dignity. You are terrified of punishment, but he offers a kiss. You fear reproach, but he prepares a banquet.[30] Let us now discuss the actual parable. EXPOSITION OF THE GOSPEL OF LUKE 7.211-12.[31]

---

[23]Ps 22:2 LXX. [24]See Lk 15:20. [25]See Lk 15:13. [26]See Rom 4:14. [27]Wis 1:13. [28]Ps 145:8 LXX. [29]Lk 15:22. [30]See Lk 15:23. [31]EHG 317**.

15:11-24 THE PRODIGAL SON

[11]And he said, "There was a man who had two sons; [12]and the younger of them said to his father, 'Father, give me the share of property that falls to me.' And he divided his living between them. [13]Not many days later, the younger son gathered all he had and took his journey into a far country, and there he squandered his property in loose living. [14]And when he had spent everything, a great famine arose in that country, and he began to be in want. [15]So he went and joined himself to one of the citizens of that country, who sent him into his fields to feed swine. [16]And he would gladly have fed on[u] the pods that the swine ate; and no one gave him anything. [17]But when he came to himself he said, 'How many of my father's hired servants have bread enough and to spare, but I perish here with hunger! [18]I will arise and go to my father, and I will say to him, "Father, I have sinned against heaven and before you; [19]I am no longer worthy to be called your son; treat me as one of your hired servants."' [20]And he arose and came to his father. But while he was yet at a distance, his father saw him and had compassion, and ran and embraced him and kissed him. [21]And the son said to him, 'Father, I have sinned against heaven and before you; I am no longer worthy to be called your son.'[v] [22]But the father said to his servants, 'Bring quickly the best robe, and put it on him; and put a ring on his hand, and shoes on his feet; [23]and bring the fatted calf and kill it, and let us eat and make merry; [24]for this my son was dead, and is alive again; he was lost, and is found.' And they began to make merry."

u Other ancient authorities read *filled his belly with*   v Other ancient authorities add *treat me as one of your hired servants*

OVERVIEW: This parable calls the Pharisees and scribes who grumbled over Jesus' table fellowship with sinners to rejoice over the repentance and restoration of sinners (CYRIL OF ALEXANDRIA). The identification of the two sons is problematic, with many suggestions offered, including the elder son representing the Jews and the prodigal the Gentiles (CYRIL OF ALEXANDRIA, PETER CHRYSOLOGUS). The younger son deserved to lose the privileges of a son (PETER CHRYSOLOGUS). To leave his father's house is to depart from himself into a far country. It is like leaving the church, separating himself from Christ to go to a land of darkness that will deprive him of his goods (AMBROSE).

To give oneself over to the realm of lustful passion is to be delivered into the kingdom of darkness (AUGUSTINE). The famine he experiences is the famine of God's word, and his hunger comes from not receiving the spiritual nourishment that leads to a full and abundant life. His desperation causes him to attach himself to a citizen of that country who must be a Gentile, since he owns pigs, a man who is the equivalent of the prince of this world (AMBROSE). The irony is that he has traded the splendor of his Father's house for a bed among swine (PETER CHRYSOLOGUS). If that is not bad enough, he is so desperate for food that he begins to desire the food of the pigs, which would be unappetizing and lack nourishment, like the food offered by the devil (AMBROSE).

Despite his sin, the Spirit has not departed from him, and he is still a son who knows the love and mercy of his father (PHILOXENUS OF MABBUG). To return to the father's house is to return to Eden and be reunited with his dear ones (EPHREM THE SYRIAN). This is his first confession in which he seeks reconciliation with the Father (AMBROSE). Following the pattern of the Lord's Prayer, the prodigal confesses that his Father in heaven knows his sins; his confession addresses both his earthly and heavenly father (PETER CHRYSOLOGUS). He is no longer worthy to be called a son, and he is willing to come as a laborer in the vineyard. One is a son through birth, a friend through virtue, a servant through labor and a slave through fear (AMBROSE).

The father initiates the restoration of the son by running to the son, falling on his neck, and giving him the kiss of reconciliation (AMBROSE).

Jesus' description of the father's actions is a portrait of complete and total grace, of unconditional love that comes to us in the Father sending his Son in the incarnation (PETER CHRYSOLOGUS).

The village would see that the son has been restored to the father's house, for he has received the ring of honor and the sandals that restore him to sonship (PETER CHRYSOLOGUS). The father has welcomed back the prodigal to the divine feast as his son (ATHANASIUS). Christ, like the fatted calf, is sacrificed only at the command of the Father to provide for us daily food (PETER CHRYSOLOGUS). Already in the incense offering of Zechariah in the temple the fatted calf is present who will be offered up for the younger son (IRENAEUS). Adam, who was lost in sin, is now found in Christ, and this even applies to the Gentiles, who were dead and are now alive (AMBROSE).

15:11-24 The Prodigal Son and His Merciful Father

THE PARABLE CALLS THE PHARISEES TO REJOICE OVER THE REPENTANCE OF SINNERS. CYRIL OF ALEXANDRIA: What is the object of the parable? Let us examine the occasion that led to it so we will learn the truth. The blessed Luke had said a little before of Christ the Savior of us all.... The Pharisees and scribes made this outcry at his gentleness and love to people. They wickedly and impiously blamed him for receiving and teaching people whose lives were impure. Christ very necessarily set before them the present parable. He clearly shows them that the God of all requires even him who is thoroughly steadfast, firm, holy, and has attained to the highest praise for sobriety of conduct to be earnest in following his will. When any are called to repentance, even if they have a bad reputation, he must rejoice rather and not give way to an unloving irritation because of them. COMMENTARY ON LUKE, HOMILY 107.[1]

IDENTIFYING THE TWO SONS. CYRIL OF ALEX-

---

[1]CGSL 433**.

ANDRIA: It is the opinion of some that the two sons signify the holy angels and us earth dwellers. The elder one, who lived soberly, represents the company of the holy angels, while the younger and prodigal son is the human race. Some among us give it a different explanation, arguing that the older and well-behaved son signifies Israel after the flesh. The other son, who chose to live in the lust of pleasures and moved far away from his father, depicts the company of the Gentiles. COMMENTARY ON LUKE, HOMILY 107.[2]

THE TWO SONS REPRESENT TWO PEOPLES.

PETER CHRYSOLOGUS: "He had two sons," that is, two peoples, the Jews and the Gentiles. Prudent knowledge of the law made the Jewish people his older son, and the folly of paganism made the Gentile world his younger son. Just as surely as wisdom brings distinguished gray hairs, so does foolishness take away the traits of an adult. Morals and not age made the Gentiles the younger son. Not years but understanding of the law made the Jews the older son. SERMON 5.[3]

WHY THE YOUNGER SON DESERVED TO LOSE THE PRIVILEGES OF A SON.

PETER CHRYSOLOGUS: "He divided his means between them." The son is as impatient as the father was kind. He is weary of his father's own life. Since he cannot shorten his father's life, he works to get possession of his property. He was not content to possess his father's wealth in company with his father, and he deserved to lose the privileges of a son.

Let us make some inquiries. What reason brought the son to such actions? What bold prospect raised his spirits to make so startling a request? What reason did he have? Clearly the Father in heaven cannot be bounded by any limit, or shut in by any time, or destroyed by any power of death. The son could not await his father's death to get his wealth, so he conceived the desire to get his pleasure from the generosity of his father while he was still alive. The father's bounty proved that the insult lay in his request. SERMON 1.[4] ,

TO LEAVE THE FATHER IS TO DEPART FROM ONESELF.

AMBROSE: You see that the divine inheritance is given to those who ask. You should not think that the Father was guilty because he gave to the younger son. There is no frail age in the kingdom of God nor is faith weighed down by years. He who made the request surely judged himself worthy. If only he had not departed from his Father, he would not have known the hindrance of age. After he went abroad, he who departed from the church squandered his inheritance. "After," it says, "leaving his home and country, he went abroad into a distant country." What is farther away than to depart from oneself, and not from a place?. . . Surely whoever separates himself from Christ is an exile from his country, a citizen of the world. We are not strangers and pilgrims, but we are "fellow citizens of the saints and of the household of God,"[5] for we who were far away have come near in the blood of Christ.[6] Let us not look down on those who return from a distant land, because we were also in a distant land, as Isaiah teaches. "To them that dwelled in the region of the shadow of death, light has risen."[7] There is a distant region of the shadow of death, but we, for whom the Spirit before our face is Christ the Lord,[8] live in the shadow of Christ. The church therefore says, "Under his shadow I desired and sat down."[9] EXPOSITION OF THE GOSPEL OF LUKE 7.213-14.[10]

CHOOSING THE WASTEFUL REALM OF LUSTFUL PASSION.

AUGUSTINE: That younger son in your Gospel did not help himself with horses, or chariots, or ships, or fly away on visible wings or journey by walking. Through prodigal living in a distant region, he wasted what you, a kind father, had given him as he set out. You were kind in making him this gift, yet kinder still to him when he returned in need. To be in the realm of lustful passion is the same as to be in the realm of darkness, and that is the same as to be far away from

---

[2]CGSL 432**. [3]FC 17:45-46*. [4]FC 17:25-26*. [5]Eph 2:19. [6]Eph 2:13. [7]Is 9:2. [8]See Lam 4:20. [9]Song 2:3. [10]EHG 317-18**.

your face. CONFESSIONS 1.18.[11]

THE PRODIGAL SUFFERS STARVATION.

AMBROSE: "A mighty famine came there in that country." It was not a famine of fasts but of good works and virtues. What hunger is more wretched? Certainly whoever departs from the Word of God hungers, because "man lives not by bread alone but by every word of God."[12] Whoever leaves treasure lacks. Whoever departs from wisdom is stupefied. Whoever departs from virtue is destroyed. It was fitting that he begin to be in need, because he abandoned the treasures of wisdom and the knowledge of God[13] and the depths of heavenly riches. He began to want and to suffer starvation, because nothing is enough for prodigal enjoyment. He who does not know how to be filled with eternal nourishment always suffers starvation. EXPOSITION OF THE GOSPEL OF LUKE 7.215.[14]

THE CITIZEN IS THE PRINCE OF THIS

WORLD. AMBROSE: "He went and attached himself to one of the citizens." Whoever attaches himself is in a snare. That citizen is the prince of this world.[15] He is sent to the farm bought by the man who excused himself from the kingdom.[16] He feeds the swine, those into which the devil sought to enter, those he cast into the sea of the world as they lived in filth and foulness.[17] EXPOSITION OF THE GOSPEL OF LUKE 7.216.[18]

A BED AMONG SWINE.

PETER CHRYSOLOGUS: "He went and joined one of the citizens of that country, who sent him to his farm to feed swine." This is the experience that comes to one who refuses to trust himself to his father but delivers himself to a stranger. He flees from a most generous provider and endures a severe judge. A deserter from affection, a refugee from fatherly love, he is assigned to the swine, sentenced to them, and given over to their service. He wallows in their muddy fodder. The rush of the restless herd bruises and soils him so he perceives how wretched and bitter it is to have lost the happiness of peace-

ful life in his father's house. SERMON 1.[19]

EMPTY OF NOURISHMENT.

AMBROSE: There are those who interpret the swine as being the flocks of demons, the husks as the lack of virtue of worthless people and the boastful words of those who cannot do good. By the empty allure of philosophy and the noisy applause for eloquence,[20] they show ostentation rather than any usefulness. These cannot be lasting pleasures. EXPOSITION OF THE GOSPEL OF LUKE 7.217.[21]

DESPITE HIS SIN, THE SPIRIT DOES NOT DEPART FROM THE SON.

PHILOXENUS OF MABBUG: It was the same with the younger son who squandered his property and wasted his father's property living among prostitutes. Despite all this, he did not lose his honorable title of son. In the land of captivity, having rejected his father, he rather remembered, "How many hired servants are at this moment in my father's house who have more than enough bread, but here am I perishing from hunger." He was still a sinner. He had sinned to such an extent that he had thrown to the winds with his misdeeds the entire inheritance he had received from his father. He still called God his father. This indicates that the grace of the Spirit, which authorizes him to call God Father, did not depart from him.

We are unable to employ this term of address and call God Father, except through the authority of the Holy Spirit who is within us. It is well known that those who have not yet become God's children by the holy rebirth of baptism are not authorized to use this term. They are not permitted to say, "Our Father, who art in heaven, hallowed be thy name." The apparent reason for this is that the Holy Spirit is not yet within them to give them this authorization. It is well known to all that, when they approach the holy mysteries, the newly baptized all repeat this prayer with

---

[11]FC 21:28-29**. [12]Lk 4:4. [13]Col 2:3. [14]EHG 318-19**. [15]See Jn 12:31; 14:30; 16:11. [16]Lk 14:18. [17]See Mt 8:31-32. [18]EHG 319**. [19]FC 17:28**. [20]See Col 2:8. [21]EHG 319*.

confidence in accordance with the tradition handed down by our Lord, and then they proceed to the holy mysteries. ON THE INDWELLING OF THE HOLY SPIRIT 1.[22]

TO RETURN TO THE FATHER'S HOUSE. EPHREM THE SYRIAN:

Jacob led out his sheep
And brought them to his father's home;
A symbol for those with discernment,
A parable for those with perception
Is to be found in this homecoming:
Let us too return to our Father's house,
My brothers, and do not become
    captivated with desire
For this transient earth
    —for your true city is in Eden.
Blessed indeed is that person
Who has seen his dear ones in its midst.
HYMNS ON PARADISE 14.7.[23]

THE FIRST CONFESSION SEEKS RECONCILIATION. AMBROSE: "Father," it says, "I have sinned against heaven, and before you." This is the first confession before the Creator of nature, the Patron of mercy, and the Judge of guilt. Although God knows all things,[24] he awaits the words of your confession. . . . Confess, so that Christ may rather intercede for you, he whom we have as an advocate with the Father.[25] Confess, so that the church may pray for you and that the people may weep for you. Do not fear that perhaps you might not receive. The advocate promises pardon. The patron offers grace. The defender promises the reconciliation with the Father's good will to you. Believe because it is the truth.[26] Consent because it is a virtue. He has a reason to intercede for you, unless he died for you in vain.[27] The Father also has a reason for forgiveness, because the Father wants what the Son wants. EXPOSITION OF THE GOSPEL OF LUKE 7.224-25.[28]

REPEATING THE "OUR FATHER." PETER CHRYSOLOGUS: He now comes back to his Father and cries, "Father, I have sinned against heaven

and before you." Every day in its prayer, the church testifies that the younger son has returned to his Father's house and is calling God his Father. [The church] prays, "Our Father, who art in heaven," "I have sinned against heaven and before you." SERMON 5.[29]

A SON THROUGH BAPTISM. AMBROSE: "I am no more worthy to be called your son." Cast down, he should not exalt himself that the merit of his humility may raise him. "Make me as one of your hired servants." He knows there is a difference between sons, friends, hired servants and slaves. You are a son through baptism, friend through virtue, hired servant through labor, and slave through fear. Friends can even come from slaves and hired servants, as it is written, "You are my friends, if you do the things that I command you. I do not now call you servants."[30] EXPOSITION OF THE GOSPEL OF LUKE 7.227.[31]

RUNNING, THE FATHER INITIATES THE RECONCILIATION. AMBROSE: Christ chooses those who stand. Rise and run to the church. Here is the Father, the Son and the Holy Spirit. He who hears you pondering in the secret places of the mind runs to you. When you are still far away, he sees you and runs to you. He sees in your heart. He runs, perhaps someone may hinder, and he embraces you. His foreknowledge is in the running, his mercy in the embrace and the disposition of fatherly love. He falls on your neck to raise one prostrate and burdened with sins and bring back one turned aside to the earthly toward heaven. Christ falls on your neck to free your neck from the yoke of slavery and hang his sweet yoke upon your shoulders.[32] EXPOSITION OF THE GOSPEL OF LUKE 7.229-30.[33]

OVERLOOKING THE SON'S TRANSGRESSIONS. PETER CHRYSOLOGUS: "He fell on his neck and

---

[22]CS 101:108-9*. [23]HOP 178*. [24]See Esther 4:37 LXX; Jn 21:17. [25]1 Jn 2:1. [26]See Jn 14:6; 1 Jn 5:6. [27]See Gal 2:21. [28]EHG 322**. [29]FC 17:49*. [30]Jn 15:14-15. [31]EHG 323*. [32]See Mt 11:30. [33]EHG 323**.

kissed him." This is how the father judges and corrects his wayward son and gives him not beatings but kisses. The power of love overlooked the transgressions. The father redeemed the sins of his son by his kiss, and covered them by his embrace, in order not to expose the crimes or humiliate the son. The father so healed the son's wounds as not to leave a scar or blemish upon him. "Blessed are they," says Scripture "whose iniquities are forgiven, and whose sins are covered."[34] SERMON 3.[35]

THE FATHER'S ACTIONS SHOW THE BLESSINGS OF THE INCARNATION. PETER CHRYSOLOGUS:
The father runs out from far away. "When we were still sinners, Christ died for us."[36] The Father runs out. He runs out in his Son, when through him he descends from heaven and comes down on earth. "With me," the Son says, "is he who sent me, the Father."[37]

He "fell upon his neck." He fell, when through Christ the whole divinity came down as ours and rested in human nature. When did he kiss him? When "mercy and truth have met each other, justice and peace have kissed."[38] "He gave the best robe," that which Adam lost, the everlasting glory of immortality. "He put a ring upon his finger." That is the ring of honor, the title of liberty, the outstanding pledge of the spirit, the seal of the faith, and the dowry of the heavenly marriage. Hear the apostle: "I engaged you to one spouse, that I might present you a chaste virgin to Christ."[39] "And sandals on his feet, etc." This is so that his feet might be in shoes when he preached the gospel, for "how beautiful are the feet of those who preach the gospel of peace."[40] SERMON 5.[41]

RESTORING HIM TO SONSHIP. PETER CHRYSOLOGUS:
"Give him a ring for his finger." The father's devotion is not content to restore only his innocence. It also brings back his former honor. "And give him sandals for his feet." He was rich when he departed, but how poor he has returned! Of all his substance, he does not even bring back shoes on his feet! "Give him sandals for his feet"

that nakedness may not disgrace even a foot and that he may have shoes when he returns to his former course of life. SERMON 3.[42]

THE FATHER WELCOMES THE PRODIGAL TO THE DIVINE FEAST AS A SON. ATHANASIUS:
Then he shall get up, come to his father, and confess to him, "I have sinned against heaven and before you. I am no longer worthy to be called your son. Treat me like one of your hired servants."

When he confesses like that, he will be considered worthy of more than that for which he prayed. His father neither takes him in like a hired servant nor treats him like a stranger. Oh no, he kisses him as a son. He accepts him as a dead man come back to life again. He counts him worthy of the divine feast and gives him the precious garment he once wore.

Now there is singing and joy in the father's home. What happened is the result of the Father's grace and loving kindness. Not only does he bring his son back from death, but also through the Spirit he clearly shows his grace. To replace corruption, he clothes him with an incorruptible robe. To satisfy hunger, he kills the fatted calf. The Father provides shoes for his feet so that he will not travel far away again. Most wonderful of all, he puts a divine signet ring upon his hand. By all these things, he begets him anew in the image of the glory of Christ. FESTAL LETTER 7.[43]

CHRIST SACRIFICED AT THE FATHER'S COMMAND. PETER CHRYSOLOGUS:
"And he killed for him the fattened calf." About that David sang: "And it shall please God better than a young calf, that brings forth horns and hoofs."[44] The calf was slain at this command of the Father, because the Christ, God as the Son of God, could not be slain without the command of his Father. Listen to the apostle: "He who has not spared even his own son

---

[34]Rom 4:7. [35]FC 17:36-37*. [36]Rom 5:8. [37]Jn 8:16. [38]Ps 84:11 LXX. [39]2 Cor 11:2. [40]Rom 10:15. [41]FC 17:49-50*. [42]FC 17:38*. [43]ARL 123*. [44]Ps 68:32 LXX.

but has delivered him for us all."[45] He is the calf who is daily and continually immolated for our food. SERMON 5.[46]

ZECHARIAH'S TEMPLE OFFERING. IRENAEUS: According to Luke, having a priestly character, the Gospel began with the priest Zechariah offering incense to God. The fatted calf was already being prepared which was to be sacrificed for the finding of the younger son. AGAINST HERESIES 3.11.8.[47]

ADAM, LOST IN SIN, NOW FOUND IN CHRIST. AMBROSE: The Father rejoices "because my son

was dead and has come to life again. He was lost and is found.""He who was, is lost." He, who was not, cannot be lost. The Gentiles are not, the Christian is, according as it is written above that, "God has chosen things that are not, that he might bring to nothing things that are."[48] It is also possible to understand here the likeness of the human race in one man. Adam was, and we were all in him. Adam was lost, and all were lost in him.[49] EXPOSITION OF THE GOSPEL OF LUKE 7.234.[50]

---

[45]Rom 8:32. [46]FC 17:50*. [47]LCC 1:382-83*. [48]1 Cor 1:28. [49]1 Cor 15:22. [50]EHG 325**.

15:25-32 THE ELDER BROTHER AND HIS FATHER

[25]"Now his elder son was in the field; and as he came and drew near to the house, he heard music and dancing. [26]And he called one of the servants and asked what this meant. [27]And he said to him, 'Your brother has come, and your father has killed the fatted calf, because he has received him safe and sound.' [28]But he was angry and refused to go in. His father came out and entreated him, [29]but he answered his father, 'Lo, these many years I have served you, and I never disobeyed your command; yet you never gave me a kid, that I might make merry with my friends. [30]But when this son of yours came, who has devoured your living with harlots, you killed for him the fatted calf!' [31]And he said to him, 'Son, you are always with me, and all that is mine is yours. [32]It was fitting to make merry and be glad, for this your brother was dead, and is alive; he was lost, and is found.'"

OVERVIEW: Although some commentators say the elder brother represents Israel, it is difficult to make that identification (CYRIL OF ALEXANDRIA). He stands outside the Gentile church like the Jews hearing the music of salvation but refusing to enter in. This elder son is always with the father, for he is part of the lineage of Old Testament saints, and it is for the elder brother that Christ was born (PETER CHRYSOLOGUS).

15:25-32 The Elder Brother and His Merciful Father

THE ELDER SON DOES NOT REPRESENT ISRAEL. CYRIL OF ALEXANDRIA: If anyone says that the virtuous and sober son signifies Israel according to the flesh, we cannot agree to this opinion. In no way is it fitting to say that Israel chose a blameless life. Throughout the whole inspired

Scripture, we see them accused of being rebels and disobedient. . . .

I think it is right to mention this also. Some refer to the person of our Savior as that fatted calf that the father killed when his son was called to conversion. . . . If any one imagines that the virtuous and sober son means the physical Israel, how can Israel honestly say that he never gave him a kid? Whether we call it calf or kid, Christ is to be understood as the sacrifice offered for sin. He was not sacrificed only for the Gentiles but also that he might redeem Israel, who by reason of his frequent transgression of the law had brought great blame on himself. The wise Paul bears witness to this, saying, "For this reason Jesus also, that he might sanctify the people by his blood, suffered outside the gate."[1] COMMENTARY ON LUKE, HOMILY 107.[2]

THE JEWS NOW STAND OUTSIDE THE GENTILE CHURCH. PETER CHRYSOLOGUS: The older brother, the older son coming from the field, the people of the law, hears the music and dancing in the Father's house, yet he does not want to enter. "The harvest indeed is abundant, but the laborers are few."[3] Every day we see this same thing happen with our own eyes. The Jewish people comes to its Father's house, the church. It stands outside because of its jealousy. It hears the harp of David echoing, and the music from the singing of the psalms, and the dancing carried on by so many assembled races. It does not wish to enter. Through jealousy, it remains outside. In horror, it judges its Gentile brother by its own ancient customs, and meanwhile, it is depriving itself of its Father's goods and excluding itself from his joys. SERMON 5.[4]

THE ELDER SON IS ALWAYS WITH THE FATHER. PETER CHRYSOLOGUS: The Father steps outside and says to his son, "Son, you are always with me." How is he with his son? In the person of Abel, Enoch, Shem, Noah, Abraham, Isaac, Jacob, Moses, and all the holy men from which stems Christ's Jewish lineage read in the Gospel when it says, "Abraham begot Isaac, Isaac begot Jacob," and so on.[5] SERMON 5.[6]

CHRIST WAS BORN FOR THE ELDER SON. PETER CHRYSOLOGUS: "All that is mine is yours." How is this? The law, prophecy, temple, priesthood, sacrifices, kingdom, and the gifts are for you. This is the greatest gift of all: Christ was born. Since you through your jealousy wish to destroy your brother, you are no longer worthy to possess your Father's banquets and joys. SERMON 5.[7]

---

[1]Heb 13:12. [2]CGSL 432-33**. [3]Lk 10:2. [4]FC 17:50**. [5]Mt 1:2. [6]FC 17:51*. [7]FC 17:51*.

16:1-13 A PARABLE ABOUT POSSESSIONS AND PRUDENCE, AND SOME APPLICATIONS

[1]*He also said to the disciples, "There was a rich man who had a steward, and charges were brought to him that this man was wasting his goods. [2]And he called him and said to him, 'What is this that I hear about you? Turn in the account of your stewardship, for you can no longer be steward.' [3]And the steward said to himself, 'What shall I do, since my master is taking the stewardship away from me? I am not strong enough to dig, and I am ashamed to beg. [4]I have decided what to do, so that people may receive me into their houses when I am put out of the stewardship.' [5]So, summoning his master's debt-*

ors one by one, he said to the first, 'How much do you owe my master?' [6]He said, 'A hundred measures of oil.' And he said to him, 'Take your bill, and sit down quickly and write fifty.' [7]Then he said to another, 'And how much do you owe?' He said, 'A hundred measures of wheat.' He said to him, 'Take your bill, and write eighty.' [8]The master commended the dishonest steward for his shrewdness; for the sons of this world[w] are more shrewd in dealing with their own generation than the sons of light. [9]And I tell you, make friends for yourselves by means of unrighteous mammon,[a] so that when it fails they may receive you into the eternal habitations.

[10]"He who is faithful in a very little is faithful also in much; and he who is dishonest in a very little is dishonest also in much. [11]If then you have not been faithful in the unrighteous mammon,[a] who will entrust to you the true riches? [12]And if you have not been faithful in that which is another's, who will give you that which is your own? [13]No servant can serve two masters; for either he will hate the one and love the other, or he will be devoted to the one and despise the other. You cannot serve God and mammon."[a]

w Greek age a *Mammon* is a Semitic word for money or riches

OVERVIEW: An interpretation of the parable of the unjust steward seeks the figurative meaning of the whole parable and not a meaning for the individual parts. The steward trusting in the mercy of his Master has his documents of sin rewritten by God's Holy Spirit through Christ's cross and the grace of baptism. So do not rewrite what God has blotted out (ORIGEN). Jesus is recommending to the disciples the steward's foresight, prudence and ingenuity (AUGUSTINE). By using the transitory things of this world which are not ours we are to purchase for ourselves those things which will not pass away (EPHREM THE SYRIAN).

If the mammon was used wisely, that is, if it was used to make friends, then when it is exhausted those friends may receive you into the eternal tents. Making friends by means of unrighteous mammon no doubt refers to almsgiving without discrimination in fulfillment of Jesus' exhortation to "sell your possessions and give alms" (AUGUSTINE).[1] Riches are a loan from God that are to be deposited with the poor so that we might receive a hundredfold reward, for they will be our friends in the eternal habitations (CHRYSOSTOM). The language of faithfulness is used here as well; for Jesus questions whether their unfaithfulness in unrighteous mammon will lead

to unfaithfulness in "what is yours," that is, "the true things" that are the divine gifts received in faith that begin to reshape the divine likeness in us (CYRIL OF ALEXANDRIA).

It is impossible to be a slave to two masters who have contrary wills and two different minds which are irreconcilable. This world and the world to come are at odds with one another, and one cannot serve the world and do the will of Christ (PSEUDO-CLEMENT OF ROME). The steward was commended because he chose to serve his lord, whom he trusted would be merciful (AMBROSE).

16:1-8 *The Parable of the Prudent Steward*

IF GOD REWRITES OUR DOCUMENTS OF SIN, DO NOT REWRITE WHAT GOD HAS BLOTTED OUT. ORIGEN: What the Gospel of "the unjust steward" says is also an image of this matter. He says to the debtor [of one hundred measures of wheat], "Take your bill, sit down, and write eighty," and the other things that are related. You see that he said to each man, "Take your bill." It is evident from this that the documents of sin are ours, but God writes documents of justice. The

[1]Lk 12:33.

apostle says, "For you are an epistle written not with ink, but with the Spirit of the living God; not in tables of stone, but in the fleshly tables of the heart."[2] You have in yourselves documents of God and documents of the Holy Spirit. If you transgress, you yourself write in yourselves the handwriting of sin. Notice that at any time when you have approached the cross of Christ and the grace of baptism, your handwriting is fastened to the cross and blotted out in the fountain of baptism. Do not rewrite later what has been blotted out or repair what has been destroyed. Preserve only the documents of God in yourself. Let only the scripture of the Holy Spirit remain in you. HOMILIES ON GENESIS 13.4.[3]

JESUS RECOMMENDS THE FORESIGHT, PRUDENCE AND INGENUITY OF THE STEWARD.

AUGUSTINE: Why did the Lord Jesus Christ present this parable to us? He surely did not approve of that cheat of a servant who cheated his master, stole from him and did not make it up from his own pocket. On top of that, he also did some extra pilfering. He caused his master further loss, in order to prepare a little nest of quiet and security for himself after he lost his job. Why did the Lord set this before us? It is not because that servant cheated but because he exercised foresight for the future. When even a cheat is praised for his ingenuity, Christians who make no such provision blush. I mean, this is what he added, "Behold, the children of this age are more prudent than the children of light." They perpetrate frauds in order to secure their future. In what life, after all, did that steward insure himself like that? What one was he going to quit when he bowed to his master's decision? He was insuring himself for a life that was going to end. Would you not insure yourself for eternal life? SERMON 359A.10.[4]

16:9-13 Teachings About God and Mammon

USING TRANSITORY THINGS FOR HEAVENLY RICHES.

EPHREM THE SYRIAN: He told another parable of the steward, who was accused in the presence of his master. The shrewdness of this unjust steward was praised in the presence of his master. He unjustly wasted the initial treasures and then unjustly and cunningly cancelled the later debts. He was praised because he acquired what was to be his by what was not his, namely, his friends and supporters. Through what was not his, Adam got something that was not his, namely, thorns and pains.[5] O children of Adam, buy for yourselves those things that do not pass away, by means of those temporary things that are not yours! COMMENTARY ON TATIAN'S DIATESSARON 14.21.[6]

DO NOT EXCLUDE FROM ALMS THOSE YOU JUDGE UNWORTHY.

AUGUSTINE: Mammon is the Hebrew word for "riches," just as in Punic the word for "profit" is mammon. What are we to do? What did the Lord command? "Make yourselves friends with the mammon of iniquity, so that they too, when you begin to fail, may receive you into eternal shelters." It is easy, of course, to understand that we must give alms and a helping hand to the needy, because Christ receives it in them. . . . We can understand that we have to give alms and that we must not really pick and choose to whom we give them, because we are unable to sift through people's hearts. When you give alms to all different types of people, then you will reach a few who deserve them. You are hospitable, and you keep your house ready for strangers. Let in the unworthy, in case the worthy might be excluded. You cannot be a judge and sifter of hearts. SERMON 359A.11-12.[7]

RICHES ARE A LOAN FROM GOD NOT TO BE LEFT IDLE.

CHRYSOSTOM: You know that many high standing people renege on repayment of a loan. They are either resistant with a bad attitude or unable to pay because of poverty, as it often happens. In the case of the Lord of all, there is no room for thinking this. On the contrary, the loan

---

[2]2 Cor 3:2-3. [3]FC 71:194*. [4]WSA 3 10:216**. [5]Gen 3:17-19. [6]ECTD 223-24**. [7]WSA 3 10:216*.

is proof against loss. He guarantees to return in good time one hundred percent of what was deposited, and he keeps life everlasting in reserve for us. In the future, what excuse will we have if we are negligent and fail to gain a hundredfold in place of the little we have, the future in place of the present, the eternal in place of the temporary? What excuse will we have if we heedlessly lock our money behind doors and barricades, and we prefer to leave it lying idle? Instead, we should make it available to the needy now, so that in the future we may count on support from them. Remember that Scripture says, "Make friends with ill-gotten gains so that, when you go down in the world, they may welcome you into their eternal dwellings." HOMILIES ON GENESIS 3.21.[8]

IF UNFAITHFUL IN WHAT IS ANOTHER'S, WHO WILL GIVE YOU WHAT IS YOUR OWN?

CYRIL OF ALEXANDRIA: Anyone may readily learn the meaning and view of the Savior's words from what follows. He said, "If you have not been faithful in what is another's, who will give you what is your own?" We again say that what is another's is the wealth we possess. We were not born with riches, but on the contrary, naked. We can truly affirm in the words of Scripture that "we neither brought anything into the world, nor can carry anything out."[9] . . .

Let those of us who possess earthly wealth open our hearts to those who are in need. Let us show ourselves faithful and obedient to the laws of God. Let us be followers of our Lord's will in those things that are from the outside and not our own. Let us do this so that we may receive what is our own, that holy and admirable beauty that God forms in people's souls, making them like himself, according to what we originally were. COMMENTARY ON LUKE, HOMILY 109.[10]

THIS WORLD AND THE WORLD TO COME ARE ENEMIES.

PSEUDO-CLEMENT OF ROME: The Lord says, "No servant can serve two masters." If we want to serve both God and money, it will do us no good. "What good does it do a man to gain the whole world and forfeit his life?"[11] This world and the world to come are enemies. This one means adultery, corruption, greed and deceit, while the other gives them up. We cannot be friends of both. To get the one, we must give the other up. We think that it is better to hate what is here, for it is trivial, temporary and perishable and to value what is there: things good and imperishable. Yes, if we do the will of Christ, we will find rest, but if not, nothing will save us from eternal punishment if we fail to heed his commands. 2 CLEMENT 6.1-7.[12]

THE STEWARD SERVES GOD BY SEEKING HIS MERCY WHILE GIVING RELIEF TO THE POOR.

AMBROSE: "No servant can serve two masters,"[13] not because there are two, but the Lord is One. Although there are those who serve mammon, he still does not possess any rights to sovereignty, but they impose on themselves the chains of slavery. Power is not just, but slavery is unjust. He says, "Make for yourself friends of the mammon of iniquity," so that by giving to the poor, we may match the grace of the angels and all the saints for ourselves. He does not rebuke the steward. By this, we learn that he does not belong to the Lord himself but to the riches of others. Although he has sinned, he is praised because he sought help for himself in the future through the Lord's mercy. He fittingly mentions the mammon of iniquity, because greed tempted our dispositions with different enticements of wealth, so that we were willing to be the slaves of riches. EXPOSITION OF THE GOSPEL OF LUKE 7.244-45.[14]

---

[8]FC 74:49-50**. [9]1 Tim 6:7 [10]CGSL 444**. [11]Mt 16:26; Mk 8:36; Lk 9:25. [12]LCC 1:195*. [13]Mt 6:24. [14]EHG 328**.

16:14-18 TEACHINGS ABOUT THE LAW, THE PROPHETS AND THE KINGDOM

¹⁴*The Pharisees, who were lovers of money, heard all this, and they scoffed at him.* ¹⁵*But he said to them, "You are those who justify yourselves before men, but God knows your hearts; for what is exalted among men is an abomination in the sight of God.*

¹⁶*"The law and the prophets were until John; since then the good news of the kingdom of God is preached, and every one enters it violently.* ¹⁷*But it is easier for heaven and earth to pass away, than for one dot of the law to become void.*

¹⁸*"Every one who divorces his wife and marries another commits adultery, and he who marries a woman divorced from her husband commits adultery."*

OVERVIEW: The Pharisees are called "lovers of money" because they demonstrate in their use of possessions their opposition to God's will. As lovers of money, the Pharisees show themselves to be hypocrites, which is manifested when the Pharisees "declare [themselves] righteous before men" and are more interested in pleasing men than pleasing God. The Law and Prophets proclaimed Jesus' death and resurrection, and the kingdom of God that is now preached includes justification by faith, baptism, worship in the Spirit, and communion of saints (CYRIL OF ALEXANDRIA). Jesus' baptism by John ended the law and John's baptism by bearing the justice of the Old Testament as sinbearer (EPHREM THE SYRIAN). With John, the old is invalidated at the same time that the new receives its validation (TERTULLIAN).

To enter the kingdom by force is to desire its hope with earnest passion (CYRIL OF ALEXANDRIA). Jesus' statement on divorce and adultery seems to be unparalleled in the Old Testament; he includes no exceptions here in Luke,[1] for everyone who divorces and then remarries commits adultery. This is even true for those who divorce because of immorality (AUGUSTINE).

In the light of our understanding of the law as Torah or gospel, Jesus' words about marriage, divorce and adultery must be understood in the context of the Old Testament metaphor of God's relationship to Israel as a bridegroom to his bride. Israel, as bride, commits adultery when she chases after false gods, just as the church is now led away from the truth by persecution or by worldly pleasures and philosophies (AMBROSE).

16:14 The Pharisees Love Money

LOVERS OF MONEY WILL NOT POSSESS THE PURSE THAT CANNOT BE TAKEN AWAY. CYRIL OF ALEXANDRIA: Being lovers of money, they repeatedly did not judge matters before them according to what was agreeable to the laws of God. On the contrary, they judged inequitably and in opposition to God's will. . . .

Since it says that the Pharisees were lovers of money, they derided Jesus for directing them by his healthful doctrines to praiseworthy conduct and making them want saintly glories. He tells them that it was their duty to sell their possessions and distribute them to the poor. They would then possess in heaven a treasure that could not be stolen, purses that could not be harmed, and wealth that would not have to be abandoned. COMMENTARY ON LUKE, HOMILY 110.[2]

---

[1]Cf. Mt 5:32. [2]CGSL 446-47**.

16:15 The Way of the Pharisees

The Pharisees Are Liars Among the Altars. Cyril of Alexandria: Let us see the cause of their wickedness. The passion of greed possessed and tyrannized their heart. Their mind was in subjection even against its will. It was humbled under the power of wickedness and bound as it were by inevitable bonds. . . .

The Savior of all spoke many things to them but saw that they would not change from their crafty purposes and passions. They preferred rather to abide in their innate folly. He began to correct them sternly, calling them by the very occasion. He shows that they are hypocrites and liars in wait among the altars. They are eager for the glory due to righteous and good people, but in reality, they are not like these. They are not eager to receive the approval of God. Commentary on Luke, Homily 110.[3]

16:16-17 Teaching About the Law and the Prophets and the Kingdom of God

The Good News of God's Kingdom Is Opened Through the Violence of Christ's Death and Resurrection. Cyril of Alexandria: He says that Moses and the company of the holy prophets announced beforehand the meaning of my mystery to the inhabitants of earth. The law declares by shadows and types that I should even endure the death of the flesh to save the world and by rising from the dead abolish corruption. The prophets also spoke words meaning the same as the writings of Moses. He says, "It is not strange or not known before, that you reject my words and despise everything that would benefit you. The word of prophecy concerning you and me extends until the holy Baptist John. From the days of John, the kingdom of heaven is preached, and everyone takes it by force."[4] The kingdom of heaven here means justification by faith, the washing away of sin by holy baptism, and sanctification by the Spirit. It also means worshiping in the Spirit, the

service that is superior to shadows and types, the honor of the adoption of children, and the hope of the glory about to be given to the saints. Commentary on Luke, Homily 110.[5]

Jesus' Baptism by John. Ephrem the Syrian: The Law and the Prophets reached as far as John did, but the Messiah is the beginning of the New Testament. Through baptism, the Lord assumed the justice of the Old Testament in order to receive the perfection of the anointing and to give it in its fullness and entirety to his disciples. He ended John's baptism and the law at the same time. He was baptized in justice, because he was sinless, but he baptized in grace because all others were sinners. Through his justice, he dispensed from the law, and through his baptism, he abolished baptism [of John]. Commentary on Tatian's Diatessaron 4.2.[6]

Old Things Pass Away. Tertullian: The Creator promised that old things would pass away because he said that new things were to arise. Christ marked the date of that passing, saying, "The law and the prophets were until John." He set up John as a boundary stone between the one order and the other, of old things thereafter coming to an end, and new things beginning. The apostle necessarily, in Christ revealed after John, also invalidates the old things while validating the new. His concern is for the faith of no other god than the Creator under whose authority it was even prophesied that the old things were to pass away. Against Marcion 5.2.[7]

To Take the Kingdom by Force. Cyril of Alexandria: He says that the kingdom of heaven is preached. The Baptist stood in the middle saying, "Prepare the way of the Lord."[8] He has also shown that he is already near and, as it were, within the doors, even the true Lamb of God who bears the sin of the world. Whoever hears and

---

[3]CGSL 447-48**. [4]Mt 11:12. [5]CGSL 448**. [6]ECTD 84*. [7]MFC 9:39-40*. [8]Lk 3:4.

loves the sacred message takes it by force. This means that he uses all his eagerness and strength in his desire to enter within the hope. He says in another place, "The kingdom of heaven is taken by violence, and the violent seize upon it."[9] COMMENTARY ON LUKE, HOMILY 110.[10]

16:18 How Words of Torah Stand in the Kingdom of God

IMMORALITY IS NOT A CONDITION FOR DIVORCE. AUGUSTINE: Who are we to say that someone commits adultery in taking another woman after he puts away his wife, and that another who, in doing this, does not commit adultery? The Gospel says that everyone who performs such an act commits adultery. If everyone who marries another woman after the dismissal of his wife commits adultery, this includes the one who puts away his wife without the cause of immorality and the one who puts away his wife for this reason. ADULTEROUS MARRIAGES 9.[11]

MARRIAGE REFLECTS THE RELATIONSHIP BETWEEN CHRIST AND HIS CHASTE AND LOVING CHURCH. AMBROSE: He had above proposed that the kingdom of God should be preached. When he had said that one tittle cannot fall from the law, he added, "Everyone who puts away his wife, and marries another, commits adultery." The apostle rightly admonishes, saying that this is a great sacrament concerning Christ and the church.[12] You find a marriage that doubtlessly was joined by God, when he himself says, "No man comes to me, unless my Father who sent me has drawn him."[13] He alone could join this marriage. Solomon mystically said, "A wife will be prepared for a man by God."[14] The man is Christ, and the wife is the church that is a wife in love and a virgin in innocence. Do not let him whom God has drawn to the Son be separated by persecution,[15] distracted by extravagance, ravaged by philosophy, tainted by Manichaeus, perverted by Arius, or infected by Sabellius.[16] God has joined; let not a Jew separate. All who desire to defile the truth of faith and wisdom are adulterers. . . . Come, Lord Jesus, to find your bride not tainted or polluted. She has not defiled your house or disregarded your commandments. Let her say to you, "I found him whom my soul loved."[17] Let her lead you into the house of wine. Wine makes glad the heart of man.[18] Let the Spirit saturate her. Let her recognize the mystery and speak the prophecy.[19] EXPOSITION OF THE GOSPEL OF LUKE 8.9-12.[20]

---

[9]Mt 11:12. [10]CGSL 448**. [11]FC 27:73**. [12]See Eph 5:32. [13]Jn 6:44. [14]Prov 19:14. [15]See Rom 8:35. [16]These were the names of infamous heretics from the early church; cf. Col 2:8. [17]Song 3:4. [18]Ps 104:15 (103:15 LXX); Song 5:1. [19]See Joel 2:28-29. [20]EHG 333-35**.

16:19-31 THE RICH MAN AND LAZARUS

[19]"There was a rich man, who was clothed in purple and fine linen and who feasted sumptuously every day. [20]And at his gate lay a poor man named Lazarus, full of sores, [21]who desired to be fed with what fell from the rich man's table; moreover the dogs came and licked his sores. [22]The poor man died and was carried by the angels to Abraham's bosom. The rich man also died and was buried; [23]and in Hades, being in torment, he lifted up his eyes, and saw Abraham far off and Lazarus in his bosom. [24]And he called out, 'Father Abraham, have mercy upon me, and send Lazarus

to dip the end of his finger in water and cool my tongue; for I am in anguish in this flame.' ²⁵But Abraham said, 'Son, remember that you in your lifetime received your good things, and Lazarus in like manner evil things; but now he is comforted here, and you are in anguish. ²⁶And besides all this, between us and you a great chasm has been fixed, in order that those who would pass from here to you may not be able, and none may cross from there to us.' ²⁷And he said, 'Then I beg you, father, to send him to my father's house, ²⁸for I have five brothers, so that he may warn them, lest they also come into this place of torment.' ²⁹But Abraham said, 'They have Moses and the prophets; let them hear them.' ³⁰And he said, 'No, father Abraham; but if some one goes to them from the dead, they will repent.' ³¹He said to him, 'If they do not hear Moses and the prophets, neither will they be convinced if some one should rise from the dead.'"

Overview: The rich man refuses to give alms to a poor man full of sores who was lying at his gate (Jerome). In contrast to the rich man, Lazarus the poor man is pathetic and pitiable (Cyril of Alexandria). Yet Jesus names this poor man, suggesting his importance in God's sight and that his name is written in heaven,[1] while the rich man's name is not recorded in Scripture or in heaven (Augustine). The name Lazarus means "one who has been helped" (Jerome). The image is striking. Jesus uses figurative language here to describe the great chasm that exists between the torment of hell with its fire and the consolation of heaven in the bosom of Abraham (Gregory of Nyssa). Lazarus, a poor man of faith, is received by Abraham, a rich man of faith (Augustine). The rich man feasted on earth, but Lazarus now feasts in heaven as his soul finds rest in the bosom of Abraham (Prudentius).

The rich man is burning in the fires of hell while he can see on the other side of the chasm the fountains of paradise (Ephrem the Syrian). The souls of the wicked clearly experience the pain of the fires of hell (Gregory the Great). Abraham, who had mercy on Sodom, is not able to show mercy to this rich man in hades (Ephrem the Syrian). He now desires a drop of water when during his life he would not give Lazarus a drop or a crumb (Peter Chrysologus). The reason the rich man does not receive mercy now— the good thing—is because he did not show mercy in his life (Augustine).

This account illuminates the story of the unrighteous steward, for saints make friends for themselves by feeding the hungry and giving drink to the thirsty. The Pharisees need to become like the unrighteous steward by seeing that their Lord is Jesus and, relying on his mercy, to give alms to people like Lazarus (Augustine). Could the five brothers be the rich man's senses who enslaved him in riches on earth and sent him to the torment of hades? (Jerome). During his life, the rich man ignored Moses and the prophets and may have even ridiculed them (Augustine). If they refuse to hear Moses and the prophets, they are refusing to hear Christ, who speaks through them (Jerome).

16:19-22 The Life and Death of the Rich Man and Lazarus

The Rich Man Does Not Give Alms. Jerome: The rich man, in purple splendor, is not accused of being greedy or of carrying off the property of another, or of committing adultery, or, in fact, of any wrongdoing. The evil alone of which he is guilty is pride. Most wretched of men, you see a member of your own body lying there outside at your gate, and have you no compassion? If the laws of God mean nothing to you, at least take pity on your own situation and be in fear, for perhaps you might become like him. Give

---

[1] Cf. Lk 10:20.

what you waste to your own member. I am not telling you to throw away your wealth. What you throw out, the crumbs from your table, offer as alms. ON LAZARUS AND DIVES.[2]

THE RICH MAN WAS FULLY AWARE OF THE NEED OF LAZARUS. JEROME: Lazarus was lying at the gate in order to draw attention to the cruelty paid to his body and to prevent the rich man from saying, "I did not notice him. He was in a corner. I could not see him. No one announced him to me." He lay at the gate. You saw him every time you went out and every time you came in. When your crowds of servants and clients were attending you, he lay there full of ulcers. ON LAZARUS AND DIVES.[3]

THE DOGS AND THE RICH MAN COMPARED. CYRIL OF ALEXANDRIA: Cut off from compassion and care, he would have gladly gathered the worthless morsels that fell from the rich man's table to satisfy his hunger. A severe and incurable disease also tormented him. Yes, it says that even the dogs licked his sores and did not injure him yet sympathized with him and cared for him. Animals relieve their own sufferings with their tongues, as they remove what pains them and gently soothe the sores. The rich man was crueler than the dogs, because he felt no sympathy or compassion for him but was completely unmerciful. COMMENTARY ON LUKE 111.[4]

LAZARUS' NAME WRITTEN IN HEAVEN. AUGUSTINE: Jesus kept quiet about the rich man's name and mentioned the name of the poor man. The rich man's name was thrown around, but God kept quiet about it. The other's name was lost in silence, and God spoke it. Please do not be surprised. God just read out what was written in his book. . . . You see, God who lives in heaven kept quiet about the rich man's name, because he did not find it written in heaven. He spoke the poor man's name, because he found it written there, indeed he gave instructions for it to be written there. SERMON 33A.4.[5]

LAZARUS MEANS "ONE WHO HAS BEEN HELPED." JEROME: "There was a certain poor man, named Lazarus." The meaning of Lazarus's name is . . . one who has been helped. He is not a helper but one who has been helped. He was a poor man, and in his poverty, the Lord came to his assistance. ON LAZARUS AND DIVES.[6]

16:23-26 Heavenly Life and Eternal

FIGURATIVE LANGUAGE DESCRIBES HEAVEN AND HELL. GREGORY OF NYSSA: I said, "What are the fire, the gulf, or the other things which are mentioned, if they are not what they are said to be?"

"It seems to me," she [Macrina] said, "that the Gospel wishes, through each of these details, to indicate some opinions concerning what we are seeking in connection with the soul. The patriarch says to the rich man, 'You had your share of goods during your life in the flesh.' He also says concerning the beggar, 'This man fulfilled his duty by his experience of hardship during his life.' By the gulf separating the one from the other, Scripture seems to me to set forth an important belief. . . . This, in my opinion, is the gulf, which is not an earthly abyss, that the judgment between the two opposite choices of life creates. Once one has chosen the pleasure of this life and has not remedied this bad choice by a change of heart, he produces for himself a place empty of good hereafter. He digs this unavoidable necessity for himself like some deep and trackless pit.

"It seems to me that Scripture uses the 'bosom of Abraham,' in which the patient sufferer finds rest, as a symbol of the good state of the soul. This patriarch was the first person recorded to have chosen the hope of things to come in preference to the enjoyment of the moment. Deprived of everything he had in the beginning of his life, living among strangers, he searched for a future

---

[2]FC 57:201*. [3]FC 57:201*. [4]CGSL 453-54**. [5]WSA 3 2:163**. [6]FC 57:201.

prosperity through present affliction. We use the word *bosom* when referring figuratively to a part of the outline of the sea. It seems to me that Scripture uses the word *bosom* as a symbol of the immeasurable goals toward which those who sail virtuously through life will come to when having departed from life. They anchor their souls in this good bosom as in a quiet harbor." ON THE SOUL AND THE RESURRECTION.[7]

FEAR NOT RICHES AS SUCH BUT GREED.

AUGUSTINE: I think that we have proved that Christ did not object to the riches of the rich man but to his impiety, infidelity, pride and cruelty. . . .

The rich must not start saying that I have agreed to be their advocate. They felt afraid, after all, when reminded of the gospel. When they heard about the rich man hurled into the pains of hell, they felt afraid. I have reassured them. They do not need to fear riches but vices. They should not fear wealth but greed. They should not be afraid of goods but of greed. Let them possess wealth like Abraham, and let them possess it with faith. Let them have it, possess it and not be possessed by it. SERMON 299E.5.[8]

THE SOUL RESTS IN THE PATRIARCH'S
BOSOM. PRUDENTIUS:

But until the perishable body
You will raise up, O God, and refashion,
What mansion of rest is made ready
For the soul that is pure and unsullied?
It shall rest in the patriarch's bosom
As did Lazarus, hedged round with flowers,
Whom Dives beheld from a distance
While he burned in the fires everlasting.

HYMN FOR EVERY DAY 10.149-56.[9]

FOUNTAINS ON ONE SIDE, FIRE ON THE
OTHER. EPHREM THE SYRIAN:

This place, despised and spurned
By the denizens of paradise,
Those who burn in Gehenna
    hungrily desire;

Their torment doubles
At the sight of its fountains,
They quiver violently
As they stand on the opposite side;
The rich man, too, begs for succor
But there is no one to wet his tongue,
For fire is within them,
While the water is opposite them.

HYMNS ON PARADISE 1.17.[10]

THE SOULS OF THE WICKED SUFFER THE PAIN
OF FIRE. GREGORY THE GREAT: From the words of Scripture, we gather that the soul suffers from the burning heat not only through its sense of sight but also by actually experiencing the pain. We know from Christ's words that the rich man was burned in hell. His prayer to Abraham declares that his soul was held in fire. He says, "Send Lazarus to dip the tip of his finger in water, and cool my tongue. I am tormented in this flame." Since Christ describes the condemned sinner Dives surrounded by the flames of hell, no one with understanding would deny that fire holds fast the souls of the wicked. DIALOGUE 4.30.[11]

THE FRUITS OF PARDON MUST BE SEEN IN
THOSE PARDONED. EPHREM THE SYRIAN: The Lord compared the priests of the people with him who was clothed in purple. Nothing is more honored than purple clothing. He compared the disciples of the cross with Lazarus. There were none more lowly than Lazarus was. He revealed the name of his beloved ones through Lazarus, his beloved one. He also wished to reveal the name of his enemies through the words, "If they do not listen to Moses and the prophets." It is not the case that all those living are alive, or that all those buried are dead.

See, the more the rich man lived sumptuously, the more Lazarus was humbled! The more Lazarus was made low, the greater was his crown.

---

[7]FC 58:232-34**. [8]*WSA* 3 8:268**. [9]FC 43:76*. [10]*HOP* 84. [11]FC 39:226*.

Why should he have seen Abraham above all the just, and Lazarus in his bosom? He saw him because Abraham loved the poor and so that we might learn that we cannot hope for pardon at the end, unless the fruits of pardon can be seen in us. If Abraham, who was friendly to strangers and had mercy on Sodom, was not able to have mercy on the one who did not show pity to Lazarus, how can we hope that there will be pardon for us? That man called him "my father," and Abraham called him "my son," but he was not able to help him. "Remember, my son, that you received good things during your life and Lazarus evil things." COMMENTARY ON TATIAN'S DIATESSARON 15.12-13.[12]

THE RICH MAN CONTINUES TO TREAT LAZARUS WITH CONTEMPT. PETER CHRYSOLOGUS:

"Send Lazarus." As I see the matter, the rich man's actions spring not from new pain but from ancient envy. This hell does not kindle his jealousy as much as Lazarus's possession of heaven. People find it a serious evil and unbearable fire to see in happiness those whom they once held in contempt. The rich man's ill will does not leave him, although he already endures its punishment. He does not ask to be led to Lazarus but wants Lazarus to be led to him. O rich man, loving Abraham cannot send to the bed of your tortures Lazarus whom you did not condescend to admit to your table. Your respective fortunes have now been reversed. You look at the glory of him whose misery you once spurned. He who wondered at you in your glory sees your tortures. SERMON 122.[13]

THE MEASURE YOU GIVE SHALL BE GIVEN TO YOU. AUGUSTINE: "Remember, son, that you received good things in your life, and Lazarus likewise bad things." He assigns pain in return for riches, refreshment in return for poverty, flames in return for purple and joy in return for nakedness. The equal balance of the scales will be maintained. The standard of measurement will not be proved false that says, "The measure you give will

be the measure you get."[14] The reason he refuses to show mercy to the rich man in his pain is that while he lived the rich man neglected to show mercy. The reason why he ignored the rich man's pleas in his torment is that he ignored the poor man's pleas on earth. SERMON 367.2.[15]

THE RICH MAN DID NOT MAKE FRIENDS WITH HIS UNRIGHTEOUS MAMMON. AUGUSTINE: Why then, rich man, do you desire too late in hell what you never hoped for while you were enjoying your luxuries? Are you not the one who ignored the person lying at your gate? Are you not the one who in your disdain for the poor man made fun of Moses and the prophets? You refused to hold faith with a neighbor in his poverty; now you do not enjoy his good times.[16] . . .

We should not hold faith with a poor neighbor in such a way that we hope riches are coming to him in due course, and so we keep faith with him in order to hold them with him. That is not the way at all. What is the way is in line with our Lord's instruction, "Make friends for yourselves with the mammon of iniquity, so that they too may receive you in the eternal dwellings."[17] There are poor people here who have no dwellings where they themselves can receive you. Make friends of them with the mammon of iniquity, the profits that iniquity calls profits. Since there are profits that justice calls profits, they are in God's treasury. . . .

"Whoever receives a prophet in the name of a prophet will receive a prophet's reward. Whoever gives one of my little ones a cup of cold water simply in the name of a disciple, truly, I say to you, he will not lose his reward."[18] He holds faith with a neighbor in his poverty, and therefore he will enjoy his good things. SERMON 41.5-6.[19]

16:27-31 On Hearing Moses and the Prophets

---

[12]ECTD 235-36**. [13]FC 17:210-11**. [14]Mt 7:2. [15]WSA 3 10:297**. [16]Sir 22:23. [17]Lk16:9. [18]Mt 10:41-42. [19]WSA 3 2:230-31*.

Loving Too Much Your Own Five Senses, You Could Not Love Your Neighbor in Need. Jerome: Your father is Abraham. How can you say, "Send him to my father's house"? You have not forgotten your father. You have not forgotten that your father destroyed you. Since he was your father, you have five brothers: sight, smell, taste, hearing and touch. These are the brothers to whom formerly you were enslaved. Since they were the brothers you loved, you could not love your brother Lazarus. Naturally you could not love him as brother, because you loved them. Those brothers have no love for poverty. Your sight, your sense of smell, your taste, and your sense of touch were your brothers. These brothers of yours loved wealth, and they had no eye for poverty. "I have five brothers, that he may testify to them." They are the brothers who sent you into these torments. They cannot be saved unless they die. "Lest they too come into this place of torments." Why do you want to save those brothers who have no love for poverty? Brothers must dwell with their brother. On Lazarus and Dives 86.[20]

The Rich Man Ignored and Ridiculed Moses and the Prophets. Augustine: He and his brothers were in the habit of making fun of the prophets. I imagine and have no doubt at all that he talked with his brothers about the prophets. He talked about their urging us to do good and forbidding us to do wrong, and their frightening us with torments to come and promising rewards to come. He made fun of all this and said with his brothers, "What life is there after death? What does rottenness in the grave remember? What do ashes feel? Everyone is carried there and buried. Whoever came back from there and was heard?" That is the reason, as he remembered his words, that he wanted Lazarus to go back to his brothers, so that now they would not say, "Whoever came back from there?" This also has a very suitable and proper answer. This man, you see, seems to have been a Jew. That is why he said, "Father Abraham." He got an excellent and fitting answer. "If they do not listen to Moses and the prophets, they will not be convinced even if one should rise from the dead." This was fulfilled with the Jews, because they did not listen to Moses and the prophets, nor did they believe Christ when he rose. Had he not foretold this to them before, "If you believed Moses, you would also believe me"?[21] Sermon 41.4.[22]

Not Hearing Christ. Jerome: "If they do not hear Moses and the prophets, they will not believe even if someone rises from the dead." "If you believed Moses, you would believe me also, for he wrote of me."[23] Do you now see what Abraham means? You do well to wait for him who will rise from the dead, but Moses and the prophets proclaim that he is the One who is going to rise from the dead. Christ, in fact, speaks in them. If you hear them, you will also hear him. On Lazarus and Dives 86.[24]

---

[20]FC 57:205*. [21]Jn 5:46. [22]WSA 3 2:229**. [23]Jn 5:46. [24]FC 57:208*.

17:1-10 MORE TEACHINGS BY JESUS
ON DISCIPLESHIP

¹*And he said to his disciples, "Temptations to sin*[x] *are sure to come; but woe to him by whom they come!* ²*It would be better for him if a millstone were hung round his neck and he were cast into the sea, than that he should cause one of these little ones to sin.*[y] ³*Take heed to yourselves; if your brother sins, rebuke him, and if he repents, forgive him;* ⁴*and if he sins against you seven times in the day, and turns to you seven times, and says, 'I repent,' you must forgive him."*

⁵*The apostles said to the Lord, "Increase our faith!"* ⁶*And the Lord said, "If you had faith as a grain of mustard seed, you could say to this sycamine tree, 'Be rooted up, and be planted in the sea,' and it would obey you.*

⁷*"Will any one of you, who has a servant plowing or keeping sheep, say to him when he has come in from the field, 'Come at once and sit down at table'?* ⁸*Will he not rather say to him, 'Prepare supper for me, and gird yourself and serve me, till I eat and drink; and afterward you shall eat and drink'?* ⁹*Does he thank the servant because he did what was commanded?* ¹⁰*So you also, when you have done all that is commanded you, say, 'We are unworthy servants; we have only done what was our duty.'"*

x Greek *stumbling blocks*   y Greek *stumble*

OVERVIEW: The meaning of "stumbling block" is any impediment that might keep a believer from confessing that Jesus is *the* stumbling block. This impediment may be a temptation to sin or the sins that individuals commit against one another that are in need of forgiveness, as the context seems to indicate (CYRIL OF ALEXANDRIA). The scandal may also be connected to the passion of Christ (PETER CHRYSOLOGUS). In either case, scandal is sin because it causes offense (JEROME). How appropriate that Jesus would follow the parable about the rich man with words about mercy (AMBROSE). To forgive your brother seven times is to bear one another's burdens and so fulfill the law of Christ[1] (CYRIL OF ALEXANDRIA).

The apostles' request for an increase in faith is to ask for strength by the Holy Spirit. Such faith was given them after Jesus' resurrection (CYRIL OF ALEXANDRIA). The mustard seed signifies the great inner strength of faith in the church

(AUGUSTINE). The apostles should be more mindful of their slave relationship to their Lord than of the powers they might manifest through faith (AMBROSE). Seeking glory through one's faith empties that faith of its benefits and renders unprofitable the servants of the Lord (CHRYSOSTOM).

17:1-2 Those Who Create Stumbling Blocks

WOE TO THOSE WHO PLACE TEMPTATIONS IN THE PATH. CYRIL OF ALEXANDRIA: The accompanying discussion that immediately follows these opening remarks and speaks of our pardoning our brothers and sisters in case they ever sin against us leads us to the idea that these were the offenses meant. What are these offenses? They are, I suppose, mean and annoying actions, fits of

---

[1]Gal 6:2.

anger whether on good grounds or without justification, insults, slander, and other stumbling blocks similar to these. He says that these temptations must come. Is this then because God, who governs all, forces people to their commission of sin? Away with the thought! Nothing that is evil comes from him. He is the fountain of all virtue. Why then must this happen? They clearly happen because of our infirmity, for all of us stumble in many things, as it is written.[2] Nevertheless he says that there will be woe to the person who lays the stumbling blocks in the way. He does not leave indifference in these things without rebuke but restrains it by fear of punishment. He still commands us to bear with patience those who cause sins to happen. Commentary on Luke, Homilies 113-16.[3]

The Scandal Here Is the Passion of Christ. Peter Chrysologus: Hear the Lord saying, "Woe to the world because of scandals!" A scandal tempts the saints, fatigues the cautious, throws down the incautious, disturbs all things and confuses all people. It is true that in this present passage the Lord is talking about the scandal of his passion. Sermon 27.[4]

Temptations Are Sins to Come. Jerome: "It is impossible," he says, "that scandals should not come." I suppose that a scandal is a sin because sin comes through scandal. "In many things we all offend."[5] Granted that I have not come to ruin, but I have certainly offended not only in one thing but also in many things. Against the Pelagians 2.15.[6]

17:3-4 Forgive Those Who Repent

Jesus Follows the Parable with Words of Mercy. Ambrose: "If your brother sins against you, reprove him." After the parable of the rich man who was tortured in punishment, how fittingly he added the command of showing mercy to those indeed who repent of their error, for fear that despair might not recall someone

from guilt! He is truly moderate, so that pardon is not difficult or leniency lax, fearing that harsh reproof might cast someone down or conspiracy might invite guilt! . . . He fittingly said, "If your brother sins against you," for it is not an equal condition to sin against people and against God.[7] The apostle, who is a true interpreter of the divine prophecy, says, "After the first admonition, avoid a person that is a heretic,"[8] because unbelief is not on a par with minor transgression. Since error very often surprises someone through ignorance, he commands that it should be rebuked, so that stubbornness is shunned and a mistake is corrected. Exposition of the Gospel of Luke 8.21-22.[9]

To Forgive Seven Times. Cyril of Alexandria: He says, "If he who sins against you repents and acknowledges his fault, you shall forgive him not only once, but very many times." We . . . must rather imitate those whose business it is to heal our bodily diseases and who do not care for a sick person once only or twice, but just as often as he happens to become ill. Let us remember that we also are liable to infirmities and overpowered by our passions. This being the case, we pray that those who have the duty to rebuke us and who have the authority to punish us may show themselves forgiving and kind to us. It is our duty, having a common feeling for our mutual infirmities, to bear one another's burdens, so we will fulfill the law of Christ.[10] Observe also that in the Gospel according to Matthew, Peter makes the inquiry, "How often will my brother sin against me, and I forgive him?"[11] The Lord then tells the apostles, "Although he sins seven times in the day," that is, frequently, "and will acknowledge his fault, you shall forgive him." Commentary on Luke, Homilies 113-16.[12]

17:5-6 Doing Great Things by Faith

---

[2]Jas 3:2. [3]CGSL 461-62**. [4]FC 17:74*. [5]Jas 3:2. [6]FC 53: 319**. [7]1 Sam 2:25. [8]Tit 3:10. [9]EHG 338-39**. [10]Gal 6:2. [11]Mt 18:21. [12]CGSL 462**.

To Increase Faith Is to Strengthen It by the Holy Spirit. CYRIL OF ALEXANDRIA: They ask, "Add faith to us." They do not ask simply for faith, for perhaps you might imagine them to be without faith. They rather ask Christ for an addition to their faith and to be strengthened in faith. Faith partly depends on us and partly is the gift of the divine grace. The beginning of faith depends on us and our maintaining confidence and faith in God with all our power. The confirmation and strength necessary for this comes from the divine grace. For that reason, since all things are possible with God, the Lord says that all things are possible for him who believes.[13] The power that comes to us through faith is of God. Knowing this, blessed Paul also says in the first epistle to the Corinthians, "For to one is given through the Spirit the word of wisdom, to another the word of knowledge according to the same Spirit, and to another faith in the same Spirit."[14] You see that he has placed faith also in the catalogue of spiritual graces. The disciples requested that they might receive this from the Savior, contributing also what was of themselves. By the descent upon them of the Holy Spirit, he granted it to them after the fulfillment of the dispensation. Before the resurrection, their faith was so feeble that they were liable even to the charge of being "little of faith." COMMENTARY ON LUKE, HOMILIES 113-16.[15]

The Great Faith of the Church. AUGUSTINE: A mustard seed looks small. Nothing is less noteworthy to the sight, but nothing is stronger to the taste. What does that signify but the very great fervor and inner strength of faith in the church? SERMON 246.3.[16]

17:7-10 *An Apostle Is a Humble Slave*

The Faithful Are Called to Humble Service. AMBROSE: You do not say to your servant, "Sit down," but require more service from him and do not thank him. The Lord also does not allow only one work or labor for you, because so long as we live we must always work.

Know that you are a servant overwhelmed by very much obedience. You must not set yourself first, because you are called a son of God. Grace must be acknowledged, but nature not overlooked. Do not boast of yourself if you have served well, as you should have done. The sun obeys, the moon complies,[17] and the angels serve. . . . Let us not require praise from ourselves nor prevent the judgment of God and anticipate the sentence of the Judge but reserve it for its own time and Judge. EXPOSITION OF THE GOSPEL OF LUKE 8.31-32.[18]

Pursuit of Human Glory. CHRYSOSTOM: He said, "When you have done everything, say, 'We are unprofitable servants,'" to warn them in his wish that they keep themselves at great distance from that destructive passion. Dearly beloved, see how the person with his mouth open for human glory and performing the works of virtue on that account has no benefit from it. Despite practicing every example of virtue, if he seems to give himself credit for it, he ends up empty-handed and bereaved of everything. HOMILY ON GENESIS 31.4.[19]

---

[13]Mk 9:23. [14]1 Cor 12:8. [15]CGSL 462-63**. [16]WSA 3 7:104*. [17]Josh 10:12-13; Let Jer 60. [18]EHG 342-43**. [19]FC 82:239-40**.

17:11-19 THE THIRD TRAVEL NOTICE, CLEANSING OF THE TEN LEPERS AND THE THANKFUL SAMARITAN

[11]On the way to Jerusalem he was passing along between Samaria and Galilee. [12]And as he entered a village, he was met by ten lepers, who stood at a distance [13]and lifted up their voices and said, "Jesus, Master, have mercy on us." [14]When he saw them he said to them, "Go and show yourselves to the priests." And as they went they were cleansed. [15]Then one of them, when he saw that he was healed, turned back, praising God with a loud voice; [16]and he fell on his face at Jesus' feet, giving him thanks. Now he was a Samaritan. [17]Then said Jesus, "Were not ten cleansed? Where are the nine? [18]Was no one found to return and give praise to God except this foreigner?" [19]And he said to him, "Rise and go your way; your faith has made you well."

OVERVIEW: Jesus sends the lepers to the priest to be cleansed spiritually because this is what the law demands, and in sending them he sends the healing, for they were made clean on the way (CYRIL OF ALEXANDRIA). The Samaritan responds in faith by blessing Jesus and glorifying him for the benefits he received (ATHANASIUS). The thankless nine do not realize the eschatological significance of what happened to them, that is, God's kingdom has arrived in Jesus (CYRIL OF ALEXANDRIA).

17:11-19 *Cleansing of the Ten Lepers*

JESUS SENT THEM TO THE PRIESTS TO FULFILL THE LAW. CYRIL OF ALEXANDRIA: Why did he not say, "I will, be cleansed,"[1] as he did in the case of another leper, instead of commanding them to show themselves to the priests? It was because the law gave directions to this effect to those who were delivered from leprosy.[2] It commanded them to show themselves to the priests and to offer a sacrifice for their cleansing. He commanded them to go as being already healed so that they might bear witness to the priests, the rulers of the Jews and always envious of his glory. They testified that wonderfully and beyond their hope, they had been delivered from their misfortune by Christ's willing that they should be healed. He did not heal them first but sent them to the priests, because the priests knew the marks of leprosy and of its healing. COMMENTARY ON LUKE, HOMILIES 113-16.[3]

BLESS THE HELPER FOR BENEFITS RECEIVED. ATHANASIUS: Today, the Lord rebukes those who keep the Passover the way the Jews did, just as he rebuked certain lepers he had cleansed. You recall that he loved the one who was thankful, but he was angry with the ungrateful ones, because they did not acknowledge their Deliverer. They thought more highly of their cure from leprosy than of him who had healed them. . . . Actually, this one was given much more than the rest. Besides being healed of his leprosy, he was told by the Lord, "Stand up and go on your way. Your faith has saved you."

You see, those who give thanks and those who glorify have the same kind of feelings. They bless their helper for the benefits they have received. That is why Paul urged everybody to "glorify God with your body."[4] Isaiah also commanded, "Give glory to God."[5] FESTAL LETTER 6.[6]

THE THANKFULNESS OF THE SAMARITAN.

---

[1]Lk 5:13. [2]See Lev 14:2. [3]CGSL 466**. [4]1 Cor 6:20. [5]Is 42:12. [6]ARL 101-2*.

CYRIL OF ALEXANDRIA: Falling into a thankless forgetfulness, the nine lepers that were Jews did not return to give glory to God. By this, he shows that Israel was hard of heart and utterly unthankful. The stranger, a Samaritan, was of foreign race brought from Assyria. The phrase "in the middle of Samaria and Galilee" has meaning. "He re-turned with a loud voice to glorify God." It shows that the Samaritans were grateful but that the Jews, even when they benefited, were ungrateful. COMMENTARY ON LUKE, HOMILIES 113-16.[7]

[7]CGSL 466**.

17:20-37 TEACHINGS ABOUT THE COMING OF THE KINGDOM

[20]*Being asked by the Pharisees when the kingdom of God was coming, he answered them, "The kingdom of God is not coming with signs to be observed;* [21]*nor will they say, 'Lo, here it is!' or 'There!' for behold, the kingdom of God is in the midst of you."*[z]

[22]*And he said to the disciples, "The days are coming when you will desire to see one of the days of the Son of man, and you will not see it.* [23]*And they will say to you, 'Lo, there!' or 'Lo, here!' Do not go, do not follow them.* [24]*For as the lightning flashes and lights up the sky from one side to the other, so will the Son of man be in his day.*[a] [25]*But first he must suffer many things and be rejected by this generation.* [26]*As it was in the days of Noah, so will it be in the days of the Son of man.* [27]*They ate, they drank, they married, they were given in marriage, until the day when Noah entered the ark, and the flood came and destroyed them all.* [28]*Likewise as it was in the days of Lot—they ate, they drank, they bought, they sold, they planted, they built,* [29]*but on the day when Lot went out from Sodom fire and sulphur rained from heaven and destroyed them all—* [30]*so will it be on the day when the Son of man is revealed.* [31]*On that day, let him who is on the housetop, with his goods in the house, not come down to take them away; and likewise let him who is in the field not turn back.* [32]*Remember Lot's wife.* [33]*Whoever seeks to gain his life will lose it, but whoever loses his life will preserve it.* [34]*I tell you, in that night there will be two in one bed; one will be taken and the other left.* [35]*There will be two women grinding together; one will be taken and the other left."*[b] [37]*And they said to him, "Where, Lord?" He said to them, "Where the body is, there the eagles*[c] *will be gathered together."*

z Or *within you*   a Other ancient authorities omit *in his day*   b Other ancient authorities add verse 36, *"Two men will be in the field; one will be taken and the other left"*   c Or *vultures*

OVERVIEW: The question of the Pharisees about the "when" of the kingdom of God shows how much they and the crowds did not understand that the kingdom had come already now in the person of Jesus and in his ministry of release to the captives. It comes through the spread of the gospel and therefore is received within us by faith (CYRIL OF ALEXANDRIA). It comes through supernatural

269

knowledge by the grace of God through faith alone (ISAAC OF NINEVEH). When the kingdom of God is within you, there is righteousness, peace and joy, and there is no room for the kingdom of Satan (JOHN CASSIAN). If we are servants of the Lord, then we will know that we are partaking of his kingdom (AMBROSE). Jesus speaks about the coming of the Son of man in order to prepare his disciples for the persecution they will experience (CYRIL OF ALEXANDRIA). If one knows what the signs are for the Lord's coming in judgment, then one will know when the end is about to come (AMBROSE). The order of the kingdom is this: first the Son of man must suffer and enter his glory, and then the end will come (CYRIL OF ALEXANDRIA).

The signs that will accompany the day of the Son of man will be not only clear but sudden, for there are great similarities between the days of Noah and Lot and the days of the Son of man in the suddenness of God's judgment (CYRIL OF ALEXANDRIA). For the flood that came upon Noah and his family was like baptism, bringing salvation to those in the ark but death to those outside. Those on the rooftops are not to come down from the roof, that is, from a life that is spiritual into one that is carnal (AUGUSTINE). They may be the rich who desire to be seen by all but will be tempted to return to their possessions in the house when the end finally comes (CYRIL OF ALEXANDRIA). Those in the field are to stay where they are, for they are sowing the Word of God (AMBROSE). They are to persevere in the work of the kingdom and not take their hands off the plow (CYRIL OF ALEXANDRIA). Remember Lot's wife, and do not look back. She looked back at Sodom, where all her possessions perished, and she lost her life (AMBROSE). Lot represents the soul that resists the temptation to look back, whereas his wife represents the flesh that returns to her possessions (ORIGEN). To resist the temptation to look back is what it means to lose your life in order to save it (CYRIL OF ALEXANDRIA).

Christ will come at night because it will be the time of darkness because of the Antichrist (AMBROSE). The man taken from the bed may be a rich man if he led a charitable life by making friends for himself with his wealth. Both women come from poverty, but only one has lived a virtuous and righteous life (CYRIL OF ALEXANDRIA). One woman represents believers; another unbelievers (AMBROSE).

The disciples will recognize the coming of the kingdom because it will be abundantly clear to them, as clear as it is when one is looking for a dead body marked by the vultures hovering over it. This will find fulfillment when Jesus' body is nailed to the cross and he is surrounded by his faithful followers like the women who gather at his tomb. The gathering place of the kingdom is the body of Christ, and it will remain so in the age of the church—the body of Christ where his saints gather around the sacrament of his body (AMBROSE).

17:20-21 *The Kingdom Is Present Now*

THE KINGDOM OF GOD COMES BY FAITH.

CYRIL OF ALEXANDRIA: These miserable men ask in mockery, "When will the kingdom of God come?" This is like saying, "Before this kingdom of which you speak comes, cross and death will seize you." What does Christ reply? He again displays his long-suffering and incomparable love to humanity. Reviled, he does not revile again. Suffering, he does not threaten.[1] He does not harshly scold them, but because of their wickedness, he does not stoop to give them an answer to their question. He says only what is for the benefit of all people: that the kingdom of God does not come by watching. "Behold, the kingdom of God is within you." He says, "Do not ask about the times in which the season of the kingdom of heaven will again arise and come. Rather, be eager that you may be found worthy of it. It is within you. That is, it depends on your own wills and is in your own power, whether or not you receive it. Everyone that has attained to justification by means of faith in Christ and decorated by every

---

[1]1 Pet 2:23.

virtue is counted worthyq of the kingdom of heaven." COMMENTARY ON LUKE, HOMILY 117.[2]

FAITH GIVES SUPERNATURAL KNOWLEDGE.

ISAAC OF NINEVEH: "The Kingdom of the Heavens is within you," and you should not hope to find it in a place, nor does it come in observation, according to the word of Christ. ASCETICAL HOMILIES 53.[3]

THE KINGDOM OF GOD IS RIGHTEOUSNESS, PEACE AND JOY.

JOHN CASSIAN: If the devil has been driven out and sin no longer reigns, then the kingdom of God is established in us. As it is written in the Gospel, "The kingdom of God does not come with observation, nor will they say, 'Lo here,' or 'Lo, there.' Truly I say to you that the kingdom of God is within you." The only thing that can be "within us" is knowledge or ignorance of the truth and the affection for righteousness or sin by which we prepare our hearts to be a kingdom of Christ or the devil. St. Paul described the nature of this kingdom in this way: "For the kingdom of God is not food and drink, but righteousness and peace and joy in the Holy Spirit."[4] If the kingdom of God is within us and is righteousness, peace and joy, then someone that remains in these is surely within the kingdom of God. Someone that remains in unrighteousness, conflict and the melancholy that kills the life of the spirit is already a citizen of the devil's kingdom, of hell and of death. These are the signs whether it is God's kingdom or the devil's. CONFERENCE 1.13.[5]

TO PARTAKE OF THE KINGDOM.

AMBROSE: Asked by the disciples when the kingdom of God would come,[6] the Lord said, "The kingdom of God is within you," through the truth of grace and not through the slavery of guilt. Let those that would be free be servants in the Lord.[7] As we share in service, we also share in the kingdom. He said, "The kingdom of God is within you." He would not say when it would come. He said there would be a day of judgment, so that he instilled in all terror of the judgment to come,[8] and he did not add the guarantee of its postponement. EXPOSITION OF THE GOSPEL OF LUKE 8.33.[9]

17:22-25 The Son of Man Must Suffer

JESUS PREPARES HIS DISCIPLES FOR PERSECUTION.

CYRIL OF ALEXANDRIA: He now speaks to the holy disciples as his true companions. He says, "The days will come when you will desire to see one of the days of the Son of man, and will not see it." . . . He would have them prepared for all that can cause people grief. He wants them ready to endure patiently so that approved they may enter the kingdom of God. He warns them that before his coming from heaven at the consummation of the world, tribulation and persecution will precede him. They will wish to see one of the days of the Son of man, such as those when they were still going around with Christ and speaking with him. COMMENTARY ON LUKE, HOMILY 117.[10]

ONE WHO KNOWS THE SIGNS KNOWS THE END.

AMBROSE: He who knows the signs of the coming judgment also knows the end. Why would he not know? He is like flashing lightning, since as the Light, the Son of God[11] illumines the inner part of the heavenly mystery. "In that hour," it says. He also knows the hour, but he knows it for himself, he does not know it for me. He then suitably asserts that the cause of the flood, fire and of the judgment proceeded from our sins, because God did not create evil, but our actions devised it for themselves. EXPOSITION OF THE GOSPEL OF LUKE 8.35-36.[12]

JESUS WILL COME IN GLORY LIKE LIGHTNING.

CYRIL OF ALEXANDRIA: At the end time of the world, he will not descend from heaven obscurely or secretly, but with godlike glory and as dwelling in the light which no one can approach.[13] He declared that his coming will be like the light-

---

[2]CGSL 467-68**. [3]AHSIS 264. [4]Rom 14:17. [5]LCC 12:202-3**. [6]Acts 1:6. [7]See 1 Cor 7:22. [8]See Mt 24:30-31. [9]EHG 343-44**. [10]CGSL 468**. [11]See Jn 1:9. [12]EHG 344-45**. [13]1 Tim 6:16.

ning. He was born indeed in the flesh of a woman, to fulfill the dispensation for our sakes. For this reason, he emptied himself, made himself poor, and no longer showed himself in the glory of the Godhead.[14] The season and the necessity of the dispensation summoned him to this humiliation. After his resurrection from the dead, ascension into heaven, and enthronement with God the Father, he will descend again. He will not descend with his glory withdrawn or in the lowliness of human nature. In the majesty of the Father with the companies of the angels guarding him, he will stand before him as God and Lord of all. He will come as the lightning, and not secretly. COMMENTARY ON LUKE, HOMILY 117.[15]

The Kingdom Must Come Through Suffering Before It Comes in Glory. CYRIL OF ALEXANDRIA: That they might know that he was about first to undergo his saving passion, abolish death by the death of his flesh, put away the sin of the world, destroy the ruler of this world, ascend to the Father and in due time appear to judge the world in righteousness, he says that he must first suffer many things.[16] COMMENTARY ON LUKE, HOMILY 117.[17]

17:26-33 The Examples of Noah and Lot

Judgment Will Come Suddenly. CYRIL OF ALEXANDRIA: To show that he will appear unexpectedly and with no one knowing it, the Lord says that the end of the world will come and be as it was in the days of Noah and Lot. He says, "They were eating and drinking, and were taking wives and being made the wives of men. They were selling and buying and building," but the coming of the waters destroyed the one, while the others were the prey and food of fire and brimstone. What does this signify? It signifies that he requires us to be always watchful and ready to make our defense before the tribunal of God. COMMENTARY ON LUKE, HOMILY 117.[18]

The Flood Was Baptism for Believers,

Death for Unbelievers. AUGUSTINE: In the days of Noah this preaching to them was futile because they did not believe when the patience of God waited for them for many years in which the ark was built. Its building was in a sense a kind of preaching. In the same way today, their imitators do not believe. They are shut up in the darkness of ignorance. They are like in a prison, looking in vain on the church being built throughout the whole world. Judgment threatens them as did the flood in which all the unbelievers perished. The Lord says, "As in the days of Noah, so will it be also in the days of the Son of man. They were eating and drinking, marrying and giving in marriage until Noah entered the ark, and the flood came and destroyed them all." Since this signified a future event, the flood also signified baptism for believers and death for unbelievers. There is also a symbol in what was spoken and not done, where it is written about the stone that signifies Christ. Two effects were foretold. It is a stumbling block for unbelievers and a building for believers. LETTER 164.[19]

Leaving a Spiritual Life for a Carnal One. AUGUSTINE: Regarding the saying, "He that is on the housetop, let him not come down to take anything out of his house, and he that is in the field, let him not go back to take his coat," can be suitably taken in a spiritual sense. In all our trials, each one must take care not to be overcome or to come down from a spiritual height to a carnal life. He who had progressed should not look back by turning toward the past or failing to reach out to the future. This is true of every trial. How much greater care must be prescribed in a trial such as that foretold for the city as "Such as has not been from the beginning, neither will be"? How much more this is true for that final tribulation which is to come on the world, that is, the church spread through the whole world? LETTER 199.32.[20]

---

[14]Phil 2:7. [15]CGSL 468-69**. [16]Ps 96:13 (95:13 LXX). [17]CGSL 469**. [18]CGSL 469**. [19]FC 20:393**. [20]FC 30:381-82**.

THE RICH ARE THOSE ON THE ROOFTOPS.

CYRIL OF ALEXANDRIA: The Savior . . . was speaking of the last day, that is, the end of this world. . . . Strengthening them to recall the last day and the end time, he commands them to disregard all earthly and temporary matters and look only to one end, the duty of everyone saving his soul. He says, "He that is on the housetop, do not let him go down to the house to carry away his goods." In these words, he apparently means the one who is at ease, living in wealth and worldly glory. Those that stand on the housetops are always conspicuous in the eyes of those who are around the house. COMMENTARY ON LUKE, HOMILY 118.[21]

THOSE WORKING IN THE FIELD ARE SOWING THE WORD OF GOD.

AMBROSE: "He that will be on the housetop, do not let him go down. He that will be in the field, do not let him turn back." How may I understand what is the field unless Jesus himself teaches me? He says, "No one putting his hand to the plough and looking back is fit for the kingdom of God."[22] The lazy person sits in the farmhouse, but the industrious person plants in the field. The weak are at the fireplace, but the strong are at the plough. The smell of a field is good, because the smell of Jacob is the smell of a full field.[23] A field is full of flowers. It is full of different fruits. Plough your field if you want to be sent to the kingdom of God. Let your field flower, fruitful with good rewards. Let there be a fruitful vine on the sides of your house and young olive plants around your table.[24] Already aware of its fertility, let your soul, sown with the Word of God and tilled by spiritual farming, say to Christ, "Come, my brother, let us go out into the field."[25] Let him reply, "I have come into my garden, my sister, my bride. I have gathered my vintage of myrrh."[26] What is better than the vintage of faith, by which the fruit of the resurrection is stored and the spring of eternal rejoicing is watered? EXPOSITION OF THE GOSPEL OF LUKE 8.43.[27]

PERSEVERE IN THE FAITH.

CYRIL OF ALEXANDRIA: He says, "Even if anyone is in the field, in the same way, do not let him turn back." That means if anyone is found devoted to work and occupied in labor, earnestly desiring spiritual fruitfulness and gathering the wages of virtuous toil, let him hold firmly to this diligence. Let him not turn back. As Christ himself has again said somewhere, "No one that puts his hand to the plough and turns back is fit also for the kingdom of heaven."[28] It is our duty to maintain our religious exertions without wavering and to persevere in them with undaunted wills or else we may suffer the kind of fate that befell the woman at Sodom. We take her as an example because he says, "Remember Lot's wife. For when she was rescued from Sodom, but would afterward have returned, she became a pillar of salt." That means she became foolish and stonelike. COMMENTARY ON LUKE, HOMILY 118.[29]

LOT'S WIFE LOOKED BACK AT HER POSSESSIONS.

AMBROSE: For this reason, the Lord says, "Remember Lot's wife," who because she looked back, lost the function of her own nature.[30] Satan[31] and Sodom are behind. Flee excess and shun extravagance. Know that not everyone can flee to the mountain. Remember that the one who did not return to his old pursuits, as if to Sodom,[32] escaped because he came to the mountain.[33] She, who was weaker since she looked back, could not come to the mountain. She remained, although her husband's help supported her. EXPOSITION OF THE GOSPEL OF LUKE 8.45.[34]

THE SOUL GOING TOWARD SALVATION MUST NOT LOOK BACKWARD.

ORIGEN: "The law is spiritual"[35] and the things that happened to the ancients "happened figuratively."[36] Let us see if perhaps Lot, who did not look back, is the rational understanding and the courageous soul. His wife here represents the flesh. The flesh al-

---

[21]CGSL 470**. [22]Lk 9:62. [23]Gen 27:27. [24]Ps 127:3 LXX. [25]Song 7:11. [26]Song 5:1. [27]EHG 347*. [28]Lk 9:62. [29]CGSL 471. [30]Gen 19:26; Wis 10:7. [31]See 1 Tim 5:15. [32]Gen 13:10. [33]Gen 19:30. [34]EHG 348**. [35]Rom 7:14. [36]1 Cor 10:11 Vulgate.

ways looks to vices. When the soul is going toward salvation, it looks backward and seeks pleasures. Concerning this, the Lord also said, "No man putting his hand to the plow and looking back is fit for the kingdom of God." He adds, "Remember Lot's wife." The fact that "she became a little statue of salt" appears to be an open indication of her foolishness. Salt represents the wisdom that she lacked. HOMILIES ON GENESIS 5.2.[37]

TO LOSE YOUR LIFE YOU SAVE IT. CYRIL OF ALEXANDRIA: Whoever loses his life shall certainty save it. This is what the blessed martyrs did, enduring conflicts even to loss of blood and life and placing on their heads as their crown their true love for Christ. Those who, from weakness of resolution and mind, denied the faith and fled from the present death of the body, became their own murderers. They will go down to hell to suffer the penalties of their wicked cowardice. The judge will descend from heaven. He will call those who with all their heart have loved him and earnestly practiced a completely virtuous life, saying, "Come, you blessed of my Father, inherit the kingdom prepared for you from the foundations of the world."[38] He will pass a severe and overwhelming sentence on those who have led careless and unrestrained lives or have not maintained the glory of faith in him, saying to them, "Depart, you cursed, into everlasting fire." COMMENTARY ON LUKE, HOMILY 118.[39]

17:34-35 Some Taken, Some Left Behind

CHRIST COMES AT NIGHT. AMBROSE: He fittingly said, "night," because the Antichrist is the hour of darkness. The Antichrist spreads darkness in the hearts of people, when he says he is the Christ. . . . Christ, like flashing lightning,[40] scatters the spheres of his light throughout the world. He does not wander through the desert. He is not enclosed in some other places, because the Lord says, "I fill heaven and earth."[41] He shines with the light of his splendor, so that we may see his glory in that night of the resurrec-

tion. EXPOSITION OF THE GOSPEL OF LUKE 8.46.[42]

A CHARITABLE LIFE. CYRIL OF ALEXANDRIA: By the two who are in one bed, he seems to hint at those who live in rest and plenty. They are equal to one another, as far as being possessed of worldly affluence. The bed is the symbol of rest. He says, "One of them will be taken, and one will be left." How is one taken? Not all those who are possessed of wealth and ease in this world are wicked and merciless. COMMENTARY ON LUKE, HOMILY 118.[43]

ONLY ONE IS RIGHTEOUS. CYRIL OF ALEXANDRIA: He says, "Two women will be grinding at a mill. The one will be taken, and the other left." By these he again seems to mean those who live in poverty and labor. Even in these, he says that there is a certain vast difference. Some have carried the burden of poverty courageously, honoring a serious and virtuous way of life. Others have been of a different character. They are planners for every wicked practice and all shamefulness. There will be even in their case a full and exact investigation of their manners. The good will be taken, and he that is not good will be left. COMMENTARY ON LUKE, HOMILY 118.[44]

BELIEVERS AND UNBELIEVERS. AMBROSE: Two people in this world, which is very often compared with a field,[45] are believers and unbelievers. One will receive the reward of their merits; therefore the faithful one is taken, but the faithless is left.[46] EXPOSITION OF THE GOSPEL OF LUKE 8.52.[47]

17:37 The Signs Will Be Clear

THE EAGLES ARE THE WOMEN WHO GATHER AROUND CHRIST'S BODY AT THE TOMB. AMBROSE: "Answering, they said, 'Where, Lord?' "

---

[37]FC 71:114**. [38]Mt 25:34. [39]CGSL 471**. [40]Mt 24:27. [41]Jer 23:24. [42]EHG 348-49**. [43]CGSL 472**. [44]CGSL 472**. [45]See Mt 13:38. [46]Mt 24:40. [47]EHG 352**.

The disciples asked this. The Lord predicted where they must flee, when they must stay, and of what they should be wary. He summarized everything in a general definition, saying, "Wherever the body will be, the eagles will be gathered together." Let us first speculate what the eagles are, so we may determine what the body is. The souls of the righteous are compared with eagles, because they seek the heights,[48] leave the depths behind, and reportedly reach a great age. David also says to his soul, "Your youth will be renewed like that of an eagle."[49] If we understood the eagles, we cannot doubt concerning the body, particularly if we remember that Joseph received the body of Christ from Pilate.[50] Does it not seem to you that the eagles around the body are Mary of Cleopas, Mary Magdalene, Mary, the mother of the Lord,[51] and the assembly of the apostles around the Lord's tomb? EXPOSITION OF THE GOSPEL OF LUKE 8.54-55.[52]

THE SAINTS GATHER AROUND THE SACRAMENT. AMBROSE: He says concerning this body, "My flesh is meat indeed, and my blood is drink indeed."[53] Around this body, eagles fly on spiritual wings. Around the body, eagles believe that Jesus has come in the flesh, because every spirit that confesses that Jesus Christ has come in the flesh is of God.[54] Where faith is, there is the sacrament and the dwelling place of holiness. The body is also the church, in which we are renewed in the spirit[55] through the grace of baptism, and the frailties of old age are restored for ages of new life. EXPOSITION OF THE GOSPEL OF LUKE 8.56.[56]

---

[48]Obad 1:4. [49]Ps 102:5 LXX. [50]Jn 19:38. [51]Jn 19:25. [52]EHG 353**. [53]Jn 6:55. [54]1 Jn 4:2. [55]See Eph 4:23. [56]EHG 353-54**.

18:1-8 THE UNRIGHTEOUS JUDGE

[1]And he told them a parable, to the effect that they ought always to pray and not lose heart. [2]He said, "In a certain city there was a judge who neither feared God nor regarded man; [3]and there was a widow in that city who kept coming to him and saying, 'Vindicate me against my adversary.' [4]For a while he refused; but afterward he said to himself, 'Though I neither fear God nor regard man, [5]yet because this widow bothers me, I will vindicate her, or she will wear me out by her continual coming.'" [6]And the Lord said, "Hear what the unrighteous judge says. [7]And will not God vindicate his elect, who cry to him day and night? Will he delay long over them? [8]I tell you, he will vindicate them speedily. Nevertheless, when the Son of man comes, will he find faith on earth?"

OVERVIEW: It is not the length of prayer that Jesus is recommending, something that he cautions against, but persistence in prayer (AUGUSTINE). Those who pray continually have an advocate with the Father, who gives them whatever they ask (ORIGEN). In the parable, a persistent widow will be blessed because she seeks out her judge with persistence. And because of her persistence, the judge shows her mercy even though he has no respect for people or fear of God, showing how much more we might expect from our merciful God (CYRIL OF ALEXANDRIA). The persistent prayer of the widow transforms the iniquity and wickedness of the judge into mercy because she was more persistent than he was (EPHREM THE SYRIAN).

As much as it may appear to himself and his society that he does not fear God or respect people, the judge, when pushed by a shameless widow, does care about his reputation. In a similar way—and this involves moving from the lesser to the greater—God will be true to himself and his Word: the time of vindication for his faithful saints will come (AUGUSTINE). God will eventually give vindication, because he has promised salvation to the elect, who cry to him day and night, from the attacks of the Satan their adversary (MARTYRIUS).

God's vindication does indeed come quickly at Christ's atonement because our enemy is none other than Satan. Our cry for vindication is for the incarnate Word of God to avenge us against the tyranny of the devil. The longsuffering God who vindicates quickly wants his elect to pray constantly and confidently: they are to ask, seek and persevere. Christ asks, "Nevertheless, when the Son of man comes, will he even find the faith on the earth?" Will there be a faithful community awaiting at the coming of the Son of man amid all the false teachings (CYRIL OF ALEXANDRIA)?

18:1 Introduction

NOT THE LENGTH OF PRAYER BUT PERSISTENCE. AUGUSTINE: [The Lord] taught us to pray[1] to receive this blessed life. He taught us not to pray with much speaking, as if we were more likely to be heard, the more words we use in our prayer. The Lord said, "He knows what is needful for us before we ask him." For this reason, it may seem strange, although he cautions us against much speaking, he still urges us to pray since he knows what is needful for us before we ask for it. He said, "We should always pray and not faint." He used the example of a certain widow who wished to be avenged of her adversary and petitioned an unjust judge so often that she made him listen to her. She made him listen not through any motive of justice or compassion, but

through weariness of her insistence. In this way, we were to learn how surely the merciful and just God hears us when we pray without ceasing. The widow, because of her continual petition, could not be treated with contempt even by an unjust and wicked judge. LETTER 130.[2]

THOSE WHO PRAY CONTINUALLY HAVE AN ADVOCATE WITH THE FATHER. ORIGEN: He prays for those who pray and appeals with those who appeal. He does not, however, pray for servants who do not pray continuously through him. He will not be the Advocate with God for his own if they are not obedient to his instructions that they always should pray and not lose heart. It says, "And he told them a parable to the effect that they should always pray and not lose heart. In a certain city there was a judge, etc." . . . Who would hesitate a moment to be persuaded to pray if he believes that the mouth of Jesus cannot lie, when he says, "Ask, and it will be given you . . . for everyone who asks, receives"?[3] ON PRAYER 10.2.[4]

18:2-5 The Parable

THE PERSISTENCE OF THE WIDOW. CYRIL OF ALEXANDRIA: The present parable assures us God will bend his ear to those who offer him their prayers, not carelessly nor negligently but with earnestness and constancy. The constant coming of the oppressed widow conquered the unjust judge that did not fear God or have any shame. Even against his will, he granted her request. How will not he who loves mercy and hates iniquity, and who always gives his helping hand to those that love him, accept those who draw near to him day and night and avenge them as his elect? COMMENTARY ON LUKE, HOMILY 119.[5]

PERSISTENT PRAYER TRANSFORMS INIQUITY AND WICKEDNESS INTO MERCY. EPHREM THE SYRIAN: How was that unjust judge immoral and

---

[1]Mt 6:7-8. [2]FC 18:387-88**. [3]Lk 11:9-10; Mt 7:7-8. [4]OSW 101**. [5]CGSL 478*.

wicked? How was the upright judge gracious and just? The first in his iniquity was not willing to vindicate the widow, and in his wickedness, he was not willing to put her mind at rest. The justice of God knows how to vindicate, and his grace discerns how to give life. The iniquity of this wicked judge was contrary to the justice of God, and the wickedness of this rebel was in opposition to the grace of the gentle One. His wickedness therefore was stubbornness, for it dared to go against the fear of God. His boldness was stubborn, for it refused the lowly person.

These two were stubborn, but persistent prayer was even more stubborn. The persistence of the widow humiliated both the iniquity that was rebelling against God and the boldness that was behaving arrogantly towards human beings. She subjected them to her will, so that they might provide her with a vindication over her adversary. Persistence transformed these two bitter branches, and they bore sweet fruit that was against their nature. The iniquity of the judge brought about a righteous judgment and a just retribution for the falsely accused woman. His wickedness gave peace to the afflicted one, although iniquity does not know how to judge, and wickedness does not know how to give refreshment. Persistence forced these two evil and bitter branches to give good fruit against their nature. If we persist in prayer, we should be even more able to prevail on the grace and justice of God to give us fruit that agrees with their nature. Let justice vindicate us, and let grace refresh us. Accordingly, the fruit of justice is the just reward of the oppressed, while the giving of refreshment to the afflicted is the fruit of grace. COMMENTARY ON TATIAN'S DIATESSARON 16.16.[6]

18:6-8 The Interpretation

NOT AN ALLEGORICAL REPRESENTATION OF GOD. AUGUSTINE:

These examples now are proposed so that important things may be suggested from things of less importance. They are like the example of the judge who feared neither God nor people and who nevertheless yielded to the widow bothering him to judge her case. He yielded not through piety or kindness but through fear of suffering annoyance. By no means does that unjust judge furnish an allegorical representation of God. The example is of an unjust man who, although he yields for the mere sake of avoiding annoyance, nevertheless cannot disregard those who bother him with continual pleadings. By this the Lord wishes us to infer how much care God bestows on those who beseech him, for God is both just and good. SERMON ON THE MOUNT 15.[7]

GOD VINDICATES US AGAINST SATAN'S ATTACKS. MARTYRIUS:

As our Savior pointed out, even the cruel and wicked judge eventually looked into the poor widow's case because she had wearied him with her insistence. It is quite clear that God does not neglect us. Even if he makes us wait, he will nonetheless answer us and see to our case all of a sudden. When we pray all the time, we should not weary. We should eagerly cry out to him day and night, begging him with a broken heart and a humble spirit. "A humble spirit is a sacrifice to God, and God will not reject a broken heart."[8] BOOK OF PERFECTION 75.[9]

THE INCARNATE WORD OF GOD AVENGES US. CYRIL OF ALEXANDRIA:

We say in our prayers to him who is able to save and drive away from us that wicked being, "Avenge me of my adversary." The only-begotten Word of God has truly done this by having become man. He has ejected the ruler of this world from his tyranny over us and has delivered and saved us and put us under the yoke of his kingdom. It is excellent to make requests through constant prayer, because Christ will receive our pleas and fulfill our petitions. COMMENTARY ON LUKE, HOMILY 119.[10]

WILL THE SON OF MAN FIND FAITH? CYRIL OF

---

[6]ECTD 250-51**. [7]FC 11:159*. [8]Ps 51:17. [9]CS 101:233**. [10]CGSL 479**.

ALEXANDRIA: People sell the word of righteousness and make many abandon sound faith. They involve them in the inventions of devilish error. As Scripture says, they belch things out of their own hearts and not out of the mouth of the Lord. He foretold this saying, "When the Son of man comes, will he find faith on the earth?" It did not escape his knowledge. How could it, since he is God, who knows all things? In his own words, he tells us that the love of many will grow cold. In the end times, some will depart from a correct and blameless faith. They will be going after seducing spirits and listening to the false words of people who have a seared conscience.[11] Against these, we come near to God as faithful servants, begging him that their wickedness and their attempts against his glory may have no effect. COMMENTARY ON LUKE, HOMILY 119.[12]

---

[11]1 Tim 4:1-2. [12]CGSL 479**.

18:9-14 THE PHARISEE AND THE TAX COLLECTOR

[9]*He also told this parable to some who trusted in themselves that they were righteous and despised others:* [10]*"Two men went up into the temple to pray, one a Pharisee and the other a tax collector.* [11]*The Pharisee stood and prayed thus with himself, 'God, I thank thee that I am not like other men, extortioners, unjust, adulterers, or even like this tax collector.* [12]*I fast twice a week, I give tithes of all that I get.'* [13]*But the tax collector, standing far off, would not even lift up his eyes to heaven, but beat his breast, saying, 'God, be merciful to me a sinner!'* [14]*I tell you, this man went down to his house justified rather than the other; for every one who exalts himself will be humbled, but he who humbles himself will be exalted."*

OVERVIEW: The parable of the Pharisee and the tax collector has clear links with the preceding parable, for it portrays a man whose prayer is evidence of the faith Christ hopes to find when he returns in judgment (AUGUSTINE). The self-loving Pharisee accuses others of what he is most guilty because of his pride and arrogance (CYRIL OF ALEXANDRIA). This Pharisee illustrates the danger of pride for all who serve God with their sacrifices of praise (MARTYRIUS). Instead of confessing his sickness through the salutary medicine of repentance, he compares his own health to the diseases of others (AUGUSTINE).

The tax collector does not even raise his eyes to the heavens (which is typical of Jews at prayer), and he beats his chest as a sign of his unworthiness. The posture of his prayer shows his humility. He asks for mercy and receives absolution (CYRIL OF ALEXANDRIA). In comparing himself with others, he does not claim to be better; rather, he knows and confesses that he is worst of all. It is always more difficult to confess one's sins than one's righteousness (EPHREM THE SYRIAN). The one who thought that he was rich in fact was very poor. Humility is the mark of a sinner. The principle of radical reversal applies: "Everyone who exalts himself will be humbled, and the one who humbles himself will be exalted" (BASIL THE GREAT).

18:9 The Introduction

FINDING FAITH IN THE PUBLICAN. AUGUS-
TINE: Does it not strike you when the Lord says
in the Gospel, "When the Son of man comes, do
you think he will find faith on earth?" Knowing
that some would arrogantly attribute this faith to
themselves, he immediately said, "To some who
seemed to themselves to be just and despised others, he spoke this parable. Two men went up into
the temple to pray: the one a Pharisee and the
other a publican, etc." LETTER 89.[1]

18:10-13 The Parable

**THE INFIRMITY OF OTHERS IS NOT A FIT
SUBJECT FOR PRAISE FOR THOSE IN GOOD
HEALTH.** CYRIL OF ALEXANDRIA: What profit is
there in fasting twice in the week if it serves only
as a pretext for ignorance and vanity and makes
you proud, haughty and selfish? You tithe your
possessions and boast about it. In another way,
you provoke God's anger by condemning and accusing other people because of this. You are
puffed up, although not crowned by the divine
decree for righteousness. On the contrary, you
heap praises on yourself. He says, "I am not as the
rest of humankind." Moderate yourself, O Pharisee. Put a door and lock on your tongue.[2] You
speak to God who knows all things. Wait for the
decree of the judge. No one who is skilled in
wrestling ever crowns himself. No one also receives the crown from himself but waits for the
summons of the referee. . . . Lower your pride, because arrogance is accursed and hated by God. It
is foreign to the mind that fears God. Christ even
said, "Do not judge, and you shall not be judged.
Do not condemn, and you will not be condemned."[3] One of his disciples also said, "There is
one lawgiver and judge. Why then do you judge
your neighbor?"[4] No one who is in good health
ridicules one who is sick for being laid up and
bedridden. He is rather afraid, for perhaps he
may become the victim of similar sufferings. A
person in battle, because another has fallen, does

not praise himself for having escaped from misfortune. The weakness of others is not a suitable
subject for praise for those who are in health.
COMMENTARY ON LUKE, HOMILY 120.[5]

THE DANGERS OF PRIDE. MARTYRIUS: Whoever offers to God sacrifices of praise, the rational
fruits of the lips that confess his name, should be
very alert for the ambushes of the evil one. Satan
lies in ambush ready to catch you by surprise at
the very time of thanksgiving. He will get up and
accuse you before God, just as he did with your
fellow Pharisee in the temple. This time, he will
not be puffing you up with pride over good
works, as he did with the Pharisee, but he will be
making you drunk with a different kind of pride.
He makes you drunk on pride in the lovely and
sweet sound of your own voice, the beauty of your
chants that are sweeter than honey and the honey-
comb. The result is that you do not realize that
these belong to God, and not to yourself. BOOK
OF PERFECTION 78.[6]

**ON REPORTING ONE'S OWN SYMPTOMS, NOT
ANOTHER'S, TO A DOCTOR.** AUGUSTINE: How
useful and necessary a medicine is repentance!
People who remember that they are only human
will readily understand this. It is written, "God
resists the proud, but gives grace to the humble."[7]
. . . The Pharisee was not rejoicing so much in his
own clean bill of health as in comparing it with
the diseases of others. He came to the doctor. It
would have been more worthwhile to inform him
by confession of the things that were wrong with
himself instead of keeping his wounds secret and
having the nerve to crow over the scars of others.
It is not surprising that the tax collector went
away cured, since he had not been ashamed of
showing where he felt pain. SERMON 351.1.[8]

THE PUBLICAN RECEIVES ABSOLUTION. CYRIL

---

[1]FC 18:34-35*. [2]Ps 140:3 LXX. [3]Lk 6:37. [4]Jas 4:12. [5]CGSL 481**.
[6]CS 101:234*. [7]1 Pet 5:5; Jas 4:6; Job 22:29; Prov 3:34. [8]WSA 3
10:118**.

of ALEXANDRIA: It says that the tax collector "stood afar off," not even venturing to raise up his eyes. You see him abstaining from all boldness of speech. He seems devoid of the right to speak and beaten down by the scorn of conscience. He was afraid that God would see him, since he had been careless in keeping his laws and had led an unchaste and uncontrolled life. You also see that he accuses his own depravity by his external manner. The foolish Pharisee stood there bold and broad, lifting up his eyes without a qualm, bearing witness of himself and boastful. The other feels shame for his conduct. He is afraid of his judge. He beats his breast. He confesses his offenses. He shows his illness as to the Physician, and he prays that he will have mercy. What is the result? Let us hear what the judge says. He says, "This man went down to his house justified rather than the other." COMMENTARY ON LUKE, HOMILY 120.[9]

IT IS MORE DIFFICULT TO CONFESS ONE'S SINS THAN ONE'S RIGHTEOUSNESS. EPHREM THE SYRIAN: In the case of that Pharisee who was praying, the things he said were true. Since he was saying them out of pride and the tax collector was telling his sins with humility, the confession of sins of the last was more pleasing to God than the acknowledgment of the almsgiving of the first. It is more difficult to confess one's sins than one's righteousness. God looks on the one who carries a heavy burden. The tax collector therefore appeared to him to have had more to bear than the Pharisee had. He went down more justified than the Pharisee did, only because of the fact he was humble. If this Pharisee had been sinful, his prayer would have added iniquity to iniquity, but the Lord purified the tax collector of his iniquity. If just by praying, the Pharisee's prayer provoked God's wrath, then as a result of that provocation, the prayer of the tax collector proved all the more potent. COMMENTARY ON TATIAN'S DIATESSARON 15.24.[10]

18:14 The Conclusion

HUMILITY IS THE MARK OF A SINNER. BASIL THE GREAT: The stern Pharisee, who in his overweening pride not only boasted of himself but also discredited the tax collector in the presence of God, made his justice void by being guilty of pride. Instead of the Pharisee, the tax collector went down justified, because he had given glory to God, the holy One. He did not dare lift his eyes but sought only to plead for mercy. He accused himself by his posture, by striking his breast, and by entertaining no other motive except propitiation. Be on your guard, therefore, and bear in mind this example of severe loss sustained through arrogance. The one guilty of insolent behavior suffered the loss of his justice and forfeited his reward by his bold self-reliance. He was judged inferior to a humble man and a sinner because in his self-exaltation he did not await the judgment of God but pronounced it himself. Never place yourself above anyone, not even great sinners. Humility often saves a sinner who has committed many terrible transgressions. ON HUMILITY.[11]

---

[9]CGSL 482**. [10]ECTD 242**. [11]FC 9:481-82**.

18:15-17 CHILDREN AND THE KINGDOM OF GOD

[15]*Now they were bringing even infants to him that he might touch them; and when the disciples saw it, they rebuked them.* [16]*But Jesus called them to him, saying, "Let the children come to me,*

and do not hinder them; for to such belongs the kingdom of God. [17]Truly, I say to you, whoever does not receive the kingdom of God like a child shall not enter it."

OVERVIEW: As Jesus draws closer and closer to Jerusalem, some persons (presumably the parents) try to bring little children to Jesus. Even now, mothers are bringing their children to Jesus in baptism. By their simplicity, innocence, humility and utter inability to come to Jesus, infants and young children demonstrate the characteristics and posture of those who enter the kingdom (CYRIL OF ALEXANDRIA). It is not childhood that is being sought but goodness that reflects the simplicity of a child (AMBROSE). "Stop preventing them" implies the mandate "Do not prevent infants or Gentiles from receiving the gifts of the King through holy baptism" (AUGUSTINE).

18:15-17 Receiving the Kingdom as a Child

MOTHERS STILL BRING INFANTS TO JESUS.
CYRIL OF ALEXANDRIA: Mothers brought their babes. They wanted his blessing and begged for their infants the touch of his holy hand. The blessed disciples rebuked them for doing this, not because they envied the babes; rather they were paying him due respect as their teacher and preventing him from getting unnecessarily tired. They placed much value on order.

Even until now, infants are brought near and blessed by Christ by means of consecrated hands. The pattern of the act continues even until this day and descends to us from the custom of Christ as its fountain. Only now, the bringing of infants does not take place in an unbecoming or disorderly manner but with proper order, solemnity and reverence. COMMENTARY ON LUKE, HOMILY 121.[1]

THE SIMPLICITY, INNOCENCE AND HUMILITY OF CHILDREN.
CYRIL OF ALEXANDRIA: What is there in babies that is worthy of imitation? Is it their lack of firmness and intelligence? It is incredible to affirm or imagine anything like this. Christ, however, does not wish us to be without

understanding but wants us perfectly to know everything that is useful and necessary for our salvation. Wisdom even promises that she will give cleverness to the simple and the beginning of sense and understanding to the young.[2] . . . How someone might at once be both simple and clever, the Savior explains to us elsewhere, saying, "Be clever as serpents and simple as doves."[3] Blessed Paul also writes, "My brothers, do not be children in your minds, but in wickedness be babies, and in your minds grown men."[4]

It is necessary to examine the meaning of being babies in wickedness and the way a person becomes a baby, but a grown person in mind. Knowing very little or nothing at all, a baby is correctly acquitted of the charge of depravity and wickedness. It is also our duty to attempt to be like them in the very same way. We must entirely put away from us habits of wickedness, that we also may be regarded as people who do not even know the path that leads to deception. Unconscious of spite and fraud, we must live in a simple and innocent manner, practicing gentleness and a priceless humility and readily avoiding wrath and spitefulness. These qualities are found in those who are still babies. COMMENTARY ON LUKE, HOMILY 121.[5]

GOODNESS RIVALING CHILDLIKE SIMPLICITY.
AMBROSE: Why does he say that children are fit for the kingdom of heaven?[6] Perhaps it is because they do not know spitefulness, have not learned to deceive, dare not strike back,[7] neglect to search for wealth, and do not work after honor and ambition. . . . Childhood is not meant, but rather goodness rivaling childlike simplicity.[8] It is not a virtue to be unable to sin, but to be unwilling to do so and to retain perseverance of will, so that the will imitates childhood and the person imi-

---

[1]*CGSL* 483**. [2]Prov 1:4. [3]Mt 10:16. [4]1 Cor 14:20. [5]*CGSL* 483-84**. [6]See Mt 19:14. [7]See 1 Pet 2:22-23. [8]See 1 Cor 4:20.

tates nature. EXPOSITION OF THE GOSPEL OF LUKE 8.57.[9]

INFANTS ENTER THE KINGDOM OF GOD THROUGH HOLY BAPTISM. AUGUSTINE: The other doctrine that your brotherhood claims they preach, that little children can attain the reward of eternal life without the grace of baptism, is very foolish. "Unless they eat of the flesh of the Son of man and drink his blood, they will not have life in them."[10] It seems to me that those who claim this for them without regeneration want to nullify baptism, since they teach that these chil-dren have what they believe is not to be bestowed on them in baptism even by themselves. If they do not want anything to stand in their way, let them confess that there is no need of rebirth and that the sacred stream of regeneration has no effect. The Lord proclaims this in the Gospel to disarm the vicious doctrine of proud people by the swift reasoning of truth. He says, "Allow the little children, and do not forbid them to come to me." LETTER 182.[11]

---

[9]EHG 354**. [10]Jn 6:54. [11]FC 30:130*.

18:18-30 THE RICH RULER

[18]*And a ruler asked him, "Good Teacher, what shall I do to inherit eternal life?"* [19]*And Jesus said to him, "Why do you call me good? No one is good but God alone.* [20]*You know the commandments: 'Do not commit adultery, Do not kill, Do not steal, Do not bear false witness, Honor your father and mother.'"* [21]*And he said, "All these I have observed from my youth."* [22]*And when Jesus heard it, he said to him, "One thing you still lack. Sell all that you have and distribute to the poor, and you will have treasure in heaven; and come, follow me."* [23]*But when he heard this he became sad, for he was very rich.* [24]*Jesus looking at him said, "How hard it is for those who have riches to enter the kingdom of God!* [25]*For it is easier for a camel to go through the eye of a needle than for a rich man to enter the kingdom of God."* [26]*Those who heard it said, "Then who can be saved?"* [27]*But he said, "What is impossible with men is possible with God."* [28]*And Peter said, "Lo, we have left our homes and followed you."* [29]*And he said to them, "Truly, I say to you, there is no man who has left house or wife or brothers or parents or children, for the sake of the kingdom of God,* [30]*who will not receive manifold more in this time, and in the age to come eternal life."*

OVERVIEW: A "certain ruler" shows his hostility toward Jesus, mixing flattery with fraud and deceit by addressing him with the neutral, noncommittal title *teacher,* a title for Jesus that is mostly used by his opponents (CYRIL OF ALEXANDRIA). No one is good except the one true God: Father, Son and Holy Spirit. When one breaks these commandments by giving into sinful pleasures, he becomes like a thorn in fruitful ground that chokes out the Word that brings eternal life. He was not able to experience the joy of charity that comes from being freed from riches (AUGUSTINE).

Over the centuries, many have attempted to explain away the striking image of a camel going through the eye of a needle. Some commentators say that it refers to a large cable used in navigation (CYRIL OF ALEXANDRIA) or even to Gentiles or publicans who enter the kingdom through confession, unlike the Pharisee who will not enter because of his arrogance (AMBROSE). Most commentators affirm that Jesus intends the hearer to take it literally. Such an extraordinary statement has caused many of the saints to follow Jesus to the letter, selling all that they have and following him in a life of self-denial (JOHN OF DAMASCUS). The apostles serve as examples of those who have left everything behind, even family, in order to follow Jesus. To be a disciple one must be willing to give up property and family so that the pain of abandoning one's possessions is great, whether those possessions be great or little (CYRIL OF ALEXANDRIA).

18:18-23 Jesus Responds to the Question

FLATTERY MIXED WITH FRAUD AND DECEIT. CYRIL OF ALEXANDRIA: The Jewish crowds . . . with their princes and teachers . . . looked at Christ as being a mere man like one of us, and not as God who had become man. They approached him to test him and lay the nets of their cleverness for him. . . .

He is called here a ruler. He fancied himself to have learned the law and supposed that he had been accurately taught it. He imagined that he could convict Christ of introducing laws of his own and of dishonoring the commandment spoken by most wise Moses. It was the Jews' goal to prove that Christ opposed and resisted the former commandments and established new laws by his own authority, in opposition to those previously existing. Their wicked conduct toward him had a false pretext. He comes near and makes a pretense of speaking kindly. He calls him "Teacher," designates him "good," and professes himself desirous of being a disciple. He says, "What shall I do to inherit eternal life?" Observe how he mixes flattery with fraud and deceit, like one who mingles vinegar with honey. He supposed that he could deceive him in this way. COMMENTARY ON LUKE, HOMILY 122.[1]

BEING UNCHANGEABLY GOOD A SPECIAL CHARACTERISTIC OF GOD. CYRIL OF ALEXANDRIA: What reply is made by the all-knowing One of whom it is written that he "takes the wise in their craftiness"?[2] "Why do you call me good? No one is good except one, God." You see how Christ proved immediately that the ruler was neither wise nor learned, although he was the ruler of a synagogue of the Jews. He says, "You did not believe that I am God, and the clothing of the flesh has led you astray. Why did you apply to me titles suitable to the supreme nature alone, while you still assume that I am a mere man like you and not superior to the limits of human nature?" In the nature that transcends all, God alone is found to be good by nature, that is, unchangeably good. . . . He says, "I do not seem to you to be truly God. Ignorantly and foolishly, you have applied to me the properties and virtues of the divine nature. Why do you then imagine that I, a mere man that never is invested with goodness but only gains it by the assent of the divine will, have the property of the unchangeable nature?" This was the meaning of what Christ spoke. COMMENTARY ON LUKE, HOMILY 122.[3]

NO ONE IS GOOD EXCEPT THE ONE GOD. AUGUSTINE: The Father is good. The Son is good. The Holy Spirit is good. Still, there are not three goods but one good. He said, "No one is good except the one God." The Lord Jesus Christ did not answer. He feared that the one who in addressing a man had said "good master" might understand him as only a man. He therefore did not say, "No one is good except the Father alone." He rather said, "No one is good except the one God." By the name *Father*, the Father makes himself known. The name *God* includes himself, as well as the Son and the Holy Spirit, because the Trinity is one God. ON THE TRINITY 8.[4]

THE JOY OF CHARITY. AUGUSTINE: The young man asked the Lord how to attain to eternal life

---

[1]CGSL 486-87**. [2]Job 5:13. [3]CGSL 487**. [4]FC 45:186**.

and heard that he must sell all his goods and distribute them to the poor and have his treasure in heaven. Why else did he go away sad, except that he had, as the Gospel says, great riches? It is one thing not to wish to hoard up what one does not have. It is another thing to scatter what has been accumulated. The former is like refusing food; the latter, like cutting off a limb. LETTER 31.[5]

18:24-30 *All Things Are Possible with God*

THE CAMEL IS A THICK CABLE USED IN SAILING. CYRIL OF ALEXANDRIA: The ruler was too weak in his intentions and could not be prevailed upon even to listen to the advice of selling his possessions, although it would have been good for him and full of reward. Our Lord lays bare the sickness that has its home in the rich, saying, "How hard it is for those that have riches to enter into the kingdom of God! I say to you, that it is easier for a camel to enter in through the eye of a needle than for a rich man into the kingdom of God." Now by a camel he means not the animal of that name but rather a thick cable. It is the custom of those well-versed in navigation to call the thicker cables "camels." COMMENTARY ON LUKE, HOMILY 123.[6]

THE CAMEL REPRESENTS THE GENTILES AND THE PUBLICANS. AMBROSE: "It is easier for a camel to pass through the eye of a needle than for a rich man to enter into the kingdom of God." This is great power. It has great weight in words. With what other words would he more vehemently express that a rich person must not boast in his riches than these by which a compassionate person is defined as against nature? . . . You can also understand it morally, about every sinner and haughty rich person. When he did not dare to raise his eyes to God, the tax collector, burdened with the awareness of his own sins, was like a camel. Through the help of his confession, he will pass more easily through the eye of a needle than the Pharisee will enter the kingdom of heaven. The Pharisee was arrogant in prayer,

boasting of innocence, and overconfident of glory. He rebuked mercy, proclaimed himself, and accused another. He would rather confront the Lord than beg him.[7] If anyone trembles at the camel, let him shudder at him whose deeds are uglier than a camel. EXPOSITION OF THE GOSPEL OF LUKE 8.70-72.[8]

A CALL TO SELF-DENIAL. JOHN OF DAMASCUS: "How hard it is for those who have riches to enter into the kingdom of God! It is easier for a camel to go through the eye of a needle than for a rich man to enter into the kingdom of God!" When all the saints heard this command, they thought they should withdraw from this hardness of riches. They parted with all their goods. By this distribution of their riches to the poor, they laid up for themselves eternal riches. They took up the cross and followed Christ. Some followed, being made perfect by martyrdom, even as I have already told you, while others by the practice of self-denial did not fall short of them in the life of the true philosophy. Know that this is a command of Christ our King and God that leads us from corruptible things and makes us partakers of everlasting things. BARLAAM AND JOSEPH 15.128-29.[9]

THE PAIN OF ABANDONING POSSESSIONS. CYRIL OF ALEXANDRIA: It says, "Peter said to him, 'Look, we have left all and followed you.'"[10] . . .

I imagine, to this some may reply, "What had the disciples given up? They were men who gained the necessities of life by their sweat and labor, being by trade fishermen, who perhaps owned a boat and nets somewhere. They did not have well-built houses or any other possessions. What did they leave, or for what did they ask a reward from Christ?" What is our answer to this? For this very reason, they made this most necessary inquiry. Since they possessed nothing except what was trifling and of slight value, they would learn how God will reward and gladden with his

---

[5]FC 12:114-15*. [6]*CGSL* 490**. [7]See Lk 18:9-41. [8]*EHG* 360-61**.
[9]LCL 34:217**. [10]Mt 19:27.

gifts those who likewise have left but little for the sake of the kingdom of God. They desired to be counted worthy of the kingdom of heaven because of their love for him. The rich man, one who has disregarded much, will confidently expect a reward. He who possessed little and abandoned it, how was it not right to ask what hopes he might entertain? For this reason, as representing those in the same condition of their having left little, they say, "Behold, we have left all and followed you."

It is further necessary to observe also this. Correctly considered, the pain of abandoning is the same whether one abandons much or little. Come and let us see the real meaning of the matter by a trivial example. Suppose two men had to stand naked. The one took off expensive clothes while the other put off only what was cheap and easy to get. Would not the pain of the nakedness be equal in both cases? What possible doubt can there be on this point? As far as regards obedience and good will, those who had different circumstances and yet practiced equal readiness and willingly sold what they had must be placed on an equal footing with the rich. The very wise Paul also takes up their cause. He wrote, "If there be a ready mind, it is accepted according to what a man has and not according to what he has not."[11] Thus inquiry of the holy apostles was not unreasonable. COMMENTARY ON LUKE, HOMILY 124.[12]

---

[11]2 Cor 8:12. [12]CGSL 492-93**.

18:31-34 THE THIRD AND FINAL PASSION PREDICTION

---

[31]And taking the twelve, he said to them, "Behold, we are going up to Jerusalem, and everything that is written of the Son of man by the prophets will be accomplished. [32]For he will be delivered to the Gentiles, and will be mocked and shamefully treated and spit upon; [33]they will scourge him and kill him, and on the third day he will rise." [34]But they understood none of these things; this saying was hid from them, and they did not grasp what was said.

OVERVIEW: As Jesus' journey to Jerusalem draws to a close, he predicts his passion and resurrection one more time. To prepare the disciples, Jesus shows his power to know what lies ahead for him in Jerusalem by predicting his death and resurrection to show them later that he was fully aware of his destiny. Only Luke adds here "all the things that have been written through the prophets," showing his interest in demonstrating that the passion and resurrection were in fulfillment of the Scriptures. The mystery of the passion and resurrection will be hidden from the disciples now, but after Jesus rises from the dead their eyes will be opened and they will fully grasp the meaning of these words (CYRIL OF ALEXANDRIA).

18:31-34 The Twelve Do Not Understand

JESUS PREDICTS HIS SUFFERING AND RESURRECTION. CYRIL OF ALEXANDRIA: To prepare the disciples' minds, the Savior of all tells them that he will suffer the passion on the cross and death in the flesh as soon as he has gone up to Jerusalem. He added that he would also rise wiping out the pain and obliterating the shame of the passion by the greatness of the miracle. It was glorious and worthy of God to be able to break the bonds of death and hurry back to life. According to the expression of wise Paul, the resurrection from the dead testifies that he is God and the Son of God.[1] COMMENTARY ON LUKE, HOMILY 125.[2]

JESUS SHOWS THAT HIS DEATH AND RESURRECTION FULFILL SCRIPTURE. CYRIL OF ALEXANDRIA: He told them beforehand what would happen so that they might be aware that he foreknew his passion. Although it was in his power easily to escape, Christ still went ahead to willingly meet it. Saying, "Behold, we go up to Jerusalem," he urgently testified and commanded them to remember what had been foretold. He necessarily added that the holy prophets had foretold all these things. As in the person of Christ, Isaiah says, "I have given my back to scourging, and my cheeks to buffetings; and I have not turned away my face from the shame of spitting."[3] In another place, the prophet says of him, "As a sheep he was led unto the slaughter, and was silent, as a lamb before its shearer."[4] "All we like sheep have gone astray: every one has gone astray in his path, and the Lord has delivered him up because of our sins."[5] In the twenty-second psalm, blessed David, painting as it were beforehand the sufferings upon the cross, set before us Jesus speaking as one already hanging on the tree. He says, "But I am a worm, and no man; scorned by men and despised by the people. All who see me mock at me, they make mouths at me, they wag their heads;

'He committed his cause to the Lord; let him deliver him, let him rescue him, for he delights in him!' "[6] Some of the Jews did shake their wicked heads at him, deriding him and saying, "If you are the Son of God, come down now from the cross, and we will believe you."[7] He said, "They divide my garments among them, and for my raiment they cast lots."[8] In another place, Christ again says of those that crucified him, "They gave gall for my food, and for my thirst they made me drink vinegar."[9] COMMENTARY ON LUKE, HOMILY 125.[10]

THE HIDDEN MYSTERY OF THE PASSION. CYRIL OF ALEXANDRIA: The Savior of all then declared these things beforehand to the holy apostles. It says, "They did not understand what was said, and the word was hid from them." They did not then know accurately what the holy prophets proclaimed. Although [Peter] who was first among the disciples heard the Savior once say that he should be crucified, die and arise, he did not yet understand the depth of the mystery. He resisted, saying: "Far be that from you, Lord. This will not happen to you."[11] He was rebuked for speaking this because he did not know the meaning of the relevant Scripture inspired by God. When Christ arose from the dead, he opened their eyes,[12] as another of the holy Evangelists wrote. They were enlightened, being enriched with the abundant participation of the Spirit. COMMENTARY ON LUKE, HOMILY 125.[13]

---

[1]Rom 1:4. [2]CGSL 496**. [3]Is 50:6. [4]Is 53:7. [5]Is 53:6. [6]Ps 22:6-8. [7]Mt 27:42. [8]Ps 22:18. [9]Ps 69:21. [10]CGSL 497**. [11]Mt 16:22. [12]Lk 24:31. [13]CGSL 498**.

18:35-43 THE HEALING OF THE BLIND MAN

³⁵*As he drew near to Jericho, a blind man was sitting by the roadside begging;* ³⁶*and hearing a multitude going by, he inquired what this meant.* ³⁷*They told him, "Jesus of Nazareth is passing by."* ³⁸*And he cried, "Jesus, Son of David, have mercy on me!"* ³⁹*And those who were in front rebuked him, telling him to be silent; but he cried out all the more, "Son of David, have mercy on me!"* ⁴⁰*And Jesus stopped, and commanded him to be brought to him; and when he came near, he asked him,* ⁴¹*"What do you want me to do for you?" He said, "Lord, let me receive my sight."* ⁴²*And Jesus said to him, "Receive your sight; your faith has made you well."* ⁴³*And immediately he received his sight and followed him, glorifying God; and all the people, when they saw it, gave praise to God.*

OVERVIEW: Luke has only one blind man as opposed to Matthew's two, but the difference in meaning is negligible (AMBROSE). Although his physical eyes are closed, he has been opened to the healing presence of Jesus as the Son of David, and therefore the Messiah, whom he pursues with persistence (CYRIL OF ALEXANDRIA). It is the title *Nazarean* that prompts the blind man's persistent cries for mercy, for it is more than a simple notice of where Jesus is from, as it designates Jesus as the miracle-working prophet from Nazareth. The blind man confesses his faith and shows his love for Christ by crying out, "Jesus, Son of David, have mercy on me." What Jesus acknowledges here is the man's faith in him as the giver of life, and the man's persistent desire to stand in the presence of Jesus, who brings a new creation by giving him sight (EPHREM THE SYRIAN). This confrontation with the presence of Jesus brings the radical great reversal for the blind man: immediately he receives his sight from him who is the true light. Set free from blindness, the healed man also becomes a disciple, following Jesus and glorifying God (CYRIL OF ALEXANDRIA).

18:35 Introduction: Blindness

THE LIGHT THAT ENLIGHTENS THE GENTILES. AMBROSE: In the Gospel according to St. Matthew, two men are depicted,[1] but Luke depicts one. Matthew depicts it as Jesus was leaving Jericho,[2] but Luke as he was approaching the city. Otherwise there is no difference. The image of the Gentile people is in this case one man who through the divine blessing received the clarity of his lost sight. It makes no difference whether the Gentile people received the healing through one or two blind men since, taking the origin from Ham and Japheth, sons of Noah,[3] they set out the two authors of their race in two blind men. EXPOSITION OF THE GOSPEL OF LUKE 8.80.[4]

18:36-39 The Blind Man's Cry for Mercy

THE BLIND MAN KNOWS THAT JESUS IS THE SON OF DAVID AND MESSIAH. CYRIL OF ALEXANDRIA: The blind man must have understood that the sight of the blind cannot be restored by human means but requires, on the contrary, a divine power and an authority such as God only possesses. With God nothing whatsoever is impossible. The blind man came near to him as to the omnipotent God. How then does he call him the Son of David? What can one answer to this? The following is perhaps the explanation. Since

[1]Mt 20:30. [2]Mt 20:29. [3]See Gen 10:1. [4]EHG 365**.

287

he was born and raised in Judaism, of course, the predictions contained in the law and the holy prophets concerning Christ had not escaped his knowledge. He heard them chant that passage in the book of the Psalms, "The Lord has sworn in truth to David, and will not annul it, saying: 'of the fruit of your loins I will set a king upon your throne.' "[5] The blind man also knew that the blessed prophet Isaiah said, "There will spring up a shoot from the root of Jesse, and from his root a flower will grow up."[6] Isaiah also said, "Behold, a virgin will conceive and bring forth a son, and they will call his name Emmanuel, which being interpreted is, God with us."[7] He already believed that the Word, being God, of his own will had submitted to be born in the flesh of the holy Virgin. He now comes near to him as to God and says, "Have mercy on me, Son of David." Christ testifies that this was his state of mind in offering his petition. He said to him, "Your faith has saved you." COMMENTARY ON LUKE, HOMILY 126.[8]

JESUS THE NAZARENE. EPHREM THE SYRIAN: While he was asking who it was, they said to him, "Jesus, the Nazarene." He knew that they were not saying that to him with love. He left what pertained to enemies and grasped hold of what pertained to friends. "Son of David, have mercy on me." They were trying to prevent him, fearing that his eyes may be opened, and the Pharisees might recognize him and be irritated. COMMENTARY ON TATIAN'S DIATESSARON 15.22.[9]

18:40-42 Jesus' Response of Healing

FAITH GIVES THE BLIND MAN LIFE AND THEN SIGHT. EPHREM THE SYRIAN: The Light came into the world to give sight to the blind and faith to those who lacked it. When he approached the blind man, he cried out and said, "Jesus, Son of David, have mercy on me." The beggar's hand was stretched out to receive a penny from human beings and found himself receiving the gift of God! "Son of David, have mercy on me."[10] He

correctly understood that Jesus was the Son of David, David who spared the blind and the lame of the Jebusites.[11] What did he then answer him? "See, your faith has saved you." Christ did not say to him, "It is your faith that has caused you to see," in order to show that faith had first given him life and then bodily sight. COMMENTARY ON TATIAN'S DIATESSARON 15.22.[12]

18:43 Conclusion: Sight

JESUS THE TRUE LIGHT GIVES SIGHT. CYRIL OF ALEXANDRIA: With supreme authority, he said, "Receive your sight." The expression is wonderful, worthy of God and transcending the bounds of human nature! Which of the holy prophets ever spoke like this or used words of so great authority? Observe that he did not ask of another the power to restore vision to him who was deprived of sight. He did not perform the divine miracle as the effect of prayer to God but rather attributed it to his own power. By his almighty will, Christ did whatever he would. "Receive," he said, "your sight." The word was light to him that was blind, because it was the word of him who is the true Light. COMMENTARY ON LUKE, HOMILY 126.[13]

HE GLORIFIES GOD AND FOLLOWS JESUS. CYRIL OF ALEXANDRIA: Now that he was delivered from his blindness, did he neglect the duty of loving Christ? He certainly did not. It says, "He followed him, offering him glory like to God." He was set free from double blindness. Not only did he escape from the blindness of the body but also from that of the mind and heart. He would not have glorified him as God, had he not possessed spiritual vision. He became the means of others giving Christ glory, for it says that all the people gave glory to God. COMMENTARY ON LUKE, HOMILY 126.[14]

---

[5]Ps 132:11 (131:11 LXX). [6]Is 11:1. [7]Mt 1:23; Is 7:14. [8]CGSL 499-500**. [9]ECTD 241*. [10]Mk 10:47. [11]2 Sam 5:6-8. [12]ECTD 241*. [13]CGSL 500-501*. [14]CGSL 501**.

19:1-10 ZACCHAEUS, THE CHIEF TAX COLLECTOR

¹He entered Jericho and was passing through. ²And there was a man named Zacchaeus; he was a chief tax collector, and rich. ³And he sought to see who Jesus was, but could not, on account of the crowd, because he was small of stature. ⁴So he ran on ahead and climbed up into a sycamore tree to see him, for he was to pass that way. ⁵And when Jesus came to the place, he looked up and said to him, "Zacchaeus, make haste and come down; for I must stay at your house today." ⁶So he made haste and came down, and received him joyfully. ⁷And when they saw it they all murmured, "He has gone in to be the guest of a man who is a sinner." ⁸And Zacchaeus stood and said to the Lord, "Behold, Lord, the half of my goods I give to the poor; and if I have defrauded any one of anything, I restore it fourfold." ⁹And Jesus said to him, "Today salvation has come to this house, since he also is a son of Abraham. ¹⁰For the Son of man came to seek and to save the lost."

OVERVIEW: As Jesus approaches Jericho, he encounters a blind man and Zacchaeus, both of whom are outcasts upon whom Jesus will show mercy (AMBROSE). Zacchaeus is the chief tax collector, and therefore a great sinner who would be included with the prostitutes by the Pharisees as examples of complete depravity (CYRIL OF ALEXANDRIA). Zacchaeus shows that it is difficult but possible for the rich to enter the kingdom of heaven (JEROME). Climbing a sycamore tree is unusual for someone of his position, but in order to see Jesus he must rise above the earth, including all the foolish sins of the world (CYRIL OF ALEXANDRIA). Like Christ, who was lifted on the cross to show the foolishness of God, Zacchaeus is willing to be foolish so that he may see Christ crucified (AUGUSTINE).

Jesus has welcomed Zacchaeus into his heart, and now he is ready to be welcomed by Zacchaeus into his house (AUGUSTINE). The Lord, who knows Zacchaeus's thoughts, calls him to come away from his life in the law and to descend into Jesus' presence so that he might become a true son of Abraham (EPHREM THE SYRIAN). These possessions became his when Zacchaeus used them for salvation, so that what had been a hindrance to him in attaining eternal life now had become a benefit when used properly (MAXIMUS OF TURIN).

Jesus is that one man without sin who came to save those who were lost because of sin (AUGUSTINE). God promises salvation for those who are the true children of Abraham, which Zacchaeus shows that he is by his almsgiving (CYPRIAN).

19:1 Introduction: Jesus Enters Jericho

ZACCHAEUS AND THE BLIND MAN RECEIVE MERCY. AMBROSE: "And, behold, there was a man named Zacchaeus." Zacchaeus in the sycamore; the blind man by the wayside.[1] The Lord waits for the one to have mercy on him and honors the other with the radiance of his visit. He questions the one before healing him[2] and attends the other's house as an uninvited guest. He knew that his host's reward was to be rich. Although Christ had not yet heard his voice of invitation, he has heard his good will. **EXPOSITION OF THE GOSPEL OF LUKE 8.82.**[3]

19:2-4 Zacchaeus Seeks Jesus

THE SINFULNESS OF ZACCHAEUS. CYRIL OF ALEXANDRIA: Zacchaeus was leader of the tax collectors, a man entirely abandoned to greed,

[1]Lk 18:35. [2]Lk 18:41. [3]EHG 366*.

whose only goal was the increase of his gains. This was the practice of the tax collectors, although Paul calls it idolatry,[4] possibly as being suitable only for those who have no knowledge of God. Since they shamelessly, openly professed this vice, the Lord very justly joined them with the prostitutes, saying to the leaders of the Jews, "The prostitutes and the tax collectors go before you into the kingdom of God."[5] Zacchaeus did not continue to be among them, but he was counted worthy of mercy at Christ's hands. He calls near those who are far away and gives light to those who are in darkness. COMMENTARY ON LUKE, HOMILY 127.[6]

A RICH MAN WHO ENTERS THE KINGDOM.

JEROME: There certainly is much truth in a certain saying of a philosopher, "Every rich man is either wicked or the heir of wickedness."[7] That is why the Lord and Savior says that it is difficult for the rich to enter the kingdom of heaven.[8] Someone may raise the objection, "How did wealthy Zacchaeus enter the kingdom of heaven?" He gave away his wealth and immediately replaced it with the riches of the heavenly kingdom. The Lord and Savior did not say that the rich would not enter the kingdom of heaven but that they will enter with difficulty. HOMILY ON PSALM 83 (84).[9]

TO SEE CHRIST. CYRIL OF ALEXANDRIA: Come

and let us see what was the method of Zacchaeus's conversion. He desired to see Jesus and therefore climbed into a sycamore tree, and so a seed of salvation sprouted within him. Christ saw this with the eyes of deity. Looking up, he also saw Zacchaeus with the eyes of humanity, and since it was his purpose for all to be saved, he extends his gentleness to him. To encourage him, he says, "Come down quickly." Zacchaeus searched to see Christ, but the multitude prevented him, not so much that of the people but of his sins. He was short of stature, not merely in a bodily point of view but also spiritually. He could not see him unless he were raised up from the earth and climbed into the sycamore, by which Christ was about to pass. The story contains a puzzle. In no other way can a person see Christ and believe in him except by climbing up into the sycamore, by making foolish his earthly members of fornication, uncleanness, etc. COMMENTARY ON LUKE, HOMILY 127.[10]

ZACCHAEUS, UNABLE TO SEE JESUS THROUGH THE CROWD, WAS UNASHAMED TO CLIMB THE TREE OF FOLLY. AUGUSTINE: Zacchaeus

climbed away from the crowd and saw Jesus without the crowd getting in his way.

The crowd laughs at the lowly, to people walking the way of humility, who leave the wrongs they suffer in God's hands and do not insist on getting back at their enemies. The crowd laughs at the lowly and says, "You helpless, miserable clod, you cannot even stick up for yourself and get back what is your own." The crowd gets in the way and prevents Jesus from being seen. The crowd boasts and crows when it is able to get back what it owns. It blocks the sight of the one who said as he hung on the cross, "Father, forgive them, because they do not know what they are doing."[11] . . . He ignored the crowd that was getting in his way. He instead climbed a sycamore tree, a tree of "silly fruit." As the apostle says, "We preach Christ crucified, a stumbling block indeed to the Jews, [now notice the sycamore] but folly to the Gentiles."[12] Finally, the wise people of this world laugh at us about the cross of Christ and say, "What sort of minds do you people have, who worship a crucified God?" What sort of minds do we have? They are certainly not your kind of mind. "The wisdom of this world is folly with God."[13] No, we do not have your kind of mind. You call our minds foolish. Say what you like, but for our part, let us climb the sycamore tree and see Jesus. The reason you cannot see Jesus is that you are ashamed to climb the sycamore tree.

---

[4]Col 3:5. [5]Mt 21:31. [6]*CGSL* 505**. [7]See Letter 120.1, PL 22:984 (821). [8]Mt 19:23. [9]FC 48:119*. [10]*CGSL* 505-6**. [11]Lk 23:34. [12]1 Cor 1:23. [13]1 Cor 3:19.

Let Zacchaeus grasp the sycamore tree, and let the humble person climb the cross. That is little enough, merely to climb it. We must not be ashamed of the cross of Christ, but we must fix it on our foreheads, where the seat of shame is. Above where all our blushes show is the place we must firmly fix that for which we should never blush. As for you, I rather think you make fun of the sycamore, and yet that is what has enabled me to see Jesus. You make fun of the sycamore, because you are just a person, but "the foolishness of God is wiser than men."[14] SERMON 174.3.[15]

19:5-8 Jesus Must Stay in Zacchaeus's Home

ZACCHAEUS WELCOMES JESUS TO HIS HOUSE. AUGUSTINE: The Lord, who had already welcomed Zacchaeus in his heart, was now ready to be welcomed by him in his house. He said, "Zacchaeus, hurry up and come down, since I have to stay in your house." He thought it was a marvelous piece of good luck to see Christ. While imagining it was a marvelous piece of luck quite beyond words to see him passing by, he was suddenly found worthy to have him in his house. Grace is poured out, and faith starts working through love. Christ, who was already dwelling in his heart, is welcomed into his house. Zacchaeus says to Christ, "Lord, half my goods I give to the poor, and if I have cheated anyone of anything, I am paying back four times over." It is as if he were saying, "The reason I am keeping back half for myself is not in order to have it, but to have something from which to pay people back."

There you are. That is really what welcoming Jesus means, welcoming him into your heart. Christ was already there. He was in Zacchaeus and spoke through him. The apostle says that this is what it means, "For Christ to dwell by faith in your hearts."[16] SERMON 174.5.[17]

ZACCHAEUS LEAVES THE LAW FOR SALVATION. EPHREM THE SYRIAN: Zacchaeus was praying in his heart as follows, "Happy the one who is worthy that this just man should enter into his dwelling." The Lord said to him, "Hurry, come down, Zacchaeus." Seeing he knew his thoughts, he said, "Just as he knows this, he knows also all that I have done." He therefore said, "All that I have unjustly received, I give back fourfold." Hurry and come down from the fig tree, because it is with you that I will be staying. The first fig tree of Adam will be forgotten, because of the last fig tree of the chief tax collector, and the name of the guilty Adam will be forgotten because of the innocent Zacchaeus. COMMENTARY ON TATIAN'S DIATESSARON 20.[18]

ZACCHAEUS USED HIS PROPERTY TO EXPRESS GRATITUDE FOR HIS SALVATION. MAXIMUS OF TURIN: Zacchaeus must be praised. His riches were unable to keep him from the royal threshold. He should be greatly praised because his riches brought him to the threshold of the kingdom. From this, we understand that wealth is not a hindrance but a help to attaining the glory of Christ. While we possess it, we should not squander it on wild living but give it away for the sake of salvation. There is no crime in possessions, but there is crime in those who do not know how to use possessions. For the foolish, wealth is a temptation to vice, but for the wise, it is a help to virtue. Some receive an opportunity for salvation, but others acquire an obstacle of condemnation. SERMONS 95-96.[19]

19:9-10 Jesus' Pronouncement About His Ministry

ONE MAN WITHOUT SIN. AUGUSTINE: "The Son of man came to seek and to save what was lost." All were lost. From the moment the one man sinned, in whom the whole race was contained, the whole race was lost. One man without sin came. He would save them from sin. SERMON 175.1.[20]

---

[14]1 Cor 1:25. [15]WSA 3 5:259-60**. [16]Eph 3:17. [17]WSA 3 5:260-61**. [18]ECTD 240-41*. [19]ACW 50:219-20**. [20]WSA 3 5:265*.

ZACCHAEUS A TRUE SON OF ABRAHAM. CYP-RIAN: Finally, he also calls sons of Abraham those whom he perceives are active in helping and nourishing the poor. Zacchaeus said, "Behold, I give one half of my possessions to the poor, and if I have defrauded anyone of anything, I restore it fourfold." Jesus responded, "Today salvation has come to this house, since he too is a son of Abraham." If Abraham believed in God and it was ac-counted to him as righteousness, then he who gives alms according to the command of God certainly believes in God. He that possesses the true faith keeps the fear of God. Moreover, he keeps the fear of God by showing mercy to the poor. WORKS AND ALMSGIVING 8.[21]

---

[21]FC 36:234.

19:11-28 THE PARABLE OF THE MINAS

[11]*As they heard these things, he proceeded to tell a parable, because he was near to Jerusalem, and because they supposed that the kingdom of God was to appear immediately.* [12]*He said therefore, "A nobleman went into a far country to receive a kingdom and then return.* [13]*Calling ten of his servants, he gave them ten pounds,[e] and said to them, 'Trade with these till I come.'* [14]*But his citizens hated him and sent an embassy after him, saying, 'We do not want this man to reign over us.'* [15]*When he returned, having received the kingdom, he commanded these servants, to whom he had given the money, to be called to him, that he might know what they had gained by trading.* [16]*The first came before him, saying, 'Lord, your pound has made ten pounds more.'* [17]*And he said to him, 'Well done, good servant! Because you have been faithful in a very little, you shall have authority over ten cities.'* [18]*And the second came, saying, 'Lord, your pound has made five pounds.'* [19]*And he said to him, 'And you are to be over five cities.'* [20]*Then another came, saying, 'Lord, here is your pound, which I kept laid away in a napkin;* [21]*for I was afraid of you, because you are a severe man; you take up what you did not lay down, and reap what you did not sow.'* [22]*He said to him, 'I will condemn you out of your own mouth, you wicked servant! You knew that I was a severe man, taking up what I did not lay down and reaping what I did not sow?* [23]*Why then did you not put my money into the bank, and at my coming I should have collected it with interest?'* [24]*And he said to those who stood by, 'Take the pound from him, and give it to him who has the ten pounds.'* [25]*(And they said to him, 'Lord, he has ten pounds!')* [26]*'I tell you, that to every one who has will more be given; but from him who has not, even what he has will be taken away.* [27]*But as for these enemies of mine, who did not want me to reign over them, bring them here and slay them before me.'"*

[28]*And when he had said this, he went on ahead, going up to Jerusalem.*

e The mina, rendered here by *pound*, was about three months' wages for a laborer

OVERVIEW: The nobleman is journeying to a "far country" to obtain a kingdom, for he is the Son of the Father, and this journey takes place when he ascends to the Father in heaven. The nobleman is first and foremost a giver of gifts, for these talents are divine gifts given to the faithful. These gifts are given partially during his ministry and fully on Pentecost to the church in the diversity of gifts (CYRIL OF ALEXANDRIA).

Since the kingdom is an ongoing reality wherever Jesus is, already during his ministry there is opposition to this kingdom when enemies struggle against him and reject his kingdom, particularly the Jewish multitudes that have continually opposed Jesus. The nobleman summons his "stewards of the mysteries" to account for their stewardship of preaching the kingdom and administering the sacraments in building up the kingdom (CYRIL OF ALEXANDRIA).

The mina given to the first servant earned ten minas more, and his reward is authority over ten towns, the equivalent to interest being paid on the Word of God (ORIGEN). What has been given is the office of investor of the Word, not collector of the interest (AUGUSTINE). When we are in the business of the Lord, the profits of the business go to us (ORIGEN). No one is immune from this responsibility, for all those who have been given this gift must dispense of it in whatever station God has placed them (AUGUSTINE). This marks the end of Jesus' teaching outside Jerusalem, and when the journey narrative concludes, Jesus enters Jerusalem, the holy city of his destiny, for his passion and the salvation of the world (CYRIL OF ALEXANDRIA).

19:11-27 Uncertainty About the Kingdom and the Parable of the Minas

JESUS ASCENDS TO A FAR COUNTRY IN HEAVEN. CYRIL OF ALEXANDRIA: The scope of the parable briefly represents the whole meaning of the dispensation that was for us and of the mystery of Christ from the beginning even to the end. The Word, being God, became man. He was made in the likeness of sinful flesh, because of this he is also called a servant. He is and was free born, because the Father unspeakably begot him. He is also God, transcending all in nature and in glory and surpassing the things of our estate, or rather even the whole creation, by his incomparable fullness. . . .

By nature God, he is said to have received from the Father the name that is above every name when he became man. We might then believe in him as God and the King of all, even in the flesh that was united to him.

When he had endured the passion on the cross for our sakes and had abolished death by the resurrection of his body from the dead, he ascended to the Father and became like a man journeying to a far country. Heaven is a different country from earth, and he ascended so that he might receive a kingdom for himself. . . . How does he who reigns over all with the Father ascend to him to receive a kingdom? The Father also gives this to the Son according to his becoming man. When he ascended into heaven, he sat down on the right hand of the Majesty on high,[1] waiting until his enemies are put under his feet.[2] COMMENTARY ON LUKE, HOMILY 128.[3]

TALENTS ARE DIVINE GIFTS GIVEN TO THE FAITHFUL. CYRIL OF ALEXANDRIA: To those who believe in him, the Savior distributes a variety of divine gifts. We affirm that this is the meaning of the talent. Truly great is the difference between those who receive the talents and those who have even completely denied his kingdom. They are rebels that throw off the yoke of his scepter, while the others are endowed with the glory of serving him. As faithful servants, therefore, they are entrusted with their Lord's wealth. They gain something by doing business. They earn the praises due to faithful service, and they are considered worthy of eternal honors. COMMENTARY ON LUKE, HOMILY 129.[4]

---

[1]Heb 1:3. [2]See Ps 110; Mt 22:44; Mk 12:36; Lk 20:43; Acts 2:35; Heb 1:13; 10:13. [3]CGSL 508-10*. [4]CGSL 511**.

THE DIVERSITY OF THE GIFTS STILL EVIDENT. CYRIL OF ALEXANDRIA: The sacred Scripture clearly shows how he distributed, who the persons are, and what the talents that he distributes signify. He continues to distribute even to this day. Blessed Paul said, "There are distributions of gifts but the same Spirit. There are distributions of ministries but the same Lord. There are distributions of things to be done but the same God who works all in every man."[5] Explaining what he said, he states the kinds of the gifts as follows: "For to one is given the word of wisdom, and to another the word of knowledge, and to another faith, and to another gifts of healing,[6] and so on. These words make plain the differences in the gifts. COMMENTARY ON LUKE, HOMILY 129.[7]

THE CITIZENS WHO HATE JESUS. CYRIL OF ALEXANDRIA: It says that his citizens hated him. Likewise, Christ admonishes the Jewish crowds, saying, "If I had not done among them the works which no one else did, they would not have sin; but now they have seen and hated both me and my Father."[8] They would not let him reign over them, and yet the holy prophets were constantly speaking predictions of Christ as a king. One of them even said, "Rejoice greatly, daughter of Zion, for your King comes to you, just, and a Savior; he is meek, and riding on a donkey, and on a new foal."[9] Blessed Isaiah says of him and of the holy apostles, "Behold, a just king shall reign, and princes shall rule with judgment."[10] Again, Christ somewhere said by the voice of the psalmist, "But I have been appointed King by him on Zion, his holy mount, and I will declare the commandment of the Lord."[11] They then denied his kingdom. When they came near to Pilate saying, "Away with him, away with him, crucify him,"[12] he asked them, or rather said to them in derision, "Shall I crucify your king?" They answered with wicked words and said, "We have no king but Caesar."

Having denied the kingdom of Christ, they fell under the dominion of Satan and brought on themselves the yoke of sin that cannot be lifted. COMMENTARY ON LUKE, HOMILY 128.[13]

THE TALENTS DISTRIBUTED TO THE APOSTLES AND THEIR SUCCESSORS. CYRIL OF ALEXANDRIA: I think that I should mention whom Christ has entrusted with these gifts, according to the measure of each one's readiness and disposition. . . . Another Evangelist is aware of a difference between the amounts of the talents distributed. To one, he gave five talents, and to another two, and to another one.[14] You see that the distribution was suitable to the measure of each one's faculties. As to those who were entrusted with them, come, and let us to the best of our ability declare who they are. They are those who are perfect in mind to whom also strong meat is fitting and whose intellectual senses are exercised for the discerning of good and evil.[15] They are those who are skilled in instructing correctly and acquainted with the sacred doctrines. They know how to direct both themselves and others to every better work. In short, the wise disciples were above all others. Next to these come those who succeeded to their ministry, or who hold it at this day, even the holy teachers that stand at the head of the holy churches. COMMENTARY ON LUKE, HOMILY 129.[16]

INTEREST ON THE WORD OF GOD. ORIGEN: Interest on the Word of God is having in life and deeds things that the Word of God has commanded. When you hear the Word, if you use it and act according to those words that you hear and live according to these words, then you are preparing interest for the Lord. Each of you can make ten talents from five. You will then hear from the Lord, "Well done, good and faithful servant, you shall have power over ten cities." Beware of this, fearing that any one of you may gather "in a napkin" or bury "in the earth" the money that has been received. You know well the nature of the outcome for this kind of man when the Lord comes. HOMILY ON EXODUS 13.1.[17]

---

[5]1 Cor 12:4-7. [6]1 Cor 12:8. [7]*CGSL* 511**. [8]Jn 15:24. [9]Zech 9:9. [10]Is 32:1. [11]Ps 2:6-7. [12]Jn 19:15. [13]*CGSL* 510**. [14]Mt 25:15. [15]Heb 5:14. [16]*CGSL* 512**. [17]FC 71:376*.

THE OFFICE OF INVESTORS. AUGUSTINE: We are well aware of the threats made by the Lord's merciful "greed." He is everywhere seeking a profitable return on his money. He says to the lazy servant, who wished to pass judgment on something he could not see, "Wicked servant, out of your own mouth I condemn you. You said I am a difficult man, reaping where I have not sown, gathering where I have not scattered. So you knew all about my greed. You, then, should have given my money to the stockbrokers. When I came, I would have demanded it with interest." We could only lay out our Lord's money. He is the one who will demand the interest on it, not only from this man but also from all of us. SERMON 279.12.[18]

WHEN IN BUSINESS FOR THE LORD, THE PROFITS GO TO US. ORIGEN: What you have offered to God you shall receive back multiplied. Something like this, although put in another way, is related in the Gospels when in a parable someone received a pound that he might engage in business, and the master of the house demanded the money. If you have caused five to be multiplied to ten, then they are given to you. Hear what Scripture says, "Take his pound, and give it to him who has ten pounds."

We therefore appear at least to engage in business for the Lord, but the profits of the business go to us. We appear to offer sacrifice to the Lord, but the things we offer are given back to us. God does not need anything, but he wants us to be rich. He desires our progress through each, individual thing. HOMILY ON GENESIS 8.[19]

EVERYONE IS ACCOUNTABLE FOR DISPENSING THE GIFTS. AUGUSTINE: In the Gospel, you have heard both the reward of the good servants and the punishment of the bad. The fault of that servant who was reproved and severely punished was this and only this: that he would not put to use what he had received. He preserved it intact, but his master was looking for a profit from it. God is greedy for our salvation. If such condemnation befalls the servant who did not use what he had received, what should they who lose it expect? We therefore are dispensers. We expend, but you receive. We expect a profit on your part—living good lives—for that is the profit from our dispensing. Do not think that you are free from the obligation of dispensing. Of course, you cannot dispense your gifts as from this higher station of ours, but you can dispense them in whatever station you happen to be. When Christ is attacked, defend him. Give an answer to those who complain. Rebuke blasphemers, but keep yourselves far from any fellowship with them. If in this way you gain anyone, you are putting your gifts to use. SERMON 94.[20]

19:28 Conclusion: Ascent to Jerusalem

JESUS TURNS FROM TEACHING TO HIS PASSION IN JERUSALEM. CYRIL OF ALEXANDRIA: As long as it was fitting that he should travel the country of the Jews trying to win by lessons and admonitions superior to the law many to the grace that is by faith, he did not cease to do so. The time was now calling Christ to the passion for the salvation of the whole world. He therefore goes up to Jerusalem to free the inhabitants of the earth from the tyranny of the enemy, to abolish death, and to destroy the sin of the world. First, he points out to the Israelites by a plain fact, that a new people from among the heathen shall be subject to him, while they themselves are rejected as the murderers of the Lord. COMMENTARY ON LUKE, HOMILY 129.[21]

---

[18]WSA 3 8:67**. [19]FC 71:146-47*. [20]FC 11:293-94. [21]CGSL 514**.

19:29-36 THE TRIUMPHANT ENTRANCE INTO JERUSALEM

²⁹*When he drew near to Bethphage and Bethany, at the mount that is called Olivet, he sent two of the disciples,* ³⁰*saying, "Go into the village opposite, where on entering you will find a colt tied, on which no one has ever yet sat; untie it and bring it here.* ³¹*If any one asks you, 'Why are you untying it?' you shall say this, 'The Lord has need of it.'"* ³²*So those who were sent went away and found it as he had told them.* ³³*And as they were untying the colt, its owners said to them, "Why are you untying the colt?"* ³⁴*And they said, "The Lord has need of it."* ³⁵*And they brought it to Jesus, and throwing their garments on the colt they set Jesus upon it.* ³⁶*And as he rode along, they spread their garments on the road.*

OVERVIEW: Jesus draws near to Bethphage and Bethany, which are right outside the city, Bethany meaning "obedience" and Bethphage "a house of jaws," that is, a place for priests (ORIGEN). Then he draws near to the descent from the Mount of Olives, where the city of Jerusalem comes into view, in order to plant new olives trees—the Gentiles—that would worship him (AMBROSE). For three years of ministry in Galilee and en route to Jerusalem Jesus is never spoken of as riding on a colt; for this short distance from the Mount of Olives into Jerusalem, much is now made of preparing for this journey on a colt (CYRIL OF ALEXANDRIA).

Jesus *is* a king, but he begins his life in humility in a manger in Bethlehem and now concludes his work by humbly riding on a colt into Jerusalem (EPHREM THE SYRIAN). There is a clear echo of the promise of Jacob to the house of Judah: "Binding his foal to the vine and his donkey's colt to the choice vine, he washes his garments in wine and his vesture in the blood of grapes."[1] The "wine" and "blood of grapes" suggest the imminent outpouring of Jesus' blood (JUSTIN MARTYR). The garments thrown over the colt represent the virtues of the disciples as they prepare the colt for Jesus, the mystic rider who will now enter Jerusalem and the hearts of the Gentile believers (AMBROSE).

19:29-36 Preparations for Jesus' Humble Entrance

THE DISCIPLES SENT TO A PLACE OF OBEDIENCE AND A PLACE FOR PRIESTS. ORIGEN: When the Savior had come "to Bethphage and Bethany near Mount Olivet," he sent two of his disciples" to untie "the foal of a donkey" that had been tied, "on which no man had ever sat." To me, this seems to apply more to the deeper sense than to the simple narrative. The donkey had been bound. Where was it bound? "Across from Bethphage and Bethany." "Bethany" means "house of obedience," and "Bethphage" means "house of jaws." Bethphage is a priestly place, because jawbones were given to priests, as the law commands.[2] The Savior sends his disciples to the place where "obedience" is and where "the place given over to priests" is, to unbind "the foal of an ass, on which no man had ever sat." HOMILY ON THE GOSPEL OF LUKE 37.1.[3]

JESUS COMES TO THE MOUNT OF OLIVES. AMBROSE: He came to the Mount of Olivet[4] so that he could plant new olive trees[5] on the heights of virtue, the mother of which is the Jerusalem

---

[1]Gen 49:11. [2]Deut 18:3. [3]FC 94:153*. [4]Lk 19:2, 9. [5]Ps 127:4 LXX.

that is above.[6] The heavenly Gardener is on this mountain so that all those who are planted in the house of the Lord[7] may say, "But I am as a fruitful olive in the house of the Lord."[8] Perhaps that mountain is Christ himself. Who else could produce such fruits, not in many round berries but in the fullness of spirit in the fruitful Gentiles? We ascend by him, and we ascend to him.[9] He is the Door[10] and the Way[11] that is opened and which opens. Those entering knock on it,[12] and those leaving worship it. EXPOSITION OF THE GOSPEL OF LUKE 9.2.[13]

WHY JESUS RIDES ON A COLT. CYRIL OF ALEXANDRIA: What then was the sign? He sat on a colt, as we have just heard the blessed Evangelist clearly telling us. Perhaps someone will say, "When he traveled all Judea—for he taught in their synagogues and added the working of miracles to his words—he did not ask for an animal on which to ride. When Christ could have purchased one, he would not, although he often was wearied by his long journeys on the way. When passing through Samaria, he was wearied with his journey,[14] as it is written. Who can make us believe that when he was going from the Mount of Olives to Jerusalem, places separated from one another by so short an interval, that he would require a colt? Since the mother accompanied the colt, why did he not take the mother instead of choosing the colt? The donkey that bore the colt was brought to him also. We learn this from the words of Matthew, who says that he sent the disciples to a village opposite them. He said to them, "You will find a donkey tied and a colt with her. Untie and bring them to me." "They brought," it says, "the donkey and the colt with her."[15] We must consider, therefore, what are the explanations and the benefits that we derive from this occurrence and how we make Christ riding on the colt a type of the calling of the Gentiles. The colt of a donkey is mounted on which none has sat, because no one before Christ called the peoples of the nations to the church. COMMENTARY ON LUKE, HOMILY 130.[16]

A MANGER AND A DONKEY. EPHREM THE SYRIAN: "Untie the donkey and bring it to me."[17] He began with a manger and finished with a donkey, in Bethlehem with a manger, in Jerusalem with a donkey. COMMENTARY ON TATIAN'S DIATESSARON 18.1.[18]

JACOB'S BLESSING ON JUDAH. JUSTIN MARTYR: People from every nation look for him who was crucified in Judea, after whose coming the country of the Jews was immediately given over to you as the loot of war. The words "tying his foal to the vine and washing his robe in the blood of the grape"[19] allegorically signified the things that would happen to Christ and the deeds he would perform. The foal of a donkey stood tied to a vine at the entrance to a village. He ordered his disciples to lead it to him. When this was done, he mounted it and sat on it and entered Jerusalem where was located the greatest Jewish temple, which you later destroyed. FIRST APOLOGY 32.[20]

CHRIST THE MYSTIC RIDER. AMBROSE: The apostles threw down their own garments before Christ. By their preaching of the gospel, they would present the glory of their action. In Holy Scripture, very often garments are virtues, which are to soften the hardness of the Gentiles to some extent by their own virtue, so that with zealous good will they may show the undisturbed obedience of a joyful passage. The Lord of the world was not happy to be carried in a public spectacle on the back of a donkey. With the generalship of piety, he subdued the accustomed disposition of the Gentile people. The mystic Rider therefore could cover the inmost places of our mind with the hidden mystery. He would take his seat in an inward possession of the secret places of the spirits, as if infused with the Godhead, ruling the

---

[6]Gal 4:26. [7]Ps 92:13 (91:14 LXX). [8]Ps 52:8 (51:10 LXX). [9]See Jn 3:13. [10]Jn 10:9. [11]Jn 14:6. [12]Mt 7:7-8; Lk 11:9-10. [13]*EHG* 371**. [14]Jn 4:6. [15]Mt 21:2. [16]*CGSL* 514-15**. [17]Mk 11:2; Mt 21:2. [18]*ECTD* 269. [19]Gen 49:11. [20]FC 6:68-69*. Addressed to the Roman emperor.

footprints of the mind and curbing the lusts of the flesh. Those who received such a Rider in their inmost hearts are happy. A heavenly bridle curbed those mouths, or else they would be unloosed in a multitude of words.[21] EXPOSITION OF THE GOSPEL OF LUKE 9.9.[22]

---

[21]See Prov 10:19. [22] EHG 373**.

19:37-48 REACTION TO JESUS' ENTRANCE AND THE FATE OF JERUSALEM

[37]*As he was now drawing near, at the descent of the Mount of Olives, the whole multitude of the disciples began to rejoice and praise God with a loud voice for all the mighty works that they had seen,* [38]*saying, "Blessed is the King who comes in the name of the Lord! Peace in heaven and glory in the highest!"* [39]*And some of the Pharisees in the multitude said to him, "Teacher, rebuke your disciples."* [40]*He answered, "I tell you, if these were silent, the very stones would cry out."*

[41]*And when he drew near and saw the city he wept over it,* [42]*saying, "Would that even today you knew the things that make for peace! But now they are hid from your eyes.* [43]*For the days shall come upon you, when your enemies will cast up a bank about you and surround you, and hem you in on every side,* [44]*and dash you to the ground, you and your children within you, and they will not leave one stone upon another in you; because you did not know the time of your visitation."*

[45]*And he entered the temple and began to drive out those who sold,* [46]*saying to them, "It is written, 'My house shall be a house of prayer'; but you have made it a den of robbers."*

[47]*And he was teaching daily in the temple. The chief priests and the scribes and the principal men of the people sought to destroy him;* [48]*but they did not find anything they could do, for all the people hung upon his words.*

OVERVIEW: As Jesus enters Jerusalem, apostles and children proclaim his divine glory, while the Pharisees call to Jesus to rebuke his disciples (CYRIL OF ALEXANDRIA). Jerusalem was in turmoil at his birth and now at his death. In both events the voices of children are intertwined. Even the stones will cry out at his crucifixion (EPHREM THE SYRIAN). Jesus tells the Pharisees that if his followers were prevented from announcing the arrival of the Messiah to the city, then even inanimate objects such as stones would react against their nature (AMBROSE) by announcing his arrival (CYRIL OF ALEXANDRIA). At Jesus' birth there is peace *on earth*. As he enters Jerusalem for his passion and resurrection, there is peace *in heaven*. Earth and heaven are joined together in peace through the incarnation and atonement of Christ (CYRIL OF ALEXANDRIA).

By weeping over this city, Jesus fulfills in himself the beatitude "blessed are those who weep."[1] Jesus weeps not only for this city but also for all believers who fall away because of sin and the evil

---

[1]Luke 6:21.

spirits that surround them (ORIGEN). Jesus prophetically describes with detailed accuracy here and later during his eschatological discourse in the temple how devastating the city's future destruction will be at the hands of Titus during the reign of Vespasian (EUSEBIUS).

The temple will become the locale for Jesus' teaching during these final days. Hence it must be cleansed so that the holiness of Jesus may dwell in a holy place. Some of the moneychangers cannot distinguish good from evil and do not realize that all money is the Lord's (AMBROSE). Casting them out is a violent act by Jesus, but no more violent than the casting out of demons (AUGUSTINE). The temple must return to its original purpose—a place of petitionary prayer for someone like the tax collector in the parable.[2] It must not be a place of sacrifice. The temple is now a place of conflict, and the chief priests and scribes are seeking to kill Jesus for cleansing the temple and teaching there (CYRIL OF ALEXANDRIA).

19:37-40 The Response to Jesus' Entrance

HIS DISCIPLES AND THE PEOPLE PRAISE JESUS. CYRIL OF ALEXANDRIA: Christ therefore sits upon the colt. Since he now came to the descent of the Mount of Olives close to Jerusalem, the disciples went before him praising him. They were called to bear witness to the wonderful works that he performed and of his godlike glory and sovereignty. We likewise should always praise him, considering who and how great he is. Another holy Evangelist mentioned that children, holding high branches of palm trees, ran before him. With the rest of the disciples, they celebrated his glory.[3] COMMENTARY ON LUKE, HOMILY 130.[4]

THE PHARISEES REBUKE THE DISCIPLES. CYRIL OF ALEXANDRIA: The Pharisees truly complained because Christ was praised. They came near and said, "Rebuke your disciples." O Pharisee, what wrong action did they do? What charge do you bring against the disciples or how would you rebuke them? They have not sinned in any

way but have rather done what is praiseworthy. They extol as King and Lord the One the law had before pointed out by many symbols and types. The ancient company of the holy prophets had preached of him. You despised him and grieved him by your great jealousy. Your duty was to join the rest in their praises. Your duty was to withdraw far from your innate wickedness and to change your way for the better. Your duty was to follow the sacred Scriptures and to thirst after the knowledge of the truth. You did not do this, but transferring your words to the contrary, you wanted to rebuke the heralds of the truth. COMMENTARY ON LUKE, HOMILY 130.[5]

JERUSALEM IN TURMOIL AT JESUS' BIRTH AND DEATH. EPHREM THE SYRIAN: The children were shouting and saying, "Hosanna to the Son of David!" This displeased the chief priests and the scribes, and they said to him, "Do you not hear what these are saying?"[6] That means, "If these praises do not please you, make them keep silent." At his birth and at his death, children were intertwined in the crown of his sufferings. When he met Christ, the infant John jumped for joy within the womb.[7] Children were murdered at his birth.[8] They were like the grapes of his wedding feast. Children also proclaimed his praise when the time of his death approached. Jerusalem was in turmoil[9] at his birth, just as it was in turmoil again and trembling[10] the day that he entered it. When the scribes heard, they were displeased, and they were saying to him, "Stop them!" he said to them, "If these become silent, the stones will cry out." The scribes preferred that the children would cry out rather than the stones. This, however, was reserved for later, because the stones were crying out at the time of his crucifixion,[11] but those with words were silent. Speechless things proclaimed his greatness. COMMENTARY ON TATIAN'S DIATESSARON 118.2.[12]

---

[2]Lk 18:9-14. [3]Mt 21:8; Mk 11:8; Jn 12:13. [4]CGSL 516**. [5]CGSL 516-17**. [6]Mt 21:15-16. [7]Lk 1:41. [8]Mt 2:16-18. [9]Mt 2:3. [10]Mt 21:10. [11]See Mt 27:51-52. [12]ECTD 271**.

Even Stones Will Praise Jesus. Ambrose: It is not strange if the rocks would respond against their nature with praises of the Lord since murderers, harder than rocks, also proclaim them. Perhaps this means when the Jews are speechless after the Lord's passion, the living stones, according to Peter, will cry out.[13] Even with mixed emotions, the crowd nevertheless leads God to his temple with praise. Exposition of the Gospel of Luke 9.16.[14]

Jesus Calls for the Stones to Praise Him. Cyril of Alexandria: What does Christ answer to these things? "I tell you that if these be silent, the stones will cry out."

It is impossible for God not to be glorified, although those of the race of Israel refuse to do so. The worshipers of idols were once as stones and hardened, but they have been delivered from their former error and rescued from the hand of the enemy. They have escaped from devilish darkness. They have been called to the light of truth. They have awakened as from drunkenness. They have acknowledged the Creator. They do not praise him secretly, in concealment, in a hidden way and silently, but with freedom of speech and a loud voice. They praise him diligently, as it were, calling out to one another and saying, "Come, let us praise the Lord and sing psalms to God our Savior." They acknowledged Christ the Savior of all. Commentary on Luke, Homily 130.[15]

Peace of Heaven and Earth. Cyril of Alexandria: The disciples praise Christ the Savior of all, calling him King and Lord, and the peace of heaven and earth. Let us also praise him, taking the psalmist's harp and saying, "How great are your works, O Lord! In wisdom you have made them."[16] Only wisdom is in his works because he guides all useful things in their proper manner and assigns to his acts the season that suits them. Commentary on Luke, Homily 130.[17]

19:41-44 The Response of Jesus to Jerusalem

Jesus Fulfills the Beatitude for Those Who Weep. Origen: When our Lord and Savior approached Jerusalem, he saw the city and wept. . . . By his example, Jesus confirms all the Beatitudes that he speaks in the Gospel. By his own witness, he confirms what he teaches. "Blessed are the meek," he says. He says something similar to this of himself: "Learn from me, for I am meek." "Blessed are the peacemakers." What other man brought as much peace as my Lord Jesus, who "is our peace," who "dissolves hostility" and "destroys it in his own flesh"?[18] "Blessed are those who suffer persecution because of justice."

No one suffered such persecution because of justice as did the Lord Jesus, who was crucified for our sins. The Lord therefore exhibited all the Beatitudes in himself. For the sake of this likeness, he wept, because of what he said, "Blessed are those who weep," to lay the foundations for this beatitude as well. He wept for Jerusalem "and said, 'If only you had known on that day what meant peace for you! But now it is hidden from your eyes,'" and the rest, to the point where he says, "Because you did not know the time of your visitation." Homily on the Gospel of Luke 38.1-2.[19]

Luke Records Jesus' Prophecies About Jerusalem's Destruction. Eusebius: These things took place in this way in the second year of the reign of Vespasian in agreement with the prophetic pronouncements of our Lord and Savior Jesus Christ. By divine power, he foresaw these events as if already present and wept over them and mourned, according to the writings of the holy Evangelists. They add his own words, when on one occasion he spoke as if to Jerusalem itself. "Would that even today you knew the things that make for peace! Now they are hid from your eyes. For the days shall come upon you, when your enemies will cast up a bank about you and surround you, and hem you in on every side, and dash you to the ground, you and

---

[13]See 1 Pet 2:5. [14]EHG 376**. [15]CGSL 517**. [16]Ps 104:24 (103:24 LXX). [17]CGSL 514*. [18]Eph 2:14-15. [19]FC 94:156-57**.

your children within you, and they will not leave one stone upon another in you; because you did not know the time of your visitation." On another occasion, as if concerning the people, he said, "There will be great distress in the land and wrath on this people. They will fall by the edge of the sword and shall be led away captives into all nations. Jerusalem will be trampled down by the Gentiles until the times of the nations be fulfilled."[20] Again he says, "When you shall see Jerusalem encircled by an army, then know that its desolation is near."[21] If one should compare the words of our Savior with the other narratives of the historian, how could he help but marvel and confess the truly divine and supernaturally wonderful foreknowledge and prophecy of our Savior? ECCLESIASTICAL HISTORY 3.7.[22]

19:45-46 Jesus Cleanses the Temple

THE HOME OF SANCTITY. AMBROSE: God does not want his temple to be a trader's lodge but the home of sanctity. He does not preserve the practice of the priestly ministry by the dishonest duty of religion but by voluntary obedience. Consider what the Lord's actions impose on you as an example of living. . . . He taught in general that worldly transactions must be absent from the temple, but he drove out the moneychangers in particular. Who are the moneychangers, if not those who seek profit from the Lord's money and cannot distinguish between good and evil? Holy Scripture is the Lord's money. EXPOSITION OF THE GOSPEL OF LUKE 9.17-18.[23]

THE CASTING OUT OF SELLERS. AUGUSTINE: In another place, when I said the following about our Lord Jesus Christ, "He did nothing by force but everything by persuasion and admonition," I forgot that he threw out the sellers and buyers from the temple by flogging them.[24] What does this matter to us? How is it important if he also cast out demons from people against their will, not by persuasive words but by force of his power?[25] RETRACTATIONS 12.6.[26]

A HOUSE OF PRAYER, NOT A PLACE OF SACRIFICE. CYRIL OF ALEXANDRIA: There was in it a crowd of merchants and others guilty of the charge of the shameful love of money. I mean moneychangers or keepers of exchange tables, sellers of oxen, dealers of sheep, and sellers of turtledoves and pigeons. All these things were used for the sacrifices according to the legal ritual. The time had now come for the shadow to draw to an end and for the truth to shine forth. The truth is the lovely beauty of Christian conduct, the glories of the blameless life and the sweet rational flavor of worship in spirit and in truth.

The Truth, Christ as One who with his Father was also honored in their temple, commanded that those things that were by the law should be carried away, even the materials for sacrifices and burning of incense. He commanded that the temple clearly should be a house of prayer. His rebuking the dealers and driving them from the sacred courts when they were selling what was wanted for sacrifice means certainly this, as I suppose, and this alone. COMMENTARY ON LUKE, HOMILY 132.[27]

19:47-48 Jesus Teaches in the Temple

THE CHIEF PRIESTS AND SCRIBES SEEK TO KILL JESUS. CYRIL OF ALEXANDRIA: As one who possessed authority over the temple, he took care of it. . . . Their duty was to worship him, as One who with God the Father was Lord of the temple. In their great folly, they did not do this, but rather being savagely eager for hatred, they set up the sharp sting of wickedness against him and hurried to murder, which is the neighbor and brother of envy. It says that they sought to destroy him but could not, because all the people were hanging on him to hear him. Does this not make the punishment of the scribes and Pharisees, and all the rulers of the Jewish ranks, heavier? The whole people, consisting of unlearned persons, hung upon the sa-

[20]Lk 21:23-24. [21]Lk 21:20. [22]FC 19:153-54*. [23]EHG 376**. [24]Mk 11:15; Mt 21:12. [25]Mt 9:32-33; Mk 1:34; 5:13. [26]FC 60:54*. [27]CGSL 522-23**.

cred doctrines and drank the saving word like the rain. They were ready to produce the fruits of faith and place their neck under his commandments. They who had the position to urge on their people to this very thing savagely rebelled and wickedly sought the opportunity for murder. With unbri-

dled violence, they ran upon the rocks, not accepting the faith and wickedly hindering others. COMMENTARY ON LUKE, HOMILY 132.[28]

---

[28]CGSL 523**.

20:1-8 THE AUTHORITY OF JESUS

[1]*One day, as he was teaching the people in the temple and preaching the gospel, the chief priests and the scribes with the elders came up* [2]*and said to him, "Tell us by what authority you do these things, or who it is that gave you this authority."* [3]*He answered them, "I also will ask you a question; now tell me, Was the baptism of John from heaven or from men?"* [5]*And they discussed it with one another, saying, "If we say, 'From heaven,' he will say, 'Why did you not believe him?'* [6]*But if we say, 'From men,' all the people will stone us; for they are convinced that John was a prophet."* [7]*So they answered that they did not know whence it was.* [8]*And Jesus said to them, "Neither will I tell you by what authority I do these things."*

OVERVIEW: Since Jesus is from the house of Judah and not from the house of Levi, he has no jurisdiction in the temple (CYRIL OF ALEXANDRIA). Jesus brings John the Baptist into the dialogue, thus putting the Sanhedrin on the horns of a dilemma, for they are more afraid of the people than they are of God (EPHREM THE SYRIAN). They continue to reject him again in fear and are sent away in confusion, for John the Baptist is like a lamp that illuminates their hypocrisy at their inability to confess who Jesus is (AUGUSTINE). They know the answer to their question concerning Jesus' authority, and they may even believe that it is true, but they reject it nonetheless, for they refuse to be taught by Jesus (CYRIL OF ALEXANDRIA).

20:1-8 Conflict over John's Baptism

JESUS WAS FROM THE HOUSE OF JUDAH, NOT LEVI, WHICH CONTROLLED ENTRY INTO THE TEMPLE. CYRIL OF ALEXANDRIA: The Savior himself admonished them, saying, "Woe to you lawyers! for you have taken away the key of knowledge; you did not enter yourselves, and you hindered those who were entering."[1] They rise up against Christ as he teaches. They wickedly and despicably shout out, "Tell us, by what authority you do these things? Who gave you this authority?" They say, "The law given by Moses and the commandment that regulates all our institutions commanded that only those who are of the lineage of Levi should approach these sacred duties. They offer the sacrifices. They regulate whatever is done in the divine temple. The office of instructing and the government of the sacred trusts are given to them. Being of another tribe, from Judah, you grab honors that have been set apart for us. Who gave you this authority?" COMMENTARY ON LUKE, HOMILY 132.[2]

---

[1]Lk 11:52. [2]CGSL 523-24*.

THE PHARISEES FEAR HUMAN BEINGS MORE THAN GOD.

EPHREM THE SYRIAN: While he was teaching the crowds and evangelizing them, the chief priests and the scribes came and said to him, "By what power are you doing this?" If it were a question of his teaching, how could they have called it a work? It is clear that he referred to his works as testimony to the truth of his words, according to what he said: "If you do not believe in me, believe at least in the works."[3] "By what power are you doing this?" They interrogated him like inquisitors, but he did not reply to them, since they did not approach him as students out of love in order to be taught but as rebels. He asked them in turn, "From where did the baptism of John come?"[4] His word pressured them in such a way that they were forced to confess that they had not believed in John. He asked, "Was it from heaven or from human beings?" They began to reflect on it in their minds and to say, "If we say that it was from heaven, he will say, 'Why did you not believe in it?' If we say, 'From human beings,' we are afraid of the crowd."[5] When they said, "If it is from heaven," they did not also say, "We are afraid of God." They were thus afraid of human beings but not of God. COMMENTARY ON TATIAN'S DIATESSARON 16.17.[6]

JOHN IS A LAMP THAT SENDS AWAY JESUS' ENEMIES.

AUGUSTINE: The Jews, to discredit him, said to the Lord, "By what authority are you doing these things? If you are the Christ, tell us openly." They were looking for a pretext, not for faith. They wanted something by which to catch him, not something by which to be liberated. Notice what answer the one who could see their hearts gave to confound them with the lamp. He said, "I will also ask you one question. Tell me, John's baptism, from where is it? Is it from heaven, or from men?" They were immediately sent staggering backward. Although the daylight was only shining gently, they were forced to fumble and blink, since they were unable to gaze at that brilliance. They took refuge in the darkness of their hearts, and there they began to get very agitated among themselves, stumbling and falling about. We might say that they said this to themselves where they were thinking, yet where he could see. If we say, "They said, 'It is from heaven,' he will say to us, 'Why did you not believe him? He testified to Christ the Lord.' If we say, 'From men,' the people will stone us, because they regarded John as a great prophet." They said, "We do not know." You do not know, because you are in darkness and are losing the light. After all, is not it much better, if darkness is occupying the human heart, to let the light in and not to lose it? When they said, "We do not know," the Lord said, "Neither do I tell you by what authority I am doing these things. You see, I know in what mind you said 'We do not know,' not because you wish to be taught, but because you are afraid to confess." SERMON 293.4.[7]

THE PHARISEES DO NOT KNOW THE TRUTH.

CYRIL OF ALEXANDRIA: They were unworthy to learn the truth and to see the pathway that leads directly to every good work. Christ answered them, "Neither do I tell you by what authority I do these things." The Jews therefore did not know the truth, and they were not taught of God,[8] that is, of Christ. Christ reveals that knowledge to us who have believed in him. We, receiving in mind and heart his divine and adorable mystery, or rather the knowledge of it, and being careful to fulfill those things which are pleasing to him, shall reign with him. COMMENTARY ON LUKE, HOMILY 133.[9]

---

[3]Jn 10:38. [4]Mt 21:25. [5]Mt 21:25-26. [6]ECTD 251**. [7]WSA 3 8:151**. [8]Is 54:13. [9]CGSL 527**.

20:9-19 THE PARABLE OF THE WORKERS
IN THE VINEYARD

⁹*And he began to tell the people this parable: "A man planted a vineyard, and let it out to tenants, and went into another country for a long while.* ¹⁰*When the time came, he sent a servant to the tenants, that they should give him some of the fruit of the vineyard; but the tenants beat him, and sent him away empty-handed.* ¹¹*And he sent another servant; him also they beat and treated shamefully, and sent him away empty-handed.* ¹²*And he sent yet a third; this one they wounded and cast out.* ¹³*Then the owner of the vineyard said, 'What shall I do? I will send my beloved son, it may be they will respect him.'* ¹⁴*But when the tenants saw him, they said to themselves, 'This is the heir; let us kill him, that the inheritance may be ours.'* ¹⁵*And they cast him out of the vineyard and killed him. What then will the owner of the vineyard do to them?* ¹⁶*He will come and destroy those tenants, and give the vineyard to others." When they heard this, they said, "God forbid!"* ¹⁷*But he looked at them and said, "What then is this that is written:*

'The very stone which the builders rejected
has become the head of the corner'?
¹⁸*Every one who falls on that stone will be broken to pieces; but when it falls on any one it will crush him."*

¹⁹*The scribes and the chief priests tried to lay hands on him at that very hour, but they feared the people; for they perceived that he had told this parable against them.*

OVERVIEW: The parable is allegorical where God is the Lord of the vineyard, which he has leased to tenants, the Jewish religious establishment (AMBROSE). God, who planted the vineyard, went abroad for a considerable amount of time. While he is abroad, God sent prophets to declare his salvific intentions and his judgment upon those who reject him. The foolishness and wickedness of the workers delude them into thinking that they will inherit the vineyard if they kill the Son, who possesses by inheritance what belongs to the Father (CYRIL OF ALEXANDRIA).

Jesus is interpreting the significance of his death for salvation history where the inheritance of the vineyard planted in Israel and given to them to nurture will be taken away and given to Gentiles (EPHREM THE SYRIAN). After Pentecost, the vineyard will be given to the apostles and teachers of the church, the new Israel (CYRIL OF ALEXANDRIA). The church is now the vineyard, the Father the husbandman, and Christ the vine, into whom we have been grafted through the wood of the cross so that we might partake of the heavenly gifts (AMBROSE).

The people's response is fear. "Let it not happen," for they know the danger inherent in Jesus' words (CYRIL OF ALEXANDRIA). Jesus gives no answer, because the events of his life in the next few days will provide the answer. But it is clear: he is the stone which the builders rejected (EPHREM THE SYRIAN). As the cornerstone, Jesus joins two people together—Jews and Gentiles—in one body, the church. The scribes and chief priests were aware that many believed his teaching, and they were afraid to arrest Jesus because of how the people might react. More important, these religious leaders saw their fleeting place in Jesus' reading of salvation history (CYRIL OF ALEX-ANDRIA).

20:9-15 *The Parable of the Workers in the Vineyard*

THE VINEYARD IS THE HOUSE OF ISRAEL LEASED TO THE JEWS. AMBROSE: Very many derive various meanings from the word *vineyard*, but Isaiah clearly stated that the vineyard of the Lord of hosts is the house of Israel.[1] Who else but God founded this vineyard? He leased it and set out to foreign places. The Lord, who is always everywhere, does not journey from place to place, but he is present to those who love him and absent from those who neglect him. He was absent for many seasons, fearing that the foreclosure might seem premature. The more indulgent the generosity, the more inexcusable is the stubbornness. ... He thus leased to the Jews his fortified, prepared and beautified vineyard. EXPOSITION OF THE GOSPEL OF LUKE 9.23-24.[2]

GOD GOES ABROAD FOR A LONG TIME. CYRIL OF ALEXANDRIA: The vineyard of the Lord of hosts is the man of Judah, a plant new and beloved.[3] He who planted the vineyard is God, who also went away for a long time. God still fills everything and in no way whatsoever is absent from anything that exists. How, therefore, did the Lord of the vineyard go away for a long time? After they saw him in the shape of fire at his descent on Mount Sinai with Moses, who spoke the law to them as the mediator, he did not again grant to them his presence in a visible way. To use a metaphor taken from human affairs, his relation to them was like one who made a long journey abroad. COMMENTARY ON LUKE, Homily 134.[4]

GOD SENT PROPHETS. CYRIL OF ALEXANDRIA: He went away, but plainly he cared for his farm and kept it in his mind. He sent faithful servants to them at three different times to receive produce or fruit from the tillers of the vineyard. There was no period in the interval, during which there were not sent by God prophets and righteous men to admonish Israel and urge it to bring forth as fruits the glories of a life in accordance with the law. They still were wicked, disobedient and callous, and their heart was hardened against admonition so that they would in no way listen to the word that would have profited them. ... Israel was guilty of the charge of apostasy and of idol worship. This is how they shamefully threw out those who were sent to them. COMMENTARY ON LUKE, Homily 134.[5]

THE FOOLISHNESS OF KILLING THE HEIR. CYRIL OF ALEXANDRIA: The lord of the vineyard thinks to himself saying, "What shall I do?" We must carefully examine in what sense he says this. Does the householder use these words because he had no more servants? He certainly did not lack other ministers of his holy will. When a physician may say of a sick man, "What shall I do?" we should understand him to mean that every resource of medical skill had been tried without success. We affirm that the lord of the vineyard, having practiced all gentleness and care with his farm but without benefiting it in any way, says, "What shall I do?" What is the result? He advances to still greater purposes. "I will send," he says, "my son, the beloved one. Perhaps they will reverence him." Observe in this, that after the servants, he sends the Son as One not numbered among the servants but as a true Son and therefore the Lord. Although he put on the form of a servant for the dispensation's sake, he was God, very Son of God the Father who possessed natural dominion. Did they honor him who was sent as Son and Lord and as One who possesses by inheritance whatever belongs to God the Father? No, they murdered him outside the vineyard, having plotted among themselves a foolish and ignorant plan full of all wickedness. They say, "Let us kill him, that the inheritance may be ours." COMMENTARY ON LUKE, Homily 134.[6]

---

[1]Is 5:7. [2]EHG 378-79**. [3]Is 5:7. [4]CGSL 531-32**. [5]CGSL 532**. [6]CGSL 532-33**.

20:16-18 *The Interpretation*

Jesus Takes the Inheritance from Israel and Gives It to Gentiles. Ephrem the Syrian: He proposed another parable. "A certain man, a householder, planted his vineyard."[7] This is like what the psalmist said, "You brought a vine out of Egypt, you drove out the nations and planted it."[8] He protected it with a hedge, the law, and prepared a pit in it for the winepresses, the altar, and built a tower there,[9] the temple, and sent his servants to bring him its fruit. The first, the next and the last were not received. Then he sent his Son.[10] He was not the last, for although he appeared at the end, he already existed. John witnessed, "A man will come after me, who is before me."[11] He did not do this because he was unaware that the ancestors were incapable of receiving the produce but to remove the detractions of these stubborn ones from their midst. They were saying that he was not able to direct and prepare everything that he wanted to by the law, so therefore he sent his Son to impose silence on them. When they saw his Son coming, they said, "Here is the heir of the vineyard. Come! Let us kill him, and the inheritance of the vineyard will be ours."[12] They killed him, but their inheritance was taken away from them and given to the Gentiles. It happened just as he had said, "For to him who has will more be given, and he will have an abundance; but from him who has not, even what he has will be taken away."[13] Commentary on Tatian's Diatessaron 16.19.[14]

The Vineyard Given to the Holy Apostles. Cyril of Alexandria: The farm was given to other farmers. Who are they? I answer the company of the holy apostles, the preachers of the evangelical commandments, the ministers of the new covenant. They were the teachers of a spiritual service, and knew how to instruct people correctly and blamelessly and to lead them most excellently to everything that is pleasing to God. . . . The God of all plainly reveals that the farm was given to other farmers and not only to the holy apostles but also to those who come after them, although they are not from Jewish blood. He says by the voice of Isaiah to the church of the Gentiles and to the remnant of Israel, "Aliens shall stand and feed your flocks, foreigners shall be your plowmen and vinedressers."[15] Many were called from the Gentiles, and holy people from their number became teachers and instructors. Even to this day, people of Gentile race hold high place in the churches. They are sowing the seeds of piety to Christ in the hearts of believers and making the nations entrusted to their care into beautiful vineyards in the sight of God. Commentary on Luke, Homily 134.[16]

The Church, the Father, Christ. Ambrose: The vineyard prefigures us, because the people of God, founded on the root of the eternal Vine, appear above the earth, bordering the lowly ground. They now grow ripe with budding flowers. They now are clothed with dense greenery and take on a gentle yoke[17] when they worship with mature branches as if with the twigs of the vine. The Father Almighty truly is the Vinedresser, and Christ is the Vine. We, not vine sprouts, are pruned by the sickle of the eternal cultivator if we do not bear fruit in Christ.[18] The people of Christ then is correctly named a vineyard, either because the sign of the cross is woven on its forehead[19] or its fruit is gathered in the last season of the year. It may also be called a vineyard because there is equal measurement in the church of God for rich and poor, humble and powerful, servants and masters. There is no difference in the church, as in all the rows of the vineyard.[20] As the vine clings to trees, so the body is joined to the soul and the soul to the body. When the vine clings, it is raised up. When it is pruned, it is not diminished, but it increases. The people of God is

---

[7]Mt 21:33. [8]Ps 80:8 (79:9 LXX). [9]Mt 21:33. [10]Mt 21:37. [11]Jn 1:15, 30. [12]Mt 21:38. [13]Mt 13:12. [14]ECTD 252-53*. [15]Is 61:5. [16]CGSL 533-34**. [17]See Mt 11:30. [18]See Jn 15:1-2. [19]See Ezek 9:4, 6. [20]See Col 3:25.

stripped when it is bound, uplifted when it is humbled, crowned when it is cut back. The tender shoot cut from an old tree is grafted onto the progeny of another root. When the scars of the old shoot are cut away, the people of God likewise grow into the wood of the cross. It is as if they are cherished in the arms of a pious parent. The Holy Spirit comes as if cast down into the deep ditches of the earth and poured into this prison of the body. With the flow of saving water, the Holy Spirit washes away whatever is filthy and raises the posture of our members to heavenly discipline. EXPOSITION OF THE GOSPEL OF LUKE 9.30.[21]

THE RELIGIOUS LEADERS UNDERSTOOD.

CYRIL OF ALEXANDRIA: What did the scribes and Pharisees say when they heard the parable? Their words were, "Heaven forbid!" One may see by this that having understood its more profound significance, they put away from them the impending suffering and were afraid of the coming danger. They however did not escape, because they could not be restrained from disobedience, nor would they submit to believe in Christ. COMMENTARY ON LUKE, HOMILY 134.[22]

JESUS IS THE STONE REJECTED BY THE BUILDERS.

EPHREM THE SYRIAN: He led them to the point of judging themselves, saying, "What do the vinedressers deserve?"[23] They made a pronouncement concerning themselves, saying, "Let him destroy the evil ones with evil."[24] He then explained this, saying, "Have you not read that the stone which the builders rejected has become the head of the corner?"[25] What stone is this? It is the one known to be as hard as lead. See, he has said, "I am setting a plumb line in the midst of the sons of Israel."[26] To show that he himself was this stone, he said concerning it, "Whoever knocks against that stone will be broken to pieces, but it will crush and destroy whomsoever it falls upon." The leaders of the people were gathered together against him and wanted his downfall because his teaching did not please them. He said, "It will

crush and destroy whomsoever it falls upon," because he got rid of idolatry along with other such things. "The stone that struck the image has become a great mountain, and the whole earth has been filled with it."[27] COMMENTARY ON TATIAN'S DIATESSARON 16.20.[28]

JESUS JOINS TWO PEOPLE TOGETHER.

CYRIL OF ALEXANDRIA: Although he was a chosen stone, those who had the duty to build up the synagogue of the Jews in everything that was edifying rejected the Savior. He still became the head of the corner. Now the sacred Scripture compares with a corner the gathering together or joining of the two people. I mean Israel and the Gentiles in the sameness of sentiment and faith. The Savior has built the two people into one new person by making peace and reconciling the two in one body to the Father.[29] This resembles a corner, which unites two walls and binds them together. Blessed David wondered at this corner or gathering together of the two people into one. He said, "The stone which the builders rejected has become the head of the corner. This [the corner] has been done by the Lord, and is marvelous in our eyes."[30] Christ has bound together the two people in the bonds of love and in the same sentiment and faith. COMMENTARY ON LUKE, HOMILY 134.[31]

20:19 The Application

THE RELIGIOUS LEADERS FEAR THE PEOPLE.

CYRIL OF ALEXANDRIA: Again the gang of Pharisees is inflamed with unbridled rage. They draw the bow of their envy. They grind their teeth at him who calls them to life. They savagely attack him who seeks to save and who humbled himself from his supreme and godlike glory to our condition. They plot the death of he who became man

---

[21]EHG 380-81**. [22]CGSL 534**. [23]See Mt 21:40. [24]See Mt 21:41. [25]Mt 21:42; Ps 118:22 (117:22 LXX). [26]Amos 7:8. [27]Dan 2:35. [28]ECTD 253*. [29]Eph 2:15-16. [30]Ps 118:22-23 (117:22-23 LXX). [31]CGSL 534**.

that he might abolish death. The wise Evangelist shows us the only cause that hindered their shameless pride. He said that they feared the people. He understood, therefore, that they were not restrained by a feeling of piety toward God. The commandment given by Moses that plainly says,

"You shall not kill the holy and the just,"[32] did not bridle their violence. They had far more respect for the fear of people than the reverence due to God. COMMENTARY ON LUKE, HOMILY 135.[33]

---

[32]Ex 23:7. [33]CGSL 537**.

20:20-47 DISCUSSIONS WITH THE RELIGIOUS ESTABLISHMENT OF JERUSALEM

[20]*So they watched him, and sent spies, who pretended to be sincere, that they might take hold of what he said, so as to deliver him up to the authority and jurisdiction of the governor.* [21]*They asked him, "Teacher, we know that you speak and teach rightly, and show no partiality, but truly teach the way of God.* [22]*Is it lawful for us to give tribute to Caesar, or not?"* [23]*But he perceived their craftiness, and said to them,* [24]*"Show me a coin.ʃ Whose likeness and inscription has it?" They said, "Caesar's."* [25]*He said to them, "Then render to Caesar the things that are Caesar's, and to God the things that are God's."* [26]*And they were not able in the presence of the people to catch him by what he said; but marveling at his answer they were silent.*

[27]*There came to him some Sadducees, those who say that there is no resurrection,* [28]*and they asked him a question, saying, "Teacher, Moses wrote for us that if a man's brother dies, having a wife but no children, the manᵍ must take the wife and raise up children for his brother.* [29]*Now there were seven brothers; the first took a wife, and died without children;* [30]*and the second* [31]*and the third took her, and likewise all seven left no children and died.* [32]*Afterward the woman also died.* [33]*In the resurrection, therefore, whose wife will the woman be? For the seven had her as wife."*

[34]*And Jesus said to them, "The sons of this age marry and are given in marriage;* [35]*but those who are accounted worthy to attain to that age and to the resurrection from the dead neither marry nor are given in marriage,* [36]*for they cannot die any more, because they are equal to angels and are sons of God, being sons of the resurrection.* [37]*But that the dead are raised, even Moses showed, in the passage about the bush, where he calls the Lord the God of Abraham and the God of Isaac and the God of Jacob.* [38]*Now he is not God of the dead, but of the living; for all live to him."* [39]*And some of the scribes answered, "Teacher, you have spoken well."* [40]*For they no longer dared to ask him any question.*

[41]*But he said to them, "How can they say that the Christ is David's son?* [42]*For David himself says in the Book of Psalms,*

'The Lord said to my Lord,

Sit at my right hand,

---

^{43}*till I make thy enemies a stool for thy feet.'*
^{44}*David thus calls him Lord; so how is he his son?"*

^{45}*And in the hearing of all the people he said to his disciples,* ^{46}*"Beware of the scribes, who like to go about in long robes, and love salutations in the market places and the best seats in the synagogues and the places of honor at feasts,* ^{47}*who devour widows' houses and for a pretense make long prayers. They will receive the greater condemnation."*

f Greek *denarius*   g Greek *his brother*

OVERVIEW: The spies sent by the Sanhedrin resemble Pharisees by their hypocrisy as they watch Jesus closely and use every false pretense to bring erroneous charges against Jesus. The Pharisees appeal to their most hated enemies, the Roman authorities, in order to trap Jesus and deliver him over to the authority of the governor (CYRIL OF ALEXANDRIA). Since these Pharisaic scribes hold in their very purses the image and inscription of Caesar, they "give back the things of Caesar to Caesar" (AMBROSE). Jesus requires obedience and submission to the rulers of this world who have been given authority over us (CYRIL OF ALEXANDRIA). This should be done joyfully, praying for them to have sound judgment, realizing that when there is disagreement, God is the eternal Judge (JUSTIN MARTYR).

Caesar may have his image on a coin, but God's image is on every human being (AUGUSTINE). To give back to Caesar what belongs to him is to put off the earthly person and his image, and to give to God what is God's is to put on the heavenly person and his image (ORIGEN). The chief priests came from the party of the Sadducees, which means "Zadokite," or "the just one," for they considered themselves such because they did not serve God for the sake of reward (EPHREM THE SYRIAN). The Pharisees believed in the resurrection of the flesh but that this resurrected life would resemble our life now (AUGUSTINE).

The Sadducees attempt to trap Jesus concerning levirate marriages, but they misunderstand the prophets and Scripture. They are equating this age with the age to come, where there will be no marriage or offspring, because there will be no

more dying or decay (AUGUSTINE). Those whom God deems worthy, that is, faithful hearers of the Word who receive Jesus' kingdom by faith, will live forever as "equal to angels . . . sons of God . . . sons of the resurrection" (CYRIL OF ALEXANDRIA). Like angels, we will be free from the desires of this world and the needs of marriage and birth produced by those desires (CLEMENT OF ALEXANDRIA). The vocation of virginity that existed before the fall will exist in the resurrection of the dead, for through virginity we are given a foretaste of the glory of heaven (CYPRIAN).

Jesus quotes from the passage about the burning bush[1]—where the Lord tells Moses that he is the God of Abraham and Isaac and Jacob—to show that at the time of Moses, the patriarchs (who had died hundreds of years previously) were still alive in God (CYRIL OF ALEXANDRIA). Jesus is essentially saying here that he is the resurrection and the life,[2] for all are living in him by the grace of baptism (PHILOXENUS OF MABBUG).

Everyone knows that the Messiah must come from "the house and family of David,"[3] but the mystery here is that he is David's Son and David's Lord (CYRIL OF ALEXANDRIA). The Messiah is David's Son and therefore should call David lord, but because the Messiah is who he is, David must call the Messiah his Lord, for the Messiah is Son of David according to his flesh and Son of God according to his divinity (AMBROSE, CYRIL OF ALEXANDRIA). The silence of the Pharisees showed that they did not want to know the truth about him and therefore rejected

---

[1]Ex 3:1-12; cf. Acts 7:30-34.   [2]Jn 11:25.   [3]See 2 Sam 7:12-16.

him. The scribes are guilty of hypocrisy, malice and greed (CYRIL OF ALEXANDRIA).

20:20-26 Controversy over Paying Taxes to Caesar

THE HYPOCRITICAL NATURE OF JESUS' OPPO-NENTS. CYRIL OF ALEXANDRIA: These bold and hardhearted men, being ready for only evil, do not entertain a good purpose, but with their mind full of the craftiness of the devil, they commit themselves to wicked plans. They lay traps for Christ, plan a trap for an accusation against him, and gather pretexts for falsely accusing him. In their bitterness, they are already meditating and plotting the lying words they spoke against him before Pilate. . . . They pretended to be kind and just. They imagined that they could deceive him who knows secrets. Having one purpose in mind and heart, they speak words totally unlike their wicked dishonesty. COMMENTARY ON LUKE, HOMILY 135.[4]

THE HYPOCRISY OF APPEALING TO CAESAR. CYRIL OF ALEXANDRIA: What do they say? "Teacher, we know that you speak and teach rightly, nor do you accept persons but teach the way of God in truth. Is it lawful for us to give tribute to Caesar, or not?" O what polluted dishonesty! The God of all certainly wanted Israel to be exempt from human rule. They trampled under foot the divine laws and totally despised the commandment given to them. They committed themselves to their own devices. They therefore fell under the hand of those who at that time ruled over them. They also imposed on them tribute, tax and the yoke of an unaccustomed slavery. The prophet Jeremiah also lamented over Jerusalem as though it had already suffered this fate, saying, "How lonely sits the city that was full of people! How like a widow has she become, she that was great among the nations! She who was a princess among the cities has become a vassal."[5]

It therefore says that their object was to deliver him to the authority of the governor, because they expected that they would hear him say, certainly and without doubt, that it was not lawful to give tribute to Caesar. COMMENTARY ON LUKE, HOMILY 135.[6]

GIVE BACK TO THE WORLD WHAT BELONGS TO THE WORLD. AMBROSE: When they questioned him about the penny, he asks about the image, because there is one image of God and another image of the world. The apostle also admonishes us, "As we have borne the image of the earthly, let us bear also the image of the heavenly."[7] Christ does not have the image of Caesar, because he is the image of God.[8] Peter does not have the image of Caesar, because he said, "We have left all things, and have followed you."[9] The image of Caesar is not found in James and John, because they are the Sons of Thunder.[10] It is found in the sea, where there are dragons with crushed heads upon the water. The large dragon itself, with its head broken, is given there as food to the Ethiopian people.[11] If he did not have the image of Caesar, why did he pay the tax? He did not give from his own but gave back to the world what was of the world. If you would not be indebted to Caesar, do not possess what belongs to the world. You have wealth; therefore you are indebted to Caesar. If you want to owe nothing to an earthly king, leave all that you have and follow Christ.[12] EXPOSITION OF THE GOSPEL OF LUKE 9.35.[13]

OBEDIENCE TO TRANSITORY AUTHORITIES. CYRIL OF ALEXANDRIA: How did Christ overcome their craftiness? "Show me," he says, "a denarius." When they showed it to him, he asks, "Whose image and superscription are on it?" They said, "Caesar's." What did Christ answer to that? "Give to Caesar the things that are Caesar's, and to God the things that are God's." Those who have the office to govern impose a tribute of money on their subjects. God does not require of us

---

[4]CGSL 538**. [5]Lam 1:1. [6]CGSL 538-39**. [7]1 Cor 15:49. [8]2 Cor 4:4; Col 1:15. [9]Mt 19:27; Mk 10:28. [10]Mk 3:17. [11]Ps 73:14 LXX. [12]See Mk 10:21; Lk 5:11, 28. [13]EHG 383**.

anything corruptible and temporary. He rather requires willing obedience, submission, faith, love and the sweet fragrance of good works. COMMENTARY ON LUKE, HOMILY 135.[14]

JOYFULLY OBEY YOUR EARTHLY LEADERS, PRAY FOR SOUND JUDGMENT. JUSTIN MARTYR: Since he has instructed us, we, before all others, try everywhere to pay your appointed officials the ordinary and special taxes. In his time some people came to him and asked if it were necessary to pay tribute to Caesar, and he replied, "Tell me, whose likeness does this coin bear?" They said, "Caesar's." He again replied, "Give therefore to Caesar the things that are Caesar's, and to God the things that are God's."[15] We worship only God, but in other things, we joyfully obey you. We acknowledge you as the kings and rulers of men. We also pray that you may have good judgment besides royal power. If you do not listen to us although we beg you and clearly explain our position, it will by no means harm us. We believe (rather, we are sure) that everyone will pay the penalty of his misdeeds in the everlasting fire. Everyone will give an account in proportion to the powers that he received from God. Christ made this known to us when he said, "To whom God has given more, of him more shall be required." FIRST APOLOGY 17.[16]

CAESAR'S IMAGE ON A COIN, GOD'S IMAGE ON HUMAN BEINGS. AUGUSTINE: These same enemies saw the miracles of the Lord,[17] and they said, "Tell us by what authority you are doing these things." They questioned him with hostile intentions, so that if he admitted what his authority was, they could hold him as guilty of blaspheming. He acted in the same way as over the coin, when they wanted to accuse him falsely. If he said, "Let tribute be paid to Caesar," it would be as though he had cursed the people of the Jews, making them subject and tributary to a foreign power. If he had said, "It should not be paid," they could trump up a charge against him before Caesar's friends and administrators that he was

forbidding its payment. He, though, said, "Show me a coin. Whose image and inscription does it carry?" They answered, "Caesar's." He said, "So pay to Caesar what is Caesar's, and to God what is God's." That amounts to saying, "If Caesar can require his image in a coin, cannot God require his image in a human being?" SERMON 308A.7.[18]

PUT OFF THE EARTHLY IMAGE AND PUT ON THE HEAVENLY ONE. ORIGEN: Some people think that the Savior spoke on a single level when he said, "Give to Caesar what belongs to Caesar"—that is, "pay the tax that you owe." Who among us disagrees about paying taxes to Caesar? The passage therefore has a mystical and secret meaning.

There are two images in humanity. One he received from God when he was made, in the beginning, as Scripture says in the book of Genesis, "according to the image and likeness of God."[19] The other image is of the earth.[20] Man received this second image later. He was expelled from Paradise because of disobedience and sin after the "prince of this world"[21] had tempted him with his enticements. Just as the coin, or denarius, has an image of the emperor of this world, so he who does the works of "the ruler of the darkness"[22] bears the image of him whose works he does. Jesus commanded that that image should be handed over and thrown away from our face. He wills us to take on that image, according to which we were made from the beginning, according to God's likeness. It then happens that we give "to Caesar what belongs to Caesar, and to God what is God's." Jesus said, "Show me a coin." For "coin," Matthew wrote "denarius."[23] When Jesus had taken it, he said, "Whose inscription does it have?" They answered and said, "Caesar's." And he said to them in turn, "Give to Caesar what is Caesar's,

---

[14]CGSL 539**. [15]Mt 22:20-21. [16]FC 6:52**. [17]He is being rather careless; it was when they saw Jesus turning the merchants and moneychangers out of the temple, which was hardly a miracle. [18]WSA 3 9:60. [19]Gen 1:27. [20]1 Cor 15:49. [21]Jn 12:31. [22]Eph 6:12. [23]Mt 22:19.

and to God what is God's." Homily on the Gospel of Luke 39.4-6.[24]

20:27-40 Controversy over the Resurrection

The Sadducees Consider Themselves Just. Ephrem the Syrian: "The Sadducees came and were saying to him, 'There is no resurrection of the dead.'"[25] They are called Sadducees, that is "the just," because they say, "We do not serve God for the sake of reward." They do not await the resurrection, and for this reason they call themselves "the just," since they say, "We should love God without a reward." Commentary on Tatian's Diatessaron 16.22.[26]

The Jewish Understanding of the Resurrection. Augustine: The Sadducees were a particular sect of the Jews that did not believe in the resurrection. When the Sadducees posed this problem, the Jews were uncertain, hesitant and could not really answer it, because they assumed that flesh and blood could possess the kingdom of God, that is, the perishable could possess imperishability. Along comes Truth. The misguided and misguiding Sadducees questioned him and posed that problem to the Lord. The Lord, who knew what he was saying and who wished us to believe what we did not know, gives an answer by his divine authority which we are to hold by faith. The apostle, for his part, explained it to the extent that it was granted him. We must try to understand this as fully as we can. Sermon 362.18.[27]

No Marriage in the Resurrection. Augustine: What did the Lord say to the Sadducees? He said, "You are mistaken, not knowing the Scriptures or the power of God. For in the resurrection they marry neither husbands nor wives; for neither do they start dying again, but they will be equal to the angels of God."[28] The power of God is great. Why do they not marry husbands or wives? They will not start dying again. When one generation departs, another is required to succeed it.[29] There will not be such li-

ability to decay in that place. The Lord passed through the usual stages of growth, from infancy to adult manhood, because he was bearing the substance of flesh that still was mortal. After he had risen again at the age at which he was buried, are we to imagine that he is growing old in heaven? He says, "They will be equal to the angels of God." He eliminated the assumption of the Jews and refuted the objection of the Sadducees, because the Jews did indeed believe the dead would rise again, but they had crude, fleshly ideas about the state of humanity after resurrection. He said, "They will be equal to the angels of God."...

It has already been stated that we are to rise again. We have heard from the Lord that we rise again to the life of the angels. In his own resurrection, he has shown us in what specific form we are to rise again. Sermon 362.18-19.[30]

The Saints Are Children of God. Cyril of Alexandria: Let us also see what Christ said to them. He says, "The children of this world that lead worldly, fleshly lives full of fleshly lust marry and are married for the procreation of children. Those who have maintained an honorable and chosen life, full of all excellence, and have been accounted worthy of attaining to a glorious and marvelous resurrection, certainly will be raised far above the life which people lead in this world. They will live as is suitable for saints who already have been brought near to God. They are equal with the angels and are the children of God. Since all fleshly lust is taken away and no place whatsoever is left in them for bodily pleasure, they resemble the holy angels, fulfilling a spiritual and not a material service suitable for holy spirits. They are at the same time counted worthy of a glory like the angels enjoy. Commentary on Luke, Homily 136.[31]

No Marriage and No Physical Desire in

---

[24]FC 94:161-62*. [25]Mt 22:34; Mk 12:18. [26]ECTD 254*. [27]WSA 3 10:254-55**. [28]Mt 22:29-30; Mk 12:24-25. [29]Much more succinct in the Latin: *ibi enim sucessor ubi decessor.* [30]WSA 3 10:254-55**. [31]CGSL 542**.

THE **RESURRECTION.** CLEMENT OF ALEXANDRIA: If anyone ponders over this answer about the resurrection of the dead, he will find that the Lord is not rejecting marriage but is purging the expectation of physical desire in the resurrection. The words "the children of this age" were not spoken in contrast to the children of some other age. It is like saying, "those born in this generation," who are children by force of birth, being born and engendering themselves, since without the process of birth no one will pass into this life. This process of birth is balanced by a process of decay and is no longer in store for the person who has once been cut off from life here. STROMATEIS 3.87.2-3.[32]

VIRGINITY GIVES A FORETASTE OF THE GLORY OF THE RESURRECTION. CYPRIAN: Virgins, persevere in what you have begun to be. Persevere in what you will be. A great reward, a glorious prize for virtue, and an excellent reward for purity are reserved for you. Do you wish to know from what misery the virtue of continence is free and what advantage it provides? "I will multiply," said God to the woman, "your sorrows and your groans, and in sorrow you will bring forth your children, and your desire shall be for your husband, and he shall have dominion over you."[33] You are free from this sentence. You do not fear the sorrows of women and their groans. You have no fear about the birth of children, nor is your husband your master, but your master and head is Christ, in the likeness of and in place of the man. Your fortune and condition are in common. The voice of the Lord says, "The children of this world give birth and are born. Those who will be found worthy of that world and of the resurrection from the dead, they neither marry nor are given in marriage. They will not die anymore, for they are equal to the angels of God since they are the children of the resurrection." What we shall be, you already have begun to be. You already have in this world the glory of the resurrection. You pass through the world without the pollution of the world. While you remain chaste and virgins, you are equal to the angels of God. THE DRESS OF VIRGINS 22.[34]

JESUS CITES MOSES TO AFFIRM THE RESURRECTION. CYRIL OF ALEXANDRIA: The Savior also demonstrated the great ignorance of the Sadducees by bringing forward their own leader Moses, who was clearly acquainted with the resurrection of the dead. He set God before us saying in the bush, "I am the God of Abraham, and the God of Isaac and the God of Jacob."[35] Of whom is he God, if, according to their argument, these have ceased to live? He is the God of the living. They certainly will rise when his almighty right hand brings them and all that are on the earth there.

For people not to believe that this will happen is worthy perhaps of the ignorance of the Sadducees, but it is altogether unworthy of those who love Christ. We believe in him who says, "I am the resurrection and the life."[36] He will raise the dead suddenly, in the twinkling of an eye, and at the last trumpet. It shall sound, the dead in Christ shall rise incorruptible, and we shall be changed.[37] For Christ our common Savior will transfer us into incorruption, glory and to an incorruptible life. COMMENTARY ON LUKE, HOMILY 136.[38]

LIVING TO CHRIST BY THE GRACE OF BAPTISM. PHILOXENUS OF MABBUG: The prophet's words are applicable to those who sin without perceiving their sin. A sinner who has received baptism, although he may be dead toward his soul because he does not perceive his sin, he is alive to God because of the grace of baptism that he possesses. This agrees with the words "God is not of the dead but of the living, for they are all living in him." ON THE INDWELLING OF THE HOLY SPIRIT 1.[39]

20:41-44 Controversy with the Scribes

---

[32]FC 85:311*. [33]Gen 3:16. [34]FC 36:50*. [35]Ex 3:6. [36]Jn 11:25. [37]1 Cor 15:52. [38]CGSL 542-43**. [39]CS 101:124*.

THE MYSTERY REVEALED. CYRIL OF ALEXAN-DRIA: The Savior asked them, "How do they say that Christ is David's son? David himself says in the book of Psalms, 'The Lord said to my Lord, "Sit on my right hand until I place your enemies as a footstool under your feet." ' David therefore calls him Lord, and how is he his son?" The beginning of understanding is faith. He says, "If you will not believe, you cannot understand."[40] The examination of important truths leads to salvation. Emmanuel is the Son and the Lord of David. If anyone would learn in what way he is to understand this, he must certainly begin the exact and blameless examination of his mystery. This was kept in silence from the foundation of the world but has been revealed in the latter ages of the world.[41] COMMENTARY ON LUKE, HOMILY 137.[42]

JESUS IS SON OF DAVID AND SON OF GOD. AMBROSE: Before summarizing his commandments, the Lord included the faith and mercy preceding his passion at the end of his testament. Faith is that we believe Christ is our Lord and God and sits at the right hand of God.[43] . . . He rebukes those who say that Christ is the Son of David. How then did that blind man deserve healing by acknowledging the Son of David?[44] How did the children, saying "Hosanna to the Son of David,"[45] give the glory of their lofty proclamation to God? Here Jesus did not rebuke them because they acknowledged the Son of David but because they do not believe him to be the Son of God. The true faith does not confess one versus the other but both. Although at the beginning we judged to know nothing but Jesus Christ and him crucified,[46] yet now since we are near the judgment, we already do not know Christ only crucified[47] but also wait for him coming in the clouds.[48] The unbeliever looks on the wounds.[49] The faithful one is taken up and runs to meet Christ in the air.[50] Let us therefore believe that Christ is God and man. EXPOSITION OF THE GOSPEL OF LUKE 10.1-3.[51]

DAVID'S LORD AND SON. CYRIL OF ALEXAN-DRIA: We also will ask the Pharisees of today a similar question. They deny that he who was born of the holy Virgin is very Son of God the Father and himself also God. They also divide the one Christ into two sons. Let these people explain to us how David's Son is his Lord, not so much as to human lordship as divine. To sit at the right hand of the Father is the assurance and pledge of supreme glory. Those who share the same throne are equal also in dignity, and those who are crowned with equal honors are understood of course to be equal in nature. To sit by God can signify nothing else than sovereign authority. The throne declares to us that Christ possesses power over everything and supremacy by right of his substance. How is the Son of David David's Lord, seated at the right hand of God the Father and on the throne of Deity? Is it not altogether according to the unerring word of the mystery that the Word as God sprung from the very substance of God the Father? Being in his likeness and equal with him, he became flesh. He became man, perfectly and yet without departing from the incomparable excellence of the divine dignities. He continued in that state in which he had always been. He still was God, although he became flesh and in form like us. He is David's Lord therefore according to that which belongs to his divine glory, nature and sovereignty. He is his son according to the flesh. COMMENTARY ON LUKE, HOMILY 137.[52]

THE PHARISEES' REJECTION OF THE FAITH. CYRIL OF ALEXANDRIA: The Pharisees did not answer Christ's question. They did this in spitefulness, or rather against their own selves, for perhaps being convicted by the inquiry the word of salvation would have shined in them. They did not wish to know the truth, but sinfully seizing for themselves the Lord's inheritance, they de-

---

[40]Is 7:9 LXX. [41]Rom 16:25. [42]*CGSL* 544**. [43]See Mt 26:64; Mk 16:19; Rom 8:34. [44]Mk 10:46-52; Lk 18:35-43. [45]Mt 21:9. [46]1 Cor 2:2. [47]2 Cor 5:16. [48]Mt 26:64. [49]See Jn 20:25, 27. [50]1 Thess 4:17. [51]*EHG* 387-88**. [52]*CGSL* 545-46**.

nied the heir, or rather wickedly murdered him. They rejected the faith because of their love of leadership, greed for profit, and for their shameful gains. . . .

To remove from them the habit of thinking and speaking of him in a derogatory and scornful manner, he asked them, "How do they say that Christ is David's Son, etc.?" As I have already remarked, they were silent from malicious motives and thereby condemned themselves as unworthy of eternal life and of the knowledge of the truth. COMMENTARY ON LUKE, HOMILY 137.[53]

20:45-47 Warnings Against the Scribes

THE SCRIBES' BEHAVIOR SHOWS THEIR UNBELIEF. CYRIL OF ALEXANDRIA: To keep the company of the holy disciples free from disgraceful faults, he usefully testifies. He says, "Beware of the scribes and Pharisees." That means do not expose yourselves to be the prey of their vices and do not be partakers of their disregard of God. What was their custom? They walked in the streets beautifully clothed, dragging with them a pompous dignity to catch the praises of those who saw them. While they were wicked and their hearts were full of all dishonesty, they falsely assumed to themselves the reputation of piety. With solemn ways not based on reality, they diligently lengthened their prayers, supposing that unless they used many words, God would not know what their requests were. The Savior of all did not permit his worshipers to act so shamefully. He said, "When you pray, do not babble as the heathen do. They think that they will be heard for their many words."[54] He commanded them to be humble and not lovers of boasting. He commanded them not to pay any regard to the desire of empty glory but rather to seek the honor that comes from above, from God. In such ways, he deposits the knowledge of his mystery. He also appoints instructors of others, as possessing an exact and blameless knowledge of the sacred doctrines. He makes them to know how David's Son is also David's Lord. We also will classify ourselves with them, God the Father illuminating us with divine light in Christ. COMMENTARY ON LUKE, HOMILY 137.[55]

---

[53]CGSL 544-45**. [54]Mt 6:7. [55]CGSL 546-47.

21:1-4 WARNINGS ABOUT PROPER USE OF POSSESSIONS: THE WIDOW'S MITE

[1]He looked up and saw the rich putting their gifts into the treasury; [2]and he saw a poor widow put in two copper coins. [3]And he said, "Truly I tell you, this poor widow has put in more than all of them; [4]for they all contributed out of their abundance, but she out of her poverty put in all the living that she had."

OVERVIEW: In the story of the widow's gift, Jesus teaches that giving to the poor is the same as giving an offspring to the Lord (CYPRIAN). The rich, whose gifts in financial terms may have been huge compared with the widow's, gave only a little out of superfluous excess (CYRIL OF ALEXANDRIA). Jesus reiterates his teachings on the proper use of possessions, for the widow represents the church as it attends to the poor (AMBROSE). Mercy and compassion are never worthless to the Lord. No one should doubt that they are too poor to support the poor (LEO THE GREAT).

21:1-4 *True Almsgiving*

ONE WHO GRIEVES THE POOR OFFERS TO GOD. CYPRIAN: You that are rich cannot do good works in the church, because your eyes, saturated with blackness and covered with the shadows of night, do not see the needy and the poor. Do you, rich and wealthy, think that you celebrate the Lord's feast? You do not at all consider the offering. You come to the Lord's feast without a sacrificial offering and take a part of the sacrifice that the poor offered. Look in the Gospel at the widow mindful of the heavenly commandments, doing good in the very middle of the pressures and hardships of poverty. She throws two mites that were her only possessions into the treasury. . . . She was a greatly blessed and glorious woman, who even before the judgment day merited to be praised by the voice of the Judge. Let the rich be ashamed of their sterility and their misfortunes. A poor widow is found with an offering. Although all things that are given are given to orphans and widows, she who should receive gives that we may know what punishment awaits the rich person. By this teaching, even the poor should do good. We should understand that these works are given to God and that whoever does these deserves well of God. Christ therefore calls these "gifts of God" and points out that the widow has placed two mites among the gifts of God, that it can be more apparent that he who pities the poor lends to God. WORKS AND ALMSGIVING 15.[1]

THE RICH GIVE ONLY A LITTLE. CYRIL OF ALEXANDRIA: This may perhaps irritate some among the rich. We will therefore address a few remarks to them. You delight, O rich person, in the abundance of your possessions. . . . You offer not so much in proportion to your means as merely that which when you give, you will never miss—out of great abundance, a little. The woman offered two farthings, but she possessed nothing more than what she offered. She had nothing left. With empty hand but a hand bountiful of the little she possessed, she went away from the treasury. Did she not therefore justly carry off the crown? Did not the decree of superiority come to her by a holy judgment? Did she not surpass your bountifulness, in regard at least of her readiness? COMMENTARY ON LUKE, HOMILY 138.[2]

THE WIDOW REPRESENTS THE CHURCH ATTENDING THE POOR. AMBROSE: While [Jesus] stood in the temple, he also gave the verdict of which we are speaking. In the following verses, you have: "Jesus spoke these words in the treasury while teaching in the temple. And no one seized him."[3] What is the treasury? It is the contribution of the faithful, the bank of the poor, and the refuge of the needy. Christ sat near this and, according to Luke, gave the opinion that the two mites of the widow were preferable to the gifts of the rich. God's word preferred love joined with zeal and generosity rather than the lavish gifts of generosity.

Let us see what comparison he made when he gave such judgment there near the treasury, for with good reason he preferred the widow who contributed the two mites. That precious poverty of hers was rich in the mystery of faith. So are the two coins that the Samaritan of the Gospels left at the inn to care for the wounds of the man who had fallen among robbers.[4] Mystically representing the church, the widow thought it right to put into the sacred treasury the gift with which the wounds of the poor are healed and the hunger of wayfarers is satisfied. LETTERS TO LAYMEN 84.[5]

MERCY AND COMPASSION NEVER WORTHLESS. LEO THE GREAT: Although the spite of some people does not grow gentle with any kind-

---

[1]FC 36:240-41*. [2]*CGSL* 552**. [3]Jn 8:20. [4]See Lk 10:35. [5]FC 26:469-70**.

ness, nevertheless the works of mercy are not fruitless, and kindness never loses what is offered to the ungrateful. May no one, dearly beloved, make themselves strangers to good works. Let no one claim that his poverty scarcely sufficed for himself and could not help another. What is offered from a little is great, and in the scale of divine justice, the quantity of gifts is not measured but the steadfastness of souls. The "widow" in the Gospel put two coins into the "treasury," and this surpassed the gifts of all the rich. No mercy is worthless before God. No compassion is fruitless. He has given different resources to human beings, but he does not ask different affections. SERMON 20.3.1.[6]

---

[6]FC 93:74*.

21:5-26 THE FIRST SIGNS OF END TIMES: DESTRUCTION AND PERSECUTION

[5]And as some spoke of the temple, how it was adorned with noble stones and offerings, he said, [6]"As for these things which you see, the days will come when there shall not be left here one stone upon another that will not be thrown down." [7]And they asked him, "Teacher, when will this be, and what will be the sign when this is about to take place?" [8]And he said, "Take heed that you are not led astray; for many will come in my name, saying, 'I am he!' and, 'The time is at hand!' Do not go after them. [9]And when you hear of wars and tumults, do not be terrified; for this must first take place, but the end will not be at once."

[10]Then he said to them, "Nation will rise against nation, and kingdom against kingdom; [11]there will be great earthquakes, and in various places famines and pestilences; and there will be terrors and great signs from heaven. [12]But before all this they will lay their hands on you and persecute you, delivering you up to the synagogues and prisons, and you will be brought before kings and governors for my name's sake. [13]This will be a time for you to bear testimony. [14]Settle it therefore in your minds, not to meditate beforehand how to answer; [15]for I will give you a mouth and wisdom, which none of your adversaries will be able to withstand or contradict. [16]You will be delivered up even by parents and brothers and kinsmen and friends, and some of you they will put to death; [17]you will be hated by all for my name's sake. [18]But not a hair of your head will perish. [19]By your endurance you will gain your lives.

[20]"But when you see Jerusalem surrounded by armies, then know that its desolation has come near. [21]Then let those who are in Judea flee to the mountains, and let those who are inside the city depart, and let not those who are out in the country enter it; [22]for these are days of vengeance, to fulfil all that is written. [23]Alas for those who are with child and for those who give suck in those days! For great distress shall be upon the earth and wrath upon this people; [24]they will fall by the edge of the sword, and be led captive among all nations; and Jerusalem will be trodden down by the

Gentiles, until the times of the Gentiles are fulfilled.

[25]"And there will be signs in sun and moon and stars, and upon the earth distress of nations in perplexity at the roaring of the sea and the waves, [26]men fainting with fear and with foreboding of what is coming on the world; for the powers of the heavens will be shaken.

OVERVIEW: Jesus' words in this final discourse of his temple teaching deal with the destruction of the temple and Jerusalem as well as the destruction of the world (AUGUSTINE). The temple of Jerusalem will be destroyed after Jesus' crucifixion because it is nothing in comparison with the mansions prepared for us in heaven (CYRIL OF ALEXANDRIA).

Jesus' words about the temple and Jerusalem are prompted by a question about a sign portending the destruction of the temple. Two things may mislead believers because of wickedness: first will come false prophets and then famine (AMBROSE). The difference between the false christs and the true Christ will be great. His hiddenness as the incarnate Son of God who gives up his life on the cross will be fully revealed when he returns as the glorified Lord (CYRIL OF ALEXANDRIA). The second danger that Jesus warns against is linked to the false teaching of these false christs. The Jews warred against Rome in 66-73 and in the Bar Kochba revolt of 132-135. Some even saw the sack of Rome in the fifth century to be a sign of the Lord's coming (AUGUSTINE). Every subsequent war is a sign that the end is coming nearer and that the kingdom of God is even closer at hand (MAXIMUS OF TURIN).

When Jesus interjects talk of persecution here, he warns his disciples that before the temple is destroyed they will suffer betrayal just as he is about to be betrayed. They must be prepared if they are to persevere to the end (CYRIL OF ALEXANDRIA). This is the reason Jesus can comfort them by saying, "A hair from your head will not perish," although he has just spoken about their possible death. Their hope is in the integrity of the body in the resurrection of all flesh. Christian faith confesses the resurrection of the body, especially in the midst of persecution (AUGUSTINE).

Jerusalem's demise will be a sign of the final consummation (CYRIL OF ALEXANDRIA). The general prophecy of "wars and insurrections" now takes a specific shape. Jesus foretells the destruction during the reign of Vespasian of the city he wept over when he was about to enter for the week before his death (EUSEBIUS).[1] In the city marked for destruction those who have dependents are to be pitied, because it will be more difficult for them to escape. The suffering of their loved ones will intensify their own pain (AMBROSE).

This destruction, moreover, comes from the Gentiles, even as the heathen nations of Assyria and Babylonia were the instruments of God's wrath in the fall of Israel (722 B.C.) and of Judah (587 B.C.), respectively.[2] These signs of the Lord's coming have been accomplished. The shift to the second part of Luke's eschatological discourse, from prophecy about the destruction of the temple and Jerusalem to predictions about the end the world,[3] is subtle. Among the Evangelists, Luke is clear about the distinction between Jerusalem's demise and the end of the world (AUGUSTINE). Nevertheless, those who possess spiritual virtues will be able to see Christ coming through the clouds (AMBROSE).

21:5-6 The Destruction of the Temple

JESUS SPEAKS OF DESTRUCTION AND HIS SECOND COMING. AUGUSTINE: The future signs that are foretold in the Gospel according to Luke are the same as those in Matthew and Mark.[4] These three tell how the Lord answered his disci-

---

[1]See comment by Eusebius at 19:41-44. [2]See 2 Kings 17:1-41; Ezek 21:1—24:27. [3]Lk 21:25-36. [4]Mt 24:4-33; Mk 13:5-29.

ples. They asked him when the events that he had foretold of the destruction of the temple would happen. They also asked him what was to be the sign of his coming and of the end of the world. There is no discrepancy in the Gospels as to facts, although one tells one detail that another passes over or describes differently. They rather supplement each other when they are compared, and they thus give direction to the mind of the reader. It would take too long to discuss them all now. The Lord answered their questions by telling what was to happen from that time on: the destruction of Jerusalem that prompted their inquiry, and his coming in the church in which he does not cease to dwell until the end. Christ is recognized when he comes to his own, while his members are daily born. He said of this coming, "Hereafter you shall see the Son of man coming in the clouds."[5] LETTER 199.[6]

THE MANSIONS IN HEAVEN. CYRIL OF ALEXANDRIA: Some of them showed Christ the mighty works that were in the temple and the beauty of the offerings. They expected that he would admire the spectacle as they did, although he is God and heaven is his throne. He did not allow any regard for these earthly buildings, since they were unimportant. Absolutely nothing compared with the mansions that are above. Dismissing the conversation about them, he turned to what was necessary for their use. Christ forewarned them that however worthy of admiration they might think the temple was, yet at a certain time it would be destroyed from its foundations. The power of the Romans would tear it down and burn Jerusalem with fire, and retribution would be required from Israel for the Lord's murder. They had to suffer these things after the Savior's crucifixion. COMMENTARY ON LUKE, HOMILY 139.[7]

21:7-11 Signs That Will Accompany the Destruction

ASKING ABOUT SIGNS. AMBROSE: There is a true saying next to the points about the temple

that Solomon founded. The enemy must first destroy this by the time of the judgment. Everything made by labor and by hand in either age will wear out or be destroyed by force or consumed by fire. . . .

When asked when the destruction of the temple would be and what would be the sign of his coming, the Lord warns of signs and does not think that the time should be made known. Matthew added a third question. The disciples asked about the times of the destruction of the temple, the sign of the coming, and the end of the world.[8] Luke thought that enough was known about the end of the world if it were learned under the topic of the Lord's coming. EXPOSITION OF THE GOSPEL OF LUKE 10.6, 9.[9]

SHORTENING OF THE DAYS TO PREVENT TRANSGRESSION. AMBROSE: Jerusalem certainly was besieged and taken by the Roman army . . . then, the desolation will be near since many will fall into error and depart from the true faith. . . . Then the day of the Lord will suitably come, and the days will be shortened for the sake of the chosen.[10] Since the Lord's first coming was to atone for sins, the second will be to prevent transgressions, fearing more might fall into the error of unbelief. False prophets[11] and then famine will come. Tell me again of the times of Elijah, and you will find prophets of confusion, Jezebel, famine and drought on earth.[12] What was the reason? Wickedness abounded, and love grew cold.[13] EXPOSITION OF THE GOSPEL OF LUKE 10.15-18.[14]

THE FIRST AND SECOND ADVENTS COMPARED. CYRIL OF ALEXANDRIA: He explains what will happen at the consummation of the world and warns them. Before our Savior Christ comes from heaven, various false christs and false prophets will appear, coming before him. They will falsely take upon themselves his person, com-

---

[5]Mt 26:64. [6]FC 30:375-76**. [7]CGSL 554**. [8]See Mt 24:3; Mk 13:4. [9]EHG 389-90**. [10]See Mt 24:22. [11]See Mt 24:11, 24. [12]See 1 Kings 18:2, 4, 19, 22. [13]Mt 24:12. [14]EHG 393-94**.

ing into the world like swirling smoke springing up from a fire about to break out. "Do not follow them," he says. The only-begotten Word of God consented to take our likeness upon himself and to endure the birth in the flesh from a woman, in order that he might save all under heaven. . . . It was necessary that Christ should remain unknown during the time that preceded his passion. His second advent from heaven, however, will not happen secretly, as did his coming at first, but will be illustrious and terrifying. In the glory of God the Father, he will descend with the holy angels guarding him to judge the world in righteousness. He therefore says, "When false christs and false prophets arise, do not go after them." Commentary on Luke, Homily 139.[15]

The Sack of Rome a Sign of the Lord's Coming. Augustine: When this type of thing was chanted to you in the temple, "The gods who protected Rome have not saved it now, because they no longer exist," you would say, "They did save it when they existed."

We, however, can show that our God is truthful. He foretold all these things. You read all of them and heard them. I am not sure whether you have remembered them, you that are upset by such words. Have you not heard the prophets, the apostles, the Lord Jesus Christ himself foretelling evils to come? When old age comes to the world and the end draws near, you heard it, brothers and sisters, we all heard it together. There will be wars, turmoil, tribulations and famines.[16] Why do we contradict ourselves? When these things are read, we believe them, but when they are fulfilled, we grumble. Sermon 296.10.[17]

The Nearness of Wars. Maximus of Turin: Perhaps you are anxious, brothers and sisters, at the fact that we hear constantly of the tumult of wars and the onsets of battles. Perhaps your love is still more anxious since these are taking place in our times. The reason is the closer we are to the destruction of the world, the closer we are to

the kingdom of the Savior. The Lord himself says, "In the last days nation will rise against nation and kingdom against kingdom. When you see wars, earthquakes and famines, know that the kingdom of God is at hand." This nearness of wars shows us that Christ is near. Sermon 85.1.[18]

21:12-19 Persecution Before the Temple Is Destroyed

Apostles Will Be Persecuted as a Sign of the Coming Consummation. Cyril of Alexandria: Jesus gives them clear and evident signs of the time when the consummation of the world draws near. He says that there will be wars, turmoil, famines and epidemics everywhere. There will be terrors from heaven and great signs. As another Evangelist says, "All the stars shall fall, and the heaven be rolled up like a scroll, and its powers will be shaken."[19]

In the middle of this, the Savior places what refers to the capture of Jerusalem. He mixes the accounts together in both parts of the narrative. Before all these things, he says, "They will lay their hands on you and persecute you, delivering you up to synagogues and to prisons and bringing you before kings and rulers for my name's sake. This will be a witness to you." Before the times of consummation, the land of the Jews was taken captive, and the Roman armies overran it. They burned the temple, overthrew their national government, and stopped the means for legal worship. They no longer had sacrifices, now that the temple was destroyed. The country of the Jews together with Jerusalem itself was totally laid waste. Before these things happened, they persecuted the blessed disciples. They imprisoned them and had a part in unendurable trials. They brought the disciples before judges and sent them to kings. Paul was sent to Rome to Caesar. . . .

Christ promises, however, that he will deliver them certainly and completely. He says that a hair

---

[15]CGSL 555**. [16]Mk 13:7-8. [17]WSA 3 8:209**. [18]ACW 50:203*. [19]Mt 24:29.

of your head will not perish. COMMENTARY ON LUKE, HOMILY 139.[20]

CHRIST REASSURES HIS MARTYRS. AUGUSTINE: Death comes to either the soul or the body. The soul cannot die, and yet it can die. It cannot die, because its consciousness is never lost. It can die, if it loses God. You see, just as the soul itself is the life of the body, so in the same way God is the life of the soul. As the body dies when the soul that is its life abandons it, in the same way when God abandons the soul, it dies. To make sure, however, that God does not abandon the soul, it must always have enough faith not to fear death for God's sake. Then God does not abandon it, and it does not die.

It remains that the death that is feared is feared for the body. Even on this point, the Lord Christ reassured his martyrs. After all, how could they be unsure of the integrity of their bodies, when they had been reassured about the number of their hairs? "He said that your hairs have all been counted."[21] In another place he says even more plainly, "For I tell you, that not a hair of your head shall perish." Truth speaks. Does weakness hesitate? SERMON 273.1.[22]

THE FAITHFUL CHRISTIAN RECOGNIZED BY BELIEF IN RESURRECTION OF THE BODY. AUGUSTINE: We should have no doubt that our mortal flesh also will rise again at the end of the world.... This is the Christian faith. This is the Catholic faith. This is the apostolic faith. Believe Christ when he says, "Not a hair of your head shall perish." Putting aside all unbelief, consider how valuable you are. How can our Redeemer despise any person when he cannot despise a hair of that person's head? How are we going to doubt that he intends to give eternal life to our soul and body? He took on a soul and body in which to die for us, which he laid down for us when he died and which he took up again that we might not fear death. SERMON 214.11-12.[23]

21:20-24 *The Destruction of Jerusalem*

A SIGN OF THE FINAL CONSUMMATION. CYRIL OF ALEXANDRIA: To make his prediction even clearer and to mark more plainly the time of its capture, Jesus says, "When you have seen Jerusalem surrounded with armies, then know that its destruction is near." Afterwards, he again transfers his words from this subject to the time of the consummation. He says, "There will be signs in sun and moon and stars, and upon the earth distress of nations in perplexity at the roaring of the sea and the waves, men fainting with fear and with foreboding of what is coming on the world; for the powers of the heavens will be shaken." Since creation begins to be changed and brings unendurable terrors on the inhabitants of earth, there will be a certain fearful tribulation. There will also be souls departing to death. The unendurable fear of those things that are coming will be sufficient for the destruction of many. COMMENTARY ON LUKE, HOMILY 139.[24]

WOE TO PREGNANT WOMEN. AMBROSE: Woe to those pregnant women, because they are heavy in body; they are too slow to escape danger. Woe to those for whom the yet unfelt pangs of future birth, by which every body is shaken, are the signs of future judgment, the beginnings of sorrows.[25] EXPOSITION OF THE GOSPEL OF LUKE 10.26.[26]

THE SIGNS HAVE BEEN ACCOMPLISHED. AUGUSTINE: The signs given in the Gospel and in prophecy and fulfilled in us show the coming of the Lord.... We know that the coming is near by the fact that we see the fulfillment of certain signs of that coming that have been accomplished.... The signs that Christ told them to look for are listed in the Gospel of Saint Luke: "Jerusalem will be trampled down by the Gentiles until the times of the nations are fulfilled." This has happened and no one doubts that it has happened.... It is plain that there is no country or place in our time

---

[20]CGSL 555-56**. [21]Mt 10:30; Lk 12:7. [22]WSA 3 8:17**. [23]FC 38:141-42**. [24]CGSL 556**. [25]Mt 24:8. [26]EHG 396**.

that is not harassed or humbled according to the words "for fear and expectation of what will come on the whole world." All the signs that the gospel describes in the earlier verses have mostly been accomplished. LETTER 198.[27]

LUKE REFERS TO THE DESTRUCTION OF JERUSALEM. AUGUSTINE: Anyone can see that he refers to that city when Christ says, "When you shall see Jerusalem surrounded by an army, then know that its desolation is near." Anyone can see that these words refer to the last coming of the Lord when he says, "When you shall see these things come to pass, know that the kingdom of God is near." When he says, "Alas for those who are with child and for those who give suck in those days! Pray that your flight may not be in winter or on a sabbath. For then there will be great tribulation, such as has not been from the beginning of the world until now, no, and never will be."[28] This passage is phrased in this way in Matthew and Mark so that it is uncertain whether it is to be understood of the destruction of the city or of the end of the world. . . . Luke has so arranged it that it seems to refer to the destruction of that city. LETTER 199.[29]

21:25-26 Signs in Heaven and Earth

SIGNS IN THE HEAVENS WHEN PEOPLE FALL

INTO UNBELIEF. AMBROSE: This is a true sequence of prophecy and a fresh cause of mystery, because the Jews will be led captive a second time to Babylon and Assyria. Those throughout the world who have denied Christ will be captive. A hostile army will trample visible Jerusalem as the sword kills Jews. All Judea will be put to the spiritual sword, the two-edged sword,[30] by the nations that will believe. There will be different signs in the sun, moon and the stars.[31] . . . When very many fall away from religion, a cloud of unbelief will darken bright faith, because for me that heavenly Sun[32] is either diminished or increased by my faith. If very many gaze on the rays of the worldly sun, the sun seems bright or pale in proportion to the capacity of the viewer, so the spiritual light is imparted to each according to the devotion of the believer. In its monthly courses, the moon, opposite the earth, wanes when it is in the sun's quarter. When the vices of the flesh obstruct the heavenly Light, the holy church also cannot borrow the brightness of the divine Light from the rays of Christ. In the persecutions, love of this life alone certainly very often shuts out the light of God. EXPOSITION OF THE GOSPEL OF LUKE 10.36-37.[33]

---

[27]FC 30:353-54**. [28]Mt 24:19-21. [29]FC 30:377-78**. [30]Heb 4:12. [31]See Joel 2:10, 30-31; 3:15. [32]See Mal 4:2. [33]EHG 399**.

21:27-38 CONCLUSION OF THE ESCHATOLOGICAL DISCOURSE

[27]"And then they will see the Son of man coming in a cloud with power and great glory. [28]Now when these things begin to take place, look up and raise your heads, because your redemption is drawing near."

[29]And he told them a parable: "Look at the fig tree, and all the trees; [30]as soon as they come out in leaf, you see for yourselves and know that the summer is already near. [31]So also, when you see

these things taking place, you know that the kingdom of God is near. [32]*Truly, I say to you, this generation will not pass away till all has taken place.* [33]*Heaven and earth will pass away, but my words will not pass away.*

[34]*"But take heed to yourselves lest your hearts be weighed down with dissipation and drunkenness and cares of this life, and that day come upon you suddenly like a snare;* [35]*for it will come upon all who dwell upon the face of the whole earth.* [36]*But watch at all times, praying that you may have strength to escape all these things that will take place, and to stand before the Son of man."*

[37]*And every day he was teaching in the temple, but at night he went out and lodged on the mount called Olivet.* [38]*And early in the morning all the people came to him in the temple to hear him.*

Overview: The conclusion to the eschatological discourse focuses on the need to prepare for the coming of the Son of man on clouds after people see the signs in the sky (DIDACHE). Christ comes in a cloud to cover the mystery of his heavenly descent, like the presence of God in the Old and New Testaments (AMBROSE). "Son of man" is the title most associated with Jesus in his passion. Now the crucified and glorified Christ comes from heaven (AUGUSTINE). When believers see him coming, they know that that the dead are about to be raised and they will receive the glorious body promised in the resurrection of all flesh (CYRIL OF ALEXANDRIA). The coming of the Son of man only intensifies the fear of unbelievers, for people will wither from suffering, and fear is a sign that the end is near (AUGUSTINE). The parable of the fig tree is a simple comparison that has a double meaning. One meaning is a signal of the presence of faith in the fruit of the trees, another of unbelief signaled by the leaves of the tree that cover the deceit of sinners (AMBROSE). The advent of the kingdom in Jesus' teaching and miracles anticipated the arrival of the kingdom in his death and resurrection. The adversity that comes on the earth after his ascension shows the world that the kingdom of God is at hand (CYPRIAN).

Jesus' final admonition now is to beware of those things in life that would not be considered gross sins but those seemingly harmless activities that cloud our awareness of his imminent return and the fast-approaching end of the world: "dissipation and drunkenness and anxieties of daily life." Drunkenness weakens soul and body and darkens the mind so that Christ's coming will not come as a snare (ORIGEN). The Evangelist concludes by telling us that the people went early to the temple where Jesus was teaching by day. Then by night, he was going out to spend the night on the Mount of Olives, a common place of lodging for pilgrims who came to Jerusalem for the Passover (CYRIL OF ALEXANDRIA).

21:27-36 The Coming of the Son of Man

WATCH AND PREPARE FOR THE COMING OF THE SON OF MAN. ANONYMOUS: "Watch" over your life. Do not let "your lamps" go out, and do not keep "your loins ungirded," but "be ready," for "you do not know the hour when our Lord is coming."[1] Meet together frequently in your search for what is good for your souls, since "a lifetime of faith will be of no advantage"[2] to you unless you prove perfect at the very end. In the final days, multitudes of false prophets and seducers will appear. Sheep will turn into wolves, and love into hatred. With the increase of iniquity, people will hate, persecute and betray each other. Then the world deceiver will appear in the disguise of God's Son. He will work "signs and wonders,"[3] and the earth will fall into his hands. He will commit outrages such as have never occurred be-

---

[1]Mt 24:42, 44; Lk 12:35. [2]*Letter of Barnabas* 4:9. [3]Mt 24:24.

fore. Then humankind will come to the fiery trial, "and many will fall away"[4] and perish. "Those who persevere in their faith will be saved"[5] by the Curse himself.[6] Then "there will appear the signs"[7] of the Truth: first the sign of stretched-out hands in heaven, then the sign of "a trumpet's blast,"[8] and third, the resurrection of the dead, but not all the dead. As it has been said, "The Lord will come and all his saints with him. Then the world will see the Lord coming on the clouds of the sky."[9] DIDACHE 16.1-7.[10]

CHRIST COMES IN A CLOUD TO COVER THE HEAVENLY MYSTERY. AMBROSE: You see him in the clouds. I certainly do not think that Christ will come in the darkness of mist and the chill of rain. The clouds are visible[11] and surely cover the heaven in foggy cold. How has he set his tabernacle in the sun[12] if his coming brings the rain? Some clouds suitably cover the radiance of the heavenly mystery. Some clouds grow moist with the dew of spiritual grace.[13] Consider the cloud in the Old Testament.[14] "He spoke to them," it says, "in a pillar of cloud."[15] . . . He comes in a calm cloud in the Song of Songs, shining with the joy of a bridegroom.[16] He also comes in a swift light cloud,[17] incarnate of the Virgin. The prophet saw him as a cloud coming from the east. He fittingly said, "a light cloud,"[18] that earthly vices would not weigh down. See the cloud upon which the Holy Spirit came and the power of the Most High overshadowed.[19] When Christ will appear in the clouds, the tribes of the earth will grieve over themselves.[20] EXPOSITION OF THE GOSPEL OF LUKE 10.41-43.[21]

WE SHALL SEE HIS CRUCIFIED AND RISEN BODY. AUGUSTINE: "Then they will see the Son of man coming in a cloud with great power and majesty." As I see it, this could be taken in two ways. One way is that he will come in the church as in a cloud. He continues to come in this way according to his word, "Hereafter you will see the Son of man sitting on the right hand of the power of God, and coming in the clouds of heaven."[22] He comes with great power and majesty because his greater power and majesty will appear in the saints to whom he will give great power, so that persecution might not overcome them. The other way in which he will come will be in his body in which he sits at the right hand of the Father.[23] In this body, he died, rose again, and ascended into heaven. It is written in the Acts of the Apostles: "When he had said these things, a cloud received him and he was taken up from their sight."[24] The angels then said, "He shall so come as you have seen him going away."[25] We have reason to believe that he will come not only in the same body but also in a cloud since he will come as he left, and a cloud received him as he went. LETTER 199.[26]

OUR BODIES SHALL BE MADE GLORIOUS. CYRIL OF ALEXANDRIA: He says that they will see the Son of man coming in a cloud with power and great glory. Christ will not come secretly or obscurely but as God and Lord in glory suitable for deity. He will transform all things for the better. He will renew creation and refashion the nature of people to what it was at the beginning. He said, "When these things come to pass, lift up your heads and look upward, for your redemption is near." The dead will rise. This earthly and infirm body will put off corruption and will clothe itself with incorruption by Christ's gift. He grants those that believe in him to be conformed to the likeness of his glorious body. COMMENTARY ON LUKE, HOMILY 139.[27]

DREADFUL HUMAN SUFFERING. AUGUSTINE: You say that our very suffering forces us to admit that the end is at hand when there is a fulfillment of what was foretold: "men withering away for

---

[4]Mt 24:10. [5]Mt 10:22; 24:13. [6]An obscure reference, but possibly meaning the Christ who suffered the death of one accursed (Gal 3:13; *Letter of Barnabas* 7:9). [7]Mt 24:30. [8]Mt 24:31. [9]Zech 14:5; cf. 1 Thess 3:13; Mt 24:30. [10]LCC 1:178-79*. [11]See Mt 24:30. [12]Ps 18:6 LXX. [13]See Is 45:8. [14]Ex 13:21; 33:9. [15]Ps 99:7 (98:7 LXX). [16]See Song 3:6, 11. [17]Is 19:1. [18]Is 19:1. [19]See Lk 1:35. [20]Rev 1:7; cf. Zech 12:10. [21]*EHG* 400-401**. [22]Mt 26:61. [23]Rom 8:34; Mk 16:19; Col 3:1. [24]Acts 1:9. [25]Acts 1:11. [26]FC 30:389**. [27]*CGSL* 556**.

fear and expectation of what shall come upon the whole world." You say, "It is plain that there is no country or place in our time that is not harassed or humbled according to the words 'for fear and expectation of what shall come upon the whole world.'" If the evils that the human race now suffers are clear signs that the Lord is about to come now, what becomes of the apostle's words: "When they shall say, 'Peace and security' "?[28] When the Gospel said, "men withering away for fear and expectation," it immediately continued, "For the powers of heaven shall be moved. And then shall they see the Son of man coming in a cloud with great power and majesty." LETTER 199.36.[29]

THE FIG TREE IS A SIGN OF FAITH AND A SIGN OF UNBELIEF. AMBROSE: The fig tree therefore has a double meaning: when the wild is tamed or when sins abound. Like the believer's faith that shriveled up before it will flower, so also sinners will glory through the grace of their transgressions. On the one hand is the fruit of faith, and on the other the lewdness of unbelief. The gardening of the Evangelist as farmer produces the fruit of the fig tree for me.[30] We must not despair if sinners cover themselves with the leaves of the fig tree as with a garment of deceit, so that they may veil their conscience. Leaves without fruit are therefore suspicious. EXPOSITION OF THE GOSPEL OF LUKE 45.[31]

ADVERSITY A SIGN THAT THE KINGDOM IS AT HAND. CYPRIAN: Beloved brothers and sisters, whoever serves as a soldier of God stationed in the camp of heaven already hopes for the divine things. He should recognize himself so that we should have no fear or dread at the storms and whirlwinds of the world. Through the encouragement of his provident voice, the Lord predicted that these things would come when he was instructing, teaching, preparing and strengthening the people of his church to endure everything to come. Christ foretold and prophesied that wars, famine, earthquakes and epidemics would arise in the various places. So that an unexpected and

new fear of destructive agencies might not shake us, he forewarned that adversity would increase in the last times. Note that the things that were spoken of are happening. Since the things that were foretold are happening, whatever he promises will also follow. The Lord himself promises, "When you shall see these things come to pass, know that the kingdom of God is at hand." The kingdom of God, beloved brothers and sisters, has drawn near. The reward of life, the joy of eternal salvation, the perpetual happiness and the possession of paradise once lost are now coming as the world passes away. ON MORTALITY 2.[32]

DRUNKENNESS WEAKENS SOUL AND BODY. ORIGEN: "But take heed to yourselves lest your hearts be weighed down with dissipation and drunkenness and cares of this life, and that day come upon you suddenly like a snare." You heard the proclamation of the eternal King. You learned the deplorable end of "drunkenness" or "intoxication." Imagine a skilled and wise physician who would say, "Beware, no one should drink too much from this or that herb. If he does, he will suddenly be destroyed." I do not doubt that everyone would keep the prescriptions of the physician's warning concerning his own health. Now the Lord, who is both the physician of souls and bodies, orders them to avoid as a deadly drink the herb "of drunkenness" and the vice "of intoxication" and also the care of worldly matters. I do not know if any one can say that he is not wounded, because these things consume him.

Drunkenness is therefore destructive in all things. It is the only thing that weakens the soul together with the body. According to the apostle, it can happen that when the body "is weak," then the spirit is "much stronger,"[33] and when "the exterior person is destroyed, the interior person is renewed."[34] In the illness of drunkenness, the body and the soul are destroyed at the same time. The spirit is corrupted equally with the flesh. All the

---

[28]1 Thess 5:3. [29]FC 30:385**. [30]See Lk 13:9. [31]EHG 402**. [32]FC 36:200**. [33]2 Cor 12:10. [34]2 Cor 4:16.

members are weakened: the feet and the hands. The tongue is loosened. Darkness covers the eyes. Forgetfulness covers the mind so that one does not know himself nor does he perceive he is a person. Drunkenness of the body has that shamefulness. HOMILIES ON LEVITICUS 7.5-6.[35]

21:37-38 Jesus Continues to Teach in the Temple

AVOIDING THE UPROARS OF THE CITY. CYRIL OF ALEXANDRIA: The crowd of the Jews and their ruler stood up against the glory of Christ and argued with the Lord of all. Anyone may perceive that those Jews prepared their snare against their own souls, because they dug for themselves pitfalls of destruction. . . .

It then says that by day he taught in the temple but lodged during the nights on the mountain called the Mount of Olives. Clearly what he taught were things that surpass the legal service. The time had come when the shadow must be changed into the reality. They also gladly heard him, for they often wondered about him, because Christ's word was with power. . . .

He stayed during the nights on the Mount of Olives, avoiding the uproars that were in the city, that in this he might also be an example to us. It is the duty of those who would lead a life quiet and calm, full of rest, to avoid as far as possible the crowd and hubbub. COMMENTARY ON LUKE, HOMILY 140.[36]

---

[35]FC 83:130-31**. [36]CGSL 561-62**.

22:1-6 PREPARATIONS FOR BETRAYAL

[1]*Now the feast of Unleavened Bread drew near, which is called the Passover.* [2]*And the chief priests and the scribes were seeking how to put him to death; for they feared the people.*

[3]*Then Satan entered into Judas called Iscariot, who was of the number of the twelve;* [4]*he went away and conferred with the chief priests and officers how he might betray him to them.* [5]*And they were glad, and engaged to give him money.* [6]*So he agreed, and sought an opportunity to betray him to them in the absence of the multitude.*

OVERVIEW: The Jewish leaders "were seeking" how to kill Jesus because of the envy instigated against Jesus by the devil. Satan entered Judas and not any of the others because of Judas's covetousness. The betrayal is arranged by Judas and the religious leaders of Israel, who exploit his covetous nature and offer consecrated money for him to betray Jesus (CYRIL OF ALEXANDRIA). God and Satan are the ultimate players in this scene. Satan was waiting for his opportune time (ORIGEN).[1]

22:1-6 Judas Agrees to Betray Jesus

SATAN INITIATES THE PLOT OF THE JEWISH RELIGIOUS LEADERS. CYRIL OF ALEXANDRIA: Let us see the course of the devil's spite and the result of his crafty plans against Christ. The devil had implanted in the leaders of the Jewish synagogue envy against Christ, which even leads to murder. This disorder always leads, so to speak, to the guilt of murder. At least, this is the natural course of this vice. It was this way with Cain and Abel, and it clearly was so in the case of Joseph

[1]Lk 4:13.

and his brothers. The divine Paul also very clearly makes these sins neighbors and relatives of one another. He spoke of some as full of envy and murder.[2] The Jewish leaders sought to murder Jesus at the instigation of Satan, who had implanted this wickedness in them and who was their captain in their wicked projects. Satan is himself the inventor of murder, the root of sin and the fountain of all wickedness. COMMENTARY ON LUKE, HOMILY 140.[3]

SATAN ENTERED JUDAS BECAUSE OF HIS BESETTING SIN.

CYRIL OF ALEXANDRIA: What was this many-headed serpent's invention? It says, "He entered Judas Iscariot, who was one of the Twelve." Why did he not rather enter blessed Peter, James, John, or some other of the rest of the apostles? Why Judas Iscariot? What did Satan find in him? Satan could not approach any of those we have mentioned here, because their heart was steadfast and their love to Christ immovable. There was a place for Satan in the traitor. The bitter disease of greed, which the blessed Paul says is the root of all evil,[4] had overpowered him. Satan is crafty in working evil. Whenever he gains possession of anyone's soul, he does not attack him by means of general vice. He rather searches for that particular passion that has power over him and by its means makes him his prey. COMMENTARY ON LUKE, HOMILY 140.[5]

BETRAYAL BY A COVETOUS JUDAS WITH CONSECRATED MONEY.

CYRIL OF ALEXANDRIA: Judas lost heaven for a little silver. He missed the crown of immortality and the desirable honor of the apostleship. He missed to be numbered among the Twelve to whom Christ somewhere said, "You are the light of the world."[6] He did not care to be a light of the world. He forgot Christ, who says, "You who have followed me in my temptations, when the Son of man shall sit upon the throne of his glory, you also will sit on twelve thrones and judge the twelve tribes of Israel."[7] Judas did not want to reign with Christ. What a confusion of error blinded the mind of that greedy man! The Evangelist says, "Satan entered him." His pathway and door was the passion of greed. "There is great gain in godliness with contentment."[8] The sacred Scripture says, "We neither brought anything into the world, nor can we carry anything out."[9] Those who seek to be rich, fall into numerous and unprofitable lusts, which sink people in pitfalls and destruction. The disciple who became a traitor is a clear proof of this, because he perished for the sake of a few miserable coins. COMMENTARY ON LUKE, HOMILY 140.[10]

THE PATTERN OF PROLIFERATION OF SIN.

ORIGEN: Jesus Christ our Savior has been crucified. The author of this crime and father of this wickedness is, without doubt, the devil. It is written: "When, however, the devil had entered the heart of Judas Iscariot that he should betray him." The devil is the father of sin. He fathered Judas as his first son in this wickedness, but Judas alone could not execute the betrayal. What then is written? "Judas departed," Scripture says, "to the scribes and Pharisees and chief priests and said to them: 'What will you give me, and I will deliver him to you?'"[11] The third and fourth generation of sin was born from Judas. HOMILIES ON EXODUS 8.6.[12]

---

[2]Rom 1:29. [3]CGSL 562**. [4]1 Tim 6:10. [5]CGSL 562**. [6]Mt 5:14. [7]Mt 19:28. [8]1 Tim 6:6. [9]1 Tim 6:7; cf. Job 1:21. [10]CGSL 562-63**. [11]Mt 26:14-15; Mk 14:10-11. [12]FC 71:330*.

22:7-13 PREPARATIONS FOR THE PASSOVER

[7]*Then came the day of Unleavened Bread, on which the passover lamb had to be sacrificed.* [8]*So Jesus[h] sent Peter and John, saying, "Go and prepare the passover for us, that we may eat it." * [9]*They said to him, "Where will you have us prepare it?" * [10]*He said to them, "Behold, when you have entered the city, a man carrying a jar of water will meet you; follow him into the house which he enters,* [11]*and tell the householder, 'The Teacher says to you, Where is the guest room, where I am to eat the passover with my disciples?'* [12]*And he will show you a large upper room furnished; there make ready." * [13]*And they went, and found it as he had told them; and they prepared the passover.*

h Greek *he*

OVERVIEW: This feast of unleavened bread falls on the day of Jesus' passion. The Passover lamb whose blood atones for all is Jesus, the Lamb of God, who takes away the sin of the world. The man's name is not given but just the sign that he will be carrying a jar of water, for Judas was seeking to betray Jesus. This sign hid from Judas the location of the supper. The water jar also signifies in a mystical way the cleansing of holy baptism, through which we receive an invitataion to the feast in the upper room. Jesus is the host of this climactic Passover; as host he takes control of the proceedings and declares his desire to eat the Pascha with them so that he might avoid arrest before the time appointed (CYRIL OF ALEXANDRIA).

22:7-13 The Upper Room Is Made Ready

JESUS IS THE PASSOVER LAMB. CYRIL OF ALEXANDRIA: By its shadows, the law prefigured from of old the mystery of Christ. He is himself the witness of this when he said to the Jews, "If you would have believed Moses, you would have also believed me, for he wrote concerning me."[1] Christ is presented everywhere by means of shadows and types, both as slain for us, as the innocent and true Lamb, and as sanctifying us by his life-giving blood. We further find the words of the holy prophets in complete agreement with those of most wise Moses. Paul says, "When the full-

ness of time was come,"[2] the only-begotten Word of God submitted to the emptying of himself, the birth in the flesh of a woman, and subjection to the law according to the measure that was fitting for human nature. He was also then sacrificed for us, as the innocent and true lamb on the fourteenth day of the first month. This feast day was called *Pascha*, a word belonging to the Hebrew language and signifying the passing over. . . .

The name of the feast on which Emmanuel bore for us the saving cross was the Pascha. COMMENTARY ON LUKE, HOMILY 141.[3]

THE SIGN HIDES FROM JUDAS THE LOCATION OF THE SUPPER. CYRIL OF ALEXANDRIA: Someone may ask, "Why did Christ not plainly mention the man to those whom he sent? He did not say, 'When you go to such and such a person, whoever it might be, there prepare the Pascha for us at his house.'" He simply gave them a sign: a man bearing a pitcher of water. What do we reply to this? Look, Judas the traitor had already promised the Jews to deliver Christ to them. Judas continued in his company to watch for a good opportunity. While still making profession of the love that was the duty of a disciple, he had admitted Satan into his heart and was travailing with the crime of murder against our common Savior

---

[1]Jn 5:46. [2]Gal 4:4. [3]CGSL 564-65**.

Christ. Jesus gives a sign to prevent Judas from learning who the man was and running to tell those who had hired him. "There will meet you," he says, "a man carrying a pitcher of water." COMMENTARY ON LUKE, HOMILY 141.[4]

THE WATER JAR SIGNIFIES THE WATERS OF HOLY BAPTISM. CYRIL OF ALEXANDRIA: Perhaps Christ speaks this as symbolizing something mystical and necessary. Wherever waters enter, the waters of holy baptism, Christ stays there. How or in what way does this happen? They free us from all impurity, and they wash us from the stains of sin. They do this so that we also might become a holy temple of God and participants in his divine nature, by participation of the Holy Spirit. So that Christ may rest and stay in us, let us receive the saving waters, also confessing the faith that justifies the wicked and raises us high so that we might be counted as an upper room. . . . He that would say that the soul of every saint is an upper room would not miss the truth. COMMENTARY ON LUKE, HOMILY 141.[5]

JESUS EATS THE PASCHA TO AVOID ARREST BEFORE THE TIME. CYRIL OF ALEXANDRIA: When the disciples had prepared the Pascha,

Christ ate it with them. Christ was patient toward the traitor, and from his infinite lovingkindness condescended to admit him to the table. Judas was already a traitor, because Satan was staying within him. What did Christ also say to the holy apostles? "I have desired a desire to eat this Pascha with you." Let us examine the deep meaning of this expression. Let us search out the meaning concealed in there, and let us search for what the Savior intended.

I have already said that the greedy disciple was seeking an opportunity to betray Christ. So Judas might not deliver him to his murderers before the feast of the Pascha, the Savior did not openly state either the house or the person with whom he would celebrate the feast. He explains to them the cause of his unwillingness to tell them openly with whom he would lodge. He says, "I have desired a desire to eat with you this Pascha," apparently meaning, "I have used every effort to enable me to escape the wickedness of the traitor, that I might not endure my passion before the time." COMMENTARY ON LUKE, HOMILY 141.[6]

---

[4]CGSL 565*. [5]CGSL 565-66**. [6]CGSL 566**.

22:14-20 THE PASSOVER OF JESUS

[14]And when the hour came, he sat at table, and the apostles with him. [15]And he said to them, "I have earnestly desired to eat this passover with you before I suffer; [16]for I tell you I shall not eat it[i] until it is fulfilled in the kingdom of God." [17]And he took a cup, and when he had given thanks he said, "Take this, and divide it among yourselves; [18]for I tell you that from now on I shall not drink of the fruit of the vine until the kingdom of God comes." [19]And he took bread, and when he had given thanks he broke it and gave it to them, saying, "This is my body which is given for you. Do this in remembrance of me." [20]And likewise the cup after supper, saying, "This cup which is poured out for you is the new covenant in my blood.[j]

i Other ancient authorities read never eat it again   j Other authorities omit, in whole or in part, verses 19b-20 (which is given . . . in my blood)

OVERVIEW: When the hour of this meal comes, Christ's passion has begun. The three days of suffering, death, burial and resurrection begin with the breaking of the bread (EPHREM THE SYRIAN). The Passover Jesus celebrates with his disciples on this night is a type of the Easter feast to which believers come prepared with reverence. The preparations of the Passover by the disciples of Jesus will make them partakers of the joys of heaven (ATHANASIUS).

Jesus begins the meal by expressing his desire to eat this Passover with the disciples before his passion, for the cross will soon follow this meal (CHRYSOSTOM). The kingdom of God comes with Christ's resurrection (EPHREM THE SYRIAN). Thus the church's preaching of the kingdom and eating and drinking of the Supper, from Easter to the parousia, is an act of table fellowship celebrating that the kingdom of God has come (CYRIL OF ALEXANDRIA). After Christ rises from the dead in his new, resurrected flesh, he will drink the new cup (IRENAEUS). The eschatological perspective looks ahead to the communion of the church at the table of the Lord. There his body and blood will be present in the bread and wine. There we receive the spiritual and bodily blessings of this table as we are made partakers of Christ (CYRIL OF ALEXANDRIA). To eat his body and drink his blood is to commemorate the Lord's obedience unto death (BASIL THE GREAT).

According to Jesus, the Word of God, by the Holy Spirit the bread is his body and the wine is his blood (JOHN OF DAMASCUS). The giving of Christ's body with the bread is just as real as the giving of his body into death on the cross. Instead of eating the meat from a lamb as in the Passover, we now eat the Word of the Father. The lintels of our heart are smeared with the blood of the new covenant (ATHANASIUS). By eating his body and drinking his blood, we have life in us. The communal meal of Christ's body and blood in this life-giving Eucharist of bread and wine is Jesus' new Passover that we now receive in faith as a divine mystery (CYRIL OF ALEXANDRIA).

22:14 *The Time of the Meal*

THE THREE DAYS OF PASSION BEGIN WITH THE BREAKING OF THE BREAD. EPHREM THE SYRIAN: From the moment when he broke his body for his disciples and gave it[1] to his apostles, three days are numbered during which he was counted among the dead, like Adam. Although Adam lived for many years after having eaten of the fruit of the tree,[2] he was still numbered among the dead for having broken the commandment. God spoke to him, "The day on which you eat of it you shall die."[3] Scripture also says, "Your descendants will dwell there for four hundred years,"[4] and the years were numbered from the day on which this word was pronounced. The same way of counting applies likewise to our Lord.[5] Alternatively, the sixth day must be counted as two and the sabbath as one. It was because he had given them his body to eat in view of the mystery of his death that he entered their bodies, as afterwards he entered the earth. Our Lord blessed and broke the bread,[6] because Adam had not blessed the fruit at the time when, as a rebel, he gathered it. The bread entered them, making up for the greed by which Adam had rejected God. The three days might also be counted from the descent into hell and the ascent: the sixth day, the sabbath, and the first day of the week. COMMENTARY ON TATIAN'S DIATESSARON 19.4.[7]

THE PASSOVER A TYPE OF THE EASTER FEAST. ATHANASIUS: Above all, however, I wish to remind you and myself along with you that the Lord does not want us to come irreverently or unprepared to the Easter feast. We must have our doctrine straight, follow the proper liturgy, and do all things properly. The historical record of Israel's feast tells us, "No foreigner, no slave purchased with money, no uncircumcised man, may

---

[1]Mt 26:26; Mk 14:22. [2]See Gen 5:5. [3]Gen 2:17. [4]Gen 15:13. [5]That is, the three days were counted from the moment when he broke his body and gave it. [6]Mt 26:26; Mk 14:22. [7]ECTD 284-85**.

eat the Passover."[8] It is not supposed to be eaten in just any house. There is a proper place. He also commands it to be done in haste, because we were once groaning under the sorrow of our "bondage to Pharaoh" and the "commands of the taskmasters." In the old days, the children of Israel were considered ready to receive the feast, which was the type, only if they had followed the instructions. That type was the forerunner of our feast, although the feast was not established because of the type.

When the Word of God was ready to establish the feast, which is the fulfillment of all, he told his disciples, "I have longed very much to eat this Passover with you." The account of how the Passover was to be celebrated, as given to us in the Scriptures,[9] presents a marvelous word picture of what the festivity must have looked like. FESTAL LETTER 11.[10]

PREPARED TO EAT THE PASCHA WITH JESUS.
ATHANASIUS: On its way to Jerusalem, Israel was purified in the wilderness and was trained to forget the customs of Egypt. Similarly the Word has graciously prescribed for us the holy fast of forty days of Lent. Let us make it a time of purification and purging, so that after the fast we will be prepared to go to the upper room and eat with him, to be partakers of the joys of heaven. There is no other way for us to be prepared to go up to Jerusalem and eat the Passover but to apply ourselves to the forty-day fast. FESTAL LETTER 6.[11]

22:15-18 The Eschatological Perspective

JESUS' PASSION WILL FOLLOW THE PASCHA.
CHRYSOSTOM: Again, in another place Christ said, "I have greatly desired to eat this Pasch with you." Why then did he say "this Pasch" even though at other times he had observed this feast with them? Why then? Because the cross would follow this Pasch. And again he said, "Father, glorify your Son so that your Son may glorify you."[12] To be sure, in many places we find him foretelling the Passion,[13] desiring that it come to pass[14] and

saying that this was the reason he had come into the world.[15] AGAINST THE ANOMOEANS 7.46.[16]

THE KINGDOM COMES AT JESUS' RESURRECTION.
EPHREM THE SYRIAN: He said, "I will not drink again of this fruit of the vine until the kingdom of my Father," to show that he foresaw his imminent departure from them. He said, "until the kingdom of my Father," that is, until his resurrection. Simon Peter revealed in the Acts of the Apostles, "After his resurrection, during a period of forty days, we ate with him and we drank,[17] on this first day of the week. This agrees with what he had said, "They will not taste death before they see the kingdom of God,"[18] and after six days that was accomplished. COMMENTARY ON TATIAN'S DIATESSARON 19.5.[19]

THE KINGDOM COMES IN THE CHURCH'S PREACHING AND EUCHARIST.
CYRIL OF ALEXANDRIA: He says, "I will no longer come near to such a Pascha as this," one that consisted in the typical eating. A lamb of the flock was killed to be the type of the true Lamb until it is fulfilled in the kingdom of God, that is, until the time has appeared in which the kingdom of heaven is preached. This is fulfilled in us, who honor the worship that is superior to the law, even the true Pascha. A lamb of the flock does not sanctify those who are in Christ. Christ sanctifies us. He was made a holy sacrifice for us, by the offering of bloodless offerings and the mystical giving of thanks, in which we are blessed and enlivened. He became for us the living bread that came down from heaven, and he gives life to the world. COMMENTARY ON LUKE, HOMILY 141.[20]

JESUS WILL DRINK A NEW CUP.
IRENAEUS: When he came to his passion, he wanted to de-

---

[8]Ex 12:43-44. [9]Ex 12:11-13. [10]ARL 178-79*. [11]ARL 109*. [12]Jn 17:1. [13]Cf. Mt 16:21; 17:22-23; 20:18-19; Mk 8:31; 9:31; 10:33-34; Lk 9:22, 44; 17:25; 18:31; Jn 10:12, 17. [14]Mt 23:37; Lk 13:34. [15]Jn 3:16, 17; 6:51; 8:12; 12:47; 13:1; 18:37. [16]FC 72:203-4. [17]Acts 10:41. [18]Mt 16:28; Mk 9:1; Lk 9:27. [19]ECTD 285**. [20]CGSL 566-67**.

clare to Abraham and those with him the good news of the opening of the inheritance. After he gave thanks while holding the cup and then drank from it . . . he promised that he would again drink of the produce of the vine with his disciples. Christ thus showed the inheritance of the earth, in which the new produce of the vine is drunk, and the physical resurrection of his disciples. The new flesh that rises again is the same that received the new cup. He cannot be understood as drinking the produce of the vine when established on high with his own, somewhere above the heavens. Those who drink it are not only spirits, because it belongs to flesh and not to spirit to receive the drink of the vine. AGAINST HERESIES 5.33.1.[21]

SPIRITUAL AND PHYSICAL BLESSINGS FROM HIS TABLE. CYRIL OF ALEXANDRIA: Christ is also within us in another way by means of our partaking in the sacrifice of bloodless offerings, which we celebrate in the churches. We received from him the saving pattern of the rite, as the blessed Evangelist plainly shows us in the passage that has just been read. He tells us that Jesus took a cup, gave thanks and said, "Take this, and divide it with one another." His giving thanks meant his speaking to God the Father in the manner of prayer. Christ signified to us that he, so to speak, shares and takes part in the Father's good pleasure in granting us the life-giving blessing that was given to us then. Every grace and every perfect gift comes to us from the Father by the Son in the Holy Spirit. This act, then, was a useful pattern for us of the prayer that should be offered whenever the grace of the mystical and life-giving sacrifice is about to be spread before him by us. Accordingly, we are accustomed to do this. First, offering up our thanksgivings and joining in our praises to God the Father, Son and the Holy Spirit, we come near to the holy tables. We believe that we receive life and blessing spiritually and physically. We receive in us the Word of the Father, who for our sakes became man and who is life and the giver of life. COMMENTARY ON LUKE, HOMILY 142.[22]

THE LORD'S OBEDIENCE UNTO DEATH. BASIL THE GREAT: We should eat the body and drink the blood of the Lord as a commemoration of the Lord's obedience unto death. They who live might then no longer live for themselves but to him who died for them and rose again. THE MORALS 21.[23]

22:19 The Breaking of the Bread and the Words of Institution

THE WORD MAKES BREAD BODY AND WINE BLOOD. JOHN OF DAMASCUS: Receive the communion of the spotless mysteries of Christ, believing in fact that they are the body and blood of Christ our God, which he gave to the faithful for the forgiveness of sins. On the same night when he was betrayed, he ordained a new covenant with his holy disciples and apostles and through them for all that should believe on him. He said, "'Take, eat, this is my body, which is broken for you, for the forgiveness of sins.' In the same way he also took the cup and gave it to them saying, 'Drink all of this. This is my blood of the new covenant, which is shed for you for the forgiveness of sins. Do this in memory of me.'" He, the Word of God, is quick, powerful and working all things by his might. He makes and transforms the bread and wine of the sacrifice through his divine operation into his own body and blood, by the visitation of the Holy Spirit, for the sanctification and enlightenment of those who eagerly participate in it. BARLAAM AND JOSEPH 19.165-66.[24]

WE EAT THE WORD OF THE FATHER. ATHANASIUS: Israel ate the meat of a dumb lamb to complete the Passover. Having done so, they smeared their doorposts with blood and laughed at the destroyer. We eat of the Word of the Father, the Son, our Savior. We have the lintels of our hearts sealed with the blood of the new covenant.[25] FESTAL LETTER 4.[26]

---

[21]LCC 1:393*. [22]CGSL 568*. [23]FC 9:102**. [24]LCL 34:279, 281**. [25]Mt 26:28. [26]ARL 82*.

22:20 *The Cup of the New Testament in Jesus' Blood*

WE HAVE LIFE IN US. CYRIL OF ALEXANDRIA: By uniting flesh that was subject to death to himself, the Word being God and life drove corruption away from it. Christ also made it to be the source of life. The body of him who is the life must be this.

Do not doubt what I have said but rather accept the word in faith, having gathered proofs from a few examples. When you place a piece of bread into wine, oil, or any other liquid, you find that it becomes charged with the quality of that particular thing. When iron is brought into contact with fire, it becomes full of its activity. While it is by nature iron, it exerts the power of fire. The life-giving Word of God, having united himself to his own flesh in a way known to himself, likewise endowed it with the power of giving life. . . . When we eat the holy flesh of Christ, the Savior of us all, and drink his precious blood, we have life in us. We are made one with him, abide in him, and possess him in us. COMMENTARY ON LUKE, HOMILY 142.[27]

CHRIST'S FLESH AND BLOOD IN THE LIFE-

GIVING EUCHARIST. CYRIL OF ALEXANDRIA: It was suitable for him to be in us divinely by the Holy Spirit. It was also suitable for him to be mingled with our bodies by his holy flesh and precious blood, which we possess as a life-giving Eucharist, in the form of bread and wine. God feared that seeing actual flesh and blood placed on the holy tables of our churches would terrify us. Humbling himself to our infirmities, God infuses into the things set before us the power of life. He transforms them into the effectiveness of his flesh, that we may have them for a life-giving participation, that the body of life thus might be found in us as a life-producing seed. Do not doubt that this is true. Christ plainly says, "This is my body. This is my blood." In faith, receive the Savior's word. Since he is the truth, he cannot lie. You will honor him. The wise John says, "He that receives his witness has set his seal that God is true. For he whom God sent speaks the words of God."[28] The words of God, of course, are true. In no way whatsoever can they be false. Although we cannot understand how God does that, yet he himself knows the way of his works. COMMENTARY ON LUKE, HOMILY 142.[29]

---

[27]CGSL 570**. [28]Jn 3:33-34. [29]CGSL 571.

22:21-27 THE PRESENT CONDITION AND FUTURE CALLING OF THE DISCIPLES

[Jesus said,] [21]"But behold the hand of him who betrays me is with me on the table. [22]For the Son of man goes as it has been determined; but woe to that man by whom he is betrayed!" [23]And they began to question one another, which of them it was that would do this.

[24]A dispute also arose among them, which of them was to be regarded as the greatest. [25]And he said to them, "The kings of the Gentiles exercise lordship over them; and those in authority over them are called benefactors. [26]But not so with you; rather let the greatest among you become as the youngest, and the leader as one who serves. [27]For which is the greater, one who sits at table, or one who serves? Is it not the one who sits at table? But I am among you as one who serves.

OVERVIEW: The unholy communion of Judas is clearly recorded by Luke as taking place after Jesus distributes the sacrament of his body and blood (AUGUSTINE). The bread that Judas receives may not be the body of Christ but the bread dipped into the dish to mark him as the betrayer, as St. John records[1] (EPHREM THE SYRIAN). Satan is using the disciples' pride to create this dispute among them. Jesus, who is equal to the Father, now takes a servant's place. The normal practice of ignorant sinners is to seek to be the greatest and lord it over each other. Jesus warns us not to be like the Gentiles, who flatter their superiors and appeal to their pride, in order to achieve status (CYRIL OF ALEXANDRIA).

22:21-23 A Word About the Betrayer

THE UNHOLY COMMUNION OF JUDAS. AUGUSTINE: Some who read carelessly ask if Judas received Christ's body. Understand that the Lord had already distributed the sacrament of his body and blood to all of them when Judas himself also was there, as holy Luke most clearly tells us. After that came this event where, according to John's narrative, the Lord most openly exposes his traitor through the morsel dipped and offered, perhaps signifying through the dipping of the bread that man's pretense. Not everything that is dipped is washed, but some are dipped to be dyed. If the dipping here signifies something good, then damnation rightly followed the one ungrateful for this good.

When the bread entered the stomach, the enemy entered the mind of the ungrateful man. Judas was not possessed by the Lord but by the devil. The full effect of so great an evil already conceived in the heart still awaited completion; the damnable intention to do it had already been effected. TRACTATES ON THE GOSPEL OF JOHN 62.3-4.[2]

JUDAS SEPARATED FROM THE APOSTLES. EPHREM THE SYRIAN: It is certain that when the Lord gave the bread to his disciples, he gave them the mystery of his body. One must also then believe that when he gave the bread to his murderer, he gave it to him as the mystery of his murdered body. He dipped it to reveal the total participation of Judas in his death,[3] for his body was destined to be dipped in his blood. He may also have dipped it to give the testament with him. He moistened it and then gave it to him. He moistened it first because it had been prepared for the testament that was to follow.

Judas' greed judged and separated him from the perfect members of the Lord, as the Life-giver showed in his gentle teaching.[4] Judas was not a member of the body of his church. He was only the dust that stuck to the feet of the disciples.[5] On the night when the Lord judged and separated him from the others, he washed the mud from their feet to teach them. He taught them that he washed Judas from the feet of the disciples with water, like manure suitable for burning. Judas was considered as the feet of the body, since he was the last of the twelve apostles. Likewise, the Lord separated Judas from the apostles by means of the water when he dipped the bread in the water and gave it to him. Judas was not worthy of the bread which, together with the wine, was given to the Twelve. It would not have been permissible for the very one who was going to hand the Lord over to death to receive that which would save him from death. COMMENTARY ON TATIAN'S DIATESSARON 19.3.[6]

22:24-27 A Call to Humble Service

SATAN USES THE DISCIPLES' PRIDE TO CREATE A DISPUTE. CYRIL OF ALEXANDRIA: "Awake and watch"[7] is one of the holy apostles' summons to us. The net of sin is spread everywhere, and Satan makes us his prey in different ways. He grabs hold of us by many passions and leads us on to a condemned mind.... The disciples had given in to human weakness and were arguing with one

---

[1]Jn 13:26. [2]FC 90:38-39**. [3]Jn 13:26. [4]See Jn 6:70; 13:18-19, 21-30. [5]See Mt 10:14. [6]ECTD 284**. [7]1 Thess 5:6.

another about who was the leader and superior of the rest. Perhaps those who held the second rank among them were not willing to give way to those who held the first. This happened, and it was recorded for our benefit. What happened to the holy apostles may prove an incentive for humility in us. Christ immediately rebukes the sickness. Like a vigorous physician, he uses an earnest and deep-reaching commandment to cut away the passion that sprang up among them. COMMENTARY ON LUKE, HOMILY 143.[8]

CHRIST TAKES A SERVANT'S PLACE. CYRIL OF ALEXANDRIA: In the passage that has just been read, Christ says, "For which is the chief, he that reclines at table, or he that serves? Is it not he that reclines? But I am in the midst of you as he that serves." When Christ says this, who can be so obstinate and unyielding as not to put away all pride and banish from his mind the love of empty honor? Christ is ministered to by the whole creation of rational and holy beings. He is praised by the seraphim. He is tended by the services of the universe. He is the equal of God the Father in his throne and kingdom. Taking a servant's place, he washed the holy apostles' feet. In another way, Jesus holds the post of service, because of the appointed time in the flesh. Blessed Paul witnesses to this. He writes, "I say that Christ was a minister of the circumcision to fulfill the promises of the fathers, and the Gentiles will praise God for mercy."[9] He who is ministered to became a minis-

ter. The Lord of glory made himself poor, leaving us an example,[10] as it is written. COMMENTARY ON LUKE, HOMILY 143.[11]

DO NOT FOLLOW THE GENTILES. CYRIL OF ALEXANDRIA: Let us avoid the love of pride and deliver ourselves from the blame attached to the desire for leadership. To act this way makes us like Christ, who submitted to empty himself for our sakes. Arrogance and haughtiness of mind make us plainly resemble the princes of the Gentiles, who always love to act arrogantly. It may even be fitting in their case. "They are called," he says, "benefactors that are flattered as such by their inferiors." Let them be like this. They are not within the pale of the sacred laws or obedient to the Lord's will. They are the victims of these afflictions. It should not be so with us. Let our exaltation rather consist in humility and our glorying in not loving glory. Let our desire be for those things that please God, while we keep in mind what the wise man says to us, "The greater you are, humble yourself the more, and you will find grace before the Lord."[12] He rejects the proud and counts the boastful as his enemies but crowns with honors the meek and lowly in mind. COMMENTARY ON LUKE, HOMILY 143.[13]

---

[8]CGSL 572**. [9]Rom 15:8. [10]2 Pet 2:21. [11]CGSL 573**. [12]Sir 3:18. [13]CGSL 573**.

22:28-34 THE NEW COMMISSION OF THE APOSTLES AND THE ROLE OF PETER

[28]"You are those who have continued with me in my trials; [29]and I assign to you, as my Father assigned to me, a kingdom, [30]that you may eat and drink at my table in my kingdom, and sit on thrones judging the twelve tribes of Israel.

31"Simon, Simon, behold, Satan demanded to have you,[k] that he might sift you[k] like wheat, 32but I have prayed for you that your faith may not fail; and when you have turned again, strengthen your brethren." 33And he said to him, "Lord, I am ready to go with you to prison and to death." 34He said, "I tell you, Peter, the cock will not crow this day, until you three times deny that you know me."

k The Greek word for *you* here is plural; in verse 32 it is singular

OVERVIEW: Jesus elaborates on the ministry to which the disciples are appointed. They will persevere with Jesus in his trials and receive the reward for fidelity to him in his trials (CYRIL OF ALEXANDRIA). The apostles will be commissioned into the ministry as stewards of the mysteries as he will shape them for spiritual judgment (AMBROSE). Christ now commissions Peter as leader of the disciples. But first, Satan will attack Peter precisely because he is the leader among the Twelve (CYRIL OF ALEXANDRIA). The threat to faith and its protection are in the hands of the Son of God (TERTULLIAN). Peter is portrayed as a sinner who falls from the faith (AMBROSE). Instead of asking for strength to endure these temptations, Peter's zeal causes him to contradict Jesus' words and announce his own courage. But even before he sins and denies his Lord, Jesus is offering forgiveness to Peter (CYRIL OF ALEXANDRIA). Peter continues to strengthen the church today through his apostolate, his martyrdom and the letters of the New Testament (AUGUSTINE). Just as Peter denied Jesus at dawn, it is at a dawn three days later that the risen Christ will restore Peter, bringing about his repentance and conversion and forgiving his sins (PRUDENTIUS).

22:28-30 The Apostles Appointed for Trials, the Kingdom and Judging

THE REWARD FOR THE DISCIPLES' FIDELITY. CYRIL OF ALEXANDRIA: The Savior therefore drives away from the holy apostles the affliction of pride. They might perhaps think among themselves and even say, "What will be the reward of faithfulness? What advantage shall we, who have waited on Christ, receive when temptations happen from time to time?" Confirmed by the hope of the blessings that are in store, they throw away from their minds all laziness in virtuous pursuits. They rather choose with an eager mind to follow him and take pleasure in labor for his sake. They also count the doing it a cause of gain, the pathway of joy, and the means of eternal glory. COMMENTARY ON LUKE, HOMILY 143.[1]

JESUS SHAPES THE APOSTLES FOR SPIRITUAL JUDGMENT. AMBROSE: The twelve thrones [are] refuges for corporeal sitting, but because Christ, according to the divine likeness, judges by discernment of hearts, not by examination of deeds, rewarding virtue and condemning wickedness. Thus also, the apostles are shaped for spiritual judgment in recompense of faith and in rebuking error by virtue and execration of unbelief, and prosecuting the blasphemers with aversion. EXPOSITION OF THE GOSPEL OF LUKE.[2]

22:31-34 Peter to Strengthen the Disciples

SATAN ATTACKS PETER AS A LEADER IN THE CHURCH. CYRIL OF ALEXANDRIA: To humble our tendency for pride and to repress ambitious feelings, Christ shows that even he who seemed to be great is nothing and infirm. He therefore passes by the other disciples and turns to him who is the foremost and sat at the head of the company. He says, "Satan has many times desired to sift you as wheat, that is, to search and try you and expose you to intolerable blows." Satan usually attacks people who are above average. Like some fierce and arrogant barbarian, Satan challenges to one-

---

[1]CGSL 573**. [2]EHG 404.

to-one combat those of high reputation in the ways of piety. He challenged Job, but his patience defeated him. The boaster fell. The endurance of that triumphant hero conquered him. Satan preys on human nature, because it is infirm and easy to overcome. He is harsh, pitiless and unappeasable in heart. As the sacred Scripture says of him, "His heart is hard as a stone, and he stands like an anvil that cannot be beaten out."[3] Christ's might, however, places him under the feet of the saints. He has said, "Behold, I have given you to tread on serpents and scorpions and upon all the power of the enemy, and nothing shall hurt you."[4] COMMENTARY ON LUKE, HOMILY 144.[5]

GOD PROTECTS OUR FAITH FROM ALL THREATS.

TERTULLIAN: The devil also asked for power to tempt the apostles, since he did not have it except with divine permission. In the Gospel, the Lord said to Peter, "Behold, Satan has desired to have you, that he may sift you as wheat; but I have prayed for you, that your faith may not fail." That is to say, the devil could not have so much power as to be able to endanger the faith of Peter. We thus see that the threat to our faith as well as its protection are in the power of God. ON FLIGHT IN TIME OF PERSECUTION 2.4.[6]

IMITATORS BUT NO EQUALS.

AMBROSE: Although Peter was ready in spirit, he still was weak in physical love. Christ rebuked him before he denied the Lord. Not even Peter could equal the steadfastness of the divine purpose. The Lord's Passion has imitators but no equals. I do not criticize Peter's denial, but I praise his weeping. The one is common to nature, but the other is peculiar to virtue. EXPOSITION OF THE GOSPEL OF LUKE 10.52.[7]

PETER ANNOUNCES HIS COURAGE INSTEAD OF ASKING FOR STRENGTH.

CYRIL OF ALEXANDRIA: In the passion of his zeal, Peter professed steadfastness and endurance to the last extremity, saying that he would courageously resist the terrors of death and count chains as nothing. In so doing, he erred from what was right. When the Savior told Peter that he would be weak and contradict the Lord, he should not have loudly protested the contrary. The Truth could not lie. Peter should have rather asked strength from Christ, either that he might not suffer this or that he might be rescued immediately from harm. He was fervent in spirit, warm in his love toward Christ, and of unrestrained zeal in rightly performing those duties which fit a disciple in his service to his master. Peter declares that he will endure to the last extremity. Christ rebuked him for foolishly speaking against what was foreknown and for his unreasonable haste in contradicting the Savior's words. For this reason he says, "Truly I tell you, that the rooster will not crow tonight, until you have three times denied me." This proved true. Let us not think highly of ourselves, even if we see ourselves greatly distinguished for our virtues. Let us rather offer the praises of our thanks to Christ who redeems us and who grants us even the desire to be able to act correctly. COMMENTARY ON LUKE, HOMILY 144.[8]

FORGIVENESS OFFERED BEFORE PETER SINS.

CYRIL OF ALEXANDRIA: Admire the beautiful skill of the passage and the surpassing greatness of the divine gentleness! He fears that Peter's impending fall would lead the disciple to desperation, as though he would be expelled from the glories of the apostleship. Peter's former following of Christ would then lose its reward, because of his inability to bear the fear of death and his denying him. Christ therefore immediately fills him with good hope. He grants him the confident assurance that he will be counted worthy of the promised blessings and gather the fruits of faithfulness. He says, "When you are converted, strengthen your brothers." O what great and incomparable kindness! The affliction of faithlessness had not yet made the disciple ill, and already

---

[3]Job 41:24 Vulgate. [4]Lk 10:19. [5]CGSL 576**. [6]FC 40:279*. [7]EHG 405**. [8]CGSL 577**.

he has received the medicine of forgiveness. COMMENTARY ON LUKE, HOMILY 144.[9]

PETER CONTINUES TO STRENGTHEN THE CHURCH. AUGUSTINE: What else does the Lord's passion present us with in our head Christ Jesus, but supremely the tests and trials of this life? That is why, as the time of his death drew near, Christ said to Peter, "Satan has asked for you all to sift you like wheat. And I have prayed, Peter, for you, that your faith should not fail. Go and strengthen your brothers." He certainly has strengthened us by his apostolate, martyrdom and letters. In them he also warned us to fear the night I am speaking of and instructed us to be carefully vigilant, having the consolation of prophecy like a light in the night. "We have," he said, "the more certain prophetic word, to which you do well to attend, as to a lamp shining in a dark place, until the day dawns, and the morning star rises in your hearts."[10] SERMON 210.6.[11]

PETER'S DENIAL OVERCOME BY JESUS' RESURRECTION. PRUDENTIUS:
The Savior once to Peter showed

What hidden power this bird may have,
And warned that ere the cock would crow
Himself three times must be denied.[12]
For evil deeds are ever done
Before that herald of the dawn
Enlightens humankind and brings
An end to error and to sin.
Forthwith he wept his bitter fall[13]
Whose lying lips denied the Christ,
The while his heart was innocent,
And steadfast faith his soul preserved.
And never more such word he spoke,
By slip of tongue or conscious fault,
For mindful of the crowing cock,
The just man ceased from ways of sin.
Hence all now hold in firm belief
That in the stillness of the night
When loudly crows the joyful cock
Our Lord came back from hell's dim shore.[14]
HYMN FOR EVERY DAY 1.49-68.[15]

---

[9]CGSL 577**. [10]2 Pet 1:19. [11]WSA 3 6:121*. [12]Mt 26:34; Mk 14:30; Jn 13:38. [13]See Mt 26:75; Mk 14:72; Lk 22:62. [14]See Mt 28:1; Jn 20:1. [15]FC 43:6**.

22:35-38 JESUS' FINAL WORDS TO HIS DISCIPLES AND THE FINAL PASSION PREDICTION

[35]And he said to them, "When I sent you out with no purse or bag or sandals, did you lack anything?" They said, "Nothing." [36]He said to them, "But now, let him who has a purse take it, and likewise a bag. And let him who has no sword sell his mantle and buy one. [37]For I tell you that this scripture must be fulfilled in me, 'And he was reckoned with transgressors'; for what is written about me has its fulfilment." [38]And they said, "Look, Lord, here are two swords." And he said to them, "It is enough."

OVERVIEW: Jesus' final words to the disciples instruct them to provide for themselves and even arm themselves for violent conflict by selling their garments and buying a sword because of the war that will take place with his passion. Jesus is counted with transgressors when he is crucified between two thieves in fulfillment of Scripture (CYRIL OF ALEXANDRIA). The meaning of the two swords has occasioned much comment, representing such things as the spiritual swords of the two Testaments or the law and the gospel (AMBROSE).

22:35-38 Reckoned with Transgressors

PREPARE FOR THE COMING WAR. CYRIL OF ALEXANDRIA: Christ foretold the war about to burst on the Jews.[1] With unendurable violence, it would spread like some river over all their land. He now says, "But now, let him who has a purse take it, and likewise a bag." The saying in appearance had reference to the apostles but in reality applied to every Jew. Christ addressed them. He did not say that the holy apostles must get a purse and bag. He said that whosoever has a purse, let him take it. This means that whoever had property in the Jewish territories should collect all that he had and flee, so that if he could save himself, he might do so. Some did not have the means of equipping themselves for travel and from extreme poverty must continue in the land. "Let such a person," Jesus says, "sell his cloak and buy a sword." From now on, the question with all those who continue in the land will not be whether they possess anything or not, but whether they can exist and preserve their lives. War will come to them with such unendurable force that nothing shall be able to stand against it. COMMENTARY ON LUKE, HOMILY 145.[2]

JESUS RECKONED WITH THIEVES IN FULFILLMENT OF SCRIPTURE. CYRIL OF ALEXANDRIA: He tells them the cause of the evil and of a tribulation so severe and irremediable befalling them. He says that according to the Scriptures, he is about to be numbered with the transgressors. Christ plainly refers to his being hung on the cross with the thieves who were crucified with him, enduring a

transgressor's punishment. . . . He will also sit on the throne of his glory, judging the world in righteousness,[3] as it is written. The prophet says, "Then they will look on him whom they pierced."[4] As these wretched beings ridiculed Christ as they saw him hang on the precious cross, they will behold him crowned with godlike glory and will fall into the pit of destruction in just retribution of their wickedness toward him. "What concerns me," he says, "has an end as far as it relates to my suffering death in the flesh." Then those things foretold by the holy prophets in olden times will happen to those who murdered him. COMMENTARY ON LUKE, HOMILY 145.[5]

THE MEANING OF THE TWO SWORDS. AMBROSE: Why do you who forbid me to wield a sword now command me to buy one? Why do you command me to have what you forbid me to draw?[6] Perhaps he may command this so that a defense may be prepared, not as a necessary revenge, but that you may be seen to have been able to be avenged but to be unwilling to take revenge. The law does not forbid me to strike back. You say to Peter when he offers two swords, "It is enough," as if it were permitted even to the gospel. . . . This seems wicked to many, but the Lord is not wicked, he who when he could take revenge chose to be sacrificed. There is also a spiritual sword, so that you may sell your inheritance and purchase the Word,[7] which clothes the innermost parts of the mind. There is also the sword of suffering, so that you may lay aside the body. . . . The disciples may have offered two swords: one of the New and one of the Old Testament, with which we are armed against the deceits of the devil.[8] Then the Lord says, "It is enough," as if nothing is lacking to him whom the teaching of each Testament has strengthened. EXPOSITION OF THE GOSPEL OF LUKE 10.53-55.[9]

---

[1]The war of 64-70, which resulted in seizure of Jerusalem and destruction of the temple. [2]CGSL 579*. [3]Is 11:4. [4]Zech 12:10 [5]CGSL 579-80*. [6]Cf. Mt 26:52. [7]See Mt 13:44-46. [8]Eph 6:11. [9]EHG 405-6**.

22:39-46 JESUS' OWN PRAYER ON
THE MOUNT OF OLIVES

[39]*And he came out, and went, as was his custom, to the Mount of Olives; and the disciples followed him.* [40]*And when he came to the place he said to them, "Pray that you may not enter into temptation."* [41]*And he withdrew from them about a stone's throw, and knelt down and prayed,* [42]*"Father, if thou art willing, remove this cup from me; nevertheless not my will, but thine, be done."[l]* [45]*And when he rose from prayer, he came to the disciples and found them sleeping for sorrow,* [46]*and he said to them, "Why do you sleep? Rise and pray that you may not enter into temptation."*

l Other ancient authorities add verses 43 and 44: [43]*And there appeared to him an angel from heaven, strengthening him.* [44]*And being in an agony he prayed more earnestly; and his sweat became like great drops of blood falling down upon the ground*

OVERVIEW: The Lukan narrative of Jesus' agony (and the disciples' sleeping) on the Mount of Olives is paralleled in Matthew and Mark, showing the mystery of Christ's grief and temptation in the garden. Jesus' prayer to the Father to "take this cup from me" referred to the cup of suffering and death (CYRIL OF ALEXANDRIA). To drink the cup is to accept martyrdom (ORIGEN). The whole purpose of Jesus' ministry, and of the gospel, is at stake in this request. But Jesus must drink the chalice to acquit the debt of everyone that even the prophets and martyrs could not pay with their death (EPHREM THE SYRIAN).

Jesus here experiences human sufferings as the incarnate Word (CYRIL OF ALEXANDRIA). It is a testimony to the fullness of Jesus' incarnation, his having been made "like his brothers in every respect,"[1] that he asks his Father to take his destiny—the cross—away from him. It is as Son of God and Son of man that Jesus chooses to drink the cup (JOHN OF DAMASCUS). He must grieve and sorrow for us so that he might overcome our sorrow and give us his joy (AMBROSE). Every human naturally and without sin may utter the same kind of prayer to avoid suffering, which Jesus does now in the lowliness and weakness with which he has clothed himself (EPHREM THE SYRIAN).

Jesus begins his prayer "if you [the Father] are

willing" and ends "not my [Jesus'] will, but may yours [the Father's] happen." The will of the Father and the Son are one (AMBROSE). Jesus subordinates his desire to have the cup taken away to his desire to fulfill the Father's will, and that will of the Father calls for Jesus to drink the cup to the very bottom (GREGORY OF NAZIANZUS). By his act of obedience, Jesus reverses the sin of Adam (EPHREM THE SYRIAN). Jesus must go the way the Father has ordained for him to accomplish the world's redemption because of his love for the world (CYRIL OF ALEXANDRIA).

The strengthening Jesus receives from heaven above accompanies his fervent prayer to the Father, and the dripping of sweat like blood to the earth beneath reveals the depth of his agony and the fullness of his humanity (HIPPOLYTUS). Jesus, strengthened by the angel, endures this bloody agony to show the depth of his feeling for our suffering and pain (JUSTIN MARTYR). Through his bloody sweat, Jesus heals Adam, who was sick with sin, and brings him back to the garden (EPHREM THE SYRIAN). The disciples are tempted when they opt for sleep instead of prayer (TERTULLIAN), for they do not yet realize that the only

[1]Heb 2:17.

path to resurrection life is through the cross.

22:39-40 Jesus Tells His Disciples to Pray

THE MYSTERY OF CHRIST'S GRIEF AND TEMPTATION. CYRIL OF ALEXANDRIA: The Savior stayed in Jerusalem during the day, evidently teaching the Israelites and revealing to them the way of the kingdom of heaven. When the evening came, he continued with the holy disciples on the Mount of Olives at a spot called Gethsemane. The wise evangelist Matthew tells us this. . . .

"Taking with him Peter and the two sons of Zebedee, he began to be sorrowful and troubled. Then he said to them, 'My soul is very sorrowful, even to death.'"[2] Going forward a little, Christ knelt and prayed, saying, "Father, if you will, put this cup away from me, but not my will but yours be done." Please see here the depths of the appointed time in the flesh and the height of that unspeakable wisdom. Focus the penetrating eye of the mind on it. If you can see the beautiful art of the mystery, you also will say, "Oh, the depth of the riches both of the wisdom and the knowledge of God! His judgments are unsearchable, and his ways past finding out."[3] COMMENTARY ON LUKE, HOMILY 146.[4]

22:41-43 Jesus Prays to His Father

JESUS SUBMITS TO THE PASSION. CYRIL OF ALEXANDRIA: You have heard Christ say, "Father, if you will, remove this cup from me." Was then his passion an involuntary act? Was the need for him to suffer or the violence of those who plotted against him stronger than his own will? We say no. His passion was a voluntary act, although in another respect it was severe, because it implied the rejection and destruction of the synagogue of the Jews. . . .

Since it was impossible for Christ not to endure the passion, he submitted to it, because God the Father so willed it with him. COMMENTARY ON LUKE, HOMILY 147.[5]

TO DRINK THE CUP IS TO ENTER MARTYRDOM. ORIGEN: Something in the passage has perhaps escaped our notice. You will find it out by noting how the cup is mentioned in the three Gospels. Matthew writes that the Lord said, "Father, if it is possible, let this cup pass from me."[6] Luke writes, "Father, if you are willing, remove this cup from me." Mark writes, "Abba, Father, all things are possible to you, remove this cup from me."[7] Every martyrdom completed by death for whatever motive is called a cup. See whether you cannot say with him, "Let this cup pass from me." . . . "The cup of salvation" in Psalms is the death of the martyrs. That is why the verse "I will take the cup of salvation and call on the name of the Lord"[8] is followed by "Precious in the sight of the Lord is the death of his saints."[9] EXHORTATION TO MARTYRDOM 29.[10]

JESUS DRINKS THE CHALICE TO CANCEL THE DEBT OF EVERYONE. EPHREM THE SYRIAN: "If it is possible, let this chalice pass from me."[11] He knew that he was going to rise on the third day, but he also knew in advance the scandal of his disciples, the denial of Simon, the suicide of Judas, the destruction of Jerusalem and the scattering of Israel. "If it is possible, let the chalice pass from me," he said. He knew what he was saying to his Father and was well aware that this chalice could pass from him. He had come to drink it for everyone, in order to cancel, through this chalice, everyone's debt, a debt that the prophets and martyrs could not pay with their death. COMMENTARY ON TATIAN'S DIATESSARON 20.2.[12]

JESUS SUFFERS AS THE INCARNATE WORD. CYRIL OF ALEXANDRIA: The passion of grief, or affliction or sore distress as we may call it, cannot have reference to the divine nature of the Word, which is not able to suffer. That is impossible since it transcends all passion. We say that the

---

[2]Mt 26:37-38. [3]Rom 11:33. [4]CGSL 581**. [5]CGSL 585-86**. [6]Mt 26:39. [7]Mk 14:36. [8]Ps 116:13. [9]Ps 116:15. [10]OSW 61**. [11]Mt 26:39. [12]ECTD 292**.

incarnate Word also willed to submit himself to the measure of human nature by suffering what belongs to it. He is said to have hungered although he is life, the cause of life and the living bread. He was also weary from a long journey although he is the Lord of powers. It also is said that he was grieved and seemed to be capable of anguish. It would not have been fitting for him who submitted himself to emptiness and stood in the measure of human nature to have seemed unwilling to endure human things. The Word of God the Father, therefore, is altogether free from all passion. For the appointed time's sake, he wisely submitted himself to the weaknesses of humankind in order that he might not seem to refuse that which the time required. He even obeyed human customs and laws. He still did not bear this in his own [divine] nature. COMMENTARY ON LUKE, HOMILY 146.[13]

Jesus, Son of God and Son of Man, Chooses to Drink the Cup. JOHN OF DAMASCUS:

Consequently, while he had naturally the power of willing as God and as man, the human will followed after and was subordinated to his will, not being motivated by its own opinion but wanting what his divine will wanted. With the permission of the divine will, he suffered what was naturally proper to him. When he begged to be spared death, he did so naturally, with his divine will wanting and permitting. He was thus in agony and afraid. Then, when his divine will wanted his human will to choose death, it freely accepted the passion. He did not freely deliver himself over to death as God alone but also as man. By this, he also gave us the grace of courage in the face of death. He says before his saving passion, "Father, if it is possible, let this cup pass from me."[14] Clearly as man and not as God, he was to drink from the chalice. Consequently, as man, he wishes the cup to pass, and these words arose from a natural fear. "Not my will, but yours be done." That is to say, "I am of another substance than yours, but also of your substance which is mine and yours in so far as I

am begotten consubstantial with you." These are words of courage. Since by his good pleasure the Lord truly became man, his soul at first experienced the weakness of nature. Through sense perception, he felt a natural pain at the thought of his soul's separation from the body. It was then strengthened by the divine will and faced death courageously. He was entirely God with his humanity and entirely man with his divinity. He as man in himself and through himself subjected his humanity to God the Father and became obedient to the Father. He thus set a most noble example and pattern for us. ORTHODOX FAITH 3.18.[15]

Jesus Took Our Sadness to Bestow on Us His Joy. AMBROSE:

Very many people have difficulty with this passage. They attribute the Savior's sorrow to a weakness implanted from the beginning, rather than received for a time. They also desire to distort the sense of a natural saying. I think that it should not be explained away. Nowhere else than here do I marvel more at his piety and majesty. It would have profited me less if he had not received my grief. He who had no reason to grieve for himself therefore grieved for me. Having set aside the delight in eternal Divinity, he is afflicted by the weariness of my weakness. He took my sadness in order to bestow on me his joy. He came down to our footprints, even to the hardship of death, in order to call us back to life in his own footprints. I confidently mention sadness, because I proclaim the cross. He did not undertake the appearance but the reality of the incarnation. He must thus also undertake the grief in order to overcome the sorrow and not exclude it. Those who have borne the numbness rather than the pain of wounds do not receive the praise of having strength. He was a man in suffering, and acquainted with the bearing of sickness.[16] EXPOSITION OF THE GOSPEL OF LUKE 10.56.[17]

---

[13]CGSL 583**. Since the divine nature, being unchangeable, cannot suffer, the incarnate word suffers in the flesh, in the human nature, yet without denying the mystery of the interpenetration of the divine and human natures. [14]Mt 26:39. [15]FC 37:319-20**. [16]Is 53:3. [17]EHG 406-7**.

JESUS EXPERIENCES FEAR AND ANXIETY.
EPHREM THE SYRIAN: "If it is possible, let this cup pass from me." He said this because of the lowliness with which he had clothed himself, not in pretence, but in reality. Since he had really become unimportant and had clothed himself in lowliness, it would have been impossible for his lowliness not to have experienced fear and not to have been upset. He took on flesh and clothed himself with weakness. He ate when hungry, became tired after working, and overcome by sleep when weary. It was necessary, when the time for his death arrived, that all these things that have to do with the flesh be fulfilled. The anguish of death in fact invaded him, to make clear his nature as a son of Adam, over whom "death reigns,"[18] according to the word of the apostle. COMMENTARY ON TATIAN'S DIATESSARON 20.4.[19]

JESUS' WILL AND THE FATHER'S WILL ARE ONE. AMBROSE: Since he then says, "Not my will but yours be done," he referred his own will to man and his Father's to the Godhead. The will of man is temporary, but the will of the Godhead is eternal. There is not one will of the Father and another of the Son. There is one will where there is one Godhead. Learn that you are subject to God, so that you may choose not what you yourself want but what you know will be pleasing to God. EXPOSITION OF THE GOSPEL OF LUKE 10.60.[20]

JESUS' HUMAN WILL IS NOT OPPOSED TO THE WILL OF THE FATHER. GREGORY OF NAZIANZUS: "Father, if it is possible, let this cup pass from me; nevertheless let not what I will but your will prevail." It is unlikely that he did not know whether it was possible or not, or that he would oppose the Father's will. This is the language of him who came down and assumed our nature. However, this is not the language of human nature.... The passage does not mean that the Son has a special will of his own besides that of the Father but that he does not have a special will. The meaning would be, "Not to do mine own

will, for there is none of mine apart from, but that which is common to me and you. Since we have one Godhead, so we have one will." ORATION 30.12, ON THE SON.[21]

JESUS REVERSES THE SIN OF ADAM. EPHREM THE SYRIAN: "Not according to my will, but yours." He said this word against Adam, who resisted the will of the Creator and followed the will of his enemy. Consequently Adam was delivered over into the mouth of his enemy. Our Lord resisted the will of the flesh to uphold the will of the Creator of flesh, because he knew that all happiness depends on the will of his Father. "Not my will but yours be done." COMMENTARY ON TATIAN'S DIATESSARON 20.9.[22]

JESUS SUFFERS BECAUSE OF HIS LOVE FOR THE WORLD. CYRIL OF ALEXANDRIA: God the Father had pity on earth's inhabitants who were in misery, caught in the snares of sin, and liable to death and corruption. A tyrant's hand made them bow and herds of devils enslaved them. He sent his Son from heaven to be a Savior and Deliverer. He was made like unto us in form. He knew he would suffer. The shame of his passion was not the fruit of his own will, but he still consented to undergo it that he might save the earth. God the Father wanted that, from his great kindness and love for humanity. He "so loved the world that he gave even his only-begotten Son, that whosoever believes in him should not perish but have everlasting life."[23] As to the disgrace of his passion, Christ did not want to suffer.... He was obedient to the Father, even to death, and the death of the cross at that. COMMENTARY ON LUKE, HOMILY 147.[24]

22:44-46 Jesus' Bloody Sweat

JESUS' BLOODY SWEAT IS A SIGN OF HIS HUMANITY. HIPPOLYTUS: Although he was God clearly revealed, he did not disown what was hu-

---

[18]Rom 5:14, 17. [19]ECTD 294**. [20]EHG 407-8**. [21]LCC 3:185**. [22]ECTD 296*. [23]Jn 3:16. [24]CGSL 586**.

man about himself as well. He is hungry and exhausted, weary and thirsty; he fears and flees and is troubled when he prays. He sleeps on a pillow, yet as God he has a nature that does not know sleeping. He asks to be excused the suffering of the cup, yet he was present in the world for this very reason. In his agony, he sweats and an angel strengthens him, yet he strengthens those who believe in him and has taught them by his example to treat death with contempt. AGAINST NOETUS 18.[25]

JESUS' BLOODY SWEAT SHOWS THE DEPTH OF HIS FEELING. JUSTIN MARTYR: "All my bones are poured out and scattered like water; my heart is become like wax melting in the midst of my belly."[26] This passage foretold what would happen on that night when they came to Mount Olivet to capture him. In the memoirs of the apostles and their successors, it is written that his perspiration poured out like drops of blood as he prayed and said, "If it is possible, let this cup pass from me." His heart and bones were evidently quaking, and his heart was like wax melting in his belly. We therefore may understand that the Father wanted his Son to endure in reality these severe sufferings for us. We may not declare that since he was the Son of God, he did not feel what was done and inflicted on him. The words "my strength is

dried up like a potsherd, and my tongue cleaves to my jaws"[27] predicted that he would remain silent. He who proved that all your teachers are without wisdom did not answer a word in his own defense. DIALOGUE WITH TRYPHO 103.[28]

JESUS' BLOODY SWEAT HEALS ADAM. EPHREM THE SYRIAN: "His sweat became like drops of blood," the Evangelist said. He sweated to heal Adam who was sick. "It is by the sweat of your brow," said God, "that you will eat your bread."[29] He remained in prayer in this garden to bring Adam back into his own garden again. COMMENTARY ON TATIAN'S DIATESSARON 20.11.[30]

THE DISCIPLES ARE TEMPTED. TERTULLIAN: The devil tempted Christ himself, and Christ pointed out the subtle director of the temptation. He later confirms this passage by his words to his apostles when he says, "Pray that you may not enter into temptation." They were so tempted to desert their Lord because they had indulged in sleep instead of prayer. The phrase that balances and interprets "lead us not into temptation" is "but deliver us from evil." ON PRAYER 8.[31]

---

[25]ANF 5:230**. [26]Ps 22:14. [27]Ps 22:15. [28]FC 6:310-11*. [29]Gen 3:19. [30]ECTD 297*. [31]FC 40:166-67**.

22:47-53 THE BETRAYAL

[47]*While he was still speaking, there came a crowd, and the man called Judas, one of the twelve, was leading them. He drew near to Jesus to kiss him;* [48]*but Jesus said to him, "Judas, would you betray the Son of man with a kiss?"* [49]*And when those who were about him saw what would follow, they said, "Lord, shall we strike with the sword?"* [50]*And one of them struck the slave of the high priest and cut off his right ear.* [51]*But Jesus said, "No more of this!" And he touched his ear and healed him.* [52]*Then Jesus said to the chief priests and officers of the temple and elders, who had come out against him, "Have you come out as against a robber, with swords and clubs?* [53]*When I was with you day after day in the temple, you did not lay hands on me. But this is your hour, and the power of darkness."*

OVERVIEW: Judas is one of the Twelve, heightening the scandal and humiliation of this betrayal (CYRIL OF ALEXANDRIA). To betray with a kiss is the deepest of ironies (AMBROSE). There is no love here, for children of Adam under Satan's power do this deed, for Judas did not have the power in and of himself to betray Jesus (EPHREM THE SYRIAN).

Violence represents the kind of kingdom the confused disciples would have brought if Jesus had permitted them to continue their ignorant endeavors. Love rather than a sword, and healing rather than violence are the way of the kingdom (CYRIL OF ALEXANDRIA). Jesus responds to this moment of arrest and violence not with power but with healing (EPHREM THE SYRIAN). Jesus' action is consistent with the portraits of Jesus in the Gospel: the Creator comes to his creation as a man to heal the creation (AMBROSE). But the soldiers, who witnessed this healing, respond to this act of mercy by arresting Jesus and taking him to his trials (EPHREM THE SYRIAN).

By treating Jesus as a robber, they place him in a category in which they belong, for they do not understand the mercy or compassion of Jesus (AMBROSE). Jesus' betrayal closes with his summation that those who have come to arrest him are simply envoys of Satan: "This is your [Satan's] hour and the power of darkness" (CYRIL OF ALEXANDRIA).

22:47-48 Judas Betrays Jesus with a Kiss

THE SHAME AND HUMILIATION OF JUDAS.

CYRIL OF ALEXANDRIA: He adds that he was one of the Twelve. This also is a matter of great importance to demonstrate more fully the guilt of the traitor's crime. The Lord equally honored him with the rest and decorated him with apostolic dignities. Christ admitted him, chosen and beloved, to the holy table and the highest honors, but this became the pathway and the means for the murderers of Christ. What dirge can be sufficient for him, or what floods of tears must not each shed from his eyes when he considers from what happi-

ness that wretched being fell into such total misery! For a worthless cent, he stopped being with Christ and lost his hope toward God. He lost the honor, crowns, life and glory prepared for Christ's true followers, and the right of reigning with the Lord. COMMENTARY ON LUKE, HOMILY 148.[1]

THE IRONY OF JUDAS'S KISS. AMBROSE: This is

a great sign of divine power and a great lesson of virtue. The intention of betrayal is revealed, and yet patience is not denied. You have shown, Lord, whom he betrayed, while you reveal the hidden things.[2] You have also shown whom he betrayed, when you say "the Son of man," because the flesh, not the Godhead, is meant. Nevertheless Christ even more refutes the ingratitude that betrayed him. Although he was the Son of God, yet for our sake he was willing to be the Son of man. It is as if he would say, "Because of you, ungrateful one, I took upon myself what you betray." Look at the hypocrisy! I think it is exposed through the question that accuses the traitor with the compassion of love: "Judas, do you betray the Son of man with a kiss?" That is like saying, "Do you wound with the pledge of love, shed blood in the duty of charity, and give death with the instrument of peace? Do you, a servant, betray your Lord, a disciple his master, a chosen one the creator?" In other words, "The wounds of a friend are more useful than the voluntary kisses of an enemy."[3] He says this to a traitor. What does Christ say to a peacemaker? "Let him kiss me with the kisses of his mouth."[4] He kissed Judas, not that Christ should teach us to pretend but that he should not appear to flee from betrayal. Hence he did not deprive Judas of the dues of love.[5] It is written, "I was peaceful among those that hate peace."[6] EXPOSITION OF THE GOSPEL OF LUKE 10.63-64.[7]

JUDAS LACKED POWER ON HIS OWN. EPHREM

THE SYRIAN: The tribe of Judah marked the beginning of the kingdom,[8] and the apostle Judas

---

[1]CGSL 587-88**. [2]Ps 50:6 LXX. [3]Prov 27:6. [4]Song 1:2. [5]See Mt 26:49. [6]Ps 120:6 (119:6 LXX). [7]EHG 409**. [8]See Gen 49:10.

marked its extinction. In deceitfully handing him over to the Romans with a kiss, he handed over to them the responsibility of avenging Jesus so that they would one day exact it from Judah. The wicked one came to dig his deep abyss, and our God explained it gently to him. He showed that he was helpful, a fountain of mercy. He said, "Judas, would you betray the Son of man with a kiss?" He showed that Judas did not have the power to hand over the Son of God. "Well then, why have you come, my friend?"[9] The Lord called animosity friendship, and he turned toward Judas. The deceitful disciple approached the true Master to kiss him. The Lord withdrew from him the Spirit that he had breathed into him. He removed it from him, not wanting the corrupting wolf to be among his sheep. He said, "That which he had has been taken away from him."[10] COMMENTARY ON TATIAN'S DIATESSARON 20.12.[11]

22:49-51 Jesus Rebukes His Supporters for Their Misunderstanding

LOVE AND HEALING INSTEAD OF VIOLENCE AND SWORDS. CYRIL OF ALEXANDRIA: The blessed disciples, wounded with the prodding of divine love, drew their swords to repel the attack. Christ would not permit this, but he rebuked Peter, saying, "Put your sword into its sheath; for all who have taken swords shall die by swords." In this, he gave us a pattern of the way in which we must hold on by our love for him and of the extent to which the burning zeal of our piety may proceed. He does not want us to use swords to resist our enemies. He would rather have us use love and prudence.... The Savior moderates the unmeasured heat of the holy apostles. By preventing the example of such an act, he declares that those who are the leaders in his religion have no need in any way whatsoever of swords. With divine dignity, Christ healed him who received the blow and gave this godlike sign for their condemnation to those who came to seize him. COMMENTARY ON LUKE, HOMILY 148.[12]

JESUS RESPONDS TO VIOLENCE WITH HEALING. EPHREM THE SYRIAN: Not fearing the power that had flattened them,[13] they stretched out their impure hands and seized him who was purifying them. "Simon cut off the ear of one of them." The good Lord in his gentleness took it and put it back in its elevated place on the body, as a figure of him who had fallen into the lower abyss because of his sins. "Put your sword back again into its place."[14] He whose word was a sword did not need a sword. Just as he restored the ear that was cut off back to its place, he could have separated the members that were joined. Unsatisfied with showing the intensity of his power with a single example, he showed it to all those who "retreated and fell backwards to the ground."[15] The one whose ear had been healed would not be the only one to benefit from grace. He allowed all that were about to apprehend him to benefit from it, so that they would certainly know whom they were going to arrest. The grace of him who had restored the ear to its place made those who "fell backwards to the ground" able to get up again. COMMENTARY ON TATIAN'S DIATESSARON 20.13.[16]

JESUS THE CREATOR HEALS THE SERVANT. AMBROSE: Comprehend, if you can, how pain passes at the contact with the Savior's hand, and wounds are healed not when sprinkled with a cure, but when covered with his touch. The clay recognizes its maker,[17] and the flesh follows the hand of the Lord who formed it, for the creator repairs his work as he wishes. Thus in another place, vision is restored to the blind man after clay is spread on his eyes,[18] as if he had returned to nature. He could have commanded but preferred to act, so that we should realize that it is he himself who from the dust of the earth fashioned the limbs of our bodies,[19] suited to different functions, and quickened us with infused strength of

---

[9]Mt 26:50. [10]Mt 13:12. [11]ECTD 298**. [12]CGSL 588-89**. [13]See Jn 18:6. [14]Mt 26:52. [15]Jn 18:6. [16]ECTD 298-99*. [17]Job 36:3. [18]Jn 9:6-7. [19]Gen 2:7; Job 38:14; Sir 17:1; 33:10.

mind. EXPOSITION OF THE GOSPEL OF LUKE.[20]

THE SOLDIERS RESPOND WITH VIOLENCE.

EPHREM THE SYRIAN: Since our Lord was the fulfillment of justice and the beginning of mercy, he put the sword in its sheath and put justice back in its place again. He then healed the ear through mercy. He put the ear back in its place and made good the imperfection of justice through fruitful mercy. He whose ear had been healed expressed his gratitude for this love with hatred. Those who had "fallen backwards to the ground" and had been raised up again through Christ, thanked him for his help with chains. "They bound him," said the Evangelist, "and led him away."[21] COMMENTARY ON TATIAN'S DIATESSARON 20.13.[22]

22:52-53 Jesus Questions His Captors

THEY DO NOT UNDERSTAND JESUS' COMPASSION.

AMBROSE: They came and they seized him. They would die a more dreadful death as a fruit of their zeal. These wretches did not understand the mystery nor revere such compassion of piety, because Christ did not let even his enemies be

wounded. They inflicted death on the righteous One, and he healed the wounds of his persecutors. EXPOSITION OF THE GOSPEL OF LUKE 10.71.[23]

THE HOUR OF DARKNESS IS THE HOUR OF

SATAN. CYRIL OF ALEXANDRIA: "You have one hour against me." That is a very short and limited time, between the precious cross and the resurrection from the dead. This also is the power given to darkness. Darkness is the name of Satan, for he is total night and darkness. Blessed Paul says that the God of this world has blinded the minds of those that do not believe, or else, the light of the gospel of the glory of Christ should shine on them.[24] God granted power to Satan and the Jews to rise up against Christ. They, however, dug for themselves the pitfall of destruction. He certainly saved all under heaven by means of his passion and rose the third day, having trampled under foot the empire of death. They brought down inevitable condemnation on their own heads in company with that traitorous disciple. COMMENTARY ON LUKE, HOMILY 148.[25]

---

[20]EHG 412. [21]Jn 18:12-13. [22]ECTD 299*. [23]EHG 411-12**. [24]2 Cor 4:4. [25]CGSL 589-90**.

22:54-62 THE DENIAL OF PETER

[54]Then they seized him and led him away, bringing him into the high priest's house. Peter followed at a distance; [55]and when they had kindled a fire in the middle of the courtyard and sat down together, Peter sat among them. [56]Then a maid, seeing him as he sat in the light and gazing at him, said, "This man also was with him." [57]But he denied it, saying, "Woman, I do not know him." [58]And a little later some one else saw him and said, "You also are one of them." But Peter said, "Man, I am not." [59]And after an interval of about an hour still another insisted, saying, "Certainly this man also was with him; for he is a Galilean." [60]But Peter said, "Man, I do not know what you are saying." And immediately, while he was still speaking, the cock crowed. [61]And the

Lord turned and looked at Peter. And Peter remembered the word of the Lord, how he had said to him, "Before the cock crows today, you will deny me three times." [62]And he went out and wept bitterly.

OVERVIEW: Peter follows Jesus to the house of the high priest because of his piety and devotion to his Lord (AMBROSE). Peter denies Jesus because of his cowardice and fear of death (CYRIL OF ALEXANDRIA). Peter denies that he is among the Galileans, denying his association with Jesus and with his fellow disciples—fellow brothers of Jesus (AMBROSE). Peter's denial comes before he was baptized with the Holy Spirit at Pentecost (AUGUSTINE).

Only Luke records the look of Jesus, which reminds Peter of Jesus' teaching at the table, so that his conscience condemns him (CYRIL OF ALEXANDRIA). By singling out Peter among his persecutors, Jesus conveys to him the humility that Peter will need when he confronts fear and anxiety over his own death (LEO THE GREAT). The look therefore also holds the promise of an absolution. Peter remembers Jesus' promise. He knows that the Lord's word is true and efficacious, calling sinners to repentance and absolving them (AMBROSE). This marvelous scene captures the whole purpose of Luke's Gospel. Through Peter's denials, absolution and restoration, he will be able to fulfill the second part of Jesus' prophetic instructions that he will turn and strengthen his brother disciples as a shepherd of Christ's flock (AUGUSTINE). Peter's bitter tears are an expression of his surprise at this guilt and heartfelt sorrow that he has so quickly rejected his Lord (AMBROSE). Peter washes away his denial by baptismal tears of repentance (AUGUSTINE).

22:54-55 Peter Follows Jesus

PETER SHOWS HIS DEVOTION. AMBROSE: One close to denial fittingly followed from afar, because he could not have denied him if he had stayed close to Christ. Perhaps we should vener-

ate him for this with the greatest admiration, because he did not forsake the Lord although he was afraid. . . . Peter follows Christ because of devotion. He denies because of sudden temptation. It is commonplace that he falls, and it is through faith that he repents. The fire was already burning in the house of the chief priest. Peter approached to warm himself,[1] because with the imprisonment of the Lord, the warmth of his mind had already cooled within him. EXPOSITION OF THE GOSPEL OF LUKE 10.72.[2]

22:56-60 The Three Denials

COWARDICE AND FEAR OF DEATH. CYRIL OF ALEXANDRIA: We do not say that the denial took place in order that Christ's words might come true. We say rather that his object was to forewarn the disciple, inasmuch as what was about to happen did not escape Christ's knowledge. The misfortune, therefore, happened to the disciple from the cowardice of human nature. Since Christ had not risen from the dead, he had not yet abolished death and wiped corruption away. The fear of undergoing death was something beyond human endurance. COMMENTARY ON LUKE, HOMILY 149.[3]

THE FIRST TO DENY JESUS. AMBROSE: What difference does it make that the maid is the first to give Peter away? The men could have recognized him instead. Perhaps this happened so that we may see that the female sex also sinned by killing the Lord, so that his passion should also redeem womankind. A woman therefore was the first to receive the mystery of the resurrection and to obey the commands,[4] so that she abolished

---

[1]Mk 14:54; Jn 18:18. [2]EHG 412**. [3]CGSL 591-92**. [4]See Jn 20:11-18.

the old error of her sin. EXPOSITION OF THE GOSPEL OF LUKE 10.73.[5]

PETER'S DENIAL COMES BEFORE PENTECOST.

AUGUSTINE: By saying that Peter did penance, we have to take care not to think that he did it as those who are properly called penitents now do it in the church. Who could bear it that we should think the first of the apostles was numbered among such penitents? He repented of having denied Christ, as his tears show, for so it is written, "he wept bitterly."[6] They had not yet been strengthened by the resurrection of the Lord, the coming of the Holy Spirit who appeared on the day of Pentecost, or by that breath which the Lord breathed on them after he rose from the dead. LETTER 265.[7]

22:61 Fulfillment of Prophecy

PETER CONDEMNED BY HIS CONSCIENCE.

CYRIL OF ALEXANDRIA: This miserable act arose from the affliction of human cowardice. The disciple's conscience condemned him. The proof of this is his grieving immediately afterwards and his tears of repentance that fell from his eyes as for a serious sin. It says, "Having gone out, he wept bitterly," after Christ had looked at him and reminded him of what he had said to Peter. COMMENTARY ON LUKE, Homily 149.[8]

THE GAZE OF TRUTH. LEO THE GREAT: Then

"the Lord looked at Peter." Christ stood in the middle of the priests' insults, the witnesses' lies, and the injuries of those that struck him and spat on him. He met the troubled disciple with his eyes, the same eyes that had foreseen that Peter would undergo a struggle. In so doing, the gaze of truth entered Peter, directed toward the place where the amendment of his heart would be grounded. It was as if the Lord's voice were echoing within Peter, saying, "What are you thinking, Peter? Why do you withdraw into yourself? Turn to me, trust in me, " and "follow me."[9] This is the time for my passion. The hour of your suffering

has not yet come. Why do you fear what you yourself will also overcome? Do not let the weakness that I have accepted disturb you. I was anxious for you, but you should not worry about me." SERMON 54.5.1.[10]

LIKE PETER, WE ARE TO REPENT. AMBROSE:

Peter also wept bitterly. He wept so that he could purge his sin with tears. If you want to deserve pardon, you should wash away your guilt with tears. At that same moment and time, Christ looks at you. If you perhaps fall into some sin, because he is a witness to your secrets, he looks at you so that you may recall and confess your error. Imitate Peter, when he says in another place for the third time, "Lord, you know that I love you."[11] Since he denied him a third time, he confesses him a third time. He denied at night, but he confesses by day. These words were written that we should know that no one must boast of himself. If Peter fell because he said, "Although others shall be scandalized in you, I shall not be scandalized,"[12] what other person can rightly take himself for granted? Since David also said, "I said in my prosperity, 'I shall never be moved,' " he admitted that his boasting had harmed him, saying, "You turned away your face, and I was troubled."[13] EXPOSITION OF THE GOSPEL OF LUKE 10.90-91.[14]

PETER'S DENIAL PREPARES HIM TO SHEPHERD CHRIST'S FLOCK. AUGUSTINE: When

fear overwhelmed him, as the Lord had predicted, he three times denies the one for whom he promised to die. As it says, "The Lord looked at him and he, for his part, wept bitterly." Remembrance of his denial was necessarily bitter, so that the grace of redemption might be even more sweet. If Christ had not left him to himself, he would not have denied. If Christ had not looked at him, he would not have wept. God hates people relying presumptuously on their

---

[5]EHG 412**. [6]Mt 26:75. [7]FC 32:277*. [8]CGSL 592**. [9]See Jn 21:22. [10]FC 93:235-36**. [11]Jn 21:15. [12]Mt 26:33 Vulgate. [13]Ps 30:6-7 (29:7-8 LXX). [14]EHG 417-18**.

own powers. Like a doctor, he lances this swollen tumor in those whom he loves. By lancing it, of course, he inflicts pain, but he also ensures health later. When he rises again, the Lord entrusts his sheep to Peter, to that one who denied him. Peter denied him because he relied on himself, but later Peter would feed his flock as a pastor, because he loved him. After all, why does he ask him three times about his love, if not to prick his conscience about his threefold denial? SERMON 285.3.[15]

22:62 Peter Weeps Bitterly

GUILT TAKES PETER BY SURPRISE. AMBROSE: Why did Peter weep? Guilt took him by surprise. I am accustomed to weep if I lack guilt, if I do not avenge myself, or do not get what I wickedly desire. Peter grieved and wept because he went astray as a man. I do not learn why he spoke, but I learn that he wept. I read of his tears, but I do not read of his explanation. What cannot be defended can be purged. Tears may wash away the offense that is a shame to confess aloud. Tears

deal with pardon and shame. Tears speak of guilt without fear and confess sin without the obstacle of shame. Tears do not demand pardon and deserve it. I learn why Peter was silent, lest a swift petition for pardon might offend even more. First he must weep, and then he must pray. EXPOSITION OF THE GOSPEL OF LUKE 10.88.[16]

A BAPTISM OF TEARS. AUGUSTINE: To wash away the sin of denial, Peter needed the baptism of tears. From where would he get this, unless the Lord gave him this too? That is why the apostle Paul gave this advice to his people concerning deviant opinions and about how they should deal with them. He said they must be "correcting his opponents with gentleness. God may perhaps grant that they will repent and come to know the truth."[17] So even repentance is a gift from God. The heart of the proud is hard ground. It is softened for repentance only if it is rained on by God's grace. SERMON 229O.I.[18]

---

[15]WSA 3 8:96-97*. [16]EHG 417**. [17]2 Tim 2:25. [18]WSA 3 6:324*.

22:63-71 THE JEWISH TRIAL BEFORE THE SANHEDRIN

[63]Now the men who were holding Jesus mocked him and beat him; [64]they also blindfolded him and asked him, "Prophesy! Who is it that struck you?" [65]And they spoke many other words against him, reviling him.

[66]When day came, the assembly of the elders of the people gathered together, both chief priests and scribes; and they led him away to their council, and they said, [67]"If you are the Christ, tell us." But he said to them, "If I tell you, you will not believe; [68]and if I ask you, you will not answer. [69]But from now on the Son of man shall be seated at the right hand of the power of God." [70]And they all said, "Are you the Son of God, then?" And he said to them, "You say that I am." [71]And they said, "What further testimony do we need? We have heard it ourselves from his own lips."

OVERVIEW: By placing this scene of the mocking and beating of Jesus as the preface to the trials,

Luke shows us the patience of Jesus as he endures the beatings and ridicule of his captors. The blindfolding of Jesus is ironic because the hearer knows that Jesus has already prophesied the temptations and failings of the disciples, as well as his own mocking, beating and humiliation. The trial revolves around the charge leveled against Jesus by the Sanhedrin as to whether he is "the Christ of God," which they know to be true. Jesus has already provided abundant evidence through his words and deeds, but they do not believe he is the Christ, and his response condemns them. One needs to recognize the evidence, to see the truth, to confess that Jesus is the Christ; the Sanhedrin refuses to do this and instead accuses him of blasphemy and seeks to put him to death (Cyril of Alexandria).

27:63-71 Jesus Is the Christ, the Son of God, the Great I Am

Jesus Endures Beatings and Ridicule.

Cyril of Alexandria: "Now the men who were holding Jesus mocked him and beat him; they also blindfolded him and asked him, 'Prophesy! Who is it that struck you?'" "When he was reviled, he did not revile in return; when he suffered, he did not threaten; but he trusted to him who judges justly."[1] We should say what the holy prophets said about certain men, "Be appalled, O heavens, at this, be shocked, be utterly desolate, says the Lord."[2] He is the Lord of earth and heaven, the Creator and Architect of all, the King of kings and Lord of lords. He is of surpassing greatness in glory and majesty, the foundation of everything, and that in which all things exist and remain. All things exist in him.[3] He is the breath of all the holy spirits in heaven. This One is despised as one of us, patiently endures beatings, and submits to the ridicule of the wicked. He offers himself to us as a perfect pattern of patience. He rather reveals the incomparable greatness of his godlike gentleness. Commentary on Luke, Homily 150.[4]

The Irony of His Captors' Call for Prophecy.

Cyril of Alexandria: Perhaps even Christ endures this to rebuke our minds'

weakness and to show that human things fall as far below the divine excellencies as our nature is inferior to his. We of earth, mere corruption and ashes, immediately attack those who would disturb us, as we have a heart full of fierceness like savage beasts. He, who in nature and glory transcends the limits of our understanding and our powers of speech, patiently endured those officers when they not only mocked but also hit him. It says, "Now the men who were holding Jesus mocked him and beat him; they also blindfolded him and asked him, 'Prophesy! Who is it that struck you?'" They ridicule, as if he were some ignorant person, him who is the giver of all knowledge and even sees what is hidden within us. He has somewhere said by one of the holy prophets, "Who is this that darkens counsel by words without knowledge?"[5] He who tries hearts and minds and is the giver of all prophecy, how could he not know who hit him? As Christ said, "Darkness has blinded their eyes, and their minds are blinded."[6] One may say of them, "Woe to them that are drunk, but not with wine! Their vine is of the vine of Sodom and of Gomorrah."[7] Commentary on Luke, Homily 150.[8]

The Sanhedrin Know That He Is the Christ.

Cyril of Alexandria: When at dawn their wicked assembly gathered, they brought into their midst the Lord of Moses and the Sender of the prophets. After illegally mocking him, they asked if he were the Christ. O senseless Pharisee, if you ask because you do not know, surely until you had learned the truth you should not hurt him, or else by chance you may hurt God. If you make pretense of ignorance, while really you know that he is the Christ, you must hear what the sacred Scripture says, "God is not mocked."[9] Commentary on Luke, Homily 150.[10]

Jesus' Response Condemns the Sanhedrin.

Cyril of Alexandria: I think that we

---

[1]1 Pet 2:23. [2]Jer 2:12. [3]Col 1:17. [4]CGSL 594**. [5]Job 38:2. [6]Jn 12:40. [7]Is 29:9; Deut 32:32. [8]CGSL 594-95**. [9]Gal 6:7. [10]CGSL 595**.

should examine the words used by Christ, because they were a correction for the lack of love to God of which the scribes and Pharisees were guilty. When they ask whether he is truly the Christ and could learn this very thing, he answers them, "If I tell you, you will not believe; and if I ask, you will not return an answer." COMMENTARY ON LUKE, HOMILY 150.[11]

THE SANHEDRIN ACCUSES JESUS OF BLAS-PHEMY. CYRIL OF ALEXANDRIA: They say, "We no longer need any testimony," as being the hearers of Christ's words. What had they heard him say? O vile and senseless people, you wanted to learn if he were the Christ! He taught you that by nature and in truth he is the Son of God the Father, and he shares the throne of Deity with him. As you confessed, you now have no need of testi-mony, because you have heard him speak. You might now have learned best that he is the Christ. This would have proved for you the pathway to faith, had you only been one of those who would know the truth. Making even the pathway of salvation an occasion for their souls' ruin, they do not understand. They senselessly slay him, keeping but one aim in view in contempt of all law. They totally disregard the divine commands. It is written, "The holy and the just you shall not kill."[12] They paid no regard whatsoever to the sacred commands but rushed down some steep hill to fall into the snares of destruction. COMMENTARY ON LUKE, HOMILY 150.[13]

---

[11]CGSL 595*. [12]Ex 23:7. [13]CGSL 597*.

23:1-5 PILATE'S FIRST TRIAL

[1]*Then the whole company of them arose, and brought him before Pilate.* [2]*And they began to accuse him, saying, "We found this man perverting our nation, and forbidding us to give tribute to Caesar, and saying that he himself is Christ a king."* [3]*And Pilate asked him, "Are you the King of the Jews?" And he answered him, "You have said so."* [4]*And Pilate said to the chief priests and the multitudes, "I find no crime in this man."* [5]*But they were urgent, saying, "He stirs up the people, teaching throughout all Judea, from Galilee even to this place."*

OVERVIEW: The Sanhedrin levels three coordinate charges against Jesus: "perverting our nation," "preventing the giving of tribute taxes to Caesar," and "saying that he himself is Christ, a king." The hearer knows immediately that the first two charges are false, especially the second one, for Jesus has argued for the paying of taxes to Caesar.[1] Hence Pilate's first verdict of innocence— "I find no legal cause in this man"—is the first of three such declarations of innocence by Pilate (CYRIL OF ALEXANDRIA).[2]

23:1-5 *Pilate's First Declaration of Jesus' Innocence*

THE SANHEDRIN BRINGS FALSE CHARGES. CYRIL OF ALEXANDRIA: You say, "We found this man perverting our people." Tell us in what this perversion consisted? Christ taught repentance. Where did he forbid giving tribute to Caesar? He said, "Give to Caesar the things that are Caesar's,

---

[1]Lk 20:20-26. [2]Lk 23:13-16, [20], 22.

and to God the things that are God's."[3] Where then did he forbid giving tribute to Caesar? Their only purpose was to bring down to death the One who was raising them to life. This was the goal of their strategy, the shameful deeds they planned, of the falsehood they invented, and the bitter words running from their wicked tongues. The law still loudly proclaims to you, "You shall not bear false witness against your neighbor,"[4] and "The holy and the just you shall not kill."[5] COMMENTARY ON LUKE, HOMILY 151.[6]

PILATE DECLARES JESUS INNOCENT. CYRIL OF ALEXANDRIA: They had no respect whatsoever for the law. Led by an uncontrolled recklessness into whatever pleased only themselves without examination of the case, they invented numerous charges heaping up against Christ accusations that were neither true nor capable of being proved. They were convicted of being even more wicked than an idolater is. Acquitting Jesus of all blame, Pilate not only once but three times openly said, "I find no crime in this man." COMMENTARY ON LUKE, HOMILY 151.[7]

---

[3]Mt 22:17. [4]Ex 20:16. [5]Ex 23:7. [6]CGSL 602**. [7]CGSL 602**.

23:6-12 HEROD'S TRIAL

[6]When Pilate heard this, he asked whether the man was a Galilean. [7]And when he learned that he belonged to Herod's jurisdiction, he sent him over to Herod, who was himself in Jerusalem at that time. [8]When Herod saw Jesus, he was very glad, for he had long desired to see him, because he had heard about him, and he was hoping to see some sign done by him. [9]So he questioned him at some length; but he made no answer. [10]The chief priests and the scribes stood by, vehemently accusing him. [11]And Herod with his soldiers treated him with contempt and mocked him; then, arraying him in gorgeous apparel, he sent him back to Pilate. [12]And Herod and Pilate became friends with each other that very day, for before this they had been at enmity with each other.

OVERVIEW: No matter how many words Herod hurls at him, Jesus remains silent as a sign that he is completely in control of the situation in his willing submission to the Father's plan and his disdain for Herod and the charges against him. Herod and his soldiers demonstrate their contempt by mocking Jesus, as the soldiers of the Sanhedrin did at the beginning of the trials by dressing Jesus in elegant clothing, not realizing that this white robe symbolizes the sinless passion of Jesus (AMBROSE). Pilate and Herod, who were enemies, are now friends through their experience with Jesus in his trials (CYRIL OF JERUSALEM).

23:6-12 Herod and Pilate Reconciled

JESUS' SILENCE IS A SIGN OF DISDAIN FOR HEROD AND THE CHARGES. AMBROSE: There follows a wonderful passage that gives human hearts the spiritual endurance to submit calmly to injustice. They accuse the Lord, and he stands mute.[1] The one that does not lack a defense is

---

[1]Mt 27:12, 14.

suitably mute. Let those who fear to being over-come seek a defense. By remaining silent, he does not confirm the accusation. By not refuting it, he despises it. A special attribute of Christ is that among wicked judges he seemed to have been un-willing rather than unable to be defended. The Lord explained why he would remain silent, say-ing, "If I should tell you, you will not believe me; and if I should also ask you, you will not answer me."[2] It is extraordinary that he chose to prove himself a king, rather than speak, so that those who confess what they taunt would have no grounds for condemnation. When Herod wanted to see him work wonders, he was silent and per-formed none because Herod's cruelty did not merit to behold the divine and the Lord shunned boasting. Perhaps Herod prefigures all the impi-ous, who if they did not believe in the law and the prophets cannot see the miraculous works of Christ in the gospel either.[3] EXPOSITION OF THE GOSPEL OF LUKE 10.97-99.[4]

JESUS' WHITE ROBE SYMBOLIZES HIS SIN-LESS PASSION. AMBROSE: It is significant that Jesus is clothed in a white garment by Herod. It denotes his sinless passion, because the Lamb of God without stain and with glory accepted the sins of the world.[5] Herod and Pilate, who became friends instead of enemies through Jesus Christ, symbolize the peoples of Israel and the Gentiles, since the future harmony of both follows from the Lord's passion.[6] First the people of the na-tions capture the Word of God and bring it to the people of the Jews, through the devotion of their faith. They clothe with glory the body of Christ, whom they had previously despised.[7] EXPOSI-TION OF THE GOSPEL OF LUKE 10.103.[8]

JESUS RECONCILES THE HEARTS OF PILATE AND HEROD. CYRIL OF JERUSALEM: Having been bound, Christ went from Caiaphas to Pilate; is this also written? Yes: "And having bound him, they led him away as a present to the King of Ja-rim."[9] But some keen listener will object: "Pilate was not a king." (Let us pass over for the time the main points of the inquiry.) "How then, having bound him, did they lead him as a present to the king?" But read the Gospel: "Pilate, hearing that he was from Galilee, sent him to Herod; for Herod was then king and was present in Jerusa-lem." Notice the exactness of the prophet, for he says that he was sent as a present. For "Herod and Pilate became friends that very day; whereas pre-viously they had been at enmity with each other." It was fitting that he, who was to restore peace between earth and heaven, should first put at peace the very men who condemned him, for the Lord himself was there present, "who reconciles the hearts of the princes of the earth."[10] Mark the exactness of the prophets and their truthful testi-mony. CATECHETICAL LECTURES 13.14.[11]

---

[2]Lk 22:67-68. [3]See Jn 5:46-47. [4]*EHG* 420**. [5]See Jn 1:29. [6]See Eph 2:13. [7]Rom 11:30-31. [8]*EHG* 421-22**. [9]Hos 10:6 LXX. The accom-modation of the Old Testament text may seem strained, but Cyril had the example of Justin (*Dialogue with Trypho* 103) before him, and Rufi-nus after him drew the same parallel. [10]Job 12:24. [11]FC 64:14-15.

23:13-25 PILATE'S SECOND TRIAL AND VERDICT

[13]*Pilate then called together the chief priests and the rulers and the people,* [14]*and said to them, "You brought me this man as one who was perverting the people; and after examining him before you, behold, I did not find this man guilty of any of your charges against him;* [15]*neither did Herod,*

for he sent him back to us. Behold, nothing deserving death has been done by him; [16]*I will therefore chastise him and release him."* [m]

[18]*But they all cried out together, "Away with this man, and release to us Barabbas"—* [19]*a man who had been thrown into prison for an insurrection started in the city, and for murder.* [20]*Pilate addressed them once more, desiring to release Jesus;* [21]*but they shouted out, "Crucify, crucify him!"* [22]*A third time he said to them, "Why, what evil has he done? I have found in him no crime deserving death; I will therefore chastise him and release him."* [23]*But they were urgent, demanding with loud cries that he should be crucified. And their voices prevailed.* [24]*So Pilate gave sentence that their demand should be granted.* [25]*He released the man who had been thrown into prison for insurrection and murder, whom they asked for; but Jesus he delivered up to their will.*

m Here, or after verse 19, other ancient authorities add verse 17, *Now he was obliged to release one man to them at the festival*

OVERVIEW: The fourth and final trial of Jesus in Luke continues to accent Jesus' innocence, contrasting his innocence, as declared by Pilate and Herod, with the demands for his death. The Jewish leaders and people accuse Jesus of sedition, demand his crucifixion, and would rather set free a convicted revolutionary and murderer like Barabbas (AMBROSE). Jesus will be crucified even though he is the innocent, suffering, righteous one, for Pilate, Herod, the thief on the cross, and the centurion will all declare him innocent (CYRIL OF JERUSALEM). Again Jesus' prophecy to his disciples after the Last Supper is coming true, "And with transgressors he was reckoned,"[1] for with their cries for crucifixion they are sending Jesus into the wilderness as a scapegoat bearing his sins (ORIGEN). Repeatedly the prophet Isaiah has foretold the betrayal of Jesus by the people and their call for his death (CYRIL OF ALEXANDRIA). Indeed, the city that called for Jesus' crucifixion will be destroyed after forty years (ORIGEN).

23:13-25 Pilate Declares Jesus Innocent a Second and Third Time

PILATE AND HEROD DECLARE JESUS INNOCENT. AMBROSE: They send Christ to Herod and then to Pilate. Although neither pronounces him guilty, both gratify the desires of strange cruelty. Pilate washes his hands but does not wash away his actions. A judge should not yield to either

envy or fear and then sacrifice the blood of the innocent.[2] Pilate's wife warned him.[3] Grace shone in the flight. The Godhead was revealed, yet he still did not abstain from a sacrilegious verdict. EXPOSITION OF THE GOSPEL OF LUKE 10.100.[4]

THE DEATH OF AN INNOCENT MAN. AMBROSE: What kind of people crucified the Lord of glory![5] Those that violently demand the death of an innocent man fittingly seek the release of a murderer. Wickedness has such laws as to hate innocence and love guilt. The interpretation of the name gives the likeness of the image, because *Barabbas* means "son of the father." He belongs to those to whom it is said, "You are of your father the devil."[6] They were about to choose the Antichrist as son of their father, rather than the Son of God. EXPOSITION OF THE GOSPEL OF LUKE 10.101-2.[7]

PILATE AND OTHERS FIND NO GUILT IN JESUS. CYRIL OF JERUSALEM: Many have been crucified throughout the world, but the demons are not afraid of any of these. These people died because of their own sins, but Christ died for the sin of others. He "did not sin, neither was deceit found in his mouth." It was not Peter, who could be suspected of partiality, who said this, but Isaiah, who, although not present in the flesh, in

---

[1]Lk 22:37, quoting Is 53:12. [2]See Mt 27:24. [3]See Mt 27:19. [4]EHG 421**. [5]See 1 Cor 2:8. [6]Jn 8:44. [7]EHG 421**.

spirit foresaw the Lord's coming in the flesh. Why do I bring only the prophet as a witness? Take the witness of Pilate himself. He passed judgment on him, by saying, "I find no guilt in this man." When he delivered him over and washed his hands, he said, "I am innocent of the blood of this just man."[8] The robber is another witness to Jesus' innocence. He is the first man to enter paradise. He rebuked his friend and said, "We are receiving what our deeds deserved, but this man has done nothing wrong, because you and I were present at his judgment."[9] CATECHETICAL LECTURES 13.3.[10]

JESUS SENT INTO THE WILDERNESS AS A
SCAPEGOAT. ORIGEN: The word of the Lord is rich, and according to the opinion of Solomon, "it must be written on the heart" not once but also twice and "three times."[11] Let us to the best of our ability also now attempt to add something to what was said long ago. Let us show how "as a type of things to come"[12] this one male goat was sacrificed to the Lord as an offering and the other one was sent away "living." Hear in the Gospels what Pilate said to the priests and the Jewish people: "Which of these two do you want me to send out to you: Jesus, who is called the Christ, or Barabbas?"[13] Then all the people cried out to release Barabbas and to hand Jesus over to be killed.[14] Look, you have a male goat who was sent "living into the wilderness." He carried with him the sins of the people who cried out and said, "Crucify, crucify!" The first is a male goat sent "living into the wilderness." The second is the male goat that was offered to God as an offering to atone for sins. Christ made a true atonement for those who believe in him. HOMILIES ON LEVITICUS 10.2.2.[15]

THE PROPHET ISAIAH FORETOLD THE CRY OF
THE CRUCIFIXION. CYRIL OF ALEXANDRIA: They brought the holy and just One to Pilate. They spoke violent and unrestrained words against him and poured out falsely invented accusations. They persisted in the ferocity with which they accused him. Pilate then ruled that it should be as they desired, although he had publicly said, "I find no wickedness in this man." It says, "They cried out, 'Away with him, crucify him!'" The Lord had rebuked this unmerciful and unlawful cry by the voice of the prophet Isaiah. It is written, "The vineyard of the Lord of hosts is the house of Israel, and the men of Judah are his pleasant planting; and he looked for justice, but behold, bloodshed; for righteousness, but behold, a cry!"[16] In another place, he said of them, "Woe to them, for they have strayed from me! Destruction to them, for they have rebelled against me! I would redeem them, but they speak lies against me."[17] It is written again, "Their princes shall fall by the sword, because of the rudeness of their tongue."[18] COMMENTARY ON LUKE, HOMILY 152.[19]

THE CITY THAT CALLED FOR JESUS' CRUCI-
FIXION IS LATER DESTROYED. ORIGEN: Celsus goes on to say that "those who killed Jesus suffered nothing for a long a time afterwards." We must inform him and all who are prone to learn the truth. The Jewish people called for the crucifixion of Jesus with shouts of "Crucify him, crucify him!" They preferred to set free the robber who had been thrown into prison for sedition and murder. They wanted Jesus, who had been delivered through envy, to be crucified. The city where all these things happened was attacked shortly after this. After a long siege, it was totally overthrown and destroyed. God judged the inhabitants of that place unworthy of living the life of citizens together. Although it may seem incredible to say, God spared this people in delivering them to their enemies. He saw that they were incurably against any improvement and were daily sinking deeper and deeper

---

[8]Mt 27:24. [9]That the two robbers were present at the judgment of Christ seems rather unlikely. Cyril assumes perhaps that they were condemned to be crucified at the same time as Christ. [10]FC 64:5-6**. [11]Prov 22:18, 20. [12]1 Cor 10:11; Heb 10:1. [13]Mt 27:17. [14]Mt 27:21-22. [15]FC 83:204-5**. [16]Is 5:7. [17]Hos 7:13. [18]Hos 7:16. [19]CGSL 604**.

into evil. All this happened to them because the blood of Jesus was shed at their instigation and on their land. The land was no longer able to bear those who were guilty of so fearful a crime against Jesus. AGAINST CELSUS 8.42.[20]

---

[20]ANCL 23:526-27.

23:26-32 THE JOURNEY TO THE CROSS

[26]*And as they led him away, they seized one Simon of Cyrene, who was coming in from the country, and laid on him the cross, to carry it behind Jesus.* [27]*And there followed him a great multitude of the people, and of women who bewailed and lamented him.* [28]*But Jesus turning to them said, "Daughters of Jerusalem, do not weep for me, but weep for yourselves and for your children.* [29]*For behold, the days are coming when they will say, 'Blessed are the barren, and the wombs that never bore, and the breasts that never gave suck!'* [30]*Then they will begin to say to the mountains, 'Fall on us'; and to the hills, 'Cover us.'* [31]*For if they do this when the wood is green, what will happen when it is dry?"*

[32]*Two others also, who were criminals, were led away to be put to death with him.*

OVERVIEW: How ironic that it is a Gentile, "Simon from Cyrene, a region in North Africa" (present-day Libya), who receives the burden of the cross from Jesus (EPHREM THE SYRIAN). Like Abraham, Jesus is carrying wood to the place of sacrifice (CYRIL OF ALEXANDRIA). Christ's death is not a reason for mourning. It is a passover to life everlasting, for he has been raised from the dead (ATHANASIUS). Jesus contrasts himself to Jerusalem and shows that the tears of the daughters of Jerusalem should not be for him but for Jerusalem and its inhabitants when the city is destroyed (CYRIL OF ALEXANDRIA). If they destroy the wood that gives fruit, what will they do to the dry wood that bears no fruit (EPHREM THE SYRIAN)? It is better to be moist wood now than dry wood then, when the fire of destruction comes.

23:26-27 Participants on the Journey

SIMON RECEIVES THE BURDEN OF THE CROSS FOR JESUS. EPHREM THE SYRIAN: After he took up the wood of his cross and set out, they found and stopped a man of Cyrene, that is, from among the Gentiles, and placed the wood of the cross on him. It was only right that they should have given the wood of the cross voluntarily to the Gentiles, since in their rebellion, the Jews rejected the coming of him who was bringing all blessings. In rejecting it themselves, in their jealousy, they threw it away to the Gentiles. They rejected it in their jealousy, and the Gentiles received it, to their even greater jealousy. The Lord approved the welcoming Gentiles and thus provoked jealousy among their contemporaries through the Gentiles' acceptance. By carrying the wood of his cross himself, Christ revealed the sign of his victory. Christ said that another person would not pressure him into death. "I have power over my life, to lay it down or to take

---

it up again."[1] Why should another person have carried the cross? This showed that he, in whom no sin could be found, went up on the cross for those who rejected him. Commentary on Tatian's Diatessaron 20.20.[2]

Like Isaac, Jesus Carries Wood to the Place of Sacrifice. Cyril of Alexandria: When blessed Abraham went up the mountain that God showed him so that he might sacrifice Isaac according to God's command, he laid the wood on the boy. Isaac was a type of Christ carrying his own cross on his shoulders and going up to the glory of his passion. Christ taught us that his passion was his glory. He said, "Now is the Son of man glorified, and in him God is glorified; if God is glorified in him, God will also glorify him in himself, and glorify him at once."[3] Commentary on Luke, Homily 152.[4]

23:28-32 Four Warnings by Jesus to the Daughters of Jerusalem

Christ's Death Is Not a Reason for Mourning. Athanasius: The Lord over death set out to abolish death. Being Lord, he accomplished his aim. We therefore have passed from death to life. The concept that the Jews and those who think like them held about the Lord was wrong. Things did not turn out at all according to their expectations, because the opposite was true. In fact, "he who sits in heaven shall laugh at them: the Lord shall have them in derision."[5]

That is the reason our Savior restrained the women from weeping when he was being led to death. He said, "Do not weep for me." He wished to show that his death was not an event for us to mourn about but rather to be joyful about, since he who died for us is alive! He was not created from nothing, but he derives his being from the Father. Festal Letter 9.[6]

The Women Will Wail When Jerusalem Is Destroyed. Cyril of Alexandria: He was go-

ing to the place of crucifixion. Weeping women, as well as many others, followed him. The female sex tends to weep often. They have a disposition that is ready to sink at the approach of anything that is sorrowful. "Daughters of Jerusalem, do not weep for me, but weep for yourselves and for your children. For behold, the days are coming when they will say, 'Blessed are the barren, and the wombs that never bore, and the breasts that never gave suck!'" How did this happen? When the war came on the country of the Jews, they all totally perished, small and great. Infants with their mothers and sons with their fathers were destroyed without distinction. He then says, "Then they will begin to say to the mountains, 'Fall on us'; and to the hills, 'Cover us.'" In extreme miseries, those less severe misfortunes become, so to speak, desirable. Commentary on Luke, Homily 152.[7]

Green and Dry Wood. Ephrem the Syrian: The Lord said, "If they do that to the green wood." He compared his divinity with the green wood and those who received his gifts to the dry wood. What is green bears fruit, as these words that he spoke testify: "For which of my works are you stoning me?[8] If I suffer to this extent, although you have found no sin in me, which of you will convict me of sin?[9] Since you have invented a pretext to dispose of me, how much more will you suffer?" Perhaps he was referring the green wood to himself, because of the miracles he had done. He called the righteous who were without virtue, the dry wood. They ate the fruit of this green wood, and they rejoiced beneath its foliage. Then they took it in hatred and destroyed it. What more will they do to the dry wood, which does not even have a sprout? What more will they do to the ordinary righteous people who do not work miracles? Commentary on Tatian's Diatessaron 20.21.[10]

---

[1]Jn 10:18. [2]ECTD 304**. [3]Jn 13:31. [4]CGSL 606**. [5]Ps 2:4. [6]ARL 160*. [7]CGSL 606**. [8]Jn 10:32. [9]Jn 8:46. [10]ECTD 304-5**.

23:33-43 JESUS' CRUCIFIXION

³³*And when they came to the place which is called The Skull, there they crucified him, and the criminals, one on the right and one on the left.* ³⁴*And Jesus said, "Father, forgive them; for they know not what they do."ⁿ And they cast lots to divide his garments.* ³⁵*And the people stood by, watching; but the rulers scoffed at him, saying, "He saved others; let him save himself, if he is the Christ of God, his Chosen One!"* ³⁶*The soldiers also mocked him, coming up and offering him vinegar,* ³⁷*and saying, "If you are the King of the Jews, save yourself!"* ³⁸*There was also an inscription over him,ᵒ "This is the King of the Jews."*

³⁹*One of the criminals who were hanged railed at him, saying, "Are you not the Christ? Save yourself and us!"* ⁴⁰*But the other rebuked him, saying, "Do you not fear God, since you are under the same sentence of condemnation?* ⁴¹*And we indeed justly; for we are receiving the due reward of our deeds; but this man has done nothing wrong."* ⁴²*And he said, "Jesus, remember me when you come intoᵖ your kingdom."* ⁴³*And he said to him, "Truly, I say to you, today you will be with me in Paradise."*

n Other ancient authorities omit the sentence And Jesus . . . what they do   o Other ancient authorities add in letters of Greek and Latin and Hebrew   p Other ancient authorities read in

OVERVIEW: The climax of the passion narrative is Jesus' arrival at the place called the Skull, where in his crucifixion he is reckoned with transgressors, becoming a curse for us (CYRIL OF ALEXANDRIA). The place called the Skull was also the location where Adam was buried (AMBROSE). The mystery of Christ's death consists in how he as the new Adam restores us to paradise and to our original condition (CYRIL OF ALEXANDRIA).

As the people cry out "Crucify him, crucify him," Jesus is praying, "Father, forgive them." Stephen's forgiveness and martyrdom in Acts will show that what Christ was able to do from the cross all Christians are able to do in him. Christ's forgiving words from the cross produce by his Spirit believers on Pentecost. Christians wear this cross on their foreheads to remind them of Christ's forgiving love as he heals them as the great physician (AUGUSTINE). Jesus takes a cross which was devised for punishment and transforms it into a stepping stone to glory by proclaiming from it absolution for all humanity (LEO THE GREAT).

The degradation of Jesus' nakedness is a significant part of the scandal of the cross, and yet it is through his nakedness that he conquers (AMBROSE). At the foot of the cross all of humanity, represented as Adam's race, now lashes out against God's Son with unbelievable malice (JUSTIN MARTYR). The inscription over the cross, though meant to mock his royal and messianic claims, speaks the truth (AMBROSE). One thief denies him; the other wins eternal glory (PRUDENTIUS). He did not save the scoffing thief by taking him down from the cross; he submitted him to the weakness of the cross (EPHREM THE SYRIAN).

The penitent evildoer's confession of sin and of faith shows the proper response to Jesus' absolution (CYRIL OF ALEXANDRIA). The penitent thief is not ashamed of Christ's suffering and does not see it as a stumbling block, and so he makes a confession of faith in the suffering, innocent Messiah. He sees on Christ's body his own wounds, and despite the reality of Christ's suffering and imminent death, he goes on to voice an even stronger confession: "Jesus, remember me when you come into your kingdom" (MAXIMUS OF TURIN).

The dying "King of the Jews" who "saved others" speaks from the cross in the unity of his two natures and says, "Truly to you I say, today with me you will be in paradise" (LEO THE GREAT). The thief will now enter paradise because Christ has opened the gates for him (CHRYSOSTOM). Jesus invites the man to participate in this forgiveness forever, for through Jesus' death he has removed the flaming sword guarding the tree of life and gives us access to paradise (ORIGEN). The road to paradise is now open and humanity is permitted to enter in Christ (PRUDENTIUS). Jesus has restored the Paradise lost by Adam by stretching out his arms on the cross and defeating Satan. From the tree of the cross, Adam hears of his return to Eden (EPHREM THE SYRIAN).

The judgment on Adam for his sin of eating from the tree was swift, and so also is the judgment of paradise swift for this thief who hangs on a tree (CYRIL OF JERUSALEM). Adorned in the robe of Christ, the thief is now welcomed into the garden in Adam's place (EPHREM THE SYRIAN). Jesus is promising to all the saints the paradise promised to the thief (ORIGEN). Jesus' words serve to incorporate the thief into the body of believers in Christ and to invite him to the ongoing feast of heaven, for life is in Christ, and wherever Christ is there is the kingdom (AMBROSE). Paradise is restored by the water and blood that flow from Jesus' side that sprinkle the penitent thief as he is baptized into Christ's death (EPHREM THE SYRIAN).

To be with Christ in paradise "today" is to be with him even when he descends into hell (AUGUSTINE). This inheritance of paradise comes through the crucified flesh of Jesus, who is offered up on the altar of the cross as a sacrifice for sins (LEO THE GREAT). It is the cross that opens the key to paradise (JEROME). For those who confess Jesus as the innocent king, such life in paradise begins now, a great comfort for sinners (EPHREM THE SYRIAN).

23:33 The Crucifixion

RECKONED WITH TRANSGRESSORS. CYRIL OF ALEXANDRIA: When he hung on the precious cross, two thieves were hung with him. What comes from this? It was truly a mockery as far as the plan of the Jews, but it was also the commemoration of prophecy. It is written, "He was also numbered with the transgressors."[1] For our sakes, he became a curse. That is, he became accursed. It is written again, "Cursed is every one that hangs on a tree."[2] His act did away with the curse that was on us. We are blessed with him and because of him. Knowing this, blessed David says, "Blessed are we of the Lord, who made heaven and earth."[3] Blessings descend to us by his sufferings. He paid our debts in our place. He bore our sins. He was stricken in our place,[4] as it is written. He took our sins in his own body on the tree,[5] because it is true that his bruises heal us.[6] He also was sick because of our sins, and we are delivered from the sicknesses of the soul. COMMENTARY ON LUKE, HOMILY 153.[7]

CHRIST'S CROSS PLANTED OVER ADAM'S GRAVE. AMBROSE: The very place of the cross is in the middle,[8] as conspicuous to all. It is above the grave of Adam, as the Hebrews truly argue.[9] It was fitting that the beginning of death occurred where the first fruits of our life were placed. EXPOSITION OF THE GOSPEL OF LUKE 10.114.[10]

THE MYSTERY OF CHRIST'S DEATH. CYRIL OF ALEXANDRIA: By becoming like us and bearing our sufferings for our sakes, Christ restores human nature to how it was in the beginning. The first man was certainly in the Paradise of delight in the beginning. The absence of suffering and of corruption exalted him. He despised the commandment given to him and fell under a curse, condemnation and the snare of death by eating

---

[1]Is 53:12. [2]Deut 21:23. [3]Ps 113:23 LXX. [4]Is 53:6. [5]1 Pet 2:24. [6]Is 53:5. [7]CGSL 609**. [8]See Jn 19:18. [9]Mt 27:33; Mk 15:22; Jn 19:17. [10]EHG 425**.

the fruit of the forbidden tree. By the very same thing, Christ restores him to his original condition. He became the fruit of the tree by enduring the precious cross for our sakes, that he might destroy death, which by means of the tree [of Adam] had invaded the bodies of humankind. COMMENTARY ON LUKE, HOMILY 153.[11]

23:34 Jesus Asks the Father to Absolve the People

THEY CRY, "CRUCIFY HIM!" HE PRAYS, "FATHER, FORGIVE." AUGUSTINE: Look at the Lord who did precisely what he commanded. After so many things the godless Jews committed against him, repaying him evil for good, did he not say as he hung on the cross, "Father, forgive them, because they do not know what they are doing"? He prayed as man, and as God with the Father, he heard the prayer. Even now he prays in us, for us and is prayed to by us. He prays in us as our high priest. He prays for us as our head. He is prayed to by us as our God. When he was praying as he hung on the cross, he could see and foresee. He could see all his enemies. He could foresee that many of them would become his friends. That is why he was interceding for them all. They were raging, but he was praying. They were saying to Pilate "Crucify," but he was crying out, "Father, forgive." He was hanging from the cruel nails, but he did not lose his gentleness. He was asking for pardon for those from whom he was receiving such hideous treatment. SERMON 382.2.[12]

STEPHEN'S FORGIVENESS AND MARTYRDOM AN EXAMPLE TO ALL CHRISTIANS. AUGUSTINE: So, brothers and sisters, let us learn above all from the example of this martyr [Stephen] how to love our enemies. We have just had the example given us of God the Father, who makes his sun rise on the good and the bad. The Son of God also said this after receiving his flesh, through the mouth of the flesh which he received for love of his enemies. After all, he came into the world as a lover of his enemies, he found absolutely all of us his enemies, he didn't find anyone a friend. It was for enemies that he shed his blood, but by his blood that he converted his enemies. With his blood he wiped out his enemies' sins; by wiping out their sins, he made friends out of enemies. One of these friends was Stephen, or rather, is and will be. Yet the Lord himself was the first to show on the cross what his instructions were. With the Jews, you see, howling at him from all sides, furious, mocking, jeering, crucifying him, he could still say, "Father, forgive them, because they do not know what they are doing; after all, it is blindness that is crucifying me." Blindness was crucifying him, and the crucified was making an eye-salve[13] for them from his blood.

But people who are reluctant to carry out the precept, eager to get the reward, who don't love their enemies but do their best to avenge themselves on them, don't pay any attention to the Lord, who would have had nobody left to praise him if he had wanted to avenge himself on his enemies. So when they hear this place in the Gospel, where the Lord says on the cross, "Father, forgive them, because they do not know what they are doing," they say to themselves, *He could do that as the Son of God, as the only Son of the Father.* Yes, it was flesh hanging there, but God was hidden within. As for us, though, what are we to do that sort of thing?

So didn't he really mean it when he gave this order? Perish the thought; he certainly meant it. If you think it is asking too much of you to imitate your Lord, look at Stephen your fellow servant....

So Stephen loved his enemies. I mean, while he stood up to pray for himself, he knelt down for them. Clearly he fulfilled what had been written.[14] He proved to be a true imitator of the

---

[11]CGSL 608**. [12]WSA 3 10:376*. [13]Rev 3:18. [14]It is difficult to see what text of Scripture Augustine had in mind here; probably it was just the Lord's command to love one's enemies. This hadn't, of course, been written and become Scripture when Stephen was martyred.

Lord's passion and a perfect disciple of Christ, completing in his own passion what he had heard from the Master. The Lord, you see, while hanging on the cross had said, "Father, forgive them because they do not know what they are doing." And the blessed Stephen, when he was already almost buried under the stones, spoke like this: "Lord Jesus, do not hold this sin against them."[15] Oh, what an apostolic man, already from being a disciple become a master! It was necessary, after all, for the first martyr of Christ to follow the teaching of the Master. He prays for the godless, he prays for blasphemers, he prays for those who are stoning him. SERMON 317.2-3, 6.[16]

CHRIST'S FORGIVENESS PRODUCES BELIEVERS ON PENTECOST. AUGUSTINE: Let me now tell you something that will help you believe what you cannot possibly understand unless you believe. Tell me, how many souls were there, in the Acts of the Apostles, who believed when they observed the miracles of the apostles? I mean those Jews who had crucified the Lord, who brought along blood stained hands, who had sacrilegious ears, whose tongues were compared with a sword. "Their teeth are weapons and arrows, and their tongue a sharp sword."[17] Christ had not prayed for them in vain. He did not say in vain, "Father, forgive them, because they do not know what they are doing." From their number, a very great many believed. As we can read, "There believed on that day," as it says, "three thousand souls."[18] There you have thousands of souls, and here so many thousand souls. The Holy Spirit came on them, through whom loved is poured out in our hearts. SERMON 229G.5.[19]

CHRIST'S HEALING BLOOD. AUGUSTINE: You are a Christian. You carry the cross of Christ on your forehead.[20] The mark stamped on you teaches you what you should profess. He was hanging on the cross, which you carry on your forehead. Do not delight in the sign of the wood but in the sign of the one hanging on it. When he was hanging on the cross, he was looking around at the people

raving against him, putting up with their insults and praying for his enemies. While they were killing him, the doctor was curing the sick with his blood. He said, "Father, forgive them, because they do not know what they are doing." These words were not futile or without effect. Later, thousands of those people believed in the one they murdered, so that they learned how to suffer for him who had suffered for them and at their hands.

Brothers and sisters, we should understand this from this sign, from this stamp that Christians receive even when they become catechumens. From this, we should understand why we are Christians. SERMON 302.3.[21]

THE MYSTERY OF OUR SALVATION. LEO THE GREAT: The very appearance of the gallows showed the criterion that he would apply when he comes to judge everyone. The believing thief's faith prefigured those who would be saved, while the blasphemer's wickedness foreshadowed those who would be condemned. Christ's passion, therefore, contains the mystery of our salvation. SERMON 55.1.[22]

JESUS CONQUERS THROUGH HIS NAKEDNESS. AMBROSE: It is important to consider what type of man ascends. I see him naked.[23] Let him who prepares to conquer this age ascend in this way so that he does not seek the help of the age. Adam, who desired clothing, was conquered.[24] He who laid down his clothes conquered. He ascended in the same way that nature formed us with God as Creator. In the same way as the first Adam lived in Paradise, the second Adam entered paradise.[25] In order not to conquer for only himself but for all, he held out his hands[26] to draw all things to himself. Having wrenched them from the bonds of death and hung them on the yoke of faith, he

---

[15]Acts 7:60. [16]WSA 3 9:143, 145. [17]Ps 57:4 (56:5 LXX). [18]Acts 2:41. [19]WSA 3 6:292**. [20]Traditionally the celebrant traces the sign of the cross on the catechumen's forehead before baptism. [21]WSA 3 8:302**. [22]FC 93:237*. [23]See Jn 19:23. [24]See Gen 3:7. [25]See 1 Cor 15:47. [26]Is 65:2; Rom 10:21.

joined those of heaven to those who before were of earth.[27] EXPOSITION OF THE GOSPEL OF LUKE 10.110.[28]

23:35-39 The Fourfold Mocking of Jesus

REPROACH AND MALICE. JUSTIN MARTYR: When the Word said, "I am a worm, and no man; the reproach of men, and the outcast of the people,"[29] he foretold what would clearly happen to him. He is everywhere a reproach to us who believe in him, and he is the outcast of the people, for he was thrown out in disgrace by your people, and he endured all the indignities which you directed toward him.... Those who saw him on the cross wagged their heads, curled their lips in scorn, turned up their noses, and sarcastically uttered the words which are recorded in the memoirs of the apostles. "He called himself the Son of God; let him come down from the cross and walk! Let God save him!"[30] DIALOGUE WITH TRYPHO 101.[31]

THE SUPERSCRIPTION SHOWS THE MAJESTY OF A KING. AMBROSE: The superscription is written and placed above, not below the cross, because the government is upon his shoulders.[32] What is this government if not his eternal power and Godhead? When asked, "Who are you?" he replied, "The beginning, who also speaks to you."[33] Let us read this superscription. "Jesus of Nazareth," it says, "The King of the Jews."[34] The superscription is fittingly above the cross because Christ's kingdom does not belong to his human body[35] but to his divine authority. The superscription is fittingly above the cross, because although the Lord Jesus was on the cross, he shines above the cross with the majesty of a king. EXPOSITION OF THE GOSPEL OF LUKE 10.112-13.[36]

23:40-42 The Second Thief Publicly Confesses Jesus

ONE THIEF DENIES CHRIST, THE OTHER WINS ETERNAL GLORY. PRUDENTIUS:

Water and blood flow out from the pierced sides of the Savior.[37]
Blood indicates the victory, and water stands for baptism.
The two robbers on crosses on each side dispute with each other.
One denies Christ is God, but the other wins heavenly glory.
SCENES FROM SACRED HISTORY 42.[38]

THE SCOFFING THIEF IS SUBMITTED TO THE WEAKNESS OF THE CROSS. EPHREM THE SYRIAN: One robber said, "Are you not the Messiah? Save yourself and us with you!" The Lord however did not take him down from the cross as he asked, in order to exalt the other robber on the right of the cross and who was believing in the crucified Savior. It would have been easy for him to use a miracle to conquer anyone as a disciple. He produced a more powerful miracle when he forced the scoffer of truth to adore him. That is why the apostle said, "That which is the weakness of God is stronger than human beings."[39] He submitted all peoples to the weakness of the cross.

Stretch out your arms toward the cross, so that the crucified Lord may stretch out his arms toward you. The one who does not stretch out his hand toward the cross cannot approach his table either. He will deprive of his table the guests who should have come to him hungry but instead came full. Do not fill yourself before going to the table of the Son. He might then make you leave the table while you are still hungry. COMMENTARY ON TATIAN'S DIATESSARON 20.23.[40]

THE CONFESSION OF THE PENITENT THIEF. CYRIL OF ALEXANDRIA: "This man," he says, "has done nothing that is hateful." O how beautiful is this confession! How wise the reasoning and how excellent the thoughts! He became the confessor

---

[27]See 1 Cor 15:48-49. [28]EHG 424**. [29]Ps 22:6. [30]Mt 27:39-43. Justin added "and walk." [31]FC 6:305-6**. [32]Is 9:6. [33]Jn 8:25 Vulgate. [34]Jn 19:19. [35]See Jn 18:36. [36]EHG 424-25**. [37]See Jn 19:34. [38]FC 52:192*. [39]1 Cor 1:25. [40]ECTD 305-6**.

of the Savior's glory and the accuser of the pride of those who crucified him. . . .

Let us look at his most beautiful confession of faith. He says, "Jesus, remember me when you come in your kingdom." You see him crucified and call him a king. You expect the One who bears scorn and suffering to come in godlike glory. You see him surrounded by a Jewish crowd, the wicked gang of the Pharisees, and Pilate's band of soldiers. All of these were mocking him, and no one confessed him. Commentary on Luke, Homily 153.[41]

Why the Penitent Thief Is Worthy of Paradise. Maximus of Turin: The suffering of the cross was a stumbling block to many, as the apostle says. "We preach Christ crucified, a stumbling block indeed to the Jews and foolishness to the Gentiles."[42]

The penitent thief considered the cross of Christ not to be a stumbling block but power rightly merits paradise. The same apostle says, "To those Jews who have been called, Christ the power of God and the wisdom of God."[43] The Lord also correctly gives paradise to him, because on the gibbet of the cross the thief confesses the one whom Judas Iscariot had sold in the garden. This is a remarkable thing. The thief confesses the one whom the disciple denied! This is a remarkable thing, I say. The thief honors the one who suffers, while Judas betrayed the one who kissed him! The one peddled flattering words of peace, and the other preached the wounds of the cross. He says, "Remember me, Lord, when you come in your kingdom." Sermons 74.1-2.[44]

The Thief Recognizes His Wounds on Christ's Body. Maximus of Turin: Although he sees his gaping wounds and observes his blood pouring forth, he believes him to be God whom he does not recognize as guilty. He acknowledges him to be righteous whom he does not think of as a sinner. He says to that other complaining thief, "We certainly are receiving what is due our deeds, but this man has done nothing wrong." He understood that Christ received these blows because of

others' sins. He sustained these wounds because of others' crimes. The thief knew that the wounds on the body of Christ were not Christ's wounds but the thief's; therefore, after he recognized his own wounds on Christ's body, he began to love all the more. Sermon 74.3.[45]

23:43 Jesus Responds by Absolving the Thief

Jesus Speaks in the Unity of His Two Natures. Leo the Great: Until now, one [thief] was the equal in all things of his companion. He was a robber on the roads and always a danger to the safety of people. Deserving the cross, he suddenly becomes a confessor of Christ. . . . "Remember me, Lord, when you enter into your kingdom." . . .

Then came the gift in which faith itself received a response. Jesus said to him, "Truly, I say to you, today you will be with me in paradise." This promise surpasses the human condition, because it did not come so much from the wood of a cross as from a throne of power. From that height, he gives a reward to faith. There he abolishes the debt of human transgression,[46] because the "form of God" did not separate itself from the "form of a servant."[47] Even in the middle of this punishment, both the inviolable divinity and the suffering human nature preserved its own character and its own oneness. Sermon 53.1.2.[48]

Christ Opens Paradise for the Thief. Chrysostom: In the beginning, God shaped man, and man was an image of the Father and the Son. God said, "Let us make man to our image and likeness."[49] Again, when he wished to bring the thief into paradise, he immediately spoke the word and brought him in. Christ did not need to pray to do this, although he had kept all people after Adam from entering there. God put there the flaming sword to guard Paradise.[50] By his au-

---

[41]CGSL 610**. [42]1 Cor 1:23. [43]1 Cor 1:24. [44]ACW 50:181-82**. [45]ACW 50:181-82**. [46]See Col 2:14. [47]Phil 2:6-7. [48]FC 93:230-31**. [49]Gen 1:26. [50]Gen 3:24.

thority, Christ opened paradise and brought in the thief. AGAINST THE ANOMOEANS 9.15.[51]

JESUS REMOVES THE FLAMING SWORD. ORIGEN: "Today you will be with me in paradise." Through saying this, he also gave to all those who believe and confess access to the entrance that Adam previously had closed by sinning. Who else could remove "the flaming turning sword which was placed to guard the tree of life" and the gates of paradise? What other sentinel was able to turn the "cherubim" from their incessant vigil, except only he to whom "was given all power in heaven and in earth"?[52] No one else besides him could do these things. HOMILIES ON LEVITICUS 9.5.[53]

HUMANITY AGAIN PERMITTED TO ENTER PARADISE. PRUDENTIUS:

We believe in thy words, O Redeemer,
Which, when triumphing over death's darkness,
Thou didst speak to thy robber companion,
Bidding him in thy footprints to follow.
Lo, now to the faithful is opened
The bright road to paradise leading;
Man again is permitted to enter
The garden he lost to the Serpent.
To that sacred abode, O great Leader,
Take, we pray thee, the soul of thy servant;
Let it rest in its native country,
Which it left, as an exile to wander.
HYMN FOR EVERY DAY 10.157-68.[54]

STRETCHING OUT HIS ARMS ON THE CROSS.
EPHREM THE SYRIAN: The hands that Adam stretched out toward the tree of knowledge, breaking the commandment, were unworthy of stretching out toward the tree of life to receive the gifts of the God that they had despised. Our Lord took these hands and attached them to the cross, so that they might kill their killer and arrive at his marvelous life. "You will be with me in the garden of delights." "Remember me in your kingdom." Since he had seen with the eyes of faith the dignity of our Lord instead of his shame

and his glory instead of his humiliation, he said, "Remember me. What is apparent now, the nails and the cross, will not make me forget what will be at the consummation and what is not yet visible: your kingdom and your glory." COMMENTARY ON TATIAN'S DIATESSARON 20.24.[55]

ADAM HEARS OF HIS RETURN TO THE GARDEN. EPHREM THE SYRIAN:

Because Adam touched the tree
he had to run to the fig;
he became like the fig tree,
being clothed in its vesture:
Adam, like some tree,
blossomed with leaves.
Then he came to that glorious
tree of the cross,
put on glory from it,
acquired radiance from it,
heard from it the truth
that he would return to Eden once more.
HYMN ON PARADISE 12.10.[56]

A TREE BROUGHT RUIN AND PARADISE. CYRIL OF JERUSALEM: The tree brought ruin to Adam. It will bring you into paradise. Do not fear the Serpent. He will not throw you out, for he has fallen from heaven. I do not say to you, 'This day you will depart,' but 'This day you will be with me.'" Take heart; you will not be thrown out. Do not fear the flaming sword, because it stands in awe of its Lord. CATECHETICAL LECTURES 13.31.[57]

THE THIEF ENTERS THE GARDEN IN ADAM'S PLACE. EPHREM THE SYRIAN:

Adam had been naked and fair,
but his diligent wife
labored and made for him
a garment covered with stains.
The garden, seeing him thus vile,
drove him forth.
Through Mary Adam had

---

[51]FC 72:239**. [52]Mt 28:18. [53]FC 83:185**. [54]FC 43:77. [55]ECTD 306**. [56]HOP 164. [57]FC 64:25**.

another robe
which adorned the thief;
   and when he became resplendent at Christ's
      promise,
the garden, looking on,
   embraced him in Adam's place.
HYMN ON PARADISE 4.5.[58]

PARADISE PROMISED TO ALL THE SAINTS.
ORIGEN: "I will recall you from there in the
end."[59] I think this means that at the end of the
ages his only-begotten Son descended even into
the nether regions,[60] for the salvation of the world
and recalled "the first-formed man"[61] from there.
Understand that what he said to the thief, "This
day you shall be with me in paradise," was not
said to him alone but also to all the saints for
whom he had descended into the nether regions.
In this man more than in Jacob the words will be
fulfilled, "I will recall you from there in the end."
HOMILY ON GENESIS 15.5.[62]

THE PENITENT THIEF IS WITH CHRIST.
AMBROSE: He asked the Lord to remember him
when he came into his kingdom, but the Lord
said, "Truly, truly, I say to you, this day you shall
be with me in paradise." For life is to be with
Christ, because where Christ is, there is the kingdom. EXPOSITION OF THE GOSPEL OF LUKE
10.121.[63]

WATER AND BLOOD OPEN PARADISE. EPHREM
THE SYRIAN: Through the mystery of the water
and blood flowing out from the Lord's side, the
robber received the sprinkling that gave him the
forgiveness of sins. "You will be with me in this
garden of delights." COMMENTARY ON TATIAN'S
DIATESSARON 20.26.[64]

TO BE WITH CHRIST IN PARADISE. AUGUS-
TINE: "Recognize to whom you are commending
yourself. You believe I am going to come, but even
before I come, I am everywhere. That is why, although I am about to descend into hell, I have
you with me in paradise today. You are with me

and not entrusted to someone else. You see, my
humility has come down to mortal human beings
and to the dead, but my divinity has never departed from paradise." SERMON 285.2.[65]

**THROUGH THE ALTAR OF THE CROSS THE
THIEF ENTERS PARADISE.** LEO THE GREAT:
This cross of Christ holds the mystery of its true
and prophesied altar. There, through the saving
victim, a sacrifice of human nature is celebrated.
There the blood of a spotless lamb dissolved the
pact of that ancient transgression. There the
whole perversity of the devil's mastery was abolished, while humility triumphed as conqueror
over boasting pride. The effect of faith was so
swift that one of the two thieves crucified with
Christ who believed in the Son of God entered
paradise justified.

   Who could explain the mystery of such a great
gift? Who could describe the power of such a marvelous transformation? In a brief moment of time,
the guilt of a longstanding wickedness was abolished. In the middle of the harsh torments of a
struggling soul, fastened to the gallows, that thief
passes over to Christ, and the grace of Christ gives
a crown to him, someone who incurred punishment for his own wickedness. SERMON 55.3.[66]

**THE CROSS OF CHRIST IS THE KEY TO PARA-
DISE.** JEROME: That flaming, flashing sword[67]
was keeping Paradise safe. No one could open the
gates that Christ closed. The thief was the first to
enter with Christ. His great faith received the
greatest of rewards. His faith in the kingdom did
not depend on seeing Christ. He did not see him
in his radiant glory or behold him looking down
from heaven. He did not see the angels serving
him. To put it plainly, he certainly did not see
Christ walking about in freedom, but on a gibbet,
drinking vinegar and crowned with thorns. He
saw him fastened to the cross and heard him beg-

---

[58]HOP 99. [59]Gen 46:4 LXX. [60]See Eph 4:9 [61]See Wis 7:1. [62]FC
71:211-12**. [63]EHG 427**. [64]ECTD 307**. [65]WSA 3 8:96** [66]FC
93:239**. [67]See Gen 3:24.

ging for help, "My God, my God, why have you forsaken me?"[68] . . . The cross of Christ is the key to paradise. The cross of Christ opened it. Has he not said to you, "The kingdom of heaven has been enduring violent assault, and the violent have been seizing it by force"?[69] Does not the One on the cross cause the violence? There is nothing between the cross and paradise. The greatest of pains produces the greatest of rewards. ON LAZARUS AND DIVES.[70]

THE COMFORT THE THIEF BRINGS TO SINNERS. EPHREM THE SYRIAN:

There came to my ear

from the Scripture which had been read
a word that caused me joy
on the subject of the thief;
it gave comfort to my soul
amidst the multitude of its vices,
telling how he had compassion on the thief.
O may he bring me too
into that garden at the sound of whose name
I am overwhelmed by joy;
my mind bursts its reins
as it goes forth to contemplate him.
HYMN ON PARADISE 8.1.[71]

---

[68]Ps 22:1 (21:1 LXX). [69]Mt 11:12. [70]FC 57:209-10. [71]HOP 131.

23:44-49 JESUS' DEATH AND THE RESPONSES

[44]*It was now about the sixth hour, and there was darkness over the whole land*[q] *until the ninth hour,* [45]*while the sun's light failed;*[r] *and the curtain of the temple was torn in two.* [46]*Then Jesus, crying with a loud voice, said, "Father, into thy hands I commit my spirit!" And having said this he breathed his last.* [47]*Now when the centurion saw what had taken place, he praised God, and said, "Certainly this man was innocent!"* [48]*And all the multitudes who assembled to see the sight, when they saw what had taken place, returned home beating their breasts.* [49]*And all his acquaintances and the women who had followed him from Galilee stood at a distance and saw these things.*

q Or *earth*   r Or *the sun was eclipsed.* Other ancient authorities read *the sun was darkened*

OVERVIEW: Luke reports an extraordinary, cosmic sign that the creation is anguished: darkness. Creation suffers with Christ in his suffering (EPHREM THE SYRIAN) and mourns for its Lord (CYRIL OF ALEXANDRIA). The darkness that God allowed to usurp authority over the world at Jesus' arrest worked death and chaos, and yet it obscures from everyone the deadly wickedness placed upon Jesus. By the darkness, Christ's enemies can now see him as he truly is: the Son of God (EPHREM THE SYRIAN).

The rending of the curtain between the Holy Place and the Holy of Holies demonstrates the division now between the two peoples—those who are in Christ and those who are not (AMBROSE). For Luke, the darkness in creation and the torn curtain in the temple are signs of judgment against the religious leaders who called for Jesus' death. The Spirit who rends the curtain in the temple comes forth from the temple to open the graves (EPHREM THE SYRIAN).

Jesus cries out with a loud voice, for he is acknowledging with his death the separation of God and humanity. The Synoptic Gospels record that at the moment of death, a Gentile centurion testifies who Jesus is (Ambrose). Jesus by his cross draws this centurion to himself so that a Gentile is the first to declare his innocence after Jesus had breathed his last (Cyril of Alexandria). Jesus' followers witness the crucifixion "at a distance" in order that the Scripture might be fulfilled (Ephrem the Syrian).

23:44-46 Jesus' Death

Creation Suffers with Christ. Ephrem the Syrian: God was victorious over the Egyptians, and he lit up the way for the Hebrews with the pillar of fire in the month of Nisan.[1] The sun became dark over them because they had returned evil for goodness. Just as God split the sea, the Spirit split the curtain in half, since they rejected and unjustly crucified the King of glory on the Skull.[2] The curtain of the temple was torn in two for this reason. Created beings suffered with him in his suffering. The sun hid its face so as not to see him when he was crucified. It retracted its light back into itself to die with him. There was darkness for three hours. The sun shined again, proclaiming that its Lord would rise from Sheol on the third day. The mountains trembled, the tombs were opened, and the curtain was torn,[3] as though grieving in mourning over the impending destruction of the place. Commentary on Tatian's Diatessaron 21.5.[4]

Creation Mourns for Its Lord. Cyril of Alexandria: When they fastened to the cross the Lord of all, the sun over their heads withdrew and the light at midday was wrapped in darkness, as the divine Amos had foretold. "There was darkness from the sixth hour until the ninth hour."[5] This was a plain sign to the Jews that the minds of those who crucified him were wrapped in spiritual darkness, for blindness in part has happened to Israel.[6] In his love for God, David even curses them, saying, "Let their eyes be darkened, that they may not see."[7]

Creation itself mourned its Lord. The sun was darkened, and the rocks were split, and the temple put on the mourners' clothes. Its veil was split from the top to the bottom. This is what God signified to us by the voice of Isaiah, saying, "I clothe the heavens with blackness, and make sackcloth their covering."[8] Commentary on Luke, Homily 153.[9]

Perhaps His Enemies Recognize Him in the Darkness. Ephrem the Syrian: If he had been the son of a foreign god, the sun would not have been eclipsed when the Lord was raised on his cross. The Creator would have spread out a more intense light, because his enemy would have been withdrawn from his sight. He would have caused his light to shine on the Jews, because they would have been doing his will. He would have clothed the temple with a curtain of glory, because its enemy's death would have purified its sad impurities, and the breaker of its law would have gone out from it. Commentary on Tatian's Diatessaron 21.3.[10]

Separation Between the Two Peoples. Ambrose: The veil is torn. This declared the division of the two peoples or the profanation of the mysteries of the synagogue. The old veil is torn,[11] so that the church may hang the new veils of its faith. The veil of the synagogue is taken away, so that we may see the inner mysteries of religion with unveiled eyes of the mind.[12] Even the centurion confesses the Son of God whom he had crucified.[13] Exposition of the Gospel of Luke 10.128.[14]

The Spirit Comes from the Temple. Ephrem the Syrian: Perhaps the Spirit, when he saw the Son hanging naked, lifted himself up[15] and tore in two the clothing. Perhaps the

---

[1]See Ex 13:4, 21-22. [2]I.e., Golgotha; see Mt 27:33. [3]See Mt 27:51-52. The Greek text reads "earth," whereas Ephrem the Syrian has "mountains." [4]ECTD 319-20**. [5]Amos 5:18. [6]Cf. Rom 11:25. [7]Ps 69:23. [8]Is 50:3. [9]CGSL 610-11**. [10]ECTD 318**. [11]Mt 27:51; Mk 15:38. [12]See 2 Cor 3:14. [13]Mt 27:54; Mk 15:39. [14]EHG 430**. [15]From its dwelling in the Holy of Holies.

symbols, when they saw the Lamb of symbols, tore the curtain apart and went out to meet him. Perhaps the spirit of prophecy, which was dwelling in the temple and had come down to herald his coming to humanity, flew away at that very instant to announce in the heights concerning our Lord's ascent into heaven. "The tombs split apart,"[16] so that he might show that he could have torn the wood of the cross apart. He did not tear apart the cross through which the kingdom would be torn from Israel. He did not shatter the cross through which sin would be chased out from the middle of the Gentiles. Instead, the Spirit tore the curtain apart. To show that the Spirit had came out from the temple, it summoned the righteous that came out of the tombs[17] as witnesses to his going out from the temple. These two departures were proclaiming each other mutually. The Spirit anointed and sanctified the kingship and the priesthood. The Spirit, wellspring of these two offices, therefore went out from there, so that it would be known that both of them had been cut off by him who had taken on both of them.

Although we know that by amputation of our finger there is healing for the person who is totally diseased, we still are unwilling to do what we know we should do. God however knew that there would be salvation for humanity through the killing of his Son, and so he did not turn away from doing this. COMMENTARY ON TATIAN'S DIATESSARON 21.6.[18]

SEPARATION OF GODHEAD AND THE FLESH. AMBROSE: "Saying this, he gave up his Spirit." He suitably "gave up" the Spirit, because he willingly gave him up. Matthew says "yielded up his Spirit,"[19] because what is yielded is spontaneous, but what is lost is unavoidable. Since this is true, he added, "with a loud voice."[20] He did this with a glorious declaration that he descended to death for our sins. I do not blush to confess what Christ did not blush to proclaim in a loud voice. This was a clear revelation of God witnessing to the separation of the Godhead and the flesh. EXPOSI-

TION OF THE GOSPEL OF LUKE 10.127.[21]

23:47 The Centurion Declares Jesus' Innocence

A GENTILE STRANGER RECOGNIZES JESUS' INNOCENCE. AMBROSE: The person who crucified the author of his salvation and afterward did not beg for forgiveness is not free from sin. Granted, he did not know previously whom he was persecuting. Nevertheless he should have recognized that the one placed on the cross was the Lord of all the elements. All the elements trembled beneath him. The sky was darkened. The sun fled away. The earth split apart. The tombs of the dead lay open, and the dead regained the company of the living. For this reason also the centurion said, "Truly this man was the Son of God." The centurion recognizes a stranger, but the Levite does not know his own. The Gentile worships him, but the Hebrew denies him. It was reasonable that the pillars of the world moved when the chief priests did not believe.[22] THE PRAYER OF JOB AND DAVID 1.5.13.[23]

JESUS DRAWS THE CENTURION TO HIMSELF. CYRIL OF ALEXANDRIA: When the centurion saw what happened, he glorified God. He said, "Truly this man was righteous." Please observe that immediately after Christ endured the passion on the cross for us, he began to win many to the knowledge of the truth. It says, "When he saw what happened, the centurion glorified God saying, 'Truly this man was righteous.'" Certain Jews also beat their chests, because their consciences doubtlessly pricked them. Their mind's eye looked up to the Lord. Perhaps they tried to clear themselves of their impious conduct against Christ by shouting against those who crucified him, although they dared not do this openly because of their rulers' impiety. Our Lord spoke the truth, saying, "When I have been

---

[16]Mt 27:51. [17]Mt 27:52-53. [18]ECTD 320**. [19]Mt 27:50. [20]Mt 27:50. [21]EHG 429**. [22]See Mt 26:60-68. [23]FC 65:336**.

lifted up from the earth, I will draw all men to myself."[24] COMMENTARY ON LUKE, HOMILY 153.[25]

JESUS' RELATIVES STAND AT A DISTANCE IN FULFILLMENT OF SCRIPTURE. EPHREM THE SYRIAN: Jesus' kinsfolk stood far off so that [the word of the psalmist] might be fulfilled: "My neighbors stood far off."[26] They killed him before the sabbath, while there was opportunity for death, and before the sabbath they buried him, while there was place for mourning. For the sabbath itself is the boundary mark for toil, and on it all distress must remain [hidden] within. There is no place for suffering on it, and neither has it any share in corruption. COMMENTARY ON TATIAN'S DIATESSARON 21.8.[27]

---

[24]Jn 7:32. [25]CGSL 611**. [26]Ps 38:11 (37:12 LXX). [27]ECTD 321.

23:50-56 JESUS' BURIAL

[50]*Now there was a man named Joseph from the Jewish town of Arimathea. He was a member of the council, a good and righteous man, [51]who had not consented to their purpose and deed, and he was looking for the kingdom of God. [52]This man went to Pilate and asked for the body of Jesus. [53]Then he took it down and wrapped it in a linen shroud, and laid him in a rock-hewn tomb, where no one had ever yet been laid. [54]It was the day of Preparation, and the sabbath was beginning.[s] [55]The women who had come with him from Galilee followed, and saw the tomb, and how his body was laid; [56]then they returned, and prepared spices and ointments.*

On the sabbath they rested according to the commandment.

s Greek *was dawning*

OVERVIEW: Joseph is a Jew from Arimathea and a council member, part of the Sanhedrin, which rejected Jesus. At Jesus' birth in a cave and his death in a tomb, a just man named Joseph oversees that his body is carefully attended to (EPHREM THE SYRIAN). Jesus will take his sabbath rest in the tomb, for the tree of life must be planted in a tomb in fulfillment of Scriptures. On the third day, he shall bring the reign of his kingdom to all creation when he rises from the dead (CYRIL OF JERUSALEM).

Joseph takes Jesus' body down from the cross and wraps it in linen, linking Jesus' birth and death, since at birth Jesus was wrapped in cloth bands. Joseph places Jesus in a rock-hewn tomb where no one else had lain, for just as Jesus died a death that was not his own, so he is laid in a borrowed tomb (MAXIMUS OF TURIN). The clean linen cloths and the tomb where no one had ever been laid show that his death and burial are as pure as the circumstances surrounding his birth (ORIGEN). Although humiliated during his journey to the cross and shamed by the crucifixion, Jesus' body is given the high honor of being laid in a new tomb, just as his body was carefully contained in the virginal womb of Mary (MAXIMUS OF TURIN).

The final preparations are by women who will be the last to the leave the tomb, the first to return to it, and the first eyewitnesses of the resurrection (AMBROSE). They return to their homes for their sabbath rest to observe the Old Testament stipulations and to prepare spices and myrrh for a dead body that they plan to anoint when the sabbath has ended, because they thought he was going to remain in the grave (CYRIL OF ALEXANDRIA).

23:50-53 Joseph of Arimathea Prepares Jesus' Body

A RIGHTEOUS JOSEPH CARES FOR HIS BODY.
EPHREM THE SYRIAN: Mary stands for Eve, and Joseph stands for another Joseph. He who asked for his corpse[1] was also named Joseph. The earlier Joseph was a righteous man who did not denounce Mary publicly.[2] The other one was also a righteous man because he did not consent to the detractors. So that it might be clear that the Lord was entrusted at the beginning to one having this name when he was born, he further allowed one with this name to prepare him for burial when he was dead. This name receives the full reward for serving him at his birth in the cave and for having served his corpse at the tomb. COMMENTARY ON TATIAN'S DIATESSARON 21.20.[3]

THE TREE OF LIFE PLANTED IN THE TOMB.
CYRIL OF JERUSALEM: We seek to know exactly where he was buried. Was his tomb made with hands? Does it rise above the ground, like the tombs of kings? Was the sepulcher made of stones joined together? What is laid upon it? O prophets, tell us exactly about his tomb. Where is it? Where should we look for it? They answer, "Look at the solid rock that you have hewn."[4] Look and see. You have in the Gospels, "In a rock-hewn tomb." What is next? What kind of door does the sepulcher have? Again, the prophet says, "They have ended my life in the pit, and they have laid a stone over me."[5] I am "the chief cornerstone, chosen, precious."[6] He that is "a stone of stumbling"[7] to the Jews but of salvation to those that believe was for a while within a stone. The tree of life was planted in the earth, to bring blessing for the earth that was cursed and to bring release for the dead. CATECHETICAL LECTURES 13.35.[8]

WRAPPED IN SWADDLING CLOTHES BY MARY, IN LINEN CLOTHS BY JOSEPH. MAXIMUS OF TURIN: Someone might say of last Sunday's sermon, in which we preached that there was no less glory in Joseph's grave receiving the Lord than in holy Mary's womb begetting him, "What comparison can there be between the womb and the grave, since the one brought forth a son from its innermost bowels while the other only gave him a place of burial?" But I say that Joseph's love was no less than Mary's, since she conceived the Lord in her womb and he did so in his heart. She offered the secret place of her inmost members to the Savior; he did not deny him the secret place for his own body. She wrapped the Lord in swaddling clothes when he was born; he wrapped him in linen cloths when he died. She anointed his blessed body with oil; he honored it with spices. Each one's service is similar and each one's love is similar; hence each one's reward must also be similar. But there is this difference: an angel called Mary to her service, but righteousness alone persuaded Joseph. SERMON 39.1.[9]

JESUS BURIED IN A BORROWED TOMB. MAXIMUS OF TURIN: Let us see why they placed the Savior in someone else's grave instead of his own. They placed him in another person's grave because he died for the salvation of others. They did not impose death on him. He endured death for us. Death did not just happen to him, but it benefited us. Why should he, who did not have his own death in himself, have his own grave? Why should he, whose dwelling remained in heaven, have a burial place on earth? Why should he have a grave? For only three days, he did not so much lie as one dead in a tomb as rest as one sleeping in a bed. The brief period of time itself certainly indicates sleep rather than death. A tomb is the

---

[1]Mt 27:58. [2]Mt 1:19. [3]ECTD 326-27**. [4]Is 51:1. [5]Lam 3:53 LXX. [6]1 Pet 2:6; cf. Is 28:16. [7]1 Pet 2:8. [8]FC 64:27-28**. [9]ACW 50:94.

dwelling of death. Christ who is life did not need a dwelling for death, nor did he who is always living require a habitation of the deceased. We have correctly laid up this life in our own tomb so that as he gives life to our death, we may rise with him from the dead. SERMON 39.3.[10]

THE PURITY OF JESUS' BIRTH AND HIS DEATH. ORIGEN: When it will be our professed purpose to treat such things, we will explain at greater length on a more suitable occasion the matters of his burial, tomb and the man who buried him. For now, it is sufficient to notice the clean linen in which the pure body of Jesus was wrapped and the new tomb that Joseph had hewn out of the rock, where "no one was yet lying." . . . It suited him, who was unlike other dead people but who even in death revealed signs of life in the water and the blood. He was, so to speak, a new dead man, laid in a new and clean tomb. His birth was purer than all the others, since he was not born in the ordinary way but of a virgin. At his burial, the new tomb where they deposited his body also symbolically indicated his purity. It was not built from stones gathered from various quarters not having natural unity. It was quarried and hewed out of one rock, united together in all its parts. AGAINST CELSUS 2.69.[11]

THE WOMB AND TOMB THAT HELD THE BODY OF JESUS. MAXIMUS OF TURIN: Let us see, then, what happens to the Lord's body after they take it down from the cross. Joseph of Arimathea, a righteous man, as the Evangelist says, took it and buried it in his new tomb in which no one had ever been laid. Blessed is the body of the Lord Christ, which in birth comes forth from a virgin's womb and in death is placed in the grave of a righteous man! Clearly this body is blessed. Virginity brought it out, and righteousness held it! Joseph's grave held him incorrupt, just as Mary's womb preserved him inviolate. In the one, a man's impurity does not touch him; in the other, death's corruption does not hurt him. In every way, holiness and virginity are bestowed on that blessed body.

A new womb conceived him, and a new grave enclosed him. The womb is the Lord's womb. It is virginal. The tomb is virginal. Should I not rather say that the tomb itself is a womb? There is, in fact, a great similarity. Just as the Lord came out from his mother's womb living, so also he rose living from Joseph's tomb. Just as he was born from the womb in order to preach, so also now he has been reborn from the tomb in order to evangelize. The last birth is more glorious than the first. The first conceived a mortal body, but the last brought out an immortal one. After the first birth, he descends to hell, but after the last birth, he returns to the heavens. The last birth is more religious than the first. The first kept the Lord of the whole world locked in the womb for nine months, but the last held him in the belly of the grave for only three days. The first offered hope to all rather slowly, but the last raised salvation for all quite quickly. SERMON 78.2.[12]

23:54-56 The Preparations of the Women

THE WOMEN ARE THE LAST TO LEAVE AND THE FIRST TO RETURN. AMBROSE: Not everyone can bury Christ. Although the pious women stand far away[13] because they are pious, they watch the place closely to bring ointments and anoint him. The anxious women are the last to leave the tomb and the first to return to it. Although stability is lacking, diligence is not. Women hesitate, and devotion cools. They are present at the time of the resurrection, and when the men were chased away, an angel commanded only the women not to be afraid.[14] First in zeal, they summon Peter,[15] but they are behind him in confidence. Then he arrives without fear, and he who had come later is the first calmly to enter[16] as he who had received the keys of the kingdom,[17] in order to open for others. The resurrection is an earthquake for the faithful, because the sluggish body awakes itself from the sleep of death.[18] It is a

---

[10]ACW 50:95**. [11]ANCL 23:72-73**. [12]ACW 50:190**. [13]Mt 27:55. [14]Mt 28:1-8. [15]Jn 20:2. [16]Jn 20:6. [17]Mt 16:19. [18]Mt 28:2.

cause of dread for the ignorant, because, disturbed by the trembling of the body and the movement of the earth, the ignorant depart from faith and belief in the resurrection. EXPOSITION OF THE GOSPEL OF LUKE 10.144-46.[19]

THE WOMEN COME TO ANOINT HIS BODY.

CYRIL OF ALEXANDRIA: Wise women followed our common Savior Christ, gathering whatever

was both useful and necessary for faith in him. When he gave his flesh as a ransom for the life of us all, they wisely committed themselves to care for his body. They supposed that the corpse would continue to remain in the grave. COMMENTARY ON LUKE, HOMILY 153.[20]

---

[19]EHG 436**. [20]CGSL 611*.

24:1-12 THE SUNDAY ANNOUNCEMENT TO THE WOMEN

[1]But on the first day of the week, at early dawn, they went to the tomb, taking the spices which they had prepared. [2]And they found the stone rolled away from the tomb, [3]but when they went in they did not find the body.[t] [4]While they were perplexed about this, behold, two men stood by them in dazzling apparel; [5]and as they were frightened and bowed their faces to the ground, the men said to them, "Why do you seek the living among the dead?[u] [6]Remember how he told you, while he was still in Galilee, [7]that the Son of man must be delivered into the hands of sinful men, and be crucified, and on the third day rise." [8]And they remembered his words, [9]and returning from the tomb they told all this to the eleven and to all the rest. [10]Now it was Mary Magdalene and Joanna and Mary the mother of James and the other women with them who told this to the apostles; [11]but these words seemed to them an idle tale, and they did not believe them.[v]

t Other ancient authorities add of the Lord Jesus u Other ancient authorities add He is not here, but has risen v Other ancient authorities add verse 12, But Peter rose and ran to the tomb; stooping and looking in, he saw the linen cloths by themselves; and he went home wondering at what had happened

---

OVERVIEW: The day of the resurrection is the eschatological, eighth day, which ushers in the new creation represented by the new week, for the shameful embarrassment of Jesus' crucifixion and the horror of his death are now surmounted as light banishes darkness at the dawn of this new day, the first day of the new era of salvation (AUGUSTINE). Having kept the sabbath according to the commandment, the women come to the tomb to anoint Jesus' body because they think Jesus is dead. To find the tomb empty may appear to find nothing, but in finding nothing, the women will

make the greatest find: the discovery that Jesus is risen and will now be present in the sacraments (BEDE).

Since angels appeared at his birth, so also they now appear at his resurrection. Jesus is not in the tomb because he is life. They are not to seek death among the One who ever lives (CYRIL OF ALEXANDRIA). The angels' announcement about the passion and resurrection of Jesus mentally transports the hearer back to Jesus' many predictions of his passion and resurrection during his ministry which were not understood (CHRYSOStom). By incorporating allusions to the other passion statements into the story of the empty tomb, the angels affirm that the sufferings and resurrection of Jesus are part of the divine plan as foretold by the ancient Scriptures and by Jesus himself (Bede).

Just as the fall of humankind came through a woman, so now the restoration is first proclaimed by women. News of Jesus' resurrection seems like nonsense in light of the horror of his death by crucifixion (Augustine). The doubts of the disciples with their anxiety and fear form the foundations of faith when the Spirit reveals the truth of the resurrection (Leo the Great). After the women's report, dismissed by the apostles as idle talk, Peter, rising up, runs to the tomb and finds only the linen cloths, for Jesus leaves his clothes behind so that Adam could enter paradise again in the state he left it—naked (Ephrem the Syrian).

24:1-8 The Angels' Announcement to the Women

Sunday, the Day of Resurrection, the First and Eighth Day. Augustine: The Lord's day is called the first of the sabbath.[1] But the first day itself falls away when the second follows it. That day, which both the eighth and the first, represents eternity. It is that day which we abandoned at the beginning by sinning in our first parents and so came down into this mortal state, and also the last and, as it were, the eighth day, to which we again look ahead after the resurrection, once our last enemy death has been destroyed.[2] Only then will this perishable thing put on imperishability and this mortal thing put on immortality.[3] The returning son [prodigal] will receive the first robe, which is to be given back to him on the last and, so to say, eighth day, after the labors of his distant exile and his feeding of pigs, and the other miseries of mortal life, and the sevenfold circulation of the wheel of time.

So it was perfectly reasonable that it should have been on the first, which is also the eighth

day—Sunday—that our Lord chose to give us an example in his own flesh of bodily resurrection. "Christ being raised from the dead will never die again; death no longer has dominion over him."[4] To this exalted state of his we must go with humility. Sermon 260c.5.[5]

The Women Come to Anoint His Dead Body. Bede: According to the Gospel reading, holy women came to see the sepulcher "after the sabbath, toward the dawn of the first day of the week." This is how we should understand this: they started to come during the evening but reached the sepulcher as the morning of Sunday was dawning; that is, they prepared the spices with which they desired to anoint our Lord's body on [Saturday] evening but brought the spices which they had prepared in the evening to the sepulcher in the morning. Matthew, for the sake of brevity, wrote this more obscurely, but the other Evangelists[6] show more distinctly the order in which it was done. After our Lord had been buried on Friday, the women went away from the tomb and prepared spices and ointments for as long as they were allowed to work. Then they refrained from any activity on the sabbath, in accord with the commandment,[7] as Luke clearly reports. When the sabbath was over, as evening was coming on, one could work again. Being unwavering in their devotion, they bought the spices which they had not prepared [earlier] (as Mark records it)[8] so that they might come and anoint him. Homilies on the Gospels 11.7.[9]

The Empty Tomb Shows Jesus Is Now Present in the Sacraments. Bede: Mystically, the rolling away of the stone implies the disclosure[10] of the divine sacraments, which were formerly hidden and closed up by the letter of the law. The law was written on stone.[11] Indeed, in

---

[1]Mt 28:1; Mk 16:2. [2]1 Cor 15:26. [3]1 Cor 15:53. [4]Rom 6:9. [5]WSA 3 7:197 **. [6]Mk16:1-2. [7]Ex 12:16; 20:8-10. [8]Mk 16:1-2. [9]CS 111 2:59-60**. [10]Disclosure: *revolutio*, a metaphorical meaning of the word translated "rolling away" earlier in the sentence. [11]Ex 24:12; 32:15; 34:1.

the case of each of us, when we acknowledge our faith in the Lord's passion and resurrection, his tomb, which had been closed, is opened up. We enter the tomb but do not find the body of the Lord, when in our hearts we carefully think back over the order [of events] of his incarnation and his passion and recall that he has risen from the dead and is no longer to be seen in his mortal flesh. But the Jew and the pagan, who ridicule the death of our Redeemer which they believe in but refuse to believe further in the triumph of his resurrection, continue to be like a tomb still closed by a stone. They are not capable of entering to see that the body of the Lord has disappeared by his rising, because by the hardness of their infidelity they are prevented from becoming aware that a dead person, who has destroyed death's right of entry and has already passed into the heights of the heavens, cannot be found on earth. HOMILIES ON THE GOSPELS II.10.[12]

ANGELS APPEAR AT HIS BIRTH AND RESURRECTION. CYRIL OF ALEXANDRIA: Angels also brought the joyful tidings of the nativity to the shepherds in Bethlehem. Now they tell of his resurrection. Heaven yields its service to proclaim him, and the hosts of the spirits which are above attend the Son as God, even though he is in the flesh. COMMENTARY ON LUKE, CHAPTER 24.[13]

JESUS IS NOT IN THE TOMB BECAUSE HE IS LIFE. CYRIL OF ALEXANDRIA: The women came to the sepulcher, and when they could not find the body of Christ—for he had risen—they were quite perplexed. And what followed? For the sake of their love and zeal for Christ, they were counted worthy of seeing holy angels who then told them the joyful news as the heralds of the resurrection, saying, "Why do you seek the living among the dead? He is not here, but is risen!" The Word of God ever lives and by his own nature is life. Yet, when he humbled and emptied himself, submitting to be made like us, he tasted death. But this proved to be the death of death, for he rose from the dead to be the way by which not so

much he himself but rather we could return to incorruption. Let no one seek among the dead him who ever lives. But if he is not here, with mortality and in the tomb, where then is he? Obviously, in heaven and in godlike glory. COMMENTARY ON LUKE, CHAPTER 24.[14]

PREDICTIONS OF CHRIST'S PASSION AND RESURRECTION WERE NOT UNDERSTOOD. CHRYSOSTOM: Do you see that they clearly understood nothing about the resurrection? The Evangelist pointed out this very thing when he said, "As yet they did not know the Scripture, that he must rise from the dead."[15] In addition to their failure to understand this, they were in much deeper ignorance about other things, such as the kingdom of heaven, that we are chosen as the first fruits, and his ascension into heaven.[16] They were still confined to the ground and not yet able to fly.

Such was the understanding they had. They expected that the kingdom would come to him immediately in Jerusalem because they had no better grasp of what the kingdom of heaven really is. Another Evangelist hinted at this when he said that they thought of it as a human kingdom. They were expecting him to enter into it but not to go to the cross and death. Even though they had heard it ten thousand times, they could not clearly understand. AGAINST THE ANOMOEANS 8.29-30.[17]

THE ANGELS RETELL THE DIVINE PLAN OF GOD. BEDE: God's Son saw fit to become Son of man to make those of us who believe in him sons of God. He was delivered into the hands of sinful human beings to separate us from the company of sinful human beings and at the same time to free us from the power of malignant spirits. He was crucified and rose on the third day, so that he might grant us the virtue of suffering for him and the hope of rising and living with him. HOMILIES ON THE GOSPELS II.10.[18]

---

[12]CS 111:90-91. [13]CGSL 615*. [14]CGSL 615**. [15]See Jn 20.9 and NAB note *ad loc.* [16]See 2 Thess 2:13. [17]FC 72:224-25. [18]CS 111:93.

24:9-11 *The Women's Report to the Apostles*

HUMANITY'S FALL THROUGH A WOMAN NOW RESTORED THROUGH WOMEN. AUGUSTINE: The women came to the tomb, but they didn't find the body in the tomb. Instead, they were told by angels that Christ had risen. The women reported this to men. And what's written? What did you hear? These things seemed in their eyes like an idle tale. How very unhappy is the human condition! When Eve related what the serpent had said, she was listened to straightaway. A lying woman was believed, and so we all died. But [the disciples] didn't believe women telling the truth so that we might live. If women are not to be trusted, why did Adam trust Eve? If women are to be trusted, why did the disciples not trust the holy women?

So in this fact we have to reflect on the goodness of the Lord's arrangements, because this, of course, was the doing of the Lord Jesus Christ that it should be the female sex which would be the first to report that he had risen again. Humanity fell through the female sex; humankind was restored through the female sex. A virgin gave birth to Christ; a woman proclaimed that he had risen again. Through a woman death, through a woman life. But the disciples didn't believe what the women had said. They thought they were raving, when in fact they were reporting the truth. SERMON 232.2.[19]

RESURRECTION NEWS SEEMS LIKE NONSENSE. AUGUSTINE: This hope, this gift, this promise, this tremendous grace—when Christ died his disciples lost it from their spirits, and on his death they fell away from hope. Here we see them receiving the news of his resurrection, and the words of the messengers seemed to them like an idle tale. Truth became like an idle tale. If ever the resurrection is proclaimed nowadays, and someone thinks it's an idle tale, doesn't everybody say he's all twisted up? Doesn't everybody loathe and detest what he says, turn away, close their ears and refuse to listen? That's what the disciples were when Christ died. What we abhor is what they were. The leading rams had the disease which the lambs shudder at. SERMON 236.2.[20]

IN THE DOUBTS OF THE DISCIPLES IS BORN THE FOUNDATION OF OUR FAITH. LEO THE GREAT: The Spirit of truth would by no means have permitted this hesitation, wavering in human weakness, to enter the hearts of his preachers, if their trembling anxiety and questioning delay were not to have established the foundations of our faith. Consequently it was our doubts and our danger that was being considered in the apostles. We, in the guise of the apostles, were being instructed against the slanders of the wicked and the proofs of earthly wisdom. Their "seeing" instructed us, their "hearing" informed us, their "touching" strengthened us.[21] Let us give thanks for the divine plan and the necessary "slowness" of the holy fathers.[22] They "doubted" so that we need not doubt. SERMON 73.1.2.444.[23]

24:12 *Peter Marvels at the Empty Tomb*

JESUS LEAVES HIS CLOTHES BEHIND. EPHREM THE SYRIAN: If he left his clothes behind in the tomb, it was so that Adam could enter into paradise without clothing, just as he had been before he had sinned.[24] In place of having to leave paradise clothed, he now had to strip himself before entering there [again]. Or [alternatively], he abandoned them to symbolize the mystery of the resurrection of the dead, for just as [the Lord] rose into glory without clothes, so we also [will rise] with our works and not with our clothes. COMMENTARY ON TATIAN'S DIATESSARON 21.23.[25]

---

[19]*WSA* 3 7:24-25*. [20]*WSA* 3 7:44*. [21]See 1 Jn 1:1-3. [22]Lk 24:25. [23]FC 93.323*. [24]See Gen 2:25. [25]ECTD 328

24:13-27 THE ROAD TO EMMAUS

^{13}*That very day two of them were going to a village named Emmaus, about seven miles^w from Jerusalem, ^{14}and talking with each other about all these things that had happened. ^{15}While they were talking and discussing together, Jesus himself drew near and went with them. ^{16}But their eyes were kept from recognizing him. ^{17}And he said to them, "What is this conversation which you are holding with each other as you walk?" And they stood still, looking sad. ^{18}Then one of them, named Cleopas, answered him, "Are you the only visitor to Jerusalem who does not know the things that have happened there in these days?" ^{19}And he said to them, "What things?" And they said to him, "Concerning Jesus of Nazareth, who was a prophet mighty in deed and word before God and all the people, ^{20}and how our chief priests and rulers delivered him up to be condemned to death, and crucified him. ^{21}But we had hoped that he was the one to redeem Israel. Yes, and besides all this, it is now the third day since this happened. ^{22}Moreover, some women of our company amazed us. They were at the tomb early in the morning ^{23}and did not find his body; and they came back saying that they had even seen a vision of angels, who said that he was alive. ^{24}Some of those who were with us went to the tomb, and found it just as the women had said; but him they did not see." ^{25}And he said to them, "O foolish men, and slow of heart to believe all that the prophets have spoken! ^{26}Was it not necessary that the Christ should suffer these things and enter into his glory?" ^{27}And beginning with Moses and all the prophets, he interpreted to them in all the scriptures the things concerning himself.*

w Greek *sixty stadia*; some ancient authorities read *a hundred and sixty stadia*

OVERVIEW: The two Emmaus disciples are not among the Eleven but could well be from among the seventy (CYRIL OF ALEXANDRIA). Jesus' identity is hidden from the Emmaus disciples, as the light of his star appeared upon humanity at his birth and then was hidden at his death (EPHREM THE SYRIAN). Their recognition of him is deferred until there is time for more catechesis on the road. The eyes of the Emmaus disciples are held from recognizing Jesus because he is now to be recognized in the breaking of the bread (AUGUSTINE).

Jesus enters their conversation in order to hear from them what they think about his death. But it is precisely these facts that caused the Emmaus disciples to stand there in sorrow, for they were scandalized by the crucifixion, even though Jesus had predicted he would die (AUGUSTINE). The

assumption of the early church's tradition, mentioned by Hegesippus (cited by EUSEBIUS), is that Cleopas is Clopas, brother of Joseph, making Cleopas the uncle of Jesus, and that the unnamed Emmaus disciple is Cleopas's son Simeon, later the second bishop of Jerusalem, the leader of the Jerusalem church after 70. Tradition reports that Simeon died a martyr's death (EUSEBIUS).

The Emmaus disciples respond with their interpretation of the events of Jesus' life, confessing to Jesus their despair and their doubts, showing that like Moses they do not fully understand God's ways. The Emmaus disciples who are scandalized by the cross need to become like the penitent thief, who through the cross saw that he might enter into the kingdom (AUGUSTINE).

Jesus must open the Scriptures for the Emmaus disciples to show them that unless he suffered and died, he could not be the Messiah (Augustine). The kerygmatic passion and resurrection formulae are supported by the scriptural foundation given by the risen Lord as he interprets for the Emmaus disciples what has remain hidden to them (Cyril of Alexandria). The implication is that the very fabric of the entire Old Testament is christological, for every thread and theme leads to and centers in the crucified and risen Christ (Augustine).

24:13-16 Conversing on the Road to Emmaus

Emmaus Disciples Come from the Seventy. Cyril of Alexandria: As two of the disciples walked to a village called Emmaus, they talked about Christ, regarding him as no longer living but mourning him as dead. As they conversed, Jesus drew near and went with them, without being recognized by them, for their eyes were restrained, so that they should not know him. You must know that these two disciples belonged to the number of the seventy, and that Cleopas's companion was Simon—not Peter or the one of Cana—but another Simon, of the seventy. Commentary on Luke, Chapter 24.[1]

Jesus' Identity Hidden. Ephrem the Syrian: At his radiant birth therefore a radiant star appeared, and at his dark death there appeared a dark gloom.[2] . . . The Lord of the star appeared in his own person to the two who were traveling with him along the road, but his identity was hidden from them. His star too was like this, for its light appeared to all humanity while its pathway was hidden from all humanity. Commentary on Tatian's Diatessaron 2.24.[3]

Recognition Is Deferred Until They Receive More Catechesis. Augustine: Here we are with two others, walking along the road and talking to each other about the things that had been happening in Jerusalem—about the iniquity of the Jews, about the death of

Christ. They were walking along, talking the matter over, grieving for him as if he were dead, not knowing he had risen again. He appeared and joined them as a third traveler, and entered into friendly conversation with them. Their eyes were held from recognizing him; their hearts, you see, needed more thorough instruction. Recognition is deferred. Sermon 232.3.[4]

Jesus Is to Be Recognized in the Breaking of the Bread. Augustine: "We," they said, "had hoped that he was the one to redeem Israel." O my dear disciples, you had hoped! So now you no longer hope? Look, Christ is alive! Is hope dead in you? Certainly, certainly, Christ is alive! Christ, being alive, found the hearts of his disciples dead, as he appeared and did not appear to their eyes. He was at one and the same time seen and concealed. I mean, if he wasn't seen, how could they have heard him questioning them and answered his questions? He was walking with them along the road like a companion and was himself the leader. Of course he was seen, but he wasn't recognized. For their eyes were restrained, as we heard, so that they wouldn't recognize him. They weren't restrained so that they wouldn't see him, but they were held so that they wouldn't recognize him.

Ah yes, brothers and sisters, but where did the Lord wish to be recognized? In the breaking of bread. We're all right, nothing to worry about—we break bread, and we recognize the Lord. It was for our sake that he didn't want to be recognized anywhere but there, because we weren't going to see him in the flesh, and yet we were going to eat his flesh. So if you're a believer, any of you, if you're not called a Christian for nothing, if you don't come to church pointlessly, if you listen to the Word of God in fear and hope, you may take comfort in the breaking of bread. The Lord's absence is not an absence. Have faith, and the one you cannot see is with you. Those two, even when the Lord was talking to them, did not have

---

[1]CGSL 616**. [2]See Mt 27:45. [3]ECTD 72. [4]WSA 3 7:25.

faith, because they didn't believe he had risen. Nor did they have any hope that he could rise again. They had lost faith, lost hope. They were walking along, dead, with Christ alive. They were walking along, dead, with life itself. Life was walking along with them, but in their hearts life had not yet been restored. SERMON 235.2-3.[5]

24:17-18 The Setting for the Catechesis on the Road

THE EMMAUS DISCIPLES SCANDALIZED BY THE CROSS. AUGUSTINE: You heard just now that the Lord Jesus, after rising from the dead, found two of his disciples on the road, talking to each other about all that had happened, and said to them, "What is this conversation you are having with each other, and why are you so sad?" . . .

So what is the benefit of this reading for us? A very considerable one, if we understand it rightly. Jesus appeared. They saw him with their eyes and did not recognize him. The Master was walking with them along the way, and he himself was the way. But they weren't yet walking along the way. He found, you see, that they had wandered off the way. After all, when he had been with them before the passion, he had foretold everything: that he was going to suffer, to die and to rise again on the third day. He had foretold it all, but his death had erased it from their memories. They were so shattered when they saw him hanging on the tree that they forgot about his teaching. They did not expect him to rise, nor did they hold on to what he had promised. SERMON 235.1-2.[6]

THE MARTYRDOM OF SIMON. EUSEBIUS: After Nero and Domitian . . . persecution was raised against us sporadically among the cities as a result of insurrection among the people. In this persecution we have learned that Simon [Symeon], the son of Clopas, whom we have shown to have been the second bishop of the church at Jerusalem, gave up his life by martyrdom. The witness of this is Hegisippus, whom we have already quoted. When relating about certain heretics, he

goes on to show that Symeon was accused by them at this time and was tortured in many ways for a great many days because he was clearly a Christian. He astonished to the highest degree both the judge himself and those with him, and won for himself an end similar to the passion of the Lord. ECCLESIASTICAL HISTORY 3.32.[7]

24:19-24 The Christology of the Emmaus Disciples

THE DOUBTS OF MOSES AND THE DOUBTS OF THE EMMAUS DISCIPLES. AUGUSTINE: So then, what kind of consideration does the doubting of Moses demand of us? . . . Moses doubted when the wood came into contact with the rock.[8] . . .

The disciples doubted when they saw the Lord crucified. He came to them after his resurrection, as they were talking to each other about this matter in a sad conversation. He kept their eyes from recognizing him, not in order to remove himself from believers but to put them off while they were still doubters. He joined in their conversation as a third party and asked them what they were talking about. They were astonished that he should be the only person not to know what had happened—to the very man, in fact, who was asking about it. "Are you," they said, "the only stranger in Jerusalem?" And they went over all that had happened to Jesus. Straightaway they proceeded to open up all the depth of their despair and, although unwittingly, they showed the doctor their wounds: "We had hoped that he was the one to redeem Israel." The doubt arose because wood had come into contact with the rock. What Moses figuratively stood for was fulfilled.[9] SERMON 352.4.[10]

---

[5]WSA 3 7:41**. [6]WSA 3 7:40-41**. [7]FC 19:190-91. [8]See Ex 15:23-25. [9]Augustine interprets the doubt of the Emmaus disciples through juxtaposition of Exodus 15:23-25 and 1 Corinthians 10:4. The rock symbolizes Christ, while the wood prefigures the cross, and therefore contact of the wood and the rock signifies crucifixion. The doubt of Moses, which Augustine reads in Exodus 15:24-25, precedes the miracle of turning water from bitter to sweet. Similarly the grief and doubts of the disciples upon crucifixion of the Lord inaugurate the joy of his resurrection. [10]WSA 3 10:142*.

Emmaus Disciples Need to Become Like the Penitent Thief.

Augustine: Recognition, though, happened only when Jesus opened up the Scriptures for them, because they had given up hope and said, "But we had hoped that he was the one to redeem Israel." O my dear disciples, you had hoped, now you don't hope? Come here, robber, give the disciples a lesson. Why have you given up hope, just because you have seen him crucified, because you've looked at him hanging there, because you have thought him weak? He was like that for the robber too, hanging on the cross beside him. The robber was sharing in his punishment but he believed straightaway and acknowledged him, while you on the other hand have forgotten he is the author of life.[11] Cry out, robber, from the cross! You, a criminal, win over the saints! What did they say? "We had hoped that he was the one to redeem Israel." What did this man say? "Jesus, remember me, when you come in your kingdom."[12] So you had hoped, had you, that it was he who would redeem Israel? O my dear disciples, if he was the one that was going to redeem Israel, it means you have defected. But he has reinstated you; he didn't abandon you. By becoming your companion on the way, he himself became for you the way. Sermon 236a.4.[13]

24:25-27 The Kerygma of the Catechetical Lectures

Christ Opens Scripture to Show Them the Christ Must Die.

Augustine: So he began to expound the Scriptures to them to help them recognize Christ precisely in the point on which they had forsaken Christ. The reason, you see, that they had despaired of Christ was that they had seen him dead. He, however, opened the Scriptures to them, so that they would realize that if he hadn't died, he couldn't be the Christ. He taught them from Moses, he taught them from the following Scriptures, he taught them from the prophets what he himself had told them: that it was necessary that the Christ

should suffer these things and enter into his glory. They listened, they were filled with joy, they breathed again, and, as they said themselves, their hearts burned within them. And still they didn't recognize the presence of the light. Sermon 236.2.[14]

Jesus Interprets the Old Testament.

Cyril of Alexandria: In this discourse the Lord shows that the law was necessary to make ready the way and the ministry of the prophets to prepare people for faith in this marvelous act, so that when the resurrection really took place, those who were troubled at its greatness might remember what was said of old and be induced to believe. He brings forward, therefore, Moses and the prophets, interpreting their hidden meaning and making plain to the worthy what to the unworthy was obscure. In this way he settles in them the ancient and hereditary faith taught them by the sacred books which they possessed. For nothing which comes from God is without its use, but all have their appointed place and service. In their due place servants were sent to make ready for the presence of the Master. They brought in beforehand prophecy as the necessary preparative for faith, so that, like some royal treasure, what had been foretold might in due season be brought forward from the concealment of its former obscurity, unveiled and made plain by the clearness of the interpretation. Commentary on Luke, Chapter 24.[15]

Everything in Scripture Speaks of Christ.

Augustine: All that we read in holy Scripture for our instruction and salvation demands an attentive ear. You have just heard how the eyes of those two disciples whom the Lord joined on their way were kept from recognizing him.[16] He found them in despair of the redemption that was in Christ, supposing him now to

---

[11]Acts 3:15. [12]Lk 23:42. [13]WSA 3 7:49**. [14]WSA 3 7:45. [15]CGSL 617*. [16]In one of the special lessons for Eastertide to which Augustine refers in the Prologue: Luke 24:13-35.

have suffered and died as a man, not imagining him to live forever as the Son of God. So he opened to them the Scriptures and showed them that it was necessary for the Christ to suffer and for all things to be fulfilled that were written concerning him in the law of Moses and the prophets and the psalms—in short, the whole of the Old

Testament. Everything in those Scriptures speaks of Christ, but only to him who has ears. He opened their minds to understand the Scriptures. And so let us pray that he will open our own. HOMILY 2.1 ON 1 JOHN.[17]

[17]LCC 8:270*.

24:28-35 RECOGNITION OF CHRIST IN THE BREAKING OF BREAD

[28]*So they drew near to the village to which they were going. He appeared to be going further, [29]but they constrained him, saying, "Stay with us, for it is toward evening and the day is now far spent." So he went in to stay with them. [30]When he was at table with them, he took the bread and blessed, and broke it, and gave it to them. [31]And their eyes were opened and they recognized him; and he vanished out of their sight. [32]They said to each other, "Did not our hearts burn within us[c] while he talked to us on the road, while he opened to us the scriptures?" [33]And they rose that same hour and returned to Jerusalem; and they found the eleven gathered together and those who were with them, [34]who said, "The Lord has risen indeed, and has appeared to Simon!" [35]Then they told what had happened on the road, and how he was known to them in the breaking of the bread.*

c Other ancient authorities omit *within us*

OVERVIEW: Only after hearing the Word of the Old Testament opened up to them does he then open their eyes to see that he is the crucified and risen Lord. Broken bread is the key to open eyes (EPHREM THE SYRIAN). The Emmaus meal is pivotal because it continues Jesus' preresurrection table fellowship and begins the church's table fellowship in celebration of Easter through the sacrament. Jesus continues to reveal himself in the breaking of the bread that has received his blessing (AUGUSTINE).

Jesus disappears from them, for from now on he will be possessed by faith in word and meal. Jesus continues to be recognized today in the breaking of the bread (AUGUSTINE). They experience burning hearts from the teaching of Jesus through the

action of the Holy Spirit (ORIGEN). The wings of fire that create the burning hearts in the disciples are the flames of the divine Scripture as they were interpreted by Jesus (AMBROSE). The Lamb who has opened Scriptures for the Emmaus disciples is the cause of their burning hearts (ORIGEN). Faith goes on to create the fire of charity that now reigns in their hearts (AUGUSTINE). It is unclear whether these disciples meet with the eleven disciples to relate what had happened at the end of this day of resurrection or on the fortieth day when Jesus was taken up (CYRIL OF ALEXANDRIA).

24:28-30 The Breaking of Bread at Emmaus

BROKEN BREAD THE KEY TO OPEN EYES.

EPHREM THE SYRIAN:
Even when the army
    surrounded Elisha
a voice proved the key
    to the eyes of the shepherd.[1]
When the disciples' eyes
    were held closed,
bread too was the key
    whereby their eyes were opened
to recognize the omniscient:
    saddened eyes beheld
a vision of joy
    and were instantly filled with happiness.
HYMNS ON PARADISE 15.4.[2]

**THE BREAKING OF THE BREAD IS THE SACRA-
MENT.** AUGUSTINE: And no one should doubt
that his being recognized in the breaking of bread
is the sacrament, which brings us together in recognizing him. LETTER 149.[3]

**JESUS REVEALS HIMSELF IN THE BREAKING
OF THE BREAD.** AUGUSTINE: Remember,
though, dearly beloved, how the Lord Jesus desired to be recognized in the breaking of bread, by
those whose eyes had been kept till then from
recognizing him. The faithful know what I'm
talking about. They know Christ in the breaking
of bread. It isn't every loaf of bread, you see, but
the one that receives Christ's blessing and becomes the body of Christ. That's where they recognized him. They were overjoyed and went
straight to the others. They found whom they already knew. By telling what they had seen, they
added to the gospel. It was all said, all done, all
written down. And it has reached us. SERMON
234.2.[4]

24:31-34 The Recognition and Return to Jerusalem

JESUS DISAPPEARED. AUGUSTINE: The Lord
Jesus was made known, and after being made
known he appeared no more. He withdrew from
them in the body, since he was held by them in

faith. That indeed is why the Lord absented himself in the body from the whole church, and ascended into heaven, for the building up of faith.
SERMON 235.4.[5]

**CHRIST CONTINUES TO BE RECOGNIZED IN
THE BREAKING OF THE BREAD.** AUGUSTINE:
He blessed the bread, broke it, and they recognized him. That's how you recognize Christ—
those of you who believe he is the Christ. But
your graces should consider what all the disciples
were like before the Lord's resurrection. I beg
their pardon for saying so, but they weren't yet
believers. They became great believers later on,
but before that they were even inferior to us. We,
I mean to say, believe that Christ has risen again,
which they didn't yet believe. But afterward they
saw, they touched, they went over him with eyes
and hands, and in that way they believed, and
their hearts were given strength from the holy
Scriptures. So they drank, they burst forth, and
they filled us up too. SERMON 236A.2.[6]

**THE HOLY SPIRIT CAUSES THE HEARTS TO
BURN.** ORIGEN: Do you want me to show you
how the fire goes out from the words of the Holy
Spirit and ignites the fire the hearts of believers?
. . . And again in the Gospel it was written, after
the Lord spoke to Cleopas, "Did not our hearts
burn within us while he talked to us on the road,
while he opened to us the Scriptures?" Where
will your burning come from? What "coals of fire"
will be found in you who are never set on fire by
the declaration of the Lord, never inflamed by the
words of the Holy Spirit? Hear also in another
place David himself saying, "My heart became hot
within me. As I mused, the fire burned."[7] HOMI-
LIES ON LEVITICUS 9.9.7.[8]

THE FLAMES OF DIVINE SCRIPTURE.
AMBROSE: Good then is love, having wings of
burning fire, that flies through the breasts and

---

[1]2 Kings 6:7. [2]HOP 183. [3]FC 20:264. [4]WSA 3 7:37*. [5]WSA 3 7:42.
[6]WSA 3 7:47-48*. [7]Ps 39:3. [8]FC 83:198.

hearts of the saints and consumes whatever is material and earthly but tests whatever is pure and with its fire makes better whatever it has touched. This fire the Lord Jesus sent upon earth.[9] Faith shone bright, devotion was enkindled, love was illuminated, and justice was resplendent. With this fire he inflamed the heart of his apostles, as Cleopas bears witness, saying, "Did not our hearts burn within us while he talked to us on the road, while he opened to us the Scriptures?" Therefore the wings of fire are the flames of the divine Scripture. ISAAC, OR THE SOUL 8.77.[10]

THE LAMB KINDLES THE HEARTS OF THE DISCIPLES.

ORIGEN: This shows that we must not only employ zeal to learn the sacred literature but also pray to the Lord and entreat "day and night"[11] that the lamb "of the tribe of Judah" may come and, himself taking "the sealed book," may deign to open it.[12] For it is he who "opening the Scriptures" kindles the hearts of the disciples so that they say, "Did not our hearts burn within us while he opened to us the scriptures?" HOMILIES ON EXODUS 12.4.[13]

BURNING HEARTS FROM THE FIRE OF CHARITY.

AUGUSTINE: Just as we are distinguished from others by faith, so let us also be distinguished by morals and by works. Let us be on fire with charity, which the demons never had. It is the fire those two also were burning with on the road. When Christ, you see, had been recognized and had left them, they said to each other, "Did not our hearts burn within us while he talked to us on the road, while he opened to us the Scrip-

tures?" Burn then, in order not to burn with the fire the demons are going to burn with.

Be on fire with the fervor of charity, in order to differentiate yourselves from demons. This fervor whirls you upward, takes you upward, lifts you up to heaven. Whatever vexations you suffer on earth, however much the enemy may humiliate Christian hearts and press them downward, the fervor of love seeks the heights. SERMON 234.3.[14]

24:34-35 The Faithful Response

THE EMMAUS DISCIPLES CONSULT WITH THE ELEVEN.

CYRIL OF ALEXANDRIA: Cleopas, it says, and his companions rose up that same hour, the same of course in which Jesus had vanished out of their sight, and returned to Jerusalem. But it does not say that they found the Eleven gathered together that same hour and told them what had happened concerning Jesus. This took place on the fortieth day after his resurrection—the day on which he was also taken up. The Evangelist therefore has omitted the events which took place in the intervening time. It was then that Cleopas and his companion found the Eleven discussing in private and saying that the Lord was risen and had been seen by Simon. Regarding this appearance, there is no mention where or when or how this took place. It was during these days that the events in Galilee also took place, which Matthew has recorded.[15] COMMENTARY ON LUKE, CHAPTER 24.[16]

---

[9]Lk 12:49. [10]FC 65:60-61. [11]Ps 1:2; Josh 1:8. [12]See Rev. 5:5. [13]FC 71:372*. [14]WSA 3 7:39*. [15]See Mt 28:16-20. [16]CGSL 617-18**.

24:36-43 THE RISEN LORD EATS
WITH HIS DISCIPLES

[36]As they were saying this, Jesus himself stood among them.[x] [37]But they were startled and frightened, and supposed that they saw a spirit. [38]And he said to them, "Why are you troubled, and why do questionings rise in your hearts? [39]See my hands and my feet, that it is I myself; handle me, and see; for a spirit has not flesh and bones as you see that I have."[y] [41]And while they still disbelieved for joy, and wondered, he said to them, "Have you anything here to eat?" [42]They gave him a piece of broiled fish, [43]and he took it and ate before them.

x Other ancient authorities add *and said to them, "Peace to you!"*   **y** Other ancient authorities add verse 40, *And when he had said this, he showed them his hands and his feet*

OVERVIEW: Jesus stands in the midst of his disciples to be present for them and to strengthen their faith. The greeting of "peace" has an extensive Old Testament background and rich overtones elsewhere in Luke, beginning with Jesus' birth, for he is the Prince of Peace (BEDE). In terror and fear, however, the disciples think that they are seeing a ghost who has passed through the walls and the closed door (AMBROSE). The certainty of faith that despises even death is now attained in Jesus' appearances to his disciples after he rose from the dead (IGNATIUS OF ANTIOCH).

The human nature of Jesus is not capable of corruption, although his hands and feet were pierced with nails (CYRIL OF ALEXANDRIA). The divine and human natures of Jesus are without division, so Jesus the Son of God is Word and flesh (LEO THE GREAT). The very wounds that Jesus shows his disciples are the wounds he will show the Father in heaven as trophies of our salvation (AMBROSE).

While rejoicing and doubting at the same time, Jesus eats the grilled fish that represents the faith of the martyrs that have gone through the fiery trials of suffering (AUGUSTINE). He puts aside all passions, for he does not need food but only uses it show that he has risen in his body (JOHN OF DAMASCUS). Thus Jesus eats before them to confirm their faith and to show that he is alive and that the body that appears before them is just like their body, with flesh and bones (CYRIL OF ALEXANDRIA).

24:36-43 Table Fellowship

CHRIST IS PRESENT TO STRENGTHEN FAITH.
BEDE: First, we must note and diligently remember that the Lord condescended to stand in the middle of his disciples who were speaking around him and to reveal his presence in a vision of himself. This is what he promised elsewhere to all the faithful, saying, "Where there are two or three gathered together in my name, there am I in their midst."[1] In order to strengthen the steadfastness of our faith, which the presence of the divine benevolence always brings, he wished sometimes to show this by the presence of a physical vision of himself. Although we are lying far below the apostles' feet, in our case we must trust that this same thing happens to us by his mercy. He is in our midst as often as we come together and gather in his name. His name is Jesus, that is, "Savior."[2] When we come together to speak about receiving our eternal salvation, it is undoubtedly true that we are gathered in the name of Jesus. It is not permissible to doubt that he is present among us as we are talking about the things that

---

[1]Mt 18:20.   [2]Cf. Jer 14:8.

he himself loves. The more truly he is present, the better we retain in a more perfect heart what we profess with our mouth. HOMILIES ON THE GOSPELS 11.9.[3]

JESUS BRINGS PEACE FROM HIS BIRTH TO HIS DEATH. BEDE: We must also see that when the Savior appeared to his disciples, he immediately imposed on them the joys of peace. He repeated that same thing that is a part of the celebrated glory of immortality that he gave as a special pledge of salvation and life when he was about to go to his passion and death. "Peace I leave to you. My peace I give you."[4] The angels seen soon after he was born also proclaimed the grace of this favor to the shepherds, praising God and saying, "Glory to God in the highest, and on earth peace to men of good will." Certainly the entire divinely arranged plan of our Redeemer's coming in the flesh is the reconciliation of the world. For this purpose, he became incarnate, suffered and was raised from the dead. He did this to lead us, who had incurred God's anger by sinning, back to God's peace by his act of reconciliation. The prophet correctly gave him the names "Father of the world to come" and "Prince of Peace."[5] The apostle also wrote about him to those from among the nations who had believed. He said, "Coming, he brought the good news of peace to you who were from far off and peace to those who were near, since through him we both have access in one Spirit to the Father."[6] HOMILIES ON THE GOSPELS 2.9.[7]

THE DISCIPLES ARE TROUBLED. AMBROSE: Persuaded by so many examples of virtue, we believe that Peter could not have doubted. It is also clear that John believed when he saw the Savior.[8] He had already believed when he saw the tomb empty of its body.[9] Why then does Luke say that they were troubled? First, the saying of a majority includes the opinion of the few. Second, although Peter had believed the resurrection, he could be troubled when he saw that the Lord appeared unexpectedly in his body in a room where the doors

were bolted and the walls solid.[10] Luke pursued details historically. One contemplated the end, and the other the course of events. By saying, "Then he opened their understanding, that they might understand the Scriptures," he also declares that the disciples believed. EXPOSITION OF THE GOSPEL OF LUKE 10.179.[11]

THE DISCIPLES DESPISED DEATH. IGNATIUS OF ANTIOCH: I myself am convinced and believe that he was in the flesh even after the resurrection. When he came to Peter and his friends, he said to them, "Take hold of me. Touch me, and see that I am not a bodiless ghost." They immediately touched him. They were convinced, clutching his body and his very breath. For this reason, they despised death itself and proved its victors. After the resurrection, he also ate and drank with them as a real human being, although in spirit he was united with the Father. LETTER TO THE SMYRNAEANS 3.1-2.[12]

JESUS SHOWS THEM HIS WOUNDS. CYRIL OF ALEXANDRIA: To convince them firmly and absolutely that he is the same one who suffered, he immediately shows that being God by nature, he knows what is hidden. The tumultuous thoughts within them do not escape him. He said, "Why are you troubled?" This is a very clear proof that the one they see before them is not some other person. He is the same one whom they saw suffering death upon the cross and laid in the tomb, even the one who sees mind and heart and from whom nothing that is in us is hid. He gives this to them as a sign: his knowledge of the tumult of thoughts that was within them. In another way, he proves that death is conquered and that human nature has put off corruption in him. He shows his hands, his feet and the holes of the nails. He permits them to touch him and in every way convince themselves that the very body that

---

[3]CS 111:79-80*. [4]Jn 14:27. [5]Is 9:6. [6]Eph 2:17-18. [7]CS 111:80*. [8]See Jn 21:7. [9]See Jn 20:8. [10]See Jn 20:19. [11]EHG 449**. [12]LCC 1:113*.

suffered was risen. Let no one quibble at the resurrection. Although you hear the sacred Scripture say that the human body is sown a physical body but raised a spiritual body,[13] do not deny the return of human bodies to incorruption. Commentary on Luke, Chapter 24.[14]

Jesus' Divine and Human Natures Are Without Division.

Leo the Great: The resurrection of the Lord was truly the resurrection of a real body, because no other person was raised than he who had been crucified and died. What else was accomplished during that interval of forty days than to make our faith entire and clear of all darkness? For a while, he spoke with his disciples and remained with them, ate with them and allowed himself to be felt with careful and inquisitive touch by those who were under the influence of doubt. This was his purpose in going in to them when the doors were shut. He gave them the Holy Ghost by his breath. After giving them the light of intelligence, he opened the secrets of holy Scripture. In his same person, he showed them the wound in the side, the prints of the nails and all the fresh tokens of the passion. He said, "See my hands and feet. It is I myself. Handle me and see. A spirit does not have flesh and bones, as you see that I have." He did all this so that we might acknowledge that the properties of the divine and the human nature remain in him without causing a division. We now may know that the Word is not what the flesh is. We may now confess that the one Son of God is Word and flesh. Tome 5.[15]

Jesus Shows the Disciples the Wounds He Will Show the Father.

Ambrose: Then, the disciples being troubled, thought they saw a spirit. To show us the appearance of the resurrection, the Lord said, "Touch, and see, for a spirit does not have flesh and bones, as you see me to have." He actually penetrated the closed and inaccessible room through the likeness of a bodily resurrection and not through a spiritual nature. They touch and handle a body, so we rise in the body. It is sown a natural body, but it rises a spiritual body.[16] The one is fine; the other is crude, since it is still hard with the nature of earthly stains. Did not the Lord offer them to touch a body that retained the signs of the wounds and the marks of the scars?[17] He not only strengthens faith but also kindles devotion, because he set his wounds accepted for our sake and refused to remove them, to show God the Father the costs of our freedom. The Father seats such a One at his right hand,[18] embracing the trophies of our salvation. Exposition of the Gospel of Luke 10.169-70.[19]

The Grilled Fish Represents the Faith of the Martyrs.

Augustine: While they were still flustered for joy, they were rejoicing and doubting at the same time. They were seeing and touching, and scarcely believing. What a tremendous favor grace has done us! We have neither seen nor touched, and we have believed. While they were still flustered for joy, he said, "Have you got here anything to eat? Certainly you can believe that I am alive and well if I join you in a meal." They offered him what they had: a portion of grilled fish. Grilled fish means martyrdom, faith proved by fire. Why is it only a portion? Paul says, "If I deliver my body to be burned, but have not love, I gain nothing."[20] Imagine a complete body of martyrs. Some suffer because of love, while others suffer out of pride. Remove the pride portion, offer the love portion. That is the food for Christ. Give Christ his portion. Christ loves the martyrs who suffered out of love. Sermon 229J.3.[21]

Jesus Puts Aside All Passions.

John of Damascus: After his resurrection from the dead, he put aside all his passions: ruin, hunger and thirst, sleep and fatigue, and the like. Although he did taste food after his resurrection, it was not

---

[13]1 Cor 15:44. [14]CGSL 618-19**. [15]LCC 3:367**. [16]1 Cor 15:44. [17]Jn 20:27. [18]See Eph 1:20. [19]EHG 444-45**. [20]1 Cor 13:3. [21]WSA 3 6:305-6**.

in obedience to any law of nature. He did not feel hunger, but at the appointed time, he confirmed the truth of the resurrection by showing that the flesh which had suffered and that which had risen were the same. ORTHODOX FAITH 4.1.[22]

JESUS EATS ROASTED FISH TO CONFIRM THEIR FAITH. CYRIL OF ALEXANDRIA: To produce in them a more firmly settled faith in his resurrection, he asked for something to eat. They brought a piece of broiled fish, which he took and ate in the presence of them all. He did this only to show them that the one risen from the dead was the same one who ate and drank with them during the whole previous period of time when he talked with them as a man, according to the prophet's voice.[23] He intended them to perceive that the human body certainly does need sustenance of this kind but a spirit does not. . . . The power of Christ surpasses human inquiry. It is not on the level of the understanding of ordinary events. He ate a piece of fish because of the resurrection. The natural consequences of eating by no means followed in the case of Christ, as the unbeliever might object, knowing that whatsoever enters the mouth must necessarily come out into the drain.[24] The believer will not admit these quibbles into his mind but leaves the matter to the power of God. COMMENTARY ON LUKE, CHAPTER 24.[25]

---

[22]FC 37:335*. [23]Bar 3:37. [24]Mt 15:17. [25]CGSL 619**.

24:44-49 THE FINAL TEACHING

[44]Then he said to them, "These are my words which I spoke to you, while I was still with you, that everything written about me in the law of Moses and the prophets and the psalms must be fulfilled." [45]Then he opened their minds to understand the scriptures, [46]and said to them, "Thus it is written, that the Christ should suffer and on the third day rise from the dead, [47]and that repentance and forgiveness of sins should be preached in his name to all nations,[z] beginning from Jerusalem. [48]You are witnesses of these things. [49]And behold, I send the promise of my Father upon you; but stay in the city, until you are clothed with power from on high."

z Or nations. Beginning from Jerusalem you are witnesses

OVERVIEW: The risen Lord asks his disciples to recall his teaching as he opens their minds to understand the Scriptures. This also encourages the hearer of the Gospel to look back into the narrative to see how Jesus had predicted his passion and to recall the Old Testament prophecies (CYRIL OF ALEXANDRIA). The faith of all the elect is the same, including the saints of the Old Testament who prophesied the Messiah's death and resurrection (BEDE). After Jesus' final passion and resurrection statement, he is talking about the church that is to be when he commands them to preach repentance and forgiveness of sins (AUGUSTINE). He must rise from the dead to show us the future that awaits us; he must also give us even now the forgiveness of sins in the administration of the sacraments (BEDE).

The proclamation of the gospel to all nations starts at Pentecost when the promise of the Father pours down upon the disciples and they are able to preach in the languages of many nations (AUGUSTINE). The church starts in Jerusalem but goes out to all the world (Bede). Jesus gives them his Spirit so that the baptism they received from John may reach its fulfillment (Cyril of Alexandria). The Spirit of Christ is the means by which the incarnate Christ's presence will attend the disciples and bestow all the gifts made possible by Christ's incarnation, suffering, death and bodily resurrection in the power of the new creation to preach the good news, heal the sick, cast out demons and raise the dead (Bede). The disciples will bear witness to the true presence of Jesus in their midst, and until they receive the power of the Spirit they are not to preach (Augustine).

24:44-49 Preaching Christ's Death and Resurrection

Jesus Recalls His Predictions and the Old Testament Prophecies. Cyril of Alexandria: When he restrained their thoughts by what he said, by the touch of their hands and by sharing food, he then opened their minds to understand that he had to suffer, even on the wood of the cross. The Lord reminds the disciples of what he said. He had forewarned them of his sufferings on the cross, according to what the prophets had long before spoken. He also opens the eyes of their hearts for them to understand the ancient prophecies. Commentary on Luke, Chapter 24.[1]

The Faith of All the Elect Is the Same. Bede: When he was about to ascend into heaven, our Lord first took care to instruct his disciples diligently concerning the mystery of faith in him. They might therefore preach it with greater certainty to the world, because they had received it from the mouth of Truth himself and recognized that the words of the prophets had long ago foreshadowed it. He appeared to them after the triumph of his resurrection, according to what we heard just now when the Gospel was read. He said, "These are the words which I spoke to you when I was still with you." That means, "When I still had a corruptible and mortal body like

yours." "Everything written about me in the law of Moses and the prophets and the psalms must be fulfilled." He said that he fulfilled the mysteries which Moses, the prophets and the psalms proclaimed. It is perfectly evident that the church is one in all its saints and that the faith of all the chosen is the same, of those who preceded and who followed his coming in the flesh. We are saved through faith in his incarnation, passion and resurrection that have been accomplished. Homilies on the Gospels 11.15.[2]

Christ Talks About the Church. Augustine: What did he tell them from the Scriptures? He said, "Repentance and forgiveness of sins should be preached in his name to all nations, beginning from Jerusalem." The disciples could not see this. They could see Christ talking about the church that would be. When Christ said something they could not see, they believed him. They could see the head, but they could not yet see the body. We can see the body, but we believe about the head. They are two: husband and wife, head and body, Christ and the church. He showed himself to the disciples and promised them the church. He showed us the church and ordered us to believe about himself. The apostles saw one thing, but they did not see the other. We also see one thing and do not see the other. Having the head there with them, they believed about the body. Having the body here with us, we should believe about the head. Sermon 229I.1.[3]

The Necessary Sequence. Bede: The disciples learned that their Maker subjected himself to countless kinds of abuses at the hands of the wicked and even to the sentence of death for their salvation. This effectively stirred them up to tolerate adversities of every kind for their salvation. They remembered that through his sacraments they had been cleansed, sanctified and united to the body of him who, when he had tasted death for them, presented an example of a speedy rising

---

[1]*CGSL* 620*. [2]*CS* 111:135**. [3]*WSA* 3 6:301**.

from death. For what other reason might they more fittingly receive the hope of their own resurrection?

"It was necessary for the Christ to suffer and rise from the dead on the third day," he said, "and for you to preach repentance and forgiveness of sins in his name among all nations." There was certainly a necessary sequence. First, Christ had to shed his blood for the redemption of the world. Then, through his resurrection and ascension, he opened to human beings the gate of the heavenly kingdom. Last, he sent those who would preach to all nations throughout the world the word of life and administer the sacraments of faith. By these sacraments, they could be saved and arrive at the joys of the heavenly fatherland, with the human being Jesus Christ. He is the very mediator between God and human beings[4] working with them. He lives and reigns forever and ever. Amen. HOMILIES ON THE GOSPELS II.9.[5]

PROCLAMATION BEGINS AT PENTECOST.

AUGUSTINE: The Lord did not only shed his blood, but he also applied his death to the preparation of the cure. He rose again to present us with a sample of resurrection. He suffered with patience all his own to teach us the patience we should have. In his resurrection, he showed us the reward of patience. As you know and we all confess, he ascended into heaven, and then he sent the Holy Spirit as he had previously promised. You remember that he said to his disciples, "Stay in the city until you are clothed with power from on high." His promise came true. The Holy Spirit came, he filled the disciples, and they started speaking with the tongues of all nations. A sign of unity was enacted in them. One person spoke then in all languages, because the unity of the church was going to speak in all languages. SERMON 175.3.[6]

PREACHING OF REPENTANCE AND FORGIVENESS BEGINS IN JERUSALEM.

BEDE: The preaching of repentance and the forgiveness of sins through confession of Christ's name appropriately started from Jerusalem. The first root of faith in him would be brought out where the splendor of his teaching and virtues, the triumph of his passion, the joy of his resurrection and ascension were accomplished. The first shoot of the blooming church, like some kind of great vine, would be planted. By an increase in the spreading of the Word, the church would extend the branches of its teaching into the whole wide world. The prophecy of Isaiah would be brought to fulfillment. He said, "The law will go forth from Zion and the word of the Lord from Jerusalem, and he will judge the nations and convict many peoples."[7] It was appropriate that the preaching of repentance and the forgiveness of sins, good news to be proclaimed to idolatrous nations and those defiled by various evil deeds, should start from Jerusalem. Perhaps some of the nations, thoroughly terrified by the magnitude of Jerusalem's offenses, might doubt the possibility of obtaining pardon if it performed fruits worthy of repentance.[8] He granted pardon even to those at Jerusalem who had blasphemed and crucified the Son of God. HOMILIES ON THE GOSPELS II.15.[9]

JESUS GIVES THEM THE HOLY SPIRIT.

CYRIL OF ALEXANDRIA: The Savior promises the disciples the descent of the Holy Spirit, which God announced of old by Joel.[10] He also promises power from above, so that they might be strong, invincible and fearlessly preach the divine mystery to people everywhere.

He says to them that they received the Spirit after the resurrection, "Receive the Holy Spirit."[11] He adds, "Wait for the promise of the Father, which you heard from me, for John baptized with water, but before many days you shall be baptized with the Holy Spirit."[12] It will not be in water any longer, because they already had received that, but it will be with the Holy Spirit. He does not add water to water but completes that which was

---

[4]1 Tim 2:5. [5]CS 111:86-87**. [6]WSA 3 5:266-67**. [7]Is 2:3-4. [8]Mt 3:8; Lk 3:8. [9]CS 111:137-38**. [10]Joel 2:28. [11]Jn 20:22. [12]Acts 1:4-5.

deficient by adding what it lacked. Commentary on Luke, Chapter 24.[13]

The Holy Spirit Will Give Them Power.

Bede: He said, "You are witnesses of these things. And I send upon you the promise of my Father." He calls the gift of the Holy Spirit "the promise of his Father." ... He added something about their promised waiting when he said, "Stay in the city until you are clothed with power from on high." He pledged that power would come down upon them from on high, because although they already possessed the Holy Spirit, they received him more fully once Christ ascended into heaven. Even before his passion, by the power of the Holy Spirit they were casting out many demons, healing many sick persons and preaching the word of life to whom they could.[14] Once he had risen from the dead, they were especially refreshed by the grace of the same Spirit. John writes, "Receive the Holy Spirit. If you forgive the sins of any, they are forgiven; if you retain the sins of any, they are retained."[15] He clothed them with his greater virtue from on high when they received him in fiery tongues ten days after the Lord's ascension.[16] They were inflamed with such great assurance of strength that any threats from the rulers could not prevent them from speaking to everyone in the name of Jesus.[17] Homilies on the Gospels 11.15.[18]

Clothed with Power from On High.

Augustine: There is still more for you to hear. He ascends into heaven, accompanied by the eyes of the disciples gazing after him. He lets them observe it, and he makes them witnesses. . . . They certainly saw, touched and felt him. They confirmed their faith by looking at him and touching him. They accompanied him with their gaze as he ascended into heaven. With attentive ears, they heard the angel's voice assuring them and foretelling that Christ would come again.

All these things were completed for them. Neither sight alone nor handling of the Lord's limbs was still enough to ensure that they would become witnesses of Christ and bravely endure everything for the preaching of the truth, fighting against falsehood even to the shedding of their blood. Who gave them such a capability? Listen to the Lord himself. "Stay in the city until you are clothed with power from on high." "You have seen and touched, but you are still not able to preach and die for what you have seen and touched, until you are clothed with power from on high. Let human beings go now and attribute it to their own powers, if they can do anything. There was Peter, and he had not yet been confirmed in the rock. He had not yet been clothed with power from on high, because "nobody can receive anything, unless it has been given him from heaven."[19] Sermon 265D.6.[20]

---

[13]CGSL 620**. [14]Mt 10:1; Mk 3:7, 15; Lk 9:1-2, 6. [15]Jn 20:22-23. [16]Acts 2:2-3. [17]Acts 4:18-21. [18]CS 111:138-39**. [19]Jn 3:27. [20]WSA 3 7:258**.

24:50-53 THE ASCENSION

[50]*Then he led them out as far as Bethany, and lifting up his hands he blessed them.* [51]*While he blessed them, he parted from them, and was carried up into heaven.*[a] [52]*And they*[b] *returned to Jerusalem with great joy,* [53]*and were continually in the temple blessing God.*

a Other ancient authorities omit *and was carried up into heaven*   b Other ancient authorities add *worshiped him, and*

OVERVIEW: Jesus leads his disciples to Bethany, the house of obedience, to give his disciples his final blessing. How appropriate that the church, the house of obedience, is created at the Mount of Olives! From there, Christ the anointed One ascends after having left himself behind in the sacraments of water and blood that flow from his pierced side (BEDE). The whole Gospel has been a catechetical journey toward this moment when the ascended Jesus creates a new pathway for us to heaven as he is worshiped by those who finally perceive that the cross and empty tomb were the goal all along (CYRIL OF ALEXANDRIA). Jesus imparts his final blessing before he ascends as he lifts up his hands to bless those who will be found worthy when he returns (BEDE). Jesus ascends in his body so that the person of Jesus, divine and human nature, is not separated (AUGUSTINE).

After worshiping him at Bethany, the disciples return to Jerusalem with great joy, for in the ascension of the flesh of Jesus to heaven they have entered there with him (LEO THE GREAT). The continuous worship of the disciples in the Jerusalem temple shows that they are worthy of the promises Jesus had given them (BEDE). After Jesus' ascension, the promised Spirit will come upon them when they are gathered together at Pentecost—not in the temple but in a house (AUGUSTINE). And so as journeying pilgrims, they continually worship Jesus, the one who has traveled "the way" on which they must now follow him.

24:50-53 *Worshiping in the Temple with Great Joy*

AT BETHANY, JESUS GIVES HIS BLESSING.

BEDE: "Then he led them out to Bethany, and lifting up his hands, he blessed them." Our Redeemer appeared in the flesh to take away sins, remove what humans deserved because of the first curse, and grant believers an inheritance of everlasting blessing. He rightly concluded all that he did in the world with words of blessing. He showed that he was the very one of whom it was said, "For indeed he who gave the law will give a blessing."[1] It

is appropriate that he led those whom he blessed out to Bethany, which is interpreted "house of obedience."[2] Contempt and pride deserved a curse, but obedience deserved a blessing. The Lord himself was made obedient to his Father even unto death,[3] so that he might restore the lost grace of blessing to the world. He gives the blessing of heavenly life only to those who strive in the holy church to comply with the divine commands. HOMILIES ON THE GOSPELS 11.15.[4]

CHRIST ASCENDS FROM THE MOUNT OF OLIVES.

BEDE: We must not pass over the fact that Bethany is on the slope of the Mount of Olives.[5] Just as Bethany represents a church obedient to the commands of the Lord, so the Mount of Olives quite fittingly represents the very person of our Lord. Appearing in the flesh, he excels all the saints, who are simply human beings, by the loftiness of his dignity and the grace of his spiritual power. We chant to him in the Psalms, "God, your God, has anointed you with the oil of happiness above your companions."[6] The present Gospel reading bears witness that he promised the favor of the same holy anointing to his companions, the faithful. He sent what he had promised, as we know, not long after that.[7] It is delightful to hear how the house of obedience, the holy church, is built on the slope of the Mount of Olives. Let us read the Gospel of John where it said that when his suffering on the cross was fulfilled, "one of the soldiers opened his side with a lance, and immediately blood and water came out."[8] These truly are the sacraments by which the church is born and nourished in Christ. These are the water of baptism that cleanses the church from sins and the blood of the Lord's chalice that confirms its gifts. It is also signed with the chrism of the Holy Spirit. The mountain on whose slope the holy city is situated, on which the gift of blessing is given, is properly called the

---

[1]Ps 83:8 Vulgate. [2]CC 72:135, 26/27. [3]Phil 2:8. [4]CS 111:139**.
[5]Jerome *De situ et nominibus locorum Hebraicorum* (PL 23:884). [6]Ps 45:7.
[7]See Acts 2:2-4. [8]Jn 19:34.

Mount of Olives that it may be capable of being perfected on the day of redemption. HOMILIES ON THE GOSPELS 11.15.[9]

CREATING A NEW PATHWAY FOR US. CYRIL OF ALEXANDRIA: Having blessed them and gone ahead a little, he was carried up into heaven so that he might share the Father's throne even with the flesh that was united to him. The Word made this new pathway for us when he appeared in human form. After this, and in due time, he will come again in the glory of his Father with the angels and will take us up to be with him. Let us glorify him.

Being God the Word, he became man for our sakes. He suffered willingly in the flesh, rose from the dead and abolished corruption. He was taken up, and he will come with great glory to judge the living and the dead, to give to every one according to his deeds. COMMENTARY ON LUKE, CHAPTER 24.[10]

JESUS ASCENDS AFTER BLESSING HIS DISCIPLES. BEDE: "While he was blessing them, he departed from them and was carried into heaven." We must note that the Savior ascended into heaven after he gave his blessing to his disciples. At the same time, we must remember that, as we read in the Acts of the Apostles, angels appeared to them as they were watching his ascension. They said to them, "He will come in the same way as you have seen him going into heaven."[11] We must labor with all eagerness to understand that the Lord will descend to judge us in the same form and substance of flesh with which he ascended. Since he departed blessing his apostles, he will also make us worthy of his blessing when he returns. He will give us the same status as those to whom he is going to say as they stand at his right hand, "Come, you who are blessed by my Father, receive the kingdom."[12] HOMILIES ON THE GOSPELS 11.15.[13]

JESUS ASCENDS TO HEAVEN IN HIS BODY, DIVINE AND HUMAN NATURE. AUGUSTINE: You heard what came to our ears just now from the Gospel: "Lifting up his hands, he blessed them. And it happened, while he was blessing them he withdrew from them, and was carried up to heaven." Who was carried up to heaven? The Lord Christ was. Who is the Lord Christ? He is the Lord Jesus. What is this? Are you going to separate the human from the divine and make one person of God, another of the man, so that there is no longer a trinity of three but a quaternary of four? Just as you, a human being, are soul and body, so the Lord Christ is Word, soul and body. The Word did not depart from the Father. He both came to us and did not forsake the Father. He both took flesh in the womb and continued to govern the universe. What was lifted up into heaven, if not what had been taken from earth? That is to say, the very flesh, the very body, about which he was speaking when he said to the disciples, "Feel, and see that a spirit does not have bones and flesh, as you can see that I have."[14] Let us believe this, brothers and sisters, and if we have difficulty in meeting the arguments of the philosophers, let us hold on to what was demonstrated in the Lord's case without any difficulty of faith. Let them chatter, but let us believe. SERMON 242.6.[15]

THE JOY OF ENTERING HEAVEN THROUGH THE FLESH OF JESUS. LEO THE GREAT: Dearly beloved, through all this time between the resurrection of the Lord and his ascension, the providence of God thought of this, taught this and penetrated their eyes and heart. He wanted them to recognize the Lord Jesus Christ as truly risen, who was truly born, truly suffered and truly died. The manifest truth strengthened the blessed apostles and all the disciples who were frightened by his death on the cross and were doubtful of his resurrection. The result was they were not only afflicted with sadness but also were filled with "great joy" when the Lord went into the heights of heaven.

[9]CS 111:139-40**. [10]CGSL 620**. [11]Acts 1:11. [12]Mt 25:34. [13]CS 111:140**. [14]Lk 24:39. [15]WSA 3 7:80*.

It was certainly a great and indescribable source of joy when, in the sight of the heavenly multitudes, the nature of our human race ascended over the dignity of all heavenly creatures. It passed the angelic orders and was raised beyond the heights of archangels. In its ascension, our human race did not stop at any other height until this same nature was received at the seat of the eternal Father. Our human nature, united with the divinity of the Son, was on the throne of his glory.

The ascension of Christ is our elevation. Hope for the body is also invited where the glory of the Head preceded us. Let us exult, dearly beloved, with worthy joy and be glad with a holy thanksgiving. Today we not only are established as possessors of paradise, but we have even penetrated the heights of the heavens in Christ. The indescribable grace of Christ, which we lost through the "ill will of the devil," prepared us more fully for that glory. Incorporated within himself, the Son of God placed those whom the violent enemy threw down from the happiness of our first dwelling at the right hand of the Father. The Son of God lives and reigns with God the Father almighty and with the Holy Spirit forever and ever. Amen. SERMON 73.3-4.[16]

CONTINUALLY IN THE TEMPLE. BEDE: "Worshiping, they returned to Jerusalem with great joy and were continually in the temple praising and blessing God." Dearly beloved brothers and sisters, we should always remember, especially in this place, our Lord's words as he was glorifying his disciples: "Blessed are the eyes that see what you see."[17] Who is truly capable of describing or of worthily imagining how with blessed sorrow they lowered to the earth the eyes with which they had looked at him whom the heavens were worshiping as their king? He was now returning to the throne of his Father's glory with the conquered mortal nature that he had taken. How sweet were the tears that they poured out when they were burning with lively hope and gladness over the prospect of their own entry into the heavenly fatherland! They knew that their God and Lord was now bringing there part of their own nature! Such a sight rightly restored them! Then they worshiped in the place where his feet stood.[18] With many tears, they wet the place where he had most recently planted his footsteps. Then they immediately returned to Jerusalem, where he ordered them to wait for the coming of the Holy Spirit. HOMILIES ON THE GOSPELS 11.15.[19]

FROM JESUS' ASCENSION TO PENTECOST. AUGUSTINE: He ascended on the fortieth day. Here we are today when everyone present is filled with the Holy Spirit as he comes upon him or her, and they speak with the tongues of all nations. He commends unity to us through the tongues of all nations. The Lord commends unity as he rises again. Christ commends it as he ascends. The Holy Spirit confirms it when he comes today. SERMON 268.4.[20]

---

[16]FC 93:324-25**. [17]Lk 10:23. [18]Ps 131:7 Vulgate. [19]CS 111:141**. [20]WSA 3 7:281.

Early Christian Writers and the Documents Cited

The following table lists all the early Christian documents cited in this volume by author, if known, or by the title of the work. The English title used in this commentary is followed in parentheses with the Latin designation and, where available, the Thesaurus Linguae Graecae (=TLG) digital reference or Cetedoc Clavis numbers. Printed sources of original language versions may be found in the bibliography of works in original languages.

Ambrose

Exposition on the Gospel of Luke (*Expositio evangelii secundum Lucam*)	Cetedoc 0143
Flight from the World (*De fuga saeculi*)	Cetedoc 0133
Isaac, or the Soul (*De Isaac vel anima*)	Cetedoc 0128
Letters (*Epistulae*)	Cetedoc 0160
On His Brother Satyrus (*De excessu fratris Satyri*)	Cetedoc 0157
The Prayer of Job and David (*De interpellatione Job et David*)	Cetedoc 0134
Six Days of Creation (*Exameron*)	Cetedoc 0123

Amphilochius

Oration 2, On the Presentation of the Lord (*In occursum domini [orat. 2]*)	TLG 2112.003

Athanasius

Festal Letters (*Epistulae festales*)	TLG 2035.x01
Life of St. Anthony (*Vita sancti Antonii*)	TLG 2035.047
On the Incarnation (*De incarnatione verbi*)	TLG 2035.002

Augustine

Admonition and Grace (*De corruptione et gratia*)	Cetedoc 0353
Adulterous Marriages (*De adulterinis coniugiis*)	Cetedoc 0302
Christian Instruction (*De doctrina christiana*)	Cetedoc 0263
City of God (*De civitate Dei*)	Cetedoc 0313
Confessions (*Confessionum libri tredecim*)	Cetedoc 0251
Enchiridion (*Enchiridion de fide, spe et caritate*)	Cetedoc 0295
Holy Virginity (*De sancta virginitate*)	Cetedoc 0300
Homilies on 1 John (*In Johannis epistulam ad Parthos tractatus*)	Cetedoc 0279
Letters (*Epistulae*)	Cetedoc 0262
On Continence (*De continentia*)	Cetedoc 0298
On Grace and Free Will (*De gratia et libero arbitrio*)	Cetedoc 0352

On the Trinity (*De Trinitate*)   Cetedoc 0329
Retractations (*Retractationum libri duo*)   Cetedoc 0250
Sermon on the Mount (*De sermone Domini in monte*)   Cetedoc 0274
Sermons (*Sermones*)   Cetedoc 0284
Tractates on the Gospel of John (*In Johannis evangelium tractatus*)   Cetedoc 0278
The Work of Monks (*De opere monachorum*)   Cetedoc 0305

Basil the Great
Concerning Baptism (*De baptismo libri duo*)   TLG 2040.052
Homilies on the Psalms (*Homiliae super Psalmos*)   TLG 2040.018
Letters (*Epistulae*)   TLG 2040.004
The Long Rules (*Asceticon magnum sive Quaestiones [regulae brevois tractatae]*)   TLG 2040.050
The Morals (*Regulae morales*)   TLG 2040.051
On Humility (*De humilitate*)   TLG 2040.036
Preface on the Judgment of God (*Prologus 7 [De judicio Dei]*)   TLG 2040.043

Bede
Exposition of the Gospel of Luke (*In Lucae evangelium expositio*)   Cetedoc 1356
Homilies on the Gospels (*Homiliarum evangelii*)   Cetedoc 1367
On the Tabernacle (*De tabernaculo et vasis eius ac vestibus sacerdotem libri iii*)   Cetedoc 1345

Benedict
Rule of St. Benedict (*Regula*)   Cetedoc 1852

Cassian, John
Conferences (*Collationes*)   Cetedoc 0512

Clement of Alexandria
Christ the Educator (*Paedagogus*)   TLG 0555.002
Stromateis (*Stromata*)   TLG 0555.004

Clement of Rome
1 Clement (*Epistula i ad Corinthios*)   TLG 1271.001

Cyprian
Exhortation to Martyrdom (*Ad Fortunatum [De exhortatione martyrii]*)   Cetedoc 0045
The Baptismal Controversy (*Epistulae*)   Cetedoc 0050
The Dress of Virgins (*De habitu virginum*)   Cetedoc 0040
The Good of Patience (*De bono patientiae*)   Cetedoc 0048
The Lapsed (*De lapsis*)   Cetedoc 0042
Letters (*Epistulae*)   Cetedoc 0050
The Lord's Prayer (*De dominica oratione*)   Cetedoc 0043
On Mortality (*De mortalitate*)   Cetedoc 0044
Works and Almsgiving (*De opere et eleemosynis*)   Cetedoc 0047

Cyril of Alexandria
Commentary on Luke (*Commentarii in Lucam [in catenis]*)   TLG 4090.108
Letters (*Epistulae 67, cf. Concilia oecumenica*)   TLG 5000.001

Cyril of Jerusalem
Catechetical Lectures (*Catecheses ad illuminandos 1-18*)   TLG 2110.003

Didache   TLG 1311.001

Ephrem the Syrian
Commentary on Tatian's Diatessaron (*In Tatiani Diatessaron*)
Homily on Our Lord (*Sermo de Domino nostro*)
Hymns on Paradise (*Hymni de paradiso*)

Eusebius
Ecclesiastical History (*Historia ecclesiastica*)   TLG 2018.002
Proof of the Gospel (*Demonstratio evangelica*)   TLG 2018.005

The Festal Menaion

Gregory of Nazianzus
Oration 29, On the Son (*De filio*)   TLG 2022.009
Oration 30, On the Son (*De filio*)   TLG 2022.010
Oration 31, On the Holy Spirit (*De spiritu sancto*)   TLG 2022.011

Gregory of Nyssa
On the Christian Mode of Life (*De instituto Christiano*)   TLG 2017.024
On the Soul and the Resurrection (*Dialogus de anima et resurrectione*)   TLG 2017.056
On Virginity (*De virginitate*)   TLG 2017.043

Gregory the Great
Dialogues (*Dialogorum libri iv*)   Cetedoc 1713
Forty Gospel Homilies (*XL Homiliarum in Evangelia*)   Cetedoc 1711

Hilary of Poitiers
On the Trinity (*De trinitate*)   Cetedoc 0433

Hippolytus
Against Noetus (*Contra haeresin Noeti*)

Ignatius of Antioch
Letter to the Smyrnaeans (*Epistulae vii genuinae*)   TLG 1443.001

Irenaeus
Against Heresies (*Adversus haereses*)   Cetedoc 1154

Isaac of Nineveh
Ascetical Homilies (*De perfectione religiosa*)

Jerome
Against the Pelagians (*Dialogi contra Pelagianos libri iii*)   Cetedoc 0615
Homilies on the Gospel of Mark (*Tractatus in Marci evangelium*)   Cetedoc 0594
Homilies on the Psalms (*Tractatus lix in psalmos*)   Cetedoc 0592
Homilies on the Psalms Alternate Series (*Tractatus in psalmos series altera*)   Cetedoc 0593
On Lazarus and Dives (*Homilia in Lucam, de Lazaro et divite*)   Cetedoc 0596
On the Gospel of John (*Homilia in Johannem evangelistam*)   Cetedoc 0597
On the Nativity of the Lord (*Homilia de nativitate Domini*)   Cetedoc 0598

John Chrysostom
Against the Anomoeans (*Contra Anomoeos*)
    Homily 7   TLG 2062.015
    Homily 8   TLG 2062.016
    Homily 9   TLG 2062.017
Baptismal Instructions (*Catechesis ultima ad baptizandos*)   TLG 2062.381
Commentary on John (*In Joannem*)   TLG 2062.015
Demonstration Against the Pagans (*Contra Judaeos et gentiles quod Christus sit deus*)   TLG 2062.372
Homilies on Genesis (*In Genesim [homiliae 1-67]*)   TLG 2062.112
Homilies on the Gospel of Matthew (*In Matthaeum [homiliae 1-90]*)   TLG 2062.152
On the Incomprehensible Nature of God (*De incomprehensibili dei natura*
    [Contra Anomoeos homiliae 1-5])   TLG 2062.012

John of Damascus
Barlaam and Joseph (*Vita Barlaam et Joasaph*)   TLG 2934.066
Orthodox Faith (*Expositio fidei*)   TLG 2934.004

Justin Martyr
Dialogue with Trypho (*Dialogus cum Tryphone*)   TLG 0645.003
First Apology (*Apologia*)   TLG 0645.001

Leo the Great
Sermons (*Tractatus septem et nonaginta*)   Cetedoc 1657
Tome (*Concilia oecumenica et generalia ecclesiae catholicae Concilium Chalcedonense a. 451*)

Martyrius
Book of Perfection

Maximus of Turin
Sermons (*Collectio sermonum antiqua*)   Cetedoc 0219a

Niceta of Remesiana
Liturgical Singing

Origen

Against Celsus (*Contra Celsum*)	TLG 2042.001
Commentary on the Gospel of John (*Commentarii in evangelium Joannis*)	TLG 2042.005
Exhortation to Martyrdom (*Exhortatio ad martyrium*)	TLG 2042.007
Fragments on Luke (*Fragmenta in Lucam*)	TLG 2042.017
Homilies on Exodus (*In Exodum homiliae*)	Cetedoc 0198
Homilies on Genesis (*In Genesim homiliae*)	Cetedoc 0198
Homilies on Leviticus (*In Leviticum homiliae*)	Cetedoc 0198
Homilies on the Gospel of Luke (*Homiliae in Lucam*)	TLG 2042.016
On First Principles (*De principiis*)	TLG 2042.002
On Prayer (*De oratione*)	TLG 2042.008

Paschasius of Dumium

Questions and Answers of the Greek Fathers (*De vitis patrum liber septimus,
sive verba seniorum auctore graeco incerto, interprete Paschasio S. R. E. Diacono*)

Peter Chrysologus

Sermons (*Collectio sermonum*)	Cetedoc 0227+

Philoxenus of Mabbug

On the Indwelling of the Holy Spirit

Prudentius

Against Symmachus (*Contra Symmachum libri duo*)	Cetedoc 1442
The Divinity of Christ (*Liber apotheosis*)	Cetedoc 1439
Hymns (*Liber cathemerinon*)	Cetedoc 1438
Scenes from Sacred History (*Tituli historiarum sive Dittochaeon*)	Cetedoc 1444

Pseudo-Clement of Rome

2 Clement (*Epistula ii ad Corinthios*)	TLG 1271.002

Pseudo-Dionysius

Celestial Hierarchy (*De caelestine hierarchia*)	TLG 2798.001

Symeon the New Theologian

Discourses (*Catecheses*)

Tertullian

Against Marcion (*Adversus Marcionem*)	Cetedoc 0014
On Flight in Time of Persecution (*De fuga in persecutione*)	Cetedoc 0025
On Idolatry (*De idololatria*)	Cetedoc 0023
On Patience (*De patientia*)	Cetedoc 0009
On Prayer (*De oratione*)	Cetedoc 0007
To Scapula (*Ad Scapulam*)	Cetedoc 0024

Theophylact

The Explanation of the Holy Gospel According to St. Luke

Biographical Sketches &
Short Descriptions
of Select Anonymous Works

This listing is cumulative, including all the authors and works cited in this series to date.

Acacius of Caesarea (d. c. 365). Pro-Arian bishop of Caesarea in Palestine, disciple and biographer of Eusebius of Caesarea, the historian. He was a man of great learning and authored a treatise on Ecclesiastes.

Alexander of Alexandria (fl. 312-328). Bishop of Alexandria and predecessor of Athanasius, upon whom he asserted considerable theological influence during the rise of Arianism. Alexander excommunicated Arius, whom he had appointed to the parish of Baucalis, in 319. His teaching regarding the eternal generation and divine substantial union of the Son with the Father was eventually confirmed at the Council of Nicaea (325).

Ambrose of Milan (c. 333-397; fl. 374-397). Bishop of Milan and teacher of Augustine who defended the divinity of the Holy Spirit and the perpetual virginity of Mary.

Ambrosiaster (fl. c. 366-384). Name given by Erasmus to the author of a work once thought to have been composed by Ambrose.

Ammonius (c. fifth century). An Aristotelian commentator and teacher in Alexandria, where he was born and of whose school he became head. Also an exegete of Plato, he enjoyed fame among his contemporaries and successors, although modern critics accuse him of pedantry and banality.

Amphilochius of Iconium (b. c. 340-345, d.c. 398-404). An orator at Constantinople before becoming bishop of Iconium in 373. He was a cousin of Gregory of Nazianzus and active in debates against the Macedonians and Messalians.

Andreas (c. seventh century). Monk who collected commentary from earlier writers to form a catena on various biblical books.

Antony (or Anthony) the Great (c. 251-c. 356). An anchorite of the Egyptian desert, well-known as a monastic father. Athanasius regarded him as the ideal of monastic life, and he has become a model for Christian hagiography.

Aphrahat (c. 270-350 fl. 337-345). "The Persian Sage" and first major Syriac writer whose work survives. He is also known by his Greek name Aphraates.

Apollinaris of Laodicea (310-c. 392). Bishop of Laodicea who was attacked by Gregory of Nazianzus, Gregory of Nyssa and Theodore for denying that Christ had a human mind.

Apostolic Constitutions (c. 381-394). Also known as *Constitutions of the Holy Apostles* and thought to be the work of the Arian bishop Julian of Neapolis. The work is divided into eight books, and is primarily a collection of and expansion on previous works such as the *Didache* (c. 140) and the

Apostolic Traditions. Book 8 ends with eighty-five canons from various sources and is elsewhere known as the *Apostolic Canons.*

Arius (fl. c. 320). Heretic condemned at the Council of Nicaea (325) for refusing to accept that the Son was not a creature but was God by nature like the Father.

Athanasius of Alexandria (c. 295-373; fl. 325-373). Bishop of Alexandria from 328, though often in exile. He wrote his classic polemics against the Arians while most of the eastern bishops were against him.

Athenagoras (fl. 176-180). Early Christian philosopher and apologist from Athens, whose only authenticated writing, *A Plea Regarding Christians,* is addressed to the emperors Marcus Aurelius and Commodus, and defends Christians from the common accusations of atheism, incest and cannibalism.

Augustine of Hippo (354-430). Bishop of Hippo and a voluminous writer on philosophical, exegetical, theological and ecclesiological topics. He formulated the Western doctrines of predestination and original sin in his writings against the Pelagians.

Babai the Great (d. 628). Syriac monk who founded a monastery and school in his region of Beth Zabday and later served as third superior at the Great Convent of Mount Izla during a period of crisis in the Nestorian church.

Basil the Great (b. c. 330; fl. 357-379). One of the Cappadocian fathers, bishop of Caesarea and champion of the teaching on the Trinity propounded at Nicaea in 325. He was a great administrator and founded a monastic rule.

Basil of Seleucia (fl. 444-468). Bishop of Seleucia in Isauria and ecclesiastical writer. He took part in the Synod of Constantinople in 448 for the condemnation of the Eutychian errors and the deposition of their great champion, Dioscurus of Alexandria.

Basilides (fl. second century). Alexandrian heretic of the early second century who is said to have believed that souls migrate from body to body and that we do not sin if we lie to protect the body from martyrdom.

Bede the Venerable (c. 672/673-735). Born in Northumbria, at the age of seven he was put under the care of the Benedictine monks of Saints Peter and Paul at Jarrow and given a broad classical education in the monastic tradition. Considered one of the most learned men of his age, he is the author of *An Ecclesiastical History of the English People.*

Benedict of Nursia (c. 480-547). Considered the most important figure in the history of Western monasticism. Benedict founded many monasteries, the most notable found at Montecassino, but his lasting influence lay in his famous Rule. The Rule outlines the theological and inspirational foundation of the monastic ideal while also legislating the shape and organization of the coenobitic life.

Book of Steps (c. 400). Written by an anonymous Syriac author, this work consists of thirty homilies or discourses which specifically deal with the more advanced stages of growth in the spiritual life.

Braulio of Saragossa (c. 585-651). Bishop of Saragossa (631-651) and noted writer of the Visigothic renaissance. His *Life* of St. Aemilianus is his crowning literary achievement.

Caesarius of Arles (c. 470-543). Bishop of Arles renowned for his attention to his pastoral duties. Among his surviving works the most important is a collection of some 238 sermons that display an ability to preach Christian doctrine to a variety of audiences.

Callistus of Rome (d. 222). Pope (217-222) who excommunicated Sabellius for heresy. It is very probable that he suffered martyrdom.

Cassia (b. c. 805, d. between 848 and 867). Nun, poet and hymnographer who founded a convent in Constanttinople.

Cassian, John (360-432). Author of a the *Institutes* and the *Conferences,* works purporting to relay the teachings of he Egyptian monastic fathers on the nature of the spiritual life which were highly influential in the development of Western monasticism.

Cassiodorus (c. 485-c. 540). Founder of Western monasticism whose writings include valuable histories and less valuable commentaries.

Chromatius (fl. 400). Bishop of Aquileia, friend of Rufinus and Jerome and author of tracts and sermons.

Clement of Alexandria (c. 150-215). A highly educated Christian convert from paganism, head of the catechetical school in Alexandria and pioneer of Christian scholarship. His major works, *Protrepticus, Paedagogus* and the *Stromata*, bring Christian doctrine face to face with the ideas and achievements of his time.

Clement of Rome (fl. c. 92-101). Pope whose *Epistle to the Corinthians* is one of the most important documents of subapostolic times.

Commodian (c. third or fifth century). Poet of unknown origin (possibly Syrian?) whose two surviving works focus on the Apocalypse and Christian apologetics.

Constitutions of the Holy Apostles. *See Apostolic Constitutions.*

Cyprian of Carthage (fl. 248-258). Martyred bishop of Carthage who maintained that those baptized by schismatics and heretics had no share in the blessings of the church.

Cyril of Alexandria (375-444; fl. 412-444). Patriarch of Alexandria whose strong espousal of the unity of Christ led to the condemnation of Nestorius in 431.

Cyril of Jerusalem (c. 315-386; fl. c. 348). Bishop of Jerusalem after 350 and author of *Catechetical Homilies*.

Cyril of Scythopolis (b. c. 525; d. after 557). Palestinian monk and author of biographies of famous Palestinian monks. Because of him we have precise knowledge of monastic life in the fifth and sixth centuries and a description of the Origenist crisis and its suppression in the mid-sixth century.

Diadochus of Photice (c. 400-474). Antimonophysite bishop of Epirus Vetus whose work *Discourse on the Ascension of Our Lord Jesus Christ* exerted influence in both the East and West through its Chalcedonian Christology. He is also the subject of the mystical *Vision of St. Diadochus Bishop of Photice in Epirus.*

Didache (c. 140). Of unknown authorship, this text intertwines Jewish ethics with Christian liturgical practice to form a whole discourse on the "way of life." It exerted an enormous amount of influence in the patristic period and was especially used in the training of catechumen.

Didymus the Blind (c. 313-398). Alexandrian exegete who was much influenced by Origen and admired by Jerome.

Diodore of Tarsus (d. c. 394). Bishop of Tarsus and Antiochene theologian. He authored a great scope of exegetical, doctrinal and apologetic works, which come to us mostly in fragments because of his condemnation as the predecessor of Nestorianism. Diodore was a teacher of John Chrysostom and Theodore of Mopsuestia.

Dionysius of Alexandria (d. c. 264). Bishop of Alexandria and student of Origen. Dionysius actively engaged in the theological disputes of his day, opposed Sabellianism, defended himself against accusations of tritheism and wrote the earliest extant Christian refutation of Epicureanism. His writings have survived mainly in extracts preserved by other early Christian authors.

Dorotheus of Gaza (fl. c. 525-540). Member of Abbot Seridos's monastery and later leader of a monastery where he wrote *Spiritual Instructions*. He also wrote a work on traditions of Palestinian monasticism.

Epiphanius of Salamis (c. 315-403). Bishop of Salamis in Cyprus, author of a refutation of eighty heresies (the *Panarion*) and instrumental in the condemnation of Origen.

Epiphanius the Latin. Author of the late fifth-century or early sixth century Latin text *Interpretation of the Gospels*. He was possibly a bishop of Benevento or Seville.

Ephrem the Syrian (b. c. 306; fl. 363-373). Syrian writer of commentaries and devotional hymns which are sometimes regarded as the greatest specimens of Christian poetry prior to Dante.

Eucherius of Lyons (fl. 420-449). Bishop of Lyons c. 435-449. Born into an aristocratic family, he, along with his wife and sons, joined the monastery at Lérins soon after its founding.

Eunomius (d. 393). Bishop of Cyzicyus who was

attacked by Basil and Gregory of Nyssa for maintaining that the Father and the Son were of different natures, one ingenerate, one generate.

Eusebius of Caesarea (c. 260/263-340). Bishop of Caesarea, partisan of the Emperor Constantine and first historian of the Christian church. He argued that the truth of the gospel had been foreshadowed in pagan writings but had to defend his own doctrine against suspicion of Arian sympathies.

Eusebius of Emesa (c. 300-c. 359). Bishop of Emesa from c. 339. A biblical exegete and writer on doctrinal subjects, he displays some semi-Arian tendencies of his mentor Eusebius of Caesarea.

Eusebius of Vercelli (fl. c. 360). Bishop of Vercelli who supported the trinitarian teaching of Nicaea (325) when it was being undermined by compromise in the West.

Euthymius (377-473). A native of Melitene and influential monk. He was educated by Bishop Otreius of Melitene, who ordained him priest and placed him in charge of all the monasteries in his diocese. When the Council of Chalcedon (451) condemned the errors of Eutyches, it was greatly due to the authority of Euthymius that most of the Eastern recluses accepted its decrees. The empress Eudoxia returned to Chalcedonian orthodoxy through his efforts.

Evagrius of Pontus (c. 345-399). Disciple and teacher of ascetic life who astutely absorbed and creatively transmitted the spirituality of Egyptian and Palestinian monasticism of the late fourth century. Although Origenist elements of his writings were formally condemned by the Fifth Ecumenical Council (Constantinople II, A.D. 553), his literary corpus continued to influence the tradition of the church.

Fastidius (c. fourth-fifth centuries). British author of *On the Christian Life*. He is believed to have written some works attributed to Pelagius.

Faustinus (fl. 380). A priest in Rome and supporter of Lucifer and author of a treatise on the Trinity.

The Festal Menaion. Orthodox liturgical text containing the variable parts of the service, including hymns, for fixed days of celebration of the life of Jesus and Mary.

Filastrius (fl. 380). Bishop of Brescia and author of a compilation against all heresies.

Fulgentius of Ruspe (c. 467-532). Bishop of Ruspe and author of many orthodox sermons and tracts under the influence of Augustine.

Gaudentius of Brescia (fl. 395). Successor of Filastrius as bishop of Brescia and author of numerous tracts.

Gennadius of Constantinople (d. 471). Patriarch of Constantinople, author of numerous commentaries and an opponent of the Christology of Cyril of Alexandria.

Gnostics. Name now given generally to followers of Basilides, Marcion, Valentinus, Mani and others. The characteristic belief is that matter is a prison made for the spirit by an evil or ignorant creator, and that redemption depends on fate, not on free will.

Gregory of Elvira (fl. 359-385). Bishop of Elvira who wrote allegorical treatises in the style of Origen and defended the Nicene faith against the Arians.

Gregory of Nazianzus (b. 329/330; fl. 372-389). Bishop of Nazianzus and friend of Basil the Great and Gregory of Nyssa. He is famous for maintaining the humanity of Christ as well as the orthodox doctrine of the Trinity.

Gregory of Nyssa (c. 335-394). Bishop of Nyssa and brother of Basil the Great, he is famous for maintaining the equality in unity of the Father, Son and Holy Spirit.

Gregory Thaumaturgus (fl. c. 248-264). Bishop of Neocaesarea and a disciple of Origen. There are at least five legendary *Lives* that recount the events and miracles which led to his being called "the wonder worker." His most important work was the *Address of Thanks to Origen*, which is a rhetorically structured panegyric to Origen and an outline of his teaching.

Gregory the Great (c. 540-604). Pope from 590, the fourth and last of the Latin "Doctors of the Church." He was a prolific author and a powerful unifying force within the Latin Church, initiating the liturgical reform that brought about the Gregorian Sacramentary and Gregorian chant.

Hesychius of Jerusalem (fl. 412-450). Presbyter and exegete, thought to have commented on the whole of Scripture.

Hilary of Arles (c. 401-449). Archbishop of Arles and leader of the Semi-Pelagian party. Hilary incurred the wrath of Pope Leo I when he removed a bishop from his see and appointed a new bishop. Leo demoted Arles from a metropolitan see to a bishopric to assert papal power over the church in Gaul.

Hilary of Poitiers (c. 315-367). Bishop of Poitiers and called the "Athanasius of the West" because of his defense (against the Arians) of the common nature of Father and Son.

Hippolytus (fl. 222-245). Recent scholarship places Hippolytus in a Palestinian context, personally familiar with Origen. Though he is known mostly for *The Refutation of All Heresies*, he was primarily a commentator on Scripture (especially the Old Testament) and other sacred texts.

Ignatius of Antioch (c. 35-107/112). Bishop of Antioch who wrote several letters to local churches while being taken from Antioch to Rome to be martyred. In the letters, which warn against heresy, he stresses orthodox Christology, the centrality of the Eucharist and unique role of the bishop in preserving the unity of the church.

Irenaeus of Lyons (c. 135-c. 202). Bishop of Lyons who published the most famous and influential refutation of Gnostic thought.

Isaac of Nineveh (d. c. 700). Also known as Isaac the Syrian or Isaac Syrus, this monastic writer served for a short while as bishop of Nineveh before retiring to live a secluded monastic life. His writings on ascetic subjects survive in the form of numerous homilies.

Isho'dad of Merv (fl. c. 850). Nestorian commentator of the ninth century. He wrote especially on James, 1 Peter and 1 John.

Isidore of Seville (c. 560-636). Youngest of a family of monks and clerics, including sister Florentina and brothers Leander and Fulgentius. He was an erudite author of comprehensive scale in matters both religious and sacred, including his encyclopedic *Etymologies*.

Jacob of Nisibis (d. 338). Bishop of Nisibis. He was present at the council of Nicaea in 325 and took an active part in the opposition to Arius.

Jacob of Sarug (c. 450-c. 520). Syriac ecclesiastical writer. Jacob received his education at Edessa. At the end of his life he was ordained bishop of Sarug. His principal writing was a long series of metrical homilies, earning him the title "The Flute of the Holy Spirit." His theological views are not certain, but it seems that he expressed a moderate monophysite position.

Jerome (c. 347-420). Gifted exegete and exponent of a classical Latin style, now best known as the translator of the Latin Vulgate. He defended the perpetual virginity of Mary, attacked Origen and Pelagius and supported extreme ascetic practices.

John Chrysostom (344/354-407; fl. 386-407). Bishop of Constantinople who was famous for his orthodoxy, his eloquence and his attacks on Christian laxity in high places.

John of Damascus (c. 650-750). Arab monastic and theologian whose writings enjoyed great influence in both the Eastern and Western Churches. His most famous writing was the *Orthodox Faith*.

John the Elder (c. eighth century) A Syriac author who belonged to monastic circles of the Church of the East and lived in the region of Mount Qardu (northern Iraq). His most important writings are twenty-two homilies and a collection of fifty-one short letters in which he describes the mystical life as an anticipatory experience of the resurrection life, the fruit of the sacraments of baptism and the Eucharist.

John the Monk. Traditional name found in *The Festal Menaion*, believed to refer to John of Damascus. *See* John of Damascus.

Josephus, Flavius (c. 37-c. 101). Jewish historian from a distinguished priestly family. Acquainted with the Essenes and Sadducees, he himself became a Pharisee. He joined the great Jewish revolt that broke out in 66 and was chosen by the Sanhedrin at Jerusalem to be commander-in-chief in Galilee. Showing great shrewdness to ingratiate himself with Vespasian by foretelling his elevation and that of his son Titus to the imperial dignity, Josephus was restored his liberty after 69 when Vespasian became emperor.

Justin Martyr (c. 100/110-165; fl. c. 148-161). Palestinian philosopher who was converted to Christianity, "the only sure and worthy philosophy." He traveled to Rome where he wrote several apologies against both pagans and Jews, combining Greek philosophy and Christian theology; he was eventually martyred.

Lactantius (c. 260-c. 330). An eloquent writer known to us through Jerome. He is acknowledged more for his technical writing skills than for his theological thought.

Leander (c. 545-c. 600). Latin ecclesiastical writer, of whose works only two survive. He was instrumental in spreading Christianity among the Visigoths, gaining significant historical influence in Spain in his time.

Leo the Great (regn. 440-461). Bishop of Rome whose *Tome to Flavian* helped to strike a balance between Nestorian and Cyrilline positions at the Council of Chalcedon in 451.

Letter of Barnabas (c. 130). An allegorical and typological interpretation of the Old Testament with a decidedly anti-Jewish tone. It was included with other New Testament works as a "Catholic epistle" at least until Eusebius of Caesarea (c. 260/263-340) questioned its authenticity.

Letter to Diognetus (c. third century). A refutation of paganism and an exposition of the Christian life and faith. The author of this letter is unknown, and the exact identity of its recipient, Diognetus, continues to elude patristic scholars.

Lucifer (d. 370/371). Bishop of Cagliari and vigorous supporter of Athanasius and the Nicene Creed. He and his followers entered into schism after refusing to acknowledge less orthodox bishops appointed by the emperor Constantius.

Luculentius (fifth century). Unknown author of a group of short commentaries on the New Testament, especially Pauline passages. His exegesis is mainly literal and relies mostly on earlier authors

such as Jerome and Augustine. The content of his writing may place it in the fifth century.

Macarius of Egypt (c. 300-c. 390). One of the Desert Fathers. Accused of supporting Athanasius, Macarius was exiled c. 374 to an island in the Nile by Lucius, the Arian successor of Athanasius. Macarius continued his teaching of monastic theology until his death.

Macrina the Younger (c. 327-379). The elder sister of Basil the Great and Gregory of Nyssa, she is known as "the Younger" to distinguish her from her paternal grandmother. She had a powerful influence on her younger brothers, especially on Gregory, who called her his teacher and relates her teaching in *On the Soul and the Resurrection*.

Manichaeans. A religious movement that originated circa 241 in Persia under the leadership of Mani but was apparently of complex Christian origin. It is said to have denied free will and the universal sovereignty of God, teaching that kingdoms of light and darkness are coeternal and that the redeemed are particles of a spiritual man of light held captive in the darkness of matter (*see* Gnostics).

Marcion (fl. 144). Heretic of the mid-second century who rejected the Old Testament and much of the New Testament, claiming that the Father of Jesus Christ was other than the Creator God (*see* Gnostics).

Marius Victorinus (b. c. 280/285; fl. c. 355-363). Grammarian who translated works of Platonists and, after his late conversion (c. 355), used them against the Arians.

Mark the Hermit (c. sixth century). Monk who lived near Tarsus and produced works on ascetic practices as well as christological issues.

Martin of Braga (fl. c. 568-579). Anti-Arian metropolitan of Braga on the Iberian peninsula. He was highly educated and presided over the provincial council of Braga in 572.

Maximus of Turin (d. 408/423). Bishop of Turin who died during the reigns of Honorius and Theodosius the Younger (408-423). Over one hundred of his sermons survive.

Maximus the Confessor (c. 580-662). Greek theologian and ascetic writer. Fleeing the Arab invasion of Jerusalem in 614, he took refuge in Constantinople and later Africa. He died near the Black Sea after imprisonment and severe suffering. His thought centered on the humanity of Christ.

Methodius of Olympus (d. 311). Bishop of Olympus who celebrated virginity in a *Symposium* partly modeled on Plato's dialogue of that name.

Minucius Felix of Rome (second or third century). Christian apologist who flourished between 160 and 300 (the exact dates are not known). His *Octavius* agrees at numerous points with the *Apologeticum* of Tertullian. His birthplace is believed to be in Africa.

Montanist Oracles. Montanism was an apocalyptic and strictly ascetic movement begun in the latter half of the second century by a certain Montanus in Phrygia, who, along with certain of his followers, uttered oracles they claimed were inspired by the Holy Spirit. Little of the authentic oracles remains and most of what is known of Montanism comes from the authors who wrote against the movement. Montanism was formally condemned as a heresy before by Asiatic synods.

Nemesius of Emesa (fl. late fourth century). Bishop of Emesa in Syria whose most important work, *Of the Nature of Man,* draws on several theological and philosophical sources and is the first exposition of a Christian anthropology.

Nestorius (c. 381-c. 451). Patriarch of Constantinople 428-431 and credited with the foundation of the heresy which says that the divine and human natures were associated, rather than truly united, in the incarnation of Christ.

Nicetas of Remesiana (fl. second half of fourth century). Bishop of Remesiana in Serbia, whose works affirm the consubstantiality of the Son and the deity of the Holy Spirit.

Novatian of Rome (fl. 235-258). Roman theologian, otherwise orthodox, who formed a schismatic church after failing to become pope. His treatise on the Trinity states the classic western doctrine.

Oecumenius (sixth century). Called the Rhetor or the Philosopher, Oecumenius wrote the earliest extant Greek commentary on Revelation.

Scholia by Oecumenius on some of John Chrysostom's commentaries on the Pauline Epistles are still extant.

Origen of Alexandria (b. 185; fl. c. 200-254). Influential exegete and systematic theologian. He was condemned (perhaps unfairly) for maintaining the preexistence of souls while denying the resurrection of the body, the literal truth of Scripture and the equality of the Father and the Son in the Trinity.

Pachomius (c. 292-347). Founder of cenobitic monasticism. A gifted group leader and author of a set of rules, he was defended after his death by Athanasius of Alexandria.

Pacian of Barcelona (c. fourth century). Bishop of Barcelona whose writings polemicize against popular pagan festivals as well as Novatian schismatics.

Palladius of Helenopolis (c. 363/364-c. 431). Bishop of Helenopolis (400-417) and then Aspuna in Galatia. A disciple of Evagrius of Pontus and admirer of Origen, Palladius became a zealous adherent of John Chrysostom and shared his troubles in 403. His *Dialogus de vita S. Johannis* is essentially a work of edification, stressing the spiritual value of the life of the desert, where he spent a number of years as a monk.

Paschasius of Dumium (c. 515-c. 580). Translator of sentences of the Desert Fathers from Greek into Latin while a monk in Dumium.

Paterius (c. sixth-seventh century). Disciple of Gregory the Great who is primarily responsible for the transmission of Gregory's works to many later medieval authors.

Paulinus of Nola (355-431). Roman senator and distinguished Latin poet whose frequent encounters with Ambrose of Milan (c. 333-397) led to his eventual conversion and baptism in 389. He eventually renounced his wealth and influential position and took up his pen to write poetry in service of Christ. He also wrote many letters to, among others, Augustine, Jerome and Rufinus.

Paulus Orosius (b. c. 380). An outspoken critic of Pelagius, mentored by Augustine. His *Seven Books of History Against the Pagans* was perhaps the first history of Christianity.

Pelagius (c. 354-c. 420). Christian teacher whose followers were condemned in 418 and 431 for maintaining that a Christian could be perfect and that salvation depended on free will.

Peter of Alexandria (d. c. 311). Bishop of Alexandria. He marked (and very probably initiated) the reaction at Alexandria against extreme doctrines of Origen. During the persecution of Christians in Alexandria, Peter was arrested and beheaded by Roman officials. Eusebius of Caesarea described him as "a model bishop, remarkable for his virtuous life and his ardent study of the Scriptures."

Peter Chrysologus (c. 380-450). Latin archbishop of Ravenna whose teachings included arguments for the supremacy of the papacy and the relationship between grace and Christian living.

Philo of Alexandria (c. 20 B.C.-c. A.D. 50). Jewish-born exegete who greatly influenced Christian patristic interpretation of the Old Testament. Born to a rich family in Alexandria, Philo was a contemporary of Jesus and lived an ascetic and contemplative life that makes some believe he was a rabbi. His interpretation of Scripture based the spiritual sense on the literal. Although influenced by Hellenism, Philo's theology remains thoroughly Jewish.

Philoxenus of Mabbug (c. 440-523). Bishop of Mabbug (Hierapolis) and a leading thinker in the early Syrian Orthodox Church. His extensive writings in Syriac include a set of thirteen *Discourses on the Christian Life*, several works on the incarnation and a number of exegetical works.

Poemen (c. fifth century). One-seventh of the sayings in the *Sayings of the Desert Fathers* are attributed to Poemen, which is Greek for shepherd. Poemen was a common title among early Egyptian desert ascetics, and it is unknown whether all of the sayings come from one person.

Polycarp of Smyrna (c. 69-155). Bishop of Smyrna who vigorously fought heretics such as the Marcionites and Valentinians. He was the leading Christian figure in Roman Asia in the middle of the second century.

Potamius of Lisbon (fl. c. 350-360). Bishop of Lisbon who joined the Arian party in 357, but later returned to the Catholic faith (c. 359?). His works from both periods are concerned with the larger Trinitarian debates of his time.

Procopius of Gaza (c. 465-c. 530). A Christian Sophist educated in Alexandria. He wrote numerous theological works and commentaries on Scripture (particularly the Hebrew Bible), the latter marked by the allegorical exegesis for which the Alexandrian school was known.

Prudentius (c. 348-c. 410). Latin poet and hymn-writer who devoted his later life to Christian writing. He wrote didactic poems on the theology of the incarnation, against the heretic Marcion and against the resurgence of paganism.

Pseudo-Dionysius the Areopagite (fl. c. 500). Author who assumed the name of Dionysius the Areopagite mentioned in Acts 17:34, and who composed the works known as the *Corpus Areopagiticum* (or *Dionysiacum*). These writings were the foundation of the apophatic school of mysticism in their denial that anything can be truly predicated of God.

Pseudo-Macarius (fl. c. 390). An imaginative writer and ascetic from Mesopotamia to eastern Asia Minor with keen insight into human nature and clear articulation of the theology of the Trinity. His work includes some one hundred discourses and homilies.

Quodvultdeus (fl. 430). Carthaginian deacon and friend of Augustine who endeavored to show at length how the New Testament fulfilled the Old Testament.

Rufinus of Aquileia (c. 345-411). Orthodox Christian thinker and historian who nonetheless translated Origen and defended him against the strictures of Jerome and Epiphanius.

Sabellius (fl. 200). Allegedly the author of the heresy which maintains that the Father and Son are a single person. The patripassian variant of this heresy states that the Father suffered on the cross.

Sahdona (fl. 635-640). Known in Greek as Martyrius, this Syriac author was bishop of Beth

Garmai for a short time. His most important work is the deeply scriptural *Book of Perfection* which ranks as one of the masterpieces of Syriac monastic literature.

Salvian the Presbyter of Marseilles (c. 400-c. 480). An important author for the history of his own time. He saw the fall of Roman civilization to the barbarians as a consequence of the reprehensible conduct of Roman Christians.

Second Letter of Clement (c. 150). The so-called *Second Letter of Clement* is the earliest surviving Christian sermon probably written by a Corinthian author, though some scholars have assigned it to a Roman or Alexandrian author.

Severian of Gabala (fl. c. 400). A contemporary of John Chrysostom, he was a highly regarded preacher in Constantinople, particularly at the imperial court, and ultimately sided with Chrysostom's accusers. His sermons are dominated by antiheretical concerns.

Severus of Antioch (fl. 488-538). A monophysite theologian, consecrated bishop of Antioch in 522. Severus believed that Christ's human nature was an annex to his divine nature and argued that if Christ were both divine and human, he would necessarily have been two persons.

Shepherd **of Hermas** (second century). Divided into five *Visions*, twelve *Mandates* and ten *Similitudes*, this Christian apocalypse was written by a former slave and named for the form of the second angel said to have granted him his visions. This work was highly esteemed for its moral value and was used as a textbook for catechumens in the early church.

Sulpicius Severus (c. 360-c. 420). An ecclesiastical writer born of noble parents. Devoting himself to monastic retirement, he became a personal friend and enthusiastic disciple of St. Martin of Tours. His ordination to the priesthood is vouched for by Gennadius, but no details of his priestly activity have reached us.

Symeon the New Theologian (c. 949-1022). Compassionate spiritual leader known for his strict rule. He believed that the divine light could be perceived and received through the practice of mental prayer.

Tertullian of Carthage (c. 155/160-225/250; fl. c. 197-222). Brilliant Carthaginian apologist and polemicist who laid the foundations of Christology and trinitarian orthodoxy in the West, though he himself was estranged from the main church by its laxity.

Theodore of Heraclea (d. c. 355). An anti-Nicene bishop of Thrace. He was part of a team seeking reconciliation between Eastern and Western Christianity. In 343 he was excommunicated at the council of Sardica. His writings focus on a literal interpretation of Scripture.

Theodore of Mopsuestia (c. 350-428). Bishop of Mopsuestia, founder of the Antiochene, or literalistic, school of exegesis. A great man in his day, he was later condemned as a precursor of Nestorius.

Theodoret of Cyr (c. 393-466). Bishop of Cyr (Cyrrhus), he was an opponent of Cyril, whose doctrine of Christ's person was finally vindicated in 451 at the Council of Chalcedon.

Theophanes (775-845). Hymnographer and bishop of Nicaea (842-845). He was persecuted during the second iconoclastic period for his support of the Seventh Council (Second Council of Nicaea, 787). He wrote many hymns in the tradition of the monastery of Mar Sabbas that were used in the *Paraklitiki*.

Theophilus of Antioch (late second century). Bishop of Antioch. His only surviving work is *Ad Autholycum*, where we find the first Christian commentary on Genesis and the first use of the term *Trinity*. Theophilus's apologetic literary heritage had influence on Irenaeus and possibly Tertullian.

Theophylact of Ohrid (c. 1050-c. 1108). Byzantine archbishop of Ohrid (or Achrida) in what is now Bulgaria. Drawing on earlier works, he wrote commentaries on several Old Testament books and all of the New Testament except for Revelation.

Valentinus (fl. c. 140). Alexandrian heretic of the mid-second century who taught that the material world was created by the transgression of God's Wisdom, or Sophia (*see* Gnostics).

Valerian of Cimiez (fl. c. 422-439). Bishop of Cimiez. He participated in the councils of Riez (439) and Vaison (422) with a view to strengthening church discipline. He supported Hilary of Arles in quarrels with Pope Leo I.

Victorius of Petovium (d. c. 304). Latin biblical exegete. With multiple works attributed to him, his sole surviving work is the *Commentary on the Apocalypse* and perhaps some fragments from *Commentary on Matthew*. Victorinus expressed strong millenarianism in his writing, though his was less materialistic than the millenarianism of Papias or Irenaeus. In his allegorical approach he could be called a spiritual disciple of Origen. Victorinus died during the first year of Diocletian's persecution, probably in 304.

Vincent of Lérins (d. 435). Monk who has exerted considerable influence through his writings on orthodox dogmatic theological method, as contrasted with the theological methodologies of the heresies.

Timeline of Writers of the Patristic Period

Location / Period	British Isles	Gaul	Spain, Portugal	Italy	Africa
					Philo of Alexandria, c. 20 B.C.-c. A.D. 50 (Greek)
2nd century		Irenaeus of Lyons, c. 135-c. 202 (Greek)		Clement of Rome, fl. c. 92-101 (Greek) Justin Martyr (Ephesus, Rome), c. 100/110-165 (Greek) Valentinus the Gnostic, fl. c. 140, (Greek) Marcion, fl. 144 (Greek)	Clement of Alexandria, c. 150-215 (Latin)
3rd century		Lactantius, c. 260- c. 330 (Latin)		Callistus of Rome, regn. 217-222 (Latin) Minucius Felix of Rome, fl. c. 218-235 (Latin) Novatian of Rome, fl. 235-258 (Latin)	Tertullian of Carthage, c. 155/160-225/250 (Latin) Origen (Alexandria, Caesaria of Palestine), 185-254 (Greek) Cyprian of Carthage, fl. 248-258 (Latin) Dionysius of Alexandria, d. c. 264 (Latin)
4th century		Hilary of Poitiers, c. 315-367 (Latin)	Potamius of Lisbon, fl. c. 350-360 (Latin) Gregory of Elvira, fl. 359-385 (Latin) Prudentius, c. 348-c. 410 (Latin)	Marius Victorinus (Rome), fl. 355-363 (Latin) Eusebius of Vercelli, fl. c. 360 (Latin) Lucifer of Cagliari (Sardinia), d. 370/371 (Latin) Faustinus (Rome), fl. 380 (Latin) Filastrius of Brescia, fl. 380 (Latin) Ambrosiaster (Italy?), fl. c. 366-384 (Latin) Gaudentius of Brescia, fl. 395 (Latin) Ambrose of Milan, c. 333-397; fl. 374-397 (Latin) Rufinus of Aquileia, c. 345-411 (Latin)	Antony the Great, c. 251-c. 355 (Greek) Arius (Alexandria), fl. c. 320 (Greek) Alexander of Alexandria, fl. 312-328 (Greek) Pachomius (Egypt), c. 292-347 (Coptic/Greek?) Athanasius of Alexandria, c. 295-373; fl. 325-373 (Greek) Macarius of Egypt, c. 300-c. 390 (Greek) Didymus (the Blind) of Alexandria, c. 313-398 (Greek) Augustine of Hippo, 354-430 (Latin)

Greece	Asia Minor	Syria	Mesopotamia, Persia	Palestine	Location Unknown
	Polycarp of Smyrna, c. 69-155 (Greek)	Ignatius of Antioch, c. 35-107/112 (Greek)			
		Theophilus of Antioch, c. late 2nd cent. (Greek)			
Athenagoras, fl. 176-180 (Greek)					
				Hippolytus (Palestine?), fl. 222-245 (Greek)	
	Gregory Thaumaturgus (Neocaesarea), fl. c. 248-264 (Greek)				
	Methodius of Olympus (Lycia), d. 311 (Greek)		Aphrahat, c. 270-350 (Syriac)	Eusebius of Caesarea (Palestine), c. 260/263-340 (Greek)	Commodian, c. 3rd or 5th cent. (Latin)
Epiphanius of Salamis (Cyprus), c. 315-403 (Greek)	Basil the Great, b. c. 330; fl. 357-379 (Greek)	Eusebius of Emesa, c. 300-c. 359 (Greek) Ephrem the Syrian, c. 306-373 (Syriac)		Acacius of Caesarea (Palestine), d. c. 365 (Greek) Cyril of Jerusalem, c. 315-386 (Greek)	
	Macrina the Younger, c. 327-379 (Greek)				
	Apollinaris of Laodicea, 310-c. 392 (Greek)				
John Chrysostom (Antioch, Constantinople), 344/354-407 (Greek)	Gregory of Nazianzus, b. 329/330; fl. 372-389 (Greek)				
	Gregory of Nyssa, c. 335-394 (Greek)				
	Amphilochius of Iconium, b. c. 340-345, d. c. 398-404 (Greek)	Nemesius of Emesa (Syria), fl. late 4th cent. (Greek)		Diodore of Tarsus, d. c. 394 (Greek) Jerome (Rome, Antioch, Bethlehem), c. 347-420 (Latin)	
	Evagrius of Pontus, c. 345-399 (Greek)				
	Theodore of Mopsuestia, c. 350-428 (Greek)				

Timeline of Writers of the Patristic Period

Location / Period	British Isles	Gaul	Spain, Portugal	Italy	Africa
5th century	Fastidius, c. 4th-5th cent. (Latin)	John Cassian (Palestine, Egypt, Constantinople, Rome, Marseilles), 360-432 (Latin) Sulpicius Severus, c. 360-c. 420 (Latin) Vincent of Lérins, d. 435 (Latin) Valerian of Cimiez, fl. c. 422-439 (Latin) Eucherius of Lyons, fl. 420-449 (Latin) Hilary of Arles, c. 401-449 (Latin) Salvian the Presbyter of Marseilles, c. 400-c. 480 (Latin)		Chromatius (Aquileia), fl. 400 (Latin) Pelagius (Britain, Rome), c. 354-c. 420 (Greek) Maximus of Turin, d. 408/423 (Latin) Paulinus of Nola, 355-431 (Latin) Peter Chrysologus (Ravenna), c. 380-450 (Latin) Leo the Great (Rome), regn. 440-461 (Latin)	Cyril of Alexandria, 375-444 (Greek) Quodvultdeus (Carthage), fl. 430 (Latin) Palladius of Helenopolis, c. 363/364-c. 431 (Greek) Ammonius of Alexandria, 5th cent. (Greek) Luculentius, 5th cent. (Latin)
6th century		Caesarius of Arles, c. 470-543 (Latin)	Paschasius of Dumium (Portugal), c. 515-c. 580 (Latin) Leander of Seville, c. 545-c. 600 (Latin) Isidore of Seville, c. 560-636 (Latin) Martin of Braga, fl. c. 568-579 (Latin) Braulio of Saragossa, c. 585-651 (Latin)	Benedict of Nursia, c. 480-547 (Latin) Cassiodorus (Calabria), c. 485-c. 540 (Latin) Gregory the Great, c. 540-604 (Latin)	Fulgentius of Ruspe, c. 467-532 (Latin)
7th century					
8th century	Bede the Venerable, c. 672/673-735 (Latin)				

Greece	Asia Minor	Syria	Mesopotamia, Persia	Palestine	Location Unknown
Nestorius (Constantinople), c. 381-c. 451 (Greek)	Basil of Seleucia, fl. 444-468 (Greek)	Severian of Gabala, fl. c. 400 (Greek)		Hesychius of Jerusalem, fl. 412-450 (Greek)	
		Theodoret of Cyr, c. 393-466 (Greek)			
Gennadius of Constantinople, d. 471 (Greek)	Diadochus of Photice, c. 400-474 (Greek)				
		Philoxenus of Mabbug, c. 440-523 (Syriac)	Jacob of Sarug, c. 450-c. 520 (Syriac)		
				Procopius of Gaza (Palestine), c. 465-c. 530 (Greek)	
		Severus of Antioch, fl. 488-538 (Greek)			
	Mark the Hermit (Tarsus), c. 6th cent. (Greek)			Dorotheus of Gaza, fl. c. 525-540 (Greek)	Pseudo-Dionysius the Areopagite, fl. c. 500 (Greek)
	Oecumenius (Isauria), 6th cent. (Greek)			Cyril of Scythopolis, b. c. 525; d. after 557 (Greek)	(Pseudo-)Constantius, before 7th cent. ? (Greek)
Maximus the Confessor (Constantinople), c. 580-662 (Greek)					Andreas, c. 7th cent. (Greek)
		Sahdona, fl. 635-640 (Syriac)			
		John of Damascus, c. 650-750 (Greek)	Isaac of Nineveh, d. c. 700 (Syriac)		
	Theophanes (Nicaea), 775-845 (Greek)		John the Elder, 8th cent. (Syriac)		
	Cassia, b. c. 805, d. c. 843-867 (Greek)				

Bibliography of Works in Original Languages

This bibliography refers readers to original language sources and supplies Thesaurus Linguae Graecae (=TLG) or Cetedoc Clavis (=CL) numbers where available. The edition listed in this bibliography may in some cases differ from the edition found in TLG or Cetedoc databases.

Ambrose. "De excessu fratris Satyri." In *Sanctii Ambrosii opera*. Edited by Karl Schenkl. CSEL 73, pp. 3-261. Vienna, Austria: Hoelder-Pichler-Tempsky, 1897. Cl. 0157.

———. "De fuga saeculi." In *Sancti Ambrosii opera*. Edited by Karl Schenkl. CSEL 32, pt. 2, pp. 163-207. Vienna, Austria: F. Tempsky; Leipzig, Germany: G. Freytag, 1897. Cl. 0133.

———. "De interpellatione Job et David." In *Sancti Ambrosii opera*. Edited by Karl Schenkl. CSEL 32, pt. 2, pp. 211-96. Vienna, Austria: F. Tempsky; Leipzig, Germany: G. Freytag, 1897. Cl. 0134.

———. "De Isaac vel anima." In *Sancti Ambrosii opera*. Edited by Karl Schenkl. CSEL 32, pt. 1, pp. 641-700. Vienna, Austria: F. Tempsky; Leipzig, Germany: G. Freytag, 1896. Cl. 0128.

———. "Epistulae." In *Sancti Ambrosii opera*. Edited by O. Faller and M. Zelzer. CSEL 82. Vienna, Austria: F. Tempsky, 1968-1990. Cl. 0160.

———. "Exameron." In *Sancti Ambrosii opera*. Edited by O. Faller. CSEL. 32, pt. 1, pp. 3-261. Vienna, Austria: Hoelder-Pichler-Tempsky, 1897. Cl. 0123.

———. "Expositio evangelii secundum Lucam." In *Sancti Ambrosii mediolanensis opera, Pars IV*. Turnhout, Belgium: Brepols, 1957. CCL 14, pp. 1-400. Cl. 0143.

Amphilochius. "In occursum domini [orat. 2]." In *Amphilochii Iconiensis opera*, pp. 37-73. Edited by C. Datema. Turnhout, Belgium: Brepols, 1978. TLG 2112. 003.

Athanasius. "De incarnatione verbi." In *Sur l'incarnation du verbe*. Edited by C. Kannengiesser. SC 199, pp. 258-468. Paris: Éditions du Cerf, 1973. TLG 2035. 002.

———. "Epistulae festales." In *Opera omnia*. PG 26. Edited by J.-P. Migne. Paris: Migne, 1857-1886. TLG 2035. x01.

———. "Vita sancti Antonii." In *Opera omnia*. PG 26, cols. 835-976. Edited by J.-P. Migne. Paris: Migne, 1857-1886. TLG 2035. 047.

Augustine. *Confessionum libri tredecim*. Edited by L. Verheijen. CCL 27. Turnhout, Belgium: Brepols, 1981. Cl. 0251.

———. "De adulterinis coniugiis." In *Sancti Aureli Augustini opera*. Edited by J. Zycha. CSEL 41, pp. 347-410. Vienna, Austria: F. Tempsky, 1900. Cl. 0302.

———. *De civitate Dei*. In *Opera*. Edited by B. Dombart and A. Kalb. CCL 47-48. Turnhout, Belgium: Brepols, 1955. Cl. 0313.

———. "De continentia." In *Sancti Aureli Augustini opera*. Edited by J. Zycha. CSEL 41, pp. 141-83. Vienna, Austria: F. Tempsky, 1900. Cl. 0298.

———. "De correptione et gratia." In *Opera omnia*. PL 44, cols. 915-46. Edited by J.-P. Migne Paris: Migne, 1845. Cl. 0353.

———. "De doctrina christiana." In *Opera*. Edited by J. Martin. CCL 32, cols. 1-167. Turnhout, Belgium: Brepols, 1962. Cl. 0263.

———. "De gratia et libero arbitrio." In *Opera omnia*. PL 44, cols. 881-912. Edited by J.-P. Migne. Paris: Migne, 1845. Cl. 0352.

———. "De opere monachorum." In *Sancti Aureli Augustini opera*. Edited by J. Zycha. CSEL 41, pp. 531-95. Vienna, Austria: F. Tempsky, 1900. Cl. 0305.

———. "De sancta virginitate." In *Sancti Aureli Augustini opera*. Edited by J. Zycha. CSEL 41, pp. 235-302. Vienna, Austria: F. Tempsky, 1900. Cl. 0300.

———. "De sermone Domini in monte." In *Sancti Aureli Augustini opera*. Edited by A. Mutzenbecher. CCL 35, pp. 1-188. Turnhout, Belgium: Brepols, 1967. Cl. 0274.

———. *De Trinitate*. In *Opera*. Edited by W. J. Mountain. CCL 50-50A. Turnhout, Belgium: Brepols, 1968. Cl. 0329.

———. "Enchiridion de fide, spe et caritate." In *Sancti Aureli Augustini opera*. Edited by E. Evans. CCL 46, pp. 49-114. Turnhout, Belgium: Brepols, 1969. Cl. 0295.

———. "Epistulae." In *Sancti Aureli Augustini opera*. Edited by A. Goldbacher. CCL 34, pts. 1, 2; 44; 57; 58. Vienna, Austria: F. Tempsky, 1895-1898. Cl. 0262.

———. "In Johannis epistulam ad Parthos tractatus." In *Opera omnia*. PL 35, cols. 1379-2062. Edited by J.-P. Migne. Paris: Migne, 1841. Cl. 0279.

———. *In Johannis evangelium tractatus*. Edited by R. Willems. CCL 36. Turnhout, Belgium: Brepols, 1954. Cl. 0278.

Basil the Great. "Asceticon magnum sive Quaestiones [regulae brevius tractatae]." In *Opera omnia*. PG 31, cols. 1052-1305. Edited by J.-P. Migne. Paris: Migne, 1885. TLG 2040. 050.

———. "De baptismo libri duo." In *Opera omnia*. PG 31, cols. 1513-1628. Edited by J.-P. Migne. Paris: Migne, 1885. TLG 2040. 052.

———. "De humilitate." In *Opera omnia*. PG 31, cols. 525-540. Edited by J.-P. Migne. Paris: Migne, 1885. TLG 2040. 036.

———. "Epistulae." In *Saint Basil: Lettres*, vol. 2, pp. 101-218; vol. 3, pp. 1-229. Edited by Y. Courtonne. Paris: Les Belles Lettres, 1961-1966. TLG 2040. 004.

———. "Homiliae super Psalmos." In *Opera omnia*. PG 29, pp. 209-494. Edited by J.-P. Migne. Paris: Migne, 1886. TLG 2040. 018.

———. "Prologus 7 [de judicio dei]." In *Opera omnia*. PG 31, cols. 653-676. Edited by J.-P. Migne. Paris: Migne, 1885. TLG 2040. 043.

———. "Regulae moralis." In *Opera omnia*. PG 31, cols. 692-869. Edited by J.-P. Migne. Paris: Migne, 1885. TLG 2040. 051.

Bede. "De tabernaculo et vasis eius ac vestibus sacerdotem libri iii." In *Opera*. Edited by D. Hurst. CCL 119A, pp. 5-139. Turnhout, Belgium: Brepols, 1969. Cl. 1345.

———. "Homiliarum evangelii." In *Opera*. Edited by D. Hurst. CCL 122, pp. 1-378. Turnhout, Belgium: Brepols, 1956. Cl. 1367.

———. "In Lucae evangelium expositio." In *Opera*. Edited by D. Hurst. CCL 120, pp. 1-425. Turnhout, Belgium: Brepols, 1960. Cl. 1356.

Benedict of Nursia. "Regula." In *La règle de saint Benoît*. Edited by Adalbert de Vogüé and Jean Neufville. 2 vols. SC 181, pp. 412-90; SC 182, pp. 508-674. Paris: Éditions du Cerf, 1971-1977. Cl. 1852.

Cassia. *See* The Festal Menaion.

Cassian, John. *Collationes*. Edited by M. Petscheig. CSEL 13. Vienna, Austria: F. Tempsky, 1886. Cl. 0512.

Clement of Alexandria. "Paedagogus." In *Le pédagogue [par] Clement d'Alexandrie*. 3 vols. Edited by M. Harl, H. Marrou, C. Matray and C. Mondésert. SC 70, pp. 108-294; SC 108, pp. 10-242; SC 58, pp. 12-190. Paris: Éditions du Cerf, 1960-1970. TLG 0555. 002.

———. "Stromata." In *Clemens Alexandrinus*, vols 2, 3rd ed. , and vol. 3, 2nd ed. Edited by O. Stählin, L. Früchtel and U. Treu. GCS 15, pp. 3-518; GCS 17, pp. 3-102. Berlin: Akademie-Verlag, 2:1960; 3:1970. TLG 0555. 004.

Clement of Rome. "Epistula i ad Corinthios." In *Clément de Rome: Épitre aux Corinthiens*. Edited by A. Jaubert. SC 167, pp. 98-204. Paris: Éditions du Cerf, 1971. TLG 1271. 001.

Cyprian. "Ad fortunatum (de exhortatione martyrii)." In *Sancti Cyprian episcopi opera*. Edited by R. Weber. CCL 3, pp. 183-216. Turnhout, Belgium: Brepols, 1972. Cl. 0045.

———. "De bono patientiae." In *Sancti Cypriani episcopi epistularium*. Edited by C. Moreschini. CCL 3A, pp. 118-33. Turnhout, Belgium: Brepols, 1976. Cl. 0048.

———. "De dominica oratione." In *Sancti Cypriani episcopi epistularium*. Edited by C. Moreschini. CCL 3A, pp. 87-113. Turnhout, Belgium: Brepols, 1976. Cl. 0043.

———. "De habitu virginum." In *S. Thasci Caecili Cypriani opera omnia*. Edited by William Hartel. CSEL 3. 1, pp. 187-205. Vienna, Austria: Gerold, 1868. Cl. 0040.

———. "De lapsis." In *Sancti Cyprian episcopi opera*. Edited by R. Weber. CCL 3, pp. 221-42. Turnhout, Belgium: Brepols, 1972. Cl. 0042.

———. "De mortalitate." In *Sancti Cypriani episcopi epistularium*. Edited by M. Simonetti. CCL 3A, pp. 15-32. Turnhout, Belgium: Brepols, 1976. Cl. 0044.

———. "De opere et eleemosynis." In *Sancti Cypriani episcopi epistularium*. Edited by M. Simonetti. CCL 3A, pp. 53-72. Turnhout, Belgium: Brepols, 1976. Cl. 0047.

———. *Epistulae*. Edited by G. F. Diercks. CCL 3B, 3C. Turnhout, Belgium: Brepols, 1994-1996. Cl. 0050.

Cyril of Alexandria. "Commentarii in Lucam." In *Opera omnia*. PG 72, cols. 476-949. Edited by J.-P. Migne. Paris: Migne, 1864. TLG 4090. 030.

———. "Epistulae." In *Concilium universale Ephesenum*. Edited by E. Schwartz. Berlin: Walter De Gruyter, 1927. TLG 5000. 001.

Cyril of Jerusalem. "Catecheses ad illuminandos 1-18." In *Cyrilli Hierosolymorum archiepiscopi opera quae supersunt omnia*, vol. 1, pp. 28-320; vol. 2, pp. 2-342. Edited by W. C. Reischl and J. Rupp. Munich: Lentner, 1848-1860. Reprint, Hildesheim: Olms, 1967. TLG 2110. 003.

Didache. In *Instructions des Apôtres*, pp. 226-242. Edited by J. P. Audet. Paris: Lecoffre, 1958. TLG 1311. 001.

Ephrem the Syrian. "Hymni de Paradiso." In *Des Heiligen Ephraem des Syrers Hymnen de Paradiso und Contra Julianum*. Edited by E. Beck. CSCO 174 (Scriptores Syri 78). Louvain, Belgium: Imprimerie Orientaliste L. Durbecq, 1957.

———. "In Tatiani Diatessaron." In *Saint Éphrem: Commentaire de l'Evangile Concordant—Text Syriaque, (Ms Chester-Beatty 709), Folios Additionnels*. Edited by L. Leloir. Chester-Beatty Monographs, no. 8, Leuven and Paris, 1990.

———. "Sermo de nomino nostro." In *Des Heilig Ephraem Sermo de Domino Nostro*. Edited by E. Beck. CSCO 270 (Scriptores Syri 116). Louvain, Belgium: Imprimerie Orientaliste L. Durbecq, 1966.

Eusebius of Caesarea. "Demonstratio evangelica." In *Eusebius Werke, Band 6: Die Demonstratio evangelica*. Edited by I. A. Heikel. GCS 23, pp. 493-96. Leipzig, Germany: Hinrichs, 1913. TLG 2018. 005.

———. "Historia ecclesiastica." In *Eusèbe de Césarée. Histoire ecclésiastique*, 3 vols. Edited by G. Bardy. SC 31, pp. 3-215; SC 41, pp. 4-231; SC 55, pp. 3-120. Paris: Éditions du Cerf, 1952-1958. TLG 2018. 002.

The Festal Menaion. *Menaion tou Martiou*. Ekklestiastike Bibliotheke. Oikos Mic. Saliberou A. E. Staliou 14, Atheneai. n.d.

Gregory of Nazianzus. "De filio [orat. 29]." In *Gregor von Nazianz. Die fünf theologischen Reden*, pp. 128-68. Edited by J. Barbel. Düsseldorf, Germany: Patmos-Verlag, 1963. TLG 2022. 009.

———. "De filio [orat. 30]." In *Gregor von Nazianz. Die fünf theologischen Reden*, pp. 170-216. Edited by J. Barbel. Düsseldorf, Germany: Patmos-Verlag, 1963. TLG 2022. 010.

———. "De spiritu sancto [orat. 31]." In *Gregor von Nazianz. Die fünf theologischen Reden*, pp. 218-76. Edited by J. Barbel. Düsseldorf, Germany: Patmos-Verlag, 1963. TLG 2022. 011.

Gregory of Nyssa. "De instituto Christiano." In *Gregorii Nysseni opera*, vol. 8. 1, pp. 40-89. Edited by W. Jaeger. Leiden: Brill, 1963. TLG 2017. 024.

———. De virginitate." In *Grégoire de Nysse. Traité de la virginité*. Edited by M. Aubineau. SC 119, pp. 246-560. Paris: Éditions du Cerf, 1966. TLG 2017. 043.

———. "Dialogus de anima et resurrectione." In *Opera omnia*. PG 46, cols. 12-160. Edited by J.-P. Migne. Paris: Migne, 1863. TLG 2017. 056.

Gregory the Great. "Dialogorum libri iv." In *Dialogues*. Edited by P. Antin. SC 260 and 265. Paris: Éditions du Cerf, 1978-80. Cl. 1713.

———. "Homiliarum xl in evangelica." In *Opera omnia*. Edited by J.-P. Migne. PL 76, cols. 1075-1312. Paris: Migne, 1857. Cl. 1711.

Hilary of Poitiers. *De trinitate*. Edited by P. Smulders. CCL 62 and 62A. Turnhout, Belgium: Brepols, 1979-1980. Cl. 0433.

Hippolytus. "Contra haeresin Noeti." In *Hippolytus of Rome. Contra Noetum*, pp. 43-93. Edited by R. Butterworth. London: Heythrop College (University of London), 1977. TLG 2115. 002.

Ignatius of Antioch. "Epistula ad Smyrnaeos (epist. 7 de vii genuinae)." In *Ignace d'Antioche, Lettres*. Edited by P. T. Camelot. SC 10, pp. 146-54. Paris: Éditions du Cerf, 1969. TLG 1443. 001.

Irenaeus. "Adversus haereses, livre 3, 5." In *Contre les hérésies*. Edited by A. Rousseau and L. Doutreleau (Book 3, 5) and C. Mercier (Book 3). SC 100, 152-53, 210-11, 263-64, 293-94. Paris: Éditions du Cerf, 1965-82. Cl. 1154 g.

[Isaac of Nineveh]. *Mar Isaacus: De perfectione religiosa*. Edited by P. Bedjan. Paris: 1900.

Jerome. *Dialogus adversus Pelagianos*. Edited by C. Moreschini. CCL 80. Turnhout, Belgium: Brepols, 1990. Cl. 0615.

———. "Homilia de nativitate Domini." In *S. Hieronymi presbyteri opera, Pars 2*. Edited by G. Morin. CCL 78, pp. 524-29. Turnhout, Belgium: Brepols, 1958. Cl. 0598.

———. "Homilia in Johannem evangelistam (1:1-14)." In *S. Hieronymi presbyteri opera, Pars 2*. Edited by G. Morin. CCL 78, pp. 517-23. Turnhout, Belgium: Brepols, 1958. Cl. 0597.

———. "Homilia in Lucam, de Lazaro et Divite." In *S. Hieronymi presbyteri opera, Pars 2*. Edited by G. Morin. CCL 78, pp. 507-16. Turnhout, Belgium: Brepols, 1958. Cl. 0596.

———. "Tractatus lix in psalmos." In *S. Hieronymi presbyteri opera, Pars 2*. Edited by G. Morin, CCL 78, pp. 3-352. Turnhout, Belgium: Brepols, 1958. Cl. 0592.

———. "Tractatus in Marci evangelium." In *S. Hieronymi presbyteri opera, Pars 2*. Edited by G. Morin. CCL 78, pp. 449-500. Turnhout, Belgium: Brepols, 1958. Cl. 0594.

———. "Tractatum in psalmos Series altera." In *S. Hieronymi presbyteri opera, Pars 2*. Edited by G. Morin. CCL 78, pp. 355-446. Turnhout, Belgium: Brepols, 1958. Cl. 0593.

John Chrysostom. "Catechesis ultima ad baptizandos." In *Varia graeca sacra*, pp. 166-75. Edited by A. Papadopoulos-Kerameus. St. Petersburg: Kirschbaum, 1909. TLG 2062. 381.

———. "Contra Anomoeos [homiliae 1-5]: De incomprehensibili dei natura." In *Jean Chrysostome. Sur l'incompréhensibilité de Dieu*. Edited by F. Cavallera, J. Danielou and R. Flaceliere. SC 28, pp. 92-322. Paris: Éditions du Cerf, 1951. TLG 2062. 012.

———. "Contra Anomoeos [homilia 7]: De consubstantiali." In *Opera omnia*. PG 48, cols. 755-68. Edited by J.-P. Migne. Paris: Migne, 1859. TLG 2062. 015.

―――. "Contra Anomoeos [homilia 8]: De petitione matris filiorum Zebedaei." In *Opera omnia*. PG 48, cols. 767-78. Edited by J.-P. Migne. Paris: Migne, 1859. TLG 2062. 016.

―――. "Contra Anomoeos [homilia 9]: In quatriduanum Lazarum." In *Opera omnia*. PG 48, cols. 779-84. Edited by J.-P. Migne. Paris: Migne, 1859. TLG 2062. 017.

―――. "Contra Judaeos et Gentiles quod Christus sit Deus, liber unus." In *Opera omnia*. PG 48, cols. 812-838. Edited by J.-P. Migne. Paris: Migne, 1859.

―――. "In Genesim homiliae 1-67." In *Opera omnia*. PG 53 cols. 21-385; PG 54 cols. 385-580. Edited by J.-P. Migne. Paris: Migne, 1862. TLG 2062. 112.

―――. "In Joannem [homiliae 1-88]." In *Opera omnia*. PG 59, cols. 23-482. Edited by J.-P. Migne. Paris: Migne, 1859. TLG 2062. 153.

―――. "In Matthaeum [homiliae 1-90]." In *Opera omnia*. PG 57 cols. 13-472; PG 58, cols. 471-794. Edited by J.-P. Migne. Paris: Migne, 1862. TLG 2062. 152.

John of Damascus. "Expositio fidei." In *Die Schriften des Johannes von Damaskos*, vol. 2, pp. 3-239. Edited by B. Kotter. Patristische Texte und Studien 12. Berlin: De Gruyter, 1973. TLG 2934. 004.

―――. "Vita Barlaam et Joasaph." In *Barlaam and Joasaph*, pp. 2-610. Edited by G. R. Woodward and H. Mattingly. Cambridge, Mass. : Harvard University Press, 1914. Reprint, 1983. TLG 2934. 066.

John the Monk. *See* The Festal Menaion.

Justin Martyr. "Apologia." In *Die ältesten Apologeten*, pp. 26-77. Edited by E. J. Goodspeed. Göttingen, Germany: Vandenhoeck & Ruprecht, 1915. TLG 0645. 001.

―――. "Dialogus cum Tryphone." In *Die ältesten Apologeten*, pp. 90-265. Edited by E. J. Goodspeed. Göttingen, Germany: Vandenhoeck & Ruprecht, 1915. TLG 0645. 003.

Leo the Great. "S. Leonis Papae I Epistola ad Flavianum Episcopum Constantinopolitanum: Adversus haeresim Eutychianam." In *Vigilius, Tapsensis Episcopus: Appendix*. Edited by J.-P. Migne. PL 72, cols. 503-508. Paris: Migne, 1863.

―――. *Tractatus septem et nonaginta*. Edited by A. Chavasse. CCL 138 and 138A. Turnhout, Belgium: Brepols, 1973. Cl. 1657.

Martyrius. "Book of Perfection" In *Martyrius (Sahdona): Oeuvres spirituelles*, part 3. Edited by A. de Halleux. CSCO 252 (Scriptores Syri 110). Louvain, Belgium : Secrétariat du Corpus Scriptorum Christianorum Orientalium, 1965.

Maximus of Turin. "Collectio sermonum antiqua." In *Maximi episcopi Taurinensis sermones*. Edited by Almut Mutzenbecher. CCL 23, pp. 1-364. Turnhout, Belgium: Brepols, 1962. Cl. 0219a.

Niceta of Remesiana. "De utilitate hymnorum." Edited by C. H. Turner. *Journal of Theological Studies* 24 (1923): 233-241

Origen. "Commentarii in evangelium Joannis [lib. 1, 2, 4, 5, 6, 10, 13]." In *Origène. Commmentaire sur saint Jean*, 3 vols. Edited C. Blanc. SC 120, pp. 56-390; SC 157 pp. 128-580; SC 222, pp. 34-282. Paris: Éditions du Cerf, 1966-1975. TLG 2042. 005.

―――. "Contra Celsum." In *Origène. Contre Celse*, 4 vols. Edited by M. Borret. SC 132 pp. 64-476; SC 136, pp. 14-434; SC 147, pp. 14-382; SC 150, pp. 14-352. Paris: Éditions du Cerf, 1967-1969. TLG 2042. 001.

―――. "De oratione." In *Origenes Werke*, vol. 2. Edited by P. Koestchau. GCS 3, pp. 297-403. Leipzig, Germany: Hinrichs, 1899. TLG 2042. 008.

―――. "De principiis." In *Origenes vier Bücher von den Prinzipien*, pp. 462-560, 668-764. Edited by H. Görgemanns and H. Karpp. Darmstadt, Germany: Wissenschaftliche Buchgesellschaft, 1976. TLG 2042. 002.

―――. "Exhortatio ad martyrium." In *Origenes Werke*, vol. 1. Edited by P. Koetschau. GCS 2, pp. 3-47.

Leipzig, Germany: Hinrichs, 1899. TLG 2042. 007.

———. "Fragmenta in Lucam [in catenis]." In *Origenes Werke*, vol. 9. Edited by M. Rauer. GCS 35, pp. 227-336. Berlin: Akademie-Verlag, 1930. TLG 2042. 017.

———. "Homiliae in Lucam." In *Opera Omnia*. PG 13, cols. 1799-1902. Edited by J.-P. Migne. Paris: Migne, 1857-1886. TLG 2042. 016.

———. "In Exodum homiliae." *Corpus Berolinense*, vol. 29, pp. 145-279. Edited by W. A. Baerhens, 1920. Cl. 0198 5.

———. "In Genesim homiliae." *Corpus Berolinense*, vol. 29, pp. 1-144. Edited by W. A. Baerhens, 1920. Cl. 0198 6.

———. "In Leviticum homiliae." *Corpus Berolinense*, vol. 29, pp. 280-507. Edited by W. A. Baerhens, 1920. Cl. 0198 3.

Paschasius of Dumin. "De vitis patrum liber septimus, sive verba seniorum auctore graeco incerto, interprete Paschasio S. R. E. Diacono." PL 73, cols 1025-1062. Edited by J.-P. Migne Paris: Migne, 1849.

Peter Chrysologus. *Sermones*. Edited by A. Olivar. CCL 24, 24A and 24B. Turnhout, Belgium: Brepols, 1975-1982. Cl. 0227+.

Philoxenus of Mabbug. "On the Indwelling of the Holy Spirit." *See* " 'Memra' de Philoxène de Mabboug sur l'inhabitation du Saint Esprit" Translated by A. Tanghe. *Le Muséon* 73 (1960): 39-71.

Prudentius. "Contra Summachum libri duo." In *Carmina Aurelii Prudentii Clementis*. Edited by M. P. Cunningham. CCL 126, pp. 182-250. Turnhout, Belgium: Brepols, 1966. Cl. 1442.

———. "Liber apotheosis." In *Carmina Aurelii Prudentii Clementis*. Edited by M. P. Cunningham. CCL 126, pp. 73-115. Turnhout, Belgium: Brepols, 1966. Cl. 1439.

———. "Liber cathemerinon." In *Carmina Aurelii Prudentii Clementis*. Edited by M. P. Cunningham. CCL 126, pp. 3-72. Turnhout, Belgium: Brepols, 1966. Cl. 1438.

———. "Tituli historiarum sive Dittochaeon." In *Carmina Aurelii Prudentii Clementis*. Edited by M. P. Cunningham. CCL 126, pp. 390-400. Turnhout, Belgium: Brepols, 1966. Cl. 1444.

Pseudo-Clement of Rome. "Epistula ii ad Corinthios." In *Die apostolischen Väter*, 3rd edition, pp. 71-81. Edited by K. Bihlmeyer and W. Schneemelcher. Tübingen, Germany: Mohr, 1970. TLG 1271. 002.

Pseudo-Dionysius. "De caelesti hierarchia." In *Denys l'Aréopagite: La hiérarchie céleste*. Edited by R. Roques, G. Heil and M. de Gandillac. SC 58, pp. 70-225. Paris: Éditions du Cerf, 1958. Reprint, 1970. TLG 2798. 001.

Symeon the New Theologian. *Catecheses 1-5*. Edited by B. Krivochéine and J. Paramelle. SC 96. Paris: Éditions du Cerf, 1963.

———. *Catecheses 6-22*. Edited by B. Krivochéine and J. Paramelle. SC 104. Paris: Éditions du Cerf, 1964.

Tertullian. "Ad Scapulam." In *Opera*. Edited by E. Dekkers. CCL 2, pp. 1127-32. Turnhout, Belgium: Brepols, 1954. Cl. 0024.

———. "Adversus Marcionem." In *Opera*. Edited by E. Kroymann. CCL 1, pp. 441-726. Turnhout, Belgium: Brepols, 1954. Cl. 0014.

———. "De fuga in persecutione." In *Opera*. Edited by J. J. Thierry. CCL 2, pp. 1135-55. Turnhout, Belgium: Brepols, 1954. Cl. 0025.

———. "De idolatria." In *Opera*. Edited by A. Reifferscheid and G. Wissowa. CCL 2, pp. 1101-24. Turnhout, Belgium: Brepols, 1954. Cl. 0023.

———. "De oratione." In *Opera*. Edited by G. F. Diercks. CCL 1, pp. 257-274. Turnhout, Belgium: Brepols, 1954. Cl. 0007.

———. "De patientia." In *Opera*. Edited by J. G. Ph. Borleffs. CCL 1, pp. 299-317. Turnhout, Belgium:

Brepols, 1954. Cl. 0009.

Theophanes. *See* The Festal Menaion.

Theophylact. "Enarratio in Evangelium Lucae." In *Theophylactus, archiepiscopus Bulgariae.* PG 123, cols. 691-1126. Edited by J.-P. Migne. Paris: Migne, 1883.

Bibliography of Works in English Translation

Ambrose. *Exposition of the Holy Gospel According to Saint Luke, with Fragments on the Prophecy of Isaias.* Translated by Theodosia Tomkinson. Etna, Calif.: Center for Traditionalist Orthodox Studies, 1998.

———. *Hexameron, Paradise, and Cain and Abel..* Translated by John J. Savage. FC 42. Washington, D.C.: The Catholic University of America Press, 1961.

———. *Letters.* Translated by Mary Melchior Beyenka. FC 26. Washington, D.C.: The Catholic University of America Press, 1954.

———. *Seven Exegetical Works.* Translated by Michael P. McHugh. FC 65. Washington, D.C.: The Catholic University of America Press, 1972.

[Ambrose]. *Funeral Orations by Saint Gregory Nazianzen and Saint Ambrose.* Translated by John J. Sullivan and Martin R. P. McGuire. FC 22. Washington, D.C.: The Catholic University of America Press, 1953.

Amphilochius. "Oration 2, On the Presentation of the Lord." In *The Sunday Sermons of the Great Fathers: Vol. 2, From the First Sunday in Lent to the Sunday After the Ascension*, pp. 173-79. Translated and edited by M. F. Toal. Swedesboro, N.J.: Preservation Press, 1996.

Athanasius. "Life of St. Anthony." In *Early Christian Biographies*, pp. 133-216. Edited by Roy J. Deferrari. FC 15. Washington, D.C.: The Catholic University of America Press, 1952.

———. *The Resurrection Letters.* Paraphrased and introduced by Jack N. Sparks. Nashville: Thomas Nelson, 1979.

———. *Select Works and Letters.* Translated by Archibald Robertson. NPNF 4. Series 2. Edited by Philip Schaff and Henry Wace. 1886-1900. Reprint, Peabody, Mass.: Hendrickson, 1994.

Augustine. *Christian Instruction; Admonition and Grace; The Christian Combat; Faith, Hope and Charity.* Translated by John J. Gavigan et al. FC 2. Washington, D.C.: The Catholic University of America Press, 1947.

———. *The City of God Books XVII-XXII.* Translated by Gerald G. Walsh and Daniel J. Honan. FC 24. Washington, D.C.: The Catholic University of America Press, 1954.

———. *Commentary on the Lord's Sermon on the Mount with Seventeen Related Sermons.* Translated by Denis J. Kavanagh. FC 11. Washington, D.C.: The Catholic University of America Press, 1951.

———. *Confessions.* Translated by Vernon J. Bourke. FC 21. Washington, D.C.: The Catholic University of America Press, 1953.

———. *Confessions and Enchiridion.* Translated and edited by Albert C. Outler. LCC 7. London: SCM Press, 1955.

———. *Later Works.* Translated by John Burnaby. LCC 8. London: SCM Press, 1955.

———. *Letters.* Translated by Sister Wilfrid Parsons and Robert B. Eno. FC 12, 18, 20, 30, 32 and 81. 6 vols. Washington, D.C.: The Catholic University of America Press, 1951-1989.

———. *The Retractations.* Translated by Mary Inez Bogan. FC 60. Washington, D.C.: The Catholic University of America Press, 1968.

———. *Sermons on the Liturgical Seasons.* Translated by Mary Sarah Muldowney. FC 38. Washington,

D.C.: The Catholic University of America Press, 1959.

———. *The Teacher, The Free Choice of the Will, Grace and Free Will*. Translated by Robert P. Russell. FC 59. Washington, D.C.: The Catholic University of America Press, 1968.

———. *Tractates on the Gospel of John 11-27*. Translated by John W. Rettig. FC 79. Washington, D.C.: The Catholic University of America Press, 1988.

———. *Tractates on the Gospel of John 55-111*. Translated by John W. Rettig. FC 90. Washington, D.C.: The Catholic University of America Press, 1994.

———. *Treatises on Marriage and Other Subjects*. Translated by Charles T. Wilcox et al. Edited by Roy J. Deferrari. FC 27. New York: Fathers of the Church, Inc., 1955.

———. *Treatises on Various Subjects*, pp. 323-94. Translated by Mary Sarah Muldowney et al. FC 16. Washington, D.C.: The Catholic University of America Press, 1952.

———. *The Trinity*. Translated by Stephen McKenna. FC 45. Washington, D.C.: The Catholic University of America Press, 1963.

———. *The Works of Saint Augustine: A Translation for the Twenty-First Century*. Edited by John E. Rotelle. Translated by Edmund Hill. Brooklyn, N.Y.: New City Press, 1990-.

Basil the Great. *Ascetic Works*. Translated by M. Monica Wagner. FC 9. New York: Fathers of the Church, Inc., 1950.

———. *Exegetic Homilies*. Translated by Agnes C. Way. FC 46. Washington, D.C.: The Catholic University of America Press, 1963.

———. *Letters*. Translated by Agnes C. Way. FC 13 and 28. 2 vols. Washington, D.C.: The Catholic University of America Press, 1951-1955.

Bede. "Christmas Day." In *The Sunday Sermons of the Great Fathers: Vol. 1, From the First Sunday of Advent to Quinquagesima*. 2 vols. Translated and edited by M. F. Toal. Swedesboro, N.J.: Preservation Press, 1996.

———. *Homilies on the Gospels*. Translated by Lawrence T. Martin and David Hurst. CS 110 and 111. 2 vols. Kalamazoo, Mich.: Cistercian Publications, 1991.

———. *On the Tabernacle*. Translated with notes and introduction by Arthur G. Holder. TTH 18. Liverpool: Liverpool University Press, 1994.

Benedict. "Rule of St. Benedict." In *Western Asceticism*, pp. 290-337. Translated by Owen Chadwick. LCC 12. Philadelphia: Westminster Press, 1958.

Cassia. *See The Festal Menaion*.

Cassian, John. "Conferences." In *Western Asceticism*, pp. 190-289. Translated by Owen Chadwick. LCC 12. Philadelphia: Westminster Press, 1958.

"A Church Manual" *[Didache]*. In *Early Christian Fathers*, pp. 171-79. Translated and edited by Cyril C. Richardson. LCC 1. Philadelphia: Westminster, 1953.

Clement of Alexandria. *Christ the Educator*. Translated by Simon P. Wood. FC 23. Washington, D.C.: The Catholic University of America Press, 1954.

———. *Stromateis: Books 1-3*. Translated by John Ferguson. FC 85. Washington, D.C.: The Catholic University of America Press, 1991.

Clement of Rome. "First Letter to the Corinthians." In *The Apostlic Fathers*, pp. 9-58. Translated by Francis X. Glimm. FC 1. New York: Christian Heritage, Inc., 1947.

Cyprian. *Treatises*. Translated and edited by Roy J. Deferrari. FC 36. Washington, D.C.: The Catholic University of America Press, 1958.

———. *Letters 1-81*. Translated by Rose Bernard Donna. FC 51. Washington, D.C.: The Catholic University of America Press, 1964.

———. "The Baptismal Controversy." In *Early Latin Theology*, pp. 147-72. Translated and edited by S. L.

Greenslade. LCC 5. Philadelphia: Westminster Press, 1956.

Cyril of Alexandria. *Commentary on the Gospel of Saint Luke*. Translated by R. Payne Smith. Long Island, N.Y.: Studion, 1983.

———. *Letters*. Translated by John I. McEnerney. FC 76 and 77. 2 vols. Washington, D.C.: The Catholic University of America Press, 1987.

Cyril of Jerusalem. *The Works of Saint Cyril of Jerusalem*. Translated by Leo P. McCauley and Anthony A. Stephenson. FC 61 and 64. 2 vols. Washington, D.C.: The Catholic University of America Press, 1969-1970.

Didache. See "A Church Manual."

Ephrem the Syrian. *Hymns on Paradise*. Translated by Sebastian Brock. Crestwood, N.Y.: St. Vladimir's Seminary Press, 1990.

———. *Saint Ephrem's Commentary on Tatian's Diatessaron*. Translated by Carmel McCarthy. Journal of Semitic Studies Supplement 2. Oxford: Oxford University Press, 1993.

———. *Selected Prose Works*. Translated by Edward G. Mathews and Joseph P. Amar. FC 91. Washington, D.C.: The Catholic University of America Press, 1994.

Eusebius. *The History of the Church from Christ to Constantine*. Translated by G. A. Williamson. New York: New York University Press, 1966.

———. *The Proof of the Gospel*. Translated by W. J. Ferrar. London: SPCK, 1920. Reprint, Grand Rapids, Mich.: Baker, 1981.

The Festal Menaion. Translated by Mother Mary and Archimandrite Kallistos Ware. Introduction by Archpriest Georges Florovsky. London: Faber and Faber, 1969.

Gregory of Nazianzus. *Faith Gives Fullness to Reasoning: The Five Theological Orations of Gregory Nazianzen*. Translated by Lionel Wickham and Frederick Williams, with introduction and commentary by Frederick W. Norris. Leiden: E. J. Brill, 1991.

———. "The Theological Orations." In *Christology of the Later Fathers*, pp. 128-214. Edited by Edward Rochie Hardy. Translated by Charles Gordon Browne and James Edward Swallow. LCC 3. Philadelphia: Westminster Press, 1954.

Gregory of Nyssa. *Ascetical Works*. Translated by Virginia Woods Callahan. FC 58. Washington, D.C.: The Catholic University of America Press, 1967.

Gregory the Great. *Dialogues*. Translated by Odo John Zimmerman. FC 39. Washington, D.C.: The Catholic University of America Press, 1959.

———. *Forty Gospel Homilies*. Translated by Dom David Hurst. CS 123. Kalamazoo, Mich.: Cistercian, 1990.

———. "St Gregory the Great: On the Feast." In *The Sunday Sermons of the Great Fathers: Vol. 1, From the First Sunday of Advent to Quinquagesima*, pp. 120-22. Translated and edited by M. F. Toal. Swedesboro, N.J.: Preservation Press, 1996.

Hilary of Poitiers. *The Trinity*. Translated by Stephen McKenna. FC 25. Washington, D.C.: The Catholic University of America Press, 1954.

[Hippolytus]. *Hippolytus, Cyprian, Caius, Novatian, Appendix*. Edited by Alexander Roberts and James Donaldson. ANF 5. 1886. Reprint, Peabody, Mass.: Hendrickson, 1994.

Ignatius of Antioch. "The Letters of Ignatius, Bishop of Antioch." In *Early Christian Fathers*, pp. 74-120. Edited and translated by Cyril C. Richardson. LCC 1. Philadelphia: Westminster Press, 1953.

Irenaeus. "Selections from the Work *Against Heresies* by Irenaeus, Bishop of Lyons." In *Early Christian Fathers*, pp. 343-97. Edited and translated by Edward Rochie Hardy. LCC 1. Philadelphia: Westminster Press, 1953.

Isaac of Nineveh. *The Ascetical Homilies of Saint Isaac the Syrian*. Translated by the Holy Transfiguration

Monastery. Boston: The Holy Transfiguration Monastery, 1984.

Jerome. *Dogmatic and Polemic Works*. Translated by John N. Hritzu. FC 53. Washington, D.C.: The Catholic University of America Press, 1965.

———. *The Homilies of Saint Jerome*. Translated by Marie L. Ewald. FC 48 and 57. 2 vols. Washington, D.C.: The Catholic University of America Press, 1964-1966.

John Chrysostom. *Apologist*. Translated by Margaret A. Schatkin and Paul W. Harkins. FC 73. Washington, D.C.: The Catholic University of America Press, 1985.

———. *Baptismal Instructions*. Translated and annotated by Paul W. Harkins. ACW 31. New York: Newman, 1963.

———. *Commentary on Saint John the Apostle and Evangelist Homilies 1-47*. Translated by Thomas Aquinas Goggin. FC 33. Washington, D.C.: The Catholic University of America Press, 1957.

———. *Homilies on Genesis*. Translated by Robert C. Hill. FC 74 and 82. 2 vols. Washington, D.C.: The Catholic University of America Press, 1986-1990.

———. *Homilies on the Gospel of Saint Matthew*. Translated by George Prevost. Revised with notes by M. B. Riddle. NPNF 10. Series 1. Edited by Philip Schaff. 1886-1889. 14 vols. Reprint, Peabody, Mass.: Hendrickson, 1994.

———. *On the Incomprehensible Nature of God*. Translated by Paul W. Harkins. FC 72. Washington, D.C.: The Catholic University of America Press, 1984.

John of Damascus. *Barlaam and Ioasaph*. Translated by G. R. Woodward and H. Mattingly. LCL 34. Cambridge, Mass.: Harvard University Press, 1937.

———. *Writings*. Translated by Frederic H. Chase. FC 37. Washington, D.C.: The Catholic University of America Press, 1958.

John the Monk. *See The Festal Menaion*.

Justin Martyr. *Writings of Saint Justin Martyr*. Translated by Thomas B. Falls. FC 6. New York: Christian Heritage, Inc., 1948.

Leo the Great. "Sermons." In *Leo the Great, Gregory the Great*, pp. 115-205. Translated by Charles Lett Feltoe. NPNF 12. Series 2. Edited by Philip Schaff and Henry Wace. 14 vols. 1886-1900. Reprint, Peabody, Mass.: Hendrickson, 1994.

———. *Sermons*. Translated by Jane P. Freeland and Agnes J. Conway. FC 93. Washington, D.C.: The Catholic University of America Press, 1996.

———. "The Tome of Leo." In *Christology of the Later Fathers*, pp. 359-70. Edited by Edward Rochie Hardy. Translated by William Bright. LCC 3. Philadelphia: Westminster Press, 1954.

Martyrius. "Martyrius (Sahdona)." In *The Syriac Fathers on Prayer and the Spiritual Life*, pp. 197-239. Translated by Sebastian Brock. CS 101. Kalamazoo, Mich.: Cistercian, 1987.

Maximus of Turin. *The Sermons of St. Maximus of Turin*. Translated and annotated by Boniface Ramsey. ACW 50. New York: Newman, 1989.

Niceta of Remesiana. "Liturgical Singing." In *Niceta of Remesiana, Sulpicius Severus, Vincent of Lerins, Prosper of Aquitaine*, pp. 65-76. Translated by Gerald G. Walsh. FC 7. New York: Fathers of the Church, Inc., 1949.

Origen. *Commentary on the Gospel According to John, Books 13-32*. Translated by Ronald E. Heine. FC 89. Washington, D.C.: The Catholic University of America Press, 1993.

———. *An Exhortation to Martyrdom, Prayer and Selected Works*. Translated by Rowan A. Greer. CWS. New York: Paulist, 1979.

———. *Homilies on Genesis and Exodus*. Translated by Ronald E. Heine. FC 71. Washington, D.C.: The Catholic University of America Press, 1982.

———. *Homilies on Leviticus*. Translated by Gary Wayne Barkley. FC 83. Washington, D.C.: The Catholic University of America Press, 1990.

———. *Homilies on Luke, Fragments on Luke*. Translated by Joseph T. Lienhard. FC 94. Washington, D.C.: The Catholic University of America Press, 1996.

———. "Sunday Outside the Octave of Christmas, and Feast of the Holy Name," In *The Sunday Sermons of the Great Fathers: Vol. 1, From the First Sunday of Advent to Quinquagesima*, pp. 186-95. Translated and edited by M. F. Toal. Swedesboro, N.J.: Preservation Press, 1996.

———. *The Writings of Origen: Volume 2, Origen Contra Celsum Books II—VIII*. Translated by Frederick Crombie. Ante-Nicene Christian Library 23. Edinburgh: T & T Clark, 1894.

Paschasius of Dumium. "Questions and Answers of the Greek Fathers." In *Iberian Fathers: Volume 1, Martin of Braga, Paschasius of Dumium, Leander of Seville*, pp. 113-71. Translated by Claude W. Barlow. FC 62. Washington, D.C.: The Catholic University of America Press, 1969.

[Peter Chrysologus]. *Saint Peter Chrysologus: Selected Sermons; and Saint Valerian: Homilies*, pp. 25-282. Translated by George E. Ganss. FC 17. Washington, D.C.: The Catholic University of America Press, 1953.

Philoxenus of Mabbug. "On the Indwelling of the Holy Spirit." In *The Syriac Fathers on Prayer and the Spiritual Life*, pp. 106-27. Translated by Sebastian Brock. CS 101. Kalamazoo, Mich.: Cistercian, 1987.

Prudentius. *Poems*. Translated by Sister M. Clement Eagan. FC 43 and 52. 2 vols. Washington, D.C.: The Catholic University of America Press, 1962-1965.

Pseudo-Clement of Rome. "An Early Christian Sermon." In *Early Christian Fathers*, pp. 183-202. Edited and translated by Cyril C. Richardson. LCC 1. Philadelphia: Westminster Press, 1953.

Pseudo-Dionysius. *The Complete Works*. Translated by Colm Luibheid. CWS. New York: Paulist, 1987.

Symeon the New Theologian. *The Discourses*. Translated by C. J. de Catanzaro. CWS. New York: Paulist, 1980.

Tertullian. *Adversus Marcionem*. Edited and translated by Ernest Evans. 2 vols. OECT. Oxford: Oxford University Press, 1972.

———. *Disciplinary, Moral and Ascetical Works*. Translated by Edwin A. Quain. FC 40. Washington, D.C.: The Catholic University of America Press, 1959.

———. "On Idolatry." In *Early Latin Theology: Selections from Tertullian, Cyprian, Ambrose and Jerome*, pp. 78-110. Edited and translated by S. L. Greenslade. LCC 5. Philadelphia: Westminster Press, 1956.

[Tertullian]. *Tertullian: Apologetical Works; and Minucius Felix: Octavius*. Translated by Rudolph Arbesmann. FC 10. Washington, D.C.: The Catholic University of America Press, 1950.

Theophanes. *See The Festal Menaion*.

Theophylact. *The Explanation by Blessed Theophylact of the Holy Gospel According to St. Luke*. Translated by Christopher Stade. House Springs, Mo.: Chrysostom Press, 1997.

Authors/Writings Index

Subject Index

Aaron, 168, 198-99
Abijah, 7
Abraham
    faith and obedience of, 188,
        204, 358
    gospel to, xx
    in Jesus' genealogy, 71
    mercy of, 263
    promise to, 61
    Zacchaeus as son of, 292
abundance, 152-53
Acts of the Apostles, 2
Adam
    among the dead, 330, 343
    garments of, 363, 376
    greed and gluttony of, 73-
        74, 330
    healing of, 344
    Jesus and, 20, 37, 42, 73,
        218, 252, 291
    poverty of, 16
    represented in parable in
        the Good Samaritan,
        179-80
    sin of, reversed, 343, 365
    Zacchaeus and, 291
adoption, 27, 45, 66
Advent, 60, 81, 319-20
agape (love feast), 237
advocate, 101, 224, 250, 276-77
Ahab, 9
Alexandria, xxiv
Alexandrian interpretation, xxii
allegory, xxii, 180
"alleluia," 183
almsgiving
    and faith, 134
    and forgiveness, xxvi, 129,
        199
    and purification, 199
    and repentance, 61
    spiritual riches through,
        211-12
    two kinds of, 110
    to the unworthy, 255
Ambrose of Milan, xvii
ancestry, 7, 32-33, 200-201, 204
angels
    announce Jesus' birth, 40
    catechetical lectures of, 40
    equality with, xxv
    as flower of the world, 210-

11
    at Jesus' resurrection, 374-
        75
    at Jesus' temptation, 42
    relation to humanity, 42
    revelation to, 8
anger, 32, 226
Anna, xxv, 48, 51-52
annunciation, xxv, 11-20
anointing, 126, 128-29
antichrist, 274-355
Antiochene interpretation, xxii
Antony and Cleopatra, 36
anxiety, 209-12, 343
apostles
    bread represents, 99
    follow Jesus, 131-32
    Jesus' feet represent, 126
    and the keys of the king-
        dom, 202
    new commission of, 335-38
    readiness of, 214-15
    spiritual judgment by, 336
    twelve, 101
    vineyard given to, 306
    See also disciples
apostolic tradition 3-4
appearance of resurrected
    Christ, 383-87
ascension of Christ, 390-93. See
    also Jesus Christ, ascension of
Aristotle, 39
Arius, 259
arrogance, 279
asceticism, 9
ask, seek, and knock, 189-90
atonement, 3-4, 356
Augustine, xviii, xix-xx, xxiv-
    xxvi
Augustus, 36-37
authority
    of apostles, 173
    given to the disciples, 176-
        77
    of Jesus, 302-3, 311
    transitory nature of, 310-11
axe, 61-62
baptism
    circumcision and, 45
    as a cross to bear, 156
    into death, 91, 130
    discipleship and, 241
    fire and, 217-18
    flood as, 272

and forgiveness of sin, 129-
    30
    God justified through, 123
    grace of, 313
    and/of the Holy Spirit, 18,
        45, 63, 217, 329, 389
    of Jesus, 44, 59, 63-68
    Passion as, 216-19
    purification and sanctifica-
        tion of, 97, 198, 329
    and rebirth, 169, 249-50,
        217, 275
    of repentance, 59
    resurrection and, 217-18
    a son through, 250
    symbolism of, 217
    of tears, 350
    Trinity and, 64
    and virgin's womb, 18
    water jar represents, 329
    See also baptism of Jesus
banquet
    entering the kingdom, 229-
        31
    Levi's, 94-98
    parable of, 237-39
baptism of Jesus, 65-68, 91,
    175-76, 218, 258
barley, 151
Barnabas, 171
barns, building bigger, 208
Barrabas, 355-56
barrenness, 7, 10
beatitudes, 103-6
Bede, the Venerable, xvii
believers and unbelievers, 274
Benedictus, 30-34
Bethany, 296, 391
Bethphage, 296
Bethlehem, 37
betrayal. See Jesus Christ,
    betrayal of
birds, 91, 210
blasphemy, 93, 352, 205
blessings, 195, 332, 392
blind man, healing of, 287-88
blood of Christ, 152, 333, 343-
    44, 361-62
boat, 88-89
body
    death of, 321
    freedom from anxiety
        about, 148
    holiness and, 275

limitation of, 160
    and mind of Christ, 196-97
    after resurrection, 204, 211
    Satan and, 204
    soul and, 199
    suffering and, 199
bosom of Abraham, 261-62
bounty of God, 111
bread
    five loaves of, 151-52
    prayer for daily, 187-88
    represents love, 190
    three loaves of, 189
    and wine, 332-33
    Word of God as, 151
bread, breaking, 330, 378-79,
    381-83
bread from heaven, 99, 146,
    157, 226
bread of life
    eternal, 237
    Jesus as, 153, 187-88, 331
    Mary and Martha feast on,
        182
bridegroom, 63, 96-97, 123
burdens, 266
burial of Jesus, 370-73
business, 241
Caesar, 310-12
Caiphas, 96, 354
Cain and Abel, 326
calf, 2, 69, 251-53
calling, divine, 168. See also Jesus
    calls and sends out
"call upon the Lord," 113
camel, 284
Capernaum, 83-86
captives, 80-81
catechesis, 133, 135, 378. See
    also catechetical lectures; Jesus
    Christ, teaching of; teaching
catechetical lectures
    Jesus' final, 387-90
    the kerygma of, 380-81
    way of life and death, 103-
        13
census, 36
centurion, 115-16, 368-70
centurion's slave, 115-17
character, 112-13
charity
    bonding through, 207
    in Christian life, xix, xxvi,
        274

427

Scripture Index